Manual for Life Style Assessment

Bernard H. Shulman, M.D.
Psychiatrist
Private Practice
Chicago

Harold H. Mosak, Ph.D.
Psychologist
Private Practice
Chicago

Brunner-Routledge
New York & London

Manual for *Life Style Assessment*

Published by
Brunner-Routledge
29 West 35th Street
New York, NY 10001

Published in Great Britain
Brunner-Routledge
11 New Fetter Lane
London EC4P 4EE

Brunner-Routledge is an imprint of the Taylor & Francis Group

6 7 8 9 10

Reprinted with modifications, June 1990 and May 1995.

Printed in the United States of America

Technical Development: Tanya Dalton
Marguerite Mader
Sheila Sheward

LCN: 87-72748

To

Rudolf Dreikurs

1897-1972

PREFACE

Rudolf Dreikurs was probably the best diagnostician of human behavior that we have ever encountered. We thought his ability was uncanny. After exchanging a few words with another person, he could make surprisingly accurate guesses about that person. But before we could learn to do this, we had to follow a learning path: to learn how to ask the appropriate questions of another human being and how to begin to sort out the meanings of traits and behaviors. We had to learn to think of a family as a social organization in which children learned about life and of each human being as a unique entity. Then, we could learn to find the uniqueness of each person.

This unique "self" was what Alfred Adler called the "unique law of movement" of the individual, or the individual's "life style". Understanding life style means we understand the person as a unique entity, separate from other entities, no matter how many traits are shared between them. The life style is a "one and only", a creation of the specific individual.

In all human endeavors where understanding another person is important, knowing that person's life style is a most helpful and useful way of knowing that person. It allows us to predict many aspects of behavior. Therapists, teachers, counselors, leaders, biographers, and students of personality can find the understanding of life style useful in their endeavors.

This manual presents the most systematic way we know of to elicit and interpret life style. Our method is based upon what we learned from Rudolf Dreikurs. We offer it as a tribute to him.

We owe thanks to Dr. Joseph W. Hollis, our publisher, for spurring us onward to complete the book. We are sincerely grateful for his firm and sympathetic hand and his belief in what we were doing. We also are grateful for the numerous typists who did these chapters over and over as we wrote and rewrote. To them, and to the thousands of subjects who provided the data upon which we based our skills, we say "Thank You."

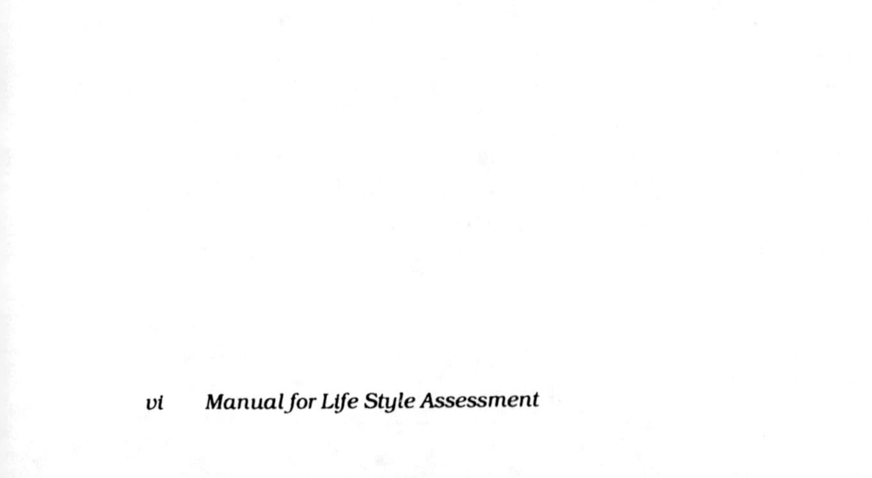

TABLE OF CONTENTS

LIST OF FIGURES

LIST OF TABLES

LIST OF TABLES (Con't)

CHAPTER 1

WHAT IS THE LIFE STYLE?

The origin and development of the term "life style" has been extensively reviewed by H.L. Ansbacher (1967). He has found references to the notion of personality style as early as *The Anatomy of Melancholy* by Robert Burton (1577-1640)—"...our style betrays us, " and in the French naturalist, Louis de Buffon (1707-1788)—"The style is the man himself" (*Bartlett's Familiar Quotations*, 1951).

Although the notion of life style as an individual personality style seems to precede its use to denote a collective manner of living, it is the latter that became more familiar through the writings of the sociologists Max Weber (1947) and Talcott Parsons (1947). They both spoke of the life style of a collective group, such as a socioeconomic class. The term has also been used to describe those of an era such as the 60s in the United States or of a social group such as the changes in the life style of women during the sexual revolution of the same era. In psychology, the notion of collective life styles is known both through the work of Alfred Adler and of other writers such as David Shapiro (1965) who described life styles of various neurotic personalities.

While Adler often used the term in a collective sense (e.g., the life style of a pampered child), he was at pains to point out that the ***life style of any individual was a singular pattern of thinking, feeling, and acting that was unique to that individual and represented the context*** **(Zusammenhang)** ***in which all specific manifestations had to be considered.***

According to Ansbacher, Adler was probably influenced by Ludwig Klages (1906) who used the phrase "the personal guiding image." Adler used this term in 1912, as well as "guiding line" and "guiding idea" (1912/1927). Two years later, he spoke of "the line a person pursues" and "life plan" (1967). Eventually, in 1933 Adler settled upon the term "life style" (1964b) and defined it as "the unique law of movement" of an individual. The life style was seen by him as a unifying principle which organized all drives, strivings, tendencies, and aspirations into a unified pattern that could be apprehended by a trained observer.

This wide ranging concept is echoed by other modern writers who considered personality as a whole. Gordon Allport spoke of "the complex propriate organization that determines the 'total posture' of a mature life system" (1961, p. 237) and J.C. Coleman spoke of "the individual's pattern of assumptions [which] leads to consistent ways of perceiving, thinking and acting—to a characteristic ***modus operandi*** or life style" (1964, p. 63).

**Why Life Style Develops—
A Biological Overview**

Some animals are instinctually programmed to such an extent that little decision making is left to the organism itself. The more complete the programming, the less creative action is required. Higher vertebrates are incompletely programmed animals. Instinctual patterns do not provide a complete program to humans on how to cope with the multitude of stimuli and challenges posed by a human life. The human is rather equipped with an ability to program self through learning. Such an ability, which requires extended development of cognitive functions such as decision making, value setting, comparing, and concluding is most highly developed in those animals which have the greatest cognitive abilities.

Where rules for coping behavior are not provided by instincts, they must be developed by other means. Rules are generalizations which permit the application of learned material to coping behavior. Without rules, each situation would require trial and error behavior. Even the primitive pleasure principle of Freudian psychology is a rule for determining behavior. The life style is the "rule of rules" for the individual. It is the cognitive blueprint for behavior which is required when no instinctual blueprint exists. But the life style is not merely a collection of rules, it is the organization of all rules into a ***pattern*** which dominates not only the rules but all coping activity.

How It Develops

Equipped with inherited receptors, processors, organizers, and effectors; born into the human Umwelt with its particular perceptual world and its numerous possibilities for extension; even before its nervous system is mature enough to permit full locomotion, the infant's learning begins. The learning starts out by trial and error of the simplest variety as the infant tries to organize its world in order to cope with it. The small child locates, reorganizes, compares, contrasts, times, sizes, tests, retests, and otherwise applies methods of learning until it develops rules which permit it to relate to the world in a less chaotic way. It studies cause and effect, good and bad, pleasant and unpleasant, desirable and undesirable, until it is able to make primitive abstractions. These early rules continue to be developed and organized into an increasingly elaborate ***pattern*** which acts as an integrator for the rules.

> An example of such empirical growth of a pattern is found in the puzzle of Rubik's cube. As continued efforts are made to solve the puzzle, the moves that seem to promise success are learned more and more smoothly and the "whole" of the problem becomes more and more clear.

The early pattern is a rule of thumb. It is constantly reinforced as the child grows until the rule of thumb is elevated to the status of a law, the "unique law of movement." This law cannot help but be reinforced by experience because it influences the pattern of perception itself, as will be described later.

Because it is a unique personal law, it receives all of the person's loyalties, as do the other familiar objects of early childhood. Because it seems to permit better coping, it becomes as a private religion or personal myth. Because it is based upon a private logic (Dreikurs, 1973), it is not influenced by common sense when that sense conflicts with the private logic. Furthermore, it is the ***only*** set of rules for coping the person has.

Eventually the ***pattern*** becomes a dominant directive in the life of the individual, a cherished Holy Writ which propounds what is required by life and how it is best achieved.

Life Style as a "Cause" of Behavior

In most scientific discussion, the word cause is used in the sense of Aristotle's ***causa efficiens;*** namely, cause as the "source of change or rest." Adlerians have also used Aristotle's concept of ***causa finalis*** when they discuss the "goal directedness of behavior" and the "purpose of symptoms." This approach is frankly teleological and Dreikurs and Sonstegard even called Adlerians "teleoanalysts" (1968). The general concept of ***cause*** is a larger one, however, and the concept of causality itself leads us to speak of cause from more than one point of view (Allport, 1955).

One type of cause discussed by Aristotle is the ***causa formalis;*** namely, the ordering or patterning of relationships that leads to specific results. In this sense the life style is a "cause" of behavior. In what ways does it act as a determiner? It (1) is a limiter in the sense that any law limits, (2) gives direction to the line of movement, but (3) also provides a feedback which reinforces or inhibits the movement. Life style is not a determiner at only one point in time or at one point in a program. It is a continuing determiner at each point in time and with each step in the progression of an event. Its causal action is continuous. It constantly defines situations and gives instructions for responding to them.

Adlerian theory holds that one always has the ability to change the life style and thus transcend the limits. In this sense the life style as ***cause*** is a "soft determiner" rather than a rigid one and behavior is not inevitable but based upon a series of choices which delimits direction of movement. The life style is transcended through the educative experience of psychotherapy or sometimes through life experiences which lead to self-awareness and recognition of subjective truths, which we may call "conversion" experiences. (See for example the story of Jean Valjean and the candlesticks in Victor Hugo's novel, *Les Miserables.*)

Components of the Life Style

If we consider the life style a pattern, then perhaps we can recognize the recurrent themes in the life of each individual that can convey to us the essence of the individual pattern. Where, however, we examine a great many individual themes, we find that they cluster around a few main elements. This is not surprising. If the life style is intended as a basic adaptive pattern, then the main elements will deal with some of the basic issues in every human life. Because these basic issues are viewed through the subjective eye of the self, one can expect to find that the life style speaks about these issues in expressed or implied ***convictions*** about them. Indeed, one way of recognizing the components of the life style is to identify the convictions according to the kinds of issues with which they are concerned. These issues seem quite basic; the meaning of life, sentiments about human relationships, an evaluation of the self, and what life requires. The expressed convictions are reducible to platitudes. This is partly because a platitude is an effective if unsophisticated way of expressing a subjectively perceived truth and partly because these convictions are formed at a time of life when simple generalization is one of the few intellectual devices available to the person. In addition, the purpose of the life style is to simplify—that is, to provide easily apprehended rules for behavior and naturally, oversimplication is a common result. Indeed oversimplification, exaggeration of one aspect of life at the expense of others and mistaking a part for the whole are three main mistakes in logic that can be found in a study of life styles.

Those convictions which we identify as component parts of the life style can be divided into two groups: those about "what is"—that is, about nature of our individual selves and the "reality" we face; and those about the values and behaviors we will pursue in our efforts to master "what is."

Convictions About "What Is": Self and the World

Carl Rogers (1961) used the term ***phenomenal field*** to mean the person's total world of experience. Parts of the phenomenal field may be conscious or unconscious. The self-concept is a differentiated part of the field. Thus, ***self*** is experienced as located in the world and interacting with it. But ***self*** is a most complex concept and the personal experience of self ranges from acute awareness of certain aspects to barely perceived consciousness of other aspects and, sometimes, even to outright surprise at what we discover in ourselves.

After Allport (1955) and Shulman (1965), the self concept can be thought of as including a number of subsets: a bodily sense (what is me), an identity (***who*** am I), a self-image (what am I), a self-regard or self-esteem (what good am I), and a self-as-object notion (what effects me). Each of these subsets is represented in the life style and can therein be identified. The statement "I am a short, fat, balding male who is good to his mother and feels guilty if he neglects her" contains all these subsets.

The continuous interaction with the world leads to continuous self-evaluation. The experience of the world includes a comparable experience of the self as interacting. Of all the subsets, the self-esteem seems to be the most vulnerable to fluctuation in the continuing interaction and attempts to preserve self-esteem are easily observed in social interactions. Congruence between self-esteem and the other subsets (self-acceptance and self-respect) has been described as an important task of life (Dreikurs & Mosak, 1967).

The bodily sense (what is me) was described by Allport (1955) as an anchor for self-awareness. It includes beliefs about the integrity of the physical body and its basic adequacy. The self-identity (who am I) is the social and cosmic ***location*** each one preempts. "I am male (not female)"; "I am black (not white)"; "I am a vegetarian (not a meat eater)"; "I am a Democrat (not Republican)" are all ways of locating the self through reference points.

Self-image (what am I) is also concerned with identity but it is more of an evaluation than a location and has implications for self-esteem (what good am I). Thus, "I am not smart enough" is a self-image statement; "Therefore, my worth is diminished" is the self-esteem conclusion. Self-image refers to abilities and status, self-esteem is the evaluation of worth. Self-image also can include convictions about one's potential—such as, "If only I had been properly loved as a child I would have been able to accomplish something in life."

Self-as-object **(what affects me)** refers to the perceived consequences to the self of its various interactions with the world. One cannot judge effects on the self without taking the world into account. One may believe "If I eat too much, I will get fat," and this statement is about "what is me" and "what I can do to me." It recognizes that we are subject to influence by the actions of both ourselves and others.

Adler's theory is a field theory. The individual has subjective convictions not only about oneself but also about the world around one and about the relation between self and world. We have chosen to call this subjective picture of the world the ***world image*** or ***Weltbild.*** The world image is a set of convictions about all items (objects, processes and locations) outside of the subjective self, and to the whole concept of "outside" in general. With the "outside" is what we are generally coping. (Sometimes we have to cope with the self). Not all aspects of the "outside" are of equal importance; some can be safely ignored, others are seen as crucial to the self. Thus, for some people a flight of birds across the sky has no personal significance. For others, it is an omen.

The concept of ***Dasein*** (Being-in-the-world) has become familiar to us through the writings of the Existentialists, notably, Ludwig Binswanger (1963). ***Dasein*** is the important subject of study for Binswanger—the way in which the person experiences self in interaction with the world, but the world is a ***unique*** world for each individual, a construct designed by the individual's own unique apprehension of his/her existence. For heuristic purposes we have discussed the self as a separate entity and examined it from several aspects. The self-as-object clearly implies that an ambient world is the surround in which the self functions. This surrounding world, as it is experienced is itself a creative product of the perceptual program of the perceiver. The "design" or image of the world is to what the person responds.

This ***Weltbild,*** again for heuristic purposes, can be divided into a picture of ***life in general*** (the basic terms of existence) and a ***social world***—the world of living among people. This division grows out of our repeated finding, when we look at the material we use to formulate a life style, that our subjects form pictures of themselves as existing under a set of conditions (a mortal human being with limited capacities subject to the laws of nature);and also as one of a class of entities (human beings) in relationship with each other. Thus, when we formulate a life style, we will find ideas about life in general—such as, "Life is unpredictable" or surprising, predestined, chaotic, malevolent, or any one of many other adjectives.

Julian Rotter's concept of ***locus of control*** is an example of such an image of life in general and its effect on oneself. Locus of control is a cognitive style. People who experience themselves as having a great deal of control over what happens in the world around them have a different world image than those who believe they have little or no control (Rotter, 1966). The first group look to themselves to cope with the world. The second group look to others, to luck, to divinity, or to other outside forces to determine the order of events.

Image of the Social World—Human Interrelationships. Subjective beliefs about the nature of society and human interaction vary widely. To a certain extent these beliefs are influenced by the context of the culture (see for example the difference between the social outlook of Western capitalist democracies and Soviet communist societies). But the most important beliefs about human relationships are individual, idiosyncratic, and grow out of personal life experiences. Many of them exist outside conscious awareness. One may believe that other humans are friends or enemies, more or less powerful, approachable or not, hostile, rejecting, uncaring, confusing, unpredictable, and so forth. Their approval and/or love and/or attention may be seen as necessities. Sometimes all human relations are seen as untrustworthy; often the different sexes are assigned different qualities. One person may feel unable to influence others in any way or may see others as operating according to arbitrary whims. Another may believe that people can be successfully appeased if one is pleasing and avoids offending at all times.

Many of these convictions define values. Thus, to please others is a positive value to some. Conversely, to overpower others is a positive value to others.

Conclusions About Behavior

Our purpose is to explain the life style and we have tried to do so by logic and analogy, by example and metaphor. We have given it one definition as a patterned set of rules or laws. It is in the conclusions about behavior, as expressed in the life style, that one can perhaps see most clearly how it is a set of rules. We have called this aspect of the life style "conclusions" but they are, like the other aspects, apparent to us as "convictions." We call this one "conclusions" for another reason. It is because one way we have of describing the life style is to say that it seems to fit into a rubric: "I am . . ., Life is . . ., therefore . . ." The ***conclusions*** about behavior are the "therefores."

Proponents of "natural law" have been wont to say that animals follow two primary urges; the urge to self-preservation and the urge to preservation of the species. Adlerians would certainly agree that such urges exist but the life style is the final arbiter of what is important and these two supposedly immutable and primal urges often operate in distorted ways, or according to personal priorities, or varying from situation to situation.

Self-preservation often comes to mean preservation of one's "face" rather than preservation of life (Cf. ***hara-kari***—a form of self-immolation to preserve honor). Preservation of the species has usually been an ideal rather than a goal. The goal has more often been preservation of the group with which one most closely identifies (perhaps the family).

What each person considers significant in life is, like the world image, influenced by the cultural context; but it is also idiosyncratic. The life style contains a prototypic statement that fits the rubric we have described: "given what I am and what life is, this is important (necessary, desirable) in order for me to have a place in the world."

The Guiding Self-ideal. Adler first used the term ***guiding self-ideal*** in 1927/1912. His theory posits such a self-created ideal as the final goal of the behavioral program of the life style. It functions as a "point of orientation" for directing the "line of movement" of the individual person. The striving in this direction is ceaseless. This final goal is the self-chosen way of fulfilling the basic psychological motivations. However, sets of ideas almost always offer a ***moral judgment*** about life and for the self, namely, how life and the self "should" be. (This aspect of the life style can be compared to the ego-ideal and super-ego of psycho-analytic theory.) Thus, "I should never sin," "I should never act cowardly," "I should always be right" are idealized demands upon the self, while "People should always play fair," "God shouldn't have let it happen" and "They should stop persecuting me" are all idealized demands upon the environment.

Like other aspects of the life style, ideals are fictions created out of the subjective frame of reference. They are private and not necessarily conscious and often not subject to consensual validation. As we said earlier, they are guides to movement and causative in a teleological sense. In Adler's words:

> The goal of the mental life becomes its governing principle, its ***causa finalis.*** Here we have the root of the unity of the personality, of the individuality. It does not matter what the source of its energies may have been. Not their origin, but their ***end,*** their ultimate goal, constitutes their individual character. (Ansbacher & Ansbacher, 1956, p. 94)

Of course, the goal is adaptive and expansive. Furthermore, the goal can always be seen as a social goal; that is, it never is able to ignore the social field in which man lives.

Typical examples of dominant goals are, "I want to be first, to be on top." "I want others to protect me and run interference for me." "I want to never lose control." "I want to be the center." Being a point of orientation it is constantly operative. It acts as the nexus of the personality structure, leads to the "unity of personality" concept of Adlerian theory.

The influence of the final or dominant goal can be seen upon examining certain central themes in psychoneurotic patients in treatment (Mosak, 1968). Although neurotic symptoms often shift during the course of treatment (obsessive-compulsives may become openly aggressive) the final goal of the patient remains the same—to keep life under control in one case, to defeat others in the second case).

In almost every description of a life style one can find the selected ideals that the particular person will value above others in achieving a place for oneself. One person will value prestige above all else, a second will value money, a third will make "love" the first choice, a fourth will value safety above all.

Moral Judgments. One corollary of this point of view is that it considers basic ethical attitudes to be much more an individual psychological matter rather than a result of mass propaganda or social systems. Ideals judge what is or is not important, good and desirable.

A typical example of a life style can then be written in shorthand fashion according to the aforementioned rubric:

I am small and weak.
Life is dangerous.
Therefore others must protect me.

Adlerians have a penchant for describing life styles in a word or phrase and would say that this is the life style of a "weak baby." A different example is

I am the rightful heir to my father's power.
Life is here to appreciate me and serve me.
Therefore, I have to be the center of attention.

We might call this the life style of a "crown prince."

Methods (How To Do It). The rubric we have devised does not specifically include all aspects of the life style and is only a shorthand expression. One could easily add a statement about methods. Many techniques of behavior change during a person's life. One learns new techniques and discards old ones as one's understanding and experience grows. These methods are not what we mean here, but only those that consistently throughout the life history of the person are used as behavioral techniques for striving toward the dominant goal, analogous to what Allport (1961) called cardinal traits. Common methods can be clearly seen in those clinical syndromes we call the personality disorders. Thus, the schizoid personality uses a method we call "distance-keeping" (Adler, 1968/1920; Credner,

1935), the dependent personality uses being needy to get service from others and so forth. Each dominant goal may have one or more methods commonly found in association with it and similar methods may be found associated with dispare goals. Thus:

"I want to be first, to be on top."

Possible methods:
"I will impress every one with my power."
"I will be the best in everything."
"If I can't be the best, I'll be the worst."

Or: "I want others to protect me."

Possible methods:
"I will charm them into loving me."
"I will only associate with those who protect me."

Long-continued patterns of behavior are often "methods" in our sense. The short phrase names the Adlerians use for life styles often describe the method as much as the goal; e.g., "weak baby" and "crown prince" are ways of describing a set of attitudinal and behavioral responses to life. If we say one has the life style of a "victim," we are saying something about the method the individual uses to achieve the desired goals as well as trying to tell the "gist" of the individual's whole pattern in one analogical phrase.

TABLE 1.1
Elements of the Life Style

Convictions about "What is"	
Self-image	(What am I?)
World image	Life in general (How does it work?)
(Weltbild)	The social world (What is the relationship between myself and others?)
Convictions about "What should be"	
(Ethical values)	
The Ideal World	(How should life be?)
Moral Judgements	(What is good and proper behavior?)
Instructions for behavior	
Dominant goal/self ideal	(What shall I pursue?) (What must I become?)
Methods	(How shall I do it?)

INFLUENCES ON THE LIFE STYLE

A developing set of concepts can be subject to many influences, more during its early plastic stages than its later rigid ones. If one could map the whole developmental history of a life style one would see at work the effects of body constitution, culture, and perhaps pure chance as well. Several of these influences deserve more extensive mention.

Ecological Factors

One may think that the very act of being human would limit the variety of life styles one would find among humans. A natural assumption is that humans would not have life styles suitable for dogs or horses. On further thought maybe biological explanations exist for the wide variety among life styles. Just as "nature" devises animals and plants to fit all but the most extreme situations, so a tendency exists for the range of life styles to expand to fit all of the available social living spaces (or social roles). The effect of the available social roles upon the developing life style will be seen more clearly in the discussion of the family constellation.

Constitutional Factors

Genetic Factors. Whether or not direct genetic influences have an effect upon the life style has not yet been conclusively answered, but no certain genetic effects appear in the life styles we have found. For the present, our answer must be that the life stlye is behavior of an order that cannot yet be measured directly for genetic factor influence.

Constitution. By the same token, the effects on life style of endocrine glands, the central nervous system, and the pituitary-hypothalamic axis cannot be directly measured except in the case of obvious physical or mental defect. Unless a child is severely feeble-minded, he/she will develop a life-style if only life is long enough. Otherwise, intelligence, whether one views it as inherited or acquired, seems to be a factor in influencing the life style since intelligence is a tool for coping behavior and the ability to cope is influenced by the tools one uses.

Constitution also influences in the following way: A very pretty girl will receive different reactions from her environment than a plain one. A muscular, athletic child will find certain opportunities that are closed to less adept counterparts. Also, the quick-witted child will see alternatives the duller child misses and is likely to win more approval from adults. But in all these factors, the response of the social situation to the constitutional "given" determines how much the constitutional trait will influence the life style; that is, how it is used in the interaction with life.

Physical defects can influence the development of the life style, depending upon the child's subjective response. That which is perceived as an inferiority functions as if it was a defect. If the child is born with a defect, acquires one during development, or imagines that he/she has one, this becomes a "given" in one's life to which the person must make some answer. Thus, Shakespeare has the hunchbacked Richard III say, "Since I cannot be a lover, I'll prove a villain." As always, the answer the person makes is his/her own creation (A. Adler, 1936).

Developmental Sequences

Adlerian psychology recognizes that critical periods occur in development. Certain human skills require practice from an early age or they cannot be learned well. Early experiences thus influence the life style. Adlerian theory holds that these early experiences are integrated by different individuals in different ways; two children can respond in different ways to the same experience. As with cultural and familial influences, the meaning one gives to a life experience can be idiosyncratic.

For purposes of understanding the adult life style, the point in development at which an experience occurred is considered less important than the late effects of the experience; namely, the way the experience was perceived and processed to fit with the growing development of the life style program. For all practical purposes, the life style prototype seems reasonably well formed by age five. Thus, experiences from before that age are in general probably more important than later ones in influencing the final life style.

Cultural Factors

Culture is seen by Adlerians as both a limiter and expander of the psychic life. Culture provides certain basic ways of looking at the world and therefore encourages certain tendencies in the development of life style. A culture which stresses individual enterprise and accomplishment will encourage different behavior from one which stresses conformity to tradition. Moreover, the values assigned to sex, age, socioeconomic status, skin color, place of birth, and so forth will all be influenced by the culture and will influence the growing child's picture of the world around self and his/her role in it. Culture therefore provides values for the growing child to use in evaluating the world and a frame of reference for ideals and goals.

Family Influences—
The Family Constellation

Each child is born into a certain family situation—an ordinal position in the family, who and what are the other family members, and what the values and atmosphere of the family are. During the course of life this specific condition may change; other siblings may be born, parents may die, crippling illness may come, and family fortunes may change. The parents may be permissive, strict, overprotective, rejecting, demanding, pampering, or inconsistent. They are, nevertheless, models who present guiding lines for the child. The family atmosphere may be oppressive or free, harmonious or full of conflict, warm and close or cold and distant, clear and simple or confusing and contradictory. Family standards may demand high performance and family myths may promise severe punishment for the child who fails to live up to expectations.

Each child responds to the situation according to subjective perceptions of it. The environment in turn responds to the activity of the child, feeding back data that the person uses to further refine his/her rules of operation. The pattern of interaction is what the Adlerian calls a "family constellation": a grouping of members playing various social roles in relation to each other. Family constellation is considered an important influence on the developing life style, but at the same time, the investigation of the family constellation is an important technique the Adlerian uses to diagnose the life style.

The main elements of the family constellation for Adlerians include sibling constellation, parent models, family values, and family atmosphere. They will be discussed at length in the next chapter.

FUNCTIONS OF THE LIFE STYLE

We have already described the life style as the cognitive blueprint, the "rule of rules" and the "unique law of movement" for each individual. We have discussed the life style as the "formal cause" of behavior, as a governor and feedback. However, we can define with more precision the functions of the life style as we see them in operation in each person.

Organizing and Simplifying Function

As previously stated, the life style provides a set of rules by which values can be assigned, a hierarchy can be established, priorities determined. Thus, it lends an overall organization to psychic activity.

Selecting Function

Actually, selecting occurs in a seven-fold function.

1. **Direction-setting.** The life style is the line of movement as the person goes through life. This line of movement can be deduced from a historical inquiry into the person's life or other observations, but the best description of the movement can be found in the life style formulation that we present in this book. Thus, the person who must avoid failure may avoid all those situations in which he/she has no guarantee of success. The ideals of the life style become beacons for the line of movement.

2. **Selective Perceiving.** Events are perceived according to the life style, and the person behaves according to these perceptions. If the life style states that others are hostile

to the person, then the individual will perceive hostility in situations where others will not.

3. **Guiding Action.** If I see myself as weak and impotent, I may most likely find myself unable to act effectively in many situations. Instead, I may be passive and/or turn to others for help. Even if I see opportunities for aggressive action, I may not take such action because I will not expect to succeed.

4. **Predicting and Anticipating.** Expectancy is in line with the life style, to the extent that it is a personality rather than a situational variable. This aspect of selection leads to the creation of self-fulfilling prophecies.

5. **Radar Function.** The life style not only permits predicting and anticipating events, it also keeps a watchful eye out for special situations. If the life style says that one will be humiliated because of one's impotence, then signals of humiliation and impotence can be watched for on a constant alert—an early warning radar system which gives ample notice. Conversely, in human relations if we meet another person who will fit into our desired ***schema*** and permit us to play the role we wish, our ability to recognize such a person is part of the radar function. When the right person comes into our sight, the alert sounds and we can begin carrying out the wished for role.

6. **Decision-making Function.** Many daily decisions are made on the basis of common sense. Where, however, common sense runs counter to the private logic of the life style, the latter prevails. Furthermore, some decisions are often not made according to common sense because sufficient data is lacking. Common examples are decisions which will have unknown consequences in an uncertain future; namely, decisions which are a gamble. Deciding to take a risk in an uncertain situation depends partly on expectancy, a cognitive variable which is influenced by the life style.

7. **Archeological Function.** This function permits us to use the earliest childhood recollections as a diagnostic device to determine the life style. Memory is selective in line with the life style and thus memories from early life are retrospectively reconstructed. The individual finds in memory historical explanations for one's own outlook.

Problem-solving Function

In a broad sense, the life style is a set of directions for the general problem of coping, of adaptation. Life can be viewed as a succession of problems to be solved. For each person, the life style sets the guidelines for problem solving.

Control of Experience

The selective perception of the life style permits an additional special kind of problem solving; namely, coping with the problem of evaluating and classifying experience. An event can become traumatic because it is so designated by the life style, since, current and past experience are perceived according to it. Moreover if the line of movement requires one to have a certain type of experience, one will arrange it. Thus, the distrustful person arranges to be betrayed and the pessimist arranges to fail in his/her endeavors.

Myth-making Function

The life style is a myth and makes myths. The self-image and world image are fictions through which the person tries to organize an understanding of the "truths" of the world. The use of such fictions to organize and apprehend experience and select responses has been discussed at length (Kelly, 1955; Vaihinger, 1965).

Reinforcing Function

The life style guides the person toward having those experiences which tend to reinforce the style itself. If the life style says "Life is dangerous," the selectivity of the life style will lead the person to experiences that reinforce this view. Thus, the life style tends to become more fixed with advancing age as it is constantly reinforced by usage.

Self-protecting Function

When events occur that would seem, objectively, to call into question the life style itself, selective perception again intervenes to filter out, reconstruct, or reinterpret the events so that they do not threaten the cherished set of rules. One cannot give up the set of rules one has until one has an alternative that is equally trustworthy. The process of reorientation in psychotherapy is largely a matter of replacing old convictions with better ones.

This self-protecting function also has been described by Sullivan (1956) who postulates the existence of a ***self system*** which functions through selective inattention to experience to filter out unwelcome information. For Sullivan, the self system is a dynamism which manages anxiety and preserves personal security by focusing awareness on what seems relevant and filtering out the irrelevant. A similar point of view has been presented by Festinger (1957) and Aronson (1972) in their discussions of ***cognitive dissonance*** as a discrepant state which motivates behavior to restore cognitive balance. In effect, when an event occurs which does not meet one's expectations, cognitive dissonance results. Aronson pointed out that all other things being equal, the balance is restored in some direction which preserves self-esteem.

Self-related Functions

Some life style functions are related to the self-concept and ideals which we have described as component part of the life style.

1. **Self-defining Function.** The life style serves to identify and define the self, its characteristics and its boundaries.

2. **Self-viewing and Judging Function.** One perceives and evaluates oneself according to one's life style. Satisfaction or dissatisfaction with the self is an evaluation dependent upon the values in the life style.

DISTORTED PERCEPTIONS IN THE LIFE STYLE (BASIC MISTAKES)

We have already said that oversimplification, exaggeration and mistaking the part for the whole are common mistakes in logic found in life styles. These distortions have been called ***basic mistakes*** by Dreikurs (1953). Mosak (1984) classified basic mistakes as follows:

Overgeneralizations.
  "People are hostile."
  "Life is dangerous."

False or impossible goals of "security."
  "One false step and you're dead."
  "I have to please everybody."

Misperceptions of life and of life's demands.
  "Life never gives me any breaks."
  "Life is so hard."

Minimization or denial of one's worth.
  "I'm stupid."
  "I'm undeserving."
  "I'm just a housewife."

Faulty values.
  "Be first even if you have to climb over others."

By what right do we presume to judge that a person has a mistaken style of life? Are we expressing our own biases when we make such judgments? Can we define a set of standards which are reasonably and commonly accepted by which we can judge a life style to be mistaken? It seems to us that these standards have already been suggested by Karen Horney (1966) in her formulation of ***overdriven attitudes.*** She has described these attitudes as the identifying characteristics of "neurotic claims." An overdriven attitude can be recognized because it is:

irrational	inappropriate	egocentric
insatiable	intolerant	vindictive
impossible	wanted without effort	compulsive

These are typical characteristics of what we have called basic mistakes. They are all misperceptions, inappropriate expectations, wrong meanings assigned to life situations, misplaced priorities and in addition lead to difficulties in living or defensively distorted approaches to life. In addition they are fueled by affective components which intensify them in the face of common sense.

Dreikurs (1957b) described basic mistakes as faulty social values related to contemporary standards, norms, and social prescriptions for behavior. Among them he included a desire for self elevation, perfectionism, a fear of making mistakes, concern with personal success, and overvaluation of reason with simultaneous devaluation of inner feelings. Thus, for Dreikurs, basic mistakes also grew out of contemporary social values which were inimical to healthy development.

The basic mistakes are usually outside of awareness. They often were more appropriate to the childhood situation than the current one. But the most obvious indicator of the basic mistake is probably the assessor's evaluation, "If one did not misinterpret life at such and such a point, one would not have this neurotic problem." Consequently, the defining of a basic mistake remains largely a matter of selection by the assessor. To overcome this difficulty, we are in the habit of using two diagnosticians rather than one to determine both life style and basic mistakes. (Two heads are more consensual than one.)

Basic mistakes can also be compared to Albert Ellis's (1962) ***irrational ideas.*** These are unconscious value assumptions about what is right, proper, and necessary in our lives. They stem from our cultural milieu, are learned early in life, and influence our expectations and goal behavior. They become subject to question only in psychotherapy or in moments of marked cognitive dissonance. Similar hypotheses also have been proposed by A.T. Beck (1976) who found faulty thinking exerting a causative influence in emotional disorders.

The mistakes themselves can be categorized further. Under each heading, we have listed some common examples:

1. **Distorted attitudes about the self** (inappropriate self-evaluations).

I am less capable than others.
An evil spirit resides in me.
I cannot face any unpleasantness.
I am someone special and unique.
I am entitled to my own way.
I am unlovable, undesirable, and unworthy.
I am an innocent victim.

2. **Distorted attitudes about the world and people.**

Life is completely unpredictable.
Life is a jungle (dog eat dog).
People are no damn good. (Men are only out for one thing. Women are too hard to please.)
Life penalizes any mistake.
Life is too confusing.
Life offers me no opportunity (doesn't give me a chance).
Life makes too many demands.
Life is unfair.

3. **Distorted goals.**

I must be without flaw (perfect).
Everyone must love me.
I must be a "good guy."
I must find perfect security.
I must never submit.
I will have my revenge on life.
I must always be in control.

4. **Distorted methods of operation.**

Finding fault in order to elevate oneself and/or keep distance.
Excessive dependency. ("Others must take care of me.")
Excessive competitiveness. ("Winning is the only thing that counts.")
Relating to others in exploiting and manipulating ways.
Distance keeping from others and life's requirements.
Antinomianism (self-deification).
Rebelling against all authority.
Making mountains out of molehills.

Putting all one's eggs in one basket.
Excessive self-indulgence.
Excessive self-control and caution. ("Nothing ventured, nothing lost.")
Distorting logic to make it compatible with one's own wishes.
Ignoring what one does not wish to confront.
Provoking life and others in order to feel justified.
Focusing only on what is wrong.

5. **Distorted ideals.**

"A 'real' man is aggressive, fearless, heroic and never defeated."
"A 'real' woman commands an entourage of men and receives gifts daily."
"The world will only be right when everyone's wishes are completely satisfied."
"I want a love deeper than the world has known before."
"Any transgression should be severely punished."
"The only thing worth being is a 'star' (or genius)."

Clinical Uses of the Life Style

We make a large claim when we say that when we understand the life style, we understand the person. Our formulation, after all, is a description of a ***leitmotif,*** a theme which runs through the person's life and lends unity to the personality by giving it a style. Any life style works itself out in various ways in different life situations and the longer we know a person, the more subsets of the guiding line of movement become apparent to us. Knowing the life style, then, is not only useful in an original assessment of the person, but it allows a continuing reference point for those who work with people over a period of time—psychotherapists, counselors, teachers, and others.

Life Style in Diagnosis

The life style provides an overview of personality in several dimensions: The concept of the self, the view of the world, the basic motivations, and the usual methods of operation.

Past events and current problems can be understood in terms of the life style. Even symptom behavior can be understood in terms of the private logic of a person who is acting according to his/her own beliefs and anticipations.

The life style can be used to predict future behaviors. It is not able to predict specific events but permits us to extrapolate future probabilities along those parameters that are issues in terms of the life style. A person with the life style of a "weak baby" will behave accordingly, even in the relationship to a therapist.

Life Style in Treatment

Part of treatment consists of revealing the life style to the patient. One discusses it with the individual, explains factors that led to it, describes the effect it would have on behavior, shows how it leads to difficulties, and exposes its internal logical and consistency.

The life style becomes a reference point for therapy. It presumes to show what is mistaken and what needs change. Interpretations of current and past behavior are made in terms of the life style and the memory of the past as well as future expectations are shown to be affected by the selective bias of the life style.

Mosak (1965) has pointed out that knowing the life style gives certain specific advantages to the therapist. It allows the latter to predict how the patient will behave in the therapeutic situation, to plan appropriate strategy, to predict the material the patient will bring to therapy, and to keep the pertinent issues in mind.

We consider change in personality structure to be a change in the life style. Thus, life style become not only a reference point, but also a focal point for any psychotherapy in which personality restructure is a goal.

The life style can be used as a tool to assess the amount of personality change from therapy. This can be determined by examining changes in the early recollections. It is a characteristic and repeated finding that the earliest childhood recollections change during successful psychotherapy, just as other perceptions of the past change.

Thus, the life style determination is a valuable aid to research about change in psychotherapy, as well as a tool which can be used to routinely check the progress of change in psychotherapy (Baruth & Eckstein, 1981; Eckstein, 1976; Mosak, 1979).

SUMMARY

The life style is a superordinate organizational pattern which directs behavior. It operates by means of selective perception, cognition, memory, and so on. It codifies rules for characteristic attitudinal positions. It becomes the intervening variable between efficient cause and effect, between the stimulation of the outside world and the responsive behavior of the person. It is formed in early childhood and is self-reinforcing through selectivity. It is self-consistent, coherent, and unified. It is constant; it does not change from time to time or situation to situation, though it is not necessarily rigid. It can be recognized by its repeated appearance as a theme in the life history or even everyday behavior of an individual. It develops through trial and error and is influenced by physical, developmental, cultural, and familial factors. It is a necessary rule for coping behavior, to bring order into one's relationship with the challenging and confronting world. It is therefore of critical significance to the clinician who wishes to understand the "whys?" of human behavior.

CHAPTER **2**

ELEMENTS OF THE FAMILY CONSTELLATION (FC)

According to Bottome (1939) and Gardner Murphy (1947), family constellation theory is one of Adler's main contributions to psychology. Adler first used the term in a 1937 paper in which he discussed the influence of family constellation on life style (Adler, 1937). In this paper, Adler discussed mainly the vicissitudes of birth order. In other writings Adler also discussed the importance of the relationship between the parents and children, how parents model behavior and the effect of certain parental behaviors such as pampering and rejection (Adler, 1958). Adler's pupils elaborated the concept. Reiss (1949) discussed the importance of family atmosphere and the mutual relationships between the parents. Friedmann (1930) described family systems which have their own dynamics and values. Finally, Dreikurs (1957a) described parental "guiding lines" and stated,

> The relationship between father and mother establishes the pattern for all interpersonal relationships in the family. If they are competitive with each other, the spirit of competition will characterize all the family relationships .... Whether parents are orderly or disorganized, cooperative or antagonistic, the family atmosphere will present its characterisitic pattern to the children as a standard of life. (1957a, p. 9)

Our own view of family constellation (FC) descends from that of Dreikurs, from what we saw him do as well as what he wrote. Among his writings he discussed the situation and tasks of each parent and grandparent, their own anxieties, expectancies, and demands they made on each other and on their children. He further described how parents model for children their own maladjustments and their cultural and psychological backgrounds which influence their child rearing methods. He also discussed the effect of rapid social change upon traditional family processes (Dreikurs, 1948).

Dreikurs' approach was to "normal" families. The misbehavior of children in such a family was a response to the behavior of the people around them. The behavior of both child and parents constituted a dyadic or triadic interpersonal event which occurred in the context of the family. Examination of the family constellation allowed Dreikurs to understand the parent child interaction and often to predict what interrelationship problems would exist in the family (Dreikurs, 1949, 1959). He also devised the first extensive questionnaire for the family constellation to be used with adults (Dreikurs, 1954) and the inventory we use (Mosak & Shulman, 1971) grows directly out of his work.

Descriptions of family constellation inventories can also be found in Eckstein, Baruth, and Mahrer (1978); Dinkmeyer, Pew, and Dinkmeyer (1979); Allen (1971); Shulman (1962); and Shulman and Nikelly (1971).

No discussion of family constellation is complete without the inclusion of the work of Toman (1969). Toman studied over 3,000 families with data collected by coworkers and assistants. He focused on birth order of parents and siblings alike and thus developed a two generation constellation. In addition, he examined the interaction of gender and birth order. Toman's findings will be examined in more detail later. First we will look at the actual elements we use to build the family constellation.

Dreikurs described the family constellation as a sociogram of the group at home during the formative years which

> reveals the field of early experiences, the circumstances under which there developed personal perspectives and biases, concepts and convictions . . . fundamental attitudes and approaches to life which are the basis for...personality. (Dreikurs, 1967, p. 137).

While the life style may be determined from any consistent pattern of behavior or may be deduced even from brief descriptions or briefly observed behavior, the most reliable method of determining the life style is from an analysis of the family constellation and the earliest childhood recollections. Family constellation is an inclusive term which contains several important elements, all a part of the child's early experiences. A complete description of the family constellation will include most of the important features found in a complete childhood history with two added features: (1) the FC includes considerable information about parents and siblings and (2) the FC investigation stresses those aspects of the childhood history which disclose the family dynamics faced by the child and its characteristic direction of movement in response. This direction of movement follows a fundamental law: the child trains itself in those qualities by which it hopes to achieve significance in the family structure (Dreikurs, 1953, p. 41).

The main elements of the family constellation are sibling constellation, family values, family atmosphere, parental behavior, and the family role played by each child.

SIBLING CONSTELLATION

Competition

According to Adler (1969a), Dreikurs (1953), and Ferguson (1958), the wish to belong and to be accepted is a basic goal of human behavior. Bowlby (1969) called the motive of this behavior ***attachment.*** The search for a place or significant status in the group has been identified by Forgus and Shulman (1979) as a differentiation of the attachment motive, although other motives such as competence and security also are served by status within the group. Animal groups that have a social hierarchy or dominance rank order show a striving for dominance or status (Lorenz, 1952; Ferguson, 1976). Human groups show this same striving. Competition among family members is understood in this sense by Adlerians; it is a striving for perceived available places in the group against those who are perceived as competitors for these places.

Open fighting between children is not necessarily a sign of real sibling rivalry. Two children may fight with each other for other reasons; such as, to win parental attention, to express anger at the parents in indirect ways, or to fulfill role enactments ("boys are expected to fight"). Competition which represents the struggle for a significant place in the family is more often shown by differences between siblings in behavioral paths, traits, and interests.

An important effect of competition is not only that siblings will develop diverse interests and traits, but also that the success of a sibling in one area may have a discouraging effect upon the competitor. One child may misbehave ***just because*** the sibling is so successful in winning parental approval through obedience. If one is an excellent student, the competitor, rather than take second place, may decide not even to try to perform well in school. The fact of competition results in a diversity of behaviors within the family—a Darwinian variation/selection process in which the child selects what seems to be the most useful variation.

Birth Order

Personality Characteristics and Birth Order. Adler's classic description of the effects of birth order contains the following features: (1) Children of the same family are not born into the same environment. The second child is born into a different psychological situation than the first. (2) It is not the actual order of birth, but the psychological situation which is important. If the eldest is feeble-minded, the second may assume the role of a first-born. (3) Marked difference in age between siblings tends to reduce competition between them. (4) Birth order is not an absolute determinant, only an influence (Adler, 1964 a., pp. 96-120).

Ordinal position refers to the actual order in which the child was born; i.e., first, second, third...tenth, eleventh, and so on. ***Birth order*** refers to five positions that Adler described which tend to have recognizable characteristics later on in life. These are the ***first-born, second, middle, youngest,*** and ***only.*** In our discussion of these positions, it is important to remember that ***psychological*** position is the important determinant (Shulman & Mosak, 1977). One child may be an only child for several years and may then find a change to the position of a first-born. The first may be overrun by the younger sibling who then becomes, in some respect, like a first born. The oldest may then function like a second born. By reason of physical illness or frailty, an older child may actually function like a youngest.

Each of these five basic positions tends to have certain characteristics related to the unique early experiences of each position. No position is better than another. Each has its advantages and disadvantages. Each has its tasks and the adult traits reflect how these tasks were answered in childhood. The most frequent characteristics of each ordinal position in normal family structure are as follows:

> ***Only Child.*** The only child never had a rival. Peers tend to be curiosities rather than competitors. However, the only child may have been pampered and never learned to share. The only child may share some features with the first born, or obversely, with the youngest.
>
> ***First-born.*** The first-born once had it all to himself/herself and would still prefer to be the first and foremost. He/she tends to feel entitled to rank and is often achievement oriented.
>
> ***Second Child.*** The second child started late and has to catch up. Someone always seems ahead of him/her, a standard bearer against whom one measures oneself.
>
> ***Middle Child.*** The middle child has a standard bearer in front and a pursuer in the rear. Surrounded by competitors, the middle child may feel squeezed into a small area in search for significance.
>
> ***Youngest Child.*** The trail is well broken for the youngest and the guidelines are clear. The youngest is never dethroned. On the other hand, he/she has much ground to cover in order to catch up.

Certain adult traits can often be found in these birth order positions. The first born is often "a great believer in power and the laws" (Adler, 1964a, p. 102). He/she tends to be conservative toward change, perhaps somewhat elitist in views. The second child is a "runner," looking for some area of success, more revolutionary in outlook, more willing to follow another's lead. The middle child tends to be sensitive to mistreatment or unfairness. The middle child is afraid of missing out on its share. The youngest, who often sets out to catch up to the others, will be very ambitious. If one has decided not to pursue, one continues in a dependent role. The only child is usually congenial and charming and has social behavior intended to please rather than to out do.

Characteristic variations also are depending upon whether the child experiences self as "successful" or not. A "failed" first born tends to give up completely. A second child, who does not feel able to catch up to the pacemaker, switches to an area of endeavor which does not compete with the eldest. A failed middle child is embittered because of being squeezed out of significance. Life is unfair. The failed youngest remains baby-like—assuming dependent and helpless roles. The failed only child is like the failed baby. Other factors making for variation including age difference, family size, and gender will be discussed shortly.

All of these so-called characteristics are probabilities only. Each case is an individual matter and may differ more or less from the mean.

Toman (1969) had something to say about each of these birth order positions and differentiates them further. Thus, a first born male with younger brothers is described by Toman as

> ... the leader, the master of other men, whether he shows it by force or cunning... He is on good terms with other males, especially when they are not older brothers themselves... He tends to be a good worker when he chooses. (1969, p. 24)

On the other hand, the oldest brother of sisters is

> ... a friend of the girls and ladies, whether sincerely or with tongue in cheek. Love of the tender sex is the most important of all concerns... He may be a good worker as long as there are female colleagues or co-workers ... (1969, p. 44)

Toman described many more traits than these for each of the eleven sibling positions he discussed. These positions are

oldest brother of brother(s)
youngest brother of brother(s)
oldest brother of sister(s)
youngest brother of sister(s)
oldest sister of sister(s)
twins
younger sister of sister(s)
oldest sister of brother(s)
youngest sister of brother(s)
intermediary sibling positions
only child

Toman warned that he was describing broad generalities and that each individual case will have it unique characteristics; e.g., siblings form subgroups, age differences may be so large that sibling relationships were not competitive, or special events may have had an important influence. Nevertheless, he believed he could predict personality traits from birth order. A reading of the Toman book will be rewarding to anyone interested in birth order factors and many of his readers will recognize themselves in his descriptions.

Forer (1976) offered views similar to Toman and, in addition, has studied birth order effects in her own clinical practice, on choice of a vocation, on sociality, choice of mate, and sexual behavior.

Social Role

Social role theory offers another useful way of viewing these birth order positions. Role is an ***"organized set of behaviors that belong to an identifiable position in the social structure and these behaviors are activated when the role is occupied"*** (Sarbin & Allen, 1968, p. 54). The psychological position of the child is its role ***location***—the way the child locates itself in the family structure. Each role carries with it a set of ***expectations*** about behavior and a set of ***demands*** for ***enactment*** of the role. How well the child enacts the role (***role skills***) and how satisfied it is with the role (***self-role***

congruence) become important in influencing the relationship between birth order and adult traits.

Factors Which Influence Birth Order and Sibling Constellation

Age Difference. Competition between siblings is most keen when they are close in age and diminishes with age difference. As a rule of thumb, children who are seven or more years apart are not in competition with each other. In a two-child family with such an age difference between them, each child will tend to function more as an only child. Much older siblings may play parental roles for the younger child.

Family Size. The rule that only five basic birth order positions exist holds true for large families as well. The family perceptions tend to classify large groups of children into older and younger groups. Thus, the third child may actually function as the first born of the second group. The technique of eliciting the family constellation will show how large families can be sorted into groups. Age difference and gender are the two most important sorting factors in normal families.

Extra-familial Competitors. In some families, children from outside the immediate family may play the role of competitors. A cousin or younger sibling of a parent may live in the house or close by and may be a competitor for the favor of one of the parenting figures. Family rearrangements, as in divorce and remarriage, may throw together children who now begin to compete. Each case is individual.

Gender Difference. In some families, the division of role demands is so complete that siblings of different sex have little need to compete with each other. The oldest girl may have her place as a first born and the oldest of the boys also may function as a first born. Each has a different role and can receive positive reinforcement from the parents for this distinction. In families where an only girl is among a group of boys, or ***vice versa,*** the position of the "one and only" is usually unique; he/she is valued for himself/herself because he/she is the only one of a kind and need not compete with siblings for a place. As Toman (1969) pointed out, relationships with sibling of the opposite sex influences the choice of a mate later in life. An older brother with younger sisters will tend to be more protective and more dominant with females later than will a younger brother with older sisters.

Death and Survivorship. A child that has lived long enough to become a significant sibling in the family and then dies, does not usually disappear from the sibling constellation. More commonly, such a child is idealized and remains an ever present standard of comparison. Because idealization elevates the status of the dead child, the surviving sibling often feels inferior by comparison. The dead child may become woven into family myths and thus affect family values and family atmosphere. The survivor may experience a ***role demand*** to somehow compensate for the death of the sibling.

> One man recalled that his older brother had been the favorite child, a good student, obedient and musically talented. The brother died of an acute illness. A relative said to him, "Now, you'll have to be a good son to your parent." His feeling was, "I'll never be able to do all those things my brother did and now I'll always be a disappointment to my parents."

Special Siblings. Various factors may create a special role for a sibling. Mental retardation, brain damage, physical defect, and prolonged illness are examples of factors which lead to a special role, requiring more attention and concern from parents. The well sibling ordinarily does not feel threatened by the sick one in these circumstances, but may feel somewhat left out when parental attention is focused on the special sibling.

Another special role occurs when a sibling is unusually talented and therefore valuable to the family for that trait alone. Special siblings do not have to compete for place; their status is assured.

We have previously mentioned that a cousin or a younger aunt or uncle who lives close by can become competitors. Family myths provide other special roles for children—the posthumous child, the first child born after several miscarriages, the child named after a dead family member, the child born out of wedlock, the child born with a caul, the child whose mother died at birth—may all receive special treatment from family members.

Favoritism. Being the favorite of a parent sometimes creates a special position. Sigmund Freud said about favoritism, "A man who has been the indisputable favorite of his mother keeps for life the feeling of a conqueror, that confidence of success that often induces real success" (Freud, 1940-1952, *Vol. 12*, p. 26). On the other hand, favoritism may weigh heavily upon the child if the parental demands are more intense for the favorite than for the others. Thus, the favorite may feel more liked or, conversely, more obligated.

Roles Available

In Chapter 1, we introduced the concept of the family as an ecological unit in which family members occupied available spaces, divided territories, and so were able to live with each other in one space yet pursue their individual goals. One small patch of prairie can hold many different species of animals provided they do not intrude upon each other too much and provide some benefits to each other. The same is true of the family, where the values and atmosphere define the available ecological niches. A family may have room for one good student, one helpful domestic child, one black-sheep child, and so on. If a second child tries to fulfill the same niche as the first born, the second child intrudes upon a sibling's territory and territorial conflict ensues which all too often does not satisfy anyone. The role of "black sheep" can be a most satisfying family role for the child who enacts it. It is a dramatic attention-getter; a way of being impressive and important in the family. The choice of this role usually means that the child is ambitious to impress and demonstrate power, and has discovered that misbehavior (and perhaps retaliation) are suitable for this purpose. Some roles are available to more than one sibling. For example, for a family to have more than one black sheep is usually possible. At other times, however, one sibling may so outshine the others in some way that the others give up and do not compete in this area at all. Some roles are more available to one sex than the other. In a family that believes "boys will be boys," mischievous behavior in a boy may be more reinforced by the parents than such behavior in a girl. On the other hand, verbal complaining and tears may be tolerated more in a girl, depending upon the values of the parents.

Thus are available roles determined and constructed; and they are perhaps the most impressive example of the creativity of the child as he/she builds his/her life.

Research on Birth Order

Early research on birth order often failed because researchers made no allowance at all for actual birth order or psychological position. Later, more sophisticated research showed some general support for Adler's theories, but even in these studies, ordinal position rather than actual birth order is treated as the variable. In one study Hilton showed that first borns are more likely to seek approval and help from their mothers and the latter are more likely to offer it (Hilton, 1967). Nisbet (1968) found that first borns are less likely to participate in dangerous sports. A study of psychiatric problems in a boot camp showed that only children were more likely than first borns to consult the psychiatrist, to be diagnosed as psychoneurotic, and to be discharged from service. Diagnoses of first borns was almost equally divided between psychoneurosis and personality disorder (Taintor, 1970). Harris's (1964) study comparing first borns and later children showed that the former have a different cognitive style from the latter. Another study (Hall & Barger, 1964) showed that in two child families (both being males), first borns tended to be conservative and interested in administrative and supervisory tasks. Younger siblings were more flexible and somewhat more gregarious. The subject population consisted of college students from intact Protestant families and is therefore a limited sample.

Altus (1966) treated birth order and ordinal position as if they were the same thing in his study. Since the two categories often are identical, especially in small families with first born sons, no surprise comes when studies on first born sons often corroborate Adler's theory. Another example of this type of research is the study by Herrell (1972). He hypothesized that first borns, because they have the right attitude for positions of power, should be over-represented among military leaders, should tolerate the military structure better than later borns (being less rebellious), and, if unhappy in subordinate roles, would be over-represented among those diagnosed as neurotic in military mental hygiene clinics. Herrell found support for these hypotheses.

Effective research on birth order will have to take into account many more variables: the actual ordinal position, the psychological position, gender of the children and parental response to them.

One study has taken into account at least one factor in addition to birth order (Mendelsohn et al., 1974). Heterosexual pairing among siblings was studied for its effects on adult heterosexual behavior. These authors found that the closer the heterosexual dyad duplicated the sibling experience of the dyad, the more likely the dyad was to be successful (an observation noted earlier by Toman, 1962).

Toman's (1969) study, as mentioned earlier, is the most extensive one on birth order and it does take the previously mentioned factors of psychological position, gender, and parental response into account. In addition, Toman recognized that large sibling groups became divided into older and younger, that age differences of over six years create a break between groups, and that loss of a parent in early life significantly influences the whole process. A study by Croake and Olson (1977) offered some evidence that both Adler's and Toman's theories have validity as determinants of personality patterns. Using the MMPI, these researchers found significant differences on various scales between all given birth order positions. They examined fifteen different combinations of brothers and sisters and found some verification for Toman's claims that the different birth order positions would have different traits, although the MMPI descriptive statement did not really match Toman's descriptions.

FAMILY VALUES—EFFECT ON SIBLING TRAITS

Family values is the term used to denote those values to which a response is demanded of the child by the family "authorities." They are usually shared by both parents. Where paternal and maternal values conflict and each parent demands a response, the response of the child depends upon with which parent the child chooses to identify, which parent is the accepted authority, and the range of alternative responses available to the child.

Family values define the issues of significance in the family. Some family values are shared by the community at large, others are unique to the family. Values are not always openly expressed but become clear to the child through interaction with the parental models. Indeed, the actual proclaimed values may be at variance with the real values and ideals of the models. Family values represent ideals and therefore demands upon the child. In some families good human relations may be a value, in others material gain. Intellectual accomplishment, social prestige, propriety, morality, rugged masculinity, and polite behavior are all examples of common family values. Some values are sex-linked, i.e., in some families men are supposed to be strong and silent while women are supposed to be emotional and talkative.

If the pressure to live up to the values is intense and the values seem excessive to the child, then he/she finds self ***oppressed*** by the values and may react by rebellion, surface submission and inner rebellion, rationalization, or other devices for dealing with an oppressive demand. Nevertheless, a response must be given to each family value that the child perceives as applying. He/she may accept and try to fulfill or may reject the value and may choose from among the thousands of techniques that human beings have developed to deal with their own ideals, those which seem to help one preserve a sense of worth in the face of an unrealized ideal.

In discussing both family values and family atmosphere Dreikurs wrote

> The family pattern by no means ***determines*** the child's behavior. It may induce quite opposite behavior patterns. Nevertheless, children of the same family... show an inclination to similar behavior, developing characteristic values and moral concepts, ***especially when these are clearly defined and accepted by both parents*** . . . similarities of character traits are an expression of the family atmosphere. (Dreikurs, 1957a, p. 9)

The particular role accepted by the child will influence which family values become more important and which less important. If the child has selected a compliant role, then obedience and pleasing others becomes a role demand for the child. For another child, impressing others may be a role demand. The child expects self to live up to the values accepted and his/her self-esteem is determined by abilities to meet these role demands.

Since values are demands as well as ideals, they act as guiding lines for aspiration and behavior. They have what Lewin (1935) called ***positive valence*** which give rise to movement toward the desired ideal. Values provide what Adler (1958) called ***the meaning of life.*** Mistaken or aberrant values can be learned from parental models or can be the result of the child's misinterpretation of parental values. What the parent is trying to teach and what the child learns are sometimes very discrepant as will be described later. Even if parents make no attempt to teach values, their own modeling behavior and their interaction with the child will present unmistakable values.

Unsatisfactory Values

Unclear (because of inconsistency) values provide unsatisfactory guiding lines and require the child to look elsewhere for its ideals. Unsatisfactory ideals are those which are obviously inappropriate even to the limited perception of the child. If the child sees a parent struggling and suffering to achieve a certain value, such as a spotless house or exemplary religious piety, the child may well consider such an ideal unsatisfactory and simply reject it, perhaps while paying lip service to it. We have previously described how the child who finds values excessive becomes oppressed. The more excessive the demand, the more discouraging it is for the child and vice versa. In these cases, the values also become unsatisfactory. On the other hand, the child may find a parental value unsatisfactory because it is insufficient, as when the child chooses stricter religious values than the parents and outdoes them in piety and ritual.

Contradictory Values

Contradictory values are cases in which the pursuit of one value negates the pursuit of an opposite value of equal significance. Common examples can be seen when the parents model diametrically opposed values and the child wants to please both of them. Walker and Belove (1982) have called this the ***loyalty dilemma.*** Another example is when the child has acquired two conflicting values such as the desire to please the parent and the desire to have complete authority over its own behavior. Such contradictory and conflicting values often lead to remarkably creative behavior as the child juggles responses to these demands and finds more or less constructive solutions.

> One man (an only child) described how his mother disapproved of rowdy behavior and did not even want him to participate in athletics. His father had been known as a town athlete and took pride in the son's athletic achievements. He tells that he went to church with his mother on Sunday and on returning home, skipped lunch so that he could immediately go to the ball field in time for the scheduled games. He adds that although he was on the basketball team all through high school and college, his mother never came to a game. In his turn, he never told his mother when he would play and never discussed athletics with her.

Sometimes, no constructive solution is apparent and the contradictory values become highly unsatisfactory. One situation of this type has been named the ***double-bind*** (Bateson, 1972). The double bind is a paradox which occurs in a relationship which by nature requires cooperation, such as that between a parent and child. It is created when the parent gives a verbal directive (makes a demand) to the child and then contradicts the directive by non-verbal behavior (the counter-demand). Now the child finds attempts to win parental approval unrewarding but feels trapped in the situation. Eventually the child becomes discouraged and stops trying to cooperate or simply does whatever must be done to escape the worst of the parental disapproval.

As can be seen, the double bind is a "no win" situation. Bateson et al. (1956) offered an example:

> A young man approaches his mother and impulsively puts his arms around her, whereupon the mother stiffens. He withdraws his arms and she asks, "Don't you love me anymore?" He blushes and she says, "Dear, you must not be so easily embarrassed and afraid of your feelings."

Bateson et al. offered this type of contradictory communication as one example of a child experience often found in the background of schizophrenics.

Another avenue open to the child where the demands of one parent contradict the values of the other, is for the child to play one parent off against the other, inducing the parents to fight among themselves; or by complaining to one about the other, win an ally. Thus the child can at least please one parent. Sometimes the child will rebel against both sets of demands and conclude that trying to please either is not worth the effort.

Values are often a function of role location and thus change with each situation. The values of a small child are largely different from those of an adolescent and these differ again from those of an adult. They change with age, environment, economic situation, cultural demands, and so forth. We are here concerned with those values which are part of the child's family situation and which continue to exist, though in changed form, in adult life.

The change in form is often a change in the symbols and behavior which express the value. If morality is the family value, the child may demonstrate it by compliant and conventional behavior; the adolescent may depreciate the parents' expression of morality and may join a religious sect and follow its rules scrupulously; the same person, now adult, may devote self to searching out and exposing corruption in religious and charitable organizations. The value—morality—remains the same. How the value is expressed and symbolized differs.

FAMILY ATMOSPHERE

Each family tends to have an atmosphere of its own which grows out of relationships and values of the family and is influenced by intercurrent events and the position of the family in the outside world. Some families live in harmony, others in conflict. In some families the members are in conflict with each other at all times except when an outside danger threatens. Some families have a democratic, some an autocratic, and others an anarchic atmosphere. Sometimes family members are close to each other, sometimes distant. They may help or ignore each other. In some, the atmosphere is confusing, contradictory, secretive, hostile, gloomy, or despondent. Initiative may be encouraged or discouraged. The overall theme may be tragic, comic, or dramatic. Oppressive standards may hang like a cloud over the family so that everyone feels like a failure.

Events which affect the family atmosphere include any sudden change such as sickness, death, divorce, economic disruption or move to a new environment. These changes may affect any or all of the three qualities we use to describe family atmosphere: ***mood, order,*** and ***relationships.***

Mood

Mood refers to the overall emotional tone present in the family most of the time and as already mentioned, it is generally an expression of the mood of one or both parents. An over-anxious parent can spread fear and tension by contagion. A disapproving, blaming parent can produce an atmosphere of mutual criticism; while a calm and supportive parent can promote a sense of security and confidence.

> One man recalled the dark mood of the whole family during his childhood. His father could not find a job during the economic depression and was frequently drunk. Father also used to say that they were all unlucky and were all destined for Hell. Mother used to cry and worry all the time. He tried to help his family by taking the coal bucket to the railroad yards to look for pieces of coal that had fallen off trains so the family could have heat in the house. He recalls that he always expected some doom at any moment.

Order

Order refers to the hierarchical relationships and the progression of events. An authoritarian hierarchy in the family is one example of a family order. Inconsistent discipline or limit setting is another example. Frequent changes in the power structure of the family, divorce and death of a parent all affect the stability of the family order. A stable order more often provides security than an unstable one.

> One woman remembers that her father, a commodities broker, was either wealthy or poor. When he did well, his mood was expansive and everyone in the family seemed happy. When he suffered reverses, he was sad and distant and the woman recalls being quiet and sad,

but trying to cheer up her father. She never knew from day to day how things would go and used to wait fearfully for him to come home. Even when things went well for a period of time, she dreaded the thought that her father might again lose his fortune. Father finally died penniless, leaving her with a deep fear of financial insecurity.

Relationships

Relationships refer to the consistent forms of interaction present in the family. A parent can consistently withhold love as a form of disapproval. Parents can be strict or overly possessive. They may show affection openly or be distant and cool. They may play favorites and indulge one child while rejecting another. They can also be mainly concerned with their own interests and pay little attention to the emotional needs of the children. Mother and Father may be in conflict with each other leaving children to feel pulled between the parents. Power contests may lead to attempts to establish dominance rather than mutual cooperation. These relationships become prototypes of all human relationships for the child and the manner of relating the child learns at home is often carried into its later life.

In Table 2.1 is a list of various types of family atmospheres and their opposites which have significant influence on the development of life style.

TABLE 2.1
Qualities of the Family Atmosphere Which Influence Life Style

MOOD	
Anxious	Calm
Excitable	Placid
Hostile	Friendly
Discouraged	Hopeful
Unhappy	Cheerful
ORDER	
Chaotic	Orderly
Strict	Permissive
Authoritarian	Democratic
Inconsistant	Consistent
Arbitrary	Logical
Confusion	Clarity
Might Makes Right	Ethical Standards
RELATIONSHIPS	
Distant	Intimate, affectionate
Competitive	Cooperative
Rejecting	Accepting
Blaming	Understanding
Concealed Feeling	Openness
Conflictual	Harmonious

Dewey Classification

Dewey (1971, 1978) has described a number of family atmospheres: the ***rejective*** atmosphere is characterized by parents who constantly criticize and disapprove; the ***authoritarian*** atmosphere is rigid and demands compliance while it denies individual initiative; ***martyrdom*** extols nobility through a display of suffering. The model suffers at the hands of another and achieves a form of moral superiority, thus gaining status. The ***inconsistent*** atmosphere limits open expression of thoughts or feelings; the ***hopeless*** atmosphere fosters discouragement, passivity, resignation and pessimism; the ***overprotective*** atmosphere does not allow children to learn to face the consequences of their own behavior or learn necessary social skills. Other atmospheres described by Dewey are ***pitying, high-standards, materialistic, disparaging, inharmonious, disorderly*** and ***excessively orderly.*** In our opinion the outcome is not always as Dewey seems to suggest. The child's own subjective conclusions are the determining factor in the outcome.

The child's early experiences with the family atmosphere influence what it will expect later in life, and especially that part of the life style which in Chapter 1 we called the ***world view.*** As we experienced life before, so we generally expect it to be in the future.

PARENTAL BEHAVIOR

Parents as Models

Parents not only interact with the child, they provide models (as do other significant adults and older children). The function of the model is to display varieties of behavior to the child who thus learns various techniques of behavior and their consequences. How men behave, how women behave, how adults relate to each other, how they meet crises, what they consider important, and what they consider proper all are displayed to the view of the child who chooses what part of the stance and behavior he/she will imitate and what will be rejected. If the models display a narrow or distorted range of behavior, the child has little opportunity to learn alternatives and tries to use the little information learned to deal with the situation. Thus, a first-born son with an indulgent and submissive mother and a dictatorial tyrannical father is very likely to become a rebellious dictatorial child himself, demanding the mother's submission and constantly enraging the father who then punishes the child and further reinforces the child's overvaluation of the importance of being the more powerful one in a relationship.

Imitation—Positive and Negative. The child may pattern self after a parent, may decide to be the opposite, or may select from each parent traits desired to emulate, always searching for values, attitudes, and techniques that enhance self and one's perceived ability to cope with life. Much imitation takes place outside the conscious awareness of the child and even the adult may not recognize that the child is imitating parental behavior. Bandura and Walters (1963) have shown that much social learning takes place through observation and imitation. Infinite variations in patterning are possible. The first born tends to pattern self after the parent of the same sex, or may pattern itself according to the values and role demands of the parent with whom the closest affiliation is established. The child may become convinced he/she cannot match the attainments of the desirable model, may fruitlessly continue attempts to do so, or may give up and switch to another form of behavior. The second child may choose to imitate the alternate parent or to try to overrun the first in imitating the same sex parent, or at least to imitate those behaviors of the parent that the first has ignored. The child may ally self with one parent against another or may even decide to outdo the parents in the same behavior.

Not only behavior is imitated, but also values and standards. Thus, a child may accept the parental dictum that children "should" be obedient, but, defining self as a naughty child, may be disobedient. The child also may reject the standards, yet imitate the behavior.

Complementary Patterning. A complementary relationship is reciprocal and mutually satisfying to parent and child.

An uneducated parent may encourage educational achievement in the child. By attaining education the child wins parental approval. In complementary patterning the value, not the behavior, is imitated.

Rebellion. Four different types of patterning may be seen in rebellious children. The child may reject both the values and behavior of the parents. The child may, on the other hand, accept the parental standards for behavior but reject their demands for conformity to those behaviors. The child may instead devise behaviors for meeting these standards or may simply define self as not being able to meet them. He/she also may misinterpret the kind of behaviors necessary to meet the standards. A third pattern for rebellion stems from the fact that rebellious behavior sometimes wins stronger reinforcement than conformity (parental attention and concern). A fourth pattern is actually a pseudo-rebellion in that it is a form of imitation. A boy may imitate a demanding, authoritarian, argumentative father and may thereby come into conflict with him.

In all cases of rebellion, the child perceives some advantage to self from so behaving. Parents may unconsciously reinforce the behavior or the behavior may give the child a feeling of power and self-esteem, even a measure of retaliation if the child is angry at the parents.

Identification. Adlerians do not use the word identification in the same sense as psychoanalytic theory which sees identification as an ego mechanism for creating an internal ego structure. Adlerians are more inclined to use a social learning model and therefore prefer the concept of ***imitation,*** of following a guiding line.

Parental Behavior Toward the Child and the Outcome

Our theory of human behavior leads us to believe that the parent-child interaction is a dyadic process with mutual feedback; therefore, the parent and child influence each other's behavior in the transaction between them. The private goals and expectancies of each person influences each one's perception of and reactions to the other. The parent who expects to be disappointed in the child is quick to perceive evidence to support that expectation and the child who expects to be rejected by the parent will equally quickly perceive evidence of rejection and often they act to arrange it in line with Merton's (1948) hypothesis of self-fulfilling prophecy. Thus, each party may experience the expected result before the other has actually done anything to warrant such a conclusion. Since each assumes that the expected has already happened (or is at least imminent), each behaves as if it has actually happened. Thus, we respond to what we think people are doing, thinking, or expecting or to what we think they will do as much as to their actual behavior. We attribute motives more in line with our own expectations rather than with reality. Relationships are full of these expectations, misattributions, and faulty conclusions. The behavior of the child in the context of the family is the result of the child's subjective appraisal of what parents seem to be doing. For this reason, we discuss and describe the parents' behavior sometimes as if that were the "cause" of the child's response and sometimes as if the child's own inner perceptions were the "cause" of its own behavior. Of course, the child's behavior is also a "cause" of the parents' response to it (Mosak, 1980). The mutual behavioral interaction provides invitation and feedback for each.

Actual Parental Behavior and Its Perception by the Child. A direct one to one relationship between the actual parental behavior and the child's experience of it does not exist. A parent may actually favor a child, yet the child may experience the parent's behavior as rejecting. A parent may be punitive but the child may feel the parent is justified. Another parent may be indulgent and yet the child may feel deprived. The child's perception of the parent's behavior toward the child is the stimulus for the response. Parental behavior is thus assigned "meanings" by the child according to the child's cognitive system.

For this reason, parents are often surprised at how the child responds to them. They may consciously intend to reinforce one set of behaviors, while actually they reinforce another. One common mistake parents make is to give "negative attention," i.e., attention for misbehavior rather than for desirable behavior. The parental attention, even though it consists of scolding and admonition, is a reinforcer.

A mother in a family education center reported an experience with her young child. She entered the kitchen and saw her child playing on the floor with some dried beans. Immediately worried, she said in a warning voice, "Don't put any of those beans up your nose!" She then went about her activities. When she returned, the child's nose was full of beans and she had to take him to the doctor to have them extracted.

Another mother wanted to teach her children to share and share alike. She tried to teach this value by very carefully giving each child the same toys and equal portions of food at the dinner table. The children did not learn to share. Instead they learned to watch each other to make certain that the other never got a larger share of anything.

A father who had been poor as a child wanted his son to have all the playthings he, himself, had wanted but been denied in his childhood. He bought countless toys for his son and was puzzled when the son broke, lost, or ignored them. The son did not value items that came to him so easily and could always be replaced. The father felt unappreciated and the son felt misunderstood.

Specific Perceptions of Behavior and Outcome. The socializing task of parents probably includes the following (adapted from Horney, 1966): (1) to provide safety and security for the child; (2) to provide it with a feeling of worth; (3) to provide an atmosphere of emotional warmth; (4) to guide the child, yet permit it the freedom to explore and make its own errors and learn from them; (5) to set limits where necessary; (6) to permit some friction so that the experience of conflict engenders problem solving behavior; and (7) to train the child in the value of cooperation. Parents use various dimensions of behavior in their attempts to perform these tasks and the child's responses are to the parental behavior as he/she perceives them. Some common dimensions of parental behavior and typical responses by the child are listed in Table 2.2. One must keep in mind that these responses by the child have a high order of probability only and also can be different from the ones listed.

TABLE 2.2

Parental Behavior and Probable Responses by Child

Dimension of Parental Behavior as Perceived by Child	Typical Responses by Child
Accepting	Positive self-image
Rejecting	Negative self-image—may look elsewhere for acceptance
Authoritarian	Submits—seeks to please or rebels—seeks power
Laissez-faire	Seeks guidance and limits
Available	Feels closer to parent
Unavailable	Feels isolated—looks elsewhere
Consistency	More trust
Inconsistency	Distrust and feeling that life is unpredictable—may become excessively orderly
Overprotection	Fearfulness or resistance to limits
Overindulgence	Does not learn to discipline self. Expects service from others

TABLE 2.2 (Continued)

Dimension of Parental Behavior as Perceived by Child	Typical Responses by Child
Excessive demands for achievement	Resentment and feelings of inferiority—becomes discouraged—may continue to try or may reject achievement orientation
Excessive moral demands	Feels like a "bad" person. May set excessive moral standards for others and depreciate them.
Excessive strictness	Seeks to please or rebels. Covert rebellion is common
Excessive criticism	Feels rejected and misunderstood. Becomes discouraged or rejects the critic
Lack of faith in the child	Tries to prove self to parent/or loses faith in self
Warmth	Feels accepted and loved
Coldness	Feels neglected or may become cold and distant himself/herself
Nurturing	Feels loved and can give love
Non-nurturing	Seeks love, may not learn how to give it
Competing	Becomes a competitor
Cooperating	Becomes a cooperator
Encouraging	Positive response
Discouraging	Tendency to give up

Attitudes Reinforced by Parental Behavior

Certain basic attitudes are considered important by Adlerians. Parental behavior influences whether or not these attitudes will develop. Dreikurs (1957b, 1973) considered these attitudes essential for human cooperation and their counterparts disruptive to it.

Table 2.3 lists these important attitudes and their polar encounterparts.

TABLE 2.3

Important Attitude Polarities Influenced by Parental Reinforcement
(Adapted from Dreikurs, 1957b, 1973, p. 103)

SOCIAL FEELING	**ANIMOSITY**
—feeling of belonging —fellow feeling —contributing —cooperation	—alienation —egocentricity/self-elevation —getting/taking —competition
Confidence in others	***Distrust and suspicion***
SELF-CONFIDENCE	**INFERIORITY FEELINGS**
self-reliance —optimism —positive self-concept —activity	—dependency —pessimism —negative self-concept —passivity
Courage	***Fear (discouragement)***

The attitudes on the left are considered healthy and prosocial. Those on the right are unhealthy and antisocial. These basic attitudes can be discovered during the assessment of the life style.

Empathy. In its original sense, empathy is ***Einfühlung,*** a primitive reflex process by which direct communication of an emotional state occurs between people. It does not necessarily mean sympathy. Sullivan uses the term to describe the way an infant can be affected by the emotional state of the caretaking adult; i.e., tension in the mother produces tension in the infant (Sullivan, 1953, p. 41). Thus the moods of parents have a direct effect on the moods of the children. This phenomenon is also often seen in clinical work. A person who is depressed tends to produce various emotional responses in the people around him/her, sometimes even depression. One who is hypomanic can produce feelings of excitement and elation in others. Experienced actors know how to deliberately produce emotional responses in the audience.

Through empathy, parents produce mood states in each other and in the children. Such mood states were previously discussed under ***family atmosphere.***

Parental Interaction

In their interaction with each other, parents provide models for human interaction, especially interaction between the sexes. The child learns from them how men and women treat each other. The child may notice that mother defers to father on the surface, but mother is the actual decision-maker in the family. The child can see the presence or absence of respect, warmth, love, and cooperation between parents. The child will tend, later in life, to desire for intimate relationship that which was thought to be good in the relationship between the child's parents and to avoid that which was thought to be bad. Parental interaction thus provides guidelines, role models, a view of marriage and parenthood, and specific interactive behavioral methods.

The emotional problems of the parents enter into their interaction with each other. A child can become caught up in the interaction between the parents with unfortunate consequences for self. One such outcome has been described by Lidz (1973) who found ***marital schism,*** a conflicted relationship between the parents, in the background of many schizophrenics. Family therapists such as Boszormenyi-Nagy (1972),

Bowen (1978), Satir (1967), and Whitaker (1978) have discussed the effects of conflict between the parents on the adaptive behavior of the child.

Absent Parents

The absence of a parent removes an important socializing agent from the child's life. The effect of a parent's death depends to a great extent upon the age of the child at the time of death, the previous relationship between the parent and the child, the amount of change in the family's life situation (e.g., economic misfortune) that ensues from the death, and the presence or absence of other parenting figures who may act as substitutes. A parent's death is usually experienced as a loss and/or abandonment. The effect of divorce can be similar, although the absent parent is usually not permanently lost after divorce. In this situation, the child may be induced to take sides in the conflict. In all these cases, the family constellation changes and the child usually experiences new role demands. The dead parent may be idealized and by comparison, the remaining parent may seem inadequate. A parent's death or a divorce may permanently change the family atmosphere. Children often feel abandoned during the dislocation that follows either death or divorce. To be an orphan also confers a special role, which is sometimes reinforced by changed reactions (positive or negative) of the people around the child.

Ineffective Parents

Sometimes a parent is incapacitated by illness, perhaps becoming a pathetic figure, losing authority and becoming like a child in status. Family concerns may center around such a sick parent so that all are affected by the atmosphere of illness and incapacity. The illness of a previously dominant parent and the mate's reaction to it may reverse the previous order of the family. Such events in the life of the family tend to leave a permanent trace on the child.

Parents are sometimes rendered ineffective by other external circumstances. A dominant father may suffer business reverses, turn to alcohol, and lose the respect of mate and children. Immigrant parents, not knowing the language or customs of the new country, may be rejected as models by the child. In each case the child responds in its unique personal way to the picture presented by parental behavior. The effect on the child need not always be negative. The child's response to an ineffective parent may be a positive one; that is, the child chooses the parent as a negative model and trains self to be an effective and responsible person.

Single parent families, stepfamilies, and blended families have always been with us but the past few decades have seen some changes in the attitude toward divorce and remarriage. The cultural change is still new enough that we do not yet know what will be the eventual effect on family values. In the case of an unwed, by choice, mother with a single child, we do not yet know what special rules may apply.

Family Myths

Family myths are usually constructed by the parents and either accepted or rejected by the child. Parents may cultivate the myth that the family is superior to other families by reason of ancestry and background. A common myth may result from the idealization of a family member who has died. Thus, a dead sibling may be thought of as having been a perfect child and all the other siblings defective by comparison. A myth is a set of fictions the family attributes to itself, more or less shared by the majority of the family members. The example previously given under the topic "family myths" about the father who asserted that they were all destined to go to Hell is one example of a myth. Sometimes, the myth is held by the parents and resisted by one or all of the children. Parents who are actually only interested in themselves may claim that they are making sacrifices for the children.

> In one family the parents described themselves as being cooperative, caring, warm, and sensitive. This self-description was belied by the behavior of the children. The oldest was exceedingly competitive and dictatorial, the second felt unloved, and the youngest felt she received no guidance. Such sibling behavior is unlikely had the parents actually been as they described themselves. All the children were highly critical of the parents.

Sometimes, the clarification and disclosure of the family myths are strongly resisted by family members.

Family Secrets

Family secrets consist of information that is known to some or all of the family members but concealed from the rest of the world. Common secrets involve a secret about a sick parent or child or an embarrassing fact. Thus, the existence of a retarded child in an institution, the fact that a parent is psychotic and has to be hospitalized from time to time or that father has spent time in jail may lead the family members to conceal such information from the world at large. The result is a feeling of conspiracy which creates distance between the family members and outsiders. Such behavior is reinforced by parents who instruct the children not to reveal secrets to neighbors. One result may be to enhance family unity, but it may also lead family members to depreciate themselves—to feel there is something wrong with them.

> A young woman had always felt that her family was different from the other people in the small town in which they lived. Her parents seldom entertained, did not encourage her to bring home playmates and always seemed secretive. She and her younger brother had been brought up in the Episcopalian Church, but her father seldom came to church and her mother always seemed angry at Father because of this. She considered herself Father's favorite and argued with her mother. She did not understand why Father did not defend himself. Brother was Mother's favorite and complied with her wishes. One day, a message came from New York that Father's brother had died. She then recalled that the brother had once visited years earlier when she was a small child, but in the intervening years no one in her family had ever mentioned that Father had relatives. Intrigued, she obtained addresses from her father and traveled to New York where she discovered a dozen relatives. She also discovered that her father had been born a Jew and that he had decided to deliberately conceal his background in deference to the wishes of his Christian wife. The family dynamics now became more

clear to her. She confronted her parents and declared that she refused to live a secret life anymore. She moved to New York and declared herself a Jewess—thus continuing to oppose her mother and champion her father.

Other Parent Figures

When extended families live in proximity, often enough parental figures are available so that each child may feel favored and experience a close relationship with an adult. Grandparents, maiden aunts, bachelor uncles, and much older siblings can all act as parental figures and provide models. A child may prefer a grandparent to a parent as a model. Adults, or even children, outside the home also may become models. Female school teachers are common models for little girls. In the determination of the family constellation, taking such models into account is always important.

FAMILY *ROLE* PLAYED BY EACH CHILD

As previously mentioned, the social role is an organized set of behaviors which belong to an identifiable position in the family. In the common family structure, parents play recognizable parental roles, sometimes divided along gender lines. Differences in roles between male and female children usually follow commonly accepted cultural patterns and children often, but not always, imitate the gender behaviors modeled by the same-sexed parent. The ecological structure of the family offers several different role locations for children, each of which provides a more or less acceptable amount of status and security for the child. Some roles receive more approval from parents than others. Some roles require more intelligence or more talent than others and not all children can meet these role demands. Some roles have more power to influence the environment than others. Some provide more self-esteem. Some roles more suitable for a small child are maladaptive if carried into adult life. Roles found in some families are not found in other families because they may be excluded by the family structure. In general, the more authoritarian and rigid the family atmosphere, the smaller will be the variety of roles found in it. The range of a role may extend over all or most behaviors of a child. However, specific behaviors may be limited to specific situations, e.g., the child behaves one way with mother, another with father, and a third way in school. Behaviors the child chooses must provide some reward or the child will never develop them. Roles and their associated behavior develop out of the child's responses to the "givens" of the situation and are fostered by imitation and reinforcement.

A role is usually given a shorthand label which suggests its main characteristics. All the birth orders are such labels since each birth order suggests that the person will display certain characteristics. Thus, traits such as responsibility and bossiness cluster more often with the first born position than with others. The complexity of roles can be seen in the permutations that surround one frequent family value—the request of the parents for compliance from the children. The following are all varieties of compliance roles:

The good child who wants to please

The child who is compliant on the surface but resents it

The child who obeys out of fear

The child who is compliant in order to get attention and who misbehaves to get attention if compliance doesn't work

The child who is good in order to have higher status than the sibling who is naughty

The child who rejects compliance as low status behavior and misbehaves and defies in order to increase feeling of status

The child who complies with stated values in order to outdo the parents and gain dominance over them, as in the child who becomes more pious than the parents and feels entitled to criticize them.

Family Stories and Relation to Role Behaviors

In some families, stories are told about one member which suggest the role the family anticipates for that member. Stories such as "How Mary won the most beautiful child contest when she was five," or "How Mother almost died when Charlie was born," if repeated often enough, create a set of expectations. Perhaps Mary will feel that she is expected to be especially pretty or Charlie may feel that he was nearly the death of Mother. The stories are "history" and become woven into the child's image of self and his/her powers or destiny.

> A fearful, socially insecure young man was often told by his grandmother that when he was three years old, he was so fearful that he ran from any animal he saw on the farm where they lived. She would gleefully tell him that he would run from tiny goslings (who instinctively chase a fleeing animal) and cry because the goslings continued to run after him. The young man thought of himself as too cowardly to face up to anything.

Each family value allows for a variety of roles which serve that value in a positive or negative sense. Thus, each role is both an answer to a set of values (demands) and a way of finding a place in the family.

SUMMARY

Family constellation provides a picture of the microcosm in which the child develops. The givens of the FC are birth order, gender, parental models, family values, and family atmosphere. The child's own reaction can be seen in his/her behavior patterns, alliances, and rivalries, areas of success and failure (where it is encouraged and where discouraged), subjective views, conformity or rebellion, and the repertoire of roles developed within the family.

CHAPTER **3**

EARLY RECOLLECTIONS (ER)

Although Munroe (1955) stated that Adler was the first to use early recollections as a projective technique, that is probably not true. Freud (1959) also used them that way, although with an entirely different emphasis as Ansbacher (1967) has pointed out. Freud emphasized that which was forgotten rather than that which was recalled and he viewed many early memories as "screens" behind which were important repressed events. Adler's own words best show his position on early recollections:

> The function of memory...[is] dominated by the necessity of adaptation. Without memories it would be impossible to exercise any precautions for the future. They are not fortuitous phenomena but speak clearly the language of encouragement and warning. There are no indifferent or nonsensical recollections... (Adler, 1957/1927, pp. 48-49)

Memory is thus an adaptive function of the mind. Memories are psychically determined for the purpose of aiding adaptation. They are used to select present and future choices of behavior; so they influence direction of goal movement. Memory functions like a vast evolutionary elaboration of a primitive orienting reflex to provide information about what direction of movement would have the most desirable results. Early childhood recollections were thought by Adler to be of especial significance since they showed the style of life in its origins and in its simplest expressions (Adler, 1958). For this reason they have become a valuable tool for eliciting the life style of an individual.

Like a cartoon drawn with a few sparse lines, the earliest recollections, in vignette form, depict the essential ingredients of a life style—the main guiding line for adapting to life and its demands. For Adler, the most important information in a memory was what was ***expressed,*** not what was ***repressed.*** Memory thus was highly selective and early recollections were selected from a vast number of experiences to be remembered because they contained adaptively useful information for the remembering individual.

IDENTIFYING CHARACTERISTICS OF EARLY RECOLLECTIONS

For most people, the time of continuous memory begins about age seven or eight. After this point, a person can recall a stream of memories which have connections to other areas of life. These later memories are recalled in a background setting; i.e., the memory is one event in a series of events. Before this time of continuous memory, most people have a handful of early memories which stand isolated. These memories are usually very short with sparse detail. An example of each type will show the difference:

> Age 5—(The doctor came to give me a shot everyday.) One day I didn't cry. (I got to be a pro at it.) He was proud of me. I felt real good about being able to take a shot without screaming.
>
> Age 3—One day I made in my pants. I was playing in the yard. I felt ashamed.

Both these memories as well as others in this chapter are taken from a collection by Mosak et al. (1980). They were given by the same person. The second memory is sparse in detail and contains no background, unlike the first. Both memories are equally valid but in the first, the background material has been put in parentheses. Background is useful in providing context, but it is not the recollection per se.

An early recollection (ER) is a vignette. It has a definite beginning and end. It usually has a visual quality so that one can visualize it as a tableau. The content of the recollection may seem important or trivial but one may extract from it a theme which is always important to the person. Often the material offered by a subject is a report rather than a recollection. An example of such a report is

> I always used to go with my father for Sunday walks. I loved the time we had together, just he and I.

While this report also has a visual quality, it does not qualify as an early recollection. It is not the description of a specific incident and does not have the here and now narrative quality of a recollection. Reports give important information about the person but do not lend themselves to the same kind of projective assessment as do the ER. The ER about the doctor's daily visit just given shows that a memory may be part report and part ER. The report part constitutes background which makes the ER more understandable, but it is only the ER part that is subject to analysis for our particular purpose.

THE DIAGNOSTIC SIGNIFICANCE OF EARLY RECOLLECTIONS

Adler (1937, 1964b) considered the discovery of the significance of early recollections to be one of the most important findings of Individual Psychology. When understood, the memories gave glimpses of profound depths within the personality structure. Admittedly, ER are not to be considered correct records of actual facts, but alterations from facts were for Adler evidence of creative tendencies in the memories which were cognitively consistent with the subject's own life goals and own private way of assigning meaning and value to the various aspects of existence. Adler drew many inferences from ER; the subject's attitude toward life, hints about why a particular line of movement in life was chosen, indications of compensatory devices developed to cope with felt inadequacies, evidence of courage or its lack, of the preference for direct or indirect methods of coping, of the type of interpersonal transactions preferred, of the presence or absence of social interest, of the values assigned to affiliation, competence behavior, status concerns, compliance and rebellion, security issues—in short, of the stance the subject adopts in order to cope with the challenges of life.

Adler used ER in order to understand the person in the present and did this by looking at the ways the ER would fit in with and explain present behavior. He used as an example the ER of a man who remembered "I was sitting in a room playing with a toy and my mother was sitting close to me." Adler made the correlation "... the patient suffers from anxiety when alone" (1964b, p. 122). The memory taken together with the symptom suggests to Adler that the patient was pampered by his mother during childhood.

From reading Adler, one deduces that he used both a nomothetic and an idiosyncratic way of looking at ER. When Adler said that ER focus on the nurturing mother are indicators of a pampered childhood or that ER which focus on danger situations are evidence of insecurity in life, he suggested that any ER with specific content may indicate a specific correlative trait or historical experience. Such a hypothesis would be relatively easy to test. On the other hand, Adler, in his anecdotal writings, often did something else. In discussing a patient, he began with the presenting situation and then examined the patient's ER in order to find guiding lines which could then explain the patient's present situation as his/her typical way of coping with life, so that the ER and present situation are seen to contain the same idiosyncratic themes. This second hypothesis does not lend itself so easily to objective measurement and thus cannot be so easily verified.

Primed And Unprimed Memories

Study of ER as a projective device probably began in the 40s when Kadis and Lazarsfeld (1948) described the differences between the material found in ER and in "images" which subjects were asked to construct of a certain specific person at a certain age. They found that the usual method of eliciting ER often did not include information about the most significant people in the person's early life. However, when prompted to recall a memory about such a person, usually a parent or sibling, the product centered specifically upon the image of the recalled person. Although Kadis and Lazarsfeld called these "images," they are actually primed ER. Usually, the examiner asks a non-priming question such as "What are your earliest memories from childhood?" Priming consists of directing a person's recall to a specific other person or event and is more likely to give information about the other person and his/her relation to the subject than to reveal in neutral terms the most basic elements of the life style.

Kadis and Lazarsfeld offer several instructive examples. One describes a 16 year old girl who stated that her older sister, who always had been kind to her, was her ideal. When asked to give her earliest image of her sister, the subject gave a primed memory:

> I was to be a flower girl at my favorite aunt's wedding. The night before the wedding my sister chopped my hair off. I couldn't go to the wedding.

"Images" (primed ER) are offered by Kadis and Lazarsfeld, as an additional assessment tool, providing information not so readily available in many unprimed ER.

Possible Sources of Contamination in Memories

Bergson (1911) had as early as 1896 stated that "The function of the body...is to choose...the useful memory, that which may complete and illuminate the present situation with a view to ultimate action." Ansbacher (1973) claimed that Bergson thus supported Adler's view that "recollections are tendentious and biased and in the service of the purposes and goals of the individual and that one may therefore infer from a person's recollections his ideals and goals."

Bartlett's (1932) classic study on memory led him to state, "Remembering appears to be far more decisively an affair of construction rather than one of mere reproduction . . . The construction . . . (is one) . . . that would justify . . . (the subject's) . . . attitude" (pp. 205-207). Edwards (1941) compared the memories of pro-New Dealers and anti-New Dealers and found that each group tended to remember in a way that harmonized with their own political attitudes. Adler himself commented on this, saying:

> The use of memories to stabilize a mood can be plainly seen in every day life. If a man suffers a defeat and is discouraged by it, he recalls previous instances of defeat... (1958, p. 74).

This raises the question of how much in the ER is an expression of a person's current mood rather than of abiding core personality. Some studies have tested the ability of ER to conform to certain clinical diagnostic entities. One such is by Eisenstein and Ryerson (1951). They examined the earliest memory of patients with certain illnesses and found concordance between the memory and the category of illness. For example the earliest memory in a case of colitis was "I was sitting on a toilet in school, sick with a stomach ache and mother having to come and get me."

A more recent study of Fogarty and Helmsley (1983) suggested that current mood is an important determinant of the mood found in ER. They used as subjects depressed outpatients compared to a crop of normal controls. Patients with depression showed an increased number of sad memories compared to normal. Improvement in depression, as measured by the *Beck Depression Inventory* showed a decrease in the sad mood of the ER.

If we could always find such a correlation, it would be very convenient, but we must ask some hard questions. Are the ER contaminated by the fact that the patient is suffering from an acute illness? Would exactly the same memory be given if the patient were examined in a period when free of symptoms? Therapists who use ER and work with depressed patients have noted that during acute depression the ER tend to have a somber mood and that these same ER become more cheerful as the depression lifts. This is more likely to signify a change in mood state rather than in any underlying character trait, as Fogarty and Helmsley said.

Similar studies by Friedman (1952) and Hafner et al. (1979) examined and compared ER of patients who were mentally ill; a neurotic vs. a psychotic cohort and normals vs. schizophrenics. Both studies found some differences between the cohorts, but in neither case was allowance made for possible contamination by the intensity of illness. Normals are different from psychotics in many different test instruments. Hafner et al. (1979) do conclude that ER cannot be used as an objective measure of differences between normals and schizophrenics if one uses content analysis as does the Manaster-Perryman Manifest Content method of scoring ER (Manaster & Perryman, 1974).

The study of Tobin and Etigson (1968) also measures the effect of current state on ER. Their cohort consisted of subjects aged 68 to 92 with a mean age of 78. Fifty-seven subjects were in the experimental group while eighty-three were in the control group. The experimental group consisted of people who were waiting for admission to a home for the aged. The control sample consisted of people living independently in the community, others also on the waiting list or residents of the homes for the aged. Both samples were asked to give ER six months to one year apart, however, the experimental group gave ER approximately four months before admission to the home and again approximately two months after admission. The independent variable was thus admission to the home and the effect of such institutionalization on ER was the object of study. The experimental group differed from controls in giving ER with more themes of loss (death, injury, interpersonal loss, etc.). Tobin and Etigson concluded that a situation change thus affects ER and that this must be taken into account by Adlerians when they interpret ER. While many of their reported ER would be considered reports rather than true ER, enough true ER were still in their sample to sound this note of caution about the contamination of ER by intercurrent life events.

THE IDIOGRAPHIC CHARACTER OF ER

Saul et al. (1956) recommended the way Adler used ER to psychoanalysts.

> Earliest memories are absolutely specific, distinctive and characteristic for each individual; moreover, they reveal, probably more clearly than any other single psychological datum the central core of each person's psychodynamics, his chief motivations, form of neurosis and emotional problem. This is the empirical observable fact. As to explaining it, it seems that the major unconscious motivations ***select*** those memories which fit them, just as the interplay of emotional forces which generates the dream selects just those events and

> memories which fit their need for expression...Memories, like all psychic functions, exist for the service of the biological motivations of the life cycle. Early memories are retained to serve present needs. . . (p. 229)

The statement by Saul et al. should help to dispel the notion that ER are a private device to be used only by followers of Alfred Adler. . . Every school of personality that postulates the existence of an organized personality structure must logically conclude that early childhood recollections have some relationship to that structure. If recollections are persistent, stable over time and situation, then these recollections must have some powerful connection with the dynamics of the personality. Furthermore, if these recollections are not about impressive events, but seem trivial and even uninteresting, that connection must be even more powerful. For Freud, these apparently trivial memories could be understood as "screens" with the repressed material clouded over. For Adler, they were expressive and creative productions and were remembered because the subject was saying something important to self, something worth remembering, perhaps a mnemonic device for unlocking a whole series of instructions for perceiving and responding to the facts of one's existence.

Mosak (1958, 1977) provided a reasonably full description of the use of ER as a projective technique which has since been used as model for many of the subsequent descriptions in the literature (e.g., Verger & Camp, 1970; Olson, 1979; Mosak, 1965; Eckstein, 1976; Kopp & Dinkmeyer, 1975; McKelvie, 1979; and others). He pointed out that ER, like dreams and free drawings, are a completely unstructured projective technique. No external stimulus is offered to the subject, unlike the Rorschach or TAT. All memories are selected and contain omissions and distortions. Whether the ER is faithful to reality or highly distorted is not of importance for the purpose of using the technique. The ER will all be consistent with each other, but complement, supplement, and elaborate each other so that ER which seem to make contradictory statements, will, when put together, prove to be statements about the same issue. The following two ER are examples of this principle:

> age 9—We had a spelling bee. I was the last one standing. It felt great.
>
> age 7—We were at a picnic and they had races for prizes. I came in second in my heat. I was crushed. (Mosak et al., 1980)

At first glance the outcome in each recollection seems different. One is a memory of winning, the other is a memory of being second best. Put together, they both make one statement: "To be number one is the only position in life that counts. Second best is not good enough."

Mosak further described how ER are interpreted both thematically and with respect to specific details, how to use a sequential analysis of a group of ER for a more rounded and complete assessment and how to reconcile contradictions. Like Ackerknecht (1976) and Dreikurs (1954), Mosak recommended the use of a series of ER rather than a single one whose interpretation is usually much more chancy and like Dreikurs he stresses the importance of paying attention to small details that profoundly affect the meaning of ER.

Subsequent to Mosak's paper, a group of papers appeared in literature in the 60s examining the use of ERs. Langs et al. (1960) developed a manual for scoring the manifest content of ER which scored 37 different items such as the feeling tone of the memory, who is mentioned in the memory, the kind of event, whether or not body parts are mentioned, and so forth. Although these authors found differences between paranoid schizophrenics and hysterical character disorders, their study added very little to the use of ER for personality assessment except to show that a wide range of scoring possibilities existed. In a later study, Langs (1965a/1965b) used ER to predict personality correlates and was more successful. Using the first ER only, he constructed 24 categories of themes and/or content in ER such as themes of illness—damage—conflict; subject's role as a pawn of others, others as subservient to the subject; moral themes; environment as unpredictable, supportive and/or traumatic; absence of interaction between subject and others; and separation or loss. Why Langs chose just these categories is not clear; presumably he found them in his group of memories and then looked for personality correlates. For each of these categories, Langs found correlates, e.g., subjects who had ER about vehicles tended to be inhibited, to be low in hostility and introspective. Langs' method of scoring tends to make ER an objective rather than a projective test and overlooks the idiosyncratic quality of ER. No matter how many trait correlations can be discovered, this is not yet the discovery of what Adler called the unique style of life of the individual.

Hedvig (1963) studied the stability of ER during exposure to experimentally manipulated experiences. The experimental conditions were success-failure and hostility-friendliness. Hedvig found that varying the experiment condition (telling the subject that he was succeeding or failing and doing so in a hostile or friendly manner) changed the TAT stories given by the subject but not the ER. Hedvig's finding is of crucial importance when we consider the effects of situational stress on ER as reported by Tobin and Etigson (1968). These two studies are in direct opposition in their conclusions and the contradiction requires further explanation.

Categorical Ratings or Gestalt Like Wholes?

Ferguson (1964) described how after three years of trying to develop rating scales for Adlerian raters to use in the study of ER, she finally gave up because none of the judges were satisfied with the scales. However, when simply asked to interpret a group of ER, all judges were able to do so in a short paragraph. Three judges were given sets of ERs and sets of interpretations and asked to match one with the other (interjudge reliability test). Each of the three judges matched ER to summary paragraphs written by the other judges. All the matchings were better than chance.

A study which was successful in using rating categories was performed by Levy and Grigg (1962). Noting that many previous ER studies had found high agreement between ER and clinical data, they decided to see if they could use ER to predict clinical and personality data. They used only the ER and the sex of the subject as their data base. In order to organize the material in the ER they developed a system similar to Murray's approach to the TAT. They considered each ER to contain a central theme which captures an "essential emotional state of the individual" (an internal attitude). Different ER from the same person could offer different themes which reflected different configurations among the themes. They devised three qualitative scales to rate these themes: Dependency/Independency, Destructive Aggression/Constructive Aggression and Sexuality. Each of these major categories had subgroups. Their own examples illustrate their scoring system:

THEME: DEPENDENCY/INDEPENDENCE
(subcategories with examples)

1. Feelings of deep seated frustration of dependency needs—complete abandonment; sense of being lost.

    Aunt came to house. Another aunt had died two years before.

    Aunt read palms and told me I would die young.

2. Feelings of temporary abandonment; separation from parents; insufficient affection; sadness over losing a real object; dissatisfaction with one's lot; birth of a sibling.

    Crying when mother took me to the first day of school.

    My brother was born and I had to go with my grandmother and stay with her until he was born.

3. Aggressive reactions to feelings of being deprived.

    Mother went out and left me and my younger brother with a twelve year old cousin. My brother and I were playing and we set the house on fire.

4. Giving rather than receiving care.

    I wanted to go to church but stayed home to take care of Mother.

5. Gratification of dependency needs.

    I got a present of a swing with a canopy from my aunt.
    (From Levy & Grigg, 1962)

While we would not use the same scoring system, nor would we interpret the ER the same way, Levy and Grigg seem to have been the first to successfully approach what Adlerian interpreters do globally by creating a system of themes and subthemes and by relating the subthemes to each other in order to find a ***configuration.*** They called their method ***thematic-configurational analysis.*** How they do it can be shown in their example of one ER.

Age 4 (male): I was on my first pair of roller skates. Mother had been going to get them for me and she had to go to the hospital for her operation. I asked her and got the skates from her before she went. I remember riding on them in the basement. All the rest were in the basement and all were laughing and it was a happy time.

In this ER, say the authors, feelings of temporary abandonment and attempts to be independent interact with each other. The inner emotional logic of the sequence of themes seems to say, "If mother abandons me, then I must strive to be independent." This is exactly the way many Adlerians would interpret this memory. The different parts of the memory are pulled together by connecting words, "If this, then that," into a Gestalt. This is the global method of interpretations we often use. Note especially Adler's (1964a/1929) interpretation of a memory:

> I went to school when I was six years old. I was not very happy. The very first day a boy attacked me. I was dreadfully afraid and trembled but...I sprang at him and threw him down. (p. 8)

Adler interpreted, "This little fragment of memory records the two typical motives of the man's life style. He trembles at first but only to overcome. And that little word 'but' holds the rich meaning of his compensation for feelings of inferiority" (1964a, p. 8).

Can a similar scoring help us to interpret ER? Levy and Grigg admit their system is not yet adequate. It simply serves to identify certain themes, not to interpret them. They find they still have to pay attention to omitted themes or persons and still have to decide whether a memory, about say the father, is to be interpreted to apply specifically to the father alone, or is a prototype (Mosak, 1958) for all father figures, authority figures, or even all males. Their scoring system does not do this for them. Furthermore, they had difficulty interpreting memories with sparse details because they could not score them. Here Adlerians with a global approach or similar method could do better. Nevertheless, this is a start at a scoring system.

Olson (1979) stated that the development of scales such as those of Levy and Grigg or Manaster and Perryman should lead to the discovery of basic nomothetic data which would enhance the value of the idiographic interpretation used by the clinician. Some of these scales will be examined in a later chapter.

Friedman and Schiffman (1962) performed a study which showed that raters could examine ER and conclude from them whether a person was a paranoid schizophrenic or a psychotic depressive. The sample contained only depressives and schizophrenics. Would these same raters have been able to distinguish those ER from those of a normal control group? Probably not. Ferguson's (1964) study and another by Hedvig (1965) showed that Adlerian and non-Adlerian judges were not able to consistently match ER with clinical diagnostic categories.

This is contrary to the claim of Eisenstein and Ryerson (1951). At this time no good evidence exists to support the concept that one can predict clinical states from ER. The usual methods of interpretation used by Adlerians are designed to assess core personality dynamics, not clinical states. They have developed no standards for trying to diagnose such clinical states from ER and to even expect to do so would run counter to Adler's theory. Knowing the life style does not mean knowing the clinical diagnosis. Other elements may be present in the ER which can lead to a diagnosis as Eisenstein and Ryerson suggested. Adler (1969a/1929) pointed out that physicians frequently have ER of sickness and death, but here he is speaking about the ***content*** of the memories, not a guiding line for coping with the world. Possibly in the future a set of templates will be developed which will allow effective correlation between certain items in ER and clinical state. One recent example is the finding by Peven and Shulman (1983) that the ER of manic-depressives show a tendency to heighten affect; that is to invest the story in the ER with extreme emotion. Another study by Jackson and Sechrest (1962) found that anxiety neurotics showed more fear, depressives showed more abandonment, and gastrointestinal patients showed more themes of gastrointestinal distress than other patients. Unfortunately, these themes did not occur often enough to be useful in diagnosis.

Taylor's (1975) review of validation studies essentially concluded that ER are a useful and rapid method of personality appraisal which correlates well with other assessment tools, but not a tool at this time to diagnose clinical psychopathology.

Mosak (1958, 1969) reminded us that ER can be studied, as Langs (1965a, 1965b) did, from a psychoanalytic point of view, to discover in them id, ego, and superego functioning; drive precipitates; and defensive operations. As Mosak pointed out, this is not the same as eliciting from them an understanding of life style—how an individual human entity creatively fashions its own subjective reality and responds to it. In later chapters we will discuss how we can interpret the ER of an individual in such a way that we can elicit the life style.

CHAPTER **4**

HOW DATA ARE COLLECTED

The ***Life Style Inventory*** (LSI) form provided in this Chapter is a skeletal guide to the material to be collected for the life style formulation. The page design grew out of long experience with the approximate amount of information elicited and requiring recording. Other designs might be even more useful, especially if the data were to be used for research. The form has appropriate places for recording information about family constellation and early recollections.

FAMILY CONSTELLATIONS (FC)

The family constellation is actually a form of life history study and a form of personality inventory. As a life history study, it is limited in two ways. The material is all autobiographical and therefore entirely subjective, with all the limitations of any subjective report. In addition, it is limited to early life history and thus is not designed to elicit the effects of significant incidents that occurred in adolescence and later, important as they may be. For life style assessment, the early experiences through puberty are the most important. Limiting the information to early life can have varied effects. Occasionally a subject who recalls childhood as exceedingly unhappy will be unwilling to give the material because doing so is accompanied by painful emotions. Other subjects may find it easier to speak of childhood because the temporal distance reduces the remembered pain. Some find it easier to admit embarrassing behavior in the past than in the present. However, if the subject offers the opinion that later life experiences were influential, our custom is to accept this information also and assess the role of these later experiences as well. In Adlerian theory, however, the basic aspects of the life style are supposedly formed by the age of five or six and thus the early life material is given much more weight.

The family constellation portion of the LSI is a personality inventory to the extent that it contains trait ratings. One difference from usual personality inventories is that a subject rates the siblings as well as oneself and thus the trait ratings are comparative rather than absolute. In effect, all family members are assigned trait ratings and all these ratings are assessed as part of the setting in which these behaviors were displayed—the situational stimulus and personal response are assessed as an interaction.

The material used in assessing family constellation (FC) consists of answers to questions asked by the assessor. While conceivably these questions could be self-administered, it is standard for an assessor to ask them and to pursue, with more specific questions, items or areas that are incompletely covered or ambiguous or need elaboration. In order for the procedure to be more suitable for self-administration, the form would require many more specific questions.

While trait ratings may lend themselves to psychometric analysis, the FC is not really an objective measurement of traits, although some attempts have been made to apply objective analysis of the person according to the trait ratings (O'Phelan, 1977). The FC is not useful for measuring current states, since it assesses traits, not states. The trait assessments are actually part of a larger analysis of the interpersonal field in the family—both role analysis (Sarbin & Allen, 1968) and group process analysis. As mentioned in Chapter 2, role analysis includes role location, expectations, demands, enactment, skills, and self-role congruence. In addition, some roles have more power than others and different roles lead to different interactions. Group process analysis examines how the family members communicate, how conflict occurs and is resolved, how people cooperate and compete, how dominance hierarchies are established, and how available roles are divided.

Early recollections (ER) are essentially a projective technique (Mosak, 1958). Sundberg (1977) asserted that Freudian theory was the driving force behind the use of projective techniques. In classical psychoanalytic theory, the important constituents of personality include unconscious id drives and ego defenses. Projective techniques are intended to elicit such unconscious psychic material. For Adlerians, projective techniques reveal the consistencies of personality—thus the life style, which is the most consistent personality aspect of all. As discussed in Chapter 3, ER are more consistent than either Rorschach or TAT over time and are less influenced by the current state of the subject than those two tests.

According to Lindzey (1961), ER are a ***construction*** technique—that is, the subject is required to produce something, in this case, early memories. Because one early memory often stimulates another, ER also have some aspects of an association technique.

Collecting information about the family constellation uses a ***structured interview*** technique. The assessor asks a series of questions in a specified order so that the data collection process remains fairly uniform from one person to another and across all settings. Some parts of this structured interview also can be considered to contain projective material. Any open-ended question such as, "What were you like as a child?" invites the subject to select his/her own preferred parameters for describing oneself. We will discuss the value of this later in the chapter.

The structured interview begins with putting the siblings in their chronological order and obtaining a short, spontaneous description of each. Then, the siblings are grouped and special circumstances which may influence family roles are investigated. Siblings are then rated against each other. Areas of physical, social, and sexual development, and school performance are then examined to see how the subject functioned in extra-familial areas. Some questions are asked about common existential issues or identity concerns; such as, what were the childhood ambitions or ideals?

Next we turn our attention to the parents, the behavior they modeled, child-parent relations, parent-parent relations, their values and the atmosphere in the home. Sometimes, grandparents and other adults play important roles as models and caretakers. That part of the structured interview dealing with the family constellation ends with questions about such adults.

The rest of the life style assessment data consists of the ER. We describe our method for collecting ER.

SIBLINGS

SIBLING CONSTELLATION (Give Childhood Descriptions)
(Oldest to Youngest) Give Age for Subject and Years Older or Younger for Others

Name: ________ Age Dif ________ M F Description:	Name: ________ Age Dif ________ M F Description:
Name: ________ Age Dif ________ M F Description:	Name: ________ Age Dif ________ M F Description:
Name: ________ Age Dif ________ M F Description:	Name: ________ Age Dif ________ M F Description:

Figure 4.1. Sibling Constellation, page 2 of the LSI Form.

Page 2 of the form (Figure 4.1) gives us information about such variables as family size, age distribution, and sexual distribution, which all may influence family climate, sibling roles, group process, and personality outcome. In the following sequence of numbering, the first number refers to the page number of the Life Style Inventory form, while the second number suggests an orderly system for proceeding to gather the information. (Thus, number 2-4 suggests the 4th step to be taken in filling out page 2.)

SIBLING CONSTELLATION

Siblings: Basic Information
(Top Part of Page 2 of the LSI Form)

2-1 In the spaces provided, list the names of all siblings in descending order of age. Include subject in order of age. Circle M or F for sex of sibling.

If there are more than six siblings, use another sheet. This permits the interviewer at a glance to observe family size, the sexual distribution, age differentials and some minor factors such as whether nicknames are used.

2-2 Include all children, living or deceased.

Note all miscarriages. Include any children who have died. This gives a truer picture of family size and may explain large gaps in age between successive children. If a child has died in childhood, it may affect the psychological position of the other siblings within the family and also may affect the parental treatment of the other children. In a two-child family, the death of a sibling may lead to special treatment of the survivor; birth order position may change or the survivor may find it necessary to compete with a dead sibling. A child born after the death of a sibling may be treated as a family treasure, pampered and overprotected. The deceased child may become an ideal model who retains a special place in the hearts of the parents and to which standard the surviving children may never attain. Furthermore, the death of a child may strongly affect the family climate. In some such families, the deceased still inhabits an important psychological position in the FC.

2-3 Place an asterisk after the name of the respondent.

The asterisk reminds us that the information given represents the ***respondent's*** view of himself and his family, not necessarily the way things actually were. If we were to interview other members of the family, we would discover that they might have different views of themselves, the others, and events. It is not uncommon when gathering such data from siblings for the interviewer to wonder whether they were truly raised in the same family.

2-4 Place the respondent's current age next to his/her name. Then list the age discrepancy, plus or minus, next to each sibling's name.

Example of an entry for Bessie

Charles +6	Matilda (+4) Died when Bessie age 5	Merton +2	Bessie* 27

Perusing this age distribution presents us with clues to subgroupings within the siblings constellation. If we cannot easily ascertain the compositions of the sub-groups from the age and sex distributions, items 2-5, 2-6 and 2-7 may provide additional information.

The age discrepancies also assist in the evaluation of the degree of competition between siblings. Siblings closer in age tend to compete more.

2-5 For siblings who are deceased, place parentheses about the age discrepancy.

Next to the parentheses, make a statement such as:

> "Died before Bessie* born." "Died when Bessie* was adult," etc.

In the space for sibling description, under each space, record a description of the dead sibling, but also note the circumstances surrounding the death, the family's reaction to it, and any changes in the subject's position. We already noted in 2-2 the importance of this information.

2-6 Starting with the oldest child, inquire, "What was he (or she) like as a child?"

Obtain the spontaneous descriptions for each child in turn, including the subject.

2-7 Inquire of the subject, "What were you like as a child?"

When we collect this spontaneous information, we avoid influencing the direction of the respondent's communication. We also learn, from what the person chooses to emphasize, what was important about each sibling or the nature of the individual and family values. Do not interfere with the spontaneous description. However, if the spontaneous description is too sparse, one may prompt by general suggestions such as, "What stands out in your mind about him/her?"

The subject can be expected to describe the childhood characteristics of self and siblings along those dimensions that are important to the subject. This aspect of the inventory can be compared to Kelly's (1955) Role Repertory Construct Test. Kelly had the subject choose three people and then describe in what way two were similar and the third differed from the other two. The subject's own choice of qualities by which to assess differences and similarities revealed the dimensions by which the subject construed people—that is, the subject's personal constructs. Here, too, the subject reveals important dimensions by which he/she assesses self and others, as well as the assessment constructs used in the family (family values).

If the subject begins the answer to 2-7 by stating, "I was fat," the assessor should then ask, "What effect did it have on you?" Thus the first construct dimensions emphasized by the subject always provide the opportunity to explore further.

SIBLING GROUPINGS	
Most different from respondent. How? Most like respondent. How? Groupings by age, sex, etc.	Relationship between siblings Who cared for and protected whom? Who played together? Who fought each other?
Sickness, surgery, or accidents?	Unusual talents or achievements?
	Childhood fears, childhood ambitions?

SHARED TRAITS AND/OR INTERESTS (Shared equally by all siblings)

Figure 4.2. Sibling Groupings, page 2 of the LSI Form.

SIBLING GROUPINGS
(Second Part of Page 2 of the LSI Form)

2-8 "Who was most different from you?"

Dreikurs (1953) held that a child is most unlike its most significant competitor in his/her way of striving for significance. If the subject's reply indicates a sibling who is not in the same sub-group, inquire as to who was the most different in the sub-group. Dreikurs' opinion also was that this competition influenced the child's search for place more than parental influence. Sometimes the child designated as most different is a child different from all the siblings, e.g., a retarded child. In that case, ask "Who was next most different?" The answer to these questions can be checked in the section on trait ratings, when similarities and differences become apparent.

2-9 "In what ways?"

While this question elaborates upon the previous question, it also expands upon the information given spontaneously on the first page. This added structure may assist inarticulate subjects to furnish information concerning the sibling configuration even when they have previously expressed inability to do so. A subject who has focused only upon similarities may here be encouraged to provide differences.

2-10 "Who was most like you?"

The reply to this question provides the clue to modeling, alliances, and family values. In this instance we permit comparison with siblings outside of the subject's group, since a young child may model self after an older sibling outside of the sub-group.

2-11 "In what ways?"

> **Example:** "Who was most like you?"
>
> "Charles was most like me. We both tried to please Mother. We would help around the house. We were both more responsible."

This answer suggests that pleasing by being helpful was a family value, that Charles and Bessie were perhaps allied and perhaps imitating one of the parents.

2-12 "Were the children grouped according to age, sex, or in any other way?"

In some families, the family consists of "older" children and "younger" children. In others the distinction is the "boys" and the "girls." Some families may be divided into the foreign-born and the native-born. Another grouping may be in terms of the children who resemble the father's family and those who resemble the mother's. Birth order only accounts for a small number of psychological positions within the family, as discussed in Chapter 2. In a family of five children, an important procedure is to determine sub-groups in order to understand the psychological position of the three middle siblings. A five-sibling family might be grouped as a 1-2-2 sibship, with the oldest actually functioning as an only child. Another possibility is a 2-3 division, with the older two forming a pair (first born and second) and the last three forming a first, middle, and youngest.

2-13 "Who cared for and protected whom?"

Because many subjects experience difficulty in dividing their families into sub-groups, questions 2-13, 2-14, and 2-15 are designed to assist in determining such groupings. The answer to the question, "Who cared for and protected whom?" may assist us in subgrouping. It also may expose whether any of the children were in a parental role. We also may learn whether nurturance and responsibility were valued in this family.

2-14 "Who played together?"

Children generally engage in peer play with members of their own sub-group. Occasionally a younger child will describe play with a very much older sibling. This is generally not peer play, but adult-child play.

2-15 "Who fought each other?"

As with Item 2-14, children generally fight, whatever form the fighting may take, with siblings within the same sub-group.

2-16 "Were any of the siblings sick? Did they have surgery or were they in an accident?"

For life style purposes, we are only interested in such events which occurred during early childhood; e.g., through the elementary school period. The inquiry also should include how the sibling or the respondent was treated by virtue of this particular event and how the respondent felt about it. Many children achieve a special place or receive special treatment by virtue of being ill, handicapped, or the victim of an accident. Some children are relieved of responsibility or given extra attention, comfort, or sympathy. Some children, learning that they can obtain special place or special treatment this way, manipulate the other family members to get this special treatment. Later in life they may expect teachers and schoolmates to continue the special treatment. One can usually assume that when the subject replies to this question, "I nearly died," that special treatment was received and that the event carries special significance.

We can learn whether any additional effects occurred from the event. An example of such additional effects can be seen in Adler's claim that physicians have recollections of illness, accident, or death (Adler, 1968). Adler's own recollections contain such events, influencing him to become a physician (Mosak & Kopp, 1973). Additional information on illness can be recorded in the section on Childhood Physical Development Item 4-1 in this manual, and top part of page 4 of the LSI form).

2-17 "Did any of the siblings possess an unusual talent or did any achieve anything special or noteworthy?"

In the search for significance in which children engage within the family structure, many children find their position within the family because they have some unusual talent or ability, positive or negative. Precociousness; being in trouble; academic, athletic, or artistic accomplishment; winning a competition; and unusual behavior all afford the child a feeling of significance. The talent is not the important determinant but rather the reinforcement received.

2-18 "What fears did you have as a child?"

The reply to this question will furnish additional information concerning the development of the child. However, subjects also may tell us a particular fear which they had as a child is retained in adult life. This information assumes special importance if we plan to engage the subject in therapy. The childhood fear is not considered the cause of the adult fear. A historical continuity may exist between childhood and adult fear, but the adult fear has a contemporaneous purpose. The childhood fear itself is of less significance than the payoff the child may have received for being afraid (Mosak et al., 1980). For example, fear of sleeping in the dark may permit the child to sleep with the parents, keeping them tied to him/her.

Some subjects will not reveal a single fear, but will describe themselves as "always fearful" or "afraid of everything, including my own shadow." Elaboration upon this theme will throw light upon their self-training in the fear response.

2-19 "What was your childhood ambition?"

The reply, "I had different ambitions at different times in my childhood," is not uncommon. While the responses may shed light upon many aspects of child development, we would have more interest in the child's goals, as reflected in recollected ambitions. A child accustomed to receiving attention may describe the childhood ambition as being an actor or fashion model. Another child may describe a childhood ambition of being a major-league pitcher because "he's in on every play." A third child relates she loved theater, and her favorite activity was being in the school and community theatre plays.

Several forms of response reveal the child's response to adult standards or expectations. The following are examples:

> "My parents always wanted me to be a doctor. They never said so, but I knew what they expected."
>
> "The nuns told me I should be a priest. I tried to be scrupulous and was always running to confession."
>
> "Anything my parents expected me to do, I did the opposite."

Other responses may give us a measure of the child's level of aspiration or self-training in certain areas.

SHARED TRAITS AND/OR INTERESTS
(Bottom Part of Page 2 of the LSI Form)

2-20 "Were any traits shared by the siblings?"

This question often elicits family values, interests, and/or behaviors. Traits or interests shared equally by all the siblings are considered to be family traits or interests, showing family values or behaviors. For example, all members in a family may have a bad temper and both parents may have modeled such behavior for the children. (See Figure 4.2.)

SIBLING RATINGS
(Page 3 of the LSI Form)

Specific Comparison Ratings of Siblings

Rating siblings comparatively on specific traits has several advantages—some subjects who have difficulty giving spontaneous descriptions are much more able to describe specific differences between themselves and other siblings when prompted with specific questions. Furthermore, sub-groupings will become even more clear if one remembers that competition is supposedly more keen between siblings in the same subgroup. When the description of the parents is taken later, it also will become clear how this modeling influenced trait selection by the various children. The comparative ratings also reveal those areas in which each child found effective ways of coping and those areas in which each became discouraged and gave up. These areas of "success" and "failure" become crucial as the child grows older, in establishing areas of interest, competency, and levels of aspiration. The child who is a poor student early may easily become discouraged in school and lose interest in becoming academically proficient. Early success in interpersonal relationships (e.g., pleasing others) reinforces interest and practice in such behavior.

The specific ratings (Figure 4.3) have been chosen because they seem to provide us with that information we find most desirable. They do not, however, constitute an absolute or exhaustive list. A much longer list would be possible, but it would make the assessment process too long. Other traits can be used for comparison rather than these, and as we describe the assessment process in subsequent chapters, we shall find occasion to demonstrate their use. In some cases, traits on the list may be omitted because they do not add appreciably to our picture of the personality (e.g., if siblings did not attend school, then asking who got the best grades is inappropriate). In some families an appropriate procedure is to ask who was the most religious, most musical, the best dresser, the most successful with the opposite sex (although this question takes us into adolescence), the most successful in scrounging for items needed by the family, the most interested in helping, and so forth.

SIBLING RATINGS
(Rate from most to least)

Intelligence	Friends
Elementary school grades	Charm
Helpful around house	Tried to please
Industrious	Had to please
Standards of achievement	Succeeded in pleasing
Actual achievement	Outgoing
Daring	Withdrawn
Assertive	Cheerful
Patient	Considerate
Methodical	Bossy
Neat	Demanded way
Persistent	Got way
Responsible	Temper
Obedient	Fighter
Mischievous	Chip on shoulder
Open rebel	Sulked
Covert rebel	Held grudges
Punished	Complained
For what?	Took advantage of others
By whom?	Stubborn
Got away with the most	Shy
Impulsive	Sensitive and easily hurt
Self-reliant	Excitement seeker
Standards of right & wrong	Idealistic
Critical of others	Materialistic
Critical of self	Pampered
Easy-going	Masculine
Sense of humor	Feminine
Excitable	Sure of self
Worried	Athletic
Other:	

Figure 4.3. Sibling Ratings, page 3 of the LSI Form.

All these questions are specific and require specific answers. This can allow respondents to be somewhat more objective than when they were providing a spontaneous description of themselves and their siblings and sometimes casts doubts on the validity of the spontaneous description by contradicting it. Subjects who tend to guard themselves for fear they will give self-derogatory information may do so less here because the average subject does not know the actual significance of most of the traits.

If Adlerians are correct in assuming the unity of personality, we should expect the subject's personality traits to cluster in such a way that consistent personality styles become apparent. Thus, the sibling who was most demanding could hardly be the one who was the most considerate and the one who was most obedient could hardly have been the most openly rebellious. Such inconsistencies beg further questioning to resolve the contradictions. As the questions are asked, they will permit the traits to cluster so that internal inconsistencies stand out.

Ratings can be asked for in two ways. With a more sophisticated subject, the request may be as follows:

3-1 "For each of the following traits, please rate your siblings and yourself from most to least."

In instances where the person has difficulty with the above instructions, the questions may be asked: *"Who was the most intelligent? Who was the least? Where would you put the others in this order?"*

Especially in larger families, the person may not be able to rank every sibling. If one cannot, the most important ranking to get is who was ***most,*** who was ***least,*** and if the subject is neither, his/her relative position in the ranking: i.e., closer to the most, next to the least.

For the neophyte life style assessor, a helpful procedure is to collect ratings for all of the siblings. Where the family is extremely large and one must economize on time, more experienced assessors may ask the subject to rate only those siblings in one's subgroup. However, remember that such shortcuts contaminate the data to some extent.

Abbreviations Used
(Top Three-Fourths of Page 12 of the LSI Form)

The requirements of recording data in a small space lead assessors to develop abbreviations. On page 12 of the LSI are the ones we use (Figure 4.4).

SIBLING RATING ABBREVIATIONS	
R,M,T,W	Initials of first name of siblings listed from most to least on a given trait.
R,M = T,W	Two siblings are rated as equal on a trait
O	No sibling with a given trait **OR** not evaluated
DR	Don't remember
?	Can't rate
R...W or R,M...	Only rated some of the siblings. Dots represent omissions
H,M,L	Rating abbreviations for High, Medium, Low
M+	Rating abbreviation for High average
ML	Rating abbreviation for Medium to Low

OTHER ABBREVIATIONS AND SYMBOLS	
K	Know
DK	Don't know
DR	Don't remember
Fa, Mo	Father, Mother
GF, PGF, MGM	Grandfather, paternal grandfather, maternal grandmother
↑ ↓	up, increase; down, decrease
——>	toward, leads to
<——	away from
<——>	between, ambivalent
< >	separated
> <	together
=	equal to, identical with
>	more than
<	less than
♂ ♀	male, female
∴	therefore
∵	because
Λ	over
V	under
c̄	with
s̄	without
ā	before
p̄	after
L	like
Ø	none, nothing

Figure 4.4. Abbreviations used in LSI recordings, page 12 of the LSI Form.

1. When siblings are rated most to least, they can be recorded in order, using the first initial of each sibling, with commas between the initials. Thus, the recording R, M, T, W states that R was the most and W the least of whichever trait is being rated. Where siblings name begin with the same letter we record as M,Ja,G,Jo.

2. When two siblings are rated as equal, an equals sign shows this equality. Thus, R, M=T, W shows that M and T were equal in their display of the trait and both between the extremes of R and W.

3. When the subject feels that the trait describes none of the siblings, place a zero after the rating. Thus   Withdrawn 0
4. Other designations such as "Doesn't remember" (DR) or "Can't rate" (?) may also be inserted.
5. If the subject can only rate some of the siblings or perhaps only "Most" or "Least," place dots between the ratings to indicate omissions, such as

   R . . . . W or R, M . . . .

6. Comments made by the subject in conjunction with the ratings are recorded so that we can have the precise nuance the subject wishes to communicate: e.g., Temper-J ("hair-trigger"), E ("slow to anger, but when he blew, he blew") . . . .
7. When we interview persons who are an only child in the family, we ask them to rate themselves "High" (above average) (H), "Medium" (average) (M), or "Low" (below average) (L). Should they inquire what the meanings of these ratings are, since we are interested in subjective impressions, we ask them to rate in terms of their appraisal of the meaning of these measurements. Some clients, given this task, will refine these measures, rating themselves as "High average" (M+) or "Medium to Low" (ML). Such ratings are not only permissible, but valuable.

Unless some child outside the family actually played some aspect of the sibling role, we do not ask the only child to compare self to friends, cousins, etc. We merely ask for the self rating.

	Charles	Matilda	Morton	Bessie	Robert
Intelligent	M	0	—	+	L
Grades	+	0	—	M	L
Helpful around house	—	0	M	M	L

M = most   + closer to M in degree the trait is expressed
L = least   — closer to L in degree the trait is expressed
0 = not evaluated

Figure 4.5. An alternate procedure to record the rating data and a list of abbreviations used.

Alternate Recording Procedure

In Figure 4.5 is a relatively quick way of determining the comparative clustering of the traits among the siblings. Often this procedure is useful as an alternative way of plotting and recording the sibling ratings.

Skewed Ratings

Skewed ratings point to underlying personality traits in the respondent. Some subjects, for example, will only describe or rate siblings according to their positive qualities, as if they are following a dictum, "If you can't say something good about a person, say nothing at all." Others overemphasize the importance of being accurate and thus give no ratings or overqualify the ones they give. Some efface themselves ("I'm just average"). Still others bend over backwards to be fair, trying to insure that they will demean no one.

TRAITS

Why These Ratings/Traits

These ratings were chosen by us as a result of our own experiences with collecting life style data. Perusal of the ratings will show that most of these traits, if not all, can be expected to elicit responses from parents, siblings, and other humans in the immediate neighborhood. They are all actually facets of interpersonal interaction.

The traits can be divided into constitutional and reactive traits. "Looks" (physical appearance) contains constitutional traits. How tall and strong a boy is and how pretty a girl is may become significant issues in personality development. Intelligence, athletic ability, and sound health are all constitutionally influenced traits. They are the "givens" which the child finds within self and to which the environment responds.

Reactive traits are the larger and more important group. They reveal the interests and preferences of the child, the direction of movement for finding one's own niche in the ecological structure of the family.

Some have misunderstood Adler, claiming that the use of a trait is more important than its possession. The intelligent child may play stupid and the frail child may play frightened. Adler did not discount the role of constitution; rather, he pointed out that a constitutional given may elicit different individual responses.

In our questions, we often may use possession language (i.e., Who had a temper?) but in our thinking we automatically translate this into the language of use or movement (What was gained by using temper?).

USE OF TRAITS TO COPE WITH DEVELOPMENTAL TASKS
(Pages 4 and 5 of the LSI Form)

Pages 4 and 5 of the LSI form provide space for obtaining additional information concerning childhood development and experience. Physical development is recorded in the first box while Adler's three life tasks are recorded in the subsequent boxes. The final box on page 4 contains responses to questions related to the fifth life task (Mosak & Dreikurs, 1967). While we are primarily interested in the subject's development, we may seek information on all of the siblings. Much of the information already will have been elicited on pages 2 and 3.

CHILDHOOD PHYSICAL DEVELOPMENT (4-1)
(Top One-Third of Page 4 of the LSI Form)

While a list of all the questions which could be asked cannot be reproduced, nor can all the kinds of information which subjects volunteer be imagined, one of the major areas explored is body image and the response of the environment to physical development, organ inferiority, and handicaps (Figure 4.6). Specific questions about sexual characteristics are asked in the section on sexual development. Typical questions on physical development include the following:

"Were you or a sibling tall, short, skinny, fat?"

CHILDHOOD PHYSICAL DEVELOPMENT
(Health, Physique, Feelings about Body, Advantages/Disadvantages, Nicknames Associated with Physique)

Figure 4.6. Childhood Physical Development, page 4 of the LSI Form.

"What effect did it have on your development?"

"Were you called any nicknames because of your physique?"

"Was physical development accelerated or retarded?"

"Were there any advantages ("I always got the cream because I was so skinny") or disadvantages ("I was such a peewee the bigger kids wouldn't let me play baseball with them.")"

"How did you regard yourself?" ("My nose was so long, I felt ugly.")

"How did others respond to your physical development?"

The value of this section is that it gives us some idea of the influence of physique and body image on the subject's personality and how it affected standing in the family constellation. In the case of any handicap we ask how the subject compensated or overcompensated for it and in what areas he/she was discouraged by it.

ELEMENTARY SCHOOL INFORMATION (4-2)
(Middle One-Third of Page 4 of the LSI Form)

ELEMENTARY SCHOOL INFORMATION
(Type of School, Grades, Subject Performance, Classroom Behavior, Relationship to Teachers, Subjects Liked and Disliked)

Figure 4.7. Elementary School Information, page 4 of the LSI Form.

The information solicited in the Elementary School Information box on page 4 (Figure 4.7) usually refers to grade school only. After the subject is afforded an opportunity to comment spontaneously, we ask questions about type of school, academic achievement, attitudes toward school, and special positions in school. Typical questions include the following:

> "What type of school (public, private, parochial) did you attend?"
>
> "What was the school climate like? Strict? Permissive? Laissez-faire? Traditional?"
>
> "What were your favorite subjects?"
>
> "What subjects did you dislike?"
>
> "In what subjects did you do best? Poorest?"
>
> "What subjects did you like best? Worst?"
>
> "How did each sibling like school?"

"How did you like the teachers?"

"How did the teachers like you?"

"What was your attendance record like?"

"Did you have a special position in school, e.g., patrol, teacher's pet, cleaning erasers?"

"Were you given any special treatment, e.g., special education, classes for gifted, speech therapy, tutoring?"

School, itself, is a challenge to the young child. It requires performance and compliance and is one source of inferiority feelings in the child who does not meet school standards. The answers to the questions give us information about the child's ability to cooperate and meet standards set by others, to develop the trait of industry, and to learn skills.

Dreikurs used to teach that the child's responses to the various challenges in school provided valuable information about personality style. How the child performed in certain subjects suggested certain traits (Mosak, Schneider, & Mosak, 1980). For example, the child whose worst subject was arithmetic and best subject was English or social studies, was often a child who lacked confidence and did not like to be pinned down. Arithmetic is a subject in which answers are either right or wrong; there is no leeway for ambiguous answers. English and social studies allow a certain flexibility in answering, so that one can be partially right. Arithmetic requires care in answering questions, an application to the task. One cannot look for answers the teacher will like, there is only one right answer.

Spelling, on the other hand, is a discipline with arbitrary rules. One must learn by memory and practice how to spell correctly. Poor spellers are supposed to have a tendency to make their own rules, rather than follow established rules. On the other hand, good spelling but poor handwriting suggests an undercover rebellion against conformity.

Compliant behavior in school suggests a desire to please by conforming. Disobedience suggests rebelliousness and school underachievement suggests discouragement about performing well in school or a bid for attention.

All these statements about a subject's specific school performance should be considered only as possibilities. Other factors can be involved. Poor spelling and reading difficuty may be the result of dyslexia or underachievement, or misbehavior may reflect problems at home. Some students will work hard when they are interested in a subject and neglect subjects they do not like. Some students will work if they like the teacher; others will work only if they smell success and give up if they do not feel they will excel.

In each case, these specific behaviors can be explored further by questions such as:

Why did you do well/poorly in that subject?

How did you react when teachers liked/disliked you?

How much did you care about school? Why?

CHILDHOOD MEANINGS GIVEN TO LIFE (4-3)
(Bottom One-Third of Page 4 of the LSI Form)

Some of the guiding ideals of the subject can be elicited by questions in this area (Figure 4.8). The answers may show whether a sense of ethics was or was not a part of the early learning. Sometimes a deep sense of pessimism or chaos can be found in these answers. The ability to come to terms with the actual conditions of existence requires flexibility, creativity, and a reasonably accurate assessment of life's possibilities. Exaggerated and rigid ideals, social isolation, and pessimistic or grandiose expectations all interfere with successful adaptation.

Some of the questions that are often asked are as follows:

"What were your expectations for yourself?"

"How would you characterize your childhood outlook on life?"

"Did you have a compelling goal in life?"

"What did you feel about right and wrong?"

"How did you feel about your religion? Your family's view of or observance of religion? Of God?"

"Did you have a favorite daydream?"

"What seemed to make life worthwhile during childhood?"

CHILDHOOD MEANINGS GIVEN TO LIFE
(Expectations, Ideals, Meaningful Goals, Favorite Daydreams, Religious Convictions)

Figure 4.8. Childhood Meaning Given to Life, page 4 of the LSI Form.

CHILDHOOD GENDER AND SEXUAL INFORMATION (5-1)
(Top One-Half of Page 5 of the LSI Form)

Inquiry centers about sexual definitions, gender identification, sex role, sex play, and the developmental aspects of sex. Typical questions might include the following and the answers recorded in the top one-half of LSI, page 5 (Figure 4.9):

CHILDHOOD GENDER AND SEXUAL INFORMATION
(Development, Source of Information, Sex Play, Reaction to Pubertal Changes, Comfort with Gender, Feelings About Sexual Activity, Sexual Abuse)

Figure 4.9. Childhood Gender and Sexual Information, page 5 of the LSI Form.

"Where and how did you obtain your sex information?"

"Did you engage in sex play?" "What kind?"

"Were you caught at it?"

"Were you a tomboy?" "A sissy?"

"Did you ever want to be a member of the other sex?"

"What were boys/girls supposed to be (do, live up to) in your family?"

"How did you feel about the size of your penis/breasts?"

"When did you begin to menstruate?" "Were you informed about it?" "How was it referred to?"

"How did you feel about it?"

"When did your body begin to develop?" "How did you feel about it?" "How did you feel about your first bra?"

"Did you masturbate?" "When did you begin?" "How did you learn about it?" "How did you feel about it?"

"How was the topic of sex treated in your family?"

"Was anyone in your family sexually abused?"

CHILDHOOD SOCIAL RELATIONSHIPS (5-2)

(Bottom One-Half of Page 5 of the LSI Form)

Again, after the subject's spontaneous observations, we inquire about such areas as social role, social affiliation, leadership-followership, and peer relationships. Such inquiry might include the following questions with responses recorded on the bottom one-half of page 5 (Figure 4.10):

CHILDHOOD SOCIAL RELATIONSHIPS
(Friends, Gangs, Availability of Peers, Role in Peer Group, Relations with Adults)

Figure 4.10. Childhood Social Relationship Information, page 5 of the LSI Form.

"Were you included or on the periphery?"

"How did the other kids regard and accept you?"

"How did your parents accept your choice of friends?"

"In what kinds of play did you engage?"

"What kinds of groups did you join?"

"Did you play with peers, younger kids, older kids, or kids of the other sex?" "What kind of kids were available?"

"Were you a 'friend to all mankind' or did you have a few close friends?"

"What was your role in the group (e.g., leader, clown, goat, idea man)?"

"How did you feel about your social life?"

"Were you different in any way from the others in your neighborhood?"

PARENTAL INFORMATION DURING SUBJECT'S CHILDHOOD
(Page 6 of the LSI Form)

Pages 6 and 7 of the form permit recording information concerning any persons who served as parents or parent-surrogates. These include step-parents, foster parents, grand-parents who actually reared the children, and so forth. The respondent may have experienced, and will describe, more than two parents. The following instructions describe the recording system used by us for page 6 (Figure 4.11).

6-1 Record father's and mother's names.

These names may disclose ethnic background. One of the children may be a "Jr." or "III," which may reveal expectations or socio-economic status (Mosak & Mosak, 1979).

PARENTAL INFORMATION DURING SUBJECT'S CHILDHOOD		
Name	FATHER ____________	MOTHER ____________
Current age even if deceased	Age ______	Age ______
At time of subject's birth	Age ______	Age ______
	Occupation ____________	Occupation ____________
(Traits, Respected, Liked, Feared)	Description:	Description:
Relations to Children		
What was most important to him/her?		
What was way to win his/her praise?		
What made him/her angry?		
In what ways did he/she influence you?		
Expectations for children		
Who was his/her favorite? Why?		
Relationship to children		
Sibling most like him/her In what ways?		
Who was closest to him/her?		
Who was most distant?		
Confided in whom?		
Took hurts to whom?		
Others:		

Subject's role in family

Subject's feeling about family

Worst possible fate for a child in the family

Other:

Figure 4.11. Parental Information During Subject's Childhood, page 6 of the LSI Form.

6-2 Record parents' current ages, even if deceased.

This permits the rapid subtractions required in Items 6-4 and 6-5.

6-3 For parents who are deceased, place parentheses about the age.

Next to the parentheses, make statements as in Item 1-5. As in that item, note the circumstances surrounding the death, the family's reaction to it, and any changes in the family climate, family fortunes. Was the family broken as a result of the death?

6-4 Compare the parents' ages.

If great disparity exists, one of the parents may have been married previously. The possibility also exists that the much younger parent may occupy psychologically the position of the oldest sibling.

6-5 Compare the parents' ages with those of the children.

In some instances, children will be reared by older, tired parents; in others, married at a young age, they are hardly more than children themselves. The older children may have been reared by young parents and the younger children by old parents.

6-6 For each parent, record his/her occupation(s).

In this context, we are primarily concerned with occupations held during the respondent's childhood. In addition to the factual information, we may derive other types of information, e.g., "My father could never hold a job." "My mother was so busy as a club-woman and raising money for charity that we never saw her."

References to work stability, responsibility, and satisfaction, alcoholism, ambition, and socio-economic status may be elicited at this point in the interview.

6-7 "When you were a child, what was your father like?"

Again, we permit the subject to give a spontaneous description. The interviewer should stress that what is wanted are the subject's perceptions when a child rather than an adult retrospective view. The latter information, while useful for other purposes, is not required for life style assessment. Information obtained here describes the parents as models for observational learning and what and how parents reinforced. When the subject completes the spontaneous description, we ask questions which will enable us to fill in whatever gaps in the data we feel still remain, such as: "What did you most like about him? Dislike?" What was his characteristic facial expression?" "What sort of remark did he usually make to you?"

One may also ask specific questions: "Was he warm, cheerful, bossy, a good provider, have good habits, etc."

These following questions (6-8 through 6-12) furnish information about standards, expectations and pressures placed upon the children. These questions give us some information about parental values and more.

6-8 "What was most important to father?"

This is an attempt to elicit what father valued. It may have been good grades, good behavior, athletic ability or cuteness.

6-9 "What was the way to win father's praise?"

Similar to 6-8, but an attempt to discover what father reinforced and who did what in trying to win praise.

6-10 "What made father angry?"

This continues the subject of 6-8 and 6-9 and gives clues to how father used anger in his relationships to the children.

6-11 "In what way did father influence you?"

Was father a positive or negative model? Did he encourage or discourage?

6-12 "What were your father's expectations for the family?"

We also may ask which of the children responded to these expectations, whether they accepted or rejected them, whether they drove themselves to achieve those goals, or whether they defaulted or withdrew and whether they wanted to or felt they could please the parents.

Some useful questions that may be asked at this point are,

"What did Father want you to be?" "Not to be?"

"When was he happy with you?" "Unhappy?"

6-13 "Who was father's favorite? Why?"

This question and subsequent ones provide information concerning parent-child relationships. Favored children often feel more secure in their place in the family. The child who was favored by no one may have felt rejected. The information permits us to discover who felt left out, which child may have been favored by all the adults, whether boys were preferred over girls, or oldest children favored by one parent and rejected by another. The last such child may later have difficulties with rejectors but relate well with those who like him. It is often useful to ask who was least favored by each parent. A parent may have had more than one favorite.

6-14 "What was the relationship between father and children like?"

The relationship between parents and children constitutes a dyadic process (Mosak, 1980). Each influences the other. We are interested in whether the parents were perceived as pampering, frightening, loving, rejecting, not available, disapproving, inconsistent, or having excessive standards. We also explore whether the children lived up to parental expectations or rebelled and whether the parents lived up to the subject's expectations.

Considerable redundance is in these questions so that one may not have to ask all of them to elicit the desired information. The redundance encourages elaboration by the subject and also picks up contradictions that need to be investigated.

After the subject's spontaneous description, we may ask,

"Were you ever afraid of him? When?"

"Were you ever confused by him? When?"

"Did you enjoy being with him or did you feel uncomfortable around him?"

"Was he home a reasonable amount of time?"

"Did you try to please him? How?"

"Did he play with you, teach you, advise you, help you, etc.?"

"Did you try to please him? How?"

Sometimes a useful procedure is to inquire, "When you were small, what did you do to get him to pay attention to you?"

6-15 "Which of the siblings was most like father and in what ways?"

The subject may state that one sibling was more like father in looks and another more like father in temperament or traits. This information helps us determine which siblings followed father's guiding line and how. Sometimes the parent is regarded as such a negative model that the respondent will say that none of the siblings was like the parent.

6-16 "Who was the closest to father?" "Did he demonstrate affection?"

As in questions 6-13 and 6-14, these questions elicit information about the family atmosphere, the kind of order, and presence or absence of warmth.

6-17 "Who was most distant from Father?"

Unless father was a negative model, the child's withdrawal from father suggests a discouragment and feeling that father will reject. It suggests problems in relating to older males later in life.

6-18 Repeat Items 6-7 through 6-17 with respect to mother.

In some families, especially those broken by death or divorce, additional parents or foster parents may be included. List them on a separate sheet and repeat items 6-7 through 6-17 for these additional parents, if it seems indicated.

When divorce occurred, we inquire when the divorce took place, what changes in living arrangements and family fortunes occurred, and how each sibling reacted.

If one parent died, the subject may have had to live with grandparents, other relatives, or foster parents. These surrogate parents should be included on page 7. The subject's reaction to this placement should be recorded. Even if the subject cannot remember a missing parent, one should inquire about that parent. In some families the dead parent is idealized and perhaps canonized.

6-19 Confided in whom?

"To whom did you go when you wanted to share a confidence?" Such information should show us which parent the child trusted more and felt closer to.

6-20 Took hurts to whom?

"To whom did you go when you were in trouble?" Sometimes the answer tells us who was more trusted, but sometimes it tells us which parent was considered to have more power—who could set things right again.

6-21 "What was your role in family?"

Record the response on bottom part of page 6 (Figure 4.11). The subject may use terms such as, "I was the baby", "I was mama's helper" if sophisticated enough. Some subjects may not be able to give such answers but can still say "I just did what I was told and minded my own business" or "I was just like other kids."

6-22 "What were your feelings about the family?"

Was the subject a critic of the family? Take a tragic view of the family? Have strong family loyalty? Become distant from family?

6-23 "What was the worst possible fate for a child in the family?"

This tells us what the family considered utter failure and disappointment in a child or what would lead the family to label the child as the most inferior family member.

NATURE OF PARENTS' RELATIONSHIP
(Top One-Third of Page 7 of the LSI Form)

7-1 "What was the nature of the relationship between your father and your mother?"

Many clients will simply indicate that it was good or poor. While this evaluative comment is important, we also wish to understand the nature as well as the quality of the parent-parent interaction while the child was young. As information is obtained, record it at the top of page 7 (Figure 4.12). We are interested in such information as shown in the heading of Figure 4.12.

NATURE OF PARENTS' RELATIONSHIP
(Description, Division of Roles, Interpersonal Relationship, Conflicts/Agreements, Marriage Happy/Unhappy)

Figure 4.12. Nature of Parents' Relationship, page 7 of the LSI Form.

Who was the dominant parent?

The decision maker?

Handled the money?

Was responsible for discipline?

We also try to learn whether the parents did things together or merely lived together under the same roof. If the parents fought, we inquire how the fights were resolved, how the children reacted, and with whom they sided.

Inconsistencies, countermanding of orders which permit a child to play off one parent against the other, also are important to ascertain. We anticipate that the relationship displayed between the parents will present a model of adult male-female relationships.

These parent-parent interactions can be described along several dimensions. After the subject has described the relationship in his/her own terms, we ask further questions to establish certain dimensions of the relationships. These will be the models (positive or negative) for many of one's future male-female relationships, one's expectancies and relationship style. The dimensions we want to discover can be seen in the following group of opposites:

pleasant-unpleasant

affectionate-unloving

close-distant

conflictful-harmonious

cooperative-each for himself

playful-lacked humor

In addition, the relationship may have been authoritarian, with one parent dominating and perhaps even tyrannizing the other. By questioning, one can investigate how each coped with the other (e.g., "Mother was the boss. Father never argued with her, but he'd just go out and get drunk.") Other specific questions will suggest themselves to the interviewer during the course of the interview.

OTHER FAMILY INFORMATION (7-2)
(Middle One-Third of Page 7 of the LSI Form)

In this space provided in middle one-third of page 7 we record such data as the following:

OTHER FAMILY INFORMATION
(Family Climate, Family Values, Socio-economic Status, Ethnicity, Religion)

Figure 4.13. Other Family Information, page 7 of the LSI Form.

1. What was the nature of the family climate? Was it a happy house? Were there many arguments? Was it peaceful or full of turmoil?

2. Was the family religious? Did the parents try to teach moral standards? Was ethical behavior important?

3. What was the family's socio-economic status? Were there any important changes in this status?

4. What was the family's cultural or ethnic background? Was it stressed by the parents?

5. What were the family values? What was stated to be important in the family? What really was important?

6. How was the family regarded in the neighborhood?

7. Were there any other family characteristics? Family myths? Family secrets?

ADDITIONAL PARENTAL FIGURES AND ADULT MODELS (7-3)

(Bottom One-Third of Page 7 of the LSI Form)

This section includes a description of any people who lived with the family during the client's childhood as well as other adults who may have played a significant role in the child's development. Such adults include grandparents, uncles and aunts, boarders, maids, an occasional teacher, Boy Scout leader, or parish priest. The information is recorded on the lower one-third of page 7 (Figure 4.14). The subject is asked to describe the client's relationship to each of these people. Some of the questions suggested on page 6 may be asked here.

ADDITIONAL PARENTAL FIGURES AND ADULT MODELS	
Who/Relationship: ______	Who/Relationship: ______

Figure 4.14. Additional Parental Figures and Adult Models, page 7 of the LSI Form.

This concludes the material that will be used in the formulation of the family constellation.

EARLY RECOLLECTIONS (ER)
(Pages 8 and 9 of the LSI Form)

8-1 **"Go as far back as you can in childhood. When you go back, what early memory comes to your mind?"** Another way to ask for early recollections is to say, **"Think back, as far back as you can. What is the first incident you can remember from your life? Something about which you can say, "One day I remember..."**

After the ER is recorded verbatim (Figure 4.10), the examiner can choose to go on to the next memory or may choose to investigate this one further. The particular method we describe here is to collect the series of ER first and then to explore them further.

EARLY RECOLLECTIONS

(Under age 10) (Description, Most Vivid Part, Feelings)

1. Age ____________:

2. Age ____________:

3. Age ____________:

4. Age ____________:

Figure 4.15. Early Recollections, page 8 of the LSI Form. (Page 9, part 2 of this section, is identical, so not shown.)

8-2 "What is your next memory?" or "What memory comes to your mind next?"

The memories need not be obtained in chronological order; the order in which the subject chooses to give them will be good enough. Continue until the subject has no more ER or begins only to recall events later than age eight or nine.

Pages 8 and 9 of the LSI form (Figure 4.15) have space for eight recollections. Additional pages may be used for additional ER but more than eight are rarely needed by the assessor. Most subjects give fewer than eight ER unless specifically primed.

How does the assessor know when one has elicited enough ER? The answer is—when the themes in the ER begin to repeat themselves. This can be best shown by giving a few examples:

Female—age 32—(the ER are presented in the order the subject gave them).

1. Age 3: I was riding on the big farm tractor with my father. I caught my foot between the wheel and the side of the tractor and it rubbed the skin off my foot. I remember my father carried me home and took me to the doctor who bandaged my foot. I cried, but I was glad my father was there.

2. Age 3: I was playing with my sister Ann and her dolls. We made a tea party and pretended we were feeding the dolls. I wanted to feed my stuffed teddy bear, but Ann said "No" because he wasn't human like a doll. I didn't feed the teddy bear, but I felt bad for him.

3. Age 5: In school I had to go to the bathroom, but I was embarrassed to ask. I sat with the older children, feeling uncomfortable. Finally, I went to the teacher and whispered it to her and she let me go.

4. Age 6 or 7: I was fighting with another girl. I don't know how it started. She hit me in the stomach and I cried. She called me a sissy and the other kids were laughing at me.

These four ER show a repetition of a theme. In ER 1 and 3, the subject experiences relationships with adults as nurturing, while in 2 and 4, relationships with peers are less satisfactory. Each theme has been repeated. If the next ER again repeats the theme, the assessor can consider this a natural stopping place.

After the series of ER is collected, a useful procedure is to review them with the subject. This gives the subject a chance to amend the recollections by changing, elaborating, or adding details.

8-3 "Are there any other details you can recall about this memory?"

Not only details, but some important background material may be elicited here. The memory in Chapter 3 of the man whose father had smothered the rest of the family is a dramatic example of how knowing background affects our interpretation of an ER.

8-4 "Do you recall how you felt at the time?"

This question is not asked if the subject has already described the feeling during the course of giving the ER. In essence, we are asking for an additional detail of a particular type. Excitement-seekers tend to recall more intense feelings than repressors. The latter, being "feeling-avoiders," may give ER in which no personal feelings are contained. Excitement-seeking is an emotional style. [Compare the sensation-seeking motive of Zuckerman (1979).]

The memory "It was Christmas. I got an electric train," would not be complete without the feeling response, "I was disappointed. I wanted a bicycle."

8-5 "What is the most vivid part of the recollection?" or "What part stands out most clearly in your mind?"

This is comparable to a "stop-action" when running a movie film. The "stop-action" contains the essence of the recollection. For example:

> "I was between two and three. Summery day. I was playing outside. I came inside and there was a drawer sticking out. I ran into it and cut my head. My mother got upset, angry and concerned. I felt I had done something wrong. I was bleeding. My mother took me to the hospital . . ."

Asked for the most vivid part of the early recollections, she responded, "The strongest is running into the house, seeing the drawer open, and not being able to stop."

The essence of the ER consists of her warning to herself of the danger of losing control over her own behavior.

When the subject cannot easily recall ER, sometimes primed ER can be elicited by asking the subject to recall a specific event. Some useful questions for priming an ER are as follows:

> ***"Do you remember when your brother (sister) was born?"***
>
> ***Do you remember your first day in school?"***
>
> ***"Do you remember a birthday? A Christmas?"***
>
> ***"Do you ever recall being sick? Frightened? Angry?"***

Knowing some details of the subject's life from the FC will often suggest other priming questions to the assessor. Remember that a primed ER is not completely spontaneous and may be less significant than spontaneous ER.

We do not ask subjects to "Make up an ER" because we do not consider such "ER" interchangeable with actual memories. They do not have the power to display the core constructs that we find in the actual memories.

SUMMARY OF FAMILY CONSTELLATION (10-1)
(Top One-Half of Page 10 of the LSI Form)

This space is provided to enable you to summarize information related to the family. See Figure 4.16.

SUMMARY OF FAMILY CONSTELLATION

Figure 4.16. Summary of Family Constellation, page 10 of the LSI Form.

SUMMARY OF EARLY RECOLLECTIONS (10-2)
(Bottom One-Half of Page 10 of the LSI Form)

This space is provided to enable you to summarize information related to early recollections. See Figure 4.17.

SUMMARY OF EARLY RECOLLECTIONS

Figure 4.17. Summary of Early Recollections, page 10 of the LSI Form.

INTERFERING ATTITUDES, BELIEFS, BEHAVIORS (11-1)
(Top One-Half of Page 11 of the LSI Form)

This space is provided to summarize attitudes, beliefs, and behaviors that may be interfering with each other and/or the client. See Figure 4.18.

INTERFERING ATTITUDES, BELIEFS, BEHAVIORS

Figure 4.18. Interfering Attitudes, Beliefs, Behaviors, page 11 of the LSI Form.

ASSETS AND STRENGTHS (11-2)
(Bottom One-Half of Page 11 of the LSI Form)

This space is provided to enable you to summarize the assets and strengths of the client. See Figure 4.19.

ASSETS AND STRENGTHS

Figure 4.19. Assets and Strengths, page 11 of the LSI Form.

DATE AND SIGNATURE (12-1)
(Bottom of Page 12 of LSI Form)

Space is provided on lower part of page 12 for you to record other comments. Then date and sign the LSI to provide a record of when and who did the interview. See Figure 4.20.

Other Comments:

Date: ______________________ Signature: ______________________

Figure 4.20. Other Comments, Date, and Signature, page 12 of the LSI Form.

SUMMARY

In Chapter 4 we have described how data are gathered and recorded on the LSI form. From time to time in this chapter we have made interpretive comments about the meaning of the data. In Chapter 5 we will describe in detail how the data are interpreted and put in logical order.

CHAPTER **5**

FAMILY CONSTELLATION (FC)

THE PROCESS AND CONTENT OF INTERPRETATION

Our purpose is to use the information from the family constellation (FC) to elicit the life style of the subject we are studying. We shall look at the subject's early life situation as a piece of that person's history which gives us information about formative influences. We will be looking for personality information. We hope to discern the terrain and the action that took place upon it, the early adventurous course of the person, and the answers that he/she gave to the meaning of life.

In order to do this we must have a set of constructs, a theory, which tells us where to look and for what to look. We must know how to recognize formative influences, how and what they influenced and what the outcome was. In our theory the family is an ecological system in which the children seek for what all children seek—nurture, recognition, affiliation, security, and guiding lines for living. However, the family is also a social system with its attendant hierarchical structure, with its jockeying for position, allies and competitors, values, dominance issues, and self-identification as a family member.

In treating early experiences as formative, we are assuming that they are more important than later experiences. We are claiming that the early learning influences later learning, that both disabling attitudes (discouragement) and enabling attitudes develop early and influence later behavior.

We have divided the content of the FC into a number of categories. Each category pays attention to a specific aspect of the FC, yet they are all interrelated in producing the final personality inventory. Each category is important in that it is either (1) a set of challenges which require a response, (2) a set of models for selecting a response style, (3) a set of contingencies which influence response, or (4) a set of responses themselves. In each category, we will try to trace developmental antecendents of the response styles and perceptual framework of the subject. These categories are birth order, constitution and gender, models, interpersonal transactions, family climate, family values, cultural values, roles, and the existential meaning of life.

Birth Order and Its Outcome

We have previously discussed the distinctions between ordinal position, birth order, and psychological position. While we may use birth order as the general term, the psychological position is what is most important to us, since the inferences we draw are based upon our perception of the subject's psychological position within the sibling array. Several examples will hopefully clarify what we can learn from birth order.

Example 5.1. A three-child family: Boy-Girl-Boy

John	Mary*	Jim
+2		-4

The subject is the only girl in the family and may have had a secure position of significance by virtue of this fact. On the other hand, the family values may have been such that the female role had less significance than the male role and she may have decided to compete with her brothers. The more significant competitor is usually the one closer in age, and thus we may expect that she would pit herself against John, either trying to outdo him or to distinguish herself by developing role-skills that were vastly different from his. In some cases, however, the family values provide equal but different role-expectations for each gender, so that what looks like competition may actually only be the different role-enactments belonging to gender differences.

John's role in the family may have given him so much preeminence that Mary may have become discouraged. In this case, her self-perception may be a negative one. If Jim also attains a preeminent role, then Mary will become a "squeezed middle child." Another common outcome is possible. In some families, boys are expected to achieve while girls are expected to behave properly. Assume that John becomes an achiever in school and Jim becomes an athlete. Mary can follow the expected gender-associated role of being the "good girl" who is kind and helpful and no doubt will receive much parental reinforcement for such behavior.

We have drawn a number of inferences from the simple diagram at the beginning of this example. Were we to continue to collect the FC data in Mary's case, we would soon learn what the actual outcome was.

Example 5.2. A six-child family: Boy-Girl-Girl-Boy-Boy-Girl

William	Alice	Cynthia	Bert	Sam*	Jewel
+10	[+8]	+4	+2		-3

Alice died when Sam was two.

The subject is the fifth of six and the youngest boy in the family. In this case, a notable discrepancy exists between the first and third which was created when the second child died. Depending on how strong the memory of the deceased remains in the family, we may find that William plays the role of an adult model rather than a sibling and in effect, for the purposes of understanding Sam, we may do better considering him the third in a sibling array of four. The only thing we can tell about William at this point is that he is the first-born son and seems to have no rivals near him. Perhaps he was overprotected after Alice died, a piece of information we will only know later. If gender roles were strongly typed and the brothers and sisters did not compete with each other, the subject is, in effect, the younger of two boys. Another possibility is that Cynthia may have played a protective role toward Sam, assisting him in his rivalry with Bert. Or, Sam and Bert may have formed an alliance against the two girls surrounding them, forming a macho male group among the siblings. We can see that a large number of outcomes may develop from the array we have diagrammed. Again, subsequent FC data will reveal the outcome. The diagram, however, permits us to start drawing inferences.

Constitution and Gender and Their Outcome

Physical disabilities, both congenital (organ inferiority) (Adler, 1917) and acquired, may stimulate the person to some kind of psychic compensation, in which case they become important in the structure of the personality. The common possible consequences of disability are (1) compensation, (2) overcompensation, (3) effects on the behavior of others toward the disability, and (4) effects on the child's own self-concept.

Compensation is the act of developing another ability to make up for a felt deficiency from a disability. Thus, a child with a club foot who cannot run may learn to excel in swimming. Such compensation may become a significant aspect of striving and is generalized to other functions.

Overcompensation is the term used to describe that situation in which an organ inferiority leads to behavior which turns a minus into a plus. Thus, the child with weak eyes becomes a painter of beautiful pictures, the one with digestive disturbances becomes a master chef, etc.

Effects on others influence how the child will be perceived by others and how the child will use the disability in interaction with others. If parents pay great attention to the disability, pamper the child, and excuse the child from certain onerous responsibilities, the child may learn to offer the disability as an excuse for requesting special exemption from tasks.

Some physical disabilities lead to pity and sympathy, others to teasing or rejection. In the LSI completion, an important step is to ask how the child responded to the disability so as to ascertain its effect on the child's self-concept.

For example, in Chapter 4 we described how a subject answered "What were you like as a child?" with the statement, "I was fat." When the spontaneous description is ended, the interviewer may ask, "What effect did it have on you?" The subject's answer may be, "I never liked my body," indicating a negative self-concept. On the other hand, "My mother always said I had a jolly disposition" points to a behavioral compensation for the feeling of inferiority associated with being fat. If the mother liked children who looked well-fed, she may well have given positive reinforcement in the form of approval. On the other hand, jibes and taunts from siblings and peers may have increased the subject's feelings of inferiority associated with being fat.

Gender. Physical disabilities are not always present, but gender is. In a patriarchal setting, with overvaluation of masculinity, what Adler (1958) termed the "masculine protest," i.e., being female may be experienced as an inferiority, with subsequent compensatory strivings. In societies which value male and female children equally, the child still must respond to the reality of gender and to the fact that humans come in two gender varieties, male and female. The FC will show what kind of gender identification each sibling made, how happy each was with his/her gender, how competent each felt in the gender role and how each defined the role.

Successful compensation for feelings of inferiority associated with disability or gender implies that the subject was not discouraged by the feeling of inferiority and adapted in a way that had positive effects on the self-concept. Some attempts to compensate do not necessarily have such a happy outcome. A less than attractive girl may compensate by developing a delightful and pleasing "personality," but in her own self-concept she may retain a negative self-image which leads her to feel discouraged about her sexual attractiveness. The effect on self-concept is perhaps the most crucial consequence of this feeling of inferiority because it will or will not lead to discouragement, the most important agent of withdrawal from life tasks.

Sibling Territories

In addition to birth order, constitution and gender, influences upon the interactions between the siblings themselves are important. We can use the model of an ecological system to conceptualize how each sibling finds a suitable territory of responses for his/her own strivings, tends to guard this territory against unwanted intrusions by others, and in turn tends to avoid areas not appropriate to self. This system is similar to that found in any social animal group. Dominance and cooperation interactions are established by the parents. The possible range of behaviors is limited by this microculture and no doubt also by human genetic programming.

The sibling trait rating list on pages two and three of the LSI form is the most convenient guide to sibling territories. Perusal of these ratings will reveal that they can be divided into several territory areas. Thus, the first two ratings, ***intelligence*** and ***grades,*** represent the academic achievement area. A later group—***daring, assertive, patient, methodical, neat, persistent***—represents an area which deals with the methods of approach to life situations. This rating list contains deliberate redundancies, as every good inventory list should, in order to increase the opportunity to elicit the sibling territories and to clarify for the examiner the confusion that may occur when the question words have different meanings for the subject than they do for the examiner.

Example 5.2 shows how the subject's answers clarify territorial divisions. In that example the subject's brother is portrayed as being more socially successful, while the subject himself avoided the territory, considering himself unsuccessful in it.

In Table 5.1 is shown how the trait ratings can be grouped into territory areas.

O'Phelan (1977) studied this rating system and found that it could be sorted into six categories of attributes, all of which would seem to have an important relationship to life style. The categories were (1) achievement, (2) social proprieties, (3) interpersonal mechanics, (4) right-wrong, (5) posture, and (6) gender.

TABLE 5.1

Trait Ratings Comprising Territory Areas Among Siblings and Typical Questions Which Help Elicit the Information

Area, and trait ratings that define it	Additional questions which help to define the area.
Academic	
intelligence grades	Who went the furthest in school?
Helpfulness	
helpful around house industrious responsible	Who liked to do things for others?
Ambitious striving	
highest standards of achievement actual achievement idealism materialism industrious	Who was the most interested in what he/she could "get?" Who was a perfectionist? Who was the hardest worker?
Method of activity	
daring assertive patient methodical neat persistent excitement seeker impulsive	Who would give up most easily when the going got tough? Who would most often finish what he/she started? Who was the most logical? Who was the most cautious?
Compliance/opposition	
responsible obedient mischievious open rebellion covert rebellion	Who gave the parents the most trouble? Who got into trouble in school?

TABLE 5.1 (Continued)

Attribute	Question
Sociability	
sociable charm pleasing outgoing cheerful considerate shy withdrawn	Who had the most friends? Who could make friends the most easily?
Personal dominance	
bossy demanded way got way temper fights chip on shoulder sulked stubborn sensitive and easily hurt critical of others complained took advantage of others would not submit to dominance	Who had to be a big shot? Who was the crybaby? Who picked on others? Who put others down? Who was the most argumentative? Who was the leader in play?
Dependence/independence	
responsible self-reliant pampered sure of self	Who took good care of his /her own things? Who struck out on his/her own the earliest?
Morality	
standards of right and wrong critical of self easy-going took advantage of others idealistic materialistic sense of humor	Who made the fuss if things weren't absolutely fair? Who just had to have his/her own way?
Control/accommodation	
excitable worried impulsive	Who got upset if plans didn't work out? Who was most irritable?
Gender areas	
masculine feminine athletic	How was each one masculine/feminine?

Trait ratings such as intelligence, grades, industry, helpfulness, and standards of achievement were in the achievement category. Social propriety included charm, pleasing, consideration, selfishness, and sociability. The category of interpersonal mechanics included assertiveness, bossiness, temper, humor, sulking, stubbornness, shyness, and sensibility. The right-wrong category included obedience, rebellion, fairness, standards of right and wrong, and critical behavior. Posture included ratings on idealism, materialism, persistence, giving up, neatness, excitement seeking, complaining, taking responsibility, withdrawal, dependency, self-reliance, hostility (chip on shoulder) and being recipient of punishment. The gender category, in addition to masculinity and femininity, included socially-typed gender behavior such as athletics, being daring, and physical appearance (looks). These are listed in Table 5.2.

Each of these areas offers the child an opportunity to carve out a personal territory of operation; that is, an area of successful striving for significance with its accompanying positive self-esteem and increased feeling of security and competence in the area. Successful striving for significance need not be identical with what we conventionally call "success." For example, a child may find an important position in the family by behaving in a dependent and helpless way and gain much parental attention thereby. Territories are avoided when they do not promise sufficient reward or the child does not feel able to cope with the area. In the latter areas, the child will either have no interest in entering the area (because it offers no reward), will actively avoid it (because it promises negative feedback), or will carve out a partial place in the territory which helps achieve one goal, but does not provide an increase in status or self-esteem. An example of the last would be the child who uses crying and sensitivity as a way of manipulating others to grant his/her wishes (power tactic). Since the child is using methods associated with dependence and insecurity, what is wanted may be obtained from others but the child may retain feelings of inferiority.

The child who avoids an area for fear of incompetence is spoken of as ***discouraged*** from the area. According to level of aspiration studies, the child will enjoy doing most what gives it the most feeling of success and will be quickly satiated (lose interest) by failure (Lewin, 1935).

TABLE 5.2
Trait Ratings Grouped by Territory Areas
(Based on study by O'Phelan, 1977)

Categories of Attributes	Traits Ratings
Achievement	Intelligence
	Grades
	Industry
	Helpfulness
	Standards of Achievement
Social	Charm
	Pleasing
	Consideration
	Selfishness
	Sociability
Interpersonal Mechanics	Assertiveness
	Bossiness
	Temper
	Humor
	Sulking
	Stubbornness
	Shyness
	Sensibility
Right-Wrong	Obedience
	Rebellion
	Fairness
	Standards of Right and Wrong
	Critical Behavior
Posture	Idealism
	Materialism
	Persistence
	Giving up
	Neatness
	Excitement Seeking
	Complaining
	Taking Responsibility
	Withdrawal
	Dependency
	Self-reliance
	Hostility (Chip on Shoulder)
	Recipient of Punishment
Gender	Masculinity
	Femininity
	Social-typed Gender
	Athletics
	Being Daring
	Physical Appearance (Looks)

In Table 5.3 is a condensed trait rating for quickly showing the territories selected by each of three siblings.

TABLE 5.3
An Example of Sibling Territories

	Merton +8	Donald +6	Lily*
Intelligence	M	L	+
Grades	+	L	M
Helped around the house (the boys worked the farm with Father)			M
Responsible	M	L	+
Considerate	M	L	+
Easy-going	L	M	—
Cheerful	L	M	+
Mischievous	L	M	—
Self-reliant	+	M	L
Temper	+	M	L

M = most
L = least
+ = the behavior was present
— = the behavior was generally lacking

In this brief survey of some of the ratings is shown that the first-born brother took responsibility, academic success and helpfulness as his territories, while the second-born took self-reliance, opposition and sociability as his. The subject easily fits into the role of the only female who did not compete with her brothers. Compliance was her territory. She added, "They teased me because I was a girl, but I learned not to mind them. I was close to Mother." She found her place in the female world and was successfully immune to the attempts of the males to depreciate her.

Parental and Other Models and Their Effects

In most families, parents model adult behavior and values for the young. However, for the child with older siblings, these also become important models at an early age. Because the life style is relatively established by the age of five or six, according to Individual Psychology, later models tend to interact with already established perceptions and more often than not, reinforce them. The behavior and values expressed by these early models will help to define all the important aspects of social roles—location, expectations, demands and so on.

Example 5.3. Parental modeling.

Subject is Lucy. Age 21.

Father: 48 years. Occupation: Engineer

Father was kind and sweet. But once in a while he used to get angry at my brother because he got bad grades in school. He was fun on family vacations. I used to wish he made more money.

Who was his favorite?

I think I was. I was the first child and he spent more time with me than with the others. We had long talks with each other.

Expectations for the children?

I think he would have liked my brother to be an engineer. When I said I wanted to be a teacher, he was happy.

Relationship to children?

He was Mr. Fixit. He could fix anything in the house and we'd ask him for help. He left the disciplining up to Mother, but he'd argue with my brother about school.

Sibling most like father?

I have a lot of his interests, but my brother has a sweet disposition like him.

Mother: 44 years. Occupation: Housewife.

Mother used to tell me to go to college and get a profession so I wouldn't have to be dependent on a man. She used to complain about father not making more money and not dressing better. She came from a more prominent family and I think she looked down on father's family. She was more of a scold, but she was always nice when we were sick or hurt. She wasn't as warm as father.

Favorite?

My brother was. He gave her more trouble, but she liked him better.

Why?

When I got older, I used to criticize her and we'd argue a lot. She wanted me to help more around the house and I was lazy. My brother helped her more.

Most like mother?

I guess I am. I criticize like she does.

Relationship between the parents?

> They used to argue because mother was always complaining. I think Mother had her way most of the time. I used to feel she was wrong in criticizing father. But, they also used to get along very well sometimes, because father was so loving.

The male model is thus a kind, loving man who can "fix" anything and can even sometimes win over the critical mother. The female model is more dominant and establishes dominance by being critical. Her dominance is tempered by Father's ability to win her over. Their interpersonal relationship thus models a balance in which each partner holds his/her own ground, knows what to do, how to maintain a good relationship and how to overcome conflict. Thus, from the information about the relationship between the parents, we can infer role definitions for each parent and a set of cognitive instructions for how men and women are supposed to behave with each other.

The subject is obviously more critical, like Mother, and accepts Mother's recommendation that she seek a profession (teacher). She learns a definition of the female role from both parents: A woman is critical of a man and is loved by him.

Example 5.4a. Sibling modeling. Learning how to be significant by watching an older sibling. Martin is 26.

Harry	Martin*
+4	

What was Harry like as a child?

> He was always in trouble. He didn't like school and he had the wrong kind of friends. When he was older, he got into trouble with the police. I felt sorry for him. Everything he did seemed to get him into trouble.

What were you like as a child?

> I was the opposite of Harry. I liked school and didn't cause my parents any trouble. They used to ask him why he couldn't be more like me, which I thought was wrong. I could see how he always got into trouble. I thought it was easy to stay on the good side of people.

In this case, Harry is a negative model for Martin. By behaving the opposite of Harry, Martin develops a significant role for himself. In this family, Harry is, of course, also significant. His difficulties make him the center of family attention.

Example 5.4b. Being discouraged by a model. Jim is 22.

Robert	Jim*
+4	

What were you like as a child?

> I never felt I could be as good as my older brother. He was a better student. He had a lot of friends and he was a good athlete. The only thing I could do was sing and dance. I used to entertain at family gatherings and that got me a lot of attention, but I was never interested in school or sports. He was a real jock, and I started to get into drugs at an early age.

A model may thus be someone to emulate or someone to avoid emulating. A model defines a role, displays role-skills and expresses role demands, which one may or may not feel able to meet.

Family Values and Their Effects

Family values define important aspects of life for the child—they help define what is significant, what ***is*** reinforced, what is success, and what is failure (when one can have a positive self-concept and when one can have a negative one). The values provide guidelines for acceptable roles in the family and later on in meeting the life tasks. Values are expressed by the models in their own behavior and in the interaction with each other and with the subject (what they actually ***do,*** rather than what they ***say***).

Individual Psychologists have never constructed an exhaustive list of family values, which is perhaps a lack in the theory. Nevertheless, they are frequently discussed in the Individual Psychology literature, both in the writings about methods of rearing children and about maladaptive deviation. For example, some parents will require obedience from their children; others will require academic excellence, helpful behavior, and so forth.

As we have previously mentioned, family values are demands upon family members which require a response from the child.

Maladaptive deviation in Individual Psychology theory is the consequence of faulty perceptions and faulty values. A common example occurs in what Individual Psychologists call overambition, e.g., "Unless I can be the best, I'm not worthwhile" or "I must never let anyone get ahead of me." The list of mistaken attitudes in Chapter 1 contains many examples of faulty family values.

Example 5.5. A clearly stated value.

What were father's ambitions for the children?

He wanted us to do well in school. He was always pleased when we brought home good grades.

Did he actually say he wanted good grades from you?

Yes. He used to tell us that unless we got an education we couldn't amount to anything. He always felt he never had enough education.

Note that the real family value was that **one should amount to something** and education was the pathway to it. Good grades became a symbol that one was on the way toward amounting to something.

Example 5.6. An unstated value.

What did your parents want you to be?

> They used to say I could be anything I wanted, but they weren't happy when I went to acting school. From the way they acted, I think they wanted me to settle down and marry the boy next door. My brothers could leave town to work, but they wanted me to stay in town.

Family Myths

Family myths are tales which confer status on the family and its members. They function to raise self-esteem, but also to give meaning to the lives of family members. They allow family members to be something special and often exemplify family values. Myths may refer to past family glories, notable ancestors, dramatic episodes in family history, and instances of special luck or special favor.

Some common examples of family myths can be seen below in the following two examples:

Example 5.7. A noted ancestor.

What was Mother's ambition for you?

> She used to tell me that I looked just like my great-uncle, Oswald, who was a famous doctor in Vienna. The whole family admired him and talked about him. She was sure that I would grow up to be a famous doctor.

Example 5.8. A prestigious family background.

What else should I know about your family that may have had an effect on you?

> My father's family was descended from the Lithuanian nobility. We always felt we were a little better than the people in our neighborhood. The family considered itself special and we were very careful whom we chose for friends. One of my aunts married a non-Lithuanian and the family didn't talk to her.

Family Climate (Atmosphere) and Its Effects

Three qualities of the family climate or atmosphere were described in Chapter 2, ***mood, order,*** and ***relationships.*** While the third quality will constantly appear when we interpret interpersonal transactions, it also affects the family climate. While one may ask direct questions about climate, these data usually appear spontaneously when we ask other questions.

Example 5.9. Family mood set by Mother's illness.

What was your mother like?

> She was very unhappy. Now that I look back, I can see that she suffered from long periods of depression. Sometimes she would cry all day. Twice she went to the hospital. It made all of us sad.

Example 5.10. Authoritarian order.

What was your father like?

> Father was very strict and stern. We never dared to disobey him. I was always frightened of him. When my brother was fifteen, he ran away from home because he didn't want to obey Father any more.

Example 5.11. Close and conflicting relationships.

> I came from a loud Italian family. Everybody talked at the top of their voices. We argued all the

time, but nobody better hurt any of us because we'd all come to that person's defense. We loved each other and we still get together every holiday and argue with each other.

Cultural Values and Social Contingencies and Their Effects

Every family exists within a cultural milieu and for better or worse is influenced by that milieu. The children of immigrant parents may not share many of the parents' cultural values, but those values are still a challenge which require a response. The cultural values in a group with a strong religious identification differ from those in a more secular group. Parents who were children during an economic depression may not understand the outlook of children who grew up during a time of affluence.

Example 5.12. A special cultural value.

What were you like as a child?

I was the first-born son in a Korean family. It is up to the first-born son to carry the family honor. My younger sister always looked up to me. I was proud of it.

Obviously, the important position of the first-born Korean son makes him someone special, who has special privileges and obligations. This is an example of a cultural value at work.

The contingencies of existence also have effects. Some of them can be seen easily in the broken family.

Example 5.13. A broken family.

I was five when my mother got sick. She died when I was seven. I missed her very much. When I was nine, my father remarried and I hated my stepmother. I felt he loved her more than he did me.

Interpersonal Transactions and Their Effects

Pampering, Neglect, and Rejection. Pampering, neglect, and rejection are mistaken ways of rearing children (Dreikurs, 1948). ***Pampering*** refers to the parent's overprotection, oversolicitousness, and overindulgence. When such parental behavior interferes with the child's development of his/her own sense of competence and independence, it is a noxious influence. The ***neglected*** child does not receive from the parents enough guidance or confirmation. Neglect is often unintentional on the part of the parent, as when the parent talks much to the child but listens little, asks the child to perform at a higher level than the child is ready for, or does not recognize other needs of the child. The child feels ***rejected*** if the parent does not seem to care about the child's welfare, but especially when the parent is abusive and critical. A pampered child may retain positive self-esteem because his/her worth is confirmed by parental solicitousness. Neglected and rejected children do not feel so valued by their parents and must look elsewhere for a positive sense of self.

Questions which elicit information about this area include the following:

For Pampering

Would they still do things for you after you were old enough to do them by yourself?

Were they excessively fearful you would get hurt?

Did you sometimes feel they underestimated you?

Were you spoiled?

For Neglect

How did you feel about not being anybody's favorite?

Did you feel neglected or overlooked in any way?

Did you feel they didn't understand you?

For Rejection

How did you feel when they got angry at you? Punished you?

Did you ever feel you couldn't please them, no matter how hard you tried?

Did you feel they expected (demanded) too much from you?

Did you wish you had different parents?

Were you physically abused?

Until now we have discussed various kinds of interpersonal transactions as they were modeled in the family and only paid peripheral attention to them as they were experienced by the subject in his/her own interactions. In Chapter 2 we discussed various dimensions of parental interaction with the child (Table 2.1) and typical responses by the child (or typical interactions in which the child was engaged). Thus, if the parent is overindulgent, the child may expect such service from others as well. Those data which show us the effects of interpersonal transactions come from the spontaneous descriptions of family members, sibling ratings, and parent-child interactions. From these data we will infer what role each family member played in the overall constellation, which figures were seen as friends and which as adversaries, what behavior was reinforced by whom, how one viewed human relationships, what techniques were used for relating, and what was the effect on one's self-image.

Example 5.14. Family roles.

What was your brother like?

He was always in trouble. My mother had to go to school almost every week because he got into fights with the other children. I wasn't a goody-goody, but, by comparison, I was a well-behaved child.

Example 5.15. Friends (allies).

How did Mother relate to the children?

She was always on our side. She protected us from father when he was angry at us. She was always there when we needed her.

Example 5.16. Adversaries.

Which children fought each other?

My older sister always used to call me stupid. I decided to show her I wasn't stupid, and I became a good student. I was best in the class.

Examples 5.15 and 5.16 may present significant figures who lead to the subject's developing ***personifications*** (Sullivan, 1953). A personification is an internal image which endows whole classes of people with attributes possessed by one of the significant figures in the subject's past. For example, all older maternal women may been seen by the subject in Example 5.15 as protective and nurturing. In Example 5.16, women may be seen as critical and needing to be put in their place.

Example 5.17. The ***Gegenspieler*** (contrapuntal relationship)

While this German word literally means "opposing player," the ***Gegenspieler*** is not always an opponent. It is the person from whom the subject takes certain cues and with whom he/she has a competitive relationship. Such relationships can often be seen in the behavior of young children.

Barry was four and Danny was two. When Barry wanted to play with the wagon, Danny would insist on playing with the wagon. Eventually,

Barry would give Danny the wagon and would go to the kiddie car. When Danny noticed this, he would lose interest in the wagon and want the kiddie car. Barry was at first annoyed, but then discovered that he could keep Danny constantly frustrated by always finding something new to play with when he permitted Danny to persuade him to relinquish the toy of the moment.

Danny had chosen Barry as his ***Gegenspieler***—the person from whom he took his cue. Barry responded by presenting Danny with a constantly changing set of cues. At one point Danny became tired of the whole thing and sat mournfully sucking his thumb. Barry then approached him and said, "Look Danny, I'm playing with the wagon. Don't you want it?"

In this competitive relationship, Barry and Danny are not necessarily adversaries, but they are ***Gegenspieler.*** They are busy watching each other in order to figure out what to do next.

Example 5.18. Reinforced behavior.

What would mother do when you hit your little sister?

She used to tell me that I should protect her and not hit her and she'd punish me. I really felt my sister used to start it to get me in trouble. She'd get into my stuff and mess up my things, and when I complained, mother would say that I should be patient because she was too little to understand.

Such behavior on the part of mother reinforces the provocative behavior of the little sister as well as the older child's feeling of being unfairly treated.

Example 5.19. Reinforced behavior.

My father always used to take me for walks with him. I loved it. My mother and sister would stay home because they thought it was too cold to take a walk. My father and I would bundle up and go out in the cold and walk. We had our best talks at that time and I would feel like I was his favorite.

Example 5.20. Success and failure experiences in various life areas.

Did you have any outstanding achievements?

I was a good swimmer. I won medals. My parents used to come and watch me. I felt proud of it.

Who had the most friends?

My brother did. Everyone liked him. I used to wish I was a popular as him, but I was shy. I had only one friend.

Who was the most responsible?

I was the one who helped the most. My brother used to get out of doing things. He always had an excuse.

The subject in this case has had both success and failure experiences—the usual case. While successful as an athlete, in engaging in constructive behavior in the home and in pleasing the parents, the subject feels like a comparative failure in the area of peer friendships.

Example 5.21. Conclusions about human relationships.

What was the relationship like between the parents?

They argued a lot. I think my father had a girl friend, and Mother would get very angry. When they argued, my father would leave the house and not come back for hours.

Did you take sides?

> All the kids took mother's side. We felt that father was being unfair. Sometimes mother would cry, and we'd feel terrible and try to be nice to her.

We can make an inference about the subject's outlook on human relationships from this material. The subject expresses a value which states that people should be "fair" to each other. Unfairness carries negative connotations. The proper way to treat a person is to "be nice," especially to a person who has suffered at the hands of others. Other possible inferences include the following: the female child is observing an undesirable model of husband-wife interaction and may conclude that a woman may suffer at the hands of a man; and a male child may conclude that males somehow do as they please, even if women are displeased, and if it's unfair, so what?

Since ER usually involve some type of human interaction, we may expect the ER of this subject to confirm at least one of the inferences we make in Example 5.21.

Example 5.22. Techniques for relating.

Sally*	Max	Warren
	-3	-6

Who tried to please the most?

> Max.

How?

> He was more willing to help when Mother asked him.

And you and Warren?

> Warren wasn't asked to help much. I did my share when I was asked. I didn't really try to please my mother, but I tried very hard to please Father. Warren just naturally pleased everybody. He was cheerful and cute.

Who used charm the most?

Warren. He was naturally charming.

The least?

Max didn't try to be charming. He was kind of gruff.

How about you?

I tried to be charming outside the house, but at home I wasn't.

Who was the most quarrelsome?

That was myself.

Who was most bossy?

I was.

Who complained the most?

I did.

These and similar questions permit us to make inferences about the techniques each child developed for relating to others. Max apparently used being helpful as a way of establishing a relationship, apparently to mother. Warren related by being cute and charming, while Sally was bossy, complained, used charm only outside the house, and tried to please Father. A few more questions will round out the picture.

Who was the best student? Best grades?

I was. I got the best grades.

What effect did that have on your position in the family?

My parents were proud of me. I used to help Max and Warren with their school work.

Who tried hardest to achieve?

I did.

Who was the most concerned about right and wrong?

I was.

Who was the most concerned about fair and unfair?

That was I.

What did you complain about?

Mostly about my brothers when they wouldn't listen to me.

Now we can see Sally's technique for relating within the family. She was the star student and the guardian of right and wrong, sitting in judgment on others. She expected a position of authority within the family as a consequence. She was the achiever and expected to be recognized as such.

Example 5.23. Prosocial and antisocial behavior.

What was Jack like?

He was always in trouble. My father was always angry at him. He ditched school and ran away from home a few times. My parents always worried about him.

What was Mary like?

She was the good one. Always responsible and always trying to help.

These descriptions do not necessary tell us how Jack and Mary will behave as adults. Jack may stop the rebellious behavior when he becomes an adult, and Mary may be a covert rebel. However, in childhood, Mary tried to be a cooperator while Jack seems to have been a defiant rebel who used noncooperation as a way of behaving. These childhood behaviors often occur only in specific contexts. The rest of the FC will tell us whether these behaviors were generalized to most situations or occurred only in particular circumstances.

Distinctions between prosocial and antisocial behavior play an important role in the Individual Psychologist's evaluation of personality to the extent that they correspond to what Adler called behavior "on the useful—versus the useless—side of life." Useless behavior is behavior which does not contribute to the general good. It is a consequence of faulty training and represents a feeling of "discouragement" about "one's chances in life." Dreikurs (1948), however, pointed out that antisocial and/or oppositional behavior in a child must be seen in context, and that this context includes not only discouragement but also the reinforcement practices of the adults. Thus, the child may misbehave to get attention rather than to express opposition, although, he adds, that personal power, revenge and the display of inadequacy are the other three common reasons for misbehavior.

Example 5.24. The effect on self-image.

We have already defined the ***self-image*** as that aspect of the self-concept which contains positive and negative self-evaluations. In this sense, it is identical with what is often called ***self-esteem.*** Self-image is inextricably associated with the person's movement toward the dominant goals of his/her life style—the guiding self-ideal. A defeat in the pursuit of the dominant goal is a threat to self-esteem—that is, to the self-image. We have already discussed the effect of pampering, neglect, and rejection on self-image.

While the best way of assessing self-image is usually through an analysis of the ER, much FC material gives clues to the self-image.

Example 5.24a.

What were you like as a child?

> Not much, I guess. My mother used to tell me my birth was an accident—that she hadn't wanted any more children.

Example 5.24b.

What role did you play with your group of friends? Were you a leader or follower or outsider or group "goat?"

> I wanted to be liked, so I tried to please everybody. I used to act like a clown so people would like me. I didn't tell them about myself because I thought they wouldn't like me if they got to know me.

Both of these examples indicate a negative self-image based upon feelings of unacceptability to others. The following example shows a positive self-image.

Example 5.24c.

> My sister was always making my mother angry. Mother was always being called to school for her misbehavior. I felt sorry for both of them. I didn't see any sense in my sister's bad behavior. I felt that I certainly wouldn't cause trouble. My mother had enough already.

Sometimes one finds that a person feels quite acceptable to others but also feels incompetent to perform tasks on his/her own or otherwise meet the challenges of life. An example can be seen in the following ER:

Example 5.25. Age 5

> My mother sent me to the store for a bottle of milk. On the way home the bag slipped out of my hand and the bottle broke. I ran home and told my mother. She was angry. I felt she shouldn't have asked such a small child to do the job.

Example 5.26. Differences between parent-child and child-child relationships.

Human relationships differ in different contexts. A mother may tell us that her child is a terror at home, while the teacher may report that the child is well-behaved in school. A child may oppose the mother but comply with the wishes of the father, who is seen as having greater status.

> **What were you like as a child?**
>
> > I was always outside. I never wanted to be home because my parents were always criticizing. I had a lot of friends and I always wanted to be with them. I usually didn't like adults.

The opposite also can be found.

> **Example 5.27.** Preference for adult companions.
>
> **Who had the most friends?**
>
> > I never had any friends my own age. I always felt different from them.
>
> **In what way?**
>
> > I was always more serious. Adults always liked me. When my father went hunting with his friends, they would take me along and I loved it, but the other kids were interested in baseball and I just wasn't. I can't even remember playing kid games. I always seemed old for my age.

Roles

As stated in Chapter 1, a ***role*** is an organized set of behaviors that belongs to an identifiable position in the social structure. In this case, the social structure is the family. Each role has a location, a set of expectations, a set of demands for enactment, and a set of role skills. In addition, self-role congruence becomes one of the determiners of self-image.

Several types of roles have already been discussed in the text—the "good child" and the "black sheep" are two examples. No single question elicits role, but it can usually be inferred from the information in the spontaneous self-description combined with the sibling ratings. The role of each family member can be so inferred.

Example 5.28. A family role.

From the information given in the sibling ratings of example 5.22, , one discovers that the subject was the most responsible, the most achieving, the bossiest, and the most critical. She was also the one most concerned with right and wrong and was punished the most for talking back to the parents.

From this information we infer that the subject sat in judgment on the behavior of others and protested when they did not meet her standards for proper behavior. The authoritarian parents objected to Sally's own authoritarian attitude. Sally's family role can be described as the "guardian of the rules of right and wrong behavior" and the "moral judge of the family."

Where such a role is found, it is likely to be an imitation of parental behavior and a form of rebellion against parental authority.

A role may have power (it affects family transactions significantly) or not. A role also confers position in the hierarchy of the family. In addition, a role carries with it a positive or negative self-esteem evaluation, irrespective of its power and position in the hierarchy. Thus, the "black sheep" role usually has considerable power and may even confer dominance over other siblings, but the person enacting this role may well have very low self-esteem.

The Meaning of Life (Adler, 1958; Mosak & Dreikurs, 1967).

> A subject recalls that his father was an embittered and unhappy man who drank himself to death. One scene stood out in his memory, in which his father angrily stated, "When we are all gathered before God on Judgment Day, our family will be off in some corner behind the door and He won't even notice us." The subject's brother also abandoned himself to despair and became alcoholic. The subject however, concluded that, grim as the world may be, it was a mistake to give in to despair because it made others (e.g., Mother) so unhappy. He felt, "Unhappy I may be, but I must never make others unhappy." He was extremely mild-

mannered, never expressed anger, and always tried to please.

Conclusions about the nature and meaning of life are often drawn more easily from the ER than the FC because the current attitude to life may be different than it was in childhood, but the special section on this topic offers important clues to the subject's philosophy of life, i.e., does one have an optimistic or pessimistic stance toward the world? Is it essentially a friendly or inimical place? Is it orderly or unpredictable, meaningful or absurd? Does one hope or despair?

The meaning the subject assigns to life affects one's motivation toward action in the world. If the world is meaningless, then one may easily abandon oneself to hedonism or despair. If life has no rules, then one's own whims are the guidelines.

For the Individual Psychologist, social interest (Adler, 1964b) provides the most important context for meaning in life—the attachment to and interest in others. One finds the meaning of one's existence through commitment to the tasks of life in interaction with others.

Example 5.29. The meaning of life.

What was your favorite way of spending time?

I always wanted to be playing with my friends. I hated to be alone. When my friends weren't around, I would make up games with imaginary companions. I always had to have something to keep my busy.

We can infer from this answer that subject finds a meaning to life in activity itself, especially activity together with others. However, the behavior described is common to many children in middle childhood, and we would seek confirmation of our inference by checking the ratings. If the subject was industrious and had many friends, we would feel more confident of our inference. If these traits are still prominent in adult life, our inference is probably correct.

One also may ask, "What would you like the epitaph on your tombstone to say? For what would you like to be remembered?" The answer may show us what meaning the person assigns to his/her own life.

Self-Concept

Some of the questions we have discussed earlier evoke self-concept. "How did you feel about yourself as a child?" "Did you like or dislike yourself?" "How would you have wanted to change yourself?" The answers tell us also how judgmental the person is about himself/herself. Self-concept is usually elicited easily from the self-description and ratings in questions 1 through 7 and the ratings in Chapter 4.

As we have seen, the process of interpretation of the FC so far has consisted of asking a series of questions, which gives us information about each of the content categories which we attempt to deduce. The answers to each of the questions often lead us to ask other questions which flesh out the picture we are constructing. From the beginning, we make inferences and, as we proceed, we are able to check and revise our inferences until we believe we have an accurate view of each content category. Since the interview format is used to collect the data, we can further check an inference by asking the subject if our guesses sound correct. The great majority of subjects will recognize when a guess is valid and will confirm or dispute the guess. Only a few defensive subjects will refuse to confirm a valid guess.

Essentially, what we wish to learn from the FC is how the subject responded to his/her early life situation and how these responses may have become elaborated into behavioral styles which became part of the personality and are still used in adult life. In order to help us do this, a useful procedure will be to have an instrument which will allow us to group the responses according to each content category and then hopefully to arrive at a global picture of the FC. In so doing we will hope that our content categories allow us to see what Keniston (1963) called the "press of history" on individual lives with its "subtle interweaving of themes" (1963, p. 60). However, the themes we find will show us how the subject construed his/her history as much or more than what the history actually was.

These construed themes are what we want to find. Sundberg (1977) reminded us of three general approaches to life history assessments: the search for themes, the search for etiology or early childhood "causes" of later events, and the search for predictors of behavior. Our system of classification will have some aspect of all three approaches but, for the understanding of personality, the themes are most important.

The system we will use will start with the "givens" of the family constellation: birth order, constitution and gender, models, parent caretaking behavior, sibling behavior, family values, family atmosphere, and ambient culture. These are the challenges which require a response, and the models. To each of these givens we will look for the response made by the child. The relationship between given and response should have both etiologic and predictive implications. The constellation of these responses should lead us to an understanding of the role selected by the child in response to the demands of the givens. Thus, our system will analyze ***responses.*** From this analysis we will perform a ***role analysis*** and a ***group process analysis.*** We will study the aim of the response and its role character, and study the group process characteristics of the response—how the response was carried out, how it was reinforced, and how it fit into the family ecology.

SUMMARIZING FAMILY CONSTELLATION

Table 5.4 is six pages of the LSI form with data collected for the FC inventory. We will use these data to show how interpretation is accomplished. Pages 4 and 5 of the LSI (Table 5.4) contain information about other aspects of early development than family constellation per se. These two pages describe some challenges of physical development, elementary school information, gender and sexual information, and social relationships. In these four areas, we look for information on how the subject responded to each challenge. Table 5.5 shows the ***givens*** we will use.

(Continued on page 159)

TABLE 5.4
The LSI Form
(Page 2)

SIBLING CONSTELLATION (Give Childhood Descriptions)
(Oldest to Youngest) Give Age for Subject and Years Older or Younger for Others

Name: Ellen Age Dif + 7 M F Description: Kind and a peacemaker. If there was an argument, she would only try to settle it and show who was at fault, calm people down and bring peace. She always had pretty clothes and had some place to go to.	Name: Olive Age Dif + 3 M F Description: Lively, conniving, intelligent. She used to manipulate me, so I figured she was intelligent. Good dancer. I always had to beware of her because she'd be the one to push me back in my place.
Name: Hans Age Dif + 3 M F Description: Was a troublemaker. He used to get in with the wrong crowd and would steal things. He would always stand up for his rights and show you how you were wrong. Always sociable. He wound up going away to a juvenile home for boys.	Name: Inga Age Dif M F Description: Appearance-wise I thought I was cute. I used to help around the house a lot. I had friends over. It felt warm and good but generally my mother didn't want me to have kids over at the house. Our house was always filled with people because of my sisters and brother.
Name: Age Dif M F Description:	Name: Age Dif M F Description:

SIBLING GROUPINGS

Most different from respondent. Hans
How? Hans was troublemaker. I was always good.
Most like respondent. Ellen
How? I tried to be kind & sympathetic like her.
Groupings by age, sex, etc.
2 - 1 - 1

Sickness, surgery, or accidents? Ø

Relationship between siblings
Who cared for and protected whom? Ellen for me.
Who played together? None
Who fought each other? Olive & Hans

Unusual talents or achievements? E - ballet
O - accordian H - make things out of wood
Childhood fears, childhood ambitions?
Marry a millionaire and have 6 children

SHARED TRAITS AND/OR INTERESTS
(Shared equally by all siblings)

None that I know

2

TABLE 5.4 (Continued)
The LSI Form
(Page 3)

SIBLING RATINGS
(Rate from most to least)

Intelligence E - O - I - H
Elementary school grades I - . . . . - H
Helpful around house I - E - H - O
Industrious O - E - I - H
Standards of achievement I - . . . . - H
Actual achievement O - E - I - H
Daring H - I - O - E They used to call me daredevil
Assertive O - E - H - I
Patient E - . . . . - H
Methodical O - E - I - H
Neat E - O - I - H
Persistent E - O - I - H
Responsible E - O - I - H
Obedient I - . . . . - H
Mischievous H - O - I - E
Open rebel H - . . . . - E
Covert rebel O - . . . . - I
Punished H - O - I - E
For what? disobedience
By whom? Mother
Got away with the most O - H - E - I
Impulsive H - . . . . - E
Self-reliant O - E - I - H
Standards of right & wrong I - . . . . - H
Critical of others O - H - I - E
Critical of self I - . . . . - E
Easy-going E - . . . . - I
Sense of humor O - E - I - H
Excitable DK
Worried I - . . . . - E
Other:

Friends O - E - I - H
Charm O . . . I
Tried to please I - E - O - H
Had to please I . . . H
Succeeded in pleasing E - O - I - H
Outgoing H - O - E - I
Withdrawn I - . . . . - H
Cheerful O - I - E - H
Considerate E - O - I - H
Bossy E - O - I - H
Demanded way H - I - O - E
Got way H - . . . . - I
Temper O - . . . . - I
Fighter O - H - I - E
Chip on shoulder I . . . E
Sulked I . . . O
Held grudges I - . . . . - E
Complained H - I - O - E
Took advantage of others O - . . . . - I
Stubborn H - O - I - E
Shy I - . . . O
Sensitive and easily hurt I - . . . . - O
Excitement seeker H - O - I - E
Idealistic I - . . . . - H
Materialistic I - . . . . - E
Pampered DK
Masculine H - O - I - E
Feminine E - I - O - H ("Frilly clothes")
Sure of self O - E - H - I
Athletic O - H - I - E

3

TABLE 5.4 (Continued)
The LSI Form
(Page 4)

CHILDHOOD PHYSICAL DEVELOPMENT
(Health, Physique, Feelings about Body, Advantages/Disadvantages, Nicknames Associated with Physique)

Before grade school, I was chunky and had bangs. I had my hair curly and lost some weight when I started first grade. I was always tall for my age. I used to get kidded about my height. I had hurt feelings. was always strong and very active. I didn't like myself when I got in the upper grades --I didn't think I was attractive. Breast development at 12 years old.* I thought it was normal. Menstruated at 12 years. I felt I was a woman then. It was a good feeling. Always concerned about my weight. It seemed to go up at certain times for no good reason and then I'd have to diet.

* Some assessors place this information under Sexual Information.

ELEMENTARY SCHOOL INFORMATION
(Type of School, Grades, Subject Performance, Classroom Behavior, Relationship to Teachers, Subjects Liked and Disliked)

I went to a Catholic school and the nuns always liked me. I was well-behaved and was good in reading. I did well in school, but I talked a lot. That was my biggest problem. I always got marks in conduct for talking when I wasn't supposed to. Got along well with the kids. Reading was my favorite subject. The worst was history--so many facts to remember. Really had to apply myself in it in order to get through. Spelling was good. Math was good. Penmanship was good.

CHILDHOOD MEANINGS GIVEN TO LIFE
(Expectations, Ideals, Meaningful Goals, Favorite Daydreams, Religious Convictions)

I wanted to grow up and marry rich. I wanted people to like me. Not very religious. I thought people should try to get along well. I didn't see why people were mean to each other.

4

TABLE 5.4 (Continued)
The LSI Form
(Page 5)

CHILDHOOD GENDER AND SEXUAL INFORMATION
(Development, Source of Information, Sex Play, Reaction to Pubertal Changes, Comfort with Gender, Feelings About Sexual Activity, Sexual Abuse)

I always liked being a girl. I think I noticed the difference between boys and girls around 4 or 5 years old. I was a tomboy--played with dolls, dress-up and planned on getting married, etc., but was considered a tomboy because I played on the monkey bars and swung upside down and did daring things for a girl. My girlfriends told me about intercourse when I was 10 years old. No problems with sex. I feel I don't have any sexual problems.

CHILDHOOD SOCIAL RELATIONSHIPS
(Friends, Gangs, Availability of Peers, Role in Peer Group, Relations with Adults)

Had friends in the neighborhood. We had a club and I was the vice president. In school I had friends. I had a boyfriend from second to fourth grade. All the kids were having boy friends and girl friends at that time. Had a couple of girls who lived down the block that I was close with. I had one good close friend throughout school and even now. (In her group, she felt like she was more of a leader than a follower.)

5

TABLE 5.4 (Continued)
The LSI Form
(Page 6)

PARENTAL INFORMATION DURING SUBJECT'S CHILDHOOD

Name	FATHER RONALD	MOTHER FRIEDA
Current age even if deceased	Age 73	Age 68
At time of subject's birth	Age 44	Age 39
	Occupation Dispatcher	Occupation Homemaker
(Traits, Respected, Liked, Feared)	Description: I didn't like him. He would scream and yell. I knew he was afraid of people. Was paranoid. Thought we were poisoning him. Sad and quiet. Thought his brother was poisoning him.	Description: Strong. Down to earth. Always had right answer. Seemed sorrowful. Sick a couple of times when I was young. Praying & crying. Hard life. Father always accused her of affairs. Fantastic cook. Clean house. Do for kids first. Wanted us to be good.
Relations to Children What was most important to him/her?		
What was way to win his/her praise?	We never tried.	
What made him/her angry?	Anything could make him angry.	Seldom angry at us, only at Father.
In what ways did he/she influence you?	I never wanted to be like him.	I wanted to be a good mother but I didn't want a husband like Father.
Expectations for children	To obey him. Good job. Be successful.	Marry a good man & have children.
Who was his/her favorite? Why?	Maybe I was. He liked to watch me.	Hans. He would show love. Would buy things for her.
Relationship to children	Tried to boss. Domineering attitude	Maternal, loving
Sibling most like him/her In what ways?	Hans, usually too sick to be wise. Drinks.	Olive--very religious Ellen--sympathetic
Who was closest to him/her?	Maybe Ellen.	Hans.
Who was most distant?	Olive ignored him. I tried to stay away. When I was 6-7 years old, he used to take me for walks, buy me candy. I liked him then.	
Confided in whom?		I would tell Mother. She was sympathetic.
Took hurts to whom?		
Others:		

Subject's role in family I tried to b helpful and please Mother.

Subject's feeling about family Too much fighting. Too much noise.

Worst possible fate for a child in the family ??

Other:

6

TABLE 5.4 (Continued)
The LSI Form
(Page 7)

NATURE OF PARENTS' RELATIONSHIP
(Description, Division of Roles, Interpersonal Relationship, Conflicts/Agreements, Marriage Happy/Unhappy)

A dead marriage. My father was always screaming and having an argument and my mother was always trying to calm things down. They separated a few times. Father thought Mother was poisoning his food and would take off and live with his friend for a couple of weeks. They disagreed about child-raising. (Fought openly in front of kids, accusing Mother of promiscuity with brother and both trying to do away with him. Argued about finances. One of the older kids would step in and stop Father from becoming violent. Father would transfer anger from Mother to one of the kids. No resolution, fights would just end and things would calm down till the next time. Inga felt depressed when parents fought.) I used to cry a lot. I felt rejected because, when they were fighting, I felt they shouldn't have had children and I shouldn't have been born. Took Mother's side.

OTHER FAMILY INFORMATION
(Family Climate, Family Values, Socio-economic Status, Ethnicity, Religion)

I don't think I expressed it as a child; I just felt it. The other kids would make a farce of the way Father behaved, so I knew it was in his mind, (accusations) not real. Father was Catholic; children went to Catholic schools. Economic Situation: Both parents worked. Always had jobs. No children went to college. Family Values: Both parents wanted their children to be successful; both valued good grades in school.

ADDITIONAL PARENTAL FIGURES AND ADULT MODELS

Who/Relationship: Mike (Father's brother)	Who/Relationship:
He was a kindly man. Always good to us. We lived with him when we came to the U.S. and always lived close to them, always felt his family was better than us--more love and more refinement than our family. I knew the accusations were baloney. I might have liked him more because of it. Because he was the underdog (innocent).	

7

TABLE 5.5
Given Content Categories of the FC

Birth Order	Parental caretaking behavior
Gender	Sibling behaviors and interaction
Constitution	Family values
Models	Family atmosphere
	Ambient culture

When we examine the responses, we will note the social role implications and ***group process*** implications of these responses. That is, each response will, in some way, fit into the eventual social role one tries to play. One can also say that the aim of the response functions as a guiding line for the method of behavior used in the response.

The group process implications point to the continuing interaction between family members and the status and security issues involved. The "process" is how each person acts, reacts, and interacts with the others. Alliances and rivalries, dominance behaviors and territorial behaviors are part of the group process.

We will examine each given in Inga's case and the responses she made.

Category 1. Birth Order

The subject is the youngest with three older siblings who serve as models. No evidence is in the data that she overran any older sibling. All the information suggests that she was an active participant in the family and did not play a dependent role. Nevertheless, she experienced herself as the youngest who had a place among her peers (see Childhood Social Relationships, Table 5.4, p. 5) but in danger of being "pushed back in her place" by the older siblings. She views herself as useful but subordinate.

Her main response to the demand of her birth order is to accept a role as youngest child and develop behaviors which allow her a significant place in the family structure. Her self-description and the trait ratings suggest that she played a compliant and useful role at home and in school. Apparently, only with her peers was she more assertive (a daring tomboy and vice president of the social club). The aims of these adaptive responses are understood by us as attempts to achieve a significant position in the social hierarchy—a basic human striving. The particular behaviors used to achieve this aim are of interest to us; she tries to be someone who counts through being helpful, not being troublesome and pleasing the caretakers, other authorities and her peers. In short, she tries to win favor by pleasing others. Such behavior can be considered a social role and, in this family, was one of the acceptable roles available to females.

We may summarize this category as follows:

Birth Order and Response

YOUNGEST OF FOUR	Two older sisters serve as models, brother serves as negative model. She plays role of a younger child and carves out her own territory
AIM	To achieve a significant position among others.
METHOD	Compliant and pleasing behavior to win favor
SOCIAL ROLE IMPLICATIONS	This is a common role for a youngest girl, especially following on the heels of a misbehaving brother (her territory).

GROUP PROCESS IMPLICATIONS	Mother and Ellen reinforced independent behavior. There is little specific information, but we speculate that Inga's behavior received positive reinforcement and fit in the family values.

As we continue to summarize the categories, we will expect them to dovetail and provide converging information.

Category 2. Gender

Sufficient data are in the inventory to show that the subject enjoyed being feminine and set a premium on feminine behavior and attractiveness. She described that others called her a tomboy because she was daring, but she does not perceive her daring behavior as non-feminine. The female models in the family are all depicted as strong, and her goal is to be a successful adult female. However, females are dependent on males ("marry a millionaire").

Gender and Response

FEMALE	Experience congruence with female role. Views females as strong, helpful, and independent. Females are not devalued.
AIM	To be a "successful" adult female.
SOCIAL ROLE IMPLICATIONS	The role demands and enactments are clearly enjoyed by her. The sexual aspects are "no problem."
GROUP PROCESS IMPLICATIONS	Inga imitates the other female models, especially Ellen, who has high status. Inga accepts the family value for feminine behavior, and acts it out.

Category 3. Constitution

This category is significant in only some subjects but can be so significant that it cannot readily be omitted. In Inga's case, several constitutional issues are mentioned: she reports she was tall for her age and sensitive to teasing about it, was concerned about her weight, and felt unattractive. However, she reported these factors as past issues and seems to have negotiated these discouragements successfully. While she felt unattractive because of her height, after puberty she felt like a "woman." In effect, her response to this given was to have a positive self-image, to see more good than bad in herself.

Category 4. Models

The most significant childhood models are parents and older siblings. Other significant figures sometimes play an important role at this stage, perhaps a teacher or other family member. For this subject we can include the uncle as a model. We will describe each model separately.

Models and Responses

MODEL		
FATHER	Tyrannical and paranoid behavior.	Disliked and pitied him. Father is a negative model who is not imitated by the subject. His behavior has low value. Note that father and mother are quite old compared to the subject, a situation which often creates distance between parent and child.
MOTHER	A strong but sorrowful figure who also models domestic excellence.	Inga does not classify herself as imitating mother, but there is some reason to suspect that she valued mother's domestic skills. Mother is also an object of pity and Inga obviously does not desire Mother's lot. How-

ever, Inga reports that she also suffered (Table 5.4, p. 2), again imitating mother.

ELLEN	The family peacemaker and model of successful femininity. Ellen is also a strong figure.	Examination of the trait ratings (Table 5.4, p. 2) shows that, while Inga puts herself in the middle on most ratings, she rates herself as being more like Ellen than anyone else in the family. She is like her in femininity, compliance, pleasing others, and responsible behavior. However, she rates herself as different from Ellen in being self-critical, more sensitive, and quick to take offense. The ratings suggest that Inga used techniques of passive rebellion and sensitivity to protest her situation. Such behavior did not violate her compliant role. Most likely, she does not feel as successful as Ellen. Note that Inga does not recognize rebellion in herself ("I don't think I rebelled.") and probably did not perceive her sensitivity, sulking, and complaining as covert rebellion.

Inga thus tried to imitate Ellen's femininity and pleasing behavior but did not achieve her first-born aplomb or effectiveness. Her techniques for protesting were those used frequently by a youngest child.

OLIVE	Another strong female who uses less honorable techniques to assert her power. Olive fights openly, while Inga uses more covert techniques.	The weight of these data suggests that Inga does not select Olive as a model to imitate, but she admires Olive's social status.
HANS	A troublemaker.	Neither of the family males is a model to imitate. Perhaps Inga would have liked to have had Hans' courage, but his disruptive behavior presents a negative model.
UNCLE	A kind man who is an innocent victim of Father's accusations. A higher status male.	Inga likes and also pities him, but, while he presented certain ideal male characteristics, she does not seem to imitate him in any way.

SOCIAL ROLE IMPLICATIONS

From a perusal of the behavior Inga imitated and that which she did not, we obtain more information about the social role she assumed. Now we can see that she was not only a pleaser but also sensitive, someone who "suffered in silence" and used techniques of weakness (suffering and sulking) to register her protests against her relative inability to assert herself. She presents herself as being more like her mother than she seems to realize.

GROUP PROCESS IMPLICATIONS

Inga describes herself as someone who tried to get her way but did not succeed. Perhaps she sees herself as the least powerful in the family. We also may detect an underlying sense of unfairness. We also can speculate from data so far analyzed that sensitivity and suffering did not have as much power to influence others as did open assertion. Why did she continue to use this behavior? Perhaps being the youngest, she could find no success in open assertion. At any rate, the use of such behaviors is usually associated with the underdog role in human relationships.

As we examine the models, we see some clear distinctions along gender lines. None of the men are described as both strong and having high status. Even the uncle is only kind and good. All the women are presented as more adequate than the men. Perhaps a key statement which shows this on p. 4 of Table 5.4: "He acted the boss, but mother really ran the house."

Category 5. Parental Caretaking Behavior

		Response
FATHER	"He used to take me for walks, buy me candy."	"I liked him then."
	"He ruled over us all."	Disapproved and rejected his authority.
MOTHER	"Maternal," "fantastic cook," "kids came first."	Admired as a model. Felt sorry for her. Wants to be like her and suffers like her.

SOCIAL ROLE IMPLICATIONS — Inga did not seem able to play the strong persons as much as mother, but she seems to have imitated mother in preferring reason over physical force, wanting to help others and in showing her rebellion by sensitivity and hurt feelings, as we have already decided.

GROUP PROCESS IMPLICATIONS — Inga probably concluded that, if things were to be straightened out, women would have to do so, but one stronger than she. Perhaps one day she can become the adequate adult female who can bring harmony and peace to others.

Category 6. Sibling Behaviors and Interactions

The interaction of the siblings with the subject is our concern here, not the siblings as models. For example, Ellen and Olive treated Inga in different ways. Ellen was an ally, Olive a rival. Hans seemed to have argued with everyone. Olive became an example of a person against whom she felt unable to assert herself. Her response was to feel hurt (suffer). One might conclude that Inga perceived people stronger than her as being either friendly or inimical, and that she could do very little about it.

Being the youngest, Inga felt less powerful within the family than she did with her peers, where she could see herself as a leader, liked and admired by others.

Other aspects of parental caretaking behavior and sibling interactions also will be seen in our discussion of family values and atmosphere.

Category 7. Family Values

The data from which family values are elicited come from the description of the behavior of the family caretakers and authorities, in this case, the parents and older siblings. Information will also come from the ratings and other parts of the collected material.

Caretakers provide guidelines (models) and feedback (reinforcement). We will examine Inga's case by looking at four aspects of caretaker behavior: what they (1) demand or expect; (2) honor (value) and how; (3) reject and punish and how they punish; and (4) permit or overlook and when. (See Table 5.6.) If the child considers some of these demands illegitimate or inappropriate, then the child will feel less obliged to meet these demands or use them to reinforce a feeling of unfairness.

If we look at the older siblings, we can see that Ellen's behavior and values seemed like those of mother, but Olive, like father, demanded that Inga play a subordinate role, and

TABLE 5.6
Parental Behavior Dimensions and Inga's Responses

Father	**Inga's Response**
Demanded: Submission	Views the demand as illegitimate but afraid to oppose openly.
Valued: material success	Accepted the value.
Rejected: (not known)	
Permitted: (not known)	
Mother	**Inga's Response**
Demanded: (not known)	
Valued: cordial relationships, helpfulness	Accepted and imitated. Helped mother in order to win her approval.
Rejected: (not known)	
Permitted: independent behavior	Independent behavior with peers. At home, she uses sensitivity and silent protest.

punished her by "putting her in her place." Neither Olive nor Hans were caretakers in the sense we are using the words.

Category 8. Family Atmosphere

We have previously said that family atmosphere can be divided into the subcategories of mood, order, and relationship (Table 2.1). In Inga's family, the family mood seems to have been excitable and unhappy because of father's explosive and dictatorial behavior. Father is described as always screaming and arguing, while Mother and the older children were always trying to calm him down. The family order seems to have been in a state of flux—Mother and Ellen tried to establish a peaceful and logical order, while Father destroyed this order with attempts to impose his own authority. Inga clearly chose Mother's side and favored ethical standards as a basis for order.

The family relationships were more complex. They were a mixture of cooperation and competition, accusing and pitying, conflictual and lacking in harmonious intimacy. Mother is described as putting the children first, but this is more a tribute to her dutiful behavior than to her warmth. The child-rearing methods were a subject of conflict between the parents.

TABLE 5.7
Family Atmosphere and Inga's Response

MOOD		
	excitable unhappy explosive	pities others and self; tries to avoid upsetting others
ORDER		
	conflict between arbitrary and ethical consistency and logic	rejects arbitrary authority; tries to be helpful
RELATIONSHIPS		
	conflictual	sides with peacemakers but pities both sides.

Table 5.7 listed several important attitude polarities which are influenced by family atmosphere and parental behaviors. We have data to suggest that certain attitudes included in that list were reinforced in Inga. These were self-reliance, cooperation, and activity. However, the data also suggest that a positive self-concept came more from her relationship with her peers than with family members.

Were we now to determine social role and group process implications, we would find that our conclusions from the data are beginning to repeat themselves. The subject's social role becomes more clearly that of a youngest girl in a conflicted family situation, rejecting arbitrary and disturbing behavior and trying to judge herself and others by ethical standards. Conflict is threatening to her and cordiality is reassuring. Her main method of interpersonal operation is to try to please and she often does not feel pleasing enough.

The group process centers around the "sick" father who makes trouble and his conflict with the long-suffering mother. Inga is a spectator of this drama, which overshadows everything else in the family. Family members are seen as victims of Father's sick behavior and as struggling successfully or otherwise to free themselves from Father's power to intimidate. The two great divisions in the family are between Father and Mother (with all the siblings on her side) and between male and female, with specific behaviors modeled by each gender.

The Response Categories

The three response categories, sibling territories, social role, and meaning of life, remain to be evaluated.

Sibling Territories. By plotting the territory of each sibling, we will be able to delineate the areas of success/encouragement and failure/discouragement for each sibling and further round out our picture of the FC. The information on pp. 2 through 5 of Table 5.4 is the most valuable for this purpose. Eleven territorial areas were listed in Table 5.1, and we shall use these for our tabulation in Table 5.8.

TABLE 5.8
Sibling Territories

	Ellen	Olive	Hans	Inga
ACADEMIC	most intelligent	intelligent		best grades
HELPFULNESS	responsible, peacemaker			responsible, helpful to mother
AMBITIOUS STRIVING				highest standard of achievement
METHOD OF ACTIVITY	easy-going methodical	industrious charm sociable outgoing	daring sought excitement troublemaker	industrious daring (sought) excitement pleasing considerate easily hurt methodical
COMPLIANCE/ OPPOSITION		covert rebel	mischief open rebel	most obedient sulked
SOCIABILITY	considerate pleasing	cheerful		cheerful shy
PERSONAL	bossy Father's favorite	retained dominance over Inga temper fighter critical of others	demanded and got his way stubborn Mother's favorite	used techniques of youngest (sensitive. sulked)
DEPENDENCE/ INDEPENDENCE	(all siblings were socialized to be independent)			
MORALITY/ ETHICAL STANDARDS				high moral standards self-critical idealistic
CONTROL/ ACCOMODATION		(no clear distinction in this area)		
GENDER ROLE	successful female	prettiest	only male	feminine

On page 2 of Table 5.4, Hans is described as always sociable. On page 2 he is rated as having the least friends and being the most withdrawn, although the most outgoing. This discrepancy remains unclarified in the data and is an example of the need for careful questioning to ascertain what the subject means. The word sociable may mean a friendly attitude, extraverted behavior, or popularity with others. When uncertain, we must clarify by asking further questions.

Data from Table 5.8 confirm our previous speculations. Ellen's areas of success are in academics, in being helpful, in cordial relationships, in being Father's favorite, and in femininity. Olive seemed to maintain her own place by being successfully social in a more assertive way. Hans played the role of rebel and Mother's favorite. Inga's territories were compliant behavior, high moral standards, pleasing others, and the use of sensitivity, sulking, and silent suffering to register her protests.

Each sibling thus had a territory in which to strive. Hans, the only boy, selected a territory in which he had no opposition from any of the girls. He is like Father in his non-cooperative behavior and in being a troublemaker. In this family, troublemaking may have been an expectation for males. Olive seems much more out for herself than her two sisters. Ellen and Inga were "good girls," and Olive shows some of the characteristics of a middle girl squeezed between two good girls and trying to make elbow room for herself by her temper and criticism. Inga's territory is that of a youngest who tries to please and fit in but feels unable to be as assertive as others, and she sees herself as being subordinate in status.

Social Role. The second of our response categories is social role, the way in which the subject actually tried to fit into the family and the larger world. Inga's social role in family is in Table 5.9 and social role with peers is in Table 5.10. This category will predict for us the similar behaviors we expect to find in the subject's adult life. It will further describe for us the methods selected by the subject to cope with the early challenges of life.

The tabulation of social role is an additional use of the data which fits smoothly with the other interpretations we have made. From our general knowledge we would expect that Inga's roles would easily fit into the family and peer ecologies in the great majority of group situations. Her behavior is not

TABLE 5.9
Inga's Social Role in the Family

Location	Youngest child, a girl, and a pleaser.
Expectations	If she helps and does not make trouble, she will please others and be accepted by them.
Enactment	By considerate and helpful behavior. By ethical standards and compassion.
Role Skills	While, objectively, relatively successful in pleasing, she is not sure of her success in this role. She does not obtain all she wants. Mother will still not let her have friends in the house as much as she would like.
Self-role Congruence	No incongruence exists between her self-perception and the role. Her enactment of the role does not impair her self-esteem. However, she hopes for a higher status in the future when she is a successful adult female.

TABLE 5.10
Inga's Social Role With Peers

Location	A tall and physically adept girl who actively seeks friends.
Expectations	If she is outgoing and pleasing, she will have status with peers.
Enactment	By friendly and even physically daring behavior.
Role Skills	Effective in having both boy friends and girl friends. Had status among peers.
Self-role Congruence	Outside of a few concerns about her height and weight, Inga feels quite comfortable in her feminine role—with both sexes.

threatening to dominants or peers, except to Olive, who wants to protect her own territory. If we consider four group process issues—the roles available in the family and with peers, reinforcements offered for these roles, models available, and the fit of the role with family and cultural values—we can see that Inga's social roles should be effective. Let us briefly discuss the four issues in regard to the family ecology:

1. **Roles available in the family.** For an ambitious youngest girl to achieve status in this family, she would have to display either some unusual and outstanding success or be compliant and pleasing, since the role of troublemaker was already conspicuously pre-empted by Hans, and no female was modeling such a role. Being the youngest, she could not successfully be a bossy dominant, nor could she assert herself openly against the older siblings, all of whom were assertive.

2. **Reinforcements offered for the role.** Compliance and helpfulness usually elicit positive reinforcement. Note that self-assertion against others provided no rewards for Inga in the family; neither did open complaining. We do not know how her sulking and sensitivity were reinforced, but she presents herself as "suffering in silence." Her only reward for this seems to have been in its confirmation of her own weakness in coping with the dominant others by open self-assertion.

3. **Models available.** In this family, male and female models are clearly distinct in behavior and function. Females are rational and have to struggle with the troublemaking behavior of males. While males can dominate for short periods, females are actually more functionally effective and are the more enduring powers (Father becomes a piteous figure and Hans goes to reform school). Inga does not imitate any of the male models; she imitates Mother and Ellen. Her reaction to the male models is to behave the opposite way, i.e., not to make trouble.

4. **Role congruence with family and cultural values.** From the female models, Inga selected a role which fit in with the power structure of the family. Her role seemingly

violated none of the family values and led her to no significant conflict with family members. In this family of Central European background, the father tried to play the role of authority but actually failed at it.

The Meaning of Life. In their efforts to cope with the demands and challenges of existence, humans ascribe various meanings to "life." They try to understand what is important, good, true. They look for guidelines to orient themselves.

The meaning given to life is a set of conclusions one draws from the ***Weltbild*** and thus a group of internal constructs. Usually to elicit these constructs from the ER is easier than the FC inventory, but often the material in the LSI will reveal to us the meaning a particular human has ascribed to "life."

In Chapter 1, we discussed how the life style contains conclusions about life and oneself in the world (Table 1.1). We discussed there various distorted attitudes or meanings that can be ascribed to life. Life can be seen as a Garden of Eden or a vale of tears. It can be seen as a creation of God or as a mindless combination of molecules with no meaning. It can be a battleground between forces of good and evil, a place to work out salvation or the brief flicker of a candle in a long dark night.

The meaning ascribed to life functions as a guiding construct, and the person, who holds the meaning, mobilizes behavior in the context of that meaning. As we perceive, so we select our responses.

If we examine Inga's inventory, we can find material which points to a meaning for life. For Inga, life is a problem in human relationships. People have the power to be helpful and please each other or to be cruel and make each other unhappy. Life is a conflict between reason/harmony/kindness and unreason/disorder/hostility in which people often become victims. She and Mother are victims of Father's irrational behavior, while Father himself is the piteous victim of his own paranoia. Life is, at its base, a tragedy.

Obviously, the interpretation of the FC requires that the examiner have the skill to recognize the pertinent issues and put the interpretation into suitable language. All of the tables in the chapter are intended to be guiding lines toward interpretation, but the final interpretation is a creative formulation of the examiner. As yet no reliability studies have shown how much uniformity exists among different interpreters of the FC, however one piece of strongly suggestive evidence is that class after class of students have learned to interpret FC to the satisfaction of the instructors. Apparently, students understood what to look for and how to describe their findings in commonly understood language.

A final formulation of the FC would include a descriptive statement from each of the categories, and this formulation could start with any one category and finish with any other. The following formulation (Table 5.11) of Inga's FC is by one examiner, in his own words. As we follow it, we can see how it touches on one category after another in order to form an understandable description of the FC in one complete statement. The remarks in brackets are inserted in order to show the category involved.

TABLE 5.11
FC Formulation Summary of Inga

Inga is the youngest of four, in some ways the youngest of three girls and in some ways a girl following an older brother [***birth order***]. Each in the family was ambitious in his or her own way [***family value***]. The adult models were an authoritarian, "sick" father who bossed but was obviously wrong and a mother who was right and competent but was intimidated by father [***parental models***]. Father's intimidation affected the whole family [***family atmosphere***]. The oldest girl imitated Mother's interest in peace and feminine pursuits. The other girl and only boy were more rebellious and out for themselves [***birth order and gender response***]. Inga compared herself in looks, social skills, and talents and felt inferior [***sibling territories***]. She found a place through compliance [***sibling territories***] and hoped that if she were pleasing enough and achieved enough [***social role***], everything would turn out well for her. However, no matter what she did, she didn't fulfill her high ambition [***meaning of life***].

Important family issues were who would have whose way and war versus peace [***family values and family atmosphere***]. The conflict seemed to spoil everything, so an atmosphere of unhappiness and wrongness existed in the family [***family atmosphere***].

Inga fought back by feeling angry and hurt and suffering silently, feeling like a righteous and suffering victim [***meaning of life***].

Note that this summary could be more complete and every reader could add more information to it. However, this example (Table 5.11) is enough to show how such a summary can be constructed.

THE PREDICTIVE VALUE OF THE FC

The relationship between childhood behavior and the family situation is easy to see from the data. But what can we predict about her current behavior? We can guess at a number of things.

Birth Order Effects

Having been a youngest who was ambitious but felt lacking, we can guess that Inga may continue in adult life to feel that all her efforts will not be good enough to allow her to attain her goals.

Constitution and Gender Effects

She may be happy in female roles but will never be sure enough of her attractiveness as a female nor of her homemaking skills.

Interpersonal Relations

She may be sensitive to any slight to her position. She may accept subordinate roles and not feel appreciated enough. She may strive for cooperation and harmony and feel unable to cope with conflict and disagreement. She may feel that others "make trouble" for her. She may try to please and hope to be liked but may not be sure how to please. Nevertheless, she will always try to make friends.

Mood

When life goes smoothly, Inga will be hopeful and compliant. But in conflict situations, where she is not successful in pleasing, she may become discouraged, especially when the conflict is with an authority. The use of "silent suffering" and sulking suggests that she may be subject to episodes of depression.

Social Role Effects

If her active compliance does not work, her undercover resentment may come to the fore. If so, she may become increasingly discouraged and suffer in silence, stopping her active efforts to please and becoming a silent accuser.

One can, of course, start with the FC as the only known data and predict the adult situation. In this case, one prediction we can make is that, for Inga, conflict with authority would be a critical situation for her. She has no effective way of coping with it. We can then examine the future course of her life to see if our prediction is valid; in this case, it is. Inga suffered a depression as a consequence of an argument with an employer. His criticism of her work enraged her, but she felt unable to do anything about it, took to her bed with a mixture of anger and depression, obsessive thoughts of suicide and angry thoughts of attacking him.

A REVIEW OF THE PROCESS

What have we done to interpret the data in the FC? First, we have listened carefully to the language which the subject has used. We have listened to descriptor terms—the adjectives and adverbs used—and to the comparisons made. By eliciting spontaneous descriptions, we have heard what areas are stressed by the subject and what emotional responses she expressed. In essence, by eliciting descriptors, we have tried to see how the subject construes life and people.

Second, we have looked for match-ups, such as the correlation between childhood behavior and the parental model of such behavior, complementary relationships, trait clusters which give us patterns of behavior, territorial trade-offs, and other matches which allow us to fit these data which must be explained because sometimes the incongruity is the missing piece which, when explained, gives us the key which allows us to see the pattern of the ***Gestalt,*** the whole picture.

In all this, we have transplanted descriptors, such as trait ratings, into movement terms. Our final description will be a description of planned adaptive behavior in a specific psychological situation—a way of meeting the tasks of life.

During this process we have constantly plotted data against theory. We began with a theory of the FC and we have expected these data to fit this theory. Our theory has been, we hope, broad enough that those data we recovered fell into the theory's domain.

Eventually, the interpretation of data according to the theory gives a set of psychodynamics which has the power to explain etiology and predict current and future behavior.

The different tables we have used have comfortably fit our theory so that, if the theory is valid, each table will likely be valid also. But we have also suggested that some consensual validity of the interpretations come from the subject's agreement with them—from the subject's verbal, facial, and postural expressions of agreement. Also the tabulation of the categories has tended to produce the same conclusions from different scales. This means that we have looked at the information from several different angles permitted by the theory and we have, by and large, come to the same conclusions each time.

CHAPTER 6

INTERPRETING EARLY RECOLLECTIONS

PERTINENT ISSUES IN INTERPRETING EARLY RECOLLECTIONS (ER)

When No ER Are Recalled

In rare cases, the subject will report that he/she recalls no ER. Sometimes this is the result of faulty interviewing techniques; the interviewer may have given unclear instructions or lacked the training to elicit ER by appropriate questions. Sometimes a suspicious subject will refuse to give ER because of not trusting the interviewer. In some of these cases, primed ER can still be obtained, but often these are curiously unsatisfactory. When ER are not forthcoming, it is as if the selective effect of memory does not include early life experiences and these subjects have no ready store of memories for easy recall. When such subjects are patients in psychotherapy, one may expect that they eventually will begin to report ER which are of the same quality one obtains from the majority of subjects.

Length of Time the ER Has Been Remembered

The subject commonly will report of an ER, "I've always remembered this." These ER are familiar to the subject and are most trustworthy in supplying information about the personality. According to the theory, they should reveal the most consistent elements in the personality. However, if a subject in psychotherapy were to say, "Here's one I haven't thought of in a long time," this ER should be considered a possible indicator of an incipient change in personality. When subjects begin to delve into their own memories, open themselves to the contents of these memories, and recall one which had once been familiar, they are reestablishing a conscious link between every day self-awareness and past experiences.

One must take into account that such ER may be no more than an additional confirmation of what the familiar ER already say. The reestablished link may only provide the same information about the meaning of life as before. Somewhat different are ER which are reported with the statement, "I didn't remember this before." These are still more likely to be indicators of a change in the memory organization and thus, in the perceptual organization of the subject.

Changes in ER

Plewa (1935) has warned that changes in the details of ER, reappearance of long forgotten ER, forgetting of previously given ER, or appearance of new ER may all be responses to the momentary attitude of the subject. If this is so, any change in ER may be a contamination by current events rather than a change in personality. However, ER often do change in the course of psychotherapy and this change seems to be in line with actual changes in the subject's outlook on life (Dreikurs, 1954; Mosak, 1958; Eckstein, 1976). Kadis (1957) has described this as part of the process of growth during psychotherapy, in which changing perceptions of the world are supported by corresponding changes in recall. Brodsky (1952) made a similar claim.

Still unclear is the issue of when a change is a significant indicator of personality change, when it is only indicative of a change in current mood (as when a depression lifts), or when it is contaminated by current life events (as when one has to make a job change). One young woman had recently acquired a new lover who admired her back. She gave a whole new group of ER in which her back was prominently featured. However, contaminants, according to our theory, should only affect contents, not the core constructs which point to the life style.

In order for us to consider the changed ER an indicator of personality change, they must show change in the basic aspects of personality structure, in the life style; that is, a change in the self-concept, the world view, the self-ideal, or dominant goal and in the major ***modus operandi*** used by the subject.

An example of such a change can be seen in the ER of a woman in the late twenties. The first set is as follows:

> Age 4—A girl cousin, a year older, came to visit. Mother brought out a big galvanized tub so we could play in it. I was thrilled. Mother turned the hose on and we played in our bathing suits. Pretty soon my cousin got bored and walked away. I also walked away. I figured if my cousin didn't think it was fun, then it wasn't.

Two years later she recalls:

> ...after a while she left. It wasn't as much fun playing alone.

Is this an insignificant change? Not necessarily. In the first recall she accepts the other's definition of the situation. In the second, she does not give the other the power to define what is fun and what is not. She relies more on her own opinion. Another example of change in the ER of this subject is:

> Age 4—Playing with a little boy in an old car. He was opening the door. He slammed it and my finger was caught. I remember blood...I remember the smell of Lysol in the doctor's office. My mother and uncle were there.

> Age 4—There was an old black car on the grass in the middle of a lot with lots of trees. I was playing with a boy. We were going to get into the car. I was intrigued by the empty car with no grown-ups around. The door was open. Maybe I opened it. I remember a pain in my finger. (I don't remember how it got hurt). I ran to tell Mother and she took me to the doctor. I didn't mind going there because he was a friend of the family. I got my hand bandaged. His office was all yellow.

This ER, in both its versions, lends itself easily to a Freudian interpretation since the sexual allusions are so prominent—

"playing with a boy," "open door," "blood"—and the air of intrigue. Mosak (1958) pointed out the ER lent themselves to many different kinds of interpretations. For the Adlerian, the sexual allusions are also there, but in order to capture life style themes, the important point is not to confound content with theme. The sexual in this ER is to be taken as a ***modus dicendi,*** a manner of speaking, a metaphor. This can be seen clearly if we look at the difference between the first and second versions. In the first version, she is victim. In the second, she is an equal causative agent of the event; she takes responsibility. Furthermore, the outcome is not all bad; she recalls the doctor's office in a pleasant way. ***Her self-image is different.***

Such a change in the details indicates a different perception of life and helps us see why research studies which have only analyzed content do not capture the kind of diagnostic factors that a thematic configurational analysis (Levy & Grigg, 1962) can.

Age Factors in ER

We noted previously that ER from earlier ages have sparser detail than those from later ages. The earliest ER often lack connecting words such as "but," "because," "however," "then," which are plentiful in later ER. Sometimes the subject offers no very early ER. Recollections after age 9 are usually less suitable for such interpretation. We have noted situations, however, in which the subject experienced an important life change during childhood as in the loss of a parent, dethronement by a sibling, or marked change in fortunes of the family. These changes can have three types of effects.

The first (not in order of importance) effect is to produce ER which show a marked "before" and "after" view of the world so that ER before the age of the event are quite different, as if to say, "Once the world was thus, but now it is different."

The second effect is to have no ER at all before the age at which the life situation changed. ER then begin with the event itself or its immediate consequences. One common example of this is when the earliest ER is a dethronement memory—the birth of a younger sibling. No ER are retrieved from before that period.

The third effect is an age gap between ER. One or two ER may be presented from a very early age, then a lapse of several years and subsequent ER from the later years. The important event, itself, may never appear in the ER at all until it is recaptured later in therapy.

Importance of Details

We have previously discussed how details change in ER and how these details affect the interpretation. Details furthermore show some of the subject's characteristic action patterns:

> First day of school. I was a little bit dumbfounded. The teacher had introduced herself and so had each child. The east wall had a blackboard and the west wall, windows. Above was a colored ball or balls against a white background with the names of the colors.

In the details with which the subject embroiders the narrative, we can detect an observer who pays attention to every detail of the setting. We shall expect the subject to continue to show this characteristic behavior.

The Omitted Detail. Occasionally one encounters an ER which on the surface seems innocuous and easily interpreted. Yet if examined more closely, a gap seems to exist, something which does not seem to be explained within the ER. Sometimes it is a gratuitous detail, which appears not necessary to the narrative. Further questioning of this detail may yield what Dreikurs (1969) called a "goldmine." One such ER has been presented previously (Mosak, 1958).

> My family and two neighbors were sitting around the dining room table. It was a festive occasion. Everyone smiling, everyone pleased. Father was home.

The narrative could stand alone without including the last sentence. Since "everyone" was there, why does he mention his father specifically? Upon inquiry, the patient informs us that his father had just been released from a sanitarium. The family was a Christian Science family and such hospitalization was frowned upon by their religious beliefs. Although the patient no longer practiced his childhood faith, vestiges of his earlier beliefs still exist as does his need to deny the existence of illness.

Another such detail can be found in the following ER:

> Age 5—Saturday morning. I'm coming out of the hospital. My uncle and aunt were there to get me.

It seemed odd to the interpreter that the patient's uncle and aunt had picked him up since he had indicated that he had parents and had lived with them. Upon further questioning he revealed that the reason he was in the hospital was because his father had smothered the rest of the family with pillows and that he was the only one to survive.

Vocational Details. Adler (1937, 1958), Orgler (1972 [1939]) and Mosak (1958) have each pointed out that people in various vocations may reveal their occupational choice in ER. Adler (1964) indicated that physicians will have at least one ER about the themes of death, illness, or injury. The recollections of Freud, Adler, and Jung (Mosak & Kopp, 1973) and of Dreikurs (Terner & Pew, 1978) confirm this hypothesis. Our clinical experience suggests that artists and those people with a strong esthetic bent will include a color detail in their ER.

A mathematician relates—

> In the hospital after surgery. Being fed intravenously. I counted the drops as they came down the tube. No feeling about it except that it was interesting.

Positional Details. Dreikurs (1954) felt that the position of the subject in the ER suggested the stance toward life taken by the subject. A memory of lying flat on one's back in the crib suggested a different life stance than one of standing upright. Sitting in the high chair, being pushed in a stroller, looking up or looking down all suggested something about the subject's attitude toward life. A man who felt like an outsider on the periphery of life recalled:

> Age 8—I was sitting on the curb watching the other kids play ball across the street. I didn't go over.

The detail in this memory is "across the street." He himself was peripheral to the scene of action, an observer from a distance who does not enter the arena of social action.

Other Details. Using this same logic one can make other predictions. Subjects who recall tactile sensations (textures) may well have a sensual response to tactile stimuli; a great attention to affective details may point to a person who is more than usually sensitive to his/her own inner feelings (Peven & Shulman, 1983); movement details suggest an active style of responding to stimuli (Hedvig, 1965) and so forth.

ER of Trivial Events

Since the ER are treated as projections, no trivial ER exist. However, what seems like the ER of a trivial event often deals with important people or issues. In the previously given ER of the cousin who was bored playing in the galvanized tub, the subject tells us that this cousin was her chief rival in childhood.

> I was in my uncle's car by myself. I was in the driver's seat and turning the wheel and pretending I was driving.

What small boy has not done this? Yet, that it is offered as an ER makes it an important issue for the patient. It suggests that his ambition is to be able to do what adult males do, but in his projection, he sees himself as "pretending" to do what men do. Trivial ER reveal as much as dramatic ones.

Sequence of ER

ER can be considered as a creative artistic product of the person, as if they were an autobiography which not only describes events but also the person's creative responses to them. They can be compared in structure to a musical composition with its themes and variations. Being an artistic product, the sequence of the memories in itself helps in their interpretation. ER from an early stage may state the theme starkly while those from a later age with added details can show elaborations on the theme. While one ER may be hard to understand, a group of ER more surely shows the common themes that run throughout.

> Age 9—We had a spelling bee. I was the last one standing. It felt great.

The second ER from this person is an elaboration on the same theme:

> Age 8—We were playing "King of the mountain." While everybody was pushing everyone around to get to the top, I sneaked around the other side and walked to the top unmolested. I don't know how long I stayed on top but it sure felt good being there.

The theme is the same, but with a variation. Winning is equated with being "on top" (a positional detail). Note that in this ER he takes a detour to get to the top through an avenue left unnoticed by the others. He uses guile rather than skill. By hook or by crook he attains the superior position.

The third ER shows another variation.

> Age 7—It was the first day of school. All the kids were crying. I felt it was silly of them.

Knowing the previous two ER, this one is clear. Here is another way in which he is superior. He acts maturely while the others act childishly. He achieves his superior position by winning directly or failing that he resorts to a roundabout route or finds some other way to look down on others. All these ER have a single theme, no matter what the variations. The sequence confirms and elaborates the theme.

Contrasting ER. The fourth ER shows a contrast.

> Age 7—We were at a picnic and they had races for prizes, I came in second in my heat. I was crushed.

The common theme in these ER can be seen by contrasting them. (Contrast is an important way to elicit the meanings of ER.) In three he wins, in the fourth he loses. The important issue for him is to be a winner. Even second place is not good enough.

Whereas the motive of the person who gives the above ER is to be superior to others, the motive in the following set is self-control. But this is not as simple a group of ER to interpret because the four ER show a contrapuntal arrangement. The first contrasts with the second; the third seems to repeat the theme of the first but when contrasted with the fourth, the latter two show a variation which actually gives us a second theme.

> Age 3—One time I made in my pants. I was playing in the yard. I felt ashamed.

> Age 5—The doctor came to give me a shot every other day. One time I didn't cry. I got to be a pro at it. He was proud of me. I felt real good about being able to take it without screaming.

If he loses self-control, he loses face. If he maintains self-control, he wins the approval of others and his self-esteem is intact. In one case he successfully endures; in the other he cannot hold out.

> Age 5—Riding with Father to the office. I threw up in the car all over myself. I got car sick. I was very upset with myself but I couldn't control it (the vomiting).

This sounds like a repeat of the first ER. Again he cannot control the behavior of his own body, but here he reports he is upset with himself rather than ashamed. This may seem like splitting hairs but the contrast with the next ER will show that the ER also compare anger at oneself versus anger at others.

> Age 4—I was in the hospital having my tonsils out. I didn't want to be there. Then I recall the ether. It was a black mask. It was scary. I didn't know what they would do to me. I woke up in my crib and was angry. I had to use the bedpan. The only thing they did that they said they'd do was to give me ice cream. I was kicking and screaming the whole time in the hospital.

Since all of these ER are concerned with illness and three of them with the digestive tract, one wonders if this person suffers from a physical illness or is inordinately concerned with health (as a physician is). The fourth memory is like the second in that illness and medical treatment are portrayed but the theme in the fourth is no longer self-control. The way in which the fourth elaborates the discomfort of medical treatment is only suggested in the second ("one time I didn't cry"). In the fourth memory he takes up for the first time the issue of his anger at others. Here the contrast with the third ER is useful. There he was angry with himself; here he is angry at others.

What determines the object of his anger? It depends on who is the source of his trouble. In the fourth memory he does not focus on self-control but on the power and control that others have over him. In the ER he is first afraid and then angry. The fear is now gone and he justifies his anger at the others ("The only thing they did that they said they'd do was give me ice cream"). This ER suggests that the chance to find fault with others is face-saving for him and compensates for his own unhappiness with his perceived fault of not keeping his own nervous system under control.

In this second set of ER, all the situations are unpleasant. Becoming angry at others because they are at fault suggests that this person may have to search for faults in others. At the same time he seems distrustful of himself and wants to control his own natural and entirely normal physical responses to situations. In contrast to the person in the first ER set, for the second person life seems precarious. The first subject can find different ways of achieving his goal of superiority. The second subject preserves his self-esteem either by self-control or with anger at others. His important issues are power and control.

The One Different ER. On occasion, one ER may be different from all others. It often can be found sequentially separate; that is, it appears as the first ER (a prologue) or the last (an epilogue). This different ER offers a contrast to the others.

> Age 3—Father brought home new tooth brushes. He taught me and all the others to brush our teeth. It was a lot of fun.

This ER is a prologue to the others. It is a memory of a pleasant occasion initiated by her father who died when the

This ER is a prologue to the others. It is a memory of a pleasant occasion initiated by her father who died when the subject was young. Father was a source of security for the whole family. The subsequent memories are all different.

> Age 3—I cried all morning. I wanted to put on overalls like my brother and Mother wouldn't let me.
>
> Age 4—An older girl came by with crochet hooks and tried to teach Sister and me to use them. Sister learned, but I was too young.
>
> Age 3—We went to the grocery store. I carried the eggs home. They were all broken when I got home.
>
> Age 5—First day in school. I wore a cotton dress. Most of the girls were in organdies or silks. I felt humiliated.
>
> Age 6—I took my new ball to school. Someone borrowed it and lost it. At the end of the day a boy brought me an old ball but it wasn't mine. It was old and battered.

First memories like this one can be thought of as "Garden of Eden" memories. They portray how life should be—happy, with good human relations and satisfying interactions. All the subsequent ER depict life as she perceives it—unfair, unrewarding, and herself as less than others. By its contrast, the first ER stands as reminder of what she feels she is missing in life and makes more poignant the disappointments in the subsequent ER.

ELEMENTS OF ER

As we have examined the attempts to categorize ER, or parts of them, we have always found some objection to the categories. Even Adler's effort to categorize some aspects of ER can be no more than a hint of what the ER may mean. Thus, when he says that early memories in which the mother is prominent suggest a pampered child, the key word is ***suggest.*** Adler's own words are as follows:

> Provided we possess the requisite experience and use the utmost care, we may in most cases discover from the earliest recollections the mistaken direction of the life path, the lack of social interest or the contrary. Much, too, comes to light through the choice of presentation of a "we" or "I" situation. Much, too, comes to light from the mention of the mother. Recollections of dangers and accidents, as well of corporal and other punishments, disclose the exaggerated tendency to keep in mind particularly the hostile side of life. The recollection of the first visit to the kindergarten or school shows the great impression produced by new situations. The recollection of sickness or death is often linked with a fear of these dangers, and occasionally with the attempt to become better equipped to meet them, possibly as a doctor or a nurse or similarly. Recollections of a stay in the country with the mother, as well as the mention of certain persons like the mother, the father, or the grandparents in a friendly atmosphere, often show not only a preference for these persons who evidently pampered the child, but also the exclusion of others. Recollections of misdeeds, thefts, and sexual misdemeanors which have been committed usually point to a great effort to keep them from occurring again. Occasionally, one learns also of other interests, such as visual, auditory, or motor interests, which may give occasion to uncover failures in school and a mistaken occupational choice, and indicate an occupation which corresponds better to the preparation for life. (1964b, pp. 210-211)

Adler's statement provides some reasonable guidelines. The various ER may indeed mean what Adler said, but he described topics and issues. How the individual responds is equally important.

Keeping this warning in mind we will classify ER according to certain content categories for the purpose of explanation and teaching and separate these from the method of interpreting the ER for the purpose of arriving at a formulation of the individual life style.

ER Thematic Topics

Levy and Grigg (1962) used three theme categories—dependency/independence, aggression, and sexuality. They then subdivided these themes according to the type of response the subject made to each of these themes. We will define "topic" as the issue being faced by the subject but we will also include other ER types such as "prologue" and "epilogue" memories to allow us a more complete development of this category. Any one set of memories may show more than one theme. This classification will not be based on the type of response the subject makes to the issue in the ER because we want to place this in a separate category. For our purpose we will use the ER we have already discussed in this chapter as well as others.

Victim. The ER given by Kadis and Lazarsfeld (1948) is an example of a victim theme. The girl could not be the flower girl at her aunt's wedding because her sister chopped her hair off. Note that we do not classify this under the theme of body injury because the ER focused on the disappointment not on the haircut. She is the victim of what someone else has done to her. Another victim ER;

> Age 6—I was playing with a Santa Claus house on the floor. A cousin stepped on it.

Competition. The two ER about winning the spelling bee and losing the race are examples of a competition theme. This theme deals with winning and losing or how well one does in comparison to others.

Separation. Separation from a parent or absence of a parent is seen in the ER in which the boy rides the skates happily in the basement while his mother is in the hospital. The response suggests a successful denial of the pain of separation.

Next is a memory of a woman whose mother placed her with foster parents when she was three.

> Age 3—I am sitting on a desk and being told that two people there are my parents and I insist that they are not...At the railroad station I said goodbye to Mother. She

> gave me some pennies tied in a handkerchief . . . Foster Father stepped off the train and took me from Mother and went back on the train . . . I was going curiously down the aisle exploring and was being brought back by Foster Father. It was like a game. . . . I was being carried by Foster Mother. Some people met us. I had the general feeling that it was all a mistake.

Disappointment. This theme is seen in the memory of the two girls playing in a galvanized tub.

> Age 4—. . . after awhile she left. It wasn't as much fun playing alone.

Bodily Injury. The memory of the same subject about her experience in the abandoned car is a bodily injury memory. However, the setting offers many sexual allusions. This could just as easily be classified as a sexual memory.

A memory from a male shows the bodily injury.

> Age 4—A puppy came in my direction. I ran and fell and hit the corner of the step and cut myself. I was bleeding like a pig and ran into the house screaming. Father and Mother took care of me. Mother quieted me down.

Obviously, the response the subject makes to the bodily injury will determine how the ER is interpreted. For the sake of brevity, we will list and describe briefly a number of other thematic issues that can be found in ER. They are listed in Table 6.1.

One memory may appear to fit into more than one category.

> Age 4—I came into the room dancing. I fell and sprained my ankle while twisting.

Is the issue a SURPRISE, LUCK, or COMPETENCE? More ER from the same subject probably would help clarify the question. Let us look at a set of ER from another subject.

(Continued on p. 195)

TABLE 6.1
Common Thematic Topics Found in ER

DETHRONEMENT—the birth of a younger sibling or the entry onto the scene of another person who takes center stage.

SURPRISES—unexpected events occur.

OBSTACLES—ER in which one's way is blocked by an obstacle or by the action of another person.

AFFILIATION—ER of pleasant bonds with others or of a distance between the self and others.

SECURITY—feelings of security or insecurity. Since affiliation is the most important basis for security in early childhood, SECURITY and AFFILIATION are often found together. Memories of being frightened can be usually classified here.

SKILL TASKS—ER of situations which require some competence.

DEPENDENCY—ER of being dependent on others or of being self-reliant.

EXTERNAL AUTHORITY—ER of being expected to comply with a set of rules.

SELF CONTROL—the issue of being or not being able to control oneself; e.g., being able to control one's own bowel movements.

STATUS—the issue of how important one is in the eyes of others, of how one becomes significant in the group.

POWER—The issue of who is in the dominant and controlling position, oneself or someone else.

MORALITY—The issues of right and wrong, fair and unfair, good and bad. MORALITY ER often show the use of a moral attitude to raise one's status, to be superior to others or to be morally inferior to others. STATUS issues are often found together with MORALITY.

TABLE 6.1 (Continued)

HUMAN INTERACTION—ER with a specific focus on how people relate to each other. This is often expressed through the POWER, MORALITY, and STATUS themes. It is a picture of the world of social transactions.

NEW SITUATIONS—The first day at school or first day in a new neighborhood are prototype ER of this issue. SEPARATION and AFFILIATION issues are often combined with NEW SITUATION issues as are COMPETENCE and SECURITY issues.

EXCITEMENT—ER which focus on the amount of excitement or commotion in a situation. The excitement may be pleasant or unpleasant.

SEXUALITY—ER of childhood sex games, encounters with adults, or of observing sexual activity.

GENDER—ER which focus on the issues of masculinity or femininity. These also may be combined with SEXUALITY.

NURTURANCE—ER which focus on receiving affection, nurture, service, attention, or gifts from others.

CONFUSION—ER which focus on ambiguity and poorly understood events.

LUCK—ER which focus on the vagaries of fate.

SICKNESS and DEATH—ER about this topic and the effect it has on others.

GARDEN OF EDEN—An ER which depicts how life should be as opposed to how it actually is. Idyllic ER.

Age 3—Playing on the floor with beads. I swallowed one. Sister picked me up and ran out to the fields to get Mother. She wasn't perturbed.

Age 3—Playing in the kitchen near trapdoor. The door fell down on my leg. Sister picked me up and cried as hard as I did.

Age 3-4—I took hold of a hot poker, burned my hand, screamed. Mother got a jar of salve. I stuck my whole hand into it.

Age 7—I had a nosebleed in class. I left the room. Teacher came out and petted me and took me home.

The main thematic content of these ER seems at first to be bodily injury but being nurtured by others is an equally important topic: Put together, it suggests that this person views bodily injury as something that automatically elicits nurturance from others.

This list of thematic topics is not exhaustive. It is a representative sample of frequently found topics in ER. This category does not attempt to classify the behavioral responses reported in the ER. For that we need another category.

ER Response Themes

Each response in an ER is a response to the particular topical issue in the ER. Thus, if the topic is EXTERNAL AUTHORITY we can expect the subject to choose from among a range of responses from willing compliance with a desire for approval to open defiance of the rules. In any idiographic interpretation we shall have to identify both the topic and the unique response the individual selects. The range of human responses is much wider than the range of topics but we shall again try to give a representative sample of frequent response themes. A few examples follow:

Age 2-3—My parents gave me a toy piano. I was delighted.

The topic is one we have called NURTURANCE. The response is to be pleased, to enjoy the gift.

> Age 6—It was the first day of the first grade. I went home at noon and told my mother I wasn't going back.

The topic may be NEW SITUATIONS or EXTERNAL AUTHORITY. The response is a refusal to comply with the demand.

> Age 2-3—I was lying in the crib, unable to move. I couldn't get up. I screamed. Mother rushed upstairs, picked me up and told me everything was okay.

The topic seems to be DEPENDENCY or SELF-CONTROL. The response is to send out an SOS which brings the desired help.

After we have categorized the topics in the ER, we still have to understand the response the person makes. The response is more important than the topic, showing the creative behaviors used by the person to cope with the various challenges implied in the topics. The following list shows common behavioral responses to a variety of topics, with representative examples.

In reviewing the list, keep in mind that clinical interpretation has a richness of nuances that is not found in mere lists and tables of categories. Categories are useful for research and teaching but they do not replace the whole pattern that the skillful clinician derives from the material. A list of representative response themes is presented in Table 6.2 and examples of response themes are presented in Table 6.3.

Perhaps this brief list (Table 6.3) can given an impression of the myriad number of responses human beings are able to make to various challenging issues in their worlds.

Life Style Elements in ER

The relationship between the thematic topic and response theme can be expressed as an "If **a,** then **b**" linear relationship. An ER will demonstrate this:

> Age 8—My brother and a friend and I got into trouble at school. We were sent into the cloak room where we ate all the lunches. The teacher beat us up. It hurt. Eating the lunches was my idea because I wanted to get even with the teacher.

TABLE 6.2
A List of Representative Response Themes

OBSERVER—a passive spectator of events.

PROBLEM-SOLVING—active problem solving behavior, sometimes quite creative.

COMPLIANCE/REBELLION—the ER show a range of behaviors from compliance to defiance.

CALL FOR HELP—overtly or covertly signaling to others that their aid is needed.

REVENGE—getting even with others, even in a self-destructive way.

SUFFERING—ER of impotent anger, unhappiness, or other forms of distress as the main and sometimes only response to a problem situation.

MANIPULATION—demanding special service from others, intimidating or forcing them.

SEEKING EXCITEMENT—voluntarily creating exciting situations.

PRETENSE—pretending to be what one is not for the purpose of concealing one's own defects or enhancing one's status.

DENIAL—solving the problem of an unpleasant situation by focusing elsewhere than on the unpleasantness.

RESOLVE—the decision to behave a certain way or do a certain thing in the future. The planned action is to increase security or self-esteem.

COMPETENCE—ER of competent or incompetent response to a skill task.

TABLE 6.2 (Continued)

SOCIAL INTEREST—the presence or absence of prosocial behavior.

ACTIVITY—whether the response is active or passive to the challenge situation.

DISTANCE KEEPING—the tendency to withdraw from and avoid challenges.

COOPERATION—the presence or absence of collaboration in the ER. It may be for good or for evil purpose, but shows the ability to collaborate with others, the resolve to or action of taking responsibility for meeting a situation.

OVERCONFIDENCE—experiencing an unpleasant result because one tried to do more than he was capable of such as being too daring and getting hurt. The topic may be called ACCEPTING LIMITS.

SELF-AGGRANDIZEMENT—making oneself more important than one really is.

CRITICISM—fault finding as a response to challenges. One type is fault finding itself, the identification of what is wrong. Another type is blaming, the attribution of responsibility for the fault.

FEELING AVOIDANCE—the tendency to avoid, suppress, and ignore affect. See also DENIAL.

TABLE 6.3
Examples of Response Themes in ER

OBSERVER and DISTANCE KEEPING . . . I was sitting on the curb watching the other kids play ball across the street, I didn't go over.

PROBLEM SOLVING . . . We were playing "King of the mountain" . . . I sneaked around the other side and walked to the top unmolested . . .

COMPLIANCE/REBELLION and REVENGE . . . My father sent me to my room because I wouldn't eat vegetables. I was irked. I opened the window and pee'd on the eave of the roof.

CALL FOR HELP . . . I ran to tell Mother and she took me to the doctor.

SUFFERING . . . Most of the girls were in organdies or silks. I felt humiliated.

MANIPULATION . . . I wanted to sit on the front seat with my father. I cried and cried until they put me in the front seat to shut me up.

SEEKING EXCITEMENT . . . I was on a swing going up as high as I could. It was exhilarating.

PRETENSE . . . I pretended to drive the car.

DENIAL . . . I counted the drops as they came down the tube.

FEELING AVOIDANCE . . . No feeling . . . it was interesting.

COMPETENCE . . . I climbed a big tree . . .

SOCIAL INTEREST . . . and threw rocks at the caretaker of the cottage . . .

ACTIVITY . . . I didn't fight back. I thought, if I weren't a cripple, I would beat him.

COOPERATION . . . My father and I were rolling a ball back and forth to each other . . .

SELF-RELIANCE . . . My mother didn't come for me when school was over. I walked home myself.

OVERCONFIDENCE . . . I climbed on the bureau. I found a razor blade. I fell off and cut my nose.

SELF-AGGRANDIZEMENT . . . I had no fear whatever. I felt like nothing could happen to me.

CRITICISM . . . I was angry . . . The only thing they did that they said they'd do was to give . . .

The linear relationship is as follows:

If ***I get into trouble,***

then ***I will be punished.***

If ***I take revenge for the punishment,***

then ***I will get into more trouble.***

This way of teasing out and then integrating the elements in the ER go a long way toward producing a final interpretation. However, life style formulation requires that we examine more elements. In Chapter I we described the life style elements as a set of convictions about "what is," a set of convictions about "what should be," and a set of instructions for behavior. (See Table 1.1.) Topics in ER afford us information about what is important and response themes about the methods to use. Now let us see if we can draw from the ER the categories of self-concept and world view.

> Age 3—I climbed to the top of the bureau. I found a razor blade there. I fell off and cut my nose.

Self-image. The self-image aspect of the self-concept is evident. What is he? He is someone who will only suffer if he climbs too high. He will tumble and be hurt.

> Age 7-8—A boy tried to beat me up. I was scared and resigned myself to being beaten up. I didn't fight back. I thought, "If I weren't a cripple (club feet), I would beat him."

What is he? He is a cripple who cannot defend himself against physical aggression by peers.

While the body sense and self-identity aspects of the self-concept tend to remain consistent, the self-image is often contingent upon circumstances as the next ER shows.

> Age 8-9—In the country. I climbed a big tree and threw rocks at the caretaker of the cottage down below. I had no fear whatsoever. I felt like nothing could happen to me.

This ER shows that his self-image depends on how high and secure he can make his location ***vis a vis*** others. If he can get high enough, he can do as he pleases to others without fear of consequences.

Self-esteem is considered a function of the self-image. Self-esteem varies in all of us and its determinants change over time. What affords self-esteem is different for a small child than an adult, for a male than for a female. Some experiences increase it, others lower it. An example is the set of ER from the child who couldn't control his bowel movements and was ashamed, but could take his injection like a "pro" and was proud of it.

World View. The ER can show us how the subject assesses the world around himself or herself.

> Age 7—Standing behind a swing awaiting my turn. The boy swung back and knocked my teeth loose.

For her, life is precarious for unwary people.

> Age 5—First day of school. The teacher was very nice. She gave us treats to eat. There were pillows to lie on. I enjoyed it.

This subject finds some new situations in life almost sybaritically pleasant.

Relationship Between Self-concept and World View. By labeling these two categories as separate we have divided something that really is an interactive unit. Self-concept and world view are two sides of the same coin, one cannot exist without the other. Any self-concept is always embedded in a setting. As one or the other emerges as a figure from the background, it becomes more discernable in an ER. Thus different ER which will highlight either self-concept or world view should always be treated like a paired unit. One without the other is essentially an incomplete picture of an internal mental construct.

Dominant Goal/Self-Ideal. As is becoming apparent, many ER show one or perhaps two aspects of the life style components. Some ER show a clear model of what is desirable to pursue in life.

> Age 5-6—Mother asked my cousin to carry me on his shoulders in the country because I was the baby and it was a long walk. I felt good that I should be carried and didn't have to walk.

Here is a person who enjoys the prerogatives of being the baby. The baby is permitted dependence and entitled to service from others. Others are to make life easier for the person. This ER reveals a self-image and a dominant goal. If one is a baby, one can achieve significance in life through being cared for by others. Note that the theme of being elevated above others (positional detail) is also present in this ER.

Any dominant goal/self ideal grows logically out of the self-image and world view, allowing us to use the rubric we mentioned in Chapter 1:

I am ____________________, Life is ____________________,

Therefore ____.

We have several times used the ER of the boy who couldn't control his bowel movement as an example and we can do so again. We can see that his self-ideal is to be able to control himself. The next two ER from another subject show another dominant goal.

> Age 4-5—We had a Christmas tree but we couldn't afford a stand for it because we were poor. We had to put it in a jar of water. I felt bad about that. At the same time it was snowing. I stood on the porch watching and wanted to play in the snow but I didn't have any galoshes.

> Age 5—First day in kindergarten. I was happy because I had my own box of crayons and felt that the other kids were silly to cry when their mothers left.

Not surprisingly, this subject's first priority in life was to have enough money so that he always would be able to have the material things he wanted.

Ethical Values. As stated in Chapter 1, the ethical values show convictions about "what should be," the ideal world and ideal behavior.

> Age 4—Cousins visiting. I was repulsed when one of the cousins chewed potatoes with his mouth open. It was almost shocking.

Proper behavior is an important topic for this subject.

> Age 8—I bet a boy my roller skates against his BB gun that I could jump four stairs. I won the bet and took his gun home. My parents wouldn't let me keep it. I thought it was unfair because I won it fair and square.

A deal is a deal, and outsiders should not interfere, as long as it was fair and square.

> Age 3—I burned my hand. I recall them sitting on the couch. Father wrapped my hand in a handkerchief. I felt safe and good because all four of us were together.

This is an ER which makes a judgment about what is one desirable situation in life. When one has suffered an injury, the good is when the significant others can all be together. That is what provides security and happiness.

Methods of Operation. Sometimes the ER will reveal the ***modus operandi*** used by the subject in meeting life. One previous example is in the ER of the subject who won the spelling bee, went around the back of the mountain in order to reach the top, and felt superior to the other children in school who were crying. Since his dominant goal/self-ideal was to be "on top," he uses direct accomplishment, taking advantage and "putting others down," whatever works in the situation (by hook or by crook) to accomplish his goal.

Another subject gives an ER which shows direct behavior with little consideration for others.

> Age 7-8—I had to go to the bathroom very badly. My sister was in there. She was sitting on the toilet. I urinated on her.

The ***modus operandi*** in the next one is to imitate the behavior of older males.

> Age 5-6—I went to a farm with my uncles and mother and father. My uncles got into the pig sty and began to kick the pigs. I tried the same thing. It was a lot of fun.

In the next one, the method is to suffer.

> Age 5—One day I was kidded by some adult relatives for liking a girl. It hurt.

We have previously discussed methods of operation when we discussed ***response themes.*** The method of operation fundamental to the life style however is that method by which the subject negotiates his relationship with life (as revealed in the world view) and which is used to achieve the dominant goal/self ideal.

Affect in the ER

We have from time to time noted the presence of affect recall in ER. In asking questions to increase our comprehension of the ER, we have asked, "Do you remember how you felt at the time?" Sometimes, the reported affect has been the crucial detail that explained the ER. Sometimes it shows us a feeling "style." When ER change over time, the change may be most evident in a change of feeling. Using the following examples, we will try to show how various aspects of affect in the ER can be interpreted.

Affect Reveals a Response to the World. The following ER are from a 35 year old woman.

> Age 2-3—There was a burglar in the house. Everyone was terrified.

> Age 4—I was hiding in the back of the door. A man was yelling, "I'll kill that damn brat. She's always crying." A woman picked me up and ran out of the door to get away from the man. I was frightened.

The ER suggest that strange men are dangerous. The ER show no ability to protect herself, a feeling of helplessness. She depends on someone else, a woman, to rescue her. The following two ER show a different picture of the world and a different response. They are the memories of an exhibitionist.

> Age 5—My friend and I were playing in the sand. He had to urinate and took off his shorts. Two older girls passed by. I told him not to put his pants back on. The girls stopped and talked to us. I got a thrill out of it.

> Age 6—I was walking home. I had my pants wide open. An older woman passed me and said, "You better stop that or I'll tell your mother." I was scared, but I didn't believe she knew my mother (feeling?). I had a thrill from being seen.

Note that he knows he is doing something considered wrong but he enjoys the mischief he performs and its power to impress women.

Affect Expresses a Value. The next two ER from a 35 year old man shows what he values highly and what he depreciates.

> Age 6—I played doctor with a girl. I examined her. Discovered she had no penis. No reaction.

> Age 6—Outside my aunt's house. Saw a naked man in a window. Shocked. Couldn't get over the size of his penis.

What men have is far more impressive than what women have.

Absence of Affect May Indicate Feeling Avoidance As a Response. Earlier in this chapter, we gave the ER of a man who recalled watching the drops in his intravenous fluid after surgery. He also recalled no feeling. Ignoring, not recalling a feeling, may point to a coping style in which distressing emotions are managed by avoiding or ignoring them.

Affective Detail Which Reveals the Meaning. The feeling may be the detail which explains the memory.

> Age 6—I grew big pumpkins. One morning I went to tend my pumpkins and the biggest was gone. I was very upset.

> Later, I found it in the alley, dropped and burst open (feeling?). I felt better, because if I couldn't have it, they shouldn't either.

Without this last detail, one would miss the enjoyment of revenge, which is a theme in this ER (Peven & Shulman, 1986).

Changing Affect in ER. We have previously mentioned that affect in ER may be contaminated by current mood in Chapter 3 and earlier in this chapter. When a depression lifts, the subject's memories will often show more light-hearted affect, but affect is not the same as theme in ER and should not be confused.

SUMMARIZING THE INTERPRETATION OF ER

Manaster and Perryman (1974) developed a scale to test the proposition that the manifest content of ER could distinguish between persons choosing different occupations. They used subjects from five different occupational categories: teaching, counseling, nursing/medical, biological science, and accounting/business. They studied mainly content variables such as which family members were mentioned, the location of the memory, whether the subject was active or passive, and so forth. Some statistically significant differences were found such as that the nursing/medical group had the highest proportion of subjects who mentioned "mother" while the teaching group had the highest proportion who mentioned "nonfamily members."

Essentially, this experiment used the content of the memory and related it to occupational choice. The ER were not interpreted idiographically nor did the experimenters look for life style material. However, some of the content categories in the scale come close to a thematic interpretation of the ER such as whether the subject showed active or passive behavior in the memory. Their scale is worthy of further research.

Kopp and Der (1979) used a different method. They collected a series of ER from the subject and formed a hypothesis about each phrase in each ER. They looked for correlations and confirming statements. What the subject confirmed was assumed to be valid. Their scale thus includes every "action every "action statement" in the series of ER. What Kopp and Der have described is a method of systematically guessing at the meaning of each phrase similar to the way Adler used to guess about the meaning of each statement in a patient's clinical history (Adler 1969b/1931).

Altman (1973) developed an Early Recollections Rating Scale containing nine bipolar attitudes divided into two groups. The first group was "subject's behavior toward environment" and the second was "subject's affective response." The nine bipolar attitudes are shown in Table 6.4.

TABLE 6.4
Eckstein's (1976) Rating Scale
(after Altman, 1973; & Quinn, 1973)

Subject's behavior toward environment
withdrawn—gregarious
passive—active
competitive—cooperative
dependent—independent
Subject's affective response
hostile—friendly
feels rejected—feels accepted
discouraged—self confident
depressed—cheerful
feels mistreated—feels befriended

Eckstein (1976) used Altman's scale (1973) modified by Quinn (1973), in a study of changes in ER after counseling. He was able to score changes in the specific bipolar attitudes using his scale. This method of scoring does not seem to have been used to elicit a life style formulation, but did seem useful in measuring change.

We shall attempt a more elaborate system in order to pick up the idiographic life style information which our theory says can be found in the ER. The list is not exhaustive but probably will cover the great majority of themes we can find in the ER. We also list a number of common response themes, which we will use. In addition we will examine the sequence construction in each set of ER to assess the sequential interaction between themes. Then we shall try to elicit from each theme certain internal cognitive constructions which are, according to our theory, component constructs of the life style.

The material we elicited from FC data was descriptions of behavior. From the behavior we inferred the existence of certain internal cognitions. Now we shall be inferring the existence of cognitions from the subject's report of ER, not only from the behavior described in the ER but also from the progress of events, from the themes chosen to be recalled, and from the message to the self inherent in the creative artistic reconstruction of the memory.

The component constructs of the life style we seek are constructs about "what is," "what should be," and "what is to be done." We have categorized these constructs as containing a self-image, a world view, and a dominant goal and/or self ideal. Sometimes, the ER will even give us information about favored methods of operation, as in the ER of the subject who tried to be superior by winning out over others either directly, by a roundabout way, or by depreciating them.

The interpretation of ER data should complement the interpretation of FC data. Dreikurs (personal communication) used to say that from knowing the FC, one may predict issues in the ER. However, the ER does not have the power to denote psychogenesis that FC has, except for the fact that an internal master plan is in itself a motivator of behavior, perhaps the most important motivator of all. We do expect the ER interpretation to have considerable predictive power as described by Adler (1964b/1929) and Mosak (1965).

Earlier, we used selected ER examples in order to discuss different aspects of ER such as age effects, the presence or absence of background information, the meaning of small connecting words, the meaning of various details, the presence or absence of affect, and so forth. Let us now take a group of ER from one subject and extensively discuss and tabulate them.

ER of Fred, age 21. An only child (the actor you love to hiss)

Age 2—I remember being carried from bed in a dark corner of the room to a table with a cold sheet wrapped around me. There was a light shining in my eyes. It was uncomfortable.

Age 5—I was sitting on the bed next to mother. I touched her breasts. It felt pleasant. Mother looked at me angrily. I was shocked. I wondered why she was angry.

Age 5—I was sitting in the kitchen on a cupboard and Mother was feeding me groats. I didn't like it.

Age 5—It was my bedtime. The room was full of people. I remember getting undressed to go to bed and standing on the bed with my butt naked. I bent over to look through my legs at the people, trying to get their attention.

Age 5—I misbehaved at the dinner table. I don't remember how. I got a look of anger from Father and I wondered why.

Age 5—I looked in the dresser drawer and found a condom. I didn't know what it was and I asked Mother. She took it away and was angry. I wondered what it was all about.

Age 7—I was in the bathroom watching Father wash his hands. I was waiting to wash. I admired all the bubbles Father was making with the soap lather. When it was my turn I tried but I couldn't make bubbles.

Age 5—I touched an electric outlet in the wall and I got a shock.

There are eight ER in this group ranging in age from two to seven. In each ER something is being done to him which he doesn't like or he tries to do something and receives unpleasant feedback. The sequence construction is simple since only these two kinds of events occur. If we had stopped collecting the ER after the first four, we would have about the same data for interpretation.

These ER contain positional details that we should note. For example, Fred is on a table with a light shining on him, sitting on a cupboard, sitting on a bed next to mother, or standing on a bed and presenting his backside to a room full of people. In every ER he is either in the center of the stage or trying to be. He is the chief protagonist of every ER, no matter what other ***dramatis personae*** are present.

Mood is also mentioned in each ER. Every event is associated with a feeling response. Each ER tells us how Fred feels about the world and his place in it.

Table 6.1 listed 22 thematic topics commonly found in ER. Several of these topics are found in this group of ER—***surprises, skill tasks, human interaction, sexuality, nurturance,*** and ***confusion.*** However, the predominant topic in this set of memories is the topic of himself in the world and the surprises and obstacles he encounters in his peregrinations through the world. Furthermore, the world is encompassed by his home and family, none of the ER events are outside the home. We can still score his response to each of the theme topics. The scoring is provided in Table 6.5.

What kind of person would have ER of this type? Such ER are more often found in an only child who had his/her major contacts with the parents. The parents in the example are the "authorities" and he is a subordinate whose main relationship to the parents is one disapproving of their nurturing attempts and eliciting their disapproval by misbehavior. Misbehavior is what captures their attention but misbehavior of a minor mischievous type, of a small boy, rather than defiant inimical behavior. As Dreikurs stated, the only child is

> like a dwarf among giants. He spends his entire childhood among persons whose capactities are far superior to his. For this reason he may try to develop techniques and qualities that will gain him the interest and approbation of grown-ups without particular achievement on his part. (1948, p. 47)

TABLE 6.5
Fred's Responses to Thematic Topics Using The Classification System

SURPRISES—Fred finds life full of unpleasant and confusing surprises but if we look closely at this theme we note that the surprise and confusion is a response and not a stimulus situation. He does not report a response to the surprise—the response *is* a surprise or shock. Even the shock from the electric outlet is not reported as eliciting a further response.

SKILL TASKS—Fred fails in his attempt to do what father does while washing his hands. The essential idea in this ER is that he fails to be as skilled as Father. It is the comparison rather than the task that is important.

HUMAN INTERACTION—This issue is found confusing by Fred. At least, Fred claims to be confused by the responses of his parents to his misbehaviors, to his sexual curiosity. The absence of peer memories seems to make all his interactions those with adult authority figures. These adults seem to control his existence, limit his activities, punish his innocent misbehaviors, and confuse him.

SEXUALITY—The ER suggest a strong interest in sex with confusion about what it means. One thing is certain, it has the power to elicit strong responses from the mother. It can be a powerful tool for getting attention, even negative attention.

NURTURANCE—This topic leads to a negative response. The feeding activity of Mother is not welcome to him. He doesn't like her food. When he turns to her for guidance or pleasure, she becomes angry at him. There is no overt complaint against her, just surprise and confusion.

CONFUSION—Like surprise, this is his response, not a challenge stimulus. He is surprised and confused by the responses of others to him.

MISBEHAVIOR—This is another topic we should include. His misbehavior is disguised by him as innocent play or exploration. The display of his backside is only an "innocent" bid for attention. Touching Mother's breast is only pleasant play. Even his misbehavior at the table is not intended to annoy. The misbehavior produces disapproval and his response to the disapproval is surprise and confusion.

Fred's ER suggest that mischieviousness is an excellent way of persuading others to pay attention to him.

In this set of ER no small connecting words seem crucial to the interpretation, no "buts" or "ifs." Background information is absent. The ER are short and pictorial. The earliest, from age two is, as expected, sketchy, only a fragment, but it says very clearly that he was taken from his warm, quiet, and dark corner, and placed in a cold and undesirable position, exposed to the bright light, thrust into a cold and unpleasant world where the subsequent ER show he tried to find some attention by keeping others busy with him but found only rejection; where he tried to be as much of a man as father but was short on skills and where his exploration only ended in shocked surprise. This interpretation is easy to reach if we take the first ER as a prologue memory—an introduction to the others. The first ER then says, "I was thrust into the limelight in a cold world" subsequent ER say, "I'm just trying to amuse the audience during my time on stage."

Life Style Elements. If possible, we would like to elicit from the ER those internal constructs we call the life style elements—the self-image, the world view, the dominant goal/self ideal, and the method of operation or main way of pursuing the dominant goal/self ideal. Can we do this with these ER? Can we not conclude that his ***self image*** is that he does not make a favorable impression on others and is not as capable as they? His ***world view*** seems to be that others will reject his self-assertions and his attempts to affiliate (they disapprove of him). His goal remains to make an impression even if he has to play the impish clown.

We can summarize this as follows:

> Self-image—less capable and unacceptable to others.
>
> World view—the world is a confusing place where others disapprove of and reject him.
>
> Dominant goal—to occupy center stage. To make an impression.
>
> Method of operation—to keep others busy with his mischief, if he cannot win their favor.

We can characterize Fred in a short statement by saying he feels like a little boy who wants to impress the big adults, doubts his ability to do it successfully, but knows that mischief will bring some recognition, albeit unpleasant.

The ability to delineate a character in one or two broad strokes is perhaps more of a literary talent than a scientific one. It consists of the ability to make a generalization which coordinates all the elements into one short statement and this requires a type of skill in the use of language which is found more often among poets than among psychologists. Perhaps doing so is the hardest skill to learn of those required for assessing a life style.

An additional bit of information about Fred may now be added. Fred was a bright student at a leading university. However, he was frequently in trouble with the faculty because he cut class, would not hand in assignments on time, or was constantly asking to take courses out of sequence (mischief). The faculty recognized his talent but disapproved of his behavior. Fred had no friends although he mixed with the other students. Those complaints for which he sought psychotherapy were that he was always wanting to impress others and so did not get along well with people and that he felt uncomfortable with strangers. He wanted to learn to get along better with others.

The next set of ER is from a woman who responded differently to the challenges she met.

ER of Louise, age 54. First born and only girl
(Things are seldom what they seem)

> Age 5—I was in the habit of visiting Grandmother on the far side of town [background]. One time I had a dime. I got on the street car and got my transfer and nickel change. I lost the nickel and the transfer blew out the window. When I got to the transfer point, I walked the other mile and a half. Grandmother was frantic (because I took so long to come).

> Age 5—Mother gave me a covered pail. I walked to Clark's and got milk in the pail. I don't know if I saw the cows or if a neighbor boy told me that the milk came from a cow. I couldn't wait to get home and tell and I said to Mother, "Don't buy milk from Clark's, it comes from a cow." Mother said, "Where do you think milk comes from?" "From a bottle," I said. Mother then explained to me.

> Age 4—Bob [younger brother] was sent to bed as punishment. He was in our parents' bedroom. I couldn't understand why he wasn't in his own room. Later, Mother wondered why he was so quiet and not protesting. She went in and Bob was peeling the wallpaper off the wall . . . It could be he was supposed to take a nap rather than being punished.

> Age 4—I had a tantrum and I don't know why. Father put me to bed as punishment. It was Sunday and unexpected guests came. I was heartbroken . . . Later Aunt (a guest) said to Father, "How could you?" I felt she sympathesized and I felt like a martyr.

This group contains four ER all from ages 4 and 5. Let us use the classification system and see what we can deduce. Of the topics in Table 6.1 we may consider ***surprises, obstacles, affiliation, human relations, external authority, morality,*** and ***confusion.*** These are summarized in Table 6.6.

Details. Unlike Fred's ER, Louise's are fuller in detail and tell more elaborate stories. Some of the details seem unimportant. Why does the last ER contain the information "It was Sunday?" Perhaps because Sunday is a common day for visiting relatives to come. It is a way of heightening some aspect of the story. Why the detail that Bob was quiet? Because if one does not pay attention to clues, then one can't solve the mystery and can more easily be tricked. We can expect Louise to grant great significance to little details. She will be a watchful person.

Mood. In the second and fourth ER the mood expressed is one of outrage at being tricked or martyred by unfairness. In the first ER, Grandmother is frantic because she does not know where Louise is. No happy mood is found.

TABLE 6.6
Louise's Responses to Thematic Topics Using the Classification System

SURPRISES—Each ER contains an unexpected situation. The unexpected situation requires some type of action response. In the first ER, Louise solves a problem; in the second, she hurries to relay her surprising information to Mother. In the third ER, Mother's action is to investigate the situation; and in the last, Louise's response is to suffer and feel like a martyr. Note that each of the surprises poses a confusing or unpleasant event. Each character in the ER has to face unpleasantness of some type except for the second in which only Louise mistakenly assumes that she has been the victim of a trick.

OBSTACLES—The first and last ER contain obstacle situations. In the first, Louise blithely overcomes the obstacle by her own self-reliance. In the last she is constrained by the authority of father.

AFFILIATION—The issue of affiliation is only indirectly addressed. It is seen most clearly in the last ER when Louise feels that her aunt is sympathetic. There is rather a "reporting" relationship between people in which the transmission of information becomes important. We shall discuss this again under other topics.

HUMAN RELATIONS—These ER show a certain distrust of what others may do. In the second ER Louise feels one can be misled by others. Clark's gives her milk from a cow rather than a bottle. Mother corrects this by giving her the right information. In the next ER, the brother misleads Mother by quietly peeling the wall paper. One has to be watchful in human relations because people play tricks.

EXTERNAL AUTHORITY—In the last ER, Louise is deprived of her pleasure by the authority of her father. The external authority is accused of unfairness and the ER is better considered under the topic of morality.

TABLE 6.6 (Continued)

MORALITY—This topic appears in the second and fourth ER. Louise takes the stand of righteousness in these two ER. She accuses Clark's of tricking her and accuses Father of being unfair. When aunt sympathizes, it is as if Louise has won a victory. Perhaps women are authorities in moral issues.

In the fourth ER she begins by saying she misbehaved and was being punished. She concludes by pointing out that she became the innocent victim of the punishment because she was not only sent to bed, but denied the right to see her aunt. She may do wrong, but what others do to her is much wronger.

CONFUSION—If people are liable to play tricks on each other then we cannot trust external appearances. As the song from Pinafore says:

Things are seldom what they seem
Skim milk masquerades as cream.

Louise and others are confused about what is really going on. Grandmother is frantic because she lacks proper information. Louise lacks information about where milk really comes from. Mother lacks information about what brother is doing. It is pictured as if mysterious things are happening and what one sees on the surface is not to be trusted.

What sort of person would have such ER? We do not find in these ER the center stage positional details we saw in Fred's ER. The same feeling is not present of wanting to impress the bigger adults or being confused by their response to her. She portrays herself as one who tries to do what is right rather than one who tries to get attention. But her basic stance to the world is not that of Fred, a little boy trying to win his membership card in adult socity; rather she is disapproving and distrusting of others. Her response is to be a moralist—"one of the good guys" who is apt to suffer at the hands of others. This moralistic stance will allow her to rise above the wrongdoers and claim a superiority to them; even if she must suffer at their hands, she can claim the status of martrydom.

The interpretation is highly suggestive but not certain from the ER that wrongdoers may more often be men than women. Thus, her brother is the mischief maker and Father is the unfair disciplinarian while Mother is the one upon whom the trick is played and Aunt is sympathetic to her when Father punishes her. Such a guess must be supported by family constellation data or by the subject's own agreement with the guess before the assessor can consider it confirmed. For the present, it would remain only a guess.

In summary form, Table 6.7 contains life style elements in Louise's ER.

TABLE 6.7
Life Style Elements in Louise's ER

SELF-IMAGE—Righteous, trying to do right, but at a disadvantage from lack of information. Being unfairly treated by authority.

WORLD VIEW—Mysteries are to be discovered. Life contains surprises.

DOMINANT GOAL/SELF IDEAL—Be righteous (more than others). Discover the truth.

METHOD OF OPERATION—Claim righteousness, look for allies, suspect, distrust, and devalue those who devalue her.

As we did with Fred, we shall now add a bit of clinical information about Louise. She came to us at the urging of her daughter and son-in-law, insisting that she had a marital problem. Her complaint was that her husband was a member of an international organization of drug smugglers. Her evidence included particular details such as the information that her husband wanted the kitchen window shade set at a certain height. Furthermore, he turned the lights on at about the same time every night, shortly after the next door neighbor turned on the lights. The diagnosis was paranoia.

We have seen that we can classify ER according to a set of thematic topics and the individual responses to these topics. From this scale we can extrapolate life style elements and incorporate them in a short description. Usually the sequence construction of the ER is repeated over and over in different variations. Sometimes the sequence itself gives us additional information. The mood expressed in the ER offers more clues. In the end we can form a global picture, a ***Gestalt,*** which uses the life style elements as a rubric: If this is "what I am" and that is "what the world is," then such and such is "what is required." In this rubric we can see the way that person has construed life.

FORMULATING BASIC MISTAKES

We have described the ***basic mistakes*** as being misperceptions—oversimplification, exaggeration, and mistaking the part for the whole. In Chapter 1, we described how Mosak (1984) classified basic mistakes into five categories and gave examples of each. We also showed how the basic mistakes matched Karen Horney's (1966) formulation of "overdriven attitudes." From our interpretation of ER we also should like to recognize the basic mistakes of the subject. Let us examine the ER of Fred to see if we can recognize such mistakes. In our formulation of Fred's responses to the topics in the ER (Table 6.5) we noted that Fred finds life unpleasant and confusing. He is shocked by it. We can consider this an overgeneralization about life as well as a misperception of it. In his memory of being unable to wash his hands like Father or please his parents, he is ***minimizing his own worth.*** In his desire to impress always and be center stage he shows a ***faulty value.***

In Chapter 1 we listed a number of distorted attitudes. Under "distorted attitudes about the self (inappropriate self-evaluations) we listed the statement "I am less capable than others" as one example. Under "distorted attitudes about the world and people" is the statement "Life is too confusing." We can say that "distorted goal" is to be the center, to keep people busy with him; the "distorted ideal" is to make a favorable impression on everyone at all times; and the "distorted method of operation" is to innocently make mischief in order to draw attention to himself and evoke a response. All of these distortions are personal myths about himself and the world, and he acts as if these myths, which may be partly true, are an accurate description of the meaning of life.

In Table 6.8 is classification of basic mistakes.

TABLE 6.8
Classification of Basic Mistakes
(Mosak, 1984)

1. OVERGENERALIZATION.

    "People are hostile."
    "Life is dangerous."

2. FALSE OR IMPOSSIBLE GOALS OF "SECURITY."

    "One false step and you're dead."
    "I have to please everybody."

3. MISPERCEPTIONS OF LIFE AND ITS DEMANDS.

    "Life never gives me a break."
    "Life is too hard."

4. MINIMIZATION OR DENIAL OF ONE'S WORTH.

    "I'm stupid."
    "I'm undeserving."
    "I'm just a housewife."

5. FAULTY VALUES.

    "Be first even if you have to climb over others."

SUMMARY

In this chapter we have described different aspects of ER that we use in eliciting life style information. We have examined various ER groupings and interpreted them in terms of theme presented and response made. We have then used our interpretation to elicit life style elements, a self-image, a world view, a dominant goal/self ideal, and a method of operation. We concluded with a description of how we can recognize basic mistakes.

We have described a variety of components that can be found in ER and have given many examples to show these components. These so-called components are actually aspects of ER which we have chosen to interpret. Perhaps other things also can be found in ER which we ignore because they do not give us the particular data we seek.

However, an important aspect to keep in mind is that we have chosen examples that are relatively easy to interpret and that not all ER may offer such promise. Nor should one expect too much from them. Sometimes one may collect a whole set of ER and find no clear statement about many of the components we have described. Not all ER reveal a self-image, a world view, ideals, or even a response style. In interpreting ER to use the data just as it is given is better than to try to infer information that is not clearly there.

Clearly we have treated ER as metaphor. ER make statements about life and one's place in it, about what is important and what is to be prized, and about what, if anything, one can do or must do about the conditions of existence.

CHAPTER 7

AN EXAMPLE

Until now we have given part examples to illustrate the technique of scoring and summarizing a life style. Now we shall give a complete example.

If the interpretation of the example seems long and arduous, it is because we are concerned with showing as well as we can the process of interpretation. The experienced interpreter will interpret the material in a much shorter time. For this occasion, however, we will go through the whole procedure.

The life style is that of a thirty-eight year old woman who came for advice about her eleven year old son who did poorly in school and was disobedient at home. He was starting to steal from the neighbors and herself, disliked school, talked back to his mother and was annoying to peers by clownish attention-seeking behavior, so that he had no friends. There were huge scenes between mother and child. Mother admitted that she had frequently beaten him because he was so disobedient. Before coming to us, she had had two years of counseling in a family agency and according to her own report, she had learned to feel much better about herself, lost her temper with her son less often and felt less guilty about her previous punishment of him. She reports that she rejected her son during his infancy and treated him with hostility although she felt love for him at the time. As an example, she reports that if he cried for his bottle, she would angrily jam the bottle in his mouth. Originally a placid child, he started to rebel at about age five and began to misbehave.

Mother and child were seen and specific suggestions were made to mother to change her behavior. She did not always follow the suggestions, but when she did she noticed considerable change in the son's behavior; e.g., he stopped stealing and tried to please her more. At this point she realized that the major source of the problem was her own behavior and asked for help in understanding herself. The life style formulation was undertaken to help her understand herself better.

Table 7.1. is information completed on the LSI during a session with the mother. In Table 7.2 is a summary of significant information drawn for the LSI.

As can be easily-seen, the tables carry redundant information. The advantage of this is that the responses repeat themselves and converge in such a way that they confirm each other. The different tables are really different ways of asking questions about the meaning of the data. The tables are a step toward correlating the data into a global picture of Nan's early social world and her chosen response to it. Where contradiction rather than confirmation appears, it must be explained. (See Chapter 4, pp. 96-97.)

FAMILY CONSTELLATION: SUMMARY

Nan was the oldest of three and only girl, for six years an only child with a doting father, living in an innocent's paradise which was shattered by the harsh attempts of father to discipline her and by the birth of the brother. She reacted to the first by complete rebellion, precipitating a love-hate relationship between herself and father with much conflict for power and a feeling that she was bad. She then abdicated her position with mother to her brother and sought her place in an exciting outside world. The two models were a doting but overpowering father and a permissive but critical and rejecting mother. She imitated father's willfulness and power tactics and felt alienated from both. She rejected any imposed values and sought to pursue her own interests.

Since the family atmosphere was chaotic and conflictual, the parents were unable to impose their order on each other or on Nan after her dethronement. She tried to restore some of her

(Continued on p. 240)

TABLE 7.1
The Life Style Inventory
(Page 2)

SIBLING CONSTELLATION (Give Childhood Descriptions)
(Oldest to Youngest) Give Age for Subject and Years Older or Younger for Others

Name: Nan @ 38 Age Dif ______ M F Description: Stubborn, ran away all the time because I wanted to see things. Thought of myself as a bad child. Talked too much. Rambunctious. Drifted through grammar school. I wanted to help around the house but didn't know how to go about it, so I went at it compulsively. After brother was born, I tried to please. Had friend. Gregarious. A tomboy. I was constantly punished for stubborness. I	Name: Phillip Age Dif -6 years M F Description: Tried hard in school. More obedient, more submissive, lovable. Very high ambitions until he had a breakdown in his teens. (Authors' note-Since the breakdown occured in the teens, it took place after the development of the life style.)
xNamexxxxxxxxxxxxxxxAge DifxxxxxxxxxxxxxxxM F xDescriptionx don't remember why I was punished but I didn't know I was supposed to please other people. Later, I wanted to please other people. Not ambitious until I got older. I just wanted to play. I cared about dogs and having adventures	Name: John Age Dif -8 years M F Description: Veru ugly. Sickly, antisocial, isolated himself. I don't remember much about him, complained a lot. Very serious.
Name: ______ Age Dif ______ M F Description:	Name: ______ Age Dif ______ M F Description:

SIBLING GROUPINGS

Most different from respondent.
How?
Most like respondent.
How?
Groupings by age, sex, etc.

Sickness, surgery, or accidents?

Relationship between siblings
Who cared for and protected whom?

Who played together?

Who fought each other?

Unusual talents or achievements?

Childhood fears, childhood ambitions?

SHARED TRAITS AND/OR INTERESTS
(Shared equally by all siblings)

2

TABLE 7.1 (Continued)
The Life Style Inventory
(Page 3)

SIBLING RATINGS
(Rate from most to least)

Intelligence	P - N & J
Elementary school grades	P - N & J
Helpful around house	
Industrious	P - N - J
Standards of achievement	P - J - N
Actual achievement	
Daring	none
Assertive	N & J - P
Patient	
Methodical	
Neat	all about equal
Persistent	
Responsible	P - N & J
Obedient	P - N & J
Mischievous	N & J - P
Open rebel	N & J - P
Covert rebel	?
Punished	N - P & J
For what?	
By whom?	
Got away with the most	
Impulsive	
Self-reliant	
Standards of right & wrong	P - N & J (tried to do right)
Critical of others	J - N - P
Critical of self	N - J - N
Easy-going	P - N - J
Sense of humor	P - N & J
Excitable	
Worried	
Other:	
Friends (most friends)	N - P - J
Charm	P - N - J
Tried to please	P - N - J
Had to please	
Succeeded in pleasing	
Outgoing	
Withdrawn	J - N - P
Cheerful	P - N - J
Considerate	all about equal
Bossy	none
Demanded way	N & J - P
Got way	N & J - P
Temper	N - J - P
Fighter	N - J - P
Chip on shoulder	J - N - P
Sulked	N - J - P
Held grudges	
Complained	
Took advantage of others	
Stubborn	N - J - P
Shy	N
Sensitive and easily hurt	J - N - P
Excitement seeker	N - P - J
Idealistic	P - N - J
Materialistic	J - N - P
Pampered	
Masculine	P
Feminine	N
Sure of self	
Athletic	none

3

TABLE 7.1 (Continued)
The Life Style Inventory
(Page 4)

CHILDHOOD PHYSICAL DEVELOPMENT
(Health, Physique, Feelings about Body, Advantages/Disadvantages, Nicknames Associated with Physique)

I was not sickly. In my teens I had encephalitis. It seems I couldn't take pressure as well after that. Sometimes I think it wasn't just encephalitis but my total rebellion.

(Author's note: The encephalitis occurred after the lifestyle was developed. However, it may have left residual effects which would influence behavior.)

ELEMENTARY SCHOOL INFORMATION
(Type of School, Grades, Subject Performance, Classroom Behavior, Relationship to Teachers, Subjects Liked and Disliked)

Average student. Good speller. Poor at math. Didn't work at school. Wanted to take part in school plays but was very shy about it. Mother discouraged it. "I didn't care for school." " I did't work because I didn't like it."

CHILDHOOD MEANINGS GIVEN TO LIFE
(Expectations, Ideals, Meaningful Goals, Favorite Daydreams, Religious Convictions)

I wasn't sure what it was all about. No particular desire to be anything. I think it was a puzzle and I tried to figure it out.

4

TABLE 7.1 (Continued)
The Life Style Inventory
(Page 5)

CHILDHOOD GENDER AND SEXUAL INFORMATION
(Development, Source of Information, Sex Play, Reaction to Pubertal Changes, Comfort with Gender, Feelings About Sexual Activity, Sexual Abuse)

I wanted to be a boy. They could do what they wanted more. Mother told me about menstruation. I never worried about things which are natural, are easy for me to accept. I had my first period when I was in a grocery store. I knew what it was and didn't let it bother me.

CHILDHOOD SOCIAL RELATIONSHIPS
(Friends, Gangs, Availability of Peers, Role in Peer Group, Relations with Adults)

I blundered through social relationships but I had close personal friends. I finally learned how to make friends. It was more fun being with people who were always telling me what to do.

5

TABLE 7.1 (Continued)
The Life Style Inventory
(Page 6)

PARENTAL INFORMATION DURING SUBJECT'S CHILDHOOD

Name	FATHER William	MOTHER Barbara
Current age even if deceased	Age 42	Age 40
At time of subject's birth	Age 21	Age 19
	Occupation Owned Property	Occupation Taught handicrafts
(Traits, Respected, Liked, Feared)	Description: Handsome. Wealthy background. Unstable, immature, opinionated. Liked to drink and spend time with "fine people". Very fond of me. Very stern and wanted me to submit and I was determined not to. I loved him very much. Not afraid of his sternness because even when he spanked her N could usually get her way. Lost all his money during the depression and was too proud to take a job and was disappointed that no one helped him. Very few real friends, as he found out after he lost everything. Many fair weather friends.	Description: Good looking. Proud and refined. Always unhappy. She could paint, write, and play piano. She sought people out and had many friends. Very critical. Nobody pleased her. I didn't feel as close to her as I did to Father. She was more distant.

TABLE 7.1 (Continued)
The Life Style Inventory
(Page 6)

Relations to Children		
What was most important to him/her?	to submit to him	good taste
What was way to win his/her praise?	to be strong-minded like him	
What made him/her angry?	my rebellion	her anger was at father, not the children
In what ways did he/she influence you?	I became like him	O. K.
Expectations for children	Nice manners	good taste, good manners
Who was his/her favorite? Why?	Nan. He was proud of me and enjoyed me.	Phil, but she had a special feeling for John, the baby.
Relationship to children	played with me & punished us	Let me do whatever I wanted
Sibling most like him/her In what ways?	Nan. Both strong-minded.	John, "not sure"
Who was closest to him/her?	Nan. I loved him very much.	Phil & John
Who was most distant?	O.K.	Nan
Confided in whom?	None	
Took hurts to whom?	None	
Others:		

Subject's role in family	I never thought of it
Subject's feeling about family	It was the only family I knew
Worst possible fate for a child in the family	Don't know
Other:	

6

TABLE 7.1 (Continued)
The Life Style Inventory
(Page 7)

NATURE OF PARENTS' RELATIONSHIP
(Description, Division of Roles, Interpersonal Relationship, Conflicts/Agreements, Marriage Happy/Unhappy)

Father couldn't handle money well and Mother took over. The family seemed disorganized. Mother and Father always argued. Nobody won. N would feel sorry for both of them and would leave the house.

OTHER FAMILY INFORMATION
(Family Climate, Family Values, Socio-economic Status, Ethnicity, Religion)

Wealthy family until depression, then they became poor and Father became bitter. He used to be a big shot in our town until the depression.

The family had a tendency to look down on people who were their social inferiors but were always courteous to them.

ADDITIONAL PARENTAL FIGURES AND ADULT MODELS

Who/Relationship: ______	Who/Relationship: ______

7

TABLE 7.1 (Continued)
The Life Style Inventory
(Page 8)

EARLY RECOLLECTIONS
(Under age 10) (Description, Most Vivid Part, Feelings)

1. Age 5: I saw a dog that belonged to some other people. It had a wire tied around its neck and it was nearly dead when I found it. I took off the wire and brought it home.
   Feeling - I was appalled by the cruelty.
   Most vivid - the wire around the poor dog's neck.

2. Age 5: Dad asked me to wash my hands and I wouldn't. He beat me a while and I still wouldn't wash my hands. I fell asleep in the bath tub. I never did wash my hands. (The whole thing upset Mother.) (It was at this age that my trouble with Dad began.)
   Feeling - I didn't give in (satisfaction).
   Most vivid - beating me

3. Age 5: (Grandfather had a stroke and couldn't talk.) One day I was catching bumble bees in a jar and Grandfather saw me and sat up in bed and called my name (after not having been able to speak since the stroke). I thought he loved me and spoke for me and no one else.
   Feeling - felt loved and special
   Most vivid - calling my name

4. Age 6: (first school) I had a friend, a boy who lived across the street. We went to school together. It was thrilling. I turned around and Mother had my baby brother up in the window, waving goodbye.
   Feeling - thrilling
   Most vivid - looking at window, brother waving.

8

TABLE 7.1 (Continued)
The Life Style Inventory
(Page 9)

---

5. Age 6: (I recall Mother being pregnant with Phil, but not his birth, Mother and I had a nice summer before Phil was born.)

(After Phil was born) A hurricane. Noise. Water was coming in the house. Mother and I were slipping around trying to shut windows.

Feeling - It was exciting.
Most vivid - noise, commotion

6. Age ________:

7. Age ________:

8. Age ________:

9

TABLE 7.2.
Summary of LSI Information

Birth order and response

BIRTH ORDER	An only child for six years; then dethroned by a boy who had a better relationship with Mother. Life changed for her and instead of thoughtlessly doing as she pleased, she began to try to please others.
AIM	The aim of her response changes with the dethronement. Until then she felt secure in her position and saw no need to make special efforts. Afterwards, she is less secure and tries to preserve status for herself.
METHOD	She resists efforts of others to force her to submit. Stubbornness and sulking are ways of expressing power. This can be seen as the effort of a discouraged child to salvage something from the dethronement and change in father.
SOCIAL ROLE IMPLICATIONS	A dethroned first born discouraged about recovering her favored position who now refuses to submit to family authority.
GROUP PROCESS IMPLICATIONS	Her rebellion suggests that the family had an arbitrary order and failed to teach the subject the rudiments of cooperation. The parents modeled conflict. Thus, in this family, a contest for power can be expected, such contests perhaps the most common form of relationship.

TABLE 7.2
Continued

Gender and Constitution and Responses

GENDER FEMALE	Reports self as tomboy and wanting to be a boy (perhaps because it seemed to offer more freedom, perhaps more power). Otherwise, she does not let any of the aspects of the female gender hamper her (such as menstruation).
AIM	Not to submit to any constraints of gender.
METHOD	Events associated with femininity have no special meaning (it was just "natural").
SOCIAL ROLE IMPLICATIONS	This category contains no special reference to gender.
GROUP PROCESS IMPLICATIONS	Men and women seem attracted to each other and they fight with each other.

Models and Responses

FATHER	He is someone who loves her greatly and enjoys her and also abuses her. He models what seems to be an arbitrary authoritarian demand for submission.
RESPONSE TO MODEL	She loves him for his devotion to her and opposes his demand for submission. In fact, she imitates father.

TABLE 7.2
Continued

MOTHER	She is a capable, resourceful, and refined person who lets the subject do things her own way, but is not close and loving like Father. Mother is critical.
RESPONSE	After brother's birth, the subject's unthinking egocentricity is stopped. She tries to please and be helpful to Mother, but feeling that Mother prefers brother, she leaves Mother to him and seeks elsewhere for her status.
SOCIAL ROLE IMPLICATIONS	Subject imitates Father in power motive. The maternal and domestic roles do not come naturally to her, but she is critical like Mother (moral superiority motive).
GROUP PROCESS	This seems to be a group of upper middle class people who only function well when they have a superior position, Father when rich and Nan when she has no rivals. Nan recovers and learns to "make friends." Intimacy seems fraught with conflict over dominance.

Family Values and Responses

PERSONAL DOMINANCE	She refuses to submit to Father's dominance. Since the specific demand by Father is that she submit to his will, she opposes her will to his and chooses to do what she wants rather than what others try to impose on her.

TABLE 7.2
Continued

MANNERS AND REFINEMENT	She feels burdened by these demands, but still wants to be pleasing. This leads to some confusion, since she wants to do her own thing and have others be pleased at the same time.

One result is that she is often at odds with herself—oversensitive to and fighting against what she perceives as imposition. Yet wanting others to like her at the same time.

Ambient culture and response

The fact that the family was wealthy may explain why the parents were more interested in refined behavior than in the work ethic. This may also be the source of Father's pride and subsequently the subject's stubborn pride. The family motto may have been "noli me tangere."

Family atmosphere and response

MOOD	The demands, criticisms and conflicts seem to have created considerable excitement in the family. In addition, Father's inconsistent behavior (the alternation between admiration and punishment) and instability added to the excitement. The subject's response was to add to the excitement herself with her own stubbornness and temper and to withdraw from the family as a scene of action and find her way outside the home.

TABLE 7.2
Continued

ORDER	Along with the excitable and changing mood is an inconsistent order in which the parents were constantly at odds. Father was stern and Mother was permissive and critical at the same time. These two guiding lines contradicted each other. Her response is to oppose the parents' order and create her own structure of order outside the house; with dogs and friends, where she could do as she pleased.
RELATIONSHIPS	Human relationships in the family were conflictual unless one submitted as brother did. She opposes any imposition and leaves the others to fight their own battles, while feeling sorry for them. The more intimate the relationship, the more conflict there is.

FAMILY CONSTELLATION: RESPONSE CATEGORIES

Social role

LOCATION	First born, only girl and Father's favorite, but not refined enough for Mother or submissive enough for Father.
EXPECTATIONS	Others should love her, but they should not impose on her or restrict her.

TABLE 7.2
Continued

	ENACTMENT	Resists the dominance of others but tries to win their love.
	ROLE SKILLS	Feels much more adequate as a fighter than as a pleaser. She tries to be helpful, but doesn't know how.
	SELF-ROLE CONGRUENCE	Being both an opponent and a pleaser introduces contradictions in the role. She will often not be sure what sort of person she really is and will feed various alternating dysphoric emotions. She will feel that she is bad but justified, and trying to be good but not succeeding.
	SOCIAL ROLE WITH PEERS	She is more successful in pleasing where authorities do not exist and relationships are less intimate.
Meaning of life		
	TRUST	Although she can feel loved, she doesn't trust intimate relationships.
	SELF-RELIANCE	This does not seem to be a significant issue for Nan, one way or the other.
	COOPERATION	She is poorly trained in cooperation.
	PESSIMISM	She experienced difficulty and conflict about intimate relationships, but can have close friends when there is no power issue.
	COURAGE	She is courageous in fighting her opponents but discouraged about successfully pleasing intimates.

TABLE 7.2
Continued

ACTIVITY	She pursues her own interests actively, but has no interest in pursuing imposed tasks (e.g., school).
SELF-CONCEPT	A contradictory and thus confused self-concept. Views self as a bad person who is trying to be good but doesn't know how to do it.
ALIENATION	She feels belonging outside the family—to dogs, friends, her own interests. Alienated from the family.

Sibling territories

	Nan	**Phil**	**John**
ACADEMIC		X	
HELPFULNESS		X	
AMBITIOUS STRIVING		X	
METHODS OF ACTIVITY	excitement seeking	industry	complaining
	trying to please	following rules	sensitivity
	doing her own thing	cheerfulness	withdrawal
	resisting order		criticism
	criticism		

TABLE 7.2
Continued

	Nan	Phil	John
COMPLIANCE		X	
OPPOSITION	X		X
SOCIABILITY	X	X	
PERSONAL DOMINANCE	X		
DEPENDENCY			X
MORALITY		X	
CONTROL	X		X
ACCOMODATION		X	
GENDER ROLE	does not become a significant family issue (the daughter can imitate Father and the son can imitate Mother)		

Note: The symbol X means that the trait was displayed by the sibling indicated, and thus was a "territory" of behavior for that sibling.

place by pleasing Mother. When this was unsuccesful, she went outside the family to find a place. The outside world was more pleasant, more harmonious, and permitted her more freedom from authoritarian demands.

She played the role of family bad girl, frustrating her frustrating parents; but this power did not bring her the love she wanted nor did her ineffective attempts to please.

DISCUSSION

Early Development Issues

The FC summary makes assumptions about how and why Nan selected her personality traits and tries to present her behavior as an understandable response to conditions as she experienced them. Father's harsh discipline must have seemed arbitrary and unfair to his favorite daughter and she turned against him in anger. While Mother used no such harsh punishment, she was verbally rejecting. Nan concluded that she was "bad" and behaved in line with her self-perception. This is not the only possible conclusion for a child to draw from such a situation, but it is a probable one.

The retreat to the outside world, her dogs and friends, is also understandable. Her idyllic life had been destroyed.

Predictions

While she will have an idealistic notion of family relationships, she may have the most trouble with these relationships. Furthermore, she will resist any order or schedule other than her own. She will probably also have high standards of manners and refinement (propriety) and will be as critical as mother was and as forceful as father, but will express this behavior openly only within the family. At the same time she will be sympathetic to the underdog and try to make it up to him. Thus she will feel both guilty and angry, have a negative self image and be confused about herself—feel like a bad person and act like one and then try to be good and act like a friend.

She will have her own interests, whatever they be, and will want to be free to pursue them.

Principle symptoms are likely to be self-doubt, temper, willfulness and acting out plus self-punitive tendencies. Depression may occur. Close family relationships may be stormy. Conversely, she may select a compliant and understanding husband and have non-conflicted family relationships.

In examining the ER, we will first look at some of their elements: positional details, sequence construction and thematic topics. We will then construct a summary as we did for the family constellation.

EARLY RECOLLECTIONS

Positional Details

Three positional details appear. In ER #2 she falls asleep in the bath tub at the scene of her contest with father. She is exhausted but victorious because she did not give in. She can be in the inferior position but still triumph (a Pyrrhic victory).

In ER #2 her grandfather is lying in bed and out of love for her, sits up (overcomes his disability) and speaks. The meaning of the detail is unclear. Does it say that love has the power to overcome handicaps? That she, herself has special power to evoke responses in others? Perhaps both meanings are present.

In ER #3 mother holds brother up in the window behind her as she is leaving. The detail shows that mother and brother are now an intimate unit and Nan goes out into the world to seek her fortune with her own companion. This recapitulates a theme in the family constellation.

Feelings

Four memories expressly state feelings while one implies it. The emotions include pity, anger, love and pleasant excitement. The subject does not suppress feelings. Her feelings are important to her in helping her interpret the world and respond to it.

Sequence Construction

This set of ER shows a definite sequence. In the first ER (the only one without human interaction) she presents herself as sympathetic to the dog who has been abused and neglected. It is a statement about the cruelty of people. But she is not cruel to dogs; she is a friend of underdogs.

The second ER depicts her as the abused child who rebels against the cruel father. The third ER presents an idyllic situation, the special power in love or in herself to break through barriers; the claim that there should be more love in the world. These first three ER form one statement about how life is and how it should be. Each ER is a melodrama with clear heroes and villains. People who abuse power are villains. People who act out of love are heroes.

The last two ER deal with a different topic, her dethronement. The last ER is prefaced by what seems irrelevant background until we realize that she orders three events. First there is an idyllic summer with mother. Then Philip is born. Last there is a hurricane. This sequence is her own construction according to her own associations. Before Philip came, life with mother was idyllic. His coming is perceived as a hurricane, chaos.

The fourth ER is also a dethronement memory. In both these ER the fact of dethronement is presented but she reacts to it by active behavior and excitement. She finds a new field of action for herself—the outside world and its adventures.

If we recall that Philip's birth is associated in time with the onset of her conflict with Father, we can guess how critical this time in her life was for her.

Thematic Topics

DETHRONEMENT—The ER show no direct memory of the brother's birth. In one ER her reaction is to leave mother and brother together while she goes off on a thrilling adventure with a male playmate. She accepts the dethronement and goes on to other areas. In the other ER, brother's birth is presented as background only and is followed by a hurricane which invades the house. Her reaction is one of excitement in trying to cope with the elemental forces. She copes with dethronement by relegating it to the background and dealing with the world at large.

AFFILIATION—Affiliation issues are present in all ER except the last but are most clearly seen in the first and third. She takes sides with the abused dog (identifies with it) but in the effect of grandfather's love for her we see this issue presented in an ideal.

EXTERNAL AUTHORITY—ER #2 portrays the struggle between herself and the external authority. She resists, will not submit, is even proud of her ability to resist to the bitter end.

POWER—This issue seems related to the EXTERNAL AUTHORITY issue. She opposes imposed power with her own power to resist. Although smaller and weaker, she has power of her own. The power to be stubborn and the power that comes from being loved. It is also the power that allows her to champion the underdog.

MORALITY—The moral statement in the ER is that abuse of power is an evil. Righteousness is on the side of the underdog.

HUMAN INTERACTION—The ER show varieties of interaction. The best and the worst of interaction are presented, but in the last two ER there is also the comradeship of people engaged in common adventures. In this task, she and others can cooperate.

NEW SITUATIONS—She meets new situations with anticipatory excitement, expecting to have new colleagues along the way.

EXCITEMENT—See NEW SITUATIONS

What sort of person would have such ER? An excitement seeker with strong feelings. An adventurer, active and opinionated who is critical of those who abuse power. She does not want to submit to others. She wants to be free. She is open to the events of the natural world and its order but will not take orders from others willingly. Her banner is Commodore Perry's flag—a snake with the motto, "Don't tread on me."

Life Style Elements

> SELF-IMAGE—There are four different presentations of the self in the five ER. In ER # 1 she is nurturing rescuer of a victim of the cruelty of others. In ER # 2 she is a stubborn rebel against imposed demands (even though the demand that she wash here hands does not seem, on the face of it, unreasonable. In ER # 3 she is special through being loved. Her admirer will do things for her that he will not do for others. In the last two ER she presents herself as avidly participating in the exciting aspects of the outside world, in cooperation with another person in the task-coping process.

Although the FC data states that she saw herself as a bad girl, the only ER in which she could likely see herself this way is the second in which she describes her refusal to submit to father's demand. In the ER she presents herself as quite powerful. Although weaker and smaller, she is not afraid of the world. Only those who would impose their will on her are threatening (abusers). She can meet the "things" which are natural (see the section on sexual information) with enthusiasm. Even hurricanes do not frighten her as much as excite her.

Shall we however interpret the hurricane as representing the chaos ensuing after Brother's birth and her attempts to cope with it or stand for her acceptance of natural events? We can do both because we can view the data as representing either or both—and this double view can give us clues to more than one underlying motive.

The preponderance of the evidence in the ER is that her self-image is one of being powerful enough to fight against abuse and win, of having power through being loved and of eagerness to deal with the natural order of the world.

This set of ER is one in which the examiner may do better to interpret the other life style elements first before attempting to determine the self-image. Let us proceed.

> WORLD VIEW—This element is easier to see. The world itself is an exciting place in which one can find may interesting pursuits (rescuing dogs, catching bumblebees, fighting hurricanes, and seeking new adventures). The family situation is the unpleasant place. People can love her but make trouble for her. But in this world, the weak can fight back, can be rescued by champions and the more they are loved, the more they are empowered.
>
> DOMINANT GOAL/SELF IDEAL—To retain her freedom to direct her own life and her behavior without interference from others, even from those she loves (see clinical information given at the beginning of this example about how she behaved with her infant child). To have no "wires" around her neck. To have the power to do her own thing.
>
> METHOD OF OPERATION—She refuses to submit to the power of others but tries to win their love (which will add to her power) by pleasing them. Life may buffet her about but it will not defeat her. A fighter and a lover.

Now it will be easier to elicit a self-image: Although she is weak, she can successfully resist others. Although this may mean she is "bad," she resists them any way. She has power—the power of refusing to submit and the power that comes from being loved (successfully pleasing people). She is here to enjoy life, not to do what others want.

In this case, the confirming data from the FC is important for guiding us through the interpretation of the ER. The scoring of positional details helps us see how the ER images portray, for example, the little girl asleep in the bath tub exhausted by her fight against Father, Grandfather sitting upright in his bed out of love for her, and how Mother elevates the brother into an intimate relationship with her, waving goodbye as Nan goes off with a friend to seek their fortune.

The feeling details suggest that Nan expresses her feelings openly and strongly, perhaps even to excess.

The sequence construction allows us to precipitate out two separate themes, the theme of power and its abuse and the theme of coping joyfully with the outside world after she has lost her cherished place at home.

The use of the thematic topics table confirms what we elicited from the sequence construction and refines it. The life style elements table and our attempt to answer the question, "What sort of person would have such ER?" now gives enough information to construct a life style rubric:

> I must go my own way. Life is a place where others may try to force me to go their way. Therefore, I must use all my powers to resist them and remain free to enjoy my life.

In this highly oversimplified rubric we hope to capture the leitmotif of Nan's life style. This is, in essence, what we did when we characterized Fred in Chapter 6, as being like a little boy trying to impress the big adults. We could also describe Louise (Chapter 6) as the person who is always watching out for tricks. As for Nan, perhaps we have already described her well by saying that her banner contains the snake and the motto "Don't tread on me."

> SUMMARY: The most important thing in life is power. I will be powerful by going my own way and resisting the efforts of others to make me submit—even if I have to go down fighting, but my refusal will be my victory.
>
> Life may present challenges and dangers but I can handle them all with a friend at my side. This challenge is exhilarating. I don't believe in being weak. I can overcome the people who try to overpower me, champion the underdog, and cope with the awesome powers of nature.
>
> Love itself can confer power in an almost miraculous way.
>
> COMMENT: There is no single way of constructing a summary and no single starting point which is always used. The summary is an artistic product which tries to

consolidate the many different facets in the ER into a unified whole in which the parts have a meaningful relationship to each other.

Predictions

We are far less likely to find developmental information in the ER than in the FC, but predictive information is available. In many cases, this information is congruent with the predictions we made after formulating the FC, such as her trouble with intimate relationships, her resistance to imposed order, and her desire to pursue her own interests. Other predictions are not necessarily confirmed. For example, the ER do not show her as admitting defeat. She saves the dog, wins out over father, effects a near miracle with grandfather, and reacts to dethronement by leaving the scene to the usurper and throwing herself into other activity. This is not the style of a person who ordinarily becomes depressed; it is rather an active compensating style, a search for new fields of action, a retreat from the scene of a defeat to avoid remaining in an inferior position and a reestablishment of her freedom in another area. We can predict that if she cannot win out in one place, she will find another place where she can.

Mosak (1965) suggested that the ER offer information which can allow one to predict how the patient would respond to the psychotherapist. The expectations and methods of operation (coping styles) of the subject will be displayed in the patient-therapist relationship. In this case we may predict that Nan will have the capacity to form a therapeutic alliance, will find therapy intriguing yet will resist attempts by the therapist to persuade her to change her behavior.

BASIC MISTAKES

Category List

SELF—The FC data implies that Nan sees herself as bad because she resists the parental order, especially when compared to Phil, who is good. The ER data stresses the power issue more than the good/bad issue. This list of common mistakes about the self in Chapter 1 contains one statement that fits our data: "I am entitled to my own way." This conviction is somewhat tempered by her decision, after dethronement, to be more pleasing to people to avoid losing their love, but we can still list this conviction as a presumptive basic mistake subject to further verification.

THE WORLD AND PEOPLE—It is not about the world, but about people that she makes a mistake. Her demand to live her own way will bring her into conflict with people. Close relationships become very difficult if one is unwilling ever to bend one's will. This was the same problem Father had in close relationships, a difficulty in coming to terms with realities. The mistake is that she confounds acceptance of and adherence to a social order with personal submission and defeat.

DISTORTED METHODS OF OPERATION—From the list we can select "Insistence of one's way" and "Rebelling against all (imposed) authority." We can expect disturbed interpersonal relationships to result from this.

DISTORTED ETHICAL IDEALS—She confounds cooperation with authority with involuntary submission to it. Also, cooperation with the social order interferes with her pursuit of her interests. The need to give the baby a bottle is experienced as an imposition, rather than just the natural order of things.

DISTORTED CONCLUSIONS (MEANING OF LIFE)

PESSIMISM—She does doubt her ability to develop satisfying, conflict-free, close relationships.

WHAT SOLVES ALL PROBLEMS?—Freedom from restraint, aided by unconditional love, solves all problems. If she could recapture the situation she had at home before brother was born and before she began to have trouble with Father, she would have no problems.

CYNICISM—No particular mistaken conviction becomes apparent in this area.

FANATICISM—The mistake is in her excess devotion to her own triumph over the rule imposers. She fights to the end for this principle even if all she has to do is wash her hands, a small item.

The Category list is useful for assessing personality assets as well as mistakes.

SELF—Nan believes that she can effect change, rescue others, fight oppressors, and collaborate with peers. She is not discouraged about meeting the tasks of life.

THE WORLD AND PEOPLE—Her openness to the world of nature, her sense of adventure in the world and her ability to cooperate are all assets for coping with life.

METHODS OF OPERATION—The data suggest that Nan is active, courageous, and does not give up easily.

ETHICAL IDEALS—She champions the underdog, (although in relation to her son, she behaves more like the authoritarian father). She genuinely believes in loving relationships.

CONCLUSIONS ABOUT LIFE—She is an optimist who believes that problems can be solved and people can get along together.

One strength is her flexibility. When a method doesn't work, she can change it. When she becomes discouraged in one area of endeavor, she can put it behind her and proceed to another.

She is rather optimistic about life and eager to meet its challenges, finding them exciting. She is courageous and active in coping with life. She is self-reliant and collaborative with others in problem solving behavior. She is not an isolate. She is aware of her feelings and knows when she is carried away by them. She has a genuine interest in good relations with others even if she often doesn't know how. The recognition that it is not good to displease people is actually a strength. Her awareness that she too may abuse power and her discomfort about it is also a strength and an indication that she is open to change.

SUMMARY

In this chapter we have presented in extensive detail a set of life style data and the process of its interpretation. We have used enough scales to create redundancy in the elicited data in order to show in detail how the interpreter assembles conclusions. These conclusions depict what we call a life style and we have depicted it as a set of convictions and chosen behaviors which are a logical outcome of the interactions between these convictions and early childhood experience. We have tried to show how the convictions themselves are a creative perceptual organization which is an understandable and adaptive processing of the information offered by the early experiences. We have all along kept in mind the theoretical dictum that knowing the life style will tell us the person's core constructs and program for coping with the environment. It will show us the personality as a unit, a ***Gestalt.***

Is going through this long procedure necessary to understand the life style? Certainly not, but it is the most reliable method we know. Need the procedure be so long? Again, no, but the procedure is a guideline which can be followed at the examiner's pleasure. Experienced interpreters will no doubt use short cuts. Creative examiners may devise other interpretive procedures. We ourselves do not find it necessary to go through all the procedural steps we have described. We do not always require such a mass of data, nor need we use all the category lists. More often, we have developed an intuitive ability to discern the life style much more quickly, but when our intuition is not good enough, when the data seems puzzling or contradictory, the category lists organize our understanding of the data and point us toward a correct conclusion.

In the end, however, formulating a life style still requires a certain amount of intuition and to achieve this, any natural talent for empathic guessing must be amplified by personal experience with the method.

CHAPTER **8**

THE PLACE OF LIFE STYLE ASSESSMENT IN THE GENERAL AREA OF ASSESSMENT

Where can we place the life style in the assessment process? Is it interview? Questionnaire? Rating scale? Projective technique? Actually, it possesses elements of each of these methods. Certainly the life style data collection derives its information through interview, and we have already alluded to interviewing issues in various chapters. While much of the data sought come from spontaneous description, we also solicit much information through specific questioning. Adler (1917) had devised a questionnaire as have other Adlerians, such as Alexandra Adler (1950/1973) and Wexberg (1929/1970), but none of these was intended specifically to lead to a life style formulation. Until the 1950s the interpretation of a life style was not a formal procedure. Therapists before that period merely listened to the patient over a period of interviews, and as the patient produced the data, the life style was formulated through accretion of interpretations of discrete data until a global pattern could be discerned and described by the therapist. Some Adlerian therapists still operate in that fashion.

The formal life style investigation emerged when Rudolf Dreikurs had occasion to teach the authors how to interpret patient life styles. Dreikurs, practicing multiple psychotherapy (Dreikurs, Shulman, & Mosak, 1984), assigned patients to us and instructed us to collect specific information concerning the patient's early development and family interactions and also to elicit early childhood memories. Then we met with him and the patient and presented the collected data which he then interpreted and summarized. To assist in the process Dreikurs (1954) developed a questionnaire which remained in use for several years. The questionnaire was later discarded when we discovered that students were following it slavishly rather than using it as a clinical tool. As replacement we constructed several life style inventories, the first formal one appearing in 1971 and culminating in the LSI which appears in this volume. In Chapter 4 is presented a suggested questionnaire which should not be adhered to over rigidly.

Page 3 of the LSI takes the form of a rating scale. We have experimented with a number of forms of ratings, changing the traits as well as the rating methods. Two forms of ratings are illustrated in Chapter 4. Thus far, we have not developed a scaling method for treating these data. Our only recourse currently is to interpret these ratings clinically (Mosak, Schneider, & Mosak, 1980).

Finally, the early recollections have long been considered a projective technique (Munroe, 1955; Lieberman, 1957; Mosak, 1958) and interpreted as such. Also the family constellation data collection appears to be a projective technique since these produced data are not completely objective but rather subject to the patient's biased apperception. What the patient narrates is often colored, modified, distorted in content, focus, and emphasis. Significant omissions, additions, and elaborations also occur on a non-conscious level. This subjectivity becomes visible when one investigates the life style of two siblings. One often wonders, listening to their disparate descriptions, whether they grew up in the same family.

Given the character of the LSI the interpreter must become proficient in interpreting a multi-faceted instrument, the number of variables limited only by the variety of personal and family traits, conditions, and interactions present in humankind.

As the development of the life style assessment process progressed, the question of what exactly was being elicited and formulated arose. Could we select a group of elements crucial to what we thought of as "life style" and filter out other elements, no matter how interesting or informative which were "not life style?" Dreikurs, from the Adlerian point of view, instructed us to always look for a self-concept hidden somewhere in the life style data. Mosak (1954), whose original training was nondirective, had also been trained by Rogers to look for the self-concept. The complexities and variations in self-concept soon became apparent. One person might seem mainly focused on the self as "adequate" or "inadequate" ("OK" or "not OK" in transactional analysis terms), a "success" or "failure." Another might center the concept of self upon relationships with others, while a third might perceive the self as a gender-determined entity, in terms of maleness and femaleness. What was being elicited was not the total concept of self which Allport (1955) had described. Ours was a unique and idiosyncratic concept founded upon idiosyncratic perceptions. Stated differently, the self-concept was a product of biased apperception. Similarly the person's perception of the world proved equally subjective and idiosyncratic. What occured to us was that we were studying ***uniqueness*** rather than combinations of traits. Through the life style method we could learn what made one person different than or like others. This conclusion was congruent with Adler's use of the term "Individual Psychology" which refers to the "individual", an indivisible unity, the whole person with his or her uniqueness rather than to a psychology of individual differences.

In teaching life style, determining the unique personality created difficulty, leading to the investigation as to whether life style "type templates" could be constructed. Adler (1964b/1929) described patients with a phrase such as "the beggar as king" and "the bloated red frog." Mosak (1984) uses a similar process called "creating images." We devised a list of 14 "types" (Mosak & Shulman, 1961) which we later extended (Mosak, 1979). This created a different problem in that any typology violates the concept of uniqueness. Following the lead of Adler (1935) we cautioned that these types were heuristic models solely and that things which were similar were not necessarily identical. Mosak (1971, 1977) has provided a brief description of these types, has discussed two of them at length (1959, 1973), and Peven (1973) has described a third. A close look at these type descriptions indicates that they refer to the Self-Ideal, e.g., "In order to have a place I should be in control" and to the Methods of Operation i.e., the cluster of possible behavioral traits utilized by people possessing such a Self-Ideal. Kern and his co-workers (Wheeler, Kern, & Curlette, 1984) have constructed some measures of what they refer to as life style. These measures might more appropriately be termed "life style type" measures.

"The trouble with types," says Sundberg (1977), "is that most people do not fit them exactly" (p.6). In order to assess the idiosyncratic qualities of an individual personality, one must take into account, Sundberg continued, the setting in which behavior takes place, the mutually interacting elements in the setting and the role taken by or assigned to the person in this setting. The family constellation study meets these criteria. While the unique, idiosyncratic personality can only be partially approached through type classifications, typing remains a useful assessment and teaching vehicle. It permits the comparing of individuals and the prediction of their possible behaviors. Thus Attarian (1978) and Manaster and Perryman (1984) have conducted research on the relationship of life style and vocational choice, Mosak (1965) has made predictions related to patient-therapist interaction, and Kern and his co-workers (Mullis et al., 1984; Wheeler et al., 1984) have sought to quantify information placing people in type categories. Their search for themes such as social interest, conformity, and exploitation remains a useful approach to studying behavior and personality.

The life style formulation is not a psychiatric diagnosis, not a mental status examination, not an assessment of psychopathology or intelligence although we may on occasion derive such information from the life style data. We can derive inferences about such personality variables as locus of control, field dependence, cognitive complexity, achievement need and the power motive, but the life style assessment is not designed to tap these. The life style is basically a statement about personality. It formulates in outline form what Allport (1955) described as "the transitive process of personality."

> Each person is an idiom into himself, an apparent isolation of the species....If there is to be a science of personality at all it should do better than it has in the past with the feature of personality that is most outstanding—its manifest uniqueness of organization. (Allport, 1955, pp.19,21)

Capturing the uniqueness of the personality, according to Adler (1927), was best accomplished through understanding the individual's pattern of movement, a dynamic rather than static view. This line of movement, self-chosen and self-guided, its direction and its pace, forms the essence of what the life style is designed to capture. In brief, to summarize what we have already described in Chapter 1, the life style is a superordinate system with several subsystems—a self-perception, a view of the world, the perceived requirements for the self to live in the world and actualize, a perception of what the ideal self and the ideal world should be, a notion of how those ideals can be approached, a ***modus operandi*** for pursuing this cardinal motive (which includes a set of rules for coping, including rules for coping with stress), and an opinion about how one is going to fare, whether one has a chance or not, whether it is all worthwhile or not. We can infer from the life style the meaning of life, the meaning of the good life, and the nature of the ethical life. All of these reflect the person's movement or lack of it, the direction, socially and personally constructive or socially and personally non-constructive, aspirations, expectations, and long range goals which we incorporate into our summary statement of the life style. The life style summary also affords us a subjective picture of the early life history, the family dynamics, and the conditions and perceptions which helped the person select his or her posture in life. Furthermore, the projective quality of the earliest childhood recollections uncovers inner perceptions outside of the subject's own awareness. We observe how the person constructs a "self-in-the-world."

Reliability studies (Colker & Slaymaker, 1984; Ferguson, 1964; Gushurst, 1971; Hedvig, 1963; Magner-Harris, Riordan, Kern, & Curlette, 1979) have demonstrated that ERs are more consistent than TAT protocols, which can be influenced by situational variables to a far greater extent. Eckstein (1976) and Savill and Eckstein (1987) have shown that in counseling and clinical populations, changes in ERs reflect changes in outlook and mental status. Though other forms exist for collecting life style data (e.g., see Baruth & Eckstein, 1981; Powers & Griffith, 1987) other than the method discussed here, as of yet no studies have been undertaken to explore reliability through alternate form testing. O'Phelan (1977) presented a statistical evaluation of attributes of our life style form upon which interested researchers may begin such comparisons.

Validity studies have been numerous. Mosak (1969) and Taylor (1975) have presented reviews of validation studies of ER. Bruhn and Davidow (1983); Friedman and Schiffman (1962); Hafner, Fakouri, Ollendick, and Corotto (1979); and Harder (1979) have demonstrated concurrent validity of ER with nosological assessments across a spectrum of categories (delinquency, schizophrenia, depression, narcissism), as have Jackson and Sechrest (1962) and Langs (1965a, 1965b). A number of studies have discussed the predictive validity of ER in diverse populations and across situations, from vocational assessment (Attarian, 1978; Manaster & Perryman, 1974); to personality assessment and diagnosis (Barrett, 1980; Ferguson, 1964; Harder, 1979); to criminal activity (Reimanis, 1974); and to college achievement (Rogers, 1977). Chesney, Fakouri, and Hafner (1986) and Colker and Slaymaker (1984) have discussed ER predictive validity with alcoholics and substance abusers. Platt, Mosalski, and Eisenman (1968) have explored the predictive value of an understanding of sex and birth order factors upon expectations of occupational success.

Construct validity, via factor analysis, has been undertaken by Mullis, Kern, and Curlette (1987); West and Bubenzer (1978); and Wheeler, Kern, and Curlette (1986) of life style themes and data. Content validity of life style data, particularly of family constellation material, has come primarily from research upon the Adlerian conception of birth order. Driscoll and Eckstein (1982) have summarized the results of over 120 different studies pertaining to birth order. Angeli (1973); Croake and Hayden (1975); Lohman, Lohman, and Christensen (1985); Pulakos (1987) and Verger (1968) have validated the Adlerian interest in exploring sibling interaction as it pertains to life style formation. Herrell (1972); Lemay (1968); Perlin and Grater (1984); Platt, Moskalski, and Eisenman (1968); Wagner and Schubert (1977); and Wark, Swanson, and Mack (1974) have validated Adlerian formulations of birth order as evident in cases of college misconduct, military adjustment, reported interpersonal behavior, expectations of occupational success, U.S. presidents, and college plans. Nield, Ward, and Edgar (1977) have clarified the birth order conceptualization by emphasizing that research be continued not from the ordinal, static perspective, but rather from the psychological, perceived vantage point of the individual. With such a stance, many methodical and outcome inconsistencies are rectified.

Though far from exhaustive, the research is encouraging and almost universally supportive of Adlerian life style conceptions. Continued research and empirical investigation will be required, however, to explore and clarify various issues and to delineate fine distinctions and differences.

BIBLIOGRAPHY

BIBLIOGRAPHY

Ackerknecht, L.K. (1976). New aspects of early recollections (ERs) as a diagnostic and therapeutic device. *Individual Psychologist, 13*, 44-54.

Adler, Alexandra (1973). *Guiding human misfits.* New York: Kraus Reprint. (Original work published 1950)

Adler, Alfred (1917). Study of organ inferiority and its psychical compensation: Contribution to clinical medicine. *Nervous and Mental Disease Monographs.* New York: Johnson Reprint. (Original work published 1907)

Adler, Alfred (1927). *The neurotic constitution.* (B. Glueck & J.W. Lind, Trans.). New York: Moffatt, Yard. (Original work published 1912)

Adler, Alfred (1935). The fundamental views of Individual Psychology. *International Journal of Individual Psychology, 1*(1), 5-8.

Adler, Alfred (1937). Position in the family constellation influences lifestyle. *International Journal of Individual Psychology, 3*(3), 211-227. Also Chapter 7 of *Problems of neurosis* (Alfred Adler, 1964a).

Adler, Alfred (1937). Significance of early recollections. *International Journal of Individual Psychology, 3*(4), 283-287.

Adler, Alfred (1957). *Understanding human nature.* (W.B. Wolfe, Trans.). Greenwich, CT: Premier Books. (Original work published 1927)

Adler, Alfred (1958). *What life should mean to you.* New York: Capricorn Books. (Original work published 1931b)

Adler, Alfred (1964a). *Problems of neurosis: A book of case histories.* New York: Harper Torchbooks. (Original work published 1929)

Adler, Alfred (1964b). *Social interest: A challenge to mankind.* (J.Linton & R. Vaughan, Trans.). New York: Capricorn Books. (Original work published 1929)

Adler, Alfred (1968). *The practice and theory of Individual Psychology.* (P. Radin, Trans.). Totowa, NJ: Littlefield, Adams. (Original work published 1920)

Adler, Alfred (1969a). *The science of living.* Doubleday Anchor Books. (Original work published 1929)

Adler, Alfred (1969b). *The case of Mrs. A: The diagnosis of a life-style, 2nd ed.* Shulman, B. (Ed.). Chicago: Alfred Adler Institute. Also in H.L. Ansbacher & R. Ansbacher, *Superiority and social interest* (pp. 159-201). Evanston, IL: Northwestern University Press. (Original work published 1931)

Adler, C.A. (1936). Richard III—his significance as a study in criminal life style. *International Journal of Individual Psychology, 2*(3), 55-60.

Allen, T.W. (1971). A life style. *The Counseling Psychologist, 3,* 25-29.

Allport, G.W. (1955). *Becoming.* New Haven: Yale University Press.

Allport, G.W. (1961). *Pattern and growth of personality.* New York: Holt, Rinehard & Winston.

Altman, K. (1973). The relationship between social interest dimensions of early recollections and selected counselor variables. Unpublished doctoral dissertation, University of South Carolina.

Altus, W.D. (1966). Birth order and its sequelae. *Science, 151,* 44-49.

Angeli, D. (1973). Immediate elder siblings as a factor in task performance. *Journal of Individual Psychology, 31,* 167-172.

Ansbacher, H.L. (1967). Life style: A historical and systematic review. *Journal of Individual Psychology, 23,* 191-212.

Ansbacher, H.L. (1973). Adler's interpretation of early recollections: Historical account. *Journal of Individual Psychology, 29,* 135-145.

Ansbacher, H.L., & Ansbacher, R. (Eds.). (1956). *The Individual Psychology of Alfred Adler: A systematic presentation in selections from his writings.* New York: Basic Books.

Aristotle. (1968). *Metaphysics.* Book 5, Chapter 2. Ann Arbor, MI: University of Michigan Press.

Aronson, E. (1972). *The social animal.* San Francisco: W.H. Freeman.

Attarian, P.J. (1978). Early recollections: Predictors of vocational choice. *Journal of Individual Psychology, 34,* 56-61.

Bandura, A., & Walters, R.H. (1963). *Social learning and personality development.* New York: Holt, Rinehart & Winston.

Barrett, D. (1980). The first memory as a predictor of personality traits. *Journal of Individual Psychology, 36,* 136-149.

Bartlett, F.C. (1932). *Remembering: A study in experimental and social psychology.* Cambridge, England: Cambridge University Press.

Bartlett, J. (1951). *Familiar quotations* (12th ed.). Boston: Little, Brown.

Baruth, L., & Eckstein, D. (1981). *Life style: Theory, practice and research* (2nd ed.). Dubuque, IA: Kendall/Hunt.

Bateson, G. (1972) *Steps to an ecology of the mind.* New York: Ballantine.

Bateson, G., Jackson, D.D., Haley, J., & Weakland, J. (1956). Toward a theory of schizophrenia. *Behavioral Science, 1,* 251-264.

Beck, A.T. (1976). *Cognitive theory and the emotional disorders.* New York: International Universities Press.

Bergson, H. (1911). *Matter and memory.* New York: Macmillan. (Original work published 1896)

Binswanger, L. (1963). *Being-in-the-world: Selected papers of Ludwig Binswanger.* New York: Basic Books.

Boszormenyi-Nagy, I. (1972). Loyalty implications of the transference model in psychotherapy. *Archives of General Psychiatry, 27,* 374-380.

Bottome, P. (1939). *Alfred Adler: A biography.* New York: Putnam.

Bowen, M. (1978) *Family therapy in clinical practice.* New York: Jason Aronson.

Bowlby, J. (1969). *Attachment and loss. Vol. 1. Attachment.* New York: Basic Books.

Brodsky, P. (1952). The diagnostic importance of early recollections. *American Journal of Psychotherapy, 6,* 484-493.

Bruhn, R., & Davidow, S. (1983). Earliest memories and dynamics of delinquency. *Journal of Personality Assessment, 47,* 476-482.

Chesney, S.M., Fakouri, M.E., & Hafner, J.L. (1986). The relationship between early recollections and willingness/unwillingness of alcoholics to continue treatment. *Journal of Individual Psychology, 42,* 395-403.

Coleman, J.C. (1964). *Abnormal psychology and modern life (3rd ed.).* Chicago: Scott, Foresman.

Colker, J.O., & Slaymaker, F.L. (1984). Reliability of idographic interpretations of early recollections and their nomothetic validation with drug abusers. *Individual Psychology, 40,* 36-44.

Crandall, J.E. (1981). *Theory and measurement of social interest: Empirical tests of Alfred Adler's concept.* New York: Columbia University Press.

Credner, L. (1935). Neurosis as a retreat from responsibility. *International Journal of Individual Psychology*, 1935, *1*(3), 33-43.

Croake, J.W., & Hayden, D.J. (1975). Trait oppositeness in siblings: Test of an Adlerian tenet. *Journal of Individual Psychology, 31*, 175-178.

Croake, J.W., & Olson, T.D. (1977). Family constellation and personality. *Journal of Individual Psychology, 33*, 9-17.

Dewey, E.A. (1971). Family atmosphere. In A.G. Nikelly (Ed.), *Techniques for behavior change* (pp. 41-48). Springfield, IL: Charles C. Thomas.

Dewey, E.A. (1978). *Basic applications of Adlerian psychology: For self-understanding and human realtionships.* Coral Springs, FL: CMTI Press.

Dinkmeyer, D.C., Pew, W.L., & Dinkmeyer, D.C., Jr. (1979). *Adlerian counseling and psychotherapy.* Monterey, CA: Wadsworth.

Dreikurs, R. (1948). *The challenge of parenthood.* New York: Duell, Sloan & Pearce.

Dreikurs, R. (1949). Counseling for family adjustment. *Individual Psychology Bulletin, 4*, 119-137.

Dreikurs, R. (1953). *Fundamentals of Adlerian psychology.* Chicago: Alfred Adler Institute. (Original work published 1935)

Dreikurs, R. (1954). The psychological interview in medicine. *American Journal of Individual Psychology, 10*, 99-122.

Dreikurs, R. (1957a). *Psychology in the classroom.* New York: Harper.

Dreikurs, R. (1957b). Psychotherapy as correction of faulty social values. *American Journal of Individual Psychology, 13*, 150-158. Also in R. Dreikurs, *Psychodynamics, psychotherapy and counseling* (pp. 37-48). Chicago: Alfred Adler Institute, 1967.

Dreikurs, R. (1959). Communication within the family. *Central States Speech Journal, 11*, 11-19

Dreikurs, R. (1967). *Psychodynamics, psychotherapy and counseling.* Chicago: Alfred Adler Institute.

Dreikurs, R. (1969), Personal Communication

Dreikurs, R. (1973). The private logic. In H.H. Mosak (Ed.), *Alfred Adler: His influence on psychology today* (pp. 19-32). Park Ridge, NJ: Noyes Press.

Dreikurs, R., & Mosak, H.H. (1967). The tasks of life II. The fourth life task. *Individual Psychologist, 4*, 51-56.

Dreikurs, R., Shulman, B.H., & Mosak, H.H. (1984). *Multiple psychotherapy: The use of two therapists with one patient.* Chicago: Alfred Adler Institute.

Dreikurs, R., & Sonstegard, M. (1968). The Adlerian or teleoanalytic approach. In G.M. Gazda (Ed.), *Basic approaches to group psychotherapy and group counseling* (pp. 197-232). Springfield, IL: Charles C. Thomas.

Driscoll, R.E., & Eckstein, D. (1982). Empirical studies of the relationship between birth order and personality. In D. Eckstein, L. Baruth, & D. Mahrer, *Lifestyle: What it is and how to do it* (pp. 51-57). Dubuque, IA: Kendall/Hunt.

Eckstein, D. (1976). Early recollection changes after counseling: A case study. *Journal of Individual Psychology, 32*, 212-223.

Eckstein, D., Baruth, L., & Mahrer, D. (1978). *Lifestyle: What is is and how to do it.* Dubuque, IA: Kendall/Hunt.

Edwards, A.L. (1941). Political frames of reference as a factor influencing recognition. *Journal of Abnormal and Social Psychology, 36*, 34-50.

Eisenstein, V.W., & Ryerson, R. (1951). Psychodynamic significance of the first conscious memory. *Bulletin of the Menninger Clinic, 15*, 213-220.

Ellis, A. (1962). *Reason and emotion in psychotherapy.* New York: Lyle Stuart.

Ferguson, E.D. (1958). The effect of sibling competition and alliance on level of aspiration, expectation and performance. *Journal of Abnormal and Social Psychology, 56*, 213-222

Ferguson, E.D. (1964). The use of early recollections for assessing life style and diagnosing psychopathology. *Journal of Projective Techniques, 28*, 403-412.

Ferguson, E.D. (1976). *Motivation: An experimental approach.* New York: Holt, Rinehart & Winston.

Festinger, L. (1957). *A theory of cognitive dissonance.* Palo Alto, CA: Stanford University Press.

Fogarty, S.J., & Helmsley, D.R. (1983). Depression and the accessibility of memories: A longitudinal study. *British Journal of Psychiatry, 142*, 232-237.

Forer, L. (1976). *The birth order factor.* New York: David McKay.

Forgus, R., & Shulman, B.H. (1979). *Personality: A cognitive view.* Englewood Cliffs, NJ: Prentice-Hall.

Freud, S. (1938). *The basic writings of Sigmund Freud.* New York: Modern Library.

Freud, S. (1940-52). *Gesammelte Werke.* London: Imago. Also in J. Strachey (Ed.) Standard Edition (1957). London: Hogarth Press.

Freud, S. (1959). Repression. In *Collected papers* (pp. 84-97). New York: Basic Books.

Friedman, A. (1952). Early childhood memories of mental patients. *Journal of Child Psychiatry, 2,* 266-269.

Friedmann, A. (1930). The family and educational guidance. In A. Adler & associates, *Guiding the child* (pp. 53-65). London: Allen & Unwin.

Friedman, J., & Schiffman, H. (1962). Early recollections of schizophrenic and depressed patients. *Journal of Individual Psychology, 18,* 57-61.

Gushurst, R.S. (1971). The technique, utility, and validity of life style analysis. *The Counseling Psychologist, 3,* 30-39.

Hafner, J.L., Fakouri, M.E., Ollendick, T.H., & Corotto, L.V. (1979). First memories of "normal" and of schizophrenic, paranoid-type individuals. *Journal of Clinical Psychology, 35,* 731-733.

Hall E., & Barger, B. (1964). Attitudinal structures of older and younger siblings. *Journal of Individual Psychology, 20,* 59-68.

Harder, D.W. (1979). The assessment of ambitious-narcissistic character style with three projective tests: The early memories, TAT, and Rorschach. *Journal of Personality Assessment, 43,* 23-32.

Harris, I.D. (1964). *The promised seed: A comparative study of eminent first and later sons.* New York: The Free Press.

Hedvig, E.B. (1963). Stability of early recollections and thematic apperception stories. *Journal of Individual Psychology, 19,* 49-54.

Hedvig, E.B. (1965). Children's early recollections as basis for diagnosis. *Journal of Individual Psychology, 21,* 187-188.

Herrell, J.M. (1972). Birth order and the military: A review from an Adlerian perspective. *Journal of Individual Psychology, 28,* 38-44.

Hilton, I. (1967). Differences in the behavior of mothers toward first and later born children. *Journal of Personality & Social Psychology, 7,* 282-290.

Horney, K. (1950). *Neurosis and human growth.* New York: Norton.

Horney, K. (1966). *Our inner conflicts.* New York: Norton.

Jackson, M., & Sechrest, L. (1962). Early recollections in four neurotic diagnostic categories. *Journal of Individual Psychology, 18,* 52-56.

Kadis, A.L. (1957). Early childhood recollections as aids in group psychotherapy. *Journal of Individual Psychology, 13*, 181-87.

Kadis, A.L., & Lazarsfeld, S. (1948). The respective role of "earliest recollections" and "images." *American Journal of Psychotherapy*, 250-55.

Kelly, G.A. (1955). *Psychology of personal constructs.* New York: Norton.

Keniston, K. (1963). Inborn: An American Ishmael. In R.W. White (Ed.), *The study of lives (pp. 44-70).* New York: Atherton.

Kern, R. (Undated). *Life style interpretation* (audiocassette with instructional pamphlet). Coral Springs, FL: CMTI Press.

Klages, L. (1906). *Das persoenliche Leitbild.* Munich: Ackermann.

Kopp, R.R., & Dinkmeyer, D. (1975). Early recollections in life-style assessment and counseling. *The School Counselor, 23*, 22-27.

Kopp, R.R., & Der, D. (1979). Humanistic psychological assessment in psychotherapy. In Olson, H.A., (Ed.), *Early recollections: Their use in diagnosis and psychotherapy* (pp. 29-38). Springfield, IL: Charles C. Thomas.

Langs, R.J. (1965a). Earliest memories and personality: A predictive study. *Archives of General Psychiatry, 12*, 379-390.

Langs, R.J. (1965b). First memories and character diagnosis. *Journal of Nervous and Mental Diseases, 141*, 318-320.

Langs, R.J., Rothenberg, M.B., Fishman, J.R., & Reiser, M.F. (1960). A method for the clinical and theoretical study of the earliest memory. *Archives of General Psychiatry, 3*, 523-534.

Lemay, M.L. (1968). Birth order and college misconduct. *Journal of Individual Psychology, 24*, 167-169.

Levy, J., & Grigg, K. (1962). Early memories, Thematic configuration. *Archives of General Psychiatry, 7*, 83-95.

Lewin, K. (1935). *A dynamic theory of personality.* New York: McGraw-Hill.

Lidz, T. (1973). *The origin and treatment of schizophrenic disorders.* New York: Basic Books.

Lieberman, M.G. (1957). Childhood memories as a projective technique. *Journal of Projective Techniques, 21*, 32-36.

Lindzey, G. (1961). *Projective techniques and cross-cultural research.* New York: Appleton-Century-Crofts.

Lohman, J.F., Lohman, T.G., & Christensen, O. (1985). Psychological position and perceived sibling differences. *Individual Psychology, 41*, 313-327.

Lorenz, K. (1952). *King Solomon's ring.* New York: Crowell.

Magner-Harris, J., Riordan, R.J., Kern, R.M., & Curlette, W.L. (1979). Reliability of life style interpretations. *Journal of Individual Psychology, 35*, 196-201.

Manaster, G.J., & Perryman, T.B. (1974). Early recollections and occupational choice. *Journal of Individual Psychology, 30*, 232-237.

McKelvie, W.H. (1979). Career counseling with early recollections. In H.A. Olson (Ed.), *Early recollections: Their use in diagnosis and psychotherapy* (pp. 243-258). Springfield, IL: Charles C. Thomas.

Mendelsohn, M.B., Linden, J., Gruen, G., & Curran, J. (1974). Heterosexual pairing and sibling configuration. *Journal of Individual Psychology*, 30, 202-210.

Merton, R.K. (1948). The self-fulfilling prophecy. *Antioch Review, 8*, 193-210.

Mosak, H.H. (1954). The psychological attitude in rehabilitation. *American Archives of Rehabilitation Therapy, 2*, 9-10.

Mosak, H.H. (1958). Early recollections as a projective technique. *Journal of Projective Techniques, 22*, 302-311. Also in H.H. Mosak, *On purpose* (pp. 60-75). Chicago: Alfred Adler Institute, 1977.

Mosak, H.H. (1959). The getting type, a parsimonious social interpretation of the oral character. *Journal of Individual Psychology, 15*, 193-198. Also in H.H. Mosak, *On purpose* (pp. 76-81). Chicago: Alfred Adler Institute, 1977.

Mosak, H.H. (1965). Predicting the relationship to the therapist from early recollections. *Journal of Individual Psychology, 21*, 77-81. Also in H.H. Mosak, *On purpose* (pp. 87-92). Chicago: Alfred Adler Institute, 1977.

Mosak, H.H. (1968). The interrrelatedness of the neuroses through central themes. *Journal of Individual Psychology, 24*, 67-70. Also in H. H. Mosak, *On purpose* (pp.138-143). Chicago: Alfred Adler Institute, 1977.

Mosak, H.H. (1969) Early recollections: Evaluation of some current research. *Journal of Individual Psychology, 25*, 56-63. Also in H. H. Mosak, *On purpose* (pp. 144-152). Chicago: Alfred Adler Institute, 1977.

Mosak, H.H. (1971). Lifestyle. In A.G. Nikelly (Ed.), *Techniques for behavior change* (pp. 77-81). Springfield, IL: Charles C. Thomas. Also in H. H. Mosak, *On purpose* (pp. 183-187). Chicago: Alfred Adler Institute, 1977.

Mosak, H.H. (1973). The controller: A social interpretation of the anal character. In H.H. Mosak (Ed.), *Alfred Adler: His influence on psychology today* (pp. 43-52). Park Ridge, NJ: Noyes Press. Also in H. H. Mosak, *On purpose* (pp. 216-227). Chicago: Alfred Adler Institute, 1977.

Mosak, H.H. (1977). *On purpose.* Chicago: Alfred Adler Institute.

Mosak, H.H. (1979). Mosak's typology: An update. *Journal of Individual Psychology, 35,* 192-195.

Mosak, H.H. (1980). *A child's guide to parent rearing.* Chicago: Alfred Adler Institute.

Mosak, H.H. (1984). Adlerian psychotherapy. In R.J. Corsini (Ed.), *Current psychotherapies* (3rd ed.) (pp. 56-107). Itasca, IL: F.E. Peacock.

Mosak, H.H. & Dreikurs, R. (1967). The life tasks: The fifth life task. *Individual Psychologist, 5,* 16-22.

Mosak, H.H., & Kopp, R.R. (1973). The early recollections of Adler, Freud, and Jung. *Journal of Individual Psychology, 29,* 157-166.

Mosak, H.H., Schneider, S., & Mosak, L.E. (1980). *Life style: A workbook.* Chicago: Alfred Adler Institute.

Mosak, H.H. & Shulman, B. H. (1961). *Introductory Individual Psychology: A syllabus.* Chicago: Alfred Adler Institute.

Mosak, H.H., & Shulman, B.H. (1971). *The life style inventory.* Chicago: Alfred Adler Institute.

Mullis, F.Y., Kern, R.M., & Curlette, W.L. (1984, May 26). Life style can be measured. Paper presented to North American Society of Adlerian Psychology, Toronto.

Mullis, F.Y., Kern, R.M., & Curlette, W.L. (1987). Life-style themes and social interest: A further factor analytic study. *Individual Psychology, 43,* 339-352.

Munroe, R.L. (1955). *Schools of psychoanalytic thought.* New York: Dryden Press.

Murphy, G. (1947). *Personality: A biosocial approach.* New York: Harper.

Nield, J., Ward, D., & Edgar, T. (1977). Two interpretations of birth order position. *Individual Psychologist, 14*(2), 46-53.

Nisbett, R.E. (1968). Birth order and participation in dangerous sports. *Journal of Personality & Social Psychology, 8,* 351-353.

Olson, H.A. (Ed.). (1979). *Early recollections: Their use in diagnosis and psychotherapy.* Springfield, IL: Charles C. Thomas.

O'Phelan, M.L. (1977). Statistical evaluation of attributes in Adlerian life style forms. *Journal of Individual Psychology, 33,* 203-212.

Orgler, H. (1972). *Alfred Adler, the man and his work: Triumph over the inferiority complex.* New York: New American Library. (Original work published 1939)

Parsons, T. (1947). Introduction. In M. Weber, *The theory of social and economic organization* (pp. 3-86). New York: Oxford University Press.

Perlin, M., & Grater, H. (1984). The relationship between birth order and reported interpersonal behavior. *Individual Psychology, 40,* 22-28.

Peven, D. (1973). The victim. *Individual Psychologist, 10,* 18-21.

Peven, D., & Shulman, B.H. (1983). The psychodynamics of bipolar affective disorder: Some empirical findings and their applications for cognitive theory. *Individual Psychologist, 39,* 2-16.

Platt, J.L., Moskalski, D.D., & Eisenman, R. (1968). Sex and birth order and future expectations of occupational status and salary. *Journal of Individual Psychology, 24,* 170-173.

Plewa, F. (1935). The meaning of childhood recollections. *International Journal of Individual Psychology, 1,* 88-101. Also in H.A. Olson (Ed.), *Early recollections* (pp. 23-26). Springfield, IL: Charles C. Thomas.

Powers, R.L., & Griffith, J. (1987). *Understanding life style: The psychoclarity process.* Chicago: Americas Institute of Adlerian Studies.

Pulakos, J. (1987). The effects of birth order on perceived family roles. *Individual Psychology, 43,* 319-328.

Quinn, J. (1973). Predicting recidivism and type of crime from early recollections of prison inmates. Unpublished doctoral dissertation, University of South Carolina.

Reimanis, G. (1974). Anomie, crime, childhood memories, and development of social interest. *Journal of Individual Psychology, 30,* 53-58.

Reiss, S. (1949). *Mental readjustment.* London: Allen & Unwin.

Rogers, C.R. (1961). *On becoming a person.* Boston: Houghton Mifflin.

Rogers, G.W. (1977). Early recollections and college achievement. *Journal of Individual Psychology, 33,* 233-239.

Rotter, J.B. (1966). Generalized expectancies for internal versus external control of reinforcement. *Psychological Monographs, 80* (1, Whole No. 609).

Sarbin, T.R., & Allen, V.L. (1968). Role theory. In G. Lindzey & E. Aronson (Eds.), *The handbook of social psychology. Vol. 1.* (pp. 488-567). Reading, MA: Addison-Wesley.

Satir, V. (1967). *Conjoint family therapy.* Palo Alto, CA: Science & Behavior Books.

Saul, L.J., Snyder, T.R., & Sheppard, E. (1956). On earliest memories. *Psychoanalytic Quarterly, 25,* 228-237.

Savill, G.E., & Eckstein, D.G. (1987). Changes in early recollections as a function of mental status. *Individual Psychology, 43,* 1-17.

Schrecker, P. (1973). Individual Psychological significance of first childhood recollections. *Journal of Individual Psychology , 29,* 146-156.

Shapiro, D. (1965). *Neurotic styles.* New York: Basic Books.

Shulman, B.H. (1962). The family constellation in personality diagnosis. *Journal of Individual Psychology, 18,* 35-47. Also in B.H. Shulman, *Contributions to Individual Psychology* (pp. 45-59). Chicago: Alfred Adler Institute, 1973.

Shulman, B.H. (1965). A comparison of Allport's and the Adlerian concepts of life style: Contributions to a psychology of the self. *Individual Psychologist, 3,* 14-21. Also in B.H. Shulman, *Contributions to Individual Psychology* (pp. 5-15). Chicago: Alfred Adler Institute, 1973.

Shulman, B.H., & Mosak, H.H. (1977). Birth order and ordinal position: Two Adlerian views. *Journal of Individual Psychology, 33,* 114-121.

Shulman, B.H., & Nikelly, A.G. (1971). Family constellation. In A.G. Nikelly (Ed.), *Techniques for behavior change* (pp. 35-40). Springfield, IL: Charles C. Thomas.

Sullivan, H.S. (1953). *The interpersonal theory of psychiatry.* New York: Norton.

Sullivan, H.S. (1956). *Clinical studies in psychiatry.* New York: Norton.

Sundberg, N.D. (1977). *Assessment of persons.* Englewood Cliffs, NJ: Prentice-Hall.

Taintor, Z. (1970). Birth order and psychiatric problems in boot camp. *American Journal of Psychiatry, 126,* 80-86.

Taylor, J.A. (1975). Early recollections as a projective technique: A review of some validation studies. *Journal of Individual Psychology, 14,* 46-53.

Terner, J., & Pew, W.L. (1978). *The courage to be imperfect: The life and work of Rudolf Dreikurs.* New York: Hawthorn.

Tobin, S.S., & Etigson, E. (1968). Effect of stress on earliest memory. *Archives of General Psychiatry, 19,* 435-443.

Toman, W. (1962). Family constellations of divorced and married couples. *Journal of Individual Psychology, 18,* 48-51.

Toman, W. (1969). *Family constellation: Its effects on personality and behavior.* New York: Springer.

Vaihinger, H. (1965). *The philosophy of "as if": A system of the theoretical, practical and religious fictions of mankind.* London: Routledge & Kegan Paul.

Verger, D. (1968). Birth order and sibling differences in interest. *Journal of Individual Psychology, 24,* 56-59.

Verger, D., & Camp, W.L. (1970). Early recollections: Reflections of the present. *Journal of Counseling Psychology, 17,* 510-515.

Wagner, M.E. , & Schubert, H.J. P. (1977). Sibship variables and United States presidents. *Journal of Individual Psychology, 24,* 56-59.

Walker, M.H., & Belove, P.L. (1982). The loyalty dilemma. *Individual Psychology, 38,* 161-172.

Wark, D.M., Swanson, E.O., & Mack, J.K. (1974). More on birth order: Intelligence and college plans. *Journal of Individual Psychology, 30,* 221-226.

Weber, M. (1947). *The theory of social and economic organization.* New York: Oxford University Press.

West, J.D., & Bubenzer, D.L. (1978). A factor analytic consideration of life style data. *Journal of Individual Psychology, 34,* 48-55.

Wexberg, E. (1970). *Individual Psychological treatment.* Revised by B. H. Shulman. Chicago: Alfred Adler Institute. (Original work published 1929).

Wheeler, M.S., Kern, R.M., & Curlette, W.L. (1984, May 26). Wheeler-Kern-Curlette life style inventory. Paper presented to North American Society of Adlerian Psychology. Toronto.

Wheeler, M.S., Kern, R.M., & Curlette, W.L. (1986). Factor analytic scales designed to measure Adlerian life style themes. *Journal of Individual Psychology, 42,* 1-16.

Whitaker, C.A. (1978). Co-therapy of chronic schizophrenia. In M. Berger (Ed.), *Beyond the double bind: Communication and family systems, theories and techniques with schizophrenics.* New York: Brunner/Mazel.

INDEX

INDEX

C

D

E

M

N

O

P

Q

R

S

T

U

V

W

ABOUT THE AUTHORS

BERNARD H. SHULMAN

Bernard H. Shulman, M.D. is a clinical professor at Northwestern Medical School and Lecturer at Rush Medical School. He has been a member of the Board of Trustees of the Alfred Adler Institute of Chicago since its inception. He is a past president of the North American Society of Adlerian Psychology and of the International Association of Individual Psychology.

While in medical school, he was fascinated by Rudolf Dreikurs, his teacher in psychiatry, and began to study with him. Several years later he joined Dreikurs in practice and soon after, Harold Mosak also joined them. Dr. Shulman is the author of ***Essays in Schizophrenia, Contributions to Individual Psychology*** and numerous other publications, some written together with Dr. Mosak.

HAROLD H. MOSAK

Harold H. Mosak, Ph.D., is a clinical psychologist in the private practice of psychotherapy in Chicago for almost four decades. He is currently Chairman of the Board of the Alfred Adler Institute of Chicago where he is also on the faculty. Carl Rogers was his first teacher in psychotherapy at the University of Chicago where Dr. Mosak gained his doctorate in 1950. Concurrently he was in the first class of Veterans Administration interns where almost all of his training and supervision was psychoanalytically-oriented. After receiving his doctorate, he was assigned to the Veterans Administration Mental Health Clinic in Denver where his training and supervision were conducted by the Adolf Meyer psychobiologists led by Franklin Ebaugh. In 1951 he joined in Adlerian practice with Rudolf Dreikurs and Bernard H. Shulman. It was here that his interest in life style emerged and the three joined in contributing to its theoretical understanding and to developing a formal method for life style assessment.

Dr. Mosak is also the author or editor of ***On Purpose, Ha Ha and Aha: The Role of Humor in Psychotherapy, Alfred Adler: His Influence on Psychology Today, A Child's Guide to Parent Rearing, The Argot of the Drug Culture*** (with Lisa and Neal Mosak), and ***Life Style: A Workbook*** (with Seymour Schneider and Lisa Mosak) as well as numerous papers in the areas of family constellation, early recollections, personality theory, psychotherapy, education, and religion.

Java in a Nutshell

A Desktop Quick Reference for Java Programmers

Java in a Nutshell

A Desktop Quick Reference for Java Programmers

David Flanagan

O'Reilly & Associates, Inc.
Bonn • Cambridge • Paris • Sebastopol • Tokyo

Java in a Nutshell

by David Flanagan

Printed in the United States of America.

Published by O'Reilly & Associates, Inc., 103 Morris Street, Suite A, Sebastopol, CA 95472.

Series Editor: Mike Loukides

Editor: Paula Ferguson

Production Editor: John Files

Printing History:

February 1996: First Edition

This book is printed on acid-free paper with 85% recycled content, 15% post-consumer waste. O'Reilly & Associates is committed to using paper with the highest recycled content available consistent with high quality.

ISBN: 1-56592-183-6 [4/96-4th]

Table of Contents

Part II: Programming with the Java API

Part III: Java Language Reference

Part V: API Cross References

How to Use This Book

If you're new to Java, you'll want to take this book off to a peaceful place and learn about the language by reading the first three sections. Later, when you have some free time, you may want to sit down and study the example code in the next six sections. Primarily, though, this book is designed to lie flat on your desk, right next to your keyboard, for quick and convenient reference while you program. Before diving right in, please read this brief overview—it tells you how to get the most out of the book.

Part I: Introducing Java

This first part of the book introduces the Java language. Section 1, *Getting Started with Java*, is an overview of Java, with some samples of Java code to give you the flavor of the language. Section 2, *How Java Differs from C*, documents how Java differs from the C programming language and Section 3, *Classes and Objects in Java*, explains object-oriented programming with Java. Sections 2 and 3 are fairly independent of each other; you can read either one first. If you already know how to program in C or C++, the first part of this book should teach you everything you need to know to start programming with Java. If you do not know C or C++ programming, you may want to find a slower-paced book to introduce you to Java programming. After you have learned Java, you can use this material as a refresher course.

Part II: Programming with the Java API

Sections 4 through 9 form the second part of the book. The bulk of these sections is Java code—practical, real-world examples of programming with Java and Java API. The text provides an overview of the code and the code itself is thoroughly commented. Overall, though, there is not much hand-holding here. Studying the examples on your own is the best way to learn about, and build real understanding of, the Java API. The examples are also an excellent starting point for your own explorations of Java, and you should feel free to adapt them to your own needs and interests.

The sections and their contents are as follows:

Section 4, *Applets*
: Starts with a simple "Hello World" applet and progresses through event handling, animation, imagemaps, and audio.

Section 5, *Graphical User Interfaces*
: Demonstrates the use of each component, and the most important layout managers in the `java.awt` package. Shows how to create custom dialog boxes and custom components.

Section 6, *Input and Output*
: Shows how to read and write files and obtain file information and directory listings. Illustrates the use of streams and the creation of your own filter stream classes. Includes a full-featured example of creating and using pipes.

Section 7, *Networking*
: Demonstrates how to download text files with the `URL` class and obtain URL information and content with the `URLConnection` class. Shows how to send and receive datagrams and how to implement clients and servers.

Section 8, *Advanced Graphics and Images*
: Illustrates smooth animation with double-buffering and clipping. Shows how to keep track of images that are being loaded and how to process and manipulate image data.

Section 9, *Advanced Threads*
: Demonstrates thread exclusion and notification with `synchronized`, `wait()`, and `notify()`. Shows how to create thread groups, how to set thread priorities, and how to query information about threads and thread groups.

The code presented in Part II can also be found online at:

http://www.ora.com/catalog/books/javanut/

Part III: Java Language Reference

Part III of this quick reference consists of eight short sections of reference material on the Java language and related topics. The sections are as follows:

Section 10, *Java Syntax*
: A quick reference of Java language constructs: tables of primitive data types, character escapes, operators, modifiers, reserved words, and documentation comments.

Section 11, *Events*

A table of Java event types, the GUI components that generate them, and the fields of the `Event` object that are set for each type.

Section 12, *Fonts, Colors, and Cursors*

Tables of font names, colors, and cursors defined by Java for platform-independence.

Section 13, *System Properties and Applet Parameters*

Documents the standard system properties, and explains how you can use properties and parameters to allow customization of your programs and applets.

Section 14, *Applet Security*

Shows what applets can and cannot do. Provides complete list of security restrictions imposed on untrusted applets.

Section 15, *Java-Related HTML and HTTP Syntax*

Covers the full syntax of the HTML `<APPLET>` tag that lets you include applets in your Web pages.

Section 16, *The Unicode Standard*

Everything you need to know about Unicode, the character set used by Java. Provides an outline of the encoding, and explains how to convert Unicode to UTF-8 form for storage and transmission.

Section 17, *JDK Development Tools*

Full documentation, in UNIX man-page format, for *java* (the interpreter), *javac* (the compiler), *appletviewer*, and the other tools in Sun's Java Developers Kit.

Part IV: API Quick Reference

Part IV is the real heart of this book. It is a *complete* quick reference for every class, method, and variable in the Java API. The first eight sections document the classes in each of the eight packages in the Java API; the ninth section collects and documents the exception and error classes from all of the packages. Except for error and exception classes, the quick reference is organized alphabetically by package and by class. To look up a class, turn to the section that documents the class's package. To look up a method, turn to the documentation for the class that defines the method.

The documentation for each package begins with an overview of the package and a class hierarchy diagram of the classes defined in the package. This material orients you and provides the context for understanding the information on the individual classes.

The documentation of each class begins with a one or two paragraph overview. This is followed by a listing of all the constants, variables, and methods defined by the class. The listing is in almost-legal Java syntax and looks very much like a Java class definition: an `extends` clause indicates the superclass of a class, and an `implements` clause lists any implemented interfaces. Similarly, method and variable declarations include `public`, `static`, `abstract`, `final`, and similar modifiers to indicate the exact type of the method or variable. Methods are listed with their return type and complete argument list. A `throws` clause indicates any exceptions that a method can throw.

The Java syntax of the class listings is augmented by comments that provide additional information about the methods. The *`//Overrides`* comment lets you know when a method overrides a method defined in a superclass. The *`//Defines`* comment is similar—that is, it tells you when a method implements an abstract method defined by a superclass. The *`//Empty`* comment tells you that the method body is empty (i.e., that the method does nothing). This is often a useful hint that the method should be overridden by a subclass. (Note, however, that methods that simply return `null` are also essentially empty, but are not commented in this way.)

Within each class, variables and methods are grouped into categories in order to better show the overall structure of the class. The categories are always listed in the following order:

1. Public constructors
2. Protected constructors
3. Constants
4. Class (or static) variables
5. Public instance variables
6. Protected instance variables
7. Class (or static) methods
8. Public instance methods
9. Protected instance methods

Within each category, fields are listed alphabetically by variable name or method name, and the start of each category is indicated with a comment. If there are no constructors defined by the class, a comment specifies the Java default constructor. If there are no non-private constructors, a comment notes this fact to indicate that the class is non-instantiable.

Unless a method is explicitly mentioned in the class overview, its documentation is limited to the method prototype. Consider, though, all the information contained in this simple and compact form:

- The name of the method, which, in the context of the class that defines it, helps make the method's purpose clear.
- The return type and argument types of the method, which definitively specify how to invoke the method.
- The argument names, which help make the purpose of each argument clear.
- The method modifiers, such as `public`, `protected`, `abstract`, `final`, `static`, and `synchronized`, which specify how the method can be used and how it works.
- The `throws` clause, which specifies any errors or abnormal exit conditions for the method.

Do keep in mind that this is a quick reference, and it cannot provide definitive descriptions of each method and variable in the API. It has the advantage, however, of being about one tenth the size of the official API documentation shipped with Java. If you can't figure out how to use a method from the information given in this book, read about the method in the online documentation. The next time you use the method, this quick reference should be the only memory jogger you need!

Note that the material in Part V of this book is designed to be used in conjunction with this API quick reference.

Part V: API Cross References

This final part of the book cross references the API documented in Part IV. The sections in this part allow "reverse lookup" of information. In Part IV, for example, you can look up the superclass of a class, or the exceptions thrown by a method. In Part V, by contrast, you can look up the subclasses of a class, or the list of methods that throw a given exception. The sections of Part V (and their uses) are as follows:

Section 27, *Class Defined-In Index*
: Look up a class name and find out the package in which it is defined. Useful when you want to look up a class's documentation but you don't know in which section of Part IV to look.

Section 28, *Method Defined-In Index*
: Look up a method name and find out what class, or classes, define that method. Useful when you want to look up a method, but you don't know whether it is defined by a class or by one of the class's superclasses.

Section 29, *Subclass Index*
: Look up a class and find a list of all its subclasses. Useful for figuring out if you are using the right version of a class, or if there is a more specific subclass that would be better suited to your task.

Section 30, *Implemented-By Index*
: Look up an interface and find a list of classes that implement that interface. Useful when you know you want to use the interface, but don't know what implementations are available.

Section 31, *Returned-By Index*
: Look up the name of a class and find a list of methods that return objects of that type. Useful when you know that you want to work with an object of a certain type, but don't know how to obtain an instance of that object.

Section 32, *Passed-To Index*
: Look up the name of a class and find a list of methods that take arguments of that type. Useful when you have an object and want to figure out what you can do with it.

Section 33, *Thrown-By Index*
: Look up the name of an exception and find a list of methods that can throw it. Useful when planning exception handling strategies, and debugging programs that mysteriously throw exceptions.

Glossary, Contents, Index, and Tabs

This book also contains a glossary following Part V. Use it to look up unfamiliar Java-related terms. Every Java keyword appears in the glossary, often with example usage, so you can use this section as a simple Java language reference. Finally, don't forget that this book has a table of contents and a subject index, which can help you locate whatever information you're looking for. Also, notice the tabs along the edge of the book. Use these to jump quickly to each part of the book.

Preface

This handbook is a desktop quick reference for Java programmers. It also includes introductory and tutorial material for C and C++ programmers who want to learn Java. Everyone who uses this book should be sure to read the *How to Use This Book* section that precedes this one; it describes the structure of the book and explains how to get the most out of it.

Java Books and Resources

O'Reilly & Associates is developing a series of Java books. The series will include an introductory volume, a language reference, a Java Virtual Machine reference, and a complete set of Java API reference manuals (i.e., manuals that document the Java API in more complete detail than is possible with the quick reference format of this book). In addition, the Java series will include volumes covering advanced topics in Java programming, such as: networking, programming with threads, and distributed computing. Refer to *http://www.ora.com/info/java/* for a complete list of current and upcoming titles in the O'Reilly & Associates Java series.

Sun Microsystems has online reference documentation for the Java API that you may find useful in conjunction with this quick reference handbook. You may want to visit *http://www.javasoft.com/* to view or download this API documentation and other useful documents.

Also, the *comp.lang.java* newsgroup is a central location for discussion about Java. The newsgroup may soon split into a number of subgroups, for more specialized discussion, so be sure to read the FAQ list to find out which groups are most appropriate for your needs.

About the Example Programs

The example programs presented in this book are available online. See *http://www.ora.com/catalog/books/javanut/* for more information on how to download them.

Some of the examples assume that you are using tools like *javac* and *appletviewer* from Sun's Java Developers Kit (JDK). If you are using a development environment or tools from some other vendor, simply follow that vendor's instructions for compiling Java code, running applications, and displaying applets.

Please bear in mind that Java is evolving very quickly. The classes in the Java API still have a number of bugs in the Java 1.0 release, and it seems new platforms and development tools are being announced every week. It's not possible to test all the examples on all platforms, and you may sometimes find that the examples don't work correctly because of bugs in the Java class library or in a particular implementation (or port) of Java. In this case, you'll have to try to find a workaround that fixes the problem on your particular platform—this is simply the price of being on the cutting edge of a new technology.

Conventions Used in This Book

Italic is used for:

- UNIX pathnames, filenames, and program names.
- New terms where they are defined.

Boldface is used for:

- Names of GUI buttons and menus.

`Typewriter Font` is used for:

- Java language keywords, classes, methods, and variables and HTML tags in the main body of the text.
- Command-line options in the main body of the text.

`Italic Typewriter Font` is used for:

- Arguments to methods, since they could be typed in code as shown but are arbitrary names that could be changed.
- Variable expressions in command-line options in the main body of the text.

Franklin Gothic Compressed is used for:

- Java and HTML code set off from the main body of the text and class definitions in the API quick reference.

Franklin Gothic Compressed Bold is used for:

- Class, method, and variable names in class definitions in the API quick reference.
- Command lines and options that should be typed verbatim on the screen.

Franklin Gothic Compressed Italic is used for:

- Arguments to methods and comments in class definitions in the API quick reference.
- Variable expressions in command lines.

Preface

Request for Comments

We invite you to help us improve the book. If you have an idea that could make this a more useful programmer's quick reference, or if you find a bug in an example program or an error in the text, let us know by sending mail to *bookquestions@ora.com.*

If we find it necessary to issue errata for this book or to release updated examples or reference information, you'll find that updated information at the site *http://www.ora.com/catalog/books/javanut.*

Acknowledgments

I am grateful for the help of all the people who worked on this book. I had the pleasure of working with my friend and colleague Paula Ferguson, who edited this book. Her careful reading and always-practical suggestions made the book stronger, clearer, and more useful. Paula also wrote Section 1, which is an excellent overview of Java and Java programming.

Mike Loukides got this whole project underway. As the series editor for this and other O'Reilly & Associates Java books, he got me started on the book and provided high-level direction and guidance while it was evolving from a rough outline. Eric Raymond and Troy Downing were technical reviewers—they helped spot my errors and omissions, and offered good advice on making the book more useful to Java programmers.

John Files was the production editor for the book. He coordinated the entire production process, entered changes from edited copy, and handled the meticulous task of fixing line and page breaks in the manuscript. Mary Ann Faughan copyedited the book, Cory Willing proofread it, and Kismet McDonough did a final quality-control check. Seth Maislin wrote the index. Norm Walsh and Stephen Spainhour helped to generate the Windows screendumps that appear in the text. Chris Reilley created the figures, including all the detailed class hierarchy diagrams in Part IV. Edie Freedman designed the cover. Nancy Priest designed the interior format of the book and Lenny Muellner carefully implemented the format in *troff.*

Sue Willing arranged a special printing for the book so that it could appear in bookstores much sooner than would otherwise be possible. Sheryl Avruch and Frank Willison, the Production Manager and Editor-in-Chief at O'Reilly & Associates, made this book a priority and expedited its production.

Part I

Introducing Java

Part I is an introduction to Java and Java programming. If you know how to program in C or C++, these sections should teach you everything you need to know to start programming with Java.

Getting Started with Java

You've probably already heard a lot about Java; you wouldn't be reading this book if you didn't think Java was an important new technology. By now, you've probably downloaded a Java-enabled version of Netscape Navigator and played around with some of the impressive applets on Sun's Java site (*http://www.javasoft.com*) and Gamelan (*http://www.gamelan.com*). And now you're itching to start writing your own applets.

Before we get started with our first Java example, it's important to give you a bit of background about the language. With all the media hype surrounding Java (and the World Wide Web and Internet in general), it's easy to lose sight of why Java is so interesting. Lots of attention has been focused on using Java to provide interactive content on Web pages. But most of the Java applets I've seen to date are toys, interesting and attention-grabbing proofs-of-concept that don't solve real-world problems.

What's exciting about Java is that it's a language designed for programming on the Internet. It's a lot more important than ultra-hip Web pages. Java enables us to write completely new kinds of applications. With Java it's possible to imagine a true document-centric system, where a colleague can send you a report packaged with the word processing, spreadsheet, and database software you need to work with it. Or a "game broker" that acts as a matchmaker between players, who then communicate directly with each other to play the game, without the server's intervention. The fact that these applications don't exist yet just means that we haven't figured out how to use the full power of Java.

Java offers the promise that the network will become the computer. If the Internet breaks down barriers, Java removes the last and most difficult of these: the barrier that prevents you from taking software from some random site and executing it on any platform.

Why Java?

Java began life as a programming language for software for consumer electronics: devices such as toasters, microwave ovens, and personal digital assistants. Software for consumer devices has some unique design requirements. For instance, the software needs to be able to work on new computer chips as they are introduced — manufacturers often change the chips they are using as new chips become more cost-effective or introduce new features. The software also needs to be extremely reliable, because when a consumer product fails, the manufacturer typically has to replace the entire device.

A small team at Sun, headed by James Gosling, that was working on this problem quickly discovered that existing programming languages like C and C++ were not up to the task. For one thing, a program written in C or C++ must be compiled for a particular computer chip. When a new chip comes out, the program must be recompiled. The complexity of C and C++ also makes it extremely difficult to write reliable software.

As a result, in 1990 Gosling started designing a new programming language that would be more appropriate for consumer electronics software. This language, originally known as Oak, was small, reliable, and architecture-independent. In 1993, as the Java team continued to work on the design of the new language, the World Wide Web appeared on the Internet and took it by storm. The Java developers realized that an architecture-neutral language like Java would be ideal for programming on the Internet, because a program could run on all of the different types of computers connected to the Internet. In fact, all of the design goals of Java made it ideally suited for Internet programming.

At that point, the development of Java took on new importance for Sun. The team wrote a Web browser, called HotJava, that was the first Web browser to support Java applets. An *applet* is a small Java program that can be embedded in another application. You can include an applet in an HTML document to provide interactive, executable content on a Web page. HotJava demonstrated the power of the Java language in a very visible fashion to programmers and to the rest of the world. And the rest is history.

Programmers started tinkering with the Alpha release of Java that Sun made available, creating all sorts of "cool" applets. Their experience and feedback helped refine the language and its application programming interface (API). At the same time that Sun released the first Beta version of the language, Netscape announced that Version 2.0 of its Web browser, Netscape Navigator, would support Java applets. This support served only to increase the already-strong interest in Java technology, both in the computing world and on the Internet. With companies like IBM, SGI, and Oracle licensing the Java technology from Sun, you can be certain that more software and hardware products will be incorporating Java technology. As this book goes to press, even Microsoft has announced its intention to license Java.

What Is Java?

In "The Java Language: A White Paper," Sun describes Java as follows:

> Java: A simple, object-oriented, distributed, interpreted, robust, secure, architecture neutral, portable, high-performance, multithreaded, and dynamic language.

Sun acknowledges that this is quite a string of buzzwords, but the fact is that they all aptly describe the language. In order to understand the full potential of Java, let's examine each of these buzzwords in terms of the design goals Sun was trying to achieve in creating the language.

Simple

Java is a *simple* language. But what exactly do we mean by simple? One design goal was to create a language that a programmer could learn quickly, so the number of language constructs has been kept small. Another design goal was to make the language look familiar to a majority of programmers for ease of migration. If you are a C or C++ programmer, you'll find that Java uses many of the same language constructs as C and C++.

In order to keep the language both small and familiar, the Java designers removed a number of features available in C and C++. These features are mostly ones that led to poor programming practices or were rarely used. For example, Java does not support the `goto` statement; instead, it provides labelled `break` and `continue` statements and exception handling. Java does not use header files and it eliminates the C preprocessor. Because Java is object-oriented, C constructs like `struct` and `union` have been removed. Java also eliminates the operator overloading and multiple inheritance features of C++.

Getting Started

Perhaps the most important simplification, however, is that Java does not use pointers. Pointers are one of the most bug-prone aspects of C and C++ programming. Since Java does not have structures, and arrays and strings are objects, there's no need for pointers. Java automatically handles the referencing and dereferencing of objects for you. Java also implements automatic garbage collection, so you don't have to worry about memory management issues. All of this frees you from having to worry about dangling pointers, invalid pointer references, and memory leaks, so you can spend your time developing the functionality of your programs.

If it sounds like Java has gutted C and C++, leaving only a shell of a programming language, hold off on that judgment for a bit. As we'll see in Section 2, *How Java Differs from C*, Java is actually a full-featured and very elegant language.

Object-Oriented

Java is an *object-oriented* programming language. As a programmer, this means that you focus on the data in your application and methods that manipulate that data, rather than thinking strictly in terms of procedures. If you're accustomed to procedure-based programming in C, you may find that you need to change how you design your programs when you use Java. Once you see how powerful this new paradigm is, however, you'll quickly adjust to it.

In an object-oriented system, a *class* is a collection of data and methods that operate on that data. Taken together, the data and methods describe the state and behavior of an *object*. Classes are arranged in a hierarchy, so that a subclass can inherit behavior from its superclass. A class hierarchy always has a root class; this is a class with very general behavior.

To take an example from the natural world, you might define a "living thing" class to be the root of your class hierarchy. This class could have two subclasses: "animal" and "plant." You might further define the "mammal" class as a subclass of "animal."

Finally, if you defined a "human" class as a subclass of "mammal," the "human" class would inherit behavior from "mammal," "animal," and "living thing".

Java comes with an extensive set of classes, arranged in *packages*, that you can use in your programs. For example, Java provides classes that create graphical user interface components (the `java.awt` package), classes that handle input and output (the `java.io` package), and classes that support networking functionality (the `java.net` package). The `Object` class (in the `java.lang` package) serves as the root of the Java class hierarchy. For more information on the Java API, see Part IV, *API Quick-Reference*.

Unlike C++, Java was designed to be object-oriented from the ground up. Most things in Java are objects; the simple numeric, character, and boolean types are the only exceptions. While Java is designed to look like C++, you'll find that Java removes many of the complexities of that language. If you are a C++ programmer, you'll want to study the object-oriented constructs in Java carefully. Although the syntax is often similar to C++, the behavior is not nearly so analogous. For a complete description of the object-oriented features of Java, see Section 3, *Classes and Objects in Java*.

Distributed

Java is designed to support applications on networks; it is a *distributed* language. Java supports various levels of network connectivity through classes in the `java.net` package. For instance, the `URL` class allows a Java application to open and access remote objects on the Internet. With Java, it's just as easy to open a remote file as it is a local file. Java also supports reliable stream network connections with the `Socket` class, so you can create distributed clients and servers. For more information about Java's networking capabilities, see Section 7, *Networking*, and Section 24, *The java.net Package*.

Interpreted

The Java compiler generates byte-codes, rather than native machine code. To actually run a Java program, you use the Java interpreter to execute the compiled byte-codes, so Java is an *interpreted* language. Java byte-codes provide an architecture-neutral object file format; the code is designed to transport programs efficiently to multiple platforms. A Java program can be run on any system that implements the Java interpreter and run-time system. Collectively, the interpreter and run-time system implement a virtual machine called the Java Virtual Machine.

In an interpreted environment, the standard "link" phase of program development pretty much vanishes. If Java has a link phase at all, it is only the process of loading new classes into the environment, which is an incremental, lightweight process. As a result, Java supports rapid prototyping and easy experimentation, which leads to faster program development. This is in sharp contrast with the more traditional and time-consuming process of compiling, linking, and testing.

Robust

Its origin as a language for software for consumer electronics means that Java has been designed for writing highly reliable or *robust* software. Java certainly doesn't eliminate the need for software quality assurance; it's still quite possible to write unreliable software. However, Java does eliminate certain types of programming errors, which makes it considerably easier to write reliable software.

Java is a strongly typed language, which allows for extensive compile-time checking for potential type-mismatch problems. Java is more strongly typed than C++, which inherits a number of compile-time laxities from C, especially in the area of method declarations. Java requires explicit method declarations; it does not support C-style implicit declarations. These stringent requirements ensure that the compiler can catch method invocation errors, which leads to more reliable programs.

One of the most significant enhancements in terms of reliability is Java's memory model. Java does not support pointers, which eliminates the possibility of overwriting memory and corrupting data. Similarly, Java's automatic garbage collection prevents memory leaks and other pernicious bugs related to dynamic-memory allocation and deallocation. The Java interpreter also performs a number of run-time checks, such as verifying that all array and string accesses are within bounds.

Exception handling is another feature in Java that makes for more robust programs. An *exception* is a signal that some sort of exceptional condition, like an error, has occured. Using the `try/catch/finally` statement, you can group all of your error handling code in one place, which greatly simplifies the task of error handling and recovery.

Secure

One of the mostly highly touted aspects of Java is that it's a *secure* language. Security is an important concern, as Java is meant to be used in networked environments. Without some assurance of security, you certainly wouldn't want to download an applet from a random site on the Internet and let it run on your computer. Java implements several security mechanisms to protect you against code that might try to create a virus or invade your file system. All of these security mechanisms are based on the premise that nothing is to be trusted.

Security actually goes hand-in-hand with robustness. Java's memory allocation model is one of its main defenses against malicious code. As we've already seen, Java does not have pointers, so a programmer cannot get behind the scenes and forge pointers to memory. More importantly, the Java compiler does not handle memory layout decisions, so a programmer cannot guess the actual memory layout of a class by looking at its declaration. Memory references in compiled Java code are resolved to real memory addresses at run-time by the Java interpreter.

Many of the defenses in Java are there to protect you from untrusted applets. The Java run-time system uses a byte-code verification process to ensure that code loaded over the network does not violate any Java language restrictions. Part of this security mechanism involves how classes are loaded from across the network. For example, loaded classes are placed in a separate namespace than local classes, to prevent a malicious applet from replacing standard Java classes with its own versions. For more information about applet security, see Section 14, *Applet Security*.

Of course, security isn't a black-and-white thing. No one can guarantee that a Java program won't contain malicious code of any form; what Sun can claim is that Java makes rogue software more difficult to write. Java anticipates and defends against most of the techniques that have historically been used to trick software into misbehaving. It's impossible to say that Java, or any system, is "perfectly secure." Sooner or later, someone will invent new ways to attack software systems and the ball will be back in Sun's court. In real life, the best you can get is "reasonably safe," where the definition of "reasonably" depends on some tradeoff between functionality and security. The Net is clearly a dangerous environment. Java offers a reasonable middle ground between ignoring the security problem and being paralyzed by it.

Architecture Neutral

As we've already seen, Java programs are compiled to an architecture neutral byte-code format. The primary advantage of this approach is that it allows a Java application to run on any system, as long as that system implements the Java Virtual Machine. Since Java was designed to create network-based applications, it is important that Java applications be able to run on all of the different kinds of systems found on the Internet.

But the architecture neutral approach is useful beyond the scope of network-based applications. As an application developer in today's software market, you probably want to develop versions of your application that can run on PCs, Macs, and UNIX workstations. With multiple flavors of UNIX, Windows 95 and Windows NT on the PC, and the new PowerPC Macintosh, it is becoming increasingly difficult to produce software for all of the possible platforms. If you write your application in Java, however, it can run on all platforms. And using the the Abstract Windowing Toolkit (the `java.awt` package, described in Section 19, *The java.awt Package*), your application can even have the appropriate appearance and behavior for each platform.

Portable

Being architecture neutral is one big part of being *portable*. But Java goes even further, by making sure that there are no "implementation-dependent" aspects of the language specification. For example, Java explicitly specifies the size of each of the primitive data types, as well as its arithmetic behavior. (These data types are described in Section 10, *Java Syntax*.)

The Java environment itself is also portable to new hardware platforms and operating systems. The Java compiler is written in Java, while the Java run-time system is written in ANSI C. The run-time system has a clean portability boundary that is essentially POSIX-compliant.

High-performance

Java is an interpreted language, so it is never going to be as fast as a compiled language like C. In fact, Java is on the average about 20 times slower than C. But before you throw up your arms in disgust, be aware that this speed is more than adequate to run interactive, GUI and network-based applications, where the application is often idle, waiting for the user to do something, or waiting for data from the network.

Of course, there are some situations where performance is critical. To support those situations, the Java designers are working on "just in time" compilers that can translate Java byte-codes into machine code for a particular CPU at run-time. The Java byte-code format was designed with these "just in time" compilers in mind, so the process of generating machine code is fairly simple and it produces reasonably good code. In fact, Sun claims that the performance of byte-codes converted to machine code is nearly as good as native C or C++.

When you are considering performance, it's important to remember where Java falls in the spectrum of available programming languages. At one end of the spectrum, there are high-level, fully-interpreted scripting languages such as Tcl and the UNIX shells. These languages are great for prototyping and they are highly portable, but they are also very slow. At the other end of the spectrum, you have low-level compiled languages like C and C++. These languages offer high performance, but they suffer in terms of reliability and portability.

Java falls in the middle of the spectrum. The performance of Java's interpreted bytecodes is much better than the high-level scripting languages (even Perl), but it still offers the simplicity and portability of those languages. And while Java isn't as fast as a compiled language, it does provide an architecture neutral environment in which it is possible to write reliable programs.

Multithreaded

In a GUI-based network application such as a Web browser, it's easy to imagine multiple things going on at the same time. A user could be listening to an audio clip while she is scrolling a page, and in the background the browser is downloading an image. Java is a *multithreaded* language; it provides support for multiple threads of execution (also called lightweight processes) that can handle different tasks.

One benefit of multithreading is that it improves the interactive performance of graphical applications for the user. Unfortunately for the programmer, writing code in C or C++ that deals with multiple threads can be quite a headache. The main difficulty lies in making sure that routines are implemented so that they can be run by multiple concurrent threads. If a routine changes the value of a state variable, for example, then only one thread can be executing the routine at a time. With C or C++, writing a multithreaded application involves acquiring locks to run certain routines and then releasing them. Writing code that explicitly handles locks is problematic and can easily lead to deadlock situations.

Java makes programming with threads much easier, by providing built-in language support for threads. The `java.lang` package provides a `Thread` class that supports methods to start a thread, run a thread, stop a thread, and check on the status of a thread. See Section 23, *The java.lang Package*, for more details.

Java's thread support also includes a set of synchronization primitives. These primitives are based on the monitor and condition variable paradigm, a widely-used synchronization scheme developed by C.A.R. Hoare. With the `synchronized` keyword, you can specify that certain methods within a class cannot be run concurrently. These methods run under the control of monitors to ensure that variables remain in a consistent state.

A number of the examples in the various sections of Part II, *Programming with the Java API*, show the use of threads.

Dynamic

The Java language was designed to adapt to an evolving environment; it is a *dynamic* language. For example, Java loads in classes as they are needed, even from across a network. Classes in Java also have a run-time representation. Unlike in C or C++, if your program is handed an object, it can find out what class it belongs to by checking the run-time type information. The run-time class definitions in Java make it possible to dynamically link classes into a running system.

A Simple Example

Enough, already! By now you should have a pretty good idea of what Java is all about. So let's stop talking about abstract buzzwords and look at some concrete Java code. Before we look at an interesting applet, though, we are going to pay tribute to that ubiquitous favorite, "Hello World."

Hello World

Example 1-1 shows the simplest possible Java program: "Hello World."

Example 1-1: Hello World

```
public class HelloWorld {
    public static void main(String[] args) {
        System.out.println("Hello World!");
    }
}
```

This program, like every Java program, consists of a public class definition. The class contains a method or procedure named `main()`, which is where the interpreter starts excecuting the program. The body of `main()` consists of only a single line, which prints out the message:

```
Hello World!
```

This program must be saved in a file with the same name as the public class plus a *.java* extension. To compile it, you would use *javac*:*

```
% javac HelloWorld.java
```

This command produces the *HelloWorld.class* file in the current directory. To run the program, you use the Java interpreter, *java*:

```
% java HelloWorld
```

Note that when you invoke the interpreter, you do not supply the *.class* extension for the file you want to run.

A Scribble Applet

Example 1-2 shows a less trivial Java program. This program is an applet, rather than a standalone Java application. It runs inside an applet viewer or Web browser, and lets the user draw (or scribble) with the mouse, as illustrated in Figure 1-1.

Example 1-2: A Java applet

```
import java.applet.*;
import java.awt.*;

public class Scribble extends Applet {
    private int last_x = 0;
    private int last_y = 0;
    private Color current_color = Color.black;
```

*Assuming you're using Sun's Java Developers Kit (JDK). If you're using a Java development package from some other vendor, follow your vendor's instructions.

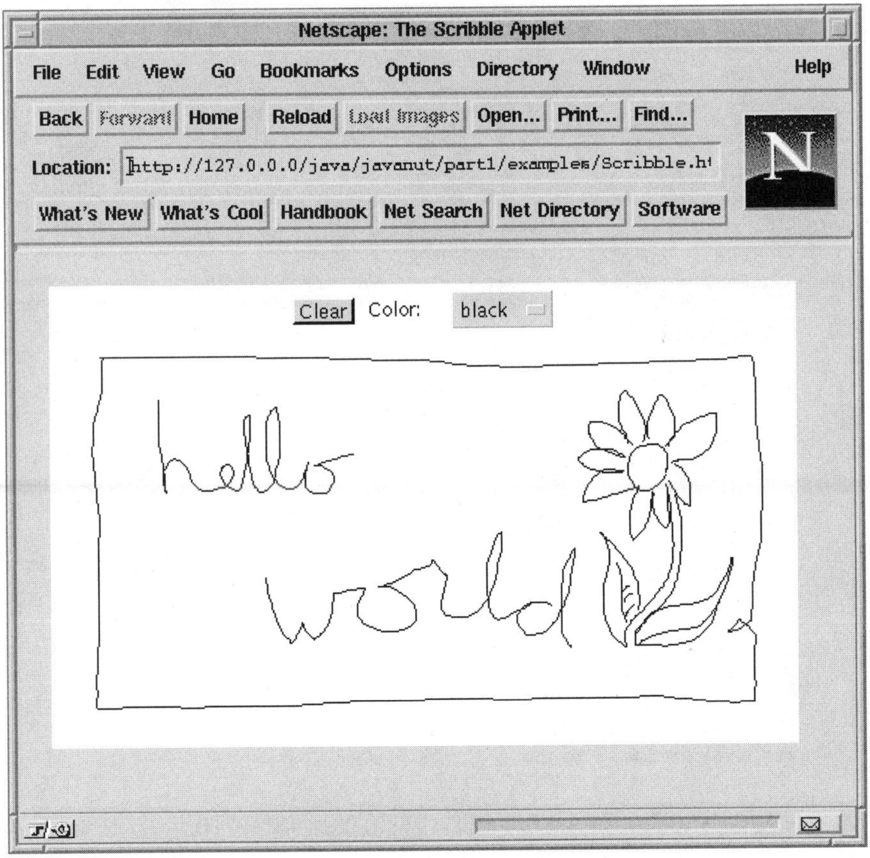

Figure 1-1: A Java applet running in a Web browser

Example 1-2: A Java applet (continued)

```
    private Button clear_button;
    private Choice color_choices;

    // Called to initialize the applet.
    public void init() {
        // Set the background color
        this.setBackground(Color.white);

        // Create a button and add it to the applet.
        // Also, set the button's colors
        clear_button = new Button("Clear");
        clear_button.setForeground(Color.black);
        clear_button.setBackground(Color.lightGray);
        this.add(clear_button);

        // Create a menu of colors and add it to the applet.
        // Also set the menus's colors and add a label.
        color_choices = new Choice();
        color_choices.addItem("black");
        color_choices.addItem("red");
        color_choices.addItem("yellow");
```

Example 1-2: A Java applet (continued)

```
            color_choices.addItem("green");
            color_choices.setForeground(Color.black);
            color_choices.setBackground(Color.lightGray);
            this.add(new Label("Color: "));
            this.add(color_choices);
        }

        // Called when the user clicks the mouse to start a scribble
        public boolean mouseDown(Event e, int x, int y)
        {
            last_x = x; last_y = y;
            return true;
        }

        // Called when the user scribbles with the mouse button down
        public boolean mouseDrag(Event e, int x, int y)
        {
            Graphics g = this.getGraphics();
            g.setColor(current_color);
            g.drawLine(last_x, last_y, x, y);
            last_x = x;
            last_y = y;
            return true;
        }

        // Called when the user clicks the button or chooses a color
        public boolean action(Event event, Object arg) {
            // If the Clear button was clicked on, handle it.
            if (event.target == clear_button) {
                Graphics g = this.getGraphics();
                Rectangle r = this.bounds();
                g.setColor(this.getBackground());
                g.fillRect(r.x, r.y, r.width, r.height);
                return true;
            }
            // Otherwise if a color was chosen, handle that
            else if (event.target == color_choices) {
                if (arg.equals("black")) current_color = Color.black;
                else if (arg.equals("red")) current_color = Color.red;
                else if (arg.equals("yellow")) current_color = Color.yellow;
                else if (arg.equals("green")) current_color = Color.green;
                return true;
            }
            // Otherwise, let the superclass handle it.
            else return super.action(event, arg);
        }
    }
```

Don't expect to be able to understand the entire applet at this point. It is here to give you the flavor of the language. In Section 2, *How Java Differs from C*, and Section 3, *Classes and Objects in Java*, we'll explain everything you need to know to understand this example. Then in Section 4, *Applets*, we'll present a number of example applets, several of which are a lot like this one.

The first thing you should notice when browsing through the code is that it looks reassuringly like C and C++. The `if` and `return` statements are familiar. Assignment of values to variables uses the expected syntax. Procedures (called "methods" in Java) are recognizable as such.

The second thing to notice is the object-oriented nature of the code. As you can see at the top of the example, the program consists of the definition of a public class. The name of the class we are defining is `Scribble`; it is an extension, or subclass, of the `Applet` class. (The full name of the `Applet` class is `java.applet.Applet`. One of the `import` statements at the top of the example allows us to refer to `Applet` by this shorter name.)

Classes are said to "encapsulate" data and methods. As you can see, our `Scribble` class contains both variable and method declarations. The methods are actually defined inside of the class. The methods of a class are often invoked through an instance of the class. Thus you see lines like:

```
color_choices.addItem("black");
```

This line of code invokes the `addItem()` method of the object referred to by the `color_choices` variable. If you're a C programmer, but not a C++ programmer, this syntax may take a little getting used to. We'll see lots more of it in Sections 2 and 3. Note that `this` is a keyword, not a variable name. It refers to the current object; in this example, it refers to the `Scribble` object.

The `init()` method of an applet is called by the Web browser or applet viewer when it is starting the applet up. In our example, this method creates a **Clear** button and a menu of color choices, and then adds these GUI components to the applet. Section 5, *Graphical User Interfaces*, demonstrates the use of these components in much more detail, and Section 19, *The java.awt Package*, contains quick reference documentation for all the GUI classes.

The `mouseDown()` and `mouseDrag()` methods are called when the user clicks and drags the mouse. These are the methods that are responsible for drawing lines as the user scribbles. The `action()` method is invoked when the user clicks on the **Clear** button or selects a color from the menu of colors. The body of the method determines which of these two "events" has occurred and handles the event appropriately. Sections 4 and 5 both contain examples that illustrate event handling with `mouseDown()`, `mouseDrag()`, `action()`, and other methods in great detail. Section 11, *Events*, contains quick reference information about events.

To compile this example, you'd save it in a file named *Scribble.java* and use *javac*:

```
% javac Scribble.java
```

This example is an applet, not a standalone program like our "Hello World" example. It does not have a `main()` method, and therefore cannot be run directly by the Java interpreter. Instead, we must reference it in an HTML file and run the applet in an applet viewer or Web browser. It is the applet viewer or Web browser that runs the Java interpreter internally to interpret the applet's compiled code. To include the applet in a Web page, we'd use an HTML fragment like the following:

```
<APPLET code="Scribble.class" width=500 height=300>
</APPLET>
```

Example 1-3 shows a complete HTML file that we might use to display the applet. Section 15, *Java-Related HTML and HTTP Syntax*, explains the HTML syntax for applets in full detail.

Getting Started

Example 1-3: An HTML file that contains an applet

```
<HTML>
<HEAD>
<TITLE>The Scribble Applet</TITLE>
</HEAD>
<BODY>
If you're using a Java-enabled browser, please scribble away
in the applet below. If your browser can't run Java
applets, you're out of luck. Sorry!
<P>
<APPLET code="Scribble.class" width=500 height=300>
</APPLET>
</BODY>
</HTML>
```

Suppose we save this example HTML file as *Scribble.html*. Then to run this applet, you could use Sun's *appletviewer* command like this:

```
% appletviewer Scribble.html
```

You could also display the applet by viewing the *Scribble.html* file in your Web browser, if your browser supports Java applets. Figure 1-1 showed the `Scribble` applet running in Netscape Navigator.*

*Some beta versions of Netscape Navigator can't run applets loaded as local files—in these buggy versions of Netscape, the HTML file must actually be downloaded from a Web server. By the time you read this, chances are good that your version of Netscape will not have this bug.

How Java Differs from C

Java vs. C

Java is a lot like C, which makes it relatively easy for C programmers to learn. But there are a number of important differences between C and Java, such as the lack of a preprocessor, the use of 16-bit Unicode characters, and the exception handling mechanism. This chapter explains those differences, so that programmers who already know C can start programming in Java right away!

This chapter also points out similarities and differences between Java and C++. C++ programmers should beware, though: While Java borrows a lot of terminology and even syntax from C++, the analogies between Java and C++ are not nearly as strong as those between Java and C. C++ programmers should be careful not to be lulled into a false sense of familiarity with Java just because the languages share a number of keywords!

One of the main areas in which Java differs from C, of course, is that Java is an object-oriented language and has mechanisms to define classes and create objects that are instances of those classes. Java's object-oriented features are a topic for a chapter of their own, and they'll be explained in detail in Section 3, *Classes and Objects in Java.*

Program Structure and Environment

A program in Java consists of one or more class definitions, each of which has been compiled into its own *.class* file of Java Virtual Machine object code. One of these classes must define a method `main()`, which is where the program starts running.*

To invoke a Java program, you run the Java interpreter, *java*, and specify the name of the class that contains the `main()` method. You should omit the *.class* extension when doing this. Note that a Java applet is not an application—it is a Java class that

**Method* is an object-oriented term for a procedure or function. You'll see it used throughout this book.

is loaded and run by already running Java application such as a Web browser or applet viewer.

The `main()` method that the Java interpreter invokes to start a Java program must have the following prototype:

```
public static void main(String argv[])
```

The Java interpreter runs until the `main()` method returns, or until the interpreter reaches the end of `main()`. If no threads have been created by the program, the interpreter exits. Otherwise, the interpreter continues running until the last thread terminates.

Command-Line Arguments

The single argument to `main()` is an array of strings, conventionally named `argv[]`. The length of this array (which would be passed as the `argc` argument in C) is available as `argv.length`, as is the case with any Java array. The elements of the array are the arguments, if any, that appeared on the interpreter command line after the class name. Note that the first element of the array is *not* the name of the class, as a C programmer might expect it to be. Example 2-1 shows how you could write a UNIX-style *echo* command (a program that simply prints out its arguments) in Java.

Example 2-1: An echo program in Java

```
public class echo {
  public static void main(String argv[]) {
    for(int i=0; i < argv.length; i++)
      System.out.print(argv[i] + " ");
    System.out.print("\n");
    System.exit(0);
  }
}
```

Program Exit Value

Note that `main()` must be declared to return `void`. Thus you cannot return a value from your Java program with a `return` statement in `main()`. If you need to return a value, call `System.exit()` with the desired integer value, as we've done in Example 2-1. Note that the handling and interpretation of this exit value are, of course, operating-system dependent. `System.exit()` causes the Java interpreter to exit immediately, whether or not other threads are running.

Environment

The Java API does not allow a Java program to read operating system environment variables because they are platform-dependent. However, Java defines a similar, platform-independent mechanism, known as the system properties list, for associating textual values with names. A Java program can look up the value of a named property with the `System.getProperty()` method:

```
String homedir = System.getProperty("user.home");
String debug = System.getProperty("myapp.debug");
```

The Java interpreter automatically defines a number of standard system properties when it starts up. You can insert additional property definitions into the list by specifying the -D option to the interpreter:

```
%java -Dmyapp.debug=true myapp
```

See Section 13, *System Properties and Applet Parameters*, for more information on system properties.

The Name Space: Packages, Classes, and Fields

As a language that is designed to support dynamic loading of modules over the entire Internet, Java takes special care to avoid name space conflicts. Global variables are simply not part of the language. Neither are "global" functions or procedures, for that matter.

No Global Variables

Java vs. C

In Java, every variable and method is declared within a class and forms part of that class. Also, every class is part of a *package*. Thus every Java variable or method may be referred to by its fully qualified name, which consists of the package name, the class name, and the field name (i.e., the variable or the method name), all separated by periods. Package names are themselves usually composed of multiple period-separated components. Thus, the fully qualified name for a method might be:

```
david.games.tetris.SoundEffects.play()
```

Packages, Classes, and Directory Structure

In Java, every compiled class is stored in a separate file. The name of this file must be the same as the name of the class, with the extension *.class* added. Thus the class SoundEffects would be stored in the file *SoundEffects.class*. This class file must be stored in a directory that has the same components as the package name. For example, if the fully qualified name of a class is david.games.tetris.SoundEffects, the full path of the class file must be *david/games/tetris/SoundEffects.class*.*

A file of Java source code should have the extension *.java*. It consists of one or more class definitions. If more than one class is defined in a *.java* file, only one of the classes may be declared public (i.e., available outside of the package), and that class must have the same name as the source file (minus the *.java* extension, of course). If a source file contains more than one class definition, those classes are compiled into multiple *.class* files.

Packages of the Java API

The Java API consists of the classes defined in the eight packages listed in Table 2-1.

*We'll use UNIX-style directory specifications in this book. If you are a Windows programmer, simply change all the forward slashes in filenames to backward slashes. Similarly, in path specifications, change colons to semicolons.

Table 2-1: The Packages of the Java API

Package name	Contents
`java.applet`	Classes for implementing applets
`java.awt`	Classes for graphics, text, windows, and GUIs
`java.awt.image`	Classes for image processing
`java.awt.peer`	Interfaces for a platform-independent GUI toolkit
`java.io`	Classes for all kinds of input and output
`java.lang`	Classes for the core language
`java.net`	Classes for networking
`java.util`	Classes for useful data types

The Java Class Path

The Java interpreter looks up its system classes in a platform-dependent default location, or relative to the directories specified by the `-classpath` argument. It looks up user-defined classes in the current directory and relative to the directories specified by the `CLASSPATH` environment variable. The directories in a class path specification should be colon-separated on a UNIX system, and semicolon-separated on a Windows system. For example, on a UNIX system, you might use:

```
setenv CLASSPATH .:~/classes:/usr/local/classes
```

This tells Java to search in and beneath the specified directories for non-system classes.

Globally Unique Package Names

The Java designers have proposed an Internet-wide unique package naming scheme that is based on the domain name of the organization at which the package is developed.

Figure 2-1 shows some fully qualified names, which include package, class, and field components.

The package Statement

The `package` statement must appear as the first statement (i.e., the first text other than comments and whitespace) in a file of Java source code, if it appears at all. It specifies which package the code in the file is part of. Java code that is part of a particular package has access to all classes (`public` and non-`public`) in the package, and to all non-`private` methods and fields in all those classes. When Java code is part of a named package, the compiled class file must be placed at the appropriate position in the `CLASSPATH` directory hierarchy before it can be accessed by the Java interpreter or other utilities.

If the `package` statement is omitted from a file, the code in that file is part of an unnamed default package. This is convenient for small test programs, or during development, because it means that the code can be interpreted from the current directory.

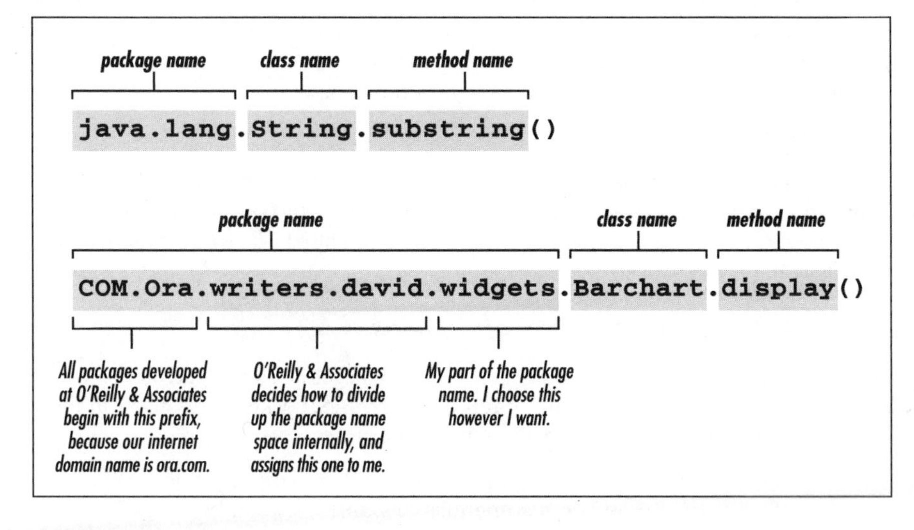

Figure 2-1: Fully qualified names in Java

Java vs. C

The import Statement

The `import` statement makes Java classes available to the current class under an abbreviated name. Public Java classes are always available by their fully qualified names, assuming that the appropriate class file can be found (and is readable) relative to the CLASSPATH environment variable. `import` doesn't actually make the class available or "read it in"; it simply saves you typing and makes your code more legible.

Any number of `import` statements may appear in a Java program. They must appear, however, after the optional `package` statement at the top of the file, and before the first class or interface definition in the file.

There are three forms of the `import` statement:

```
import package ;
import package.class ;
import package.* ;
```

The first form allows the specified package to be known by the name of its last component. For example, the following `import` statement allows `java.awt.image.ImageFilter` to be called `image.ImageFilter`:

```
import java.awt.image;
```

The second form allows the specified class in the specified package to be known by its class name alone. Thus, this `import` statement allows you to type `Hashtable` instead of `java.util.Hashtable`:

```
import java.util.Hashtable;
```

Finally, the third form of the `import` statement makes all classes in a package available by their class name. For example, the following `import` statement is implicit (you need not specify it yourself) in every Java program:

```
import java.lang.*;
```

It makes the core classes of the language available by their unqualified class names. If two packages imported with this form of the statement contain classes with the same name, it is an error to use either of those ambiguous classes without using its fully qualified name.

Access to Packages, Classes, and Fields

Java has the following rules about access to packages, classes, and fields within classes. Note that the `public`, `private`, and `protected` keywords used in these rules will be explained in more detail in the next chapter.

- A package is accessible if the appropriate files and directories are accessible (e.g., if local files have appropriate read permissions, or if they can be downloaded via the network).
- All classes and interfaces in a package are accessible to all other classes and interfaces in the same package. It is not possible to define classes in Java that are visible only within a single file of source code.
- A class declared `public` in one package is accessible within another package, assuming that the package itself is accessible. A non-`public` class is not accessible outside of its package.
- Fields (variables or methods) within a class are accessible from a different class within the same package, as long as they are not declared `private` or `private protected`. `private` fields are accessible only within their own class and `private protected` fields are accessible only within their own class and within subclasses.
- Fields within a class are accessible from a different package as long as the class is accessible, and the field is declared `public`, or the field is declared `protected` or `private protected` and the access is from a subclass of that class.
- All fields of a class are accessible from within that class.

Local Variables

The name space rules we've been describing apply to packages, classes, and the fields within classes. Java also supports local variables, declared within method definitions. These local variables behave just like local variables in C—they do not have globally unique hierarchical names, nor do they have access modifiers like `public` and `private`.

Comments

Java supports three types of comments:

- A standard C-style comment that begins with `/*` and continues until the next `*/`. As in most implementations of C, this style of comment cannot be nested.
- A C++-style comment that begins with `//` and continues until the end of the line.
- A special "doc comment" that begins with `/**` and continues until the next `*/`. These comments may not be nested. Doc comments are specially processed by the *javadoc* program to produce simple online documentation from the Java source code. See Section 10, *Java Syntax*, for more information on the doc comment syntax, and Section 17, *JDK Development Tools*, for more information on the *javadoc* program.

Java vs. C

Since C-style comments do not nest, it is a good idea to use C++-style `//` comments for most of your short comments within method bodies. This allows you to use `/* */` comments to comment out large blocks of code when you need to do that during development. This is especially important because, as you will see, Java does not support a preprocessor that allows you to use `#if 0` to comment out a block.

No Preprocessor

Java does not include any kind of preprocessor like the C *cpp* preprocessor. It may seem hard to imagine programming without `#define`, `#include`, and `#ifdef`, but in fact, Java really does not require these constructs.

Defining Constants

Any variable declared `final` in Java is a constant—its value must be specified with an initializer when it is declared, and that value may never be changed. The Java equivalent of a C `#define`'ed constant is a `static final` variable declared within a class definition. If the compiler can compute the value of such a `static final` variable at compile-time, it uses the computed value to pre-compute other compile-time constants that refer to the value. The variable `java.lang.Math.PI` is an example of such a constant. It is declared like this:

```
public final class Math {
   ...
   public static final double PI = 3.14159.....;
   ...
}
```

Note two things about this example. First, the C convention of using CAPITAL letters for constants is also a Java convention. Second, note the advantage Java constants have over C preprocessor constants: Java constants have globally unique hierarchial names, while constants defined with the C preprocessor always run the risk of a name collision. Also, Java constants are strongly typed and allow better type-checking by the compiler than C preprocessor constants.

Defining Macros

The C preprocessor allows you to define macros—a construct that looks like a function invocation but that is actually replaced directly with C code, saving the overhead of a function call. Java has no equivalent to this sort of macro, but compiler technology has advanced to a point where macros are rarely necessary any more. A good Java compiler should automatically be able to "inline" short Java methods where appropriate.

Including Files

Java does not have a `#include` directive, but it does not need one. Java defines a mapping of fully qualified class names (like `java.lang.Math`) to a directory and file structure (like *java/lang/Math.class*). This means that when the Java compiler needs to read in a specified class file, it knows exactly where to find it and does not need a special directive to tell it where to look.

Furthermore, Java does not make the distinction between *declaring* a variable or procedure and *defining* it that C does. This means that there is no need for C-style header files or function prototypes—a single Java object file serves as the interface definition and implementation for a class.

Java does have an `import` statement, which is superficially similar to the C preprocessor `#include` directive. What this statement does, however, is tell the compiler that the current file is using the specified classes, or classes from the specified package, and allows us to refer to those classes with abbreviated names. For example, since the compiler implicitly `import`s all the classes of the `java.lang` package, we can refer to the constant `java.lang.Math.PI` by the shorter name `Math.PI`.

Conditional Compilation

Java does not have any form of the C `#ifdef` or `#if` directives to perform conditional compilation. In theory, conditional compilation is not necessary in Java since it is a platform-independent language, and thus there are no platform dependencies that require the technique. In practice, however, conditional compilation is still often useful in Java—to provide slightly different user interfaces on different platforms, for example, or to support optional inclusion of debugging code in programs.

While Java does not define explicit constructs for conditional compilation, a good Java compiler (such as Sun's *javac*) performs conditional compilation implicitly—that is, it does not compile code if it can prove that the code will never be executed. Generally, this means that code within an `if` statement testing an expression that is always `false` is not included. Thus, placing code within an `if (false)` block is equivalent to surrounding it with `#if 0` and `#endif` in C.

Conditional compilation also works with constants, which, as we saw above, are `static final` variables. A class might define the constant like this:

```
private static final boolean DEBUG = false;
```

With such a constant defined, any code within an `if (DEBUG)` block is not actually compiled into the class file. To activate debugging for the class, it is only necessary to change the value of the constant to `true` and recompile the class.

Unicode and Character Escapes

Java characters, strings, and identifiers (e.g., variable, method, and class names) are composed of 16-bit Unicode characters. This makes Java programs relatively easy to internationalize for non-English-speaking users. It also makes the language easier to work with for non-English-speaking programmers—a Thai programmer could use the Thai alphabet for class and method names in her Java code.

If two-byte characters seem confusing or intimidating to you, fear not. The Unicode character set is compatible with ASCII and the first 256 characters (0x0000 to 0x00FF) are identical to the ISO8859-1 (Latin-1) characters 0x00 to 0xFF. Furthermore, the Java language design and the Java `String` API make the character representation entirely transparent to you. If you are using only Latin-1 characters, there is no way that you can even distinguish a Java 16-bit character from the 8-bit characters you are familiar with. For more information on Unicode, see Section 16, *The Unicode Standard*.

Most platforms cannot display all 34,000 currently defined Unicode characters, so Java programs may be written (and Java output may appear) with special Unicode escape sequences. Anywhere within a Java program (not only within character and string literals), a Unicode character may be represented with the Unicode escape sequence `\u`*xxxx*, where *xxxx* is a sequence of one to four hexadecimal digits.

Java also supports all of the standard C character escape sequences, such as `\n`, `\t`, and `\`*xxx* (where *xxx* is three octal digits). Note, however, that Java does not support line continuation with \ at the end of a line. Long strings must either be specified on a single long line, or they must be created from shorter strings using the string concatenation (+) operator. (Note that the concatenation of two constant strings is done at compile-time rather than at run-time, so using the + operator in this way is not inefficient.)

There are two important differences between Unicode escapes and C-style escape characters. First, as we've noted, Unicode escapes can appear anywhere within a Java program, while the other escape characters can appear only in character and string constants.

The second, and more subtle, difference is that Unicode `\u` escape sequences are processed before the other escape characters, and thus the two types of escape sequences can have very different semantics. A Unicode escape is simply an alternative way to represent a character that may not be displayable on certain (non-Unicode) systems. Some of the character escapes, however, represent special characters in a way that prevents the usual interpretation of those characters by the compiler. The following examples make this difference clear. Note that `\u0022` and `\u005c` are the Unicode escapes for the double-quote character and the backslash character.

```
// \" represents a " character, and prevents the normal
// interpretation of that character by the compiler.
// This is a string consisting of a double-quote character.
String quote = "\"";

// We can't represent the same string with a single Unicode escape.
// \u0022 has exactly the same meaning to the compiler as ".
// The string below turns into """: an empty string followed
// by an unterminated string, which yields a compilation error.
String quote = "\u0022";
```

```
// Here we represent both characters of an \" escape as
// Unicode escapes. This turns into "\"", and is the same
// string as in our first example.
String quote = "\u005c\u0022";
```

Primitive Data Types

Java adds byte and boolean primitive types to the standard set of C types. In addition, it strictly defines the size and signedness of its types. In C, an int may be 16, 32, or 64 bits, and a char may act signed or unsigned depending on the platform. Not so in Java. In C, an uninitialized local variable usually has garbage as its value. In Java, all variables have guaranteed default values, though the compiler may warn you in places where you rely, accidentally or not, on these default values. Table 2-2 lists Java's primitive data types. The subsections below provide details about these types.

Table 2-2: Java Primitive Data Types

Type	Contains	Default	Size	Min Value / Max Value
boolean	true or false	false	1 bit	N.A. N.A.
char	Unicode character	\u0000	16 bits	\u0000 \uFFFF
byte	signed integer	0	8 bits	-128 127
short	signed integer	0	16 bits	-32768 32767
int	signed integer	0	32 bits	-2147483648 2147483647
long	signed integer	0	64 bits	-9223372036854775808 9223372036854775807
float	IEEE 754 floating-point	0.0	32 bits	±3.40282347E+38 ±1.40239846E-45
double	IEEE 754 floating-point	0.0	64 bits	±1.79769313486231570E+308 ±4.94065645841246544E-324

The boolean Type

boolean values are not integers, may not be treated as integers, and may never be cast to or from any other type. To perform C-style conversions between a boolean value b and an int i, use the following code:

```
b = (i != 0);     // integer-to-boolean: non-0 -> true; 0 -> false;
i = (b)?1:0;      // boolean-to-integer: true -> 1; false -> 0;
```

The char Type

Values of type `char` do not have a sign. If a `char` is cast to a `byte` or a `short`, a negative value may result.

The `char` type in Java holds a two-byte Unicode character. While this may seem intimidating to those not familiar with Unicode and the techniques of program internationalization, it is in fact totally transparent. Java does not provide a way to compute the size of a variable, nor does it allow any sort of pointer arithmetic. What this means is that if you are only using ASCII or Latin-1 characters, there is no way to distinguish a Java `char` from a C `char`.

Integral Types

All integral types, other than `char`, are signed. There is no `unsigned` keyword as there is in C.

It is not legal to write `long int` or `short int` as it is in C.

A `long` constant may be distinguished from other integral constants by appending the character `l` or `L` to it.

Integer division by zero or modulo zero causes an `ArithmeticException` to be thrown.*

Floating-Point Types

Floating-point literals may be specified to be of type `float` by appending an `f` or `F` to the value; they may be specified to be of type `double` by appending a `d` or `D`.

`float` and `double` types have special values that may be the result of certain floating-point operations: positive infinity, negative infinity, negative zero and not-a-number. The `java.lang.Float` and `java.lang.Double` classes define some of these values as constants: `POSITIVE_INFINITY`, `NEGATIVE_INFINITY`, and `NaN`.

`NaN` is unordered—comparing it to any other number, including itself, yields `false`. Use `Float.isNaN()` or `Double.isNaN()` to test for `NaN`.

Negative zero compares equal to regular zero (positive zero), but the two zeros may be distinguished by division: one divided by negative zero yields negative infinity; one divided by positive zero yields positive infinity.

Floating-point arithmetic never causes exceptions, even in the case of division by zero.

Reference Data Types

The non-primitive data types in Java are objects and arrays. These non-primitive types are often called "reference types" because they are handled "by reference"—in other words, the address of the object or array is stored in a variable, passed to methods, and so on. By comparison, primitive types are handled "by value"—the actual primitive values are stored in variables and passed to methods.

*Exceptions signal errors in Java. Exception handling is described later in this chapter.

In C, you can manipulate a value by reference by taking its address with the & operator, and you can "dereference" an address with the * and -> operators. These operators do not exist in Java. Primitive types are always passed by value; arrays and objects are always passed by reference.

Because objects are passed by reference, two different variables may refer to the same object:

```
Button a, b;
p = new Button();            // p refers to a Button object
q = p;                       // q refers to the same Button.
p.setLabel("Ok");            // A change to the object through p...
String s = q.getLabel();     // ...is also visible through q.
                             // s now contains "Ok".
```

This is not true of primitive types, however:

```
int i = 3;                   // i contains the value 3.
int j = i;                   // j contains a copy of the value in i.
i = 2;                       // Changing i doesn't change j.
                             // Now, i == 2 and j == 3.
```

Copying Objects

Because reference types are not passed by value, assigning one object to another in Java does not copy the value of the object. It merely assigns a reference to the object. Consider the following code:

```
Button a = new Button("Okay");
Button b = new Button("Cancel");
a = b;
```

After these lines are executed, the variable `a` contains a reference to the object that `b` refers to. The object that `a` used to refer to is lost.

To copy the data of one object into another object, use the `clone()` method:

```
Vector b = new Vector;
c = b.clone();
```

After these lines run, the variable `c` refers to an object that is a duplicate of the object referred to by `b`. Note that not all types support the `clone()` method. Only classes that implement the `Cloneable` interface may be cloned. Look up `java.lang.Cloneable` and `java.lang.Object.clone()` in Section 23, *The java.lang Package*, for more information on cloning objects.

Arrays are also reference types, and assigning an array simply copies a reference to the array. To actually copy the values stored in an array, you must assign each of the values individually or use the `System.arraycopy()` method.

Checking Objects for Equality

Another implication of passing objects by reference is that the == operator tests whether two variables refer to the same object, not whether two objects contain the same values. To actually test whether two separate objects are the same, you must use a specially written method for that object type (just as you might use `strcmp()`

to compare C strings for equality). In Java, a number of classes define an `equals()` method that you can use to perform this test.

Java Has No Pointers

The referencing and dereferencing of objects is handled for you automatically by Java. Java does not allow you to manipulate pointers or memory addresses of any kind:

- It does not allow you to cast object or array references into integers or vice-versa.
- It does not allow you to do pointer arithmetic.
- It does not allow you to compute the size in bytes of any primitive type or object.

There are two reasons for these restrictions:

- Pointers are a notorious source of bugs. Eliminating them simplifies the language and eliminates many potential bugs.
- Pointers and pointer arithmetic could be used to sidestep Java's run-time checks and security mechanisms. Removing pointers allows Java to provide the security guarantees that it does.

To a C programmer, the lack of pointers and pointer arithmetic may seem an odious restriction in Java. But once you get used to the Java object-oriented programming model, it no longer seems like a serious restriction at all. The lack of pointers does mean that you probably can't do things like write UNIX device drivers in Java (at least not without using native methods written in C). But big deal—most of us never have to do this kind of low-level programming anyway.

null

The default value for variables of all reference types is `null`. `null` is a reserved value that indicates "an absence of reference"—i.e., that a variable does not refer to any object or array.

In Java, `null` is a reserved keyword, unlike `NULL` in C, where it is just a constant defined to be 0. `null` is an exception to the strong typing rules of Java—it may be assigned to any variable of reference type (i.e., any variable which has a class, interface, or array as its type).

`null` cannot be cast to any primitive type, including integral types and `boolean`. It should not be considered equal to zero (although it may well be implemented this way).

Reference Type Summary

The distinction between primitive types passed by value, and objects and arrays passed by reference is a crucial one in Java. Be sure you understand the following:

- All objects and arrays are handled by reference in Java.
- The = and == operators assign and test references to objects. Use `clone()` and `equals()` to actually copy or test the objects themselves.

- The necessary referencing and dereferencing of objects and arrays is handled automatically by Java.
- A reference type can never be cast to a primitive type.
- A primitive type can never be cast to a reference type.
- There is no pointer arithmetic in Java.
- There is no `sizeof` operator in Java.
- `null` is a special value that means "no object" or indicates an absence of reference.

Objects

Now that you know objects are passed by reference, we should discuss how they are created, used, and destroyed. The following subsections provide a very brief overview of objects. Section 3, *Classes and Objects in Java*, explains classes and objects in much greater detail.

Creating Objects

Declaring a variable to hold an object does not create the object itself; the variable only holds the reference to the object. To actually create an object, you must use the `new` keyword. This is followed by the object's class (i.e., its type) and an optional argument list in parentheses. These arguments are passed to the constructor method for the class, which serves to initialize internal fields in the new object. For example:

```
java.awt.Button b = new java.awt.Button();
ComplexNumber c = new ComplexNumber(1.0, 1.414);
```

There are actually two other ways to create an object. First, you can create a `String` object simply by enclosing characters in double quotes:

```
String s = "This is a test";
```

Because strings are used so frequently, the Java compiler provides this technique as a shortcut. The second alternative way to create objects is by calling the `newInstance()` method of a `Class` object. This technique is generally used only when dynamically loading classes, so we won't discuss it here.

The memory for newly created objects is dynamically allocated. Creating an object with `new` in Java is like calling `malloc()` in C to allocate memory for an instance of a `struct`. It is also, of course, a lot like using the `new` operator in C++. (Below, though, we'll see where this analogy to `malloc()` in C and `new` in C++ breaks down.)

Accessing Objects

As you've probably noticed in various example code fragments by now, the way you access the fields of an object is with a dot:

```
ComplexNumber c = new ComplexNumber();
c.x = 1.0;
c.y = -1.414;
```

This syntax is reminiscent of accessing the fields of a struct in C. Recall, though, that Java objects are always accessed by reference, and that Java performs any necessary dereferencing for you. Thus, the dot in Java is more like -> in C. Java hides the fact that there is a reference here in an attempt to make your programming easier.

The other difference between C and Java when accessing objects is that in Java you refer to an object's methods as if they were fields in the object itself:

```
ComplexNumber c = new ComplexNumber(1.0, -1.414);
double magnitude = c.magnitude();
```

Garbage Collection

Objects in Java are created with the new keyword, but there is no corresponding old or delete keyword or free() method to get rid of them when they are no longer needed. If creating an object with new is like calling malloc() in C or using new in C++, then it would seem that Java is full of memory leaks, because we never call free() or use the delete operator.

In fact, this isn't the case. Java uses a technique called *garbage collection* to automatically detect objects that are no longer being used (an object is no longer in use when there are no more references to it) and to free them. This means that in our programs, we never need to worry about freeing memory or destroying objects—the garbage collector takes care of that.

If you are a C or C++ programmer, it may take some getting used to to just let allocated objects go without worrying about reclaiming their memory. Once you get used to it, however, you'll begin to appreciate what a nice feature this is. We'll discuss garbage collection in more detail in the next chapter.

Arrays

Most of what we learned in the previous sections about reference types and objects applies equally well to arrays in Java:

- Arrays are manipulated by reference.
- They are dynamically created with new.
- They are automatically garbage collected when no longer referred to.

The following subsections explain these and other details.

Creating and Destroying Arrays

There are two ways to create arrays in Java. The first uses new, and specifies how large the array should be:

```
byte octet_buffer[] = new byte[1024];
Button buttons[] = new Button[10];
```

Since creating an array does not create the objects that are stored in the array, there is no constructor to call, and the argument list is omitted with this form of the new keyword. The elements of an array created in this way are initialized to the default value for their type. The elements of an array of `int` are initialized to `0`, for example, and the elements of an array of objects are initialized to `null`.

The second way to create an array is with a static initializer, which looks just like it does in C:

```
int lookup_table[] = {1, 2, 4, 8, 16, 32, 64, 128};
```

This syntax dynamically creates an array and initializes its elements to the specified values. The elements specified in an array initializer may be arbitrary expressions. This is different than in C, where they must be constant expressions.

Arrays are automatically garbage collected, just like objects are.

Multidimensional Arrays

Java also supports multidimensional arrays. These are implemented as arrays-of-arrays, as they are in C. You specify a variable as a multidimensional array type simply by appending the appropriate number of `[]` pairs after it. You allocate a multidimensional array with `new` by specifying the appropriate number of elements (between square brackets) for each dimension. For example:

```
byte TwoDimArray[][] = new byte[256][16];
```

This statement does three things:

- Declares a variable named `TwoDimArray`. This variable has type `byte[][]` (array-of-array-of-`byte`).
- Dynamically allocates an array with 256 elements. The type of this newly allocated array is `byte[][]`, so it can be assigned to the variable we declared. Each element of this new array is of type `byte[]`—a single-dimensional array of `byte`.
- Dynamically allocates 256 arrays of bytes, each of which holds 16 bytes, and stores a reference to these 256 `byte[]` arrays into the 256 elements of the `byte[][]` array allocated in the second step. The 16 bytes in each of these 256 arrays are initialized to their default value of `0`.

When allocating a multidimensional array, you do not have to specify the number of elements that are contained in each dimension. For example:

```
int threeD[][][] = new int[10][][];
```

This expression allocates an array that contains ten elements, each of type `int[][]`. It is a single-dimensional allocation, although when the array elements are properly initialized to meaningful values, the array will be multidimensional. The rule for this sort of array allocation is that the first n dimensions (where n is at least one) must have the number of elements specified, and these dimensions may be followed by m additional dimensions with no dimension size specified. The following is legal:

```
String lots_of_strings[][][][] = new String[5][3][][];
```

This is not:

```
double temperature_data[][][] = new double[100][][10];    // illegal
```

Multidimensional arrays can also be allocated and initialized with nested initializers. For example, you might declare the following multidimensional array of strings for use by the `getParameterInfo()` method of an applet:

```
String param_info[][] = {
  {"foreground",        "Color",       "foreground color"},
  {"background",        "Color",       "background color"},
  {"message",           "String",      "the banner to display"}
};
```

Note that since Java implements multidimensional arrays as arrays-of-arrays, multidimensional arrays need not be "rectangular." For example, this is how you could create and initialize a "triangular array":

```
short triangle[][] = new short[10][];          // a single-dimensional array
for(int i = 0; i < triangle.length; i++) {     // for each element of that array
  triangle[i] = new short[i+1];                // allocate a new array
  for(int j=0; j < i+1; j++)                   // for each element of the new array
    triangle[i][j] = i + j;                    // initialize it to a value.
}
```

Java vs. C

You can also declare and initialize non-rectangular arrays with nested initializers:

```
static int[][] twodim = {{1, 2}, (3, 4, 5}, {5, 6, 7, 8}};
```

To simulate multiple dimensions within a single-dimensional array, you'd use code just as you would in C:

```
final int rows = 600;
final int columns = 800;
byte pixels[] = new byte[rows*columns];

// access element [i,j] like this:
byte b = pixels[i + j*columns];
```

Accessing Array Elements

Array access in Java is just like array access in C—you access an element of an array by putting an integer-valued expression between square brackets after the name of the array:

```
int a[] = new int[100];
a[0] = 0;
for(int i = 1; i < a.length; i++) a[i] = i + a[i-1];
```

Notice how we computed the number of elements of the array in this example—by accessing the `length` field of the array. This is the only field that arrays support. Note that it is a read-only field—any attempt to store a value into the `length` field of an array will fail.

In all Java array references, the index is checked to make sure it is not too small (less than zero) or too big (greater than or equal to the array length). If the index is out of bounds, an `ArrayIndexOutOfBoundsException` is thrown.* This is another way that Java works to prevent bugs (and security problems).

*The discussion of exceptions and exception handling is still to come.

Are Arrays Objects?

It is useful to consider arrays to be a separate kind of reference type from objects. In some ways, though, arrays behave just like objects. As we saw, arrays use the object syntax `.length` to refer to their length. Arrays may also be assigned to variables of type `Object`, and the methods of the `Object` class may be invoked for arrays. (`Object` is the root class in Java, which means that all objects can be assigned to a variable of type `Object` and all objects can invoke the methods of `Object`.)

The evidence suggests that arrays are, in fact, objects. Java defines enough special syntax for arrays, however, that it is still most useful to consider them a different kind of reference type than objects.

Declaring Array Variables and Arguments

In C, you declare an array variable or array function argument by placing square brackets next to the variable name:

```
void reverse(char strbuf[], int buffer_size) {
    char buffer[500];
      ...
}
```

In Java, you would have to declare `buffer` as an array variable, and then allocate the array itself with `new`, but otherwise you could use the same syntax, with the array brackets after the variable or argument name.

However, Java also allows you to put the array brackets after the type name instead. So you could rewrite this code fragment to look something like this:

```
void reverse(char[] strbuf, int buffer_size) {
    char[] buffer = new char[500];
      ...
}
```

In a lot of ways, this new array syntax is easier to read and easier to understand. (It doesn't work in C, by the way, because pointers make C's type declaration syntax a real mess.) The only problem with this new syntax is that if you get in the habit of using it, it will make it harder for you when you (hopefully only occasionally!) have to switch back and program in C.

Java even allows you to mix the declaration styles, which is something you may find occasionally useful (or frequently confusing!) for certain data structures or algorithms. For example:

```
// row and column are arrays of byte.
// matrix is an array of an array of bytes.
byte[] row, column, matrix[];

// This method takes an array of bytes and an
// array of arrays of bytes
public void dot_product(byte[] column, byte[] matrix[]) { ... }
```

A final point to note about array declarations is that (as we've seen throughout this section) the size of an array is not part of its type as it is in C. Thus, you can declare a variable to be of type `String[]`, for example, and assign any array of `String` objects to it, regardless of the length of the array:

```
String[] strings;               // this variable can refer to any String array
strings = new String[10];       // one that contains 10 Strings
strings = new String[20];       // or one that contains 20.
```

Strings

Strings in Java are *not* null-terminated arrays of characters as they are in C. Instead, they are instances of the `java.lang.String` class. Java strings are unusual, in that the compiler treats them almost as if they were primitive types—for example, it automatically creates a `String` object when it encounters a double-quoted constant in the program. And, the language defines an operator that operates on `String` objects—the + operator for string concatenation.

An important feature of `String` objects is that they are immutable—i.e., there are no methods defined that allow you to change the contents of a `String`. If you need to modify the contents of a `String`, you have to create a `StringBuffer` object from the `String` object, modify the contents of the `StringBuffer`, and then create a new `String` from the contents of the `StringBuffer`.

Note that it is moot to ask whether Java strings are terminated with a NUL character (\u0000) or not. Java performs run-time bounds checking on all array and string accesses, so there is no way to examine the value of any internal terminator character that appears after the last character of the string.

Both the `String` and `StringBuffer` classes are documented in Section 23, *The java.lang Package*, and you'll find a complete set of methods for string handling and manipulation there. Some of the more important `String` methods are: `length()`, `charAt()`, `equals()`, `compareTo()`, `indexOf()`, `lastIndexOf()`, and `substring()`.

Operators

Java supports almost all of the standard C operators. These standard operators have the same precedence and associativity in Java as they do in C. They are listed in Table 2-3 and also in quick reference form in Section 10, *Java Syntax*.

Table 2-3: Java Operators

Prec.	Operator	Operand Type(s)	Assoc.	Operation Performed
1	`++`	arithmetic	R	pre-or-post increment (unary)
	`--`	arithmetic	R	pre-or-post decrement (unary)
	`+, -`	arithmetic	R	unary plus, unary minus
	`~`	integral	R	bitwise complement (unary)
	`!`	boolean	R	logical complement (unary)
	`(`*type*`)`	any	R	cast
2	`*, /, %`	arithmetic	L	multiplication, division, remainder
3	`+, -`	arithmetic	L	addition, subtraction
	`+`	String	L	string concatenation
4	`<<`	integral	L	left shift
	`>>`	integral	L	right shift with sign

Table 2-3: Java Operators (continued)

Prec.	Operator	Operand Type(s)	Assoc.	Operation Performed
				extension
	>>>	integral	L	right shift with zero extension
5	<, <=	arithmetic	L	less than, less than or equal
	>, >=	arithmetic	L	greater than, greater than or equal
	instanceof	object, type	L	type comparison
6	==	primitive	L	equal (have identical values)
	!=	primitive	L	not equal (have different values)
	==	object	L	equal (refer to same object)
	!=	object	L	not equal (refer to different objects)
7	&	integral	L	bitwise AND
	&	boolean	L	boolean AND
8	^	integral	L	bitwise XOR
	^	boolean	L	boolean XOR
9	|	integral	L	bitwise OR
	|	boolean	L	boolean OR
10	&&	boolean	L	conditional AND
11	||	boolean	L	conditional OR
12	?:	boolean, any, any	R	conditional (ternary) operator
13	=	variable, any	R	assignment
	*=, /=, %=, +=, -=, <<=, >>=, >>>=, &=, ^=, |=,	variable, any	R	assignment with operation

Note the following Java operator differences from C. Java does not support the comma operator for combining two expressions into one (although the `for` statement simulates this operator in a useful way). Since Java does not allow you to manipulate pointers directly, it does not support the reference and dereference operators `*` and `&`, nor the `sizeof` operator. Further, Java doesn't consider `[]` (array access) and `.` (field access) to be operators, as C does.

Java also adds some new operators:

+

The + operator applied to `String` values concatenates them.* If only one operand of + is a `String`, the other one is converted to a string. The conversion is done automatically for primitive types, and by calling the `toString()` method of non-primitive types. This `String` + operator has the same precedence as the arithmetic + operator. The += operator works as you would expect for `String` values.

`instanceof`

The `instanceof` operator returns `true` if the object on its left-hand side is an instance of the class (or implements the interface) specified on its right-hand side. `instanceof` returns `false` if the object is not an instance of the specified class or does not implement the specified interface. It also returns `false` if the specified object is `null`. The `instanceof` operator has the same precedence as the <, <=, >, and >= operators.

>>>

Because all integral types in Java are signed values, the Java >> operator is defined to do a right shift with sign extension. The >>> operator treats the value to be shifted as an unsigned number and shifts the bits right with zero extension. The >>>= operator works as you would expect.

& and |

When & and | are applied to integral types in Java, they perform the expected bitwise AND and OR operations. Java makes a strong distinction between integral types and the `boolean` type, however. Thus, if these operators are applied to `boolean` types, they perform logical AND and logical OR operations. These logical AND and logical OR operators always evaluate both of their operands, even when the result of the operation is determined after evaluating only the left operand. This is useful when the operands are expressions with side effects (such as method calls) and you always want the side effects to occur. However, when you do not want the right operand evaluated if it is not necessary, you can use the && and || operators, which perform "short-circuited" logical AND and logical OR operations just as in C. The &= and |= operators perform a bitwise or logical operation depending on the type of the operators, as you would expect.

Statements

Many of Java's control statements are similar or identical to C statements. This section lists and, where necessary, explains Java's statements. Note that the topic of exceptions and the `try/catch/finally` statement is substantial enough that it is covered later in a section of its own.

*To C++ programmers, this looks like operator overloading. In fact, Java does not support operator overloading—the language designers decided (after much debate) that overloaded operators were a neat idea, but that code that relied on them became hard to read and understand.

The if/else, while, and do/while Statements

The `if`, `else`, `do`, and `while` statements are exactly the same in Java as they are in C. The only substantial difference arises because the Java `boolean` type cannot be cast to other types. In Java, the values `0` and `null` are not the same as `false`, and non-zero and non-`null` values are not the same as `true`.

The conditional expression that is expected by the `if`, the `while`, and the `do/while` statements must be of `boolean` type in Java. Specifying an integer type or a reference type won't do. Thus, the following C code is not legal in Java:

```
int i = 10;
while(i--) {
  Object o = get_object();
  if (o) {
    do { ... } while(j);
  }
}
```

In Java, you must make the condition you are testing for clear by explictly testing your value against `0` or `null`. Use code like the following:

```
int i = 10;
while(i-- > 0) {
  Object o = get_object();
  if (o != null) {
    do { ... } while(j != 0);
  }
}
```

The switch Statement

The `switch` statement is the same in Java as it is in C. You may use `byte`, `char`, `short`, `int`, or `long` types as the values of the `case` labels, and you may also specify a `default` label just as you do in C.

The for Loop

The `for` statement is perhaps the most useful looping construct available in Java. There are only two differences between the Java `for` loop and the C `for` loop. The first difference is that although Java does not support the C comma operator (which allows multiple expressions to be joined into a single expression), the Java `for` loop simulates it by allowing multiple comma-separated expressions to appear in the initialization and increment sections, but not the test section, of the loop. For example:

```
int i;
String s;
for(i=0, s = "testing";                // initialize variables
    (i < 10) && (s.length() >= 1);     // test for continuation
    i++, s = s.substring(1))           // increment variables
{
    System.out.println(s);             // loop body
}
```

As you can see, this "difference" between the Java and C `for` loops is really a similarity.

The second difference is the addition of the C++ ability to declare local loop variables in the initialization section of the loop:

```
for(int i = 0; i < my_array.length; i++)
   System.out.println("a[" + i + "] = " + my_array[i]);
```

Variables declared in this way have the `for` loop as their scope. In other words, they are only valid within the body of the `for` loop and within the initialization, test, and increment expressions of the loop. Variables with the same name outside of the loop are not changed.

Note that because variable declaration syntax also uses the comma, the Java syntax allows you to either specify multiple comma-separated initialization expressions or to declare and initialize multiple comma-separated variables of the same type. You may not mix variable declarations with other expressions. For example, the following `for` loop declares and initializes two variables that are valid only within the `for` loop. Variables by the same name outside of the loop are not changed.

```
int j = -3;          // this j remains unchanged.
for(int i=0, j=10; i < j; i++, j--) System.out.println("k = " + i*j);
```

Java
vs. C

Labelled break and continue Statements

The `break` and `continue` statements, used alone, behave the same in Java as they do in C. However, in Java, they may optionally be followed by a label that specifies an enclosing loop (for `continue`) or any enclosing statement (for `break`). The labelled forms of these statements allow you to "break" and "continue" any specified statement or loop within a method definition, not only the nearest enclosing statements or loop.

The `break` statement, without a label, transfers control out of ("breaks out of" or terminates) the nearest enclosing `for`, `while`, `do` or `switch` statement, exactly as in C. If the `break` keyword is followed by an identifier that is the label of an arbitrary enclosing statement, execution transfers out of that enclosing statement. After the `break` statement is executed, any required `finally` clauses are executed, and control resumes at the statement following the terminated statement. (The `finally` clause and the `try` statement it is associated with are exception handling constructs and are explained in the next section.) For example:

```
test: if (check(i)) {
   try {
      for(int j=0; j < 10; j++) {
         if (j > i) break;            // terminate just this loop
         if (a[i][j] == null)
            break test;               // do the finally clause and
      }                               // terminate the if statement.
   }
   finally { cleanup(a, i, j); }
}
```

Without a label, the `continue` statement works exactly as in C: It stops the iteration in progress and causes execution to resume after the last statement in the `while`, `do`, or `for` loop, just before the loop iteration is to begin again. If the `continue` keyword is followed by an identifier that is the label of an enclosing loop, execution skips to the end of that loop instead. If there are any `finally` clauses between the continue statement and the end of the appropriate loop, these clauses are executed before control is transferred to the end of the loop.

The following code fragment illustrates how the continue statement works in its labelled and unlabelled forms.

```
big_loop: while(!done) {
  if (test(a,b) == 0) continue;        // control goes to point 2.
  try {
    for(int i=0; i < 10; i++) {
      if (a[i] == null)
        continue;                      // control goes to point 1.
      else if (b[i] == null)
        continue big_loop;             // control goes to point 2,
                                       // after doing the finally block.
      doit(a[i],b[i]);
                                       // point 1. Increment and start loop again with the test.
    }
  }
  finally { cleanup(a,b); }
                                       // point 2. Start loop again with the (!done) test.
}
```

Note the non-intuitive feature of the labelled continue statement: The loop label must appear at the top of the loop, but continue causes execution to transfer to the very bottom of the loop.

No goto Statement

goto is a reserved word in Java, but the goto statement is not currently part of the language. Labelled break and continue statements replace some important and legitimate uses of goto, and the try/catch/finally statement replaces the others.

The synchronized Statement

Since Java is a multithreaded system, care must often be taken to prevent multiple threads from modifying objects simultaneously in a way that might leave the object's state corrupted. Sections of code that must not be executed simultaneously are known as "critical sections." Java provides the synchronized statement to protect these critical sections. The syntax is:

```
synchronized (expression) statement
```

expression is an expression that must resolve to an object or an array. The *statement* is the code of the critical section, which is usually a block of statements (within { and }). The synchronized statement attempts to acquire an exclusive lock for the object or array specified by *expression*. It does not execute the critical section of code until it can obtain this lock, and in this way, ensures that no other threads can be executing the section at the same time.

Note that you do not have to use the synchronized statement unless your program creates multiple threads that share data. If only one thread ever accesses a data structure, there is no need to protect it with synchronized. When you do have to use it, it might be in code like the following:

```
public static void SortIntArray(int[] a) {
        // Sort the array a. This is synchronized so that some other
        // thread can't change elements of the array while we're sorting it.
        // At least not other threads that protect their changes to the
        // array with synchronized.
  synchronized (a) {
        // do the array sort here.
  }
}
```

The `synchronized` keyword is more often used as a method modifier in Java. When applied to a method, it indicates that the entire method is a critical section. For a `synchronized` class method (a static method), Java obtains an exclusive lock on the class before executing the method. For a `synchronized` instance method, Java obtains an exclusive lock on the class instance. (Class methods and instance methods are discussed in the next chapter.)

Java vs. C

The package and import Statements

The `package` statement, as we saw earlier in the chapter, specifies the package that the classes in a file of Java source code are part of. If it appears, it must be the first statement of a Java file. The `import` statement, which we also saw earlier, allows us to refer to classes by abbreviated names. `import` statements must appear after the `package` statement, if any, and before any other statements in a Java file. For example:

```
package games.tetris;

import java.applet.*;
import java.awt.*;
```

Exceptions and Exception Handling

Exception handing is a significant new feature of Java.* There are a number of new terms associated with exception handling. First, an *exception* is a signal that indicates that some sort of exceptional condition (such as an error) has occurred. To *throw* an exception is to signal an exceptional condition. To *catch* an exception is to handle it—to take whatever actions are necessary to recover from it.

Exceptions propagate up through the lexical block structure of a Java method, and then up the method call stack. If an exception is not caught by the block of code that throws it, it propagates to the next higher enclosing block of code. If it is not caught there, it propagates up again. If it is not caught anywhere in the method, it propagates to the invoking method, where it again propagates through the block structure. If an exception is never caught, it propagates all the way to the `main()` method from which the program started, and causes the Java interpreter to print an error message and a stack trace and exit.

As we'll see in the subsections below, exceptions make error handling (and "exceptional condition" handling) more regular and logical by allowing you to group all your exception handling code into one place. Instead of worrying about all of the things that can go wrong with each line of your code, you can concentrate on the

*It is similar to, but not quite the same as, exception handling in C++.

algorithm at hand and place all your error handling code (that is, your exception catching code) in a single place.

Exception Objects

An exception in Java is an object that is an instance of some subclass of `java.lang.Throwable`. `Throwable` has two standard subclasses: `java.lang.Error` and `java.lang.Exception`.* Exceptions that are subclasses of `Error` generally indicate linkage problems related to dynamic loading, or virtual machine problems such as running out of memory. They should almost always be considered unrecoverable, and should not be caught. While the distinction is not always clear, exceptions that are subclasses of `Exception` indicate conditions that may be caught and recovered from. They include such exceptions as `java.io.EOFException`, which signals the end of a file and `java.lang.ArrayAccessOutOfBounds`, which indicates that a program has tried to read past the end of an array.

Since exceptions are objects, they can contain data and define methods. The `Throwable` object, at the top of the exception class hierarchy, includes a `String` message in its definition and this field is inherited by all exception classes. This field is used to store a human-readable error message that describes the exceptional condition. It is set when the exception object is created by passing an argument to the constructor method. The message can be read from the exception with the `Throwable.getMessage()` method. Most exceptions contain only this single message, but a few add other data. The `java.io.InterruptedIOException`, for example, adds the following field:

```
public int bytesTransferred;
```

This field specifies how much of the I/O was complete before the exceptional condition occurred.

Exception Handling

The `try/catch/finally` statement is Java's exception handling mechanism. `try` establishes a block of code that is to have its exceptions and abnormal exits (through `break`, `continue`, `return`, or exception propagation) handled. The `try` block is followed by zero or more `catch` clauses that catch and handle specified types of exceptions. The `catch` clauses are optionally followed by a `finally` block that contains "clean-up" code. The statements of a `finally` block are guaranteed to be executed, regardless of how the code in the `try` block exits. A detailed example of the `try/catch/finally` syntax is shown in Example 2-2.

Example 2-2: The try/catch/finally statement

```
try {
        // Normally this code runs from the top of the block to the bottom
        // without problems. But it sometimes may raise exceptions or
        // exit the block via a break, continue, or return statement.
}
catch (SomeException e1) {
        // Handle an exception object e1 of type SomeException
        // or of a subclass of that type.
```

*We'll use the term "exception" to refer to any subclass of `Throwable`, whether it is actually an `Exception` or an `Error`.

```
}
catch (AnotherException e2) {
        // Handle an exception object e2 of type AnotherException
        // or of a subclass of that type.
}
finally {
        // Always execute this code, after we leave the try clause,
        // regardless of whether we leave it:
        //   1) Normally, after reaching the bottom of the block.
        //   2) With an exception that is handled by a catch.
        //   3) With an exception that is not handled.
        //   4) Because of a break, continue, or return statement.
}
```


try

The `try` clause simply establishes a block of code that is to have its exceptions and abnormal exits (through `break`, `continue`, `return`, or exception propagation) handled. The `try` clause by itself doesn't do anything interesting; it is the `catch` and `finally` clauses that do the exception handling and clean-up operations.

catch

A `try` block may be followed by zero or more `catch` clauses that specify code to handle various types of exceptions. `catch` clauses have an unusual syntax: each is declared with an argument, much like a method argument. This argument must be of type `Throwable` or a subclass. When an exception occurs, the first `catch` clause that has an argument of the appropriate type is invoked. The type of the argument must match the type of the exception object, or it must be a superclass of the exception. This `catch` argument is valid only within the `catch` block, and refers to the actual exception object that was thrown.

The code within a `catch` block should take whatever action is necessary to cope with the exceptional condition. If the exception was a `java.io.FileNotFoundException` exception, for example, you might handle it by asking the user to check his or her spelling and try again. Note that it is not required to have a `catch` clause for every possible exception—in some cases the correct response is to allow the exception to propagate up and be caught by the invoking method. In other cases, such as a programming error signaled by `NullPointerException`, the correct response is to not catch the exception at all, but to allow it to propagate and to have the Java interpreter exit with a stack trace and an error message.

finally

The `finally` clause is generally used to clean up (close files, release resources, etc.) after the `try` clause. What is useful about the `finally` clause is that the code in a `finally` block is guaranteed to be executed, if any portion of the `try` block is executed, regardless of how the code in the `try` block completes. In the normal case, control reaches the end of the `try` block and then proceeds to the `finally` block, which performs any necessary cleanup.

If control leaves the try block because of a return, continue, or break statement, the contents of the finally block are executed before control transfers to its new destination.

If an exception occurs in the try block and there is a local catch block to handle the exception, control transfers first to the catch block, and then to the finally block. If there is not a local catch block to handle the exception, control transfers first to the finally block, and then propagates up to the nearest catch clause that can handle the exception.

Note that if a finally block itself transfers control with a return, continue, or break statement, or by raising an exception, the pending control transfer is abandoned, and this new transfer is processed.

Also note that try and finally can be used together without exceptions or any catch clauses. In this case, the finally block is simply cleanup code that is guaranteed to be executed regardless of any break, continue, or return statements within the try clause.

Declaring Exceptions

Java requires that any method that can cause a "normal exception" to occur must either catch the exception or specify the type of the exception with a throws clause in the method declaration.* Such a throws clause might look like these:

```
public void open_file() throws IOException {
        // Statements here that might generate an uncaught java.io.IOException
}

public void myfunc(int arg) throws MyException1, MyException2 {
   ...
}
```

Note that the exception class specified in a throws clause may be a superclass of the exception type that is actually thrown. Thus if a method throws exceptions a, b, and c, all of which are subclasses of d, the throws clause may specify all of a, b, and c, or it may simply specify d.

We said above that the throws clause must be used to declare any "normal exceptions." This oxymoronic phrase refers to any subclass of Throwable that is not a subclass of Error or a subclass of RuntimeException. Java does not require these types of exceptions to be declared because practically any method can conceivably generate them, and it would quickly become tedious to properly declare them all. For example, every method running on a buggy Java interpreter can throw an InternalError exception (a subclass of Error) and it doesn't make sense to have to declare this in a throws clause for every method. Similarly, as far as the Java compiler is concerned, any method that accesses an array can generate an ArrayIndexOutOfBoundsException exception (a subclass of RuntimeException).

The standard exceptions that you often have to declare are java.io.IOException and a number of its more specific subclasses. java.lang.InterruptedException and several other less commonly used exceptions must also be declared. How

*C++ programmers note that Java uses throws where C++ uses throw.

do you know when you have to declare a `throws` clause? One way is to pay close attention to the documentation for the methods you call—if any "normal exceptions" can be thrown, either catch them or declare them. Another way to know what exceptions you've got to declare is to declare none and wait for the compilation errors—the compiler will tell you what to put in your `throws` clause!

Defining and Generating Exceptions

You can signal your own exceptions with the `throw` statement. The `throw` keyword must be followed by an object that is `Throwable` or a subclass. Often, exception objects are allocated in the same statement that they are thrown in:

```
throw new MyException("my exceptional condition occurred.");
```

When an exception is thrown, normal program execution stops and the interpreter looks for a `catch` clause that can handle the exception. Execution propagates up through enclosing statements and through invoking functions until such a handler is found. Any `finally` blocks that are passed during this propagation are executed.

Using exceptions is a good way to signal and handle errors in your own code. By grouping all your error handling and recover code together within the `try/catch/finally` structure, you will end up with cleaner code that is easier to understand. Sometimes, when you are throwing an exception, you can use one of the exception classes already defined by Java API. Often, though, you will want to define and throw your own exception types.

Example 2-3 shows how you can define your own exception types, throw them, and handle them. It also helps clarify how exceptions propagate. It is a long example, but worth studying in some detail. You'll know you understand exception handling if you can answer the following: What happens when this program is invoked with no argument; with a string argument; and with integer arguments 0, 1, 2, and 99?

Example 2-3: Defining, throwing, and handling exceptions

```
// Here we define some exception types of our own.
// Exception classes generally have constructors but no data or
// other methods. All these do is call their superclass constructors.
class MyException extends Exception {
  public MyException() { super(); }
  public MyException(String s) { super(s); }
}
class MyOtherException extends Exception {
  public MyOtherException() { super(); }
  public MyOtherException(String s) { super(s); }
}
class MySubException extends MyException {
  public MySubException() { super(); }
  public MySubException(String s) { super(s); }
}

public class throwtest {
      // This is the main() method. Note that it uses two
      // catch clauses to handle two standard Java exceptions.
  public static void main(String argv[]) {
    int i;
```

Java vs. C

```
        // First, convert our argument to an integer
        // Make sure we have an argument and that it is convertible.
    try {
      i = Integer.parseInt(argv[0]);
    }
    catch (ArrayIndexOutOfBoundsException e) { // argv is empty
      System.out.println("Must specify an argument");
      return;
    }
    catch (NumberFormatException e) { // argv[0] isn't an integer
      System.out.println("Must specify an integer argument.");
      return;
    }

        // Now, pass that integer to method a().
    a(i);
  }

        // This method invokes b(), which is declared to throw
        // one type of exception. We handle that one exception.
  public static void a(int i) {
    try {
      b(i);
    }
    catch (MyException e) {                    // Point 1.
              // Here we handle MyException and
              // its subclass MyOtherException
      if (e instanceof MySubException)
        System.out.print("MySubException: ");
      else
        System.out.print("MyException: ");
      System.out.println(e.getMessage());
      System.out.println("Handled at point 1");
    }
  }

        // This method invokes c(), and handles one of the
        // two exception types that that method can throw. The other
        // exception type is not handled, and is propagated up
        // and declared in this method's throws clause.
        // This method also has a finally clause to finish up
        // the work of its try clause. Note that the finally clause
        // is executed after a local catch clause, but before
        // a containing catch clause or one in an invoking procedure.
  public static void b(int i) throws MyException {
    int result;
    try {
      System.out.print("i = " + i);
      result = c(i);
      System.out.print(" c(i) = " + result);
    }
    catch (MyOtherException e) {               // Point 2
              // Handle MyOtherException exceptions:
      System.out.println("MyOtherException: " + e.getMessage());
      System.out.println("Handled at point 2");
    }
```

Example 2-3: Defining, throwing, and handling exceptions (continued)

```
    finally {
                    // Terminate the output we printed above with a newline.
      System.out.print("\n");
    }
  }

        // This method computes a value or throws an exception.
        // The throws clause only lists two exceptions, because
        // one of the exceptions thrown is a subclass of another.
  public static int c(int i) throws MyException, MyOtherException {
    switch (i) {
      case 0: // processing resumes at point 1 above
        throw new MyException("input too low");
      case 1: // processing resumes at point 1 above
        throw new MySubException("input still too low");
      case 99:// processing resumes at point 2 above
        throw new MyOtherException("input too high");
      default:
        return i*i;
    }
  }
}
```


Miscellaneous Differences

A number of miscellaneous differences between Java and C are described in the sections that follow. Miscellaneous differences that were mentioned elsewhere, such as the lack of the `goto` statement and the `sizeof` operator, are not repeated here.

Local Variable Declarations

A feature that Java has borrowed from C++ is the ability to declare and initialize local variables anywhere in a method body or other block of code. Declarations and their initializers no longer have to be the first statements in any block—you can declare them where it is convenient and fits well with the structure of your code.

Don't let this freedom make you sloppy, however! For someone reading your program, it is nice to have variable declarations grouped together in one place. As a rule of thumb, put your declarations at the top of the block, unless you have some good organizational reason for putting them elsewhere.

Forward References

For compiler efficiency, C requires that variables and functions must be defined, or at least declared, before they can be used or called. That is, forward references are not allowed in C. Java does not make this restriction, and by lifting it, it also does away with the whole concept of a variable or function declaration that is separate from the definition.

Java allows very flexible forward references. A method may refer to a variable or another method of its class, regardless of where in the current class the variable or method are defined. Similarly, it may refer to any class, regardless of where in the current file (or outside of the file) that class is defined. The only place that forward references are not allowed is in variable initialization. A variable initializer (for local variables, class variables, or instance variables) may not refer to other variables that have not yet been declared and initialized.

Method Overloading

A technique that Java borrows from C++ is called *method overloading*. Overloaded methods are methods that have the same name, but have different signatures. In other words, they return different values or they take different types of arguments, a different number of arguments, or the same type of arguments in different positions in the argument list. Method overloading is commonly used in Java to define a number of related functions with the same name, but different arguments. Overloaded methods usually perform the same basic operation, but allow the programmer to specify arguments in different ways depending on what is convenient in a given situation. Method overloading is discussed in more detail in the next chapter.

The void Keyword

The `void` keyword is used in Java, as in C, to indicate that a function returns no value. (As we will see in the next section, constructor methods are an exception to this rule.)

Java differs from C (and is similar to C++) in that methods that take no arguments are declared with empty parentheses, not with the `void` keyword. Also unlike C, Java does not have any `void *` type, nor does it require a `(void)` cast in order to correctly ignore the result returned by a call to a non-`void` method.

Modifiers

Java defines a number of modifier keywords that may be applied to variable and/or method declarations to provide additional information or place restrictions on the variable or method:

`final`
: The `final` keyword is a modifier that may be applied to classes, methods, and variables. It has a similar, but not identical meaning in each case. A `final` class may never be subclassed. A `final` method may never be overridden. A `final` variable may never have its value set. This modifier is discussed in more detail in the next chapter.

`native`
: `native` is a modifier that may be applied to method declarations. It indicates that the method is implemented elsewhere in C, or in some other platform-dependent fashion. A `native` method should have a semicolon in place of its body.

`synchronized`
: We saw the `synchronized` keyword in a previous section where it was a statement that marked a critical section of code. The same keyword can also be used as a modifier for class or instance methods. It indicates that the method modifies the internal state of the class or the internal state of an instance of the class in a way that is not thread-safe. Before running a `synchronized` class method, Java obtains a lock on the class, to ensure that no

other threads can be modifiying the class concurrently. Before running a `synchronized` instance method, Java obtains a lock on the instance that invoked the method, ensuring that no other thread can be modifying the object at the same time.

`transient`

The `transient` keyword is a modifier that may be applied to instance variables in a class. It specifies that the variable is not part of the persistent state of the object. This modifier is not currently used by any part of Java. Eventually it will be used to indicate things like scratch variables that are not part of an object's state, and thus never need to be saved to disk.

`volatile`

The `volatile` keyword is a modifier that may be applied to variables. It specifies that the variable changes asynchronously (e.g., it may be a memory-mapped hardware register on a peripheral device), and that the compiler should not attempt to perform optimizations with it. For example, it should read the variable's value from memory every time and not attempt to save a copy of it in a register.

No Structures or Unions

Java does not support C `struct` or `union` types. Note, however that a `class` is essentially the same thing as a `struct`, but with more features. And you can simulate the important features of a `union` by subclassing.

No Enumerated Types

Java does not support the C `enum` keyword for defining types that consist of one of a specified number of named values. This is somewhat surprising for a strongly-typed language like Java. Enumerated types can be partially simulated with the use of `static final` constant values.

No Bitfields

Java does not support the C ability to define variables that occupy particular bits within `struct` and `union` types. This feature of C is usually only used to interface directly to hardware devices, which is never necessary with Java's platform-independent programming model.

No typedef

Java does not support the C `typedef` keyword to define aliases for type names. Java has a much simpler type naming scheme than C does, however, and so there is no need for something like `typedef`.

No Variable-Length Argument Lists

Java does not allow you to define methods that take a variable number of arguments, as C does. This is because Java is a strongly typed language and there is no way to do appropriate type checking for a method with variable arguments. Method overloading allows you to simulate C "varargs" functions for simple cases, but there is no general replacement for this C feature.

Classes and Objects in Java

Java is an *object-oriented* language. "Object-oriented" is a term that has become so commonly used as to have practically no concrete meaning. This section explains just what "object-oriented" means for Java. It covers:

- Classes and objects in Java
- Creating objects
- Garbage collection to free up unused objects
- The difference between class (or static) variables and instance variables, and the difference between class (or static) methods and instance methods
- Extending a class to create a subclass
- Overiding class methods and dynamic method lookup
- Abstract classes
- Interface types and their implementation by classes

If you are a C++ programmer, or have other object-oriented programming experience, many of the concepts in this list should be familiar to you. If you do not have object-oriented experiece, don't fear: This section assumes no knowledge of object-oriented concepts.

We saw in the last section that close analogies can be drawn between Java and C. Unfortunately for C++ programmers, the same is not true for Java and C++. Java uses object-oriented programming concepts that are familiar to C++ programmers, and it even borrows from C++ syntax in a number of places, but the analogies between

Java and C++ are not nearly as strong as those between Java and C.* C++ programmers should forget all they know about C++ and read this section carefully, as beginners, to learn Java without the preconceptions that might come with knowing C++.

Introduction to Classes and Objects

A *class* is a collection of data and methods that operate on that data.† The data and methods, taken together, usually serve to define the contents and capabilities of some kind of *object.*

For example, a circle can be described by the x, y position of its center and by its radius. There are a number of things we can do with circles: compute their circumference, compute their area, check whether points are inside them, and so on. Each circle is different (i.e., has a different center or radius), but as a *class*, circles have certain intrinsic properties that we can capture in a definition. Example 3-1 shows how we could partially define the class of circles in Java. Notice that the class definition contains data and methods (procedures) within the same pair of curly brackets.‡

Example 3-1: The class of circles, partially captured in Java code

```
public class Circle {
   public double x, y;            // the coordinates of the center
   public double r;               // the radius

   // Methods that return the circumference and area of the circle
   public double circumference() { return 2 * 3.14159 * r; }
   public double area() { return 3.14159 * r*r; }
}
```

Objects Are Instances of a Class

Now that we've defined (at least partially) the class `Circle`, we want to do something with it. We can't do anything with the class of circles itself—we need a particular circle to work with. We need an *instance* of the class, a single circle object.

By defining the `Circle` class in Java, we have created a new data type. We can declare variables of that type:

```
Circle c;
```

But this variable `c` is simply a name that *refers to* a circle object; it is not an object itself. In Java, all objects must be created dynamically. This is almost always done with the `new` keyword:

```
Circle c;
c = new Circle();
```

*As we'll see, Java supports garbage collection and dynamic method lookup. This actually makes it a closer relative, beneath its layer of C-like syntax, to languages like Smalltalk than to C++.

†A *method* is the object-oriented term for a procedure or a function. You'll see it used a lot in this book. Treat it as a synonym for "procedure."

‡C++ programmers should note that methods go inside the class definition in Java, not outside with the a `::` operator as they usually do in C++.

Now we have created an instance of our `Circle` class—a circle object—and have assigned it to the variable `c`, which is of type `Circle`.

Accessing Object Data

Now that we've created an object, we can use its data fields. The syntax should be familiar to C programmers:

```
Circle c = new Circle();
// initialize our circle to have center (2, 2) and radius 1.0.
c.x = 2.0;
c.y = 2.0;
c.r = 1.0;
```

Using Object Methods

This is where things get interesting! To access the methods of an object, we use the same syntax as accessing the data of an object:

```
Circle c = new Circle();
double a;
c.r = 2.5;
a = c.area();
```

Take a look at that last line. We did not say:

```
a = area(c);
```

We said:

```
a = c.area();
```

This is why it is called "object-oriented" programming; the object is the focus here, not the function call. This is probably the single most important feature of the object-oriented paradigm.

Note that we don't have to pass an argument to `c.area()`. The object we are operating on, `c`, is implicit in the syntax. Take a look at Example 3-1 again: you'll notice the same thing in the definition of the `area()` method—it doesn't take an argument. It is implicit in the language that a method operates on an instance of the class within which it is defined. Thus our `area()` method can use the `r` field of the class freely—it is understood that it is referring to the radius of whatever `Circle` instance invokes the method.

How It Works

What's going on here? How can a method that takes no arguments know what data to operate on? In fact, the `area()` method does have an argument! `area()` is implemented with an implicit argument that is not shown in the method declaration. The implicit argument is named `this`, and refers to "this object"—the `Circle` object through which the method is invoked. `this` is often called the "this pointer."*

The implicit `this` argument is not shown in method signatures because it is usually not needed—whenever a Java method accesses the fields in its class, it is implied that it is accessing fields in the object referred to by the `this` argument. The same is

* "this pointer" is C++ terminology. Since Java does not support pointers, I prefer the term "this reference."

true, as we'll see, when a method in a class invokes other methods in the class—it is implicit that the methods are being invoked for the `this` object.

We can use the `this` keyword explicitly when we want to make explicit that a method is accessing its own variables and/or methods. For example, we could rewrite the `area()` method like this:

```
public double area() { return 3.14159 * this.r * this.r; }
```

In a method this simple, it is not necessary to be explicit. In more complicated cases, however, you may find that it increases the clarity of your code to use an explicit `this` where it is not strictly required.

An instance where the `this` keyword *is* required is when a method argument or a local variable in a method has the same name as one of the fields of the class. In this case, you must use `this` to access the field. If you used the field name alone, you would end up accessing the argument or local variable with the same name. We'll see examples of this in the next section.

Object Creation

Take another look at how we've been creating our circle object:

```
Circle c = new Circle();
```

What are those parentheses doing there? They make it look like we're calling a function! In fact, that is exactly what we're doing. Every class in Java has at least one *constructor* method, which has the same name as the class. The purpose of a constructor is to perform any necessary initialization for the new object. Since we didn't define one for our `Circle` class, Java gave us a default constructor that takes no arguments and performs no special initialization.

The way it works is this: The `new` keyword creates a new dynamic instance of the class—i.e., it allocates the new object. The constructor method is then called, passing the new object implicitly (a `this` reference, as we saw above), and passing the arguments specified between parentheses explicitly.

Defining a Constructor

There is some obvious initialization we could do for our circle objects, so let's define a constructor. Example 3-2 shows a constructor that lets us specify the initial values for the center and radius of our new `Circle` object. The example also shows a use of the `this` keyword, as described in the previous section.

Example 3-2: A constructor for the circle class

```
public class Circle {
  public double x, y, r;    // the center and the radius

  // Our constructor method.
  public Circle(double x, double y, double r)
  {
    this.x = x;
    this.y = y;
    this.r = r;
  }
```

Example 3-2: A constructor for the circle class (continued)

```
    public double circumference() { return 2 * 3.14159 * r; }
    public double area() { return 3.14159 * r*r; }
}
```

With the old, default constructor, we had to write code like this:

```
Circle c = new Circle();
c.x = 1.414;
c.y = -1.0;
c.r = .25;
```

With this new constructor the initialization becomes part of the object creation step:

```
Circle c = new Circle(1.414, -1.0, .25);
```

There are two important notes about naming and declaring constructors:

- The constructor name is always the same as the class name.
- The return type is implicitly an instance of the class. No return type is specified in constructor declarations, nor is the `void` keyword used. The `this` object is implicitly returned; a constructor should not use a `return` statement to return a value.

Multiple Constructors

Sometimes you'll want to be able to initialize an object in a number of different ways, depending on what is most convenient in a particular circumstance. For example, we might want to be able to initialize the radius of a circle without initializing the center, or we might want to initialize a circle to have the same center and radius as another circle, or we might want to initialize all the fields to default values. Doing this is no problem: A class can have any number of constructor methods. Example 3-3 shows how.

Example 3-3: Multiple circle constructors

```
public class Circle {
    public double x, y, r;

    public Circle(double x, double y, double r) {
        this.x = x; this.y = y; this.r = r;
    }
    public Circle(double r) { x = 0.0; y = 0.0; this.r = r; }
    public Circle(Circle c) { x = c.x; y = c.y; r = c.r; }
    public Circle() { x = 0.0; y = 0.0; r = 1.0; }

    public double circumference() { return 2 * 3.14159 * r; }
    public double area() { return 3.14159 * r*r; }
}
```

Method Overloading

The surprising thing in this example (not so surprising if you're a C++ programmer) is that all the constructor methods have the same name! So how can the compiler tell them apart? The way that you and I tell them apart is that the four methods take different arguments and are useful in different circumstances. The compiler tells them apart in the same way. In Java, a method is distinguished by its name, return type, and by the number, type, and position of its arguments. This is not limited to constructor methods—any two methods are not the same unless they have the same name, the same return type, and the same number of arguments of the same type passed at the same position in the argument list. When you call a method and there is more than one method with the same name, the compiler automatically picks the one that matches the data types of the arguments you are passing.

Defining methods with the same name and different argument or return types is called *method overloading*. It can be a convenient technique, as long as you only give methods the same name when they perform similar functions on slightly different forms of input data, or when they return slightly different forms of output data. Don't confuse method overloading with *method overriding*, which we'll discuss later.

this Again

There is a specialized use of the `this` keyword that arises when a class has multiple constructors—it can be used from a constructor to invoke one of the other constructors of the same class. So we could rewrite the additional constructors from Example 3-3 in terms of the first one like this:

```
public Circle(double x, double y, double r) {
  this.x = x; this.y = y; this.r = r;
}
public Circle(double r) { this(0.0, 0.0, r); }
public Circle(Circle c) { this(c.x, c.y, c.r); }
public Circle() { this(0.0, 0.0, 1.0); }
```

Here, the `this()` call refers to whatever constructor of the class takes the specified type of arguments. This would be a more impressive example, of course, if the first constructor that we were invoking did a more significant amount of initialization, as it might, for example, if we were writing a more complicated class.

There is a very important restriction on this `this` syntax: it may only appear as the first statement in a constructor. It may, of course, be followed by any additional initialization that a particular version of the constructor needs to do. The reason for this restriction involves the automatic invocation of superclass constructor methods, which we'll explore later in this chapter.

Class Variables

In our `Circle` class definition, we declared three "instance" variables: `x`, `y`, and `r`. Each instance of the class—each circle—has its own copy of these three variables. These variables are like the fields of a `struct` in C—each instance of the `struct` has a copy of the fields. Sometimes, though, we want a variable of which there is only one copy—something like a global variable in C.

The problem is that Java doesn't allow global variables. (Actually, those in the know consider this is a feature!) Every variable in Java must be declared inside a class. So Java uses the `static` keyword to indicate that a particular variable is a *class variable* rather than an *instance variable*. That is, that there is only one copy of the variable, associated with the class, rather than many copies of the variable associated with each instance of the class. The one copy of the variable exists regardless of the number of instances of the class that are created—it exists and can be used even if the class is never actually instantiated.

This kind of variable, declared with the `static` keyword is often called a *static variable*. I prefer (and recommend) the name "class variable" because it is easily distinguished from its opposite, "instance variable." We'll use both terms in this book.

An Example

As an example (a somewhat contrived one), suppose that while developing the `Circle` class we wanted to do some testing on it and determine how much it gets used. One way to do this would be to count the number of `Circle` objects that are instantiated. To do this we obviously need a variable associated with the class, rather than with any particular instance. Example 3-4 shows how we can do it—we declare a `static` variable and increment it each time we create a `Circle`.

Example 3-4: Static variable example

```
public class Circle {
    static int num_circles = 0;          // class variable: how many circles created
    public double x, y, r;               // instance vars: the center and the radius

    public Circle(double x, double y, double r) {
        this.x = x; this.y = y; this.r = r;
        num_circles++;
    }
    public Circle(double r) { this(0.0, 0.0, r); }
    public Circle(Circle c) { this(c.x, c.y, c.r); }
    public Circle() { this(0.0, 0.0, 1.0); }

    public double circumference() { return 2 * 3.14159 * r; }
    public double area() { return 3.14159 * r*r; }
}
```

Accessing Class Variables

Now that we are keeping track of the number of `Circle` objects created, how can we access this information? Because `static` variables are associated with the class rather than with an instance, we access them through the class rather than through the instance. Thus, we might write:*

```
System.out.println("Number of circles created: " + Circle.num_circles);
```

Notice that in our definition of the constructor method in Example 3-4, we just used `num_circles` instead of `Circle.num_circles`. We're allowed to do this within the class definition of `Circle` itself. Anywhere else, though, we must use the class name as well.

---

*Recall that `System.out.println()` prints a line of text, and that the string concatenation operator, +, converts non-string types to strings as necessary.

Global Variables?

Earlier we said that Java does not support global variables. In a sense, though, `Circle.num_circles` behaves just like one. What is different from a global variable in C is that there is no possibility of name conflicts. If we use some other class with a class variable named `num_circles`, there won't be a "collision" between these two "global" variables, because they must both be referred to by their class names. Since each class variable must be part of a class and must be referred to with its class name, each has a unique name. Furthermore, each class has a unique name because, as we saw in Section 2, *How Java Differs from C*, it is part of a package with a unique name.

Constants: Another Class Variable Example

Let's try a less forced example of why you might want to use a class variable with the `Circle` class. When computing the area and circumference of circles, we use the value π. Since we use the value frequently, we don't want to keep typing out 3.14159, so we'll define it as a class variable that has a convenient name:

```
public class Circle {
    public static final double PI = 3.14159265358979323846;
    public double x, y, r;
    // ... etc....
}
```

Besides the `static` keyword that we've already seen, we use the `final` keyword, which means that this variable can never have its value changed. This prevents you from doing something stupid like:

```
Circle.PI = 4;
```

which would tend to give you some pretty square-looking circles.

The Java compiler is smart about variables declared `static` and `final`—it knows that they have constant values. So when you write code like this:

```
double circumference = 2 * Circle.PI * radius;
```

the compiler precomputes the value `2 * Circle.PI`, instead of leaving it for the interpreter.

Java does not have a preprocessor with a C-style `#define` directive. `static final` variables are Java's substitute for C's `#define`'d constants. Note that the C convention of capitalizing constants has been carried over into Java.

Class Methods

Let's define a new method in our `Circle` class. This one tests whether a specified point falls within the defined circle:

```
public class Circle {
    double x, y, r;

    // is point (a,b) inside this circle?
    public boolean isInside(double a, double b)
    {
        double dx = a - x;
        double dy = b - y;
```

```
        double distance = Math.sqrt(dx*dx + dy*dy);
        if (distance < r) return true;
        else return false;
    }
        .
        . // Other methods omitted
        .
}
```

What's this `Math.sqrt()` thing? It looks like a method call and, given its name and its context, we can guess that it is computing a square root. But the method calls we've discussed are done through an object. `Math` isn't the name of an object that we've declared, and there aren't any global objects in Java, so this must be a kind of method call that we haven't seen before.

Classes and Objects

static Methods

What's going on here is that `Math` is the name of a class. `sqrt()` is the name of a *class method* (or static method) defined in `Math`. It differs from the *instance methods*, such as `area()` in `Circle`, that we've seen so far.

Class methods are like class variables in a number of ways:

- Class methods are declared with the `static` keyword.
- Class methods are often referred to as "static methods."
- Class methods are invoked through the class rather than through an instance. (Although within the class they may be invoked by method name alone.)
- Class methods are the closest Java comes to "global" methods. Because they must be referred to by the class name, there is no danger of name conflicts.

No this

Class methods differ from instance methods in one important way: they are not passed an implicit `this` reference. Thus, these `this`-less methods are not associated with any instance of the class and may not refer to any instance variables or invoke instance methods.

Since class methods are not passed a `this` reference, and are not invoked through an object, they are the closest thing that Java offers to the "normal" C procedures that you may be accustomed to, and may therefore seem familiar and comforting. If you're sick and tired of this object-oriented business, it is perfectly possible to write complete Java programs using only class methods, although this does defeat an important purpose of using the language!

But don't think that class methods are somehow cheating—there are perfectly good reasons to declare a method `static`. And indeed, there are classes like `Math` that declare all their methods (and variables) `static`. Since `Math` is a collection of functions that operate on floating-point numbers, which are a primitive type, there are no objects involved, and no need for instance methods. `System` is another class that defines only class methods—it provides a varied collection of system functions for which there is no appropriate object framework.

A Class Method for Circles

Example 3-5 shows two (overloaded) definitions of a method for our `Circle` class. One is an instance method and one is a class method.

Example 3-5: A class method and an instance method

```
public class Circle {
  public double x, y, r;

  // an instance method. Returns the bigger of two circles.
  public Circle bigger(Circle c) {
    if (c.r > r) return c; else return this;
  }
  // a class method. Returns the bigger of two circles
  public static Circle bigger(Circle a, Circle b) {
    if (a.r > b.r) return a; else return b;
  }
    .
    . // other methods omitted here.
    .
}
```

You would invoke the instance method like this:

```
Circle a = new Circle(2.0);
Circle b = new Circle(3.0);
Circle c = a.bigger(b);          // or, b.bigger(a);
```

And you would invoke the class method like this:

```
Circle a = new Circle(2.0);
Circle b = new Circle(3.0);
Circle c = Circle.bigger(a,b);
```

Neither of these is the "correct" way to implement this method. One or the other will seem more natural, depending on circumstances.

A Mystery Explained

Now that we understand class variables, instance variables, class methods, and instance methods, we are in a position to explore that mysterious method call we saw in our very first Java "Hello World" example:

```
System.out.println("Hello world!");
```

One hypothesis is that `println()` is a class method in a class named `out`, which is in a package named `System`. Syntactically, this is perfectly reasonable (except perhaps that class names always seem to be capitalized by convention, and `out` isn't capitalized). But if you look at the API documentation, you'll find that `System` is not a package name; it is the name of a class (which is in the `java.lang` package, by the way). Can you figure it out?

Here's the story: `System` is a class. It has a class variable named `out`. `out` refers to an object of type `PrintStream`. The object `System.out` has an instance method named `println()`. Mystery solved!

Static Initializers

Both class and instance variables can have initializers attached to their declarations. For example:

```
static int num_circles = 0;
float r = 1.0;
```

Class variables are initialized when the class is first loaded. Instance variables are initialized when an object is created.

Sometimes we need more complex initialization than is possible with these simple variable initializers. For instance variables, there are constructor methods, which are run when a new instance of the class is created. Java also allows you to write an initialization method for class variables. Such a method is called a *static initializer*.

The syntax of static initializers gets kind of bizarre. Consider that a static initializer is invoked automatically by the system when the class is loaded. Thus there are no meaningful arguments that can be passed to it (unlike the arguments we can pass to a constructor method when creating a new instance). There is also no value to return. So a static initializer has no arguments and no return value. Furthermore, it is not really necessary to give it a name, since the system calls the method automatically for us. What part of a method declaration is left? Just the `static` keyword and the curly brackets!

Classes and Objects

Example 3-6 shows a class declaration with a static initializer. Notice that the class contains a regular static variable initializer of the kind we've seen before, and also a static initializer—an arbitrary block of code between `{` and `}`.

Example 3-6: A static initializer

```
// We can draw the outline of a circle using trigonometric functions.
// Trigonometry is slow though, so we pre-compute a bunch of values
public class Circle {
  // Here are our static lookup tables, and their own simple initializers.
  static private double sines[] = new double[1000];
  static private double cosines[] = new double[1000];

  // Here's a static initializer "method" that fills them in.
  // Notice the lack of any method declaration!
  static {
    double x, delta_x;
    int i;
    delta_x = (Circle.PI/2)/(1000-1);
    for(i = 0; x = 0.0; i < 1000; i++, x += deltax) {
      sines[i] = Math.sin(x);
      cosines[i] = Math.cos(x);
    }
  }
    .
    . // The rest of the class omitted.
    .
}
```

The syntax gets even a little stranger than this. Java allows any number of static initializer blocks of code to appear within a class definition. What the compiler actually does is to internally produce a single class initialization routine that combines all the static variable initializers and all of the static initializer blocks of code, in the order that they appear in the class declaration. This single initialization procedure is run automatically, one time only, when the class is first loaded.

One common use of static initializers is for classes that implement `native` methods—i.e., methods written in C. The static initializer for such a class should call `System.load()` or `System.loadLibrary()` to read in the native library that implements these native methods.

Object Destruction

Now that we've seen how you can create and use objects, the next obvious question, a question that C and C++ programmers have been itching to have answered, is how do you destroy objects when they are no longer needed?

The answer is: You don't! Objects are not passed to any `free()` method, as allocated memory in C is. And there is no `delete` operator as there is in C++. Java takes care of object destruction for you, and lets you concentrate on other, more important things, like the algorithm you're working on.

Garbage Collection

The technique Java uses to get rid of objects once they are no longer needed is called *garbage collection*. It is a technique that has been around for years in languages such as Lisp. The Java interpreter knows what objects it has allocated. It can also figure out which variables refer to which objects, and which objects refer to which other objects. Thus, it can figure out when an allocated object is no longer referred to by any other object or variable. When it finds such an object, it knows that it can destroy it safely, and does so.

The Java garbage collector runs as a low-priority thread, and does most of its work when nothing else is going on. Generally, it runs during idle time while waiting for user input in the form of keystrokes or mouse events. The only time the garbage collector must run while something high-priority is going on (i.e., the only time it will actually slow down the system) is when the interpreter has run out of memory. This doesn't happen often because there is that low-priority thread cleaning things up in the background.

This scheme may sound extremely slow and wasteful of memory. Actually though, good garbage collectors can be surprisingly efficient. No, garbage collection will never be as efficient as explicit, well-written memory allocation and deallocation. But it does make programming a lot easier and less prone to bugs. And for most real-world programs, rapid development, lack of bugs, and easy maintenance are more important features than raw speed or memory efficiency.

Putting the Trash Out

What garbage collection means for your programs is that when you are done with an object, you can just forget about it—the garbage collector finds it and takes care of it. Example 3-7 shows an example.

Example 3-7: Leaving an object out for garbage collection

```
String processString(String s)
{
    // Create a StringBuffer object to process the string in
    StringBuffer b = new StringBuffer(s);

    // process it somehow

    // return it as a String.
    // Just forget about the StringBuffer object--
    //  it will be automatically garbage collected.
    return b.toString();
}
```

If you're a C or C++ programmer, conditioned to allocating and deallocating your own dynamic memory, you may at first feel a nagging sense of misgiving when you write procedures that allocate and then forget objects. You'll get used to it though, and even learn to love it!

There is an instance where you may want to take some action to help the garbage collection process along by "forgetting quickly." Example 3-8 explains.

Example 3-8: Forced forgetting of an object

```
public static void main(String argv[])
{
    int big_array[] = new int[100000];

    // do some computations with big_array and get a result
    int result = compute(big_array);

    // We no longer need big_array. It will get garbage collected when
    // there are no more references. Since big_array is a local variable,
    // it refers to the array until this method returns. But this
    // method doesn't return. So we've got to get rid of the reference
    // ourselves, just to help out the garbage collector.
    big_array = null;

    // loop forever, handling the user's input
    for(;;) handle_input();
}
```

Object Finalization

Just as a constructor method performs initialization for an object, a Java *finalizer* method performs finalization for an object.

Garbage collection automatically frees up the memory resources used by objects. But objects may hold other kinds of resources, such as file descriptors or sockets, as well. The garbage collector can't free these resources up for you, so you should write a finalizer method that takes care of things like closing open files, terminating network connections, and so on.

Example 3-9 shows the finalizer method from the Java FileOutputStream class. Note that a finalizer is an instance method (i.e., non-static), takes no arguments, returns no value (i.e., void), and must be named finalize().*

Example 3-9: A finalizer method

```
/**
 * Closes the stream when garbage is collected.
 * Checks the file descriptor first to make sure it is not already closed.
 */
protected void finalize() throws IOException {
    if (fd != null) close();
}
```

There are some additional things to be aware of about finalizers:

- If an object has a finalizer, that method is invoked before the system garbage collects the object.
- The Java interpreter may exit without garbage collecting all outstanding objects, so some finalizers may never be invoked. In this case, though, any outstanding resources are usually freed by the operating system.
- Java makes no guarantees about when garbage collection will occur, or what order objects will be collected in. Therefore, Java can make no guarantees about when a finalizer will be invoked, or in what order finalizers will be invoked, or what thread will execute finalizers.
- After a finalizer is invoked, objects are not freed right away. This is because a finalizer method may "resurrect" an object by storing the this pointer somewhere, so that the object once again has references. Thus, after finalize() is called, an object must once again be determined to be unreferenced before it can actually be garbage collected. Even if an object is "resurrected," the finalizer method is never invoked more than once.
- The finalizer shown in Example 3-9 declares that it may throw an exception (exceptions are described in detail in Section 2). If an uncaught exception actually occurs in a finalizer method, however, the exception is ignored by the system.

Subclasses and Inheritance

The Circle class we've defined is good for abstract mathematical manipulation. For some applications this is exactly what we need. For other applications, we want to be able to manipulate circles *and* draw them on the screen. This means we need a new class, GraphicCircle, that has all the functionality of Circle, but also has the ability to be drawn.

We want to implement GraphicCircle so that it can make use of the code we've already written for Circle. One way to do that is the following:

*C++ programmers, take note! Although Java constructor methods are named like C++ constructors, Java finalization methods are not named like C++ destructor methods.

```
public class GraphicCircle {
    public Circle c; // here's the mathematical circle
    // Here are the old methods
    public double area() { return c.area(); }
    public double circumference() { return c.circumference(); }

    // The new graphic variables and methods go here
    public Color outline, fill;
    public void draw(DrawWindow dw) { /* code omitted */ }
}
```

This approach would work, but it is not particularly elegant. The problem is that we have to write stubs for methods like `area()` and `circumference()` that have nothing to do with drawing circles. It would be nice if we didn't have to do this.

Extending a Class

In fact, we don't have to do it this way. Java allows us to define `GraphicCircle` as an extension, or *subclass* of `Circle`. Example 3-10 shows how. Note that this example assumes we have two other classes of objects defined: `Color`, which represents a color, and `DrawWindow`, a class that has the window into which drawing is done and that defines the primitive methods to do the drawing.

Example 3-10: Subclassing a class

```
public class GraphicCircle extends Circle {
    // we automatically inherit the variables and methods of
    // Circle, so we only have to put the new stuff here.
    // We've omitted the GraphicCircle constructor, for now.
    Color outline, fill;
    public void draw(DrawWindow dw) {
        dw.drawCircle(x, y, r, outline, fill);
    }
}
```

The `extends` keyword tells Java that `GraphicCircle` is a subclass of `Circle`, and that it *inherits* the variables and methods of that class.* The definition of the `draw()` method shows variable inheritance—this method uses the `Circle` variables `x`, `y`, and `r` as if they were defined right in `GraphicCircle` itself.

`GraphicCircle` also inherits the methods of `Circle`. Thus, if we have a `GraphicCircle` object referred to by variable `gc`, we can say:

```
double area = gc.area();
```

This works just as if the `area()` method were defined in `GraphicCircle` itself.

Another feature of subclassing is that every `GraphicCircle` object is also a perfectly legal `Circle` object. Thus, if `gc` refers to a `GraphicCircle` object, we can assign it to a `Circle` variable and forget all about its extra graphic capabilities:

```
Circle c = gc;
```

*Except for the `private` variables and methods. We'll talk about `private` fields of a class later. C++ programmers should note that `extends` is the Java equivalent of the `:` operator in C++—both indicate the superclass of a class.

final classes

When a class is declared with the `final` modifier, it means that it cannot be extended or subclassed. `java.lang.System` is an example of a `final` class. Declaring a class `final` prevents unwanted extensions to the class. But it also allows the compiler to make some optimizations when invoking the methods of a class. We'll explore this in more detail when we talk about method overriding later in this section.

Superclasses, Object, and the Class Hierarchy

In our example, `GraphicCircle` is a subclass of `Circle`. We can also say that `Circle` is the *superclass* of `GraphicCircle`. The superclass of a class is specified in its `extends` clause:

```
public class GraphicCircle extends Circle { ... }
```

Every class you define has a superclass. If you do not specify the superclass with an `extends` clause, the superclass is the class `Object`. `Object` is a special class for a couple of reasons:

- It is the only class that does not have a superclass
- The methods defined by `Object` can be called by any Java object

Because every class has a superclass, classes in Java form a *class hierarchy*, which can be represented as a tree with `Object` at its root. Figure 3-1 shows a class hierarchy diagram which includes our `Circle` and `GraphicCircle` classes, as well as some of the standard classes from the Java API.

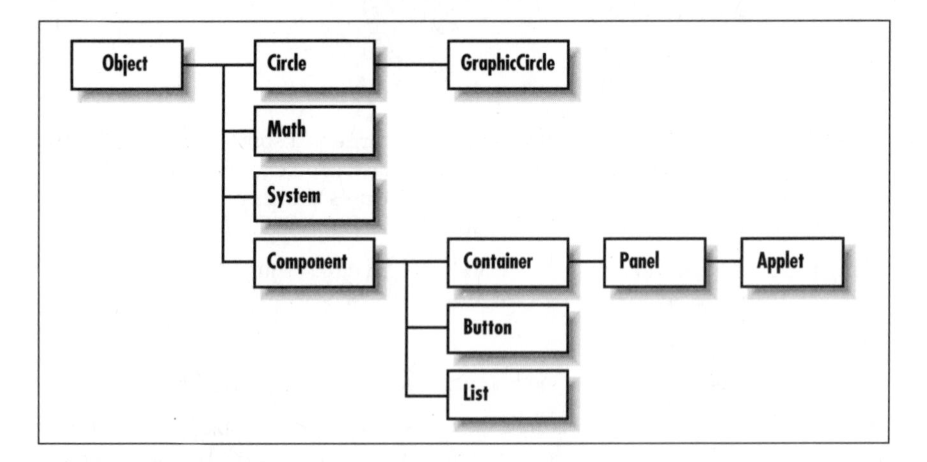

Figure 3-1: A class hierarchy diagram

The complete class hierarchy for the Java API is diagrammed in the figures of Part IV, *API Quick Reference*.

Subclass Constructors

In Example 3-10 we left out the constructor method for our new `GraphicCircle` class. Let's implement that now. Here's one way:

```
public GraphicCircle(double x, double y, double r,
            Color outline, Color fill)
  {
    this.x = x;
    this.y = y;
    this.r = r;
    this.outline = outline;
    this.fill = fill;
  }
```

This constructor relies on the fact that `GraphicCircle` inherits all of the variables of `Circle` and simply initializes those variables itself. But this duplicates the code of the `Circle` constructor, and if `Circle` did more elaborate initialization, it could become quite wasteful. What we want is a way of calling a `Circle` constructor from within our `GraphicCircle` constructor. Example 3-11 shows how we can do this.

Classes and Objects

Example 3-11: Invoking a superclass's constructor

```
public GraphicCircle(double x, double y, double r,
            Color outline, Color fill)
  {
    super(x, y, r);
    this.outline = outline;
    this.fill = fill;
  }
```

`super` is a reserved word in Java. One of its uses is that shown in the example—to invoke the constructor method of a superclass. Its use is analogous to the use of the `this` keyword to invoke one constructor method of a class from within another. Using `super` to invoke a constructor is subject to the same restrictions as using `this` to invoke a constructor:

- `super` may only be used in this way within a constructor method.
- The call to the superclass constructor must appear as the first statement within the constructor method. It must appear even before variable declarations.

Constructor Chaining

When you define a class, Java guarantees that the class's constructor method is called whenever an instance of that class is created. It also guarantees that the constructor is called when an instance of any subclass is created. In order to guarantee this second point, Java must ensure that every constructor method calls its superclass constructor method. If the first statement in a constructor is not an explicit call to a constructor of the superclass with the `super` keyword, then Java implicitly inserts the call `super()`—that is, it calls the superclass constructor with no arguments. If the superclass does not have a constructor that takes no arguments, this causes a compilation error.

There is one exception to the rule that Java invokes `super()` implicitly if you do not do so explicitly. If the first line of a constructor is a call to another constructor in the same class using the `this()` syntax that we saw earlier, Java does not implicitly call the superclass constructor. But note that if the constructor invoked with the `this()` syntax does not invoke `super()` (or invoke `this()` again) explicitly, Java does invoke `super()` implicitly. So while constructor methods within a class may invoke each other, eventually one of them must invoke (explicitly or implicitly) the superclass constructor method.

Consider what happens when we create a new instance of the `GraphicCircle` class. First, the `GraphicCircle` constructor shown in Example 3-11 is invoked. This constructor explicitly invokes a `Circle` constructor and that `Circle` constructor implicitly calls `super()` to invoke the constructor of its superclass, `Object`. The body of the `Object` constructor runs first, followed by the body of the `Circle` constructor, and finally followed by the body of the `GraphicCircle` constructor.

What this all means is that constructor calls are "chained"—any time an object is created, a sequence of constructor methods are invoked, from subclass to superclass on up to `Object` at the root of the class hierarchy. Because a superclass constructor is always invoked as the first statement of its subclass constructor, the body of the `Object` constructor always runs first, followed by the body of its subclass, and on down the class hierarchy to the class that is being instantiated.

The Default Constructor

There is one missing piece in the description of constructor chaining above. If a constructor does not invoke a superclass constructor, Java does so implicitly. But what if a class is declared without a constructor? In this case, Java implicitly adds a constructor to the class. This default constructor does nothing but invoke the superclass constructor.

For example, if we did not declare a constructor for the `GraphicCircle` class, Java would have implicitly inserted this constructor:

```
public GraphicCircle() { super(); }
```

It can be confusing when Java implicitly calls a constructor or inserts a constructor definition into a class—something is happening that does not appear in your code! Therefore, it is good coding style, whenever you rely on an implicit superclass constructor call or on a default constructor, to insert a comment noting this fact. Your comments might look like those in the following example:

```
class A {
  int i;
  public A() {
    // implicit call to super(); here.
    i = 3;
  }
}

class B extends A {
  // default constructor: public B() { super(); }
}
```

Finalizer Chaining?

You might assume that since Java chains constructor methods that it also automatically chains the finalizer methods for an object. In other words, you may think that the finalizer method of a class automatically invokes the finalizer of its superclass. In fact, Java does *not* do this. In practice, finalizer methods are relatively rare, and the need for finalizer chaining rarely arises. If a class B with a finalizer method is a subclass of a class A with its own finalizer method, then B's finalizer should be sure to invoke A's finalizer, explicitly creating a chain of finalizers. This is a little tricky, since finalizers always have the same name (finalize()), and we haven't yet learned how to invoke a method in the superclass when that method is also defined in the subclass. We'll return to the issue of finalizer chaining when we learn how.

Shadowed Variables

Suppose that our GraphicCircle class has a new variable that specifies the resolution, in dots per inch, of the DrawWindow object in which it is going to be drawn. And further, suppose that it names that new variable r:

```
public class GraphicCircle extends Circle {
  Color outline, fill;
  float r; // New variable. Resolution in dots-per-inch.
  public GraphicCircle(double x, double y, double radius, Color o, Color f) {
    super(x, y, radius); outline = o; fill = f;
  }
  public void setResolution(float resolution) { r = resolution; }
  public void draw(DrawWindow dw) { dw.drawCircle(x, y, r, outline, fill); }
}
```

Now, with this resolution variable declared, when we use the variable r in the GraphicCircle class, we are no longer referring to the radius of the circle. The resolution variable r in GraphicCircle *shadows* the radius variable r in Circle.*

So, how can we refer to the radius variable defined in the Circle class when we need it? Recall that using a variable, such as r, in the class in which it is defined is shorthand for:

```
this.r // refers to the GraphicCircle resolution variable
```

As you might guess, you can refer to a variable r defined in the superclass like this:

```
super.r // refers to the Circle radius variable.
```

Another way you can do this is to cast this to the appropriate class and then access the variable:

```
((Circle) this).r
```

This cast is exactly what the super keyword does when used like this. You can use this casting technique when you need to refer to a shadowed variable defined in a class that is not the immediate superclass. For example, if C is a subclass of B, which

*This is a contrived example, of course—we could simply rename the variable and avoid the issue.

is a subclass of A, and class C shadows a variable x that is also defined in classes A and B, then you can refer to these different variables from class C as follows:

```
x                  // variable x in class C
this.x             // variable x in class C
super.x            // variable x in class B
((B)this).x        // variable x in class B
((A)this).x        // variable x in class A
super.super.x      // illegal; does not refer to x in class A.
```

Note that you cannot refer to a shadowed variable x in the superclass of a superclass with super.super.x. Java does not recognize this syntax.

Shadowed Methods?

Just as a variable defined in one class can shadow a variable with the same name in a superclass, you might expect that a method in one class could shadow a method with the same name (and same arguments) in a superclass. In a sense, they do: "shadowed" methods are called overridden methods. But method overriding is significantly different than variable shadowing; it is discussed in the sections that follow.

Overriding Methods

When a class defines a method using the same name, return type, and arguments as a method in its superclass, the method in the class *overrides* the method in the superclass. When the method is invoked for an object of the class, it is the new definition of the method that is called, not the superclass' old definition.

Method overriding is an important and useful technique in object-oriented programming. Suppose we define a subclass Ellipse of our Circle class.* Then it would be important for Ellipse to override the area() and circumference() methods of Circle. Ellipse would have to implement new versions of these functions because the formulas that apply to circles don't work for ellipses.

Before we go any further with the discussion of method overriding, be sure that you understand the difference between method overriding and method overloading, which we discussed earlier. As you probably recall, method overloading refers to the practice of defining multiple methods (in the same class) with the same name but with differing argument lists or return types. This is very different from method overriding, and it is important not to get them confused!

Overriding Is Not Shadowing

Although Java treats the variables and methods of a class analogously in many ways, method overriding is not like variable shadowing at all: You can refer to shadowed variables simply by casting an object to the appropriate type. You cannot invoke overridden methods with this technique, however. Example 3-12 illustrates this crucial difference.

*This is admittedly a strange thing to do, since, mathematically, a circle is a kind of ellipse, and not the other way around. Nevertheless, it is a useful example here.

Example 3-12: Method overriding vs. variable shadowing

```
class A {
  int i = 1;
  int f() { return i; }
}

class B extends A {
  int i = 2;                    // shadows variable i in class A.
  int f() { return -i; }        // overrides method f in class A.
}

public class override_test {
  public static void main(String args[]) {
    B b = new B();
    System.out.println(b.i);        // refers to B.i; prints 2.
    System.out.println(b.f());      // refers to B.f(); prints -2

    A a = (A) b;                    // cast b to an instance of class A.
    System.out.println(a.i);        // now refers to A.i; prints 1;
    System.out.println(a.f());      // still refers to B.f(); prints -2;
  }
}
```


While this difference between method overriding and variable shadowing may seem surprising at first, a little thought makes the purpose clear. Suppose we have a bunch of `Circle` and `Ellipse` (a subclass of `Circle`) objects that we are manipulating. To keep track of the circles and ellipses, we store them in an array of type `Circle[]`, casting all the `Ellipse` objects to `Circle` objects before we store them. Then, when we loop through the elements of this array, we don't have to know or care whether the element is actually a `Circle` or an `Ellipse`. What we do care very much about, however, is that the correct value is computed when we invoke the `area()` method of any element of the array. That is, we don't want to use the formula for the area of a circle when the object is actually an ellipse!

Seen in this context, it is not surprising at all that method overriding is handled differently by Java than variable shadowing.

final Methods

If a method is declared `final`, it means that the method declaration is the "final" one—that it cannot be overridden. All `static` methods and `private` methods (which we haven't learned about yet) are implicitly final, as are all methods of a `final` class. If a method is explicitly or implicitly `final`, the compiler may perform certain optimizations on it, as we'll see below.

Dynamic Method Lookup

If we have an array of `Circle` and `Ellipse` objects, how does the compiler know to call the `Circle area()` method or the `Ellipse area()` method for any given item in the array? The compiler does not know this; it can't. The compiler knows that it does not know, however, and produces code that uses "dynamic method lookup" at run-time. The Java interpreter does know which objects in the array are of class `Circle` and which are of class `Ellipse`, so it is able to determine the appropriate `area()` method to call for each of the objects.*

Dynamic method lookup is fast, but it is not as fast as invoking a method directly. Fortunately, there are a number of cases in which Java does not need to use dynamic method lookup. `static` methods cannot be overridden, so they are always invoked directly. `private` methods (which we haven't learned about yet) are not inherited by subclasses and so cannot be overridden by subclasses; this means the Java compiler can safely invoke them without dynamic method lookup as well. Finally, `final` methods and methods in `final` classes are also invoked directly. These `static`, `final`, and `private` methods that can be invoked directly are also candidates for inlining—i.e., if the methods are short, the compiler may simply insert the method body into the code rather than inserting a call to the method.

Invoking an Overridden Method

We've seen the important differences between method overriding and variable shadowing. Nevertheless, the Java syntax for invoking an overridden method is very similar to the syntax for accessing a shadowed variable: both use the `super` keyword. Example 3-13 illustrates this.

Example 3-13: Invoking an overridden method

```
class A {
  int i = 1;
  int f() { return i; }           // A very simple method
}
class B extends A {
  int i;                          // This variable shadows i in A.
  int f() {                       // This method overrides f() in A.
    i = super.i + 1;              // It retrieves A.i this way.
    return super.f() + i;         // And it invokes A.f() this way.
  }
}
```

Recall that when you use `super` to refer to a shadowed variable, it is the same as casting `this` to the superclass type and accessing the variable through that. On the other hand, using `super` to invoke an overridden method is not the same as casting `this`. In this case, `super` has the special purpose of turning off dynamic method lookup and invoking the specific method that the superclass defines or inherits.

In Example 3-13 we use `super` to invoke an overridden method that is actually defined in the immediate superclass. `super` also works perfectly well to invoke overridden methods that are defined further up the class hierarchy. This is because the overridden method is inherited by the immediate superclass, and so the `super` syntax does in fact refer to the correct method. To make this more concrete, sup-

*C++ programmers should note that dynamic method lookup is what C++ does for `virtual` functions. A very important difference between Java and C++ is that Java does not have a `virtual` keyword; methods in Java are "virtual" by default.

pose class A defines method f, and that B is a subclass of A, and that C is a subclass of B that overrides method f. Then you can still use:

```
super.f()
```

to invoke the overridden method from within class C. This is because class B inherits method f from class A. If classes A, B, and C all define method f, however, then calling super.f() in class C invokes class B's definition of the method. In this case, there is no way to invoke A.f() from within class C. super.super.f() is not legal Java syntax!

It is important to note that super can only be used to invoke overridden methods from within the class that does the overriding. With our Circle and ellipse classes, for example, there is no way to write a program (with or without super) that invokes the Circle area() method on an object of type Ellipse. The only way to do this is to use super in a method within the Ellipse class.

Finally, note that this form of super does not have to occur in the first statement in a method, as it does when used to invoke a superclass constructor method.

Finalizer Chaining Revisited

Now that we've discussed method overriding and how to invoke an overridden method, we can return to the issue of the finalizer method that we left dangling earlier on.

In Java, constructor methods are automatically chained, but finalizer methods are not. If you define a finalize() method to free resources allocated by your class, you may be overriding a finalize() method in a superclass that frees resources allocated by that class. If your finalizer method does not invoke the superclass finalizer, the superclass finalizer never gets called, and resources are not deallocated when they should be.

To prevent this, you should be sure to invoke the superclass finalize() method. The best time to do this is usually after your finalize() method has done all of its deallocation. It is a good idea to add the following call:

```
super.finalize();
```

as the last line of all your finalizer methods. You should do this even if you know that none of your class's superclasses have finalizer methods, because future implementations of the class may include one.

Data Hiding and Encapsulation

We started this section by describing a class as "a collection of data and methods." One of the important object-oriented techniques that we haven't discussed so far is hiding the data within the class, and making it available only through the methods. This technique is often known as *encapsulation*, because it seals the class's data safely inside the "capsule" of the class, where it can be accessed only by trusted users—i.e., by the methods of the class.

Why would you want to do this? One reason is to protect your class against accidental or willful stupidity. A class often contains a number of variables that are interdependent and must be in a consistent state. If you allow a programmer (this may be you yourself) to manipulate those variables directly, he may change one variable without changing important related variables, thus leaving the class in an inconsistent state. If, instead, he had to call a method to change the variable, that method can be sure to do everything necessary to keep the state consistent.

Here's another way to think about encapsulation: When all of a class's variables are hidden, the class's methods define the only possible operations that can be performed on objects of that class. Once you have carefully tested and debugged your methods, you can be confident that the class will work as expected. On the other hand, if all the variables can be directly manipulated, the number of possibilities you have to test becomes unmanageable.

There are other reasons to hide data, too:

- Internal variables that are visible externally to the class just clutter up your class's API. Keeping visible variables to a minimum keeps your class tidy and elegant.
- If a variable is visible in your class, you have to document it. Save time by hiding it instead!

Visibility Modifiers

In most of our examples so far, you've probably noticed the `public` keyword being used. When applied to a class, it means that the class is visible everywhere. When applied to a method or variable, it means that the method or variable is visible everywhere.

To hide variables (or methods, for that matter) you just have to declare them `private`:

```
public class Laundromat {          // people can use this class
    private Laundry[] dirty;       // they can't see this internal variable
    public void wash();            // but they can use these public methods.
    public void dry();             // to manipulate the internal variable.
}
```

A `private` variable of a class is visible only in methods defined within that class. Similarly, a `private` method may only be invoked by methods within the class. Private methods and variables are not visible within subclasses, and are *not* inherited by subclasses as other methods and variables are. (Of course, non-`private` methods that invoke `private` methods internally are inherited and are visible in subclasses.)

Besides `public` and `private`, Java has three other visibility levels: `private protected`, `protected`, and the default visibility level, which applies if none of the `public`, `private`, and `protected` keywords are used.

A `private protected` method or variable is only visible within its own class and within subclasses. A `protected` method or variable is visible within the class where it is defined, of course, and within all subclasses of the class, and also within all classes that are in the same package as that class. A `protected` field is like a `private protected` field except that it is also visible throughout the package of the class in which it is defined. You should use `protected` or `private protected` visibility when you want to hide methods and variables from code that use your class, but want those methods and variables to be fully accessible to code that extends your class.

Somewhat counter-intuitively, the default visibility is *more* strict than `protected`. If a variable or method is not declared with any of the `public`, `private`, or `protected` keywords, it is visible only within the class that defines it, and within classes that are part of the same package. It is not visible to subclasses (unless they are subclasses in the same package).

A note about packages: A package is a group of related and possibly cooperating classes. All non-`private` variables and methods of all classes in the package are visible to all other classes in the package. This is okay because the classes are assumed to know about, and trust, each other.* The only time difficulty arises is when you write programs without a `package` statement. These classes are thrown into the default package with every other `package`-less class, and all their non-`private` fields are visible throughout the package.

There is an important point to make about subclass access to `private protected` and `protected` fields. Subclasses inherit `private protected` and `protected` fields, but they can't access those fields in instances of the superclass itself. For example, if class `A` has `private protected` fields, and `B` is a subclass of `A`, then `B` inherits those fields and can access them in instances of itself or in instances of subclasses of itself. `B` cannot access those `private protected` fields in instances of `A`, however. The same applies to `protected` fields when the subclass is not part of the same package as the superclass.

Table 3-1 shows the circumstances under which fields of the various visibility types are accessible and the circumstances under which they are inherited by subclasses.

Table 3-1: Java Field Visibility

Situation	public	default	protected	private protected	private
Accessible to non-subclass from same package?	yes	yes	yes	no	no
Accessible to subclass from same package?	yes	yes	yes	no	no
Accessible to non-subclass from different package?	yes	no	no	no	no
Accessible to subclass from different package?	yes	no	no	no	no
Inherited by subclass in same package?	yes	yes	yes	yes	no
Inherited by subclass in different package?	yes	no	yes	yes	no

All the details of field visibility in Java can become quite confusing. Here are some simple rules of thumb for using visibility modifiers:

- Use `private` for methods and variables that are only used inside the class and should be hidden everywhere else.

*If you are a C++ programmer, you might say that classes within the same package are `friend`-ly to each other.

- Use public for methods, constants, and other important variables that should be visible everywhere.
- Use private protected for methods and variables that aren't necessary to use the class, but that may be of interest to anyone extending the class. Use protected instead if you want classes in the same package to have access to those fields.
- Use the default visibility for methods and variables that you want to be hidden outside of the package, but which you want cooperating classes within the same package to have access to. Use protected instead, if you also want those fields to be visible to subclasses outside of the package.
- Use the package statement to group your classes into related packages.

Also see Section 10, *Java Syntax*, for a table that summarizes the Java visibility modifiers and other modifiers.

Data Access Methods

In the Circle example we've been using, we've declared the circle position and radius to be public fields. In fact, the Circle class is one where it may well make sense to keep those visible—it is a simple enough class, with no dependencies between the variables.

On the other hand, suppose we wanted to impose a maximum radius on objects of the Circle class. Then it would be better to hide the r variable so that it could not be set directly. Instead of a visible r variable, we'd implement a setRadius() method that verifies that the specified radius isn't too large and then sets the r variable internally. Example 3-14 shows how we might implement Circle with encapsulated data and a restriction on radius size. For convenience, we use protected fields for the radius and position variables. This means that subclasses of Circle, or cooperating classes within the shapes package are able to access these variables directly. To any other classes, however, the variables are hidden. Also, note the private constant and method used to check whether a specified radius is legal. And finally, notice the public methods that allow you to set and query the values of the class variables.

Example 3-14: Hiding variables in the Circle class

```
package shapes;                                // specify a package for the class.

public class Circle {                          // Note that the class is still public!
  protected double x, y;                       // position is hidden, but visible to subclasses
  protected double r;                          // radius is hidden, but visible to subclasses
  private static final double MAXR = 100.0;    // maximum radius
  private boolean check_radius(int r) { return (r <= MAXR); }

  // public constructors
  public Circle(double x, double y, double r) {
    this.x = x; this.y = y;
    if (check_radius(r)) this.r = r;
    else this.r = MAXR;
  }
  public Circle(double r) { this(0.0, 0.0, r); }
  public Circle() { this(0.0, 0.0, 1.0); }
```

```
    // public data access methods
    public void moveto(double x, double y) { this.x = x; this.y = y;}
    public void move(double dx, double dy) { x += dx;  y += dy; }
    public void setRadius(double r) { this.r = (check_radius(r))?r:MAXR; }

    // declare these trivial methods final so we don't get dynamic
    // method lookup and so that they can be inlined by the compiler.
    public final double getX() { return x; };
    public final double getY() { return y; };
    public final double getRadius() { return r; };
}
```


Abstract Classes and Interfaces

In Example 3-14, we declared our `Circle` class to be part of a package named `shapes`. Suppose we plan to implement a number of shape classes: `Rectangle`, `Square`, `Ellipse`, `Triangle`, and so on. We'll give all of these shape classes our two basic `area()` and `circumference()` methods. Now, to make it easy to work with an array of shapes, it would be helpful if all our shape classes have a common superclass, `Shape`. We want `Shape` to encapsulate whatever features all our shapes have in common. In this case, what they have in common is the `area()` and `circumference()` methods. But our generic `Shape` class can't actually implement these methods, since it doesn't represent any actual shape. Java handles this case with abstract methods.

Abstract Methods

Java lets us define a method without implementing it by making the method `abstract`. An `abstract` method has no body; it simply has a signature definition followed by a semicolon.* Here are the rules about `abstract` methods, and the `abstract` classes that contain them:

- Any class with an `abstract` method is automatically `abstract` itself; an `abstract` class must have at least one `abstract` method in it.
- An `abstract` class cannot be instantiated.
- A subclass of an `abstract` class can be instantiated if it overrides each of the `abstract` methods of its superclass and provides an implementation (i.e., a method body) for all of them.
- If a subclass of an `abstract` class does not implement all of the `abstract` methods it inherits, that subclass is itself `abstract`.

That description of the `abstract` keyword was pretty abstract! Example 3-15 is more concrete. It shows an `abstract Shape` class and two non-`abstract` subclasses of it.

*An `abstract` method in Java is something like a "pure virtual function" in C++ (i.e., a virtual function that is declared = 0). In C++, a class that contains a pure virtual function is called an "abstract class" and may not be instantiated. The same is true of Java classes that contain `abstract` methods.

Example 3-15: An abstract class and subclasses

```
public abstract class Shape {
  public abstract double area();
  public abstract double circumference();
}

public class Circle extends Shape {
  protected double r;
  protected static final double PI = 3.14159265358979323846;
  public Circle() { r = 1.0; }
  public Circle(double r) { this.r = r; }
  public double area() { return PI * r * r; }
  public double circumference() { return 2 * PI * r; }
  public double getRadius() { return r; }
}

public class Rectangle extends Shape {
  protected double w, h;
  public Rectangle() { w = 0.0; h = 0.0; }
  public Rectangle(double w, double h) { this.w = w;  this.h = h; }
  public double area() { return w * h; }
  public double circumference() { return 2 * (w + h); }
  public double getWidth() { return w; }
  public double getHeight() { return h; }
}
```

Note that the `abstract` methods in `Shape` have a semicolon right after their parentheses. There are no curly braces, and no method body is defined. Using the classes defined in Example 3-15, we can now write code like this:

```
Shape[] shapes = new Shape[3];              // create an array to hold shapes
shapes[0] = new Circle(2.0);                // fill in the array...
shapes[1] = new Rectangle(1.0, 3.0);
shapes[2] = new Rectangle(4.0, 2.0);

double total_area = 0;
for(int i = 0; i < shapes.length; i++)
  total_area += shapes[i].area();           // compute the area of the shapes
```

There are two important points to notice here:

- Subclasses of `Shape` can be assigned to elements of an array of `Shape`. No cast is necessary.
- You can invoke the `area()` and `circumference()` methods for `Shape` objects, even through `Shape` does not define a body for these methods, because `Shape` declared them `abstract`. If `Shape` did not declare them at all, the code would cause a compilation error.

Interfaces

Let's extend our `shapes` package further. Suppose we now want to implement a number of shapes that can be drawn on the screen. We could define an abstract `DrawableShape` class, and then implement various subclasses of it, such as `DrawableCircle`, `DrawableRectangle`, and so on. This would work fine.

But suppose we want our drawable shape types to support the area() and circumference() methods. We don't want to have to re-implement these methods, so we'd like to make DrawableCircle a subclass of Circle, for example, and DrawableRectangle a subclass of Rectangle. But classes in Java can only have one superclass. If DrawableCircle extends Circle, then it cannot also extend DrawableShape!*

Java's solution to this problem is called an *interface*. An interface looks a lot like an abstract class, except that it uses the keyword interface instead of the words abstract and class. Example 3-16 shows an interface named Drawable.

Example 3-16: An interface definition

```
public interface Drawable {
   public void setColor(Color c);
   public void setPosition(double x, double y);
   public void draw(DrawWindow dw);
}
```


While an abstract class may define some abstract methods and some non-abstract methods, all the methods defined within an interface are implicitly abstract. We've omitted the abstract keyword in this example, but it is perfectly legal to use it if you want to belabor the abstractness of interface methods. A further restriction on interfaces is that any variables declared in an interface must be static and final—that is, they must be constants.

So what can we do with an interface? Just as a class extends its superclass, it also optionally implements an interface. implements is a Java keyword that can appear in a class declaration following the extends clause. implements should be followed by the name of the interface that the class implements. In order to implement an interface, a class must first declare the interface in an implements clause, and then it must provide an implementation (i.e., a body) for all of the abstract methods of the interface.†

Example 3-17 shows how we can define a DrawableRectangle class that extends our Rectangle class and implements the Drawable interface we defined in Example 3-16. The example assumes that a Color class and a DrawWindow class are defined elsewhere, and that DrawWindow knows how to convert floating-point coordinates to pixel coordinates and knows how to draw primitive shapes.

Example 3-17: Implementing an interface

```
public class DrawableRectangle extends Rectangle implements Drawable {
   // new instance variables
   private Color c;
   private double x, y;
```

*C++ allows classes to have more than one superclass, using a technique known as "multiple inheritance." Multiple inheritance opens up a can of worms, so Java replaces it with what many believe is a more elegant solution.

†This is the real difference between multiple inheritance in C++ and interfaces in Java. In C++, a class can inherit method implementations from more than one superclass. In Java, a class can inherit actual implementations only from one superclass. It can inherit additional abstract methods from interfaces, but it must provide its own implementation of those methods. It is rare, however, to actually be able to use C++ multiple inheritance to inherit useful, non-trivial implementations from more than one class. The elegance and simplicity of Java's interface more than compensate for the inability to inherit implementations from more than one class.

Example 3-17: Implementing an interface (continued)

```
    // A constructor
    public DrawableRectangle(double w, double h) { super(w, h); }

    // Here are implementations of the Drawable methods
    // We also inherit all the public methods of Rectangle.
    public void setColor(Color c) { this.c = c; }
    public void setPosition(double x, double y) { this.x = x; this.y = y; }
    public void draw(DrawWindow dw) {
      dw.drawRect(x, y, w, h, c);
    }
}
```

Using Interfaces

Suppose we implement `DrawableCircle` and `DrawableSquare` just as we implemented `DrawableRectangle` in Example 3-17. As we saw earlier, instances of these classes can be treated as instances of the abstract `Shape` class. They can also be treated as instances of the `Drawable` interface. Example 3-18 demonstrates this.

Example 3-18: Casting objects to their interface type

```
Shape[] shapes = new Shape[3];              // create an array to hold shapes
Drawable[] drawables = new Drawable[3];   // and an array to hold drawables.

// Create some drawable shapes
DrawableCircle dc = new DrawableCircle(1.1);
DrawableSquare ds = new DrawableSquare(2.5);
DrawableRectangle dr = new DrawableRectangle(2.3, 4.5);

// The shapes can be assigned to both arrays
shapes[0] = dc;  drawables[0] = dc;
shapes[1] = ds;  drawables[1] = ds;
shapes[2] = dr;  drawables[2] = dr;

// Compute total area and draw the shapes by invoking
// the Shape and the Drawable abstract methods.
double total_area = 0;
for(int i = 0; i < shapes.length; i++) {
  total_area += shapes[i].area();              // compute the area of the shapes
  drawables[i].setPosition(i*10.0, i*10.0);
  drawables[i].draw(draw_window);              // assume draw_window defined somewhere
}
```

What this example demonstrates is that interfaces are data types in Java, just as classes are, and that when a class implements an interface, instances of that class can be assigned to variables of the interface type. Don't interpret this example to imply that you must assign a `DrawableRectangle` object to a `Drawable` variable before you can invoke the `draw()` method or that you must assign it to a `Shape` variable before you can invoke the `area()` method. `DrawableRectangle()` defines `draw()` and inherits `area()` from its `Rectangle` superclass, and so you can always invoke these methods.

Implementing Multiple Interfaces

Suppose we wanted shapes that could be scaled to be larger or smaller. One way we could do this is by defining a `Scalable` interface and implementing subclasses of `DrawableRectangle` and the other classes. To do this, though, the new subclass would have to implement both the `Drawable` interface and the `Scalable` interface. This is no problem. You may specify a list of comma-separated interfaces in the `implements` clause of any class:

```
public class DrawableScalableRectangle extends DrawableRectangle
        implements Drawable, Scalable {
  // The methods of the Scalable interface go here
}
```

Constants in Interfaces

As we noted above, constants may appear in interface definitions. What does it mean to implement an interface that contains constants? It simply means that the class that implements the interface "inherits" the constants (in a sense) and can use them as if they were defined directly in the class. There is no need to prefix them with the name of the interface:

```
class A { static final int CONSTANT1 = 3; }
interface B { static final int CONSTANT2 = 4; }
class C implements B {
  void f() {
    int i = A.CONSTANT1;        // have to use the class name here
    int j = CONSTANT2;          // No class name here, because we implement
  }                             // the interface that defines this constant.
}
```

When you have a lot of constants, used in classes throughout a package, one thing you might do is to define a class `Constants` that contains all the constants. Then in your code, you would refer to constants with names like `Constants.PI` and `Constants.MAX_ARRAY_SIZE`. Another way to handle the constants is to declare them in an interface `Constants`, and then declare all the classes that use constants to implement that interface. Then you can just use constant names like `PI` and `MAX_ARRAY_SIZE`.

Extending Interfaces

Interfaces can have sub-interfaces, just like classes can have subclasses. A sub-interface inherits all the abstract methods and constants of its super-interface, and may define new abstract methods and constants. Interfaces are different from classes in one very important way, however. An interface can extend more than one interface at a time:

```
public interface Transformable extends Scalable, Rotateable, Reflectable {}
public interface DrawingObject extends Drawable, Transformable {}
public class Shape implements DrawingObject { ... }
```

An interface that extends more than one interface inherits all the abstract methods and constants from each of those interfaces, and may define its own additional abstract methods and constants. A class that implements such an interface must implement the abstract methods defined in the interface itself as well as all the abstract methods inherited from all of the super-interfaces.

C++ Features Not Found in Java

Throughout this section, we've noted similarities and differences between Java and C++ in footnotes. Java shares enough concepts and features with C++ to make it an easy language for C++ programmers to pick up. There are several features of C++ that have no parallel in Java, however. In general, Java does not adopt those features of C++ that make the language significantly more complicated. These omissions from Java (or simplifications of C++) are described below.

C++ supports "multiple inheritance" of method implementations from more than one superclass at a time. While this seems like a very useful feature, adding it to the language actually turns out to introduce many complexities. The Java language designers chose to avoid the added complexity by using interfaces instead. Thus, a class in Java can only inherit method implementations from a single superclass, but it can inherit method declarations from any number of interfaces. In practice, this is not any particular hardship.

C++ supports (though not yet in a very standardized way) templates that allow you, for example, to implement a `Stack` class and then instantiate it as `Stack<int>` or `Stack<double>` to produce two separate types: a stack of integers and a stack of floating-point values. Java has no such facility. However, the fact that every class in Java is a subclass of `Object` means that every object can be cast to an instance of `Object`. Thus, in Java, it is often sufficient to define a data structure (such as a `Stack` class) that operates on `Object` values—the objects can be cast back to their actual type whenever necessary.

C++ allows you to define operators that perform arbitrary operations on instances of your classes. In effect, it allows you to extend the syntax of the language. This is a nifty feature, called operator overloading, that makes for very elegant examples. In practice however, it tends to make code hard to understand. After much debate, the Java language designers decided to omit such "operator overloading" from the language. Note, though, that the use of the + operator for string concatenation in Java is at least reminiscent of operator overloading.

C++ allows you to define "conversion functions" for a class that automatically invoke an appropriate constructor method when a value is assigned to a variable of that class. This is simply a syntactic shortcut (similar to overriding the assignment operator) and is not included in Java.

In C++, objects are by default manipulated by value; you must use `&` to specify a variable or function argument that is automatically manipulated by reference. In Java, all objects are manipulated by reference, so there is no need for this `&` syntax.

Section Summary

This has been a long and detailed section. The following list summarizes the most important points of the section. This summary is not intended to simplify the complex material we've covered, but it may allow you to test your comprehension of the material now, and to help jog your memory later:

- A class is a collection of data and methods that operate on that data.
- An object is a particular instance of a class.
- Object fields (variables and methods) are accessed with a dot between the object name and the field name.

- Instance (non-static) variables occur in each instance of a class.
- Class (static) variables are associated with the class. There is one copy of a class variable regardless of the number of instances of a class.
- Instance (non-static) methods of a class are passed an implicit `this` argument that identifies the object being operated on.
- Class (static) methods are not passed a `this` argument and therefore cannot use the instance methods or instance variables of the class.
- Objects are created with the `new` keyword, which invokes a class constructor method with a list of arguments.
- Objects are not explicitly freed or destroyed in any way. The Java garbage collector automatically reclaims objects that are no longer being used.
- If the first line of a constructor method does not invoke another constructor with a `this()` call, or a superclass constructor with a `super()` call, Java automatically inserts a call to the superclass constructor that takes no arguments. This enforces "constructor chaining."
- If a class does not define a constructor, Java provides a default constructor.
- A class may inherit the non-`private` methods and variables of another class by "subclassing"—i.e., by declaring that class in its `extends` clause.
- `java.lang.Object` is the default superclass for a class. It is the root of the Java class hierarchy and has no superclass itself. All Java classes inherit the methods defined by `Object`.
- Method overloading is the practice of defining multiple methods which have the same name but have different return types or argument lists.
- Method overriding occurs when a class redefines a method inherited from its superclass.
- Dynamic method lookup ensures that the correct method is invoked for an object, even when the object is an instance of a class that has overridden the method.
- `static`, `private`, and `final` methods cannot be overridden and are not subject to dynamic method lookup. This allows compiler optimizations such as inlining.
- You can explicitly invoke an overridden method with the `super` keyword.
- You can explictly refer to a shadowed variable with the `super` keyword.
- Data and methods may be hidden or encapsulated within a class by specifying the `private`, `private protected`, or `protected` visibility modifiers. Fields declared `public` are visible everywhere. Fields with no visibility modifiers are visible only within the package.
- An abstract method has no method body (i.e. no implementation).
- An abstract class contains abstract methods. The methods must be implemented in a subclass before the subclass can be instantiated.

- An interface is a collection of abstract methods and constants (`static final` variables). Declaring an interface creates a new data type.
- A class implements an interface by declaring the interface in its `implements` clause and by providing a method body for each of the abstract methods in the interface.

Part II

Programming with the Java API

The sections in Part II present real-world examples of programming with Java. You can study and learn from the examples, and you can adapt them for use in your own programs.

The example code in these chapters is available for downloading. See *http://www.ora.com/catalog/books/javanut.*

Applets

This chapter demonstrates the techniques of applet writing. It proceeds from a trivial "Hello World" applet to quite sophisticated applets. Along the way, it shows you how to:

- Draw graphics and display images in your applet.
- Handle and respond to user input from the mouse or keyboard.
- Read and use values of applet parameters, allowing customization of an applet.
- Add push buttons to an applet.
- Create and manage a thread to display animation.
- Play audio clips.

Study the examples carefully. They are the important part of this chapter! You may find it useful to refer to the quick reference in Section 18, *The java.applet Package*, while reading these examples.

A First Applet

Figure 4-1 shows what is probably the simplest possible applet you can write in Java. Example 4-1 lists its code. This example introduces the `paint()` method, which is invoked by the applet viewer (or Web browser) when the applet needs to be drawn. This method should perform graphical output—such as drawing text or lines or displaying images—for your applet. The argument to `paint()` is a `Graphics` object that you use to do the drawing.

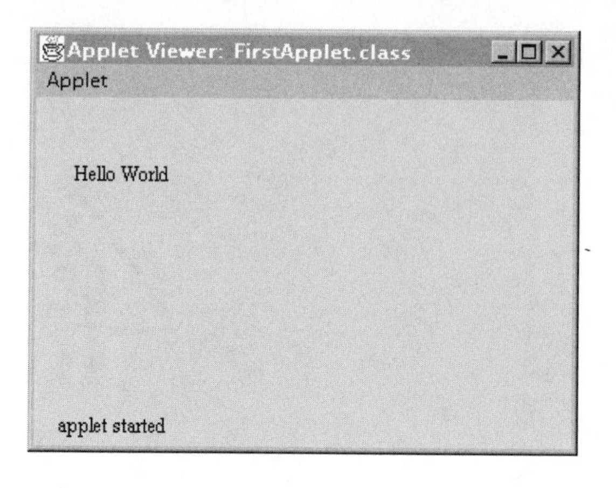

Figure 4-1: A simple applet

Example 4-1: The simplest applet

```
import java.applet.*;          // Don't forget this import statement!
import java.awt.*;             // Or this one for the graphics!

public class FirstApplet extends Applet {
    // This method displays the applet.
    // The Graphics class is how you do all drawing in Java.
    public void paint(Graphics g) {
        g.drawString("Hello World", 25, 50);
    }
}
```

To display an applet, you need an HTML file that references it. Here is an HTML fragment that can be used with our first applet:

```
<APPLET code="FirstApplet.class" width=150 height=100>
</APPLET>
```

With an HTML file that references the applet, you can now view the applet with an applet viewer or Web browser. For the rest of this chapter, we will generally not show the HTML files for our applets. See Section 15, *Java-Related HTML and HTTP Syntax*, for more details on the HTML `<APPLET>` tag.

Drawing Graphics

Example 4-2 shows an extension to our simple applet. As you can see from Figure 4-2, we've made the graphical display more interesting. This applet also does all of its drawing in the `paint()` method. It demonstrates the use of `Font` and `Color` objects. See Section 12, *Fonts, Colors, and Cursors*, for more information on fonts and colors in Java.

This example also introduces the `init()` method, which is used to perform any one-time initialization that is necessary when the applet is first created. The `paint()` method may be invoked many times in the life of an applet, so this example uses `init()` to create the `Font` object that `paint()` uses.

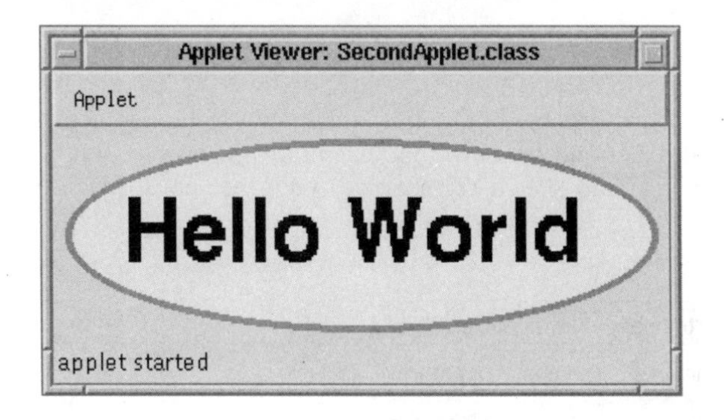

Figure 4-2: A fancier applet

Example 4-2: An applet with fancier graphics

```
import java.applet.*;
import java.awt.*;

public class SecondApplet extends Applet {
    static final String message = "Hello World";
    private Font font;

    // One-time initialization for the applet
    public void init() {
        font = new Font("Helvetica", Font.BOLD, 48);
    }

    // Draw the applet whenever necessary.  Do some fancy graphics.
    public void paint(Graphics g) {
        // The pink oval
        g.setColor(Color.pink);
        g.fillOval(10, 10, 330, 100);

        // The red outline.  java doesn't support wide lines, so we
        // try to simulate a 4-pixel wide line by drawing four ovals
        g.setColor(Color.red);
        g.drawOval(10,10, 330, 100);
        g.drawOval(9, 9, 332, 102);
        g.drawOval(8, 8, 334, 104);
        g.drawOval(7, 7, 336, 106);

        // The text
        g.setColor(Color.black);
        g.setFont(font);
        g.drawString(message, 40, 75);
    }
}
```

Applets

Handling Events

The previous two applets have only displayed output. If an applet is to be interactive in any way, it has to receive and respond to user input. Example 4-3 shows a simple applet that lets the user do a freehand sketch (or scribble) with the mouse. Figure 4-3 shows such a scribble.

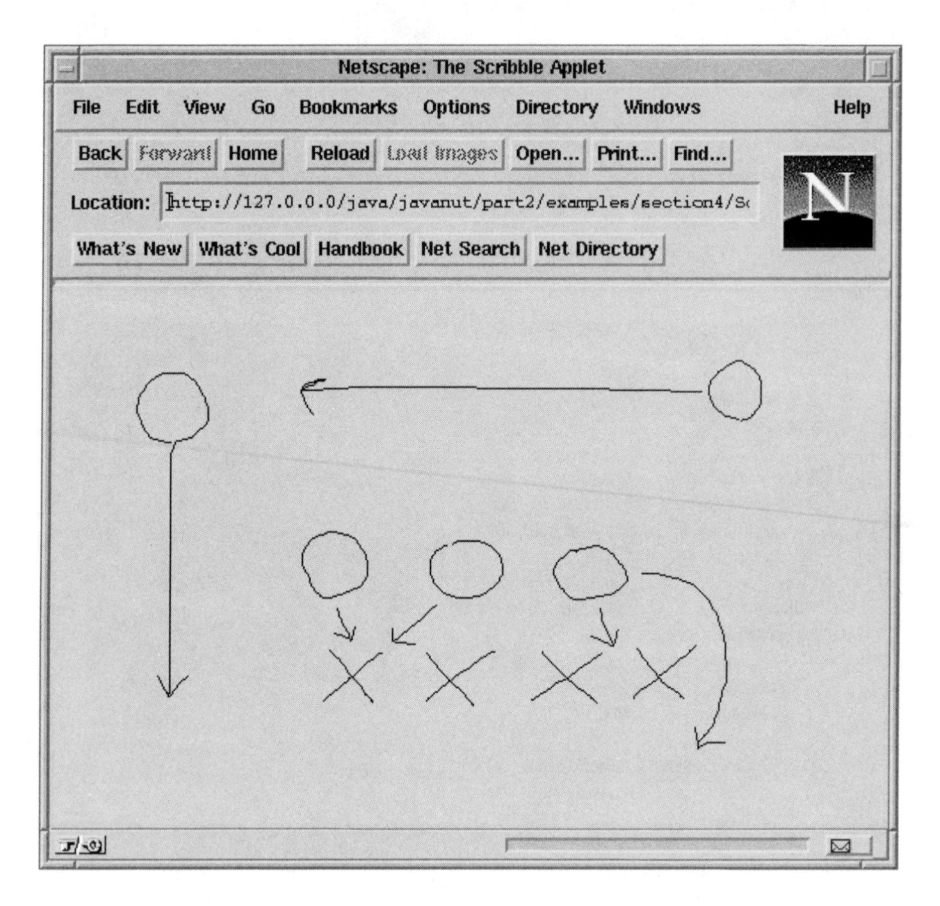

Figure 4-3: Scribbling with the Scribble applet

The `mouseDown()` and `mouseDrag()` methods are called by the system when the user presses a mouse button and moves the mouse with the button down, respectively. This applet draws lines directly in response to these events. It does not have a `paint()` method, which means that the user's scribble is lost any time that the applet is redrawn (for example, when a Web browser scrolls down a page and then scrolls back up again).

Note that both `mouseDown()` and `mouseUp()` return `true`. This is to tell the system that they've handled the `Event` object that was passed to them, and that the event should not be processed any further. The next section demonstrates event handling in more detail.

Example 4-3: The Scribble applet

```
import java.applet.*;
import java.awt.*;

public class Scribble extends Applet {
    private int last_x = 0;
    private int last_y = 0;

    // called when the user clicks
    public boolean mouseDown(Event e, int x, int y)
    {
        last_x = x; last_y = y;
        return true;
    }

    // called when the mouse moves with the button down
    public boolean mouseDrag(Event e, int x, int y)
    {
        Graphics g = getGraphics();
        g.drawLine(last_x, last_y, x, y);
        last_x = x;
        last_y = y;
        return true;
    }
}
```


Events in Detail

Example 4-4 is an applet that displays simple instructions in an otherwise blank window; it is not pictured. Whenever user events (mouse and keyboard events, mainly) occur in the applet's window, it describes the event in the applet viewer's (or Web browser's) status line. This example uses the `Applet showStatus()` method to display the messages in the status line. More importantly, though, it defines a number of methods to handle events. These methods are invoked by the system when the events occur. When you define one of these methods, you should handle the specified event and return `true`. Or, if you determine that it is not an appropriate event for your code to handle, you should return `false` so that it is passed on to other event handling code.

The `keyDown()` and `keyUp()` methods are of particular interest. Notice how they distinguish regular keys from function keys, and how they determine which key has been pressed, with what keyboard modifiers.

Notice from the mouse event handling code that Java assumes a one-button mouse—the lowest-common denominator for all platforms. The `Event` class does not have any kind of `mouseButton` field to indicate which mouse button has been pressed. Instead, on systems with two or three-button mice, using the right mouse button generates mouse events that have the META keyboard modifier set. Similarly, on three-button mice, the middle mouse button generates mouse events that have the ALT modifier set. This technique allows platforms with one and two-button mice to simulate two and three-button mice by using them in conjunction with the keyboard. See Section 11, *Events*, for more details about events, modifiers, keys, and mouse buttons in Java.

Example 4-4: Handling applet events

```
import java.applet.*;
import java.awt.*;

public class EventTester extends Applet {
    // display the instructions
    public void paint(Graphics g) {
        g.drawString("Click, drag, and type in this window.", 10, 20);
    }

    // Handle mouse events
    public boolean mouseDown(Event e, int x, int y) {
        showStatus(modifier_key_names(e.modifiers) +
                "Mouse Down: [" + x + "," + y + "]");
        return true;
    }
    public boolean mouseUp(Event e, int x, int y) {
        showStatus(modifier_key_names(e.modifiers) +
                "Mouse Up: [" + x + "," + y + "]");
        return true;
    }
    public boolean mouseDrag(Event e, int x, int y) {
        showStatus(modifier_key_names(e.modifiers) +
                "Mouse Drag: [" + x + "," + y + "]");
        return true;
    }
    public boolean mouseEnter(Event e, int x, int y) {
        showStatus("Mouse Enter: [" + x + "," + y + "]");
        return true;
    }
    public boolean mouseExit(Event e, int x, int y) {
        showStatus("Mouse Exit: [" + x + "," + y + "]");
        return true;
    }

    // Handle focus events
    public boolean gotFocus(Event e, Object what) {
        showStatus("Got Focus");
        return true;
    }
    public boolean lostFocus(Event e, Object what) {
        showStatus("Lost Focus");
        return true;
    }

    // Handle key down and key up events
    public boolean keyDown(Event e, int key) {
        int flags = e.modifiers;
        if (e.id == Event.KEY_PRESS)          // a regular key
            showStatus("Key Down: "
                    + modifier_key_names(flags)
                    + key_name(e));
        else if (e.id == Event.KEY_ACTION)    // a function key
            showStatus("Function Key Down: "
                    + modifier_key_names(flags)
                    + function_key_name(key));
        return true;
```

```
    }
    public boolean keyUp(Event e, int key) {
        int flags = e.modifiers;
        if (e.id == Event.KEY_PRESS)          // a regular key
            showStatus("Key Up: "
                    + modifier_key_names(flags)
                    + key_name(e));
        else if (e.id == Event.KEY_ACTION)   // a function key
            showStatus("Function Key Up: "
                    + modifier_key_names(flags)
                    + function_key_name(key));
        return true;
    }

    // The remaining methods help us sort out the various key events

    // Return the current list of modifier keys
    private String modifier_key_names(int flags) {
        String s = "[ ";
        if (flags == 0) return "";
        if ((flags & Event.SHIFT_MASK) != 0) s += "Shift ";
        if ((flags & Event.CTRL_MASK) != 0) s += "Control ";
        if ((flags & Event.META_MASK) != 0) s += "Meta ";
        if ((flags & Event.ALT_MASK) != 0) s += "Alt ";
        s += "] ";
        return s;
    }

    // Return the name of a regular (ASCII) key.
    private String key_name(Event e) {
        char c = (char) e.key;

        // If CTRL flag is set, handle ASCII control characters.
        if (e.controlDown()) {
            if (c < ' ') {
                c += '@';
                return "^" + c;
            }
        }
        else {
            // If CTRL flag is not set, then certain ASCII
            // control characters have special meaning.
            switch (c) {
                case '\n': return "Return";
                case '\t': return "Tab";
                case '\033': return "Escape";
                case '\010': return "Backspace";
            }
        }

        // Handle the remaining possibilities.
        if (c == '177') return "Delete";
        else if (c == ' ') return "Space";
        else return String.valueOf(c);
    }
```

Applets

Example 4-4: Handling applet events (continued)

```
        // Return the name of a function key.
        private String function_key_name(int key) {
            switch(key) {
                case Event.HOME: return "Home";
                case Event.END: return "End";
                case Event.PGUP: return "Page Up";
                case Event.PGDN: return "Page Down";
                case Event.UP: return "Up Arrow";
                case Event.DOWN: return "Down Arrow";
                case Event.LEFT: return "Left Arrow";
                case Event.RIGHT: return "Right Arrow";
                case Event.F1: return "F1";    case Event.F2: return "F2";
                case Event.F3: return "F3";    case Event.F4: return "F4";
                case Event.F5: return "F5";    case Event.F6: return "F6";
                case Event.F7: return "F7";    case Event.F8: return "F8";
                case Event.F9: return "F9";    case Event.F10: return "F10";
                case Event.F11: return "F11";  case Event.F12: return "F12";
            }
            return "Unknown Function Key";
        }
    }
```

Reading Applet Parameters

Example 4-5 shows an extension to our earlier `Scribble` applet. The `ColorScribble` class is a subclass of `Scribble` that adds the ability to scribble in a configurable foreground color over a configurable background color. (The `ColorScribble` applet looks a lot like the `Scribble` applet of Figure 4-3 and is not pictured here.)

`ColorScribble` has an `init()` method that reads the value of two "applet parameters" that can be optionally specified with the <PARAM> tag in the applet's HTML file. The returned string values are converted to colors and specified as the default foreground and background colors for the applet. Note that the `init()` method invokes its superclass's `init()` method, just in case a future version of `Scribble` defines that method to perform initialization.

This example also introduces the `getAppletInfo()` and `getParameterInfo()` methods. These methods provide textual information about the applet (its author, its version, its copyright, etc.) and the parameters that it can accept (the parameter names, their types, and their meanings). An applet should generally define these methods. Most Web browsers and applet viewers let the user examine the applet and parameter information, and some even let the user interactively specify parameter values for an applet.

Example 4-5: Reading applet parameters

```
import java.applet.*;
import java.awt.*;

public class ColorScribble extends Scribble {
    // Read in two color parameters and set the colors.
    public void init() {
        super.init();
```

```
        Color foreground = getColorParameter("foreground");
        Color background = getColorParameter("background");
        if (foreground != null) this.setForeground(foreground);
        if (background != null) this.setBackground(background);
    }

    // Read the specified parameter.  Interpret it as a hexadecimal
    // number of the form RRGGBB and convert it to a color.
    protected Color getColorParameter(String name) {
        String value = this.getParameter(name);
        int intvalue;
        try { intvalue = Integer.parseInt(value, 16); }
        catch (NumberFormatException e) { return null; }
        return new Color(intvalue);
    }

    // Return info about the supported parameters.  Web browsers and applet
    // viewers should display this information, and may also allow users to
    // set the parameter values.
    public String[][] getParameterInfo() {
        String[][] info = {
            // Array of arrays of strings describing each parameter.
            // Format: parameter name, parameter type, parameter description
            {"foreground", "hexadecimal color value", "foreground color"},
            {"background", "hexadecimal color value", "background color"}
        };
        return info;
    }

    // Return information suitable for display in an About dialog box.
    public String getAppletInfo() {
        return "Scribble v. 0.02.0ritten by David Flanagan.";
    }
}
```

The following HTML fragment references the applet, and demonstrates how parameter values can be set with the <PARAM> tag.

```
<APPLET code="ColorScribble.class" width=300 height=300>
<PARAM name="foreground" value="0000FF">
<PARAM name="background" value="FFCCCC">
</APPLET>
```

Adding a Button

Example 4-6 shows another extension to our `Scribble` applet. This one, pictured in Figure 4-4, adds a **Clear** button to the applet. Clicking on the button erases any scribbles that have been drawn.

The `ClearableScribble` applet is a subclass of the `ColorScribble` class we saw in Example 4-5. It creates the **Clear** button in its `init()` method, after first invoking the `ColorScribble init()` method. The button is created with `new` and added to the applet with the `add()` method. We set the foreground and background colors of the button so that they are distinct from the foreground and background scribble colors specified by parameters.

The `action()` method is invoked by the system when the user clicks on the button we've added to the applet. Note that we first check whether our button was the one clicked (this is useful when there is more than one button), and then proceed to clear the scribble area. If the event was not for our button, we pass it on to the `action()` method of the superclass. (The superclass, the `ColorScribble` applet, does not currently have buttons and does not define an `action()` method, but future versions of it might.)

We'll discuss adding user interface components and handling user interaction in much greater detail in Section 5, *Graphical User Interfaces.*

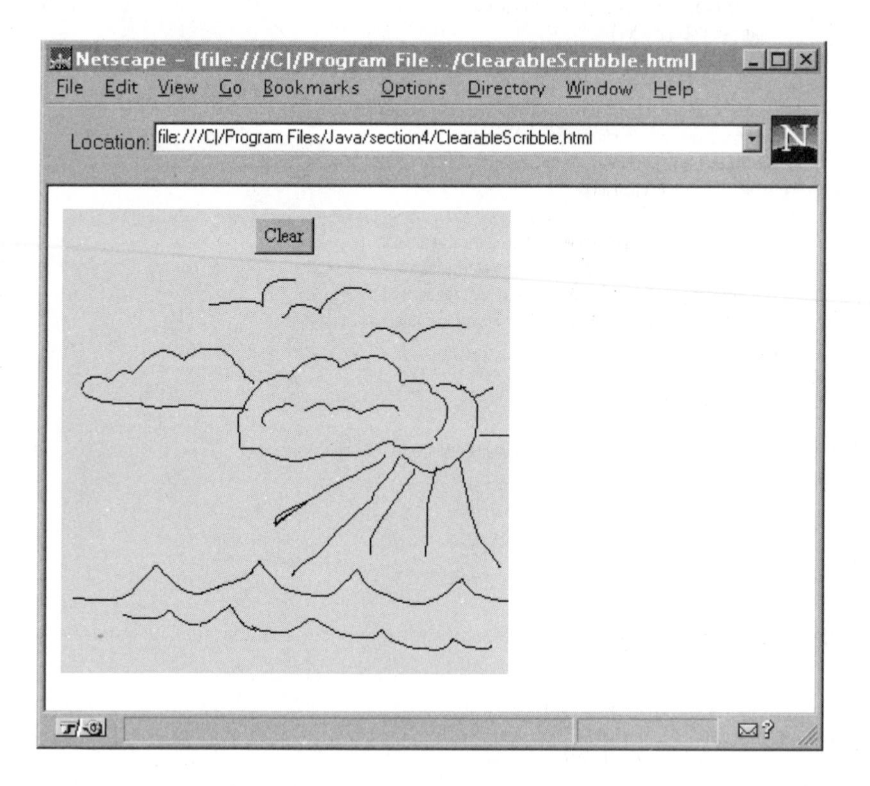

Figure 4-4: An applet with a button

Example 4-6: Adding a button to an applet

```
import java.applet.*;
import java.awt.*;

public class ClearableScribble extends ColorScribble {
    private Button clear_button;

    public void init() {
        // do ColorScribble initialization first
        super.init();
```

```
            // Create a button and add it to the applet.
            clear_button = new Button("Clear");
            clear_button.setForeground(Color.black);
            clear_button.setBackground(Color.lightGray);
            this.add(clear_button);
        }

        public boolean action(Event event, Object arg) {
            // If our button was clicked on, handle it.
            // Otherwise, let our superclass handle it if it wants to.
            if (event.target == clear_button) {
                Graphics g = this.getGraphics();
                Rectangle r = this.bounds();
                g.setColor(this.getBackground());
                g.fillRect(r.x, r.y, r.width, r.height);
                g.setColor(this.getForeground());
                return true;
            }
            else return super.action(event, arg);
        }
    }
```

Applets

An Imagemap

Example 4-7 shows a Java applet that implements an imagemap, like that shown in Figure 4-5. That is, it displays a specified image and responds to mouse clicks on specified regions of the image. This provides an extremely flexible "client-side imagemap" capability in Web pages. (Conventional HTML supports "server-side" image maps, which require custom CGI programming and are much less convenient.)

The `init()` method of this applet looks up the parameter named "image" to find the name of the image to display. Then it reads in that image, using the `Applet getImage()` method and assuming that the image name is relative to the URL of the HTML document that references the applet.

The `init()` method also reads in properties that specify a number of rectangular regions and associated URLs for each region. It uses a helper function to parse the parameters, as well as an internal class and the `java.util.Vector` class to store these rectangle specifications. The following HTML fragment shows an example of the properties read by this applet:

```
<APPLET code="Imagemap.class" width=150 height=50>
<PARAM name="image" value="images/map.gif">
<PARAM name="rect0" value="0,0,50,50,Scribble.html">
<PARAM name="rect1" value="50,0,50,50,EventTester.html">
<PARAM name="rect2" value="100,0,50,50,NoSuchFile.html">
</APPLET>
```

The applet's `paint()` method displays the image. The `update()` method overrides the default applet `update()` method. The default method clears the applet background and then calls `paint()`. Our new definition doesn't clear the background, to reduce flickering. The `destroy()` method is automatically called by the system

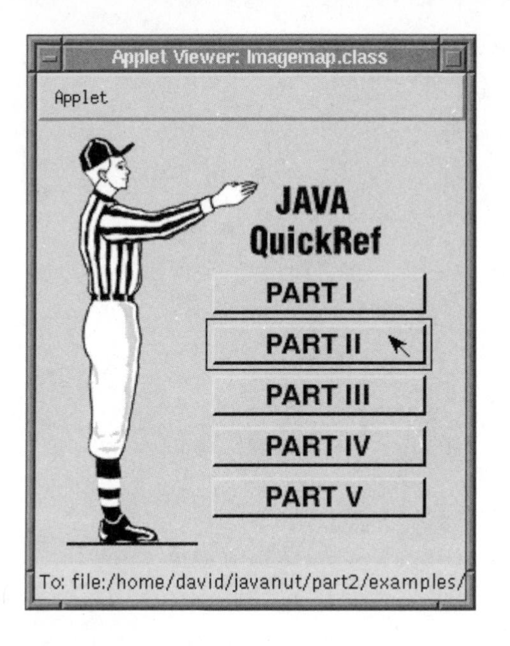

Figure 4-5: An imagemap applet

when the applet is being "unloaded" from the applet viewer or Web browser. Once `destroy()` has been called, the `start()` method will never be called again. `destroy()` is the complement of the `init()` method, but is less commonly used. In this case, it helps to free up memory used for the image (which might be quite large).

The `mouseDown()` method detects when the mouse button is pressed. If it is pressed within one of the defined rectangles, the method highlights that rectangle using XOR mode drawing (which can be erased by redrawing). The method also uses `showStatus()` to display the URL that the selected rectangle refers to in the applet viewer status line.

The `mouseUp()` method detects when the mouse button is released. If it is released in the same rectangle in which it was pressed, then this method calls `showDocument()` to ask the Web browser or applet viewer to display the document at the URL associated with the rectangle. This method also clears the status line and erases the highlighting drawn by `mouseDown()`.

Example 4-7: An imagemap applet

```
import java.applet.*;
import java.awt.*;
import java.net.*;
import java.util.*;

public class Imagemap extends Applet {
    protected Image image;        // image to display.
    protected Vector rects;       // list of rectangles in it.

    public void init() {
        // load the image to be displayed.
        image = this.getImage(this.getDocumentBase(),
```

```
                this.getParameter("image"));
        // lookup a list of rectangular areas and the URLs they map to.
        rects = new Vector();
        ImagemapRectangle r;
        int i = 0;
        while((r = getRectangleParameter("rect" + i)) != null) {
            rects.addElement(r);
            i++;
        }
    }

    // Called when the applet is being unloaded from the system.
    // We use it here to "flush" the image. This may result in memory
    // and other resources being freed quicker than they otherwise would.
    public void destroy() { image.flush(); }

    // Display the image.
    public void paint(Graphics g) {
        g.drawImage(image, 0, 0, this);
    }

    // We override this method so that it doesn't clear the background
    // before calling paint().  Makes for less flickering in some situations.
    public void update(Graphics g) { paint(g); }

    // find the rectangle we're inside
    private ImagemapRectangle findrect(int x, int y) {
        int i;
        ImagemapRectangle r = null;
        for(i = 0; i < rects.size(); i++)  {
            r = (ImagemapRectangle) rects.elementAt(i);
            if (r.inside(x, y)) break;
        }
        if (i < rects.size()) return r;
        else return null;
    }

    private ImagemapRectangle lastrect;

    // On button down, highlight the rectangle, and display a message
    public boolean mouseDown(Event e, int x, int y) {
        ImagemapRectangle r = findrect(x, y);
        if (r == null) return false;
        Graphics g = this.getGraphics();
        g.setXORMode(Color.red);
        g.drawRect(r.x, r.y, r.width, r.height);
        lastrect = r;
        this.showStatus("To: " + r.url);
        return true;
    }

    // On button up, unhighlight the rectangle.
    // If still inside the rectangle go to the URL
    public boolean mouseUp(Event e, int x, int y) {
        if (lastrect != null) {
            Graphics g = this.getGraphics();
```

```
            g.setXORMode(Color.red);
            g.drawRect(lastrect.x, lastrect.y, lastrect.width, lastrect.height);
            this.showStatus("");
            ImagemapRectangle r = findrect(x,y);
            if ((r != null) && (r == lastrect))
                this.getAppletContext().showDocument(r.url);
            lastrect = null;
        }
        return true;
    }

    // Parse a comma-separated list of rectangle coordinates and a URL.
    protected ImagemapRectangle getRectangleParameter(String name) {
        int x, y, w, h;
        URL url;
        String value = this.getParameter(name);
        if (value == null) return null;

        try {
            StringTokenizer st = new StringTokenizer(value, ",");
            x = Integer.parseInt(st.nextToken());
            y = Integer.parseInt(st.nextToken());
            w = Integer.parseInt(st.nextToken());
            h = Integer.parseInt(st.nextToken());
            url = new URL(this.getDocumentBase(), st.nextToken());
        }
        catch (NoSuchElementException e) return null;
        catch (NumberFormatException e) return null;
        catch (MalformedURLException e) return null;

        return new ImagemapRectangle(x, y, w, h, url);
    }
}

// A helper class. Just like java.awt.Rectangle, but with a new URL field.
// The constructor lets us create them from parameter specifications.
class ImagemapRectangle extends Rectangle {
    URL url;
    public ImagemapRectangle(int x, int y, int w, int h, URL url) {
        super(x, y, w, h);
        this.url = url;
    }
}
```

Animation

Example 4-8 is an applet, `Animator`, that displays a simple animation. The `init()` method uses `getParameter()` to look up the number of images in the animation and the base name of each image. The base name is a file specification relative to the URL of the current document. `init()` forms the name of each image from the base name and the image number and reads in the images using `getImage()`.

The `start()` and `stop()` methods are called by the system to tell an applet to start and to stop whatever it does. They are like the `init()` and `destroy()` methods, but may be called multiple times throughout the applet's life. (For example, an applet might be stopped when it scrolls off the current page of a Web browser.) In this case, the `start()` method starts the animation and the `stop()` method stops it.

All the applets we've seen so far have been passive—they respond to user events and to methods called by the system, but take no action on their own. Animation is active; we need to draw something over and over again. We can't use `init()`, `paint()`, or any of the other standard applet methods to do this—those methods are supposed to do a simple job and then return to the system. So to perform our animation, we need to create a `Thread` object to create a separate thread of execution. The `start()` method creates this animation thread and starts it by calling the thread's `start()` method. The `stop()` method stops the thread by calling `stop()` on it.

Note how the thread is created. The `Applet` object (`this`) is passed to the thread constructor. This creates a thread that, when started, executes the code in the `run()` method of the applet. That method performs the actual animation—it draws an image, calls `Thread.sleep()` to wait 200 milliseconds, and then loops to draw the next image.

Example 4-8: The Animator applet

```
/**
 * This applet displays an animation. It doesn't handle errors while
 * loading images. It doesn't wait for all images to be loaded before
 * starting the animation. These problems will be addressed later.
 **/
import java.applet.*;
import java.awt.*;
import java.net.*;
import java.util.*;

public class Animator extends Applet implements Runnable {
    protected Image[] images;
    protected int current_image;

    // Read the basename and num_images parameters.
    // Then read in the images, using the specified base name.
    // For example, if basename is images/anim, read images/anim0,
    // images/anim1, etc. These are relative to the current document URL.
    public void init() {
        String basename = this.getParameter("basename");
        int num_images;
        try { num_images = Integer.parseInt(this.getParameter("num_images")); }
        catch (NumberFormatException e) { num_images = 0; }

        images = new Image[num_images];
        for(int i = 0; i < num_images; i++) {
            images[i] = this.getImage(this.getDocumentBase(), basename + i);
        }
    }

    // This is the thread that runs the animation, and the methods
    // that start it and stop it.
    private Thread animator_thread = null;
```

```
    public void start() {
        if (animator_thread == null) {
            animator_thread = new Thread(this);
            animator_thread.start();
        }
    }
    public void stop() {
        if ((animator_thread != null) && animator_thread.isAlive())
            animator_thread.stop();
        // We do this so the garbage collector can reclaim the Thread object.
        // Otherwise it might sit around in the Web browser for a long time.
        animator_thread = null;
    }

    // This is the body of the thread--the method that does the animation.
    public void run() {
        while(true) {
            if (++current_image >= images.length) current_image = 0;
            this.getGraphics().drawImage(images[current_image], 0, 0, this);
            try { Thread.sleep(200); } catch (InterruptedException e) ;
        }
    }
}
```

Sound

Example 4-9 shows a subclass of our animator applet, `AudioAnimator`, that adds the ability to play an audio clip when the applet starts up. In this simple example, the sound is not synchronized with the animation in any way—it is simply played at some point not too long after the applet starts. It is a technique that could be used to add some sort of a "welcome" sound to a Web page, for example.

The `init()` method first calls the superclass initialize method, as we've seen in previous examples. Then it reads the "sound" property to find the name of the sound to download. Instead of downloading and playing the sound directly, however, it creates a thread to handle this, so that it does not delay the start of the animation. (On the other hand, if it is important that the sound begin before the animation starts, then creating this thread would not be a good technique.)

The `SoundPlayer` class is the thread that plays the sound. Its `run()` method uses the `Applet play()` method to download and play the specified sound. The constructor method for the `SoundPlayer` object calls `start()` to start the thread running. Note that this is an example of a thread created by subclassing `Thread` directly, rather than writing a class that implements `Runnable`, as we did in the `Animator` example.

Note that the `run()` method that performs the animation is not listed here. It is inherited from the `Animator` superclass.

Example 4-9: Playing a sound

```
import java.applet.*;
import java.awt.*;

public class AudioAnimator extends Animator {
    public void init() {
        // do Animator initialization first
        super.init();

        // look up the name of a sound, and then
        // load and play it (just once), in a separate thread.
        String soundname = this.getParameter("sound");
        new SoundPlayer(this, soundname);
    }
}

// This is the thread class that loads and plays the sound
class SoundPlayer extends Thread {
    private Applet applet;
    private String sound_url;
    // Store the information the run() method needs, and start it.
    public SoundPlayer(Applet app, String url) {
        applet = app;
        sound_url = url;
        this.start();
    }
    // This is the code the thread runs to load and play the sound
    public void run() { applet.play(applet.getDocumentBase(), sound_url); }
}
```


Standalone Applets

Example 4-10, the final example of this chapter, begins a transition from Java applets to Java applications. It is a trivial subclass of the `Scribble` applet that adds a `main()` method that allows it to run as a standalone Java application. The `main()` method creates an instance of the applet and then creates a window to put it in. The window is an instance of the `AppletFrame` class, which is also shown here. The `AppletFrame` creates a menu bar with a **File** menu and a **Quit** button. (The next chapter contains examples of using these and other GUI components.) The `Applet-Frame` displays the applet and calls its `init()` and `start()` methods. The `action()` method calls `System.exit()` when the user selects **Quit** from the menu.

This `AppletFrame` object only works for very simple applets and is certainly no replacement for a real applet viewer. It has many restrictions: the applet cannot use `getParameter()`, `showStatus()`, `showDocument()`, `getImage()`, or other `Applet` methods that depend on the `AppletContext`. On the other hand, it is a useful example because it demystifies applets and shows how they can be manipulated.

Example 4-10: Running an applet as an application

```
import java.applet.*;
import java.awt.*;

// This is a simple example of allowing an applet to run as a standalone
// Java application. The only problem is that when running standalone,
// it can't read applet parameters.
public class StandaloneScribble extends Scribble {
        public static void main(String args[]) {
                Applet applet = new StandaloneScribble();
                Frame frame = new AppletFrame("Scribble", applet, 300, 300);
        }
}

class AppletFrame extends Frame {
        public AppletFrame(String title, Applet applet, int width, int height) {
                // create the Frame with the specified title.
                super(title);

                // Add a menu bar, with a File menu, with a Quit button.
                MenuBar menubar = new MenuBar();
                Menu file = new Menu("File", true);
                menubar.add(file);
                file.add("Quit");
                this.setMenuBar(menubar);

                // Add the applet to the window. Set the window size. Pop it up.
                this.add("Center", applet);
                this.resize(width, height);
                this.show();

                // Start the applet.
                applet.init();
                applet.start();
        }

        // Handle the Quit menu button.
        public boolean action(Event e, Object arg)
        {
                if (e.target instanceof MenuItem) {
                        String label = (String) arg;
                        if (label.equals("Quit")) System.exit(0);
                }
                return false;
        }
}
```

Graphical User Interfaces

Graphical Interfaces

The examples in this section demonstrate how to build graphical user interfaces with Java. They show you how to:

- Create interface components and add them to containers.
- Arrange components within a container using various layout managers.
- Create simple dialog boxes.
- Receive and handle notification from user interface components that the user has interacted with them.
- Work with scrollbars.
- Create new components of your own.

The examples all use the classes of the `java.awt` package. Read the introduction to Section 19, *The java.awt Package*, for a useful overview of the classes in this package. You may also want to refer to the class descriptions in that section while reading these examples.

An Information Dialog

Example 5-1 shows how you can create a dialog box, like the one pictured in Figure 5-1, to display information to the user.

The constructor method creates a window with the specified title for the dialog box. It also creates a `MultiLineLabel` component to display the message and an **Okay** button that the user can use to dismiss the dialog. The `MultiLineLabel` class is a

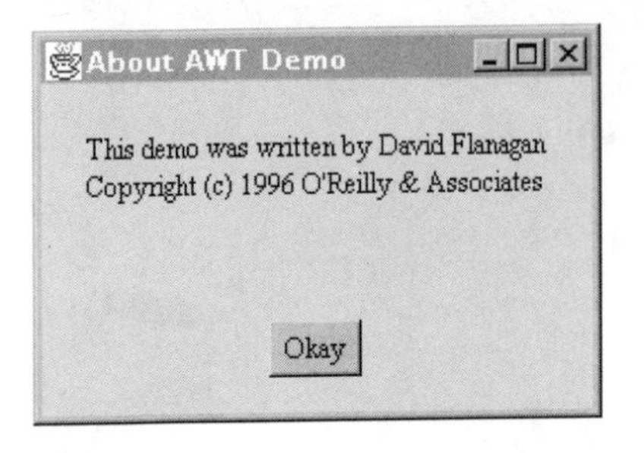

Figure 5-1: An information dialog

custom component that will be defined in a later example. It behaves much like the `java.awt.Label` object, but can display multiple lines of text.

This example shows the use of two different layout managers. A layout manager is an object that arranges Java components within their containers. Different subclasses of `LayoutManager` arrange components in a container in different ways. As you read through this example, pay particular attention to the use of the `BorderLayout` and `FlowLayout` objects.

Note that this example is a Java application, not an applet. The `main()` method tests and demonstrates the `InfoDialog` class, but this class could also be used within other, larger applications, or within applets.

Example 5-1: An information dialog

```
import java.awt.*;

public class InfoDialog extends Dialog {
    protected Button button;
    protected MultiLineLabel label;

    public InfoDialog(Frame parent, String title, String message)
    {
        // Create a dialog with the specified title
        super(parent, title, false);

        // Create and use a BorderLayout manager with specified margins
        this.setLayout(new BorderLayout(15, 15));

        // Create the message component and add it to the window
        label = new MultiLineLabel(message, 20, 20);
        this.add("Center", label);

        // Create an Okay button in a Panel; add the Panel to the window
        // Use a FlowLayout to center the button and give it margins.
        button = new Button("Okay");
        Panel p = new Panel();
        p.setLayout(new FlowLayout(FlowLayout.CENTER, 15, 15));
        p.add(button);
        this.add("South", p);

        // Resize the window to the preferred size of its components
        this.pack();
    }
```

Example 5-1: An information dialog (continued)

```
    // Pop down the window when the button is clicked.
    public boolean action(Event e, Object arg)
    {
        if (e.target == button) {
            this.hide();
            this.dispose();
            return true;
        }
        else return false;
    }

    // When the window gets the keyboard focus, give it to the button.
    // This allows keyboard shortcuts to pop down the dialog.
    public boolean gotFocus(Event e, Object arg) {
        button.requestFocus();
        return true;
    }

    public static void main(String[] args) {
        Frame f = new Frame("InfoDialog Test");
        f.resize(100, 100);
        f.show();
        InfoDialog d = new InfoDialog(f, "About AWT Demo",
                            "This demo was written by David Flanagan\n" +
                            "Copyright (c) 1996 O'Reilly & Associates");
        d.show();
    }
}
```

Graphical Interfaces

The constructor method creates a `BorderLayout` layout manager and uses the `setLayout()` method to tell the dialog to use it. The `BorderLayout` manager works by positioning four components against the four edges of the container and positioning another in the center, where it receives all the remaining space in the container. The position of components is specified to the `BorderLayout` by giving them specific names. In this case, we use the `BorderLayout` to position the button against the bottom edge by giving it the name "South," and we position the label in the center by giving it the name "Center." Note the use of the `add()` method to add a component to a container and to specify a name for it.

If you followed the code closely, you noticed that we do not add the button directly to the window. If we did that, the `BorderLayout` layout manager would force it to expand horizontally to fill the entire bottom of the dialog. Instead, we want it centered along the bottom of the dialog, with space on either side. To achieve this, we create a new container, a `Panel`, with a `FlowLayout` layout manager, and place the button in this new container. The `FlowLayout` layout manager arranges its components in rows. We create a `FlowLayout` that centers each row. Since there is only one component (the button) in this panel, the `FlowLayout` centers the button in the panel. Note that there is no need to specify a name for the button when calling the panel's `add()` method—the `FlowLayout` does not care about component names. With the button centered in the panel, it is the panel itself that we add to the dialog container, with the name "South" so that the `BorderLayout` positions it correctly.

The final call of interest in the constructor method is `pack()`. `Dialog` and `Frame` containers support this method. It sets the size of the window to the preferred size of all of the components of the window—i.e., it makes the window just big enough to display everything comfortably. You'll use this method frequently just before making a window visible.

The `action()` method handles the button click. When the **Okay** button is pressed, it first pops the window down with the `hide()` method and then "destroys" any window system resources associated with the dialog by calling `dispose()`. Once `dispose()` has been called, the window may never be used again.

The `gotFocus()` method is called by the system when the window gets the keyboard focus—i.e., when keystrokes are delivered to that window instead of any other window. Here, the method simply asks to pass the focus on to the **Okay** button. On many platforms, this allows the **Okay** button to be invoked by typing SPACE or RETURN at the keyboard.

Finally, the `main()` method demonstrates how this `InfoDialog` class might be used—a dialog is created with a specified title and message for a specified `Frame`, and is popped up with the `show()` method. One enhancement that we might add to this class is the ability to display an image along with the message (perhaps against the left side of the window, using a "West" layout of the `BorderLayout`). Another enhancement might be the ability to reuse the dialog by removing the `dispose()` call and defining methods to allow the title and message to be changed.

A Dialog with User Response

The `InfoDialog` class we saw in the previous example only displays information. The user can dismiss the dialog, but the program never has to respond when the user dismisses it. Many other dialogs, however, require the program to respond to the user's input. Example 5-2 shows the `YesNoDialog` class that can be used to create dialogs like that shown in Figure 5-2.

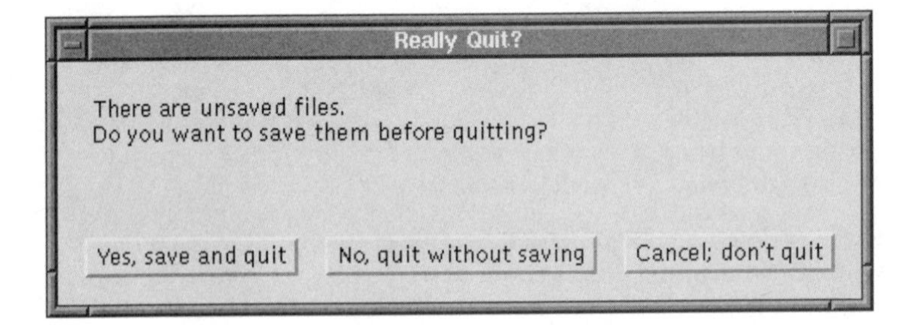

Figure 5-2: A yes-or-no dialog

As you can see, the `YesNoDialog` constructor method is much like that of the `InfoDialog` class, except that it creates three buttons, with specified labels, rather than a single **Okay** button. The difference between these two dialog types is in the `action()` method. In this case, the `action()` method checks which button the user clicked and passes that information to the `answer()` method, which calls the `yes()`, `no()`, or `cancel()` method, as appropriate.

Example 5-2: A yes-or-no dialog

```
import java.awt.*;

public class YesNoDialog extends Dialog {
    public static final int NO = 0;
    public static final int YES = 1;
    public static final int CANCEL = -1;

    protected Button yes = null, no = null, cancel = null;
    protected MultiLineLabel label;

    public YesNoDialog(Frame parent, String title, String message,
               String yes_label, String no_label, String cancel_label)
    {
        // Create the window.
        super(parent, title, true);

        // Specify a LayoutManager for it
        this.setLayout(new BorderLayout(15, 15));

        // Put the message label in the middle of the window.
        label = new MultiLineLabel(message, 20, 20);
        this.add("Center", label);

        // Create a panel of buttons, center the row of buttons in
        // the panel, and put the pane at the bottom of the window.
        Panel p = new Panel();
        p.setLayout(new FlowLayout(FlowLayout.CENTER, 15, 15));
        if (yes_label != null) p.add(yes = new Button(yes_label));
        if (no_label != null)  p.add(no = new Button(no_label));
        if (cancel_label != null) p.add(cancel = new Button(cancel_label));
        this.add("South", p);

        // Set the window to its preferred size.
        this.pack();
    }

    // Handle button events by calling the answer() method.
    // Pass the appropriate constant value, depending on the button.
    public boolean action(Event e, Object arg)
    {
        if (e.target instanceof Button) {
            this.hide();
            this.dispose();
            if (e.target == yes) answer(YES);
            else if (e.target == no) answer(NO);
            else answer(CANCEL);
            return true;
        }
        else return false;
    }

    // Call yes(), no(), and cancel() methods depending on the button the
    // user clicked.  Subclasses define how the answer is processed by
    // overriding this method or the  yes(), no(), and cancel() methods.
    protected void answer(int answer) {
        switch(answer) {
```

Example 5-2: A yes-or-no dialog (continued)

```
                case YES: yes(); break;
                case NO:  no(); break;
                case CANCEL: cancel(); break;
            }
        }
        protected void yes() {}
        protected void no() {}
        protected void cancel() {}
    }
```

Notice that the constructor method for this class allows us to omit button labels for the **Yes**, **No**, and **Cancel** buttons. If a label is omitted, the button simply won't be created.

In the `YesNoDialog` class itself, the `yes()`, `no()`, and `cancel()` methods don't do anything. To actually respond to the user's input, the Java programming model requires us to subclass `YesNoDialog` and provide our own custom definitions of these three methods. Example 5-3 shows such a subclass. Notice that there is no `main()` method in this example that shows how the `ReallyQuitDialog` class is created and used. We'll see it used in an example later in this chapter.

Example 5-3: A subclass of the dialog

```
import java.awt.*;

public class ReallyQuitDialog extends YesNoDialog {
    TextComponent status;
    // Create the kind of YesNoDialog we want
    // And store away a piece of information we need later.
    public ReallyQuitDialog(Frame parent, TextComponent status) {
        super(parent, "Really Quit?", "Really Quit?", "Yes", "No", null);
        this.status = status;
    }
    // Define these methods to handle the user's answer
    public void yes() { System.exit(0); }
    public void no() {
        if (status != null) status.setText("Quit cancelled.");
    }
}
```

All Java GUI Components

Example 5-4 shows the code required to create each of the GUI components supported by Java. Figure 5-3 shows the resulting interface on a UNIX/Motif platform; Figure 5-4 shows the interface on a Windows platform.

This example introduces the `GridBagLayout` layout manager and shows how you can use it to arrange components into more complicated arrangements than we've seen before. This layout manager is a powerful and quite confusing one. It is explained following the example code. You may also want to refer to the API quick reference material for more information about `GridBagLayout` and `GridBagConstraints`.

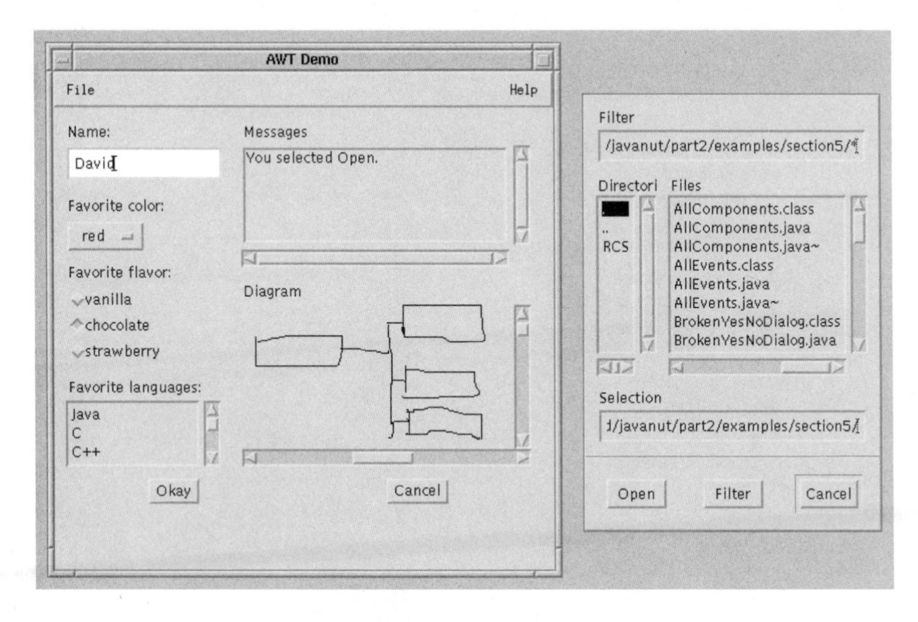

Figure 5-3: Java GUI components in Motif

Example 5-4: Creating all the Java GUI components

```
import java.awt.*;

public class AllComponents extends Frame {
    MenuBar menubar;                    // The menu bar
    Menu file, help;                    // Menu panes
    Button okay, cancel;                // Buttons
    List list;                          // A list of choices
    Choice choice;                      // A menu of choices
    CheckboxGroup checkbox_group;       // A group of button choices
    Checkbox[] checkboxes;              // The buttons to choose from
    TextField textfield;                // One line of text input
    TextArea  textarea;                 // A text window
    ScrollableScribble scribble;        // An area to draw in
    FileDialog file_dialog;

    Panel panel1, panel2 ;              // Sub-containers for all this stuff.
    Panel buttonpanel;

    // The layout manager for each of the containers.
    GridBagLayout gridbag = new GridBagLayout();

    public AllComponents(String title) {
        super(title);

        // Create the menu bar.  Tell the frame about it.
        menubar = new MenuBar();
        this.setMenuBar(menubar);
        // Create the file menu.  Add two items to it. Add to menu bar.
        file = new Menu("File");
        file.add(new MenuItem("Open"));
        file.add(new MenuItem("Quit"));
        menubar.add(file);
```

```
// Create Help menu; add an item; add to menu bar
help = new Menu("Help");
help.add(new MenuItem("About"));
menubar.add(help);
// Display the help menu in a special reserved place.
menubar.setHelpMenu(help);

// Create pushbuttons.
okay = new Button("Okay");
cancel = new Button("Cancel");

// Create a menu of choices.
choice = new Choice();
choice.addItem("red");
choice.addItem("green");
choice.addItem("blue");

// Create checkboxes, and group them.
checkbox_group = new CheckboxGroup();
checkboxes = new Checkbox[3];
checkboxes[0] = new Checkbox("vanilla", checkbox_group, false);
checkboxes[1] = new Checkbox("chocolate", checkbox_group, true);
checkboxes[2] = new Checkbox("strawberry", checkbox_group, false);

// Create a list of choices.
list = new List(4, true);
list.addItem("Java"); list.addItem("C"); list.addItem("C++");
list.addItem("Smalltalk"); list.addItem("Lisp");
list.addItem("Modula-3"); list.addItem("Forth");

// Create a one-line text field, and multiline text area.
textfield = new TextField(15);
textarea = new TextArea(6, 40);
textarea.setEditable(false);

// Create a scrolling canvas to scribble in.
scribble = new ScrollableScribble();

// Create a file selection dialog box.
file_dialog = new FileDialog(this, "Open File", FileDialog.LOAD);

// Create a Panel to contain all the components along the
// left-hand side of the window.  Use a GridBagLayout for it.
panel1 = new Panel();
panel1.setLayout(gridbag);

// Use several versions of the constrain() convenience method
// to add components to the panel and to specify their
// GridBagConstraints values.
constrain(panel1, new Label("Name:"), 0, 0, 1, 1);
constrain(panel1, textfield, 0, 1, 1, 1);
constrain(panel1, new Label("Favorite color:"), 0, 2, 1, 1,
        10, 0, 0, 0);
constrain(panel1, choice, 0, 3, 1, 1);
constrain(panel1, new Label("Favorite flavor:"), 0, 4, 1, 1,
        10, 0, 0, 0);
```

```
        constrain(panel1, checkboxes[0], 0, 5, 1, 1);
        constrain(panel1, checkboxes[1], 0, 6, 1, 1);
        constrain(panel1, checkboxes[2], 0, 7, 1, 1);
        constrain(panel1, new Label("Favorite languages:"), 0, 8, 1, 1,
                10, 0, 0, 0);
        constrain(panel1, list, 0, 9, 1, 3, GridBagConstraints.VERTICAL,
                GridBagConstraints.NORTHWEST, 0.0, 1.0, 0, 0, 0, 0);

        // Create a panel for the items along the right side.
        // Use a GridBagLayout, and arrange items with constrain(), as above.
        panel2 = new Panel();
        panel2.setLayout(gridbag);

        constrain(panel2, new Label("Messages"), 0, 0, 1, 1);
        constrain(panel2, textarea, 0, 1, 1, 3, GridBagConstraints.HORIZONTAL,
                GridBagConstraints.NORTH, 1.0, 0.0, 0, 0, 0, 0);
        constrain(panel2, new Label("Diagram"), 0, 4, 1, 1, 10, 0, 0, 0);
        constrain(panel2, scribble, 0, 5, 1, 5, GridBagConstraints.BOTH,
                GridBagConstraints.CENTER, 1.0, 1.0, 0, 0, 0, 0);

        // Do the same for the buttons along the bottom.
        buttonpanel = new Panel();
        buttonpanel.setLayout(gridbag);
        constrain(buttonpanel, okay, 0, 0, 1, 1, GridBagConstraints.NONE,
                GridBagConstraints.CENTER, 0.3, 0.0, 0, 0, 0, 0);
        constrain(buttonpanel, cancel, 1, 0, 1, 1, GridBagConstraints.NONE,
                GridBagConstraints.CENTER, 0.3, 0.0, 0, 0, 0, 0);

        // Finally, use a GridBagLayout to arrange the panels themselves
        this.setLayout(gridbag);
        // And add the panels to the toplevel window
        constrain(this, panel1, 0, 0, 1, 1, GridBagConstraints.VERTICAL,
                GridBagConstraints.NORTHWEST, 0.0, 1.0, 10, 10, 5, 5);
        constrain(this, panel2, 1, 0, 1, 1, GridBagConstraints.BOTH,
                GridBagConstraints.CENTER, 1.0, 1.0, 10, 10, 5, 10);
        constrain(this, buttonpanel, 0, 1, 2, 1, GridBagConstraints.HORIZONTAL,
                GridBagConstraints.CENTER, 1.0, 0.0, 5, 0, 0, 0);
    }

    // This is the main constrain() method.
    // It has arguments for all constraints.
    public void constrain(Container container, Component component,
                    int grid_x, int grid_y, int grid_width, int grid_height,
                    int fill, int anchor, double weight_x, double weight_y,
                    int top, int left, int bottom, int right)
    {
        GridBagConstraints c = new GridBagConstraints();
        c.gridx = grid_x; c.gridy = grid_y;
        c.gridwidth = grid_width; c.gridheight = grid_height;
        c.fill = fill; c.anchor = anchor;
        c.weightx = weight_x; c.weighty = weight_y;
        if (top+bottom+left+right > 0)
            c.insets = new Insets(top, left, bottom, right);

        ((GridBagLayout)container.getLayout()).setConstraints(component, c);
```

```
            container.add(component);
    }

    // This version of constrain() specifies the position of a component
    // that does not grow and does not have margins.
    public void constrain(Container container, Component component,
                    int grid_x, int grid_y, int grid_width, int grid_height) {
            constrain(container, component, grid_x, grid_y,
                    grid_width, grid_height, GridBagConstraints.NONE,
                    GridBagConstraints.NORTHWEST, 0.0, 0.0, 0, 0, 0, 0);
    }

    // This version of constrain() positions a component that does
    // not grow, but does have margins.
    public void constrain(Container container, Component component,
                    int grid_x, int grid_y, int grid_width, int grid_height,
                    int top, int left, int bottom, int right) {
            constrain(container, component, grid_x, grid_y,
                    grid_width, grid_height, GridBagConstraints.NONE,
                    GridBagConstraints.NORTHWEST,
                    0.0, 0.0, top, left, bottom, right);
    }

    public static void main(String[] args) {
            Frame f = new AllComponents("AWT Demo");
            f.pack();
            f.show();
    }
}
```

The constructor method in this example is a long one—it does all the component creation and layout. Creating the components is straightforward; study the example to see how it is done. Arranging the components with the `GridBagLayout` layout manager is more confusing. Before proceeding further, read about `GridBagLayout` and `GridBagConstraints` in the quick reference section of this book.

The `GridBagLayout` arranges components as specified by the values in a `GridBagConstraints` object associated with each component. In this example, the various `constrain()` methods simplify the use of the `GridBagLayout`. We use them to combine the process of specifying constraints for a component and adding the component to its container.

Note that the components in this example are arranged in three separate panels, and that the panels are all arranged within a `Frame`; each of these containers is separately laid out by a `GridBagLayout` manager. Nesting the components within panels in this way is not strictly necessary, but greatly simplifies the layout—we specify four relatively simple layouts instead of one very complicated one. Notice that a single `GridBagLayout` object is used to lay out all of the containers—the layout specifications are contained in the constraints, not in the layout manager itself, so a single manager can be used for many containers.

Recall that the `GridBagLayout` manager divides the container into rows and columns, which may each be a different size. Each column is as wide as the widest component it contains, and each row is as tall as the tallest component it contains.

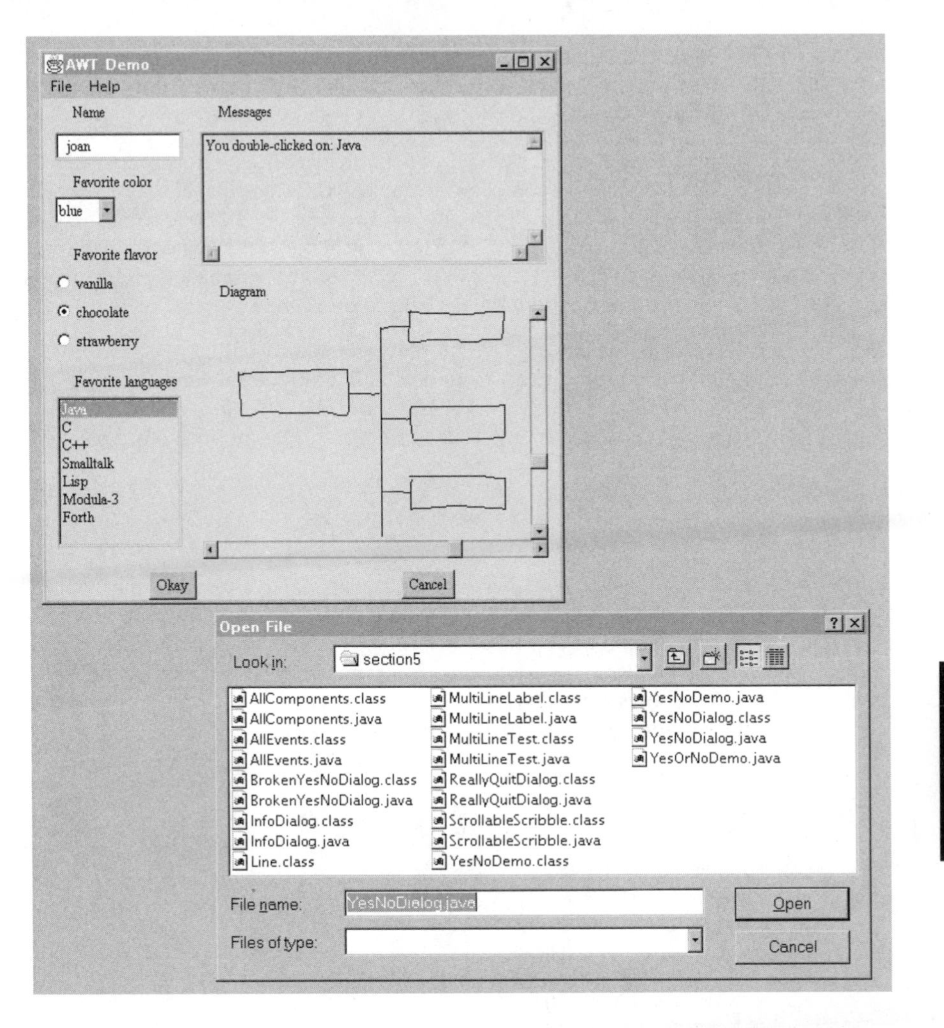

Figure 5-4: Java GUI components in Windows

Components are placed within the cells of this row/column grid, and they are allowed to span multiple rows or columns. Therefore, the four most important constraint values that specify a component's position in a `GridBagLayout` are the component's position in the grid, its width in columns, and its height in rows. All versions of the `constrain()` method require these four constraints to be specified.

Another important constraint is the `fill` value, which specifies whether the component should grow to fill any extra space available to it in the grid. Legal values are the `GridBagConstraints` constants `HORIZONTAL` (grow to fill horizontal space), `VERTICAL` (grow to fill vertical space), `BOTH` (grow in both directions) and `NONE` (never grow at all). For components that do not grow in both directions, the `anchor` constraint specifies how they should be positioned within their grid cells when there is extra space.

The `weightx` and `weighty` constraints specify how rows and columns in the grid should resize when the whole container is resized. When a container is made larger, the rows and columns of the grid receive the extra space in proportion to their relative weights. If all the items in a column have a weightx of 0.0, then that column will never become any wider when the container grows. If all the items in a row have a weighty of 0.0, then the row will never get any taller.

Finally, the optional top, left, bottom, and right arguments to constrain() specify margins for each side of each component. The GridBagLayout allocates the specified amount of extra space on each side of the component. Specifying margins is useful to prevent components from appearing squished together. The four optional margin arguments to constrain() are used to create an Insets object, which is specified as the insets constraint in the GridBagConstraints object.

The GridBagLayout is the most powerful and generally useful of the Java layout managers. It is difficult, but important to understand. Study the example; reread the explanation above; refer back to Figure 5-4; draw sketches if you need to. Whatever you do, it is important to take the time to be sure you understand exactly how each component is laid out in the window.

Handling GUI Events

In the previous example, we created lots of GUI components. None of the components actually did anything, however. When a user interacts with a Java GUI component (e.g., clicks on a button or selects an item in a list), the component generates an Event object. In order to respond to the user's interaction, we must handle the event. Example 5-5 shows how this can be done for each of the Java components that we created in the previous example.

Example 5-5: Handling GUI events

```
import java.awt.*;

public class AllEvents extends AllComponents {
    public AllEvents(String title) {
        super(title);
    }
    // This method handles all the events generated by all the components.
    public boolean handleEvent(Event event) {
        switch(event.id) {
        // Most components generate ACTION_EVENT
        // We test the target field to find out which component.
        case Event.ACTION_EVENT:
            if (event.target == textfield) {
                textarea.setText("Your name is: " + (String)event.arg + "\n");
            }
            else if (event.target == choice) {
                textarea.setText("Your favorite color is: " +
                                 (String) event.arg + "\n");
            }
            else if ((event.target == checkboxes[0]) ||
                     (event.target == checkboxes[1]) ||
                     (event.target == checkboxes[2])) {
                textarea.setText("Your favorite flavor is: " +
                                 checkbox_group.getCurrent().getLabel() + "\n");
            }
            else if (event.target == list) {
                textarea.setText("You double-clicked on: " +
                                 (String)event.arg + "\n");
            }
```

```
            else if (event.target == okay) {
                textarea.setText("Okay button clicked.\n");
            }
            else if (event.target == cancel) {
                textarea.setText("Cancel button clicked.\n");
            }
            else if (event.target instanceof MenuItem) {
                // Since we didn't save references to each of the menu objects,
                // we check which one was pressed by comparing labels.
                // Note that we respond to these menu items by
                // popping up dialog boxes.
                if (((String)event.arg).equals("Quit")) {
                    YesNoDialog d = new ReallyQuitDialog(this, textarea);
                    d.show();
                }
                else if (((String)event.arg).equals("Open")) {
                    textarea.setText("You selected Open.\n");
                    // Use the dialog box created by our superclass.
                    file_dialog.pack();     // bug workaround
                    file_dialog.show();     // blocks until user selects a file
                    textarea.setText("You selected file: " +
                                     file_dialog.getFile());
                }
                else if (((String)event.arg).equals("About")) {
                    InfoDialog d;
                    d = new InfoDialog(this, "About AWT Demo",
                                       "This demo was written by David Flanagan\n" +
                                       "Copyright (c) 1996 O'Reilly & Associates");
                    d.show();
                    textarea.setText("You selected About.\n");
                }
            }
            else {
                textarea.setText("Unknown action event.");
            }
            break;

        // Double-clicking on a list generates an action event.
        // But list selection and deselection are separate event types.
        case Event.LIST_SELECT:
            textarea.setText("You selected: " +
                             list.getItem(((Integer)event.arg).intValue()) + "\n");
            break;
        case Event.LIST_DESELECT:
            textarea.setText("You deselected: " +
                             list.getItem(((Integer)event.arg).intValue()) + "\n");
            break;

        // These are some events pertaining to the window itself.
        case Event.WINDOW_DESTROY:
            textarea.setText("Window Destroy\n");
            break;
        case Event.WINDOW_ICONIFY:
            textarea.setText("Window iconify\n");
            break;
        case Event.WINDOW_DEICONIFY:
```

```
                textarea.setText("Window deiconify\n");
                break;
            case Event.WINDOW_MOVED:
                textarea.setText("Window moved\n");
                break;

            // We print a message about each of these mouse and key events,
            // but return false after so that they can still
            // be properly handled by their correct recipient.
            case Event.MOUSE_DOWN:
                textarea.setText("Mouse down: [" + event.x + "," + event.y + "]\n");
                return false;
            case Event.MOUSE_UP:
                textarea.setText("Mouse up: [" + event.x + "," + event.y + "]\n");
                return false;
            case Event.MOUSE_DRAG:
                textarea.setText("Mouse drag: [" + event.x + "," + event.y + "]\n");
                return false;
            case Event.KEY_PRESS:
            case Event.KEY_ACTION:
                textarea.setText("Key press\n");
                return false;
            case Event.KEY_RELEASE:
            case Event.KEY_ACTION_RELEASE:
                textarea.setText("Key release\n");
                return false;

            // We ignore these event types.
            case Event.GOT_FOCUS:
            case Event.LOST_FOCUS:
            case Event.MOUSE_ENTER:
            case Event.MOUSE_EXIT:
            case Event.MOUSE_MOVE:
                return false;

            // We shouldn't ever get this...
            default:
                textarea.setText("Unexpected Event type: " + event + "\n");
                break;
            }
            return true;
        }

        // Here's the method that lets us run and test this class.
        public static void main(String[] args) {
            Frame f = new AllEvents("AWT Demo");
            f.pack();
            f.show();
        }
    }
```

The event-handling code in this example is a single long `switch` statement within the `handleEvent()` method. `handleEvent()` is invoked by the system when an event is generated. In this example, `handleEvent()` detects all of the possible events and displays an appropriate message in the text area of the window.

(Actually, scrollbar events are not handled here; scrollbars and scrolling events are the subject of the next example.) Study the code to find out what kinds of events are generated by what kinds of components and to learn how these events can be handled. You might also want to look at Section 11, *Events*, which contains a quick reference table of components and the event types they generate.

The `id` field of an `Event` specifies the type of the event. The `Event.ACTION_EVENT` type is generated by a GUI component (though components can generate other types of events as well) and means that the user has clicked a button, selected an item from a menu, entered text in a text field, and so on. The `target` field of an `Event` specifies the particular component that generated the event. The `arg` field often specifies additional useful information about the event. For example, when a button is clicked, the `arg` field contains the label of the button. `arg` is of type `Object`; you have to cast it to the appropriate type before using it. See Section 11 for full information about how the `arg` and other `Event` fields are used for each event type.

Note that you do not always have to override `handleEvent()` to handle events in Java. In the previous chapter, we saw examples that overrode `action()`, `mouseDown()`, and other methods specific to a particular event type. The problem with this approach is that it does not work for all event types. For example, there is no special method you can override to handle the `Event.LIST_SELECT` event type. Thus, for fully general-purpose event handling, you need to override the `handleEvent()` method. If you also want the convenience of being able to override `action()` and other specific event handling methods, be sure to invoke the superclass `handleEvent()` method at the end of your own `handleEvent()` method:

```
if (event_handled) return true;
else return super.handleEvent(e);
```

You must do this because it is the default implementation of `handleEvent()` that invokes `action()` and the other specific event handling methods. If you override `handleEvent()` without invoking the superclass `handleEvent()` method, then `action()` and the other methods will never be invoked.

Remember that an event handling method should return `true` if it has fully handled the event and the event needs no more processing. The method should return `false` if it did not handle the event and the event should be passed on to some other container for handling.

Working with Scrollbars

Figure 5-4 above showed a scrollable area that a user could scribble in. Example 5-4 created that area as an instance of the `ScrollableScribble` class. Now, Example 5-6 shows the definition of that class and demonstrates how to use scrollbars in your Java programs.

Example 5-6: Working with scrollbars

```
import java.awt.*;

public class ScrollableScribble extends Panel {
    Canvas canvas;
    Scrollbar hbar, vbar;
    java.util.Vector lines = new java.util.Vector(100, 100);
```

```
    int last_x, last_y;
    int offset_x, offset_y;
    int canvas_width, canvas_height;

    // Create a canvas and two scrollbars and lay them out in the panel.
    // Use a BorderLayout to get the scrollbars flush against the
    // right and bottom sides of the canvas. When the panel grows,
    // the canvas and scrollbars will also grow appropriately.
    public ScrollableScribble() {
        // implicit super() call here creates the panel
        canvas = new Canvas();
        hbar = new Scrollbar(Scrollbar.HORIZONTAL);
        vbar = new Scrollbar(Scrollbar.VERTICAL);
        this.setLayout(new BorderLayout(0, 0));
        this.add("Center", canvas);
        this.add("South", hbar);
        this.add("East", vbar);
    }

    // Draw the scribbles that we've saved in the Vector.
    // The offset_x and offset_y variables specify which portion of
    // the larger (1000x1000) scribble is to be displayed in the
    // relatively small canvas. Moving the scrollbars changes these
    // variables, and thus scrolls the picture. Note that the Canvas
    // component automatically does clipping; we can't accidentally
    // draw outside of its borders.
    public void paint(Graphics g) {
        Line l;
        Graphics canvas_g = canvas.getGraphics();
        for(int i = 0; i < lines.size(); i++) {
            l = (Line)lines.elementAt(i);
            canvas_g.drawLine(l.x1 - offset_x, l.y1 - offset_y,
                              l.x2 - offset_x, l.y2 - offset_y);
        }
    }

    // Handle user's mouse scribbles. Draw the scribbles
    // and save them in the vector for later redrawing.
    public boolean mouseDown(Event e, int x, int y)
    {
        last_x = x; last_y = y;
        return true;
    }
    public boolean mouseDrag(Event e, int x, int y)
    {
        Graphics g = canvas.getGraphics();
        g.drawLine(last_x, last_y, x, y);
        lines.addElement(new Line(last_x + offset_x, last_y + offset_y,
                                  x + offset_x, y + offset_y));
        last_x = x;
        last_y = y;
        return true;
    }
    // handle mouse up, too, just for symmetry.
    public boolean mouseUp(Event e, int x, int y) { return true; }
```

```
        // This method handles the scrollbar events.  It updates the
        // offset_x and offset_y variables that are used by the paint()
        // method, and then calls update(), which clears the canvas and
        // invokes the paint() method to redraw the scribbles.
        public boolean handleEvent(Event e) {
            if (e.target == hbar) {
                switch(e.id) {
                case Event.SCROLL_LINE_UP:
                case Event.SCROLL_LINE_DOWN:
                case Event.SCROLL_PAGE_UP:
                case Event.SCROLL_PAGE_DOWN:
                case Event.SCROLL_ABSOLUTE:
                    offset_x = ((Integer)e.arg).intValue(); break;
                }
                this.update(canvas.getGraphics());
                return true;
            }
            else if (e.target == vbar) {
                switch(e.id) {
                case Event.SCROLL_LINE_UP:
                case Event.SCROLL_PAGE_UP:
                case Event.SCROLL_LINE_DOWN:
                case Event.SCROLL_PAGE_DOWN:
                case Event.SCROLL_ABSOLUTE:
                    offset_y = ((Integer)e.arg).intValue(); break;
                }
                this.update(canvas.getGraphics());
                return true;
            }

            // If we didn't handle it above, pass it on to the superclass
            // handleEvent routine, which will check its type and call
            // the mouseDown(), mouseDrag(), and other methods.
            return super.handleEvent(e);
        }

        // This method is called when our size is changed.  We need to
        // know this so we can update the scrollbars
        public synchronized void reshape(int x, int y, int width, int height) {
            // do the real stuff
            super.reshape(x, y, width, height);
            // Update our scrollbar page size
            Dimension hbar_size = hbar.size();
            Dimension vbar_size = vbar.size();
            canvas_width = width - vbar_size.width;
            canvas_height = height - hbar_size.height;
            hbar.setValues(offset_x, canvas_width, 0, 1000-canvas_width);
            vbar.setValues(offset_y, canvas_height, 0, 1000-canvas_height);
            hbar.setPageIncrement(canvas_width/2);
            vbar.setPageIncrement(canvas_height/2);
            this.update(canvas.getGraphics());

        }
    }

    // This class stores the coordinates of one line of the scribble.
```

Example 5-6: Working with scrollbars (continued)

```
class Line {
    public int x1, y1, x2, y2;
    public Line(int x1, int y1, int x2, int y2) {
        this.x1 = x1; this.y1 = y1; this.x2 = x2; this.y2 = y2;
    }
}
```

`ScrollableScribble` is a subclass of `Panel`. The constructor method creates a `Canvas` component and horizontal and vertical scrollbars. These components are laid out within the panel with a `BorderLayout` layout manager, which is perfect for getting the scrollbars flush against the edges of the canvas.

In this example, the `mouseDown()` and `mouseDrag()` methods are used to detect the user's scribbles. When the user drags the mouse, `mouseDrag()` draws the appropriate line. It also saves the coordinates of the line so that it can be redrawn later. It creates a `Line` object to hold the coordinates and adds each `Line` to a `Vector` object. The `Vector` class implements an array that can grow to have an arbitrary number of elements. Elements are added in `mouseDrag()` with `addElement()`, and are extracted in `paint()` with `elementAt()`.

The `handleEvent()` method handles events from the scrollbars. As we described for the previous example, it invokes its superclass `handleEvent()` method so that non-scrollbar events are properly dispatched to the `mouseDown()` and `mouseDrag()` methods.

The scrollbars are used to display a large (1000 pixels by 1000 pixels) drawing (or scribble) within a much smaller canvas. The example is thoroughly commented. Study it, and you'll understand how the scrolling is done.

Defining a Custom Component

At the beginning of this chapter, our `InfoDialog` and `YesNoDialog` examples used a `MultiLineLabel` class to display their message, because the standard Java `Label` component can only display a single line of text. Example 5-7 shows the definition of the `MultiLineLabel` class. By studying it, you can learn how to create custom Java components of your own.

Example 5-7: A custom component

```
import java.awt.*;
import java.util.*;

public class MultiLineLabel extends Canvas {
    public static final int LEFT = 0;      // Alignment constants
    public static final int CENTER = 1;
    public static final int RIGHT = 2;
    protected String[] lines;              // The lines of text to display
    protected int num_lines;               // The number of lines
    protected int margin_width;            // Left and right margins
    protected int margin_height;           // Top and bottom margins
    protected int line_height;             // Total height of the font
    protected int line_ascent;             // Font height above baseline
    protected int[] line_widths;           // How wide each line is
    protected int max_width;               // The width of the widest line
```

```
protected int alignment = LEFT;        // The alignment of the text.

// This method breaks a specified label up into an array of lines.
// It uses the StringTokenizer utility class.
protected void newLabel(String label) {
    StringTokenizer t = new StringTokenizer(label, "\n");
    num_lines = t.countTokens();
    lines = new String[num_lines];
    line_widths = new int[num_lines];
    for(int i = 0; i < num_lines; i++) lines[i] = t.nextToken();
}

// This method figures out how large the font is, and how wide each
// line of the label is, and how wide the widest line is.
protected void measure() {
    FontMetrics fm = this.getFontMetrics(this.getFont());
    // If we don't have font metrics yet, just return.
    if (fm == null) return;

    line_height = fm.getHeight();
    line_ascent = fm.getAscent();
    max_width = 0;
    for(int i = 0; i < num_lines; i++) {
        line_widths[i] = fm.stringWidth(lines[i]);
        if (line_widths[i] > max_width) max_width = line_widths[i];
    }
}

// Here are four versions of the constructor.
// Break the label up into separate lines, and save the other info.
public MultiLineLabel(String label, int margin_width, int margin_height,
                int alignment) {
    newLabel(label);
    this.margin_width = margin_width;
    this.margin_height = margin_height;
    this.alignment = alignment;
}
public MultiLineLabel(String label, int margin_width, int margin_height) {
    this(label, margin_width, margin_height, LEFT);
}
public MultiLineLabel(String label, int alignment) {
    this(label, 10, 10, alignment);
}
public MultiLineLabel(String label) {
    this(label, 10, 10, LEFT);
}

// Methods to set the various attributes of the component
public void setLabel(String label) {
    newLabel(label);
    measure();
    repaint();
}
public void setFont(Font f) {
    super.setFont(f);
    measure();
```

```
            repaint();
        }
        public void setForeground(Color c) {
            super.setForeground(c);
            repaint();
        }
        public void setAlignment(int a) { alignment = a; repaint(); }
        public void setMarginWidth(int mw) { margin_width = mw; repaint(); }
        public void setMarginHeight(int mh) { margin_height = mh; repaint(); }
        public int getAlignment() { return alignment; }
        public int getMarginWidth() { return margin_width; }
        public int getMarginHeight() { return margin_height; }

        // This method is invoked after our Canvas is first created
        // but before it can actually be displayed.  After we've
        // invoked our superclass's addNotify() method, we have font
        // metrics and can successfully call measure() to figure out
        // how big the label is.
        public void addNotify() { super.addNotify(); measure(); }

        // This method is called by a layout manager when it wants to
        // know how big we'd like to be.
        public Dimension preferredSize() {
            return new Dimension(max_width + 2*margin_width,
                        num_lines * line_height + 2*margin_height);
        }

        // This method is called when the layout manager wants to know
        // the bare minimum amount of space we need to get by.
        public Dimension minimumSize() {
            return new Dimension(max_width, num_lines * line_height);
        }

        // This method draws the label (applets use the same method).
        // Note that it handles the margins and the alignment, but that
        // it doesn't have to worry about the color or font--the superclass
        // takes care of setting those in the Graphics object we're passed.
        public void paint(Graphics g) {
            int x, y;
            Dimension d = this.size();
            y = line_ascent + (d.height - num_lines * line_height)/2;
            for(int i = 0; i < num_lines; i++, y += line_height) {
                switch(alignment) {
                case LEFT:
                    x = margin_width; break;
                case CENTER:
                default:
                    x = (d.width - line_widths[i])/2; break;
                case RIGHT:
                    x = d.width - margin_width - line_widths[i]; break;
                }
                g.drawString(lines[i], x, y);
            }
        }
    }
```

Much of the code in this example is taken up with the mechanics of breaking the label up into separate lines, using the useful `java.util.StringTokenizer` class. And also with figuring out how wide the lines are using the `FontMetrics` class. But the most important code for this example is in several required methods that make this custom component work correctly.

The most important method of any custom component is the `paint()` method, which actually draws the component. (This is the same method you use to draw an applet, by the way). The `preferredSize()` and `minimumSize()` methods are also very important. These methods must be defined, or layout managers won't be able to arrange your custom component correctly.

The `addNotify()` method is also sometimes important. The system invokes this method when it wants a component to create the platform-dependent object (e.g., a Motif widget on a UNIX platform or a Windows control on a Windows platform) that actually implements the component. `addNotify()` is misleadingly named, and should probably be called `createPeer()`.

Our custom component is platform-independent; so we don't need to create a peer object. We use it, however, as a way to find out when our superclass's peer is created. The first thing our version of `addNotify()` does is to invoke the superclass version of the function. Once that call returns, we know that the peer has been created. What this means for the `MultiLineLabel` is that font metrics are now available and we can call the `measure()` method to figure out how big the lines of the label are. We need to ensure that the `measure()` method is called sometime before the `paint()` or `preferredSize()` methods are called, but not before font metrics are available. Our overridden `addNotify()` method does exactly this.

Input and Output

The examples in this chapter demonstrate how to use the Java input and output facilities. They show you how to:

- List directories.
- Read and write files.
- Use various Java stream classes.
- Define filter streams to process input data

The examples in this chapter use the classes in the `java.io` package. The introduction to Section 22, *The java.io Package*, gives a good overview of this package. You may also want to refer to the quick reference material of that section while studying the examples in this section.

Reading and Displaying Files

Example 6-1 combines the use of the `File` class with the GUI techniques we saw from the previous section. This `FileViewer` class reads in the contents of a file with the `read()` method of a `FileInputStream` and displays the file in a `TextArea` component. The `FileViewer` class is designed to be used by other classes. It also has its own `main()` method, however, so that it can be run as a standalone program. To do this, just invoke it with the name of the file specified, like this

```
%java FileViewer foo.java
```

Figure 6-1 shows a `FileViewer` window.

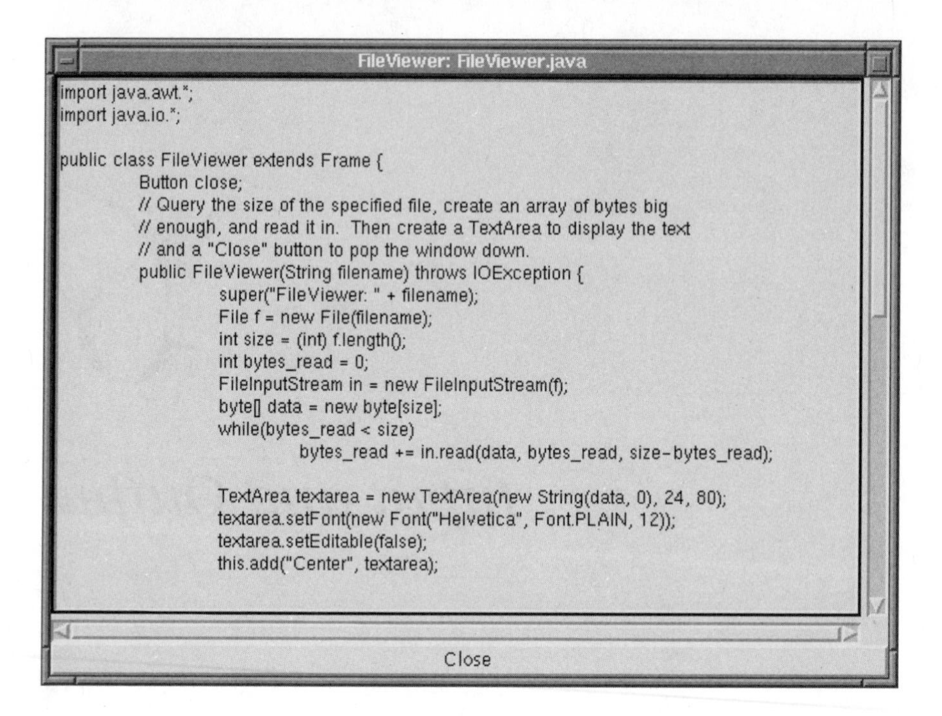
FileViewer: FileViewer.java
import java.awt.*;
import java.io.*;
public class FileViewer extends Frame {
Button close;
// Query the size of the specified file, create an array of bytes big
// enough, and read it in. Then create a TextArea to display the text
// and a "Close" button to pop the window down.
public FileViewer(String filename) throws IOException {
super("FileViewer: " + filename);
File f = new File(filename);
int size = (int) f.length();
int bytes_read = 0;
FileInputStream in = new FileInputStream(f);
byte[] data = new byte[size];
while(bytes_read < size)
bytes_read += in.read(data, bytes_read, size-bytes_read);
TextArea textarea = new TextArea(new String(data, 0), 24, 80);
textarea.setFont(new Font("Helvetica", Font.PLAIN, 12));
textarea.setEditable(false);
this.add("Center", textarea);
Close

Figure 6-1: A FileViewer window

Example 6-1: Displaying file contents

```
import java.awt.*;
import java.io.*;

public class FileViewer extends Frame {
    Button close;
    // Query the size of the specified file, create an array of bytes big
    // enough, and read it in. Then create a TextArea to display the text
    // and a "Close" button to pop the window down.
    public FileViewer(String filename) throws IOException {
        super("FileViewer: " + filename);
        File f = new File(filename);
        int size = (int) f.length();
        int bytes_read = 0;
        FileInputStream in = new FileInputStream(f);
        byte[] data = new byte[size];
        while(bytes_read < size)
            bytes_read += in.read(data, bytes_read, size-bytes_read);

        TextArea textarea = new TextArea(new String(data, 0), 24, 80);
        textarea.setFont(new Font("Helvetica", Font.PLAIN, 12));
        textarea.setEditable(false);
        this.add("Center", textarea);

        close = new Button("Close");
        this.add("South", close);
        this.pack();
        this.show();
    }
```

```
        // Handle the close button by popping this window down
        public boolean action(Event e, Object what) {
            if (e.target == close) {
                this.hide();
                this.dispose();
                return true;
            }
            return false;
        }

        // The FileViewer can be used by other classes, or it can be
        // used standalone with this main() method.
        static public void main(String[] args) throws IOException {
            if (args.length != 1) {
                System.out.println("Usage: java FileViewer <filename>");
                System.exit(0);
            }
            try Frame f = new FileViewer(args[0]);
            catch (IOException e) System.out.println(e);
        }
    }
```


Getting Directory and File Information

Just as the `FileViewer` class displays the contents of a file in a `TextArea` component, the `FileLister` class, shown in Example 6-2, displays the contents of a directory in a `List` component. When you select a file or directory name from the list, it displays information (size, modification date, etc.) about the file or directory in a `TextField` component. When you double-click on a directory, it displays the contents of that directory. When you double-click on a file, it displays the contents of the file in a `FileViewer` object. Figure 6-2 shows a `FileLister` window.

This example also demonstrates the use of the `FilenameFilter` interface for specifying what files in a directory should be listed. And it shows how you can get the current directory by querying the `user.dir` property. Note the frequent use of `try` and `catch` to handle possibilities of exceptions.

Like the `FileViewer` class, the `FileLister` can be used by other classes, or it can be invoked as a standalone program. To use it standalone, invoke it with an optional directory name and an optional `-e` argument specifying a file extension.

Example 6-2: Directory listings and file information

```
import java.awt.*;
import java.io.*;

public class FileLister extends Frame {
    private List list;
    private TextField infoarea;
    private Panel buttons;
    private Button parent, quit;
    private FilenameFilter filter;
```

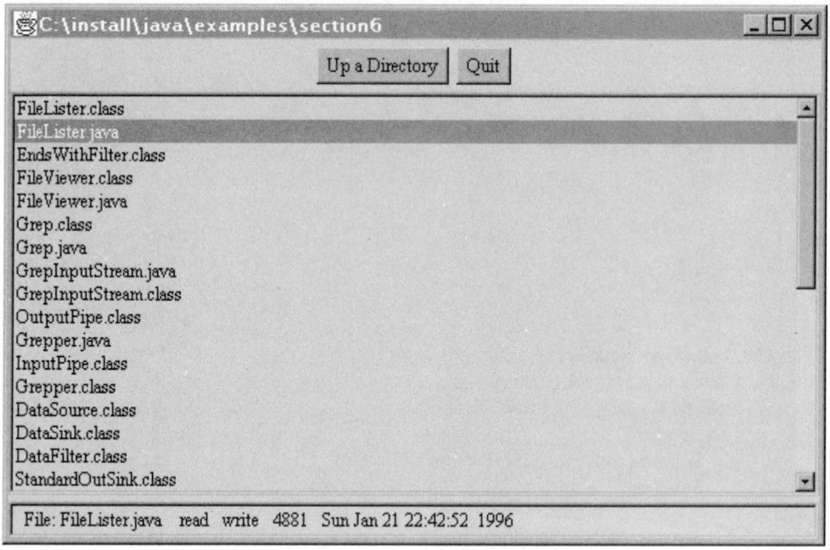

C:\install\java\examples\section6

Up a Directory Quit

FileLister.class
FileLister.java
EndsWithFilter.class
FileViewer.class
FileViewer.java
Grep.class
Grep.java
GrepInputStream.java
GrepInputStream.class
OutputPipe.class
Grepper.java
InputPipe.class
Grepper.class
DataSource.class
DataSink.class
DataFilter.class
StandardOutSink.class

File: FileLister.java read write 4881 Sun Jan 21 22:42:52 1996

Figure 6-2: A FileLister window

Example 6-2: Directory listings and file information (continued)

```
    private File cwd;
    private String[] entries;

    // Create the graphical user interface, and list the initial directory.
    public FileLister(String directory, FilenameFilter filter) throws IOException
    {
        super("File Lister");
        this.filter = filter;
        list = new List(12, false);
        infoarea = new TextField();
        infoarea.setEditable(false);
        buttons = new Panel();
        parent = new Button("Up a Directory");
        quit = new Button("Quit");
        buttons.add(parent);
        buttons.add(quit);
        this.add("Center", list);
        this.add("South", infoarea);
        this.add("North", buttons);
        this.resize(550, 350);
        this.show();

        // list the initial directory.
        list_directory(directory);
    }

    // This method uses the list() method to get all entries in a directory
    // and then displays them in the List component.
    public void list_directory(String directory) throws IOException {
        File dir = new File(directory);

        if (!dir.isDirectory())
```

```
                throw new IllegalArgumentException("FileLister: no such directory");
            list.clear();
            cwd = dir;
            this.setTitle(directory);

            entries = cwd.list(filter);
            for(int i = 0; i < entries.length; i++)
                list.addItem(entries[i]);
        }

        // This method uses various File methods to obtain information about
        // a file or directory. Then it displays that info in a TextField.
        public void show_info(String filename) throws IOException {
            File f = new File(cwd, filename);
            String info;

            if (!f.exists())
                throw new IllegalArgumentException("FileLister.show_info(): " +
                                                   "no such file or directory");

            if (f.isDirectory()) info = "Directory: ";
            else info = "File: ";

            info += filename + "    ";

            info += (f.canRead()?"read   ":"        ") +
                    (f.canWrite()?"write   ":"        ") +
                        f.length() + "   " +
                            new java.util.Date(f.lastModified());

            infoarea.setText(info);
        }

        // This method handles the buttons and list events.
        public boolean handleEvent(Event e) {
            if (e.target == quit) System.exit(0);
            else if (e.target == parent) {
                String parent = cwd.getParent();
                if (parent == null) parent = "/";        // Bug workaround
                try list_directory(parent);
                catch (IllegalArgumentException ex)infoarea.setText("Already at top");
                catch (IOException ex) infoarea.setText("I/O Error");
                return true;
            }
            else if (e.target == list) {
                // when an item is selected, show its info.
                if (e.id == Event.LIST_SELECT) {
                    try show_info(entries[((Integer)e.arg).intValue()]);
                    catch (IOException ex) infoarea.setText("I/O Error");
                }
              // When the user double-clicks, change to the selected directory
              // or display the selected file.
                else if (e.id == Event.ACTION_EVENT) {
                    try {
                        String item = new File(cwd, (String)e.arg).getAbsolutePath();
                        try list_directory(item);
```

Input and Output

```
                        catch (IllegalArgumentException ex) new FileViewer(item);
                    }
                    catch (IOException ex) infoarea.setText("I/O Error");
                }
                return true;
            }
            return super.handleEvent(e);
        }

        public static void usage() {
            System.out.println("Usage: java FileLister [directory_name] " +
                        "[-e file_extension]");
            System.exit(0);
        }
        // Parse command line arguments and create the FileLister object.
        // If an extension is specified, create a FilenameFilter for it.
        // If no directory is specified, use the current directory.
        public static void main(String args[]) throws IOException {
            FileLister f;
            FilenameFilter filter = null;
            String directory = null;

            for(int i = 0; i < args.length; i++) {
                if (args[i].equals("-e")) {
                    i++;
                    if (i >= args.length) usage();
                    filter = new EndsWithFilter(args[i]);
                }
                else {
                    if (directory != null) usage();    // Already set
                    else directory = args[i];
                }
            }

            // if no directory specified, use the current directoy
            if (directory == null) directory = System.getProperty("user.dir");
            // Create the FileLister object
            f = new FileLister(directory, filter);
        }
    }
    // This class is a simple FilenameFilter.  It defines the required accept()
    // method to determine whether a specified file should be listed.  A file
    // will be listed if its name ends with the specified extension, or if
    // it is a directory.
    class EndsWithFilter implements FilenameFilter {
        private String extension;
        public EndsWithFilter(String extension) {
            this.extension = extension;
        }
        public boolean accept(File dir, String name) {
            if (name.endsWith(extension)) return true;
            else return (new File(dir, name)).isDirectory();
        }
    }
```

Copying a File

Example 6-3 shows a FileCopy class that you can use to copy the contents of one file to another. This example uses a number of the classes from the java.io package. For example, it uses File to make sure that the source file exists and is readable. It also uses File to make sure either that the destination file exists and is writable or that the directory exists and is writable. It uses the FileInputStream and FileOutputStream classes to read bytes from the source file and write them to the destination file.

The example also shows how you can read lines of user input from System.in by creating a DataInputStream. Finally, it uses System.out and System.err, which are both instances of the PrintStream class.

The copy() method implements the functionality of the class. This method is heavily commented, so that you can follow the steps it takes. First it verifies that the source file exists and is readable. Then it checks on the destination file. If that file exists and is writable, the method asks if it is okay to overwrite the existing file. If everything checks out, the method copies the file. Note how the example throws exceptions and uses the finally statement to clean up.

The FileCopy.copy() method can be used directly by any program. FileCopy also provides a main() method so that it can be used as a standalone program. To use it this way, pass the source file name and the destination file name on the command line, like this:

```
%java FileCopy foo.java bar.java
```

Example 6-3: Copying a file

```
import java.io.*;

public class FileCopy {
    public static void copy(String source_name, String dest_name)
        throws IOException
    {
        File source_file = new File(source_name);
        File destination_file = new File(dest_name);
        FileInputStream source = null;
        FileOutputStream destination = null;
        byte[] buffer;
        int bytes_read;

        try {
            // First make sure the specified source file
            // exists, is a file, and is readable.
            if (!source_file.exists() || !source_file.isFile())
                throw new FileCopyException("FileCopy: no such source file: " +
                                            source_name);
            if (!source_file.canRead())
                throw new FileCopyException("FileCopy: source file " +
                                            "is unreadable: " + source_name);

            // If the destination exists, make sure it is a writable file
            // and ask before overwriting it. If the destination doesn't
            // exist, make sure the directory exists and is writable.
```

Input and Output

```
        if (destination_file.exists()) {
            if (destination_file.isFile()) {
                DataInputStream in = new DataInputStream(System.in);
                String response;

                if (!destination_file.canWrite())
                    throw new FileCopyException("FileCopy: destination " +
                                    "file is unwritable: " + dest_name);

                // Tell the user the file already exists
                // and ask if it is okay to overwrite it.
                System.out.print("File " + dest_name +
                        " already exists.  Overwrite? (Y/N): ");
                System.out.flush();
                // Read the user's response.  Note that we use
                // a DataInputStream created from System.in
                // in order to read lines rather than characters.
                response = in.readLine();
                if (!response.equals("Y") && !response.equals("y"))
                    throw new FileCopyException("FileCopy: copy cancelled.");
            }
            else
                throw new FileCopyException("FileCopy: destination "
                                + "is not a file: " +  dest_name);
        }
        else {
            File parentdir = parent(destination_file);
            if (!parentdir.exists())
                throw new FileCopyException("FileCopy: destination "
                                + "directory doesn't exist: " + dest_name);
            if (!parentdir.canWrite())
                throw new FileCopyException("FileCopy: destination "
                                + "directory is unwritable: " + dest_name);
        }

        // If we've gotten this far, then everything is okay;
        // we can go ahead and copy the file.
        // Create an input stream from the source file and an ouput
        // stream to the destination file.  Then read arrays of bytes
        // from one and write them to the other.  When the read() method
        // returns -1, we've reached the end of the file and can stop.
        source = new FileInputStream(source_file);
        destination = new FileOutputStream(destination_file);
        buffer = new byte[1024];
        while(true) {
            bytes_read = source.read(buffer);
            if (bytes_read == -1) break;
            destination.write(buffer, 0, bytes_read);
        }
    }
    // No matter what happens, always close any streams we've opened.
    finally {
        if (source != null)
            try source.close(); catch (IOException e) ;
        if (destination != null)
            try destination.close(); catch (IOException e) ;
```

```
            }
        }

        // File.getParent() can return null when the file is specified without
        // a directory or is in the root directory.
        // This method handles those cases.
        private static File parent(File f) {
            String dirname = f.getParent();
            if (dirname == null) {
                if (f.isAbsolute()) return new File(File.separator);
                else return new File(System.getProperty("user.dir"));
            }
            return new File(dirname);
        }

        public static void main(String[] args) {
            if (args.length != 2)
                System.err.println("Usage: java FileCopy " +
                                   "<source file> <destination file>");
            else {
                try copy(args[0], args[1]);
                catch (IOException e) System.err.println(e.getMessage());
            }
        }
    }

    class FileCopyException extends IOException {
        public FileCopyException(String msg) { super(msg); }
    }
```


Filtering Input

Example 6-4 demonstrates how you can define a subclass of `FilterInputStream` to do custom filtering of input data. The `GrepInputFilter` approximates the behavior of the UNIX *fgrep* command—it filters out all lines that do not contain a specified substring.

Note that this filter stream must be created with a `DataInputStream` specified, so that it has a stream from which to read lines of text. A regular `InputStream` will not work. The filter is extremely simple—the `readLine()` method reads lines from the specified `DataInputStream`, but only returns those that match the specified substring. Note that this filter only filters data read with the `readLine()` call. Data read through the `read()` call, for example, is not filtered.

Example 6-4: A grep-style filter stream

```
import java.io.*;

// This class is a FilterInputStream that filters out all lines that
// do not contain the specified substring.
public class GrepInputStream extends FilterInputStream {
    String substring;
    DataInputStream in;
```

Example 6-4: A grep-style filter stream (continued)

```
        public GrepInputStream(DataInputStream in, String substring) {
                super(in);
                this.in = in;
                this.substring = substring;
        }

        // This is the filter: read lines from the DataInputStream,
        // but only return the lines that contain the substring.
        // When the DataInputStream returns null, we return null.
        public final String readLine() throws IOException {
                String line;
                do {
                        line = in.readLine();
                }
                while ((line != null) && line.indexOf(substring) == -1);
                return line;
        }
}
```

Example 6-5 shows how you might use the `GrepInputStream` class to implement a *grep*-like command with Java. You invoke this program by specifying the substring to search for and the name of the file to search on the command line, like this:

```
%java Grep needle haystack.txt
```

Example 6-5: Using the GrepInputStream

```
import java.io.*;

// This class demonstrates the use of the GrepInputStream class.
// It prints the lines of a file that contain a specified substring.
public class Grep {
        public static void main(String args[]) {
                if ((args.length == 0) || (args.length > 2)) {
                        System.out.println("Usage: java Grep <substring> [<filename>]");
                        System.exit(0);
                }

                try {
                        DataInputStream d;
                        if (args.length == 2)
                                d = new DataInputStream(new FileInputStream(args[1]));
                        else
                                d = new DataInputStream(System.in);

                        GrepInputStream g = new GrepInputStream(d, args[0]);

                        String line;
                        for(;;) {
                                line = g.readLine();
                                if (line == null) break;
                                System.out.println(line);
                        }
                        g.close();
                }
```

```
                catch (IOException e) System.err.println(e);
        }
    }
```

Pipes

The Java `PipedInputStream` and `PipedOutputStream` classes allow separate threads to read and write data from and to each other. Example 6-6 shows how you might make use of this ability. It is a long and complicated example, but will repay detailed study.

The code in this example allows you to set up UNIX-style "pipes"—data flows from a "source," through any number of "filters," and then into a "sink." For example, the source might be a file, the filter might be one that performs a search-and-replace operation on the data, and the sink might be another file or the `System.out` stream. The source, filters, and sink of a pipe are all implemented as separate threads, which means that they work independently of each other, running when data is available to be read in the pipe, and blocking when there is no data available.

This example defines `PipeSource`, `PipeSink`, and `PipeFilter` interfaces that define the methods necessary for data sources, sinks, and filters. It defines two simple classes, `StreamPipeSource` and `StreamPipeSink`, that use input streams and output streams, respectively, as data sources and sinks. The example later uses these classes to set up a file as a data source and to set up `System.out` as a data sink.

The example also defines a `BasicPipeFilter` filter class that defines most of the functionality needed for a data filter. The only thing this `abstract` class leaves out is a `filter()` method. The example defines two subclasses of `BasicPipeFilter`, `GrepFilter`, and `Rot13Filter` to perform two different filtering operations on data.

The best place to start studying this example is at the end, where the class `Pipes` and its `main()` method show how all these other classes are used. `main()` shows the creation of a source, three filters, and a sink. It connects them to each other, and then starts the various threads on their tasks.

Example 6-6: Pipes in Java

```
import java.io.*;

// This interface defines the methods that the source of data for a pipe
// must define.  These methods are used to allow the source to easily be
// connected to a sink.
// Note that a PipeSource is Runnable--it is a thread body.
interface PipeSource extends Runnable {
        abstract PipedOutputStream getPipedOutputStream();
        abstract void connectOutputTo(PipeSink sink) throws IOException;
        abstract PipeSink getSink();
        abstract void start();
}
// This interface defines the methods required for a sink of data from
// a pipe.  The methods are used when connecting a source to the sink.
```

Input and Output

```
// A PipeSink is also Runnable.
interface PipeSink extends Runnable {
	abstract PipedInputStream getPipedInputStream();
	abstract void connectInputTo(PipeSource source) throws IOException;
}
// A filter in a pipe behaves like both a source of data and a sink of data.
interface PipeFilter extends PipeSource, PipeSink {
};
// This is an implementation of the PipeSource interface that uses an
// InputStream as the source of data.  It creates a PipedOutputStream
// to write the data to.  The run() method copies data from the stream
// to the pipe.
class StreamPipeSource implements PipeSource {
	protected PipedOutputStream out = new PipedOutputStream();
	protected InputStream in;
	protected PipeSink sink;

	public StreamPipeSource(InputStream in) { this.in = in; }
	public PipedOutputStream getPipedOutputStream() { return out; }
	public PipeSink getSink() { return sink; }
	public void connectOutputTo(PipeSink sink) throws IOException {
		this.sink = sink;
		out.connect(sink.getPipedInputStream());
		sink.connectInputTo(this);
	}

	public void start() {
		// Start ourselves
		new Thread(this).start();

		// If our output is a filter, then call its start() method.
		// otherwise, just start our sink
		if (sink instanceof PipeFilter) ((PipeFilter)sink).start();
		else new Thread(sink).start();
	}

	public void run() {
		byte[] buffer = new byte[512];
		int bytes_read;
		try {
			for(;;) {
				bytes_read = in.read(buffer);
				if (bytes_read == -1) { return; }
				out.write(buffer, 0, bytes_read);
			}
		}
		catch (IOException e) {
			if (e instanceof EOFException) return;
			else System.out.println(e);
		}
		finally { try out.close(); catch (IOException e); }
	}
}
// This is an implementation of the PipeSink interface that uses an output
// stream as the source of data.  It creates a PipedInputStream to read
// data from the pipe.  The run() method reads data from that pipe and
```

```
// writes it to the output stream (which might be a file or System.out, e.g.)
class StreamPipeSink implements PipeSink {
	protected PipedInputStream in = new PipedInputStream();
	protected OutputStream out;

	public StreamPipeSink(OutputStream out) {
		this.out = out;
	}

	public PipedInputStream getPipedInputStream() { return in; }
	public void connectInputTo(PipeSource source) throws IOException {
		in.connect(source.getPipedOutputStream());
	}

	public void run() {
		byte[] buffer = new byte[512];
		int bytes_read;
		try {
			for(;;) {
				bytes_read = in.read(buffer);
				if (bytes_read == -1) return;
				out.write(buffer, 0, bytes_read);
			}
		}
		catch (IOException e) {
			if (e instanceof EOFException) return;
			else System.out.println(e);
		}
		finally { try in.close(); catch (IOException e); }
	}
}
// This is an abstract implementation of the PipeFilter interface.
// It creates both a PipedInputStream to read from and a PipedOutputStream
// to write to. The abstract method filter() needs to be defined by
// a subclass to read data from one pipe, filter it, and write the filtered
// data to the other pipe.
abstract class BasicPipeFilter implements PipeFilter {
	protected PipedInputStream in = new PipedInputStream();
	protected PipedOutputStream out = new PipedOutputStream();
	protected PipeSink sink;
	public PipedInputStream getPipedInputStream() { return in; }
	public PipedOutputStream getPipedOutputStream() { return out; }

	public void connectOutputTo(PipeSink sink) throws IOException {
		this.sink = sink;
		out.connect(sink.getPipedInputStream());
		sink.connectInputTo((PipeSource) this);
	}

	public void start() {
		// Start ourselves
		new Thread(this).start();

		// If our output is a filter, then call its start() method.
		// otherwise, just start our sink
		if (sink instanceof PipeFilter) ((PipeFilter)sink).start();
```

```
            else new Thread(sink).start();
    }

    public PipeSink getSink() { return sink; }

    public void connectInputTo(PipeSource source) throws IOException {
        in.connect(source.getPipedOutputStream());
    }

    public void run() {
        try { filter(); }
        catch (IOException e) {
            if (e instanceof EOFException) return;
            else System.out.println(e);
        }
        finally {
            try { out.close(); in.close(); }
            catch (IOException e) ;
        }
    }

    abstract public void filter() throws IOException;
}
// This is a non-abstract implementation of the PipeFilter interface.
// It uses the GrepInputStream we defined elsewhere to do the filtering.
class GrepFilter extends BasicPipeFilter {
    protected GrepInputStream gis;
    protected PrintStream pout = new PrintStream(out);

    public GrepFilter(String pattern) {
        gis = new GrepInputStream(new DataInputStream(in), pattern);
    }

    public void filter() throws IOException {
        String line;
        for(;;) {
            line = gis.readLine();
            if (line == null) return;
            pout.println(line);
        }
    }
}
// This is another implementation fo PipeFilter. It implements the
// trival rot13 cypher on the letters A-Z and a-z.
class Rot13Filter extends BasicPipeFilter {
    public void filter() throws IOException {
        byte[] buffer = new byte[512];
        int bytes_read;

        for(;;) {
            bytes_read = in.read(buffer);
            if (bytes_read == -1) return;
            for(int i = 0; i < bytes_read; i++) {
                if ((buffer[i] >= 'a') && (buffer[i] <= 'z')) {
                    buffer[i] = (byte) ('a' + ((buffer[i]-'a') + 13) % 26);
                }
```

```
                    if ((buffer[i] >= 'A') && (buffer[i] <= 'Z')) {
                        buffer[i] = (byte) ('A' + ((buffer[i]-'A') + 13) % 26);
                    }
                }
                out.write(buffer, 0, bytes_read);
            }
        }
}
// This class demonstrates how you might use these pipe classes.
// It is another implementation of a UNIX-like grep command.
// Note that it frivolously passes the output of the grep pipe through two
// rot13 pipes (which, combined, leave the output unchanged).
// With the source, filter, and sink infrastructure defined above, it
// is easy to define new filters and create pipes to perform many useful
// operations. Other filter possibilities include sorting lines, removing
// duplicate lines, and doing search-and-replace.
public class Pipes {
    public static void main(String[] args) throws IOException {
        if (args.length != 2) {
            System.out.println("Usage: java Pipes <pattern> <filename>");
            System.exit(0);
        }

        // Create a source, three filters, and a sink for the pipe.
        PipeSource source =
            new StreamPipeSource(new FileInputStream(args[1]));
        PipeFilter filter = new GrepFilter(args[0]);
        PipeFilter filter2 = new Rot13Filter();
        PipeFilter filter3 = new Rot13Filter();
        PipeSink sink = new StreamPipeSink(System.out);

        // Connect them all up.
        source.connectOutputTo(filter);
        filter.connectOutputTo(filter2);
        filter2.connectOutputTo(filter3);
        filter3.connectOutputTo(sink);

        // And start their threads running.
        source.start();
    }
}
```

7

Networking

The examples in this section demonstrate Java's networking capabilities at a number of different levels of abstraction. They show you how to:

- Use the URL class.
- Use the `URLConnection` class to gain more control over the downloading of network resources.
- Write servers and clients that communicate over the Net.
- Send and receive low-overhead datagram packets.

The introduction to Section 24, *The java.net Package*, gives a good overview of the classes in the `java.net` package; the quick reference material in that section may be useful while you study the examples in this section.

Downloading the Contents of a URL

Example 7-1 shows the simplest possible use of the URL class. It creates a URL from a specified WWW address and then downloads the contents of the URL with the `getContent()` method. This technique relies on resident "content handlers" that know how to parse the incoming data and convert it to an appropriate object. The standard Java distribution does not have many of these content handlers installed. Thus, the `fetch()` method shown here only works for URLs with content type of "text/plain" and the `fetchimage()` method only works for image URLs of type "image/gif," "image/jpeg," and a few other standard types.

Note that it is possible to define your own content handler to parse any kind of data you want. This capability is usually used by Web browsers, like Sun's HotJava browser, that need the ability to download and display many different types of data. Most applications do not need to define content handlers—if they need to parse a particular type of data, they can simply write the code that does that. In the next example, we'll see how you can use a `URLConnection` to download arbitrary data from a URL.

Example 7-1: Fetching a URL

```
import java.awt.*;
import java.io.*;
import java.net.*;

// The fetch() method in this class only works for fetching text/plain
// data, and a few standard image types. The standard Java distribution
// doesn't contain content handlers for other types (such as text/html),
// so this code exits with an exception.
public class Fetch {
    // Get the contents of a URL and return it as a string.
    public static String fetch(String address)
      throws MalformedURLException, IOException
    {
        URL url = new URL(address);
        return (String) url.getContent();
    }

    // Get the contents of a URL and return it as an image
    public static String fetchimage(String address)
      throws MalformedURLException, IOException
    {
        URL url = new URL(address);
        return (Image) url.getContent();
    }

    // Test out the fetch() method.
    public static void main(String[] args)
      throws MalformedURLException, IOException
    {
        System.out.println(fetch(args[0]));
    }
}
```

Using a URLConnection

You can gain a lot more control over downloading the contents of a URL by using that object's associated `URLConnection` object. Example 7-2 shows how to use a `URLConnection` to obtain the content type, size, last-modified date, and other information about the resource referred to by a URL. It also shows how you can use a stream to download the contents of a URL, regardless of its type. Note the use of the `DataInputStream` to read lines of text from the `URLConnection`, and the use of the `java.util.Date` class to convert a `long` timestamp to a textual form.

Example 7-2: Getting information about a URL

```
import java.net.*;
import java.io.*;
import java.util.*;
```

```
public class GetURLInfo {
    public static void printinfo(URLConnection u) throws IOException {
        // Display the URL address, and information about it.
        System.out.println(u.getURL().toExternalForm() + ":");
        System.out.println("  Content Type: " + u.getContentType());
        System.out.println("  Content Length: " + u.getContentLength());
        System.out.println("  Last Modified: " + new Date(u.getLastModified()));
        System.out.println("  Expiration: " + u.getExpiration());
        System.out.println("  Content Encoding: " + u.getContentEncoding());

        // Read and print out the first five lines of the URL.
        System.out.println("First five lines:");
        DataInputStream in = new DataInputStream(u.getInputStream());
        for(int i = 0; i < 5; i++) {
            String line = in.readLine();
            if (line == null) break;
            System.out.println("  " + line);
        }
    }

  // Create a URL from the specified address, open a connection to it,
  // and then display information about the URL.
    public static void main(String[] args)
        throws MalformedURLException, IOException {
            URL url = new URL(args[0]);
            URLConnection connection = url.openConnection();
            printinfo(connection);
        }
}
```


Sending and Receiving Datagrams

Example 7-3 and Example 7-4 show how you can implement simple network communication using datagrams. Datagram communication is sometimes called "UDP"—unreliable datagram protocol. Sending datagrams is fast, but the tradeoff is that that they are not guaranteed to reach their destination, and separate datagrams are not even guaranteed to reach their destination in the order in which they were sent. Communication with datagrams is useful when you want low-overhead communication of non-critical data and when a stream model of communication is not necessary.

To send and receive datagrams, you use the `DatagramPacket` and `DatagramSocket` classes. These objects are created and initialized differently depending on whether they are to be used to send or receive. Example 7-3 shows how to send a datagram. Example 7-4 shows how to receive a datagram, and to find out who sent it.

To send a datagram, you first create a `DatagramPacket`, specifying the data to be sent, the length of the data, the host that the packet is to be sent to, and the port on the host that it is to be sent to. You then use the `send()` method of a `DatagramSocket` to send the packet. The `DatagramSocket` is a generic one, created with no arguments. It can be reused to send any packet to any address and port.

Example 7-3: Sending a datagram

```
import java.io.*;
import java.net.*;

// This class sends the specified text as a datagram to port 6010 of the
// specified host.
public class UDPSend {
    static final int port = 6010;
    public static void main(String args[]) throws Exception {
        if (args.length != 2) {
            System.out.println("Usage: java UDPSend <hostname> <message>");
            System.exit(0);
        }

        // Get the internet address of the specified host
        InetAddress address = InetAddress.getByName(args[0]);
        // Convert the message to an array of bytes
        int msglen = args[1].length();
        byte[] message = new byte[msglen];
        args[1].getBytes(0, msglen, message, 0);
        // Initilize the packet with data and address
        DatagramPacket packet = new DatagramPacket(message, msglen,
                                    address, port);
        // Create a socket, and send the packet through it.
        DatagramSocket socket = new DatagramSocket();
        socket.send(packet);
    }
}
```

To receive a datagram, you must first create a `DatagramSocket` that listens on a particular port of the local host. This socket can only be used to receive packets sent to that particular port. Then, you must create a `DatagramPacket` with a buffer specified to receive the data. Finally, the `DatagramSocket receive()` method blocks until data is received and stores the data into the packet's buffer. The Internet address and port of the sender are also stored in the `DatagramPacket`.

Example 7-4: Receiving a datagram

```
import java.io.*;
import java.net.*;

// This program waits to receive datagrams sent to port 6010.
// When it receives one, it displays the sending host and port,
// and prints the contents of the datagram as a string.
public class UDPReceive {
    static final int port = 6010;
    public static void main(String args[]) throws Exception
    {
        byte[] buffer = new byte[1024];
        String s;
        // Create a packet with an empty buffer to receive data
        DatagramPacket packet = new DatagramPacket(buffer, buffer.length);
        // Create a socket to listen on the port.
        DatagramSocket socket = new DatagramSocket(port);
```

```
            for(;;) {
                // Wait to receive a datagram
                socket.receive(packet);
                // Convert the contents to a string
                s = new String(buffer, 0, 0, packet.getLength());
                // And display them
                System.out.println("UDPReceive: received from " +
                        packet.getAddress().getHostName() + ":" +
                        packet.getPort() + ": " + s);
            }
        }
    }
```

Implementing a Server

For more reliable communication than is possible with datagrams, you need to use the `Socket` class, which implements a reliable stream network connection. A common model for network communication is for one or more clients to send requests to a single server program. Example 7-5 shows how you might implement such a server.

The server uses the `ServerSocket` class to accept connections from clients. When a client connects to the port that a `ServerSocket` is listening on, the `ServerSocket` allocates a new `Socket` object (connected to some new port) for the client to communicate through. The server can then go back to listening on the `ServerSocket` for additional client connections.

Note that this server is multithreaded. The `Server` object itself is a thread. Its `run()` method loops forever, listening for connections from clients. Each time a client connects, the `ServerSocket` creates a new `Socket` and the server creates a new thread (in this example, a new `Connection` object) to handle communication over the `Socket`. This new `Connection` object handles all communication with the client. The constructor method for the `Connection` object initializes streams for communication through the `Socket` object and starts the thread running. The `run()` method of the `Connection` object does all the communication with the client, and performs the "service" that this server provides. In this case, it simply reads a line of text from the client, reverses it, and sends it back.

Example 7-5: A server

```
import java.io.*;
import java.net.*;

public class Server extends Thread {
    public final static int DEFAULT_PORT = 6789;
    protected int port;
    protected ServerSocket listen_socket;

    // Exit with an error message, when an exception occurs.
    public static void fail(Exception e, String msg) {
        System.err.println(msg + ": " + e);
        System.exit(1);
    }
```

```
        // Create a ServerSocket to listen for connections on;  start the thread.
        public Server(int port) {
            if (port == 0) port = DEFAULT_PORT;
            this.port = port;
            try { listen_socket = new ServerSocket(port); }
            catch (IOException e) fail(e, "Exception creating server socket");
            System.out.println("Server: listening on port " + port);
            this.start();
        }

        // The body of the server thread.  Loop forever, listening for and
        // accepting connections from clients.  For each connection,
        // create a Connection object to handle communication through the
        // new Socket.
        public void run() {
            try {
                while(true) {
                    Socket client_socket = listen_socket.accept();
                    Connection c = new Connection(client_socket);
                }
            }
            catch (IOException e) fail(e, "Exception while listening for connections");
        }

        // Start the server up, listening on an optionally specified port
        public static void main(String[] args) {
            int port = 0;
            if (args.length == 1) {
                try port = Integer.parseInt(args[0]);
                catch (NumberFormatException e) port = 0;
            }
            new Server(port);
        }
    }

    // This class is the thread that handles all communication with a client
    class Connection extends Thread {
        protected Socket client;
        protected DataInputStream in;
        protected PrintStream out;

        // Initialize the streams and start the thread
        public Connection(Socket client_socket) {
            client = client_socket;
            try {
                in = new DataInputStream(client.getInputStream());
                out = new PrintStream(client.getOutputStream());
            }
            catch (IOException e) {
                try client.close(); catch (IOException e2) ;
                System.err.println("Exception while getting socket streams: " + e);
                return;
            }
            this.start();
        }
```

```
        // Provide the service.
        // Read a line, reverse it, send it back.
        public void run() {
            String line;
            StringBuffer revline;
            int len;
            try {
                for(;;) {
                    // read in a line
                    line = in.readLine();
                    if (line == null) break;
                    // reverse it
                    len = line.length();
                    revline = new StringBuffer(len);
                    for(int i = len-1; i >= 0; i--)
                        revline.insert(len-1-i, line.charAt(i));
                    // and write out the reversed line
                    out.println(revline);
                }
            }
            catch (IOException e) ;
            finally try client.close(); catch (IOException e2) ;
        }
    }
```


Implementing a Client

Example 7-6 shows a client that communicates with the server of Example 7-5. The client creates a `Socket` object to establish the connection to the server. Then, it creates a `DataInputStream` to read lines of text from the socket's `InputStream` and a `PrintStream` to write lines of text to the socket's `OutputStream`. Finally, it reads lines from the standard input, writes them to the server, reads the reply from the server, and writes that reply to the standard output. The client exits when it detects the end-of-file on either the socket input stream or on the standard input stream.

To use this client program, run it with the name of the server host specified on the command line. You may also optionally specify the port to use as the second argument:

```
%java Client oxymoron.ora.com 5001
```

Example 7-6: A client

```
import java.io.*;
import java.net.*;

public class Client {
    public static final int DEFAULT_PORT = 6789;
    public static void usage() {
        System.out.println("Usage: java Client <hostname> [<port>]");
        System.exit(0);
    }
```

```
    public static void main(String[] args) {
        int port = DEFAULT_PORT;
        Socket s = null;

        // Parse the port specification
        if ((args.length != 1) && (args.length != 2)) usage();
        if (args.length == 1) port = DEFAULT_PORT;
        else {
            try port = Integer.parseInt(args[1]);
            catch (NumberFormatException e) usage();
        }

        try {
            // Create a socket to communicate to the specified host and port
            s = new Socket(args[0], port);
            // Create streams for reading and writing lines of text
            // from and to this socket.
            DataInputStream sin = new DataInputStream(s.getInputStream());
            PrintStream sout = new PrintStream(s.getOutputStream());
            // Create a stream for reading lines of text from the console
            DataInputStream in = new DataInputStream(System.in);

            // Tell the user that we've connected
            System.out.println("Connected to " + s.getInetAddress()
                        + ":"+ s.getPort());

            String line;
            while(true) {
                // print a prompt
                System.out.print("> ");
                System.out.flush();
                // read a line from the console; check for EOF
                line = in.readLine();
                if (line == null) break;
                // Send it to the server
                sout.println(line);
                // Read a line from the server.
                line = sin.readLine();
                // Check if connection is closed (i.e. for EOF)
                if (line == null) {
                    System.out.println("Connection closed by server.");
                    break;
                }
                // And write the line to the console.
                System.out.println(line);
            }
        }
        catch (IOException e) System.err.println(e);
        // Always be sure to close the socket
        finally {
            try if (s != null) s.close(); catch (IOException e2) ;
        }
    }
}
```

An Applet Client

Example 7-7 shows another client for the server we developed. This one has a graphical user interface that sends input from a `TextField` component to the server and displays results from the server in a `TextArea` component. If you provide some kind of service from your host, you might want to include a simple client applet like this one on your home page so that people can try out the service. (Remember, though, that applets can only open network connections to the host that they came from—so don't try to create applet clients that connect to other machines.) Note that this applet uses a separate thread to read (and wait for) data from the server and display it in the text area.

Example 7-7: Another client

```
import java.applet.*;
import java.awt.*;
import java.io.*;
import java.net.*;

public class AppletClient extends Applet {
    public static final int PORT = 6789;
    Socket s;
    DataInputStream in;
    PrintStream out;
    TextField inputfield;
    TextArea outputarea;
    StreamListener listener;

    // Create a socket to communicate with a server on port 6789 of the
    // host that the applet's code is on. Create streams to use with
    // the socket. Then create a TextField for user input and a TextArea
    // for server output. Finally, create a thread to wait for and
    // display server output.
    public void init() {
        try {
            s = new Socket(this.getCodeBase().getHost(), PORT);
            in = new DataInputStream(s.getInputStream());
            out = new PrintStream(s.getOutputStream());

            inputfield = new TextField();
            outputarea = new TextArea();
            outputarea.setEditable(false);
            this.setLayout(new BorderLayout());
            this.add("North", inputfield);
            this.add("Center", outputarea);

            listener = new StreamListener(in, outputarea);

            this.showStatus("Connected to "
                        + s.getInetAddress().getHostName()
                        + ":" + s.getPort());
        }
        catch (IOException e) this.showStatus(e.toString());
    }
```

Networking

```
        // When the user types a line, send it to the server.
        public boolean action(Event e, Object what) {
            if (e.target == inputfield) {
                out.println((String)e.arg);
                inputfield.setText("");
                return true;
            }
            return false;
        }
    }

    // Wait for output from the server on the specified stream, and display
    // it in the specified TextArea.
    class StreamListener extends Thread {
        DataInputStream in;
        TextArea output;
        public StreamListener(DataInputStream in, TextArea output) {
            this.in = in;
            this.output = output;
            this.start();
        }
        public void run() {
            String line;
            try {
                for(;;) {
                    line = in.readLine();
                    if (line == null) break;
                    output.setText(line);
                }
            }
            catch (IOException e) output.setText(e.toString());
            finally output.setText("Connection closed by server.");
        }
    }
```

Advanced Graphics and Images

Advanced Graphics

The examples in this section demonstrate several important techniques for animation and image processing. They show you how to:

- Use double-buffering to produce smoother animation.
- Use clipping to produce smoother animation.
- Use the `MediaTracker` class to force images to be loaded and verify that there were no errors while loading.
- Modify the colors of an image using the `FilteredImageSource` and `RGBImageFilter` classes.

The examples in this section use classes in the `java.awt` and `java.awt.image` packages. The introductions to Section 19, *The java.awt Package*, and Section 20, *The java.awt.image Package*, describe these packages in more detail. You may find it useful to refer to the quick reference class descriptions in those sections while reading through the examples here.

Smooth Animation

Example 8-1 animates a line of text by moving it smoothly over a complex background. Figure 8-1 shows a snapshot of the animation. This example demonstrates two very important techniques for smooth animation: double-buffering and clipping. Some animation is automatically smooth—when it is done in one place, over a blank background, there is no need for these techniques. But when the object being animated moves across a non-blank background, special care is needed to prevent bad flickering.

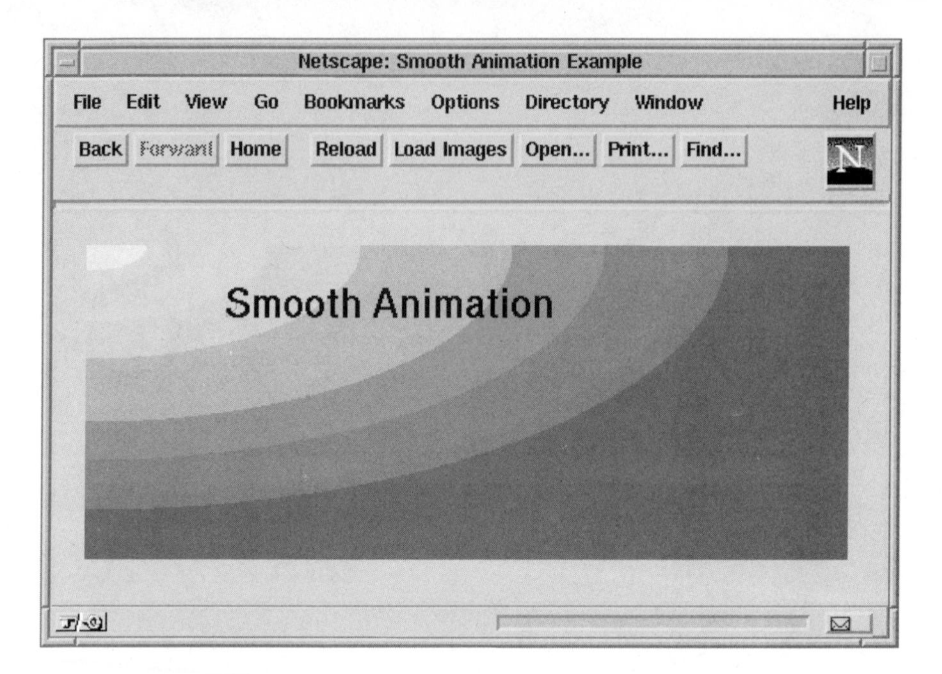

Figure 8-1: An animation in progress

Double-buffering is the practice of doing all your drawing into an offscreen "buffer," and then copying the contents of the buffer to the screen all at once. This prevents flicker that would otherwise result from erasing and redrawing the figure. In Java, our "buffer" is an offscreen `Image`, created with one of the `Component createImage()` methods. To draw into an offscreen image, you simply use its `Graphics` object, which is obtained with the `Image getGraphics()` method. In our example applet, we pass this `Graphics` object to the `paint()` method to fool the applet into drawing in the offscreen image, rather than on the screen.

Once the drawing is complete in the offscreen image, we use the `Component getGraphics()` method to get the `Graphics` object for the applet, and use that `Graphics` object to copy the offscreen image onto the screen. Note that we create the offscreen image the first time it is needed, and that we are careful to make sure that it is always the same size as the applet.

Clipping is the second important technique for making animations smooth and speedy. Animation often involves erasing and redrawing only a small region of a larger area. Unfortunately, typical `paint()` methods only know how to redraw the entire applet, not small regions of it. What we can do, though, is to set a rectangular "clipping region" in the `Graphics` objects we use. Such a clip region tells the system that it only needs to draw within a specified rectangle and that it can ignore any drawing requested outside of that rectangle. When we know the area of an applet that needs to be redrawn, we can specify a clip rectangle that surrounds that area and do a full redraw, knowing that the applet will only be redrawn inside the clip rectangle. This is usually quite efficient and much faster than doing the full redraw without clipping.

Our example applet uses this technique. Note that it is careful in the `init()` method to measure the text it animates. This way it can know exactly what region of the picture needs to be redrawn. In the `run()` method, it creates two `Rectangle` objects, which represent the area of the screen to be erased (where text currently is) and the new area where the text will be drawn. It uses the `Rectangle union()` method to find the smallest rectangle that contains both these rectangles, and uses this combined rectangle as the clipping region. It uses the rectangle both when drawing to the offscreen image and when copying the offscreen image to the screen.

A final interesting point about this example is that clicking the mouse button stops and restarts the animation. The animation is not stopped by actually calling `stop()` for the `animator` thread. Doing that might leave the screen in a partially drawn state, so instead we simply set a `please_stop` variable that the `animator` thread checks after each complete redraw.

Example 8-1: Implementing smooth animation

```
import java.applet.*;
import java.awt.*;

public class Smooth extends Applet implements Runnable {
    static final int deltax = 4;
    static final int deltay = 2;
    static final String message = "Smooth Animation";
    int x = 0;
    int y = 0;
    Color c1 = new Color(0x0000ff);
    Color c2 = new Color(0xffffff);
    Font font = new Font("Helvetica", Font.BOLD, 24);
    Image offscreen;
    int imagewidth, imageheight;
    int stringwidth, stringheight, stringascent;
    Thread animator = null;
    boolean please_stop = false;

    // Measure the size of the text we'll be animating.  We need this
    // information later to do clipping.
    public void init() {
        FontMetrics fm = this.getFontMetrics(font);
        stringwidth = fm.stringWidth(message);
        stringheight = fm.getHeight();
        stringascent = fm.getAscent();
    }

    // Start the animation
    public void start() {
        animator = new Thread(this);
        animator.start();
    }
    // Stop it.
    public void stop() {
        if (animator != null) animator.stop();
        animator = null;
    }
    // Stop and start animating on mouse clicks.
    public boolean mouseDown(Event e, int x, int y) {
        // if running, stop it.  Otherwise, start it.
        if (animator != null) please_stop = true;
```

Advanced Graphics

```
        else { please_stop = false; start(); }
        return true;
    }

    // Draw a fancy background.  Because this background is time-consuming
    // to draw, our animation techniques must be efficient to avoid bad
    // flickering.
    void drawBackground(Graphics gr, Color c1, Color c2, int numsteps) {
        int r, g, b;
        int dr = (c2.getRed() - c1.getRed())/numsteps;
        int dg = (c2.getGreen() - c1.getGreen())/numsteps;
        int db = (c2.getBlue() - c1.getBlue())/numsteps;
        Dimension size = this.size();
        int w = size.width, h = size.height;
        int dw = size.width/numsteps;
        int dh = size.height/numsteps;

        gr.setColor(c1);
        gr.fillRect(0, 0, w, h);

        for(r = c1.getRed(), g = c1.getGreen(), b = c1.getBlue();
          h > 0;
          h -= dh, w -= dw, r += dr, g += dg, b += db) {
            gr.setColor(new Color(r, g, b));
            gr.fillArc(-w, -h, 2*w, 2*h, 0, -90);
        }
    }

    // This method draws the background and  text at its current position.
    public void paint(Graphics g) {
            drawBackground(g, c1, c2, 25);
            g.setColor(Color.black);
            g.setFont(font);
            g.drawString(message, x, y);
    }

    // The body of the animator thread.
    public void run() {
        while(!please_stop) {
            Dimension d = this.size();

            // Make sure the offscreen image is created and is the right size.
            if ((offscreen == null) ||
              ((imagewidth != d.width) || (imageheight != d.height))) {
                // if (offscreen != null) offscreen.flush();
                offscreen = this.createImage(d.width, d.height);
                imagewidth = d.width;
                imageheight = d.height;
            }

            // Set up clipping.  We only need to draw within the
            // old rectangle that needs to be cleared and the new
            // one that is being drawn.

            // the old rectangle
            Rectangle oldrect = new Rectangle(x, y-stringascent,
```

```
                                    stringwidth, stringheight);
            // Update the coordinates for animation.
            x = ((x + deltax)%d.width);
            y = ((y + deltay)%d.height);

            // the new rectangle
            Rectangle newrect = new Rectangle(x, y-stringascent,
                                    stringwidth, stringheight);
            // Compute the union of the rectangles
            Rectangle r = newrect.union(oldrect);

            // Use this rectangle as the clipping region when
            // drawing to the offscreen image, and when copying
            // from the offscreen image to the screen.
            Graphics g = offscreen.getGraphics();
            g.clipRect(r.x, r.y, r.width, r.height);
            // Draw into the offscreen image.
            paint(g);
            // Copy it all at once to the screen, using clipping.
            g = this.getGraphics();
            g.clipRect(r.x, r.y, r.width, r.height);
            g.drawImage(offscreen, 0, 0, this);

            // wait a tenth of a second, then draw it again!
            try Thread.sleep(100); catch (InterruptedException e);
        }
        animator = null;
    }
}
```


Keeping Track of Images

In Section 4, *Applets*, we saw a simple animator applet that displayed a sequence of images one after the other. (This is the kind of simple animation that does not require the double-buffering or clipping techniques described above.) There were some problems with that simple animator applet, however. It would start animating before the images were all loaded, which meant that the first cycle of animations went very slowly. Also, it had no provisions for handling errors while loading images. Example 8-2 is a new animator applet that addresses these problems.

The secret is to use a `MediaTracker` object. This class lets you register images and then call a method that blocks until they have completed loading. It also allows you to check for errors in the loading process. The `init()` method creates all the `Image` objects and stores them in an array. The method also registers the images with the `MediaTracker` object. Then the `run()` method uses the `MediaTracker` to force each image to be loaded, and to check whether it loaded sucessfully. This method displays image loading results in the status line.

Note that instead of registering and loading images individually, we could instead have registered all the images with the same integer identifier. In this case, a single call to the `MediaTracker waitForID()` method would have loaded all the images, and a single call to `isErrorID()` would have specified whether there were errors with any of the images. The drawback to this approach is that you can't provide feedback in the status line for each individual image. The potentially important advantage, however, is that the MediaTracker can attempt to download the images in parallel. This could be useful, for example, over a slow network connection.

Example 8-2: Tracking image loading

```
// This applet displays an animation. It uses the MediaTracker class to
// load the images and verify that there are no errors.
import java.applet.*;
import java.awt.*;
import java.net.*;
import java.util.*;

public class Animator2 extends Applet implements Runnable {
    protected Image[] images;
    protected int num_images;
    protected int current_image;
    protected MediaTracker tracker;

    // Read the basename and num_images parameters.
    // Then read in the images, using the specified base name.
    // For example, if basename is images/anim, read images/anim0,
    // images/anim1, etc. These are relative to the current document URL.
    public void init() {
        String basename = this.getParameter("basename");
        try { num_images = Integer.parseInt(this.getParameter("num_images")); }
        catch (NumberFormatException e) { num_images = 0; }

        // getImage() creates an Image object from a URL specification,
        // but it doesn't actually load the images; that is done
        // asynchronously. Store all the images in a MediaTracker
        // so we can wait until they have all loaded (in run()).
        tracker = new MediaTracker(this);
        images = new Image[num_images];
        for(int i = 0; i < num_images; i++) {
            images[i] = this.getImage(this.getDocumentBase(), basename + i);
            tracker.addImage(images[i], i);
        }
    }

    // This is the thread that runs the animation, and the methods
    // that start it and stop it.
    private Thread animator_thread = null;
    public void start() {
        if (animator_thread == null) {
            animator_thread = new Thread(this);
            animator_thread.start();
        }
    }
    public void stop() {
        if ((animator_thread != null) && animator_thread.isAlive())
            animator_thread.stop();
        animator_thread = null;
    }

    // This is the body of the thread--the method that does the animation.
    public void run() {
```

Example 8-2: Tracking image loading (continued)

```
            // First, force all the images to be loaded, and wait until
            // they have all loaded completely.
            for (int i = 0; i < num_images; i++) {
                this.showStatus("Loading image: " + i);
                // The argument is the same one we passed to addImage()
                try tracker.waitForID(i); catch (InterruptedException e) ;
                // Check for errors loading it.
                if (tracker.isErrorID(i)) {
                    this.showStatus("Error loading image " + i + "; quitting.");
                    return;
                }
            }
            this.showStatus("Loading images: done.");

            // Now do the animation
            while(true) {
                if (++current_image >= images.length) current_image = 0;
                this.getGraphics().drawImage(images[current_image], 0, 0, this);
                try { Thread.sleep(200); } catch (InterruptedException e) ;
            }
        }
    }
```


Filtering Images

A common way to specify that a button in a graphical interface is currently inactive is to "gray it out." When a button displays an image, this means that we need a "grayed out" version of the image. Example 8-3 is an applet that demonstrates a simple way to created grayed-out images. Figure 8-2 shows an image and the grayed-out version created by this applet.

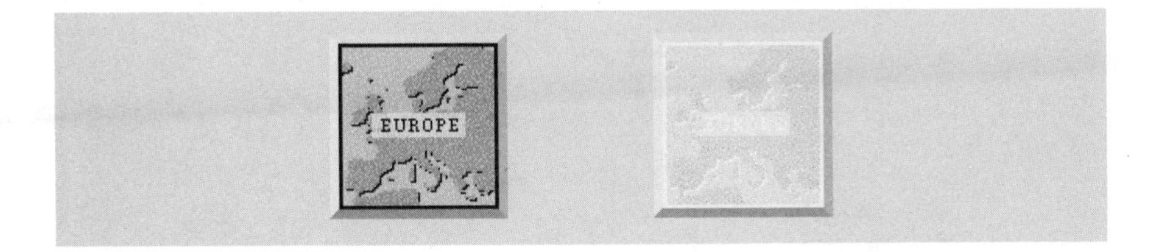

Figure 8-2: Filtered image colors

The `init()` method of this example demonstrates how you can use a source image, a `FilteredImageSource` object, and an `ImageFilter` object to produce a new, filtered image. The contents of this new image depend, of course, on the image filter. In this example, we define a `GrayFilter` as a subclass of `RGBImageFilter`. The body of this filter is the `filterRGB()` method which takes an RGB color value as input, averages it with white, and returns the result. This makes all the colors in the image more gray. Note that we are careful in this example not to modify the alpha transparency value stored in the top eight bits of the color value.

Note that the `filterRGB()` method does not use its `x` and `y` arguments. The filtering it performs is position independent, which means that the filter can be used more efficiently on the entries of a colormap instead of on each pixel of the image. To indicate that our `GrayFilter` is position independent, we set the `canFilterIndexColorModel` variable to `true` in the constructor method. On the other hand, if we were implementing an `RGBImageFilter` that produced a blurring effect, for example, the filter would be position dependent, and we would have to set `canFilterIndexColorModel` to `false`.

Finally, note that the `CropImageFilter` is another useful kind of image filter. It allows you to extract a rectangular region from a larger image.

Example 8-3: Producing a grayed out image

```
import java.applet.*;
import java.awt.*;
import java.awt.image.*;

public class GrayButton extends Applet {
    Image i, gray;

    // Load an image from a file. Create a new image that is a grayer
    // version of it, using a FilteredImageSource ImageProducer and a
    // GrayFilter ImageFilter.
    public void init() {
        i = this.getImage(this.getDocumentBase(), "images/button.gif");
        ImageFilter f = new GrayFilter();
        ImageProducer producer = new FilteredImageSource(i.getSource(), f);
        gray = this.createImage(producer);
    }

    // Display the image
    public void update(Graphics g) {
        g.drawImage(i, 0, 0, this);
    }

    // When the user clicks, display the gray image
    public boolean mouseDown(Event e, int x, int y) {
        Graphics g = this.getGraphics();
        Dimension d = this.size();
        g.clearRect(0, 0, d.width, d.height);
        g.drawImage(gray, 0, 0, this);
        return true;
    }
    // And restore the normal one when the mouse goes up.
    public boolean mouseUp(Event e, int x, int y) {
        update(this.getGraphics());
        return true;
    }
}

// Filter an image by averaging all of its colors with white.
// This washes it out and makes it grayer.
class GrayFilter extends RGBImageFilter {
    public GrayFilter() { canFilterIndexColorModel = true; }
    public int filterRGB(int x, int y, int rgb) {
        int a = rgb & 0xff000000;
        int r = ((rgb & 0xff0000) + 0xff0000)/2;
```

Example 8-3: Producing a grayed out image (continued)

```
            int g = ((rgb & 0x00ff00) + 0x00ff00)/2;
            int b = ((rgb & 0x0000ff) + 0x0000ff)/2;
            return a | r | g | b;
        }
    }
```

9

Advanced Threads

The use of threads is basic to the Java programming model. We've used them in applets to perform animations and in network servers to serve more than one client at once. The examples in this section demonstrate some advanced uses of threads:

- Obtaining information about threads and thread groups
- Specifying the name, group, and priority of a thread
- Using `synchronized` to prevent simultaneous access by multiple threads to critical data structures
- Using `wait()` to make a thread wait until some condition occurs
- Using `notify()` to tell a waiting thread that a condition has occurred

You may want to refer to the quick reference descriptions of the `Thread`, `ThreadGroup`, and `Object` classes, in Section 23, *The java.lang Package*, while studying these examples.

Threads and Thread Groups

Example 9-1 is a `ThreadLister` class, with a public `listAllThreads()` method that does just that—lists all threads (and all of their thread groups) that are running on the Java interpreter. Recall that every Java `Thread` belongs to some `ThreadGroup`, and that every `ThreadGroup` is also contained in some "parent" `ThreadGroup`. Figure 9-1 shows the output of the `listAllThreads()` method displayed in an applet.

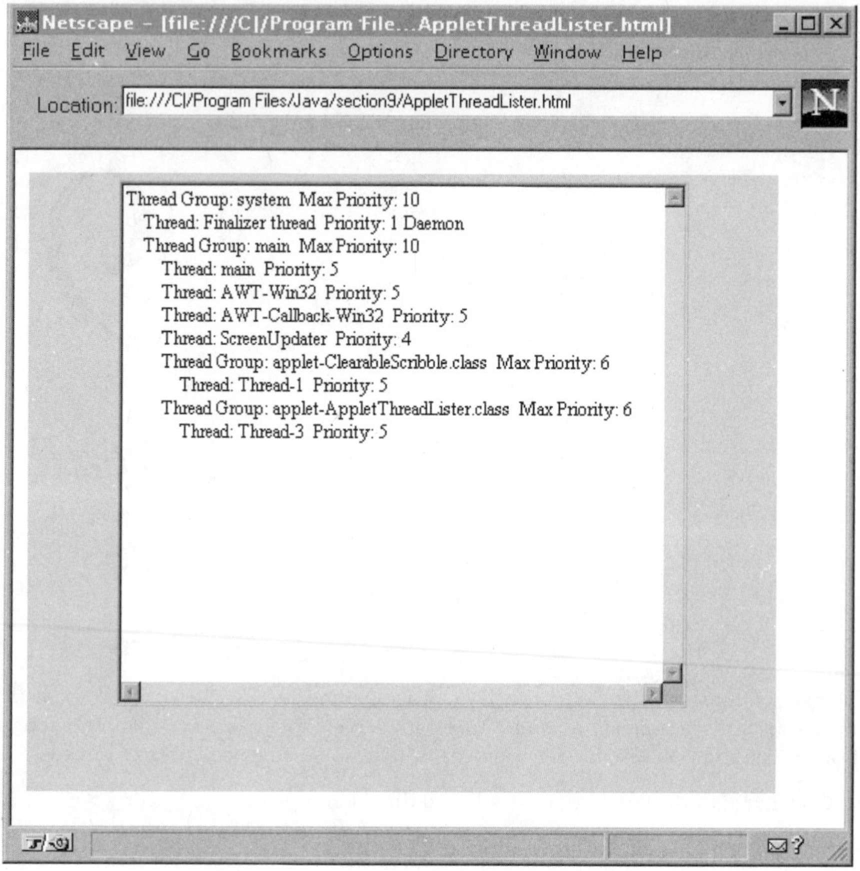

Figure 9-1: A thread-listing applet

Example 9-1: Listing all threads and thread groups

```
import java.io.*;

public class ThreadLister {
    // Display info about a thread.
    private static void print_thread_info(PrintStream out, Thread t,
                                          String indent) {
        if (t == null) return;
        out.println(indent + "Thread: " + t.getName() +
                    "  Priority: " + t.getPriority() +
                    (t.isDaemon()?" Daemon":"") +
                    (t.isAlive()?"":" Not Alive"));
    }

    // Display info about a thread group and its threads and groups
    private static void list_group(PrintStream out, ThreadGroup g,
                                   String indent) {
        if (g == null) return;
        int num_threads = g.activeCount();
        int num_groups = g.activeGroupCount();
```

```
            Thread[] threads = new Thread[num_threads];
            ThreadGroup[] groups = new ThreadGroup[num_groups];

            g.enumerate(threads, false);
            g.enumerate(groups, false);

            out.println(indent + "Thread Group: " + g.getName() +
                    " Max Priority: " + g.getMaxPriority() +
                    (g.isDaemon()?" Daemon":""));

            for(int i = 0; i < num_threads; i++)
                print_thread_info(out, threads[i], indent + "    ");
            for(int i = 0; i < num_groups; i++)
                list_group(out, groups[i], indent + "    ");
        }

        // Find the root thread group and list it recursively
        public static void listAllThreads(PrintStream out) {
            ThreadGroup current_thread_group;
            ThreadGroup root_thread_group;
            ThreadGroup parent;

            // Get the current thread group
            current_thread_group = Thread.currentThread().getThreadGroup();

            // Now go find the root thread group
            root_thread_group = current_thread_group;
            parent = root_thread_group.getParent();
            while(parent != null) {
                root_thread_group = parent;
                parent = parent.getParent();
            }

            // And list it, recursively
            list_group(out, root_thread_group, "");
        }


        public static void main(String[] args) {
            ThreadLister.listAllThreads(System.out);
        }
    }
```


The `listAllThreads()` method uses the `Thread` static method `currentThread()` to obtain the current thread, and uses `getThreadGroup()` to find the thread group of that thread. It then uses the `ThreadGroup getParent()` method to move through the thread group hierarchy until it finds the "root" thread group, the thread group that contains all other threads and thread groups.

`listAllThreads()` then calls the private `ThreadLister list_group()` method to display the contents of the root thread group, and to recursively display the contents of all thread groups it contains. `list_group()`, and the `print_thread_info()` method it calls, use various `Thread` and `ThreadGroup` methods to obtain information about the threads and their groups. Note that the `isDaemon()` method returns whether a thread is a "daemon thread" or not. Daemon threads are expected to run in the background and are not expected to exit. The Java interpreter exits when all non-daemon threads have quit.

The `ThreadLister` class has a `main()` method so that it can be run alone. It is more interesting, of course, to invoke the `listAllThreads()` method from within another program or applet—it can help you to figure out problems you are having with threads.

Example 9-2 is a short listing that shows how the `ThreadLister` output can be displayed in an applet window, as we saw in Figure 9-1. Note the use of a `ByteArrayOutputStream` to capture the `ThreadLister` output and convert it to a string for display.

Example 9-2: Listing threads in an applet

```
import java.applet.*;
import java.awt.*;
import java.io.*;

public class AppletThreadLister extends Applet {
    TextArea textarea;

    // Create a text area to put our listing in
    public void init() {
        textarea = new TextArea(20, 60);
        this.add(textarea);
        Dimension prefsize = textarea.preferredSize();
        this.resize(prefsize.width, prefsize.height);
    }

    // Do the listing.  Note the cool use of ByteArrayOutputStream.
    public void start() {
        ByteArrayOutputStream os = new ByteArrayOutputStream();
        PrintStream ps = new PrintStream(os);
        ThreadLister.listAllThreads(ps);
        textarea.setText(os.toString());
    }
}
```

synchronized, wait(), and notify()

Example 9-3 is an extended version of the `Server` class we saw in Section 7, *Networking*. As you may recall, that class creates a new thread to handle each connection to a client. We've made the following changes to the server:

- It creates a `ThreadGroup` to contain all of the client connection threads it creates.
- It gives a descriptive name to each of the threads it creates.
- It assigns each client connection thread a priority that is lower than the default, so that they cannot end up overloading the system and preventing other threads from running.
- It displays a list of all current connections in a window.

- It creates a new thread, which it calls a "vulture," that waits for the connection threads to die (i.e., to exit), and then removes them from the list of current connections.

Creating the new thread group and giving the threads names and priorities is straightforward. You can see how it is done in the code. The last two changes are a little more tricky. First, the server has to ensure that it is not adding a new thread to the list while the "vulture" thread is removing one. The way to provide "mutual exclusion" (i.e., to prevent simultaneous access to a resource) is with `synchronized` methods or `synchronized` blocks of code. The example demonstrates this technique.

The second tricky change is having the "vulture" thread wait for the other threads to exit. We do this by having the vulture call its own `wait()` method, (`wait()` is a method of the `Object` class) and having each of the connection threads invoke the vulture's `notify()` method just before they exit. The `notify()` call "wakes up" the vulture thread, which can then check the list for threads that are no longer alive and remove them. Note that the code acquires a lock on the vulture thread (i.e., is in a `synchronized` method or block) before calling the `wait()` and `notify()` methods. This is required for them to work correctly.

Example 9-3: Using synchronized, wait(), and notify()

```
import java.net.*;
import java.io.*;
import java.awt.*;
import java.util.*;

public class Server extends Thread {
    public final static int DEFAULT_PORT = 6789;
    protected int port;
    protected ServerSocket listen_socket;
    protected ThreadGroup threadgroup;
    protected List connection_list;
    protected Vector connections;
    protected Vulture vulture;

    // Exit with an error message, when an exception occurs.
    public static void fail(Exception e, String msg) {
        System.err.println(msg + ": " + e);
        System.exit(1);
    }

    // Create a ServerSocket to listen for connections on; start the thread.
    public Server(int port) {
        // Create our server thread with a name.
        super("Server");
        if (port == 0) port = DEFAULT_PORT;
        this.port = port;
        try { listen_socket = new ServerSocket(port); }
        catch (IOException e) fail(e, "Exception creating server socket");
        // Create a thread group for our connections
         threadgroup = new ThreadGroup("Server Connections");
```

Advanced Threads

Example 9-3: Using synchronized, wait(), and notify() (continued)

```
        // Create a window to display our connections in
        Frame f = new Frame("Server Status");
        connection_list = new List();
        f.add("Center", connection_list);
        f.resize(400, 200);
        f.show();

        // Initialize a vector to store our connections in
        connections = new Vector();

        // Create a Vulture thread to wait for other threads to die.
        // It starts itself automatically.
        vulture = new Vulture(this);

        // Start the server listening for connections
        this.start();
    }

    // The body of the server thread.  Loop forever, listening for and
    // accepting connections from clients.  For each connection,
    // create a Connection object to handle communication through the
    // new Socket.  When we create a new connection, add it to the
    // Vector of connections, and display it in the List.  Note that we
    // use synchronized to lock the Vector of connections.  The Vulture
    // class does the same, so the vulture won't be removing dead
    // connections while we're adding fresh ones.
    public void run() {
        try {
            while(true) {
                Socket client_socket = listen_socket.accept();
                Connection c = new Connection(client_socket, threadgroup,
                                              3, vulture);
                // prevent simultaneous access.
                synchronized (connections) {
                    connections.addElement(c);
                    connection_list.addItem(c.toString());
                }
            }
        }
        catch (IOException e) fail(e, "Exception while listening for connections");
    }

    // Start the server up, listening on an optionally specified port
    public static void main(String[] args) {
        int port = 0;
        if (args.length == 1) {
            try port = Integer.parseInt(args[0]);
            catch (NumberFormatException e) port = 0;
        }
        new Server(port);
    }
}
```

```
// This class is the thread that handles all communication with a client
// It also notifies the Vulture when the connection is dropped.
class Connection extends Thread {
    static int connection_number = 0;
    protected Socket client;
    protected Vulture vulture;
    protected DataInputStream in;
    protected PrintStream out;

    // Initialize the streams and start the thread
    public Connection(Socket client_socket, ThreadGroup threadgroup,
                int priority, Vulture vulture)
    {
        // Give the thread a group, a name, and a priority.
        super(threadgroup, "Connection-" + connection_number++);
        this.setPriority(priority);
        // Save our other arguments away
        client = client_socket;
        this.vulture = vulture;
        // Create the streams
        try {
            in = new DataInputStream(client.getInputStream());
            out = new PrintStream(client.getOutputStream());
        }
        catch (IOException e) {
            try client.close(); catch (IOException e2) ;
            System.err.println("Exception while getting socket streams: " + e);
            return;
        }
        // And start the thread up
        this.start();
    }

    // Provide the service.
    // Read a line, reverse it, send it back.
    public void run() {
        String line;
        StringBuffer revline;
        int len;

        // Send a welcome message to the client
        out.println("Line Reversal Server version 1.0");
        out.println("A service of O'Reilly & Associates");

        try {
            for(;;) {
                // read in a line
                line = in.readLine();
                if (line == null) break;
                // reverse it
                len = line.length();
                revline = new StringBuffer(len);
                for(int i = len-1; i >= 0; i--)
                    revline.insert(len-1-i, line.charAt(i));
```

```
                    // and write out the reversed line
                    out.println(revline);
                }
            }
            catch (IOException e) ;
            // When we're done, for whatever reason, be sure to close
            // the socket, and to notify the Vulture object.  Note that
            // we have to use synchronized first to lock the vulture
            // object before we can call notify() for it.
            finally {
                try client.close(); catch (IOException e2) ;
                synchronized (vulture) vulture.notify();
            }
        }

        // This method returns the string representation of the Connection.
        // This is the string that will appear in the GUI List.
        public String toString() {
            return this.getName() + " connected to: "
                + client.getInetAddress().getHostName()
                + ":" + client.getPort();
        }
    }

    // This class waits to be notified that a thread is dying (exiting)
    // and then cleans up the list of threads and the graphical list.
    class Vulture extends Thread {
        protected Server server;

        protected Vulture(Server s) {
            super(s.threadgroup, "Connection Vulture");
            server = s;
            this.start();
        }

        // This is the method that waits for notification of exiting threads
        // and cleans up the lists.  It is a synchronized method, so it
        // acquires a lock on the 'this' object before running.  This is
        // necessary so that it can call wait() on 'this'.  Even if the
        // the Connection objects never call notify(), this method wakes up
        // every five seconds and checks all the connections, just in case.
        // Note also that all access to the Vector of connections and to
        // the GUI List component are within a synchronized block as well.
        // This prevents the Server class from adding a new connection while
        // we're removing an old one.
        public synchronized void run() {
            for(;;) {
                try this.wait(5000); catch (InterruptedException e) ;
                // prevent simultaneous access
                synchronized(server.connections) {
                    // loop through the connections
                    for(int i = 0; i < server.connections.size(); i++) {
                        Connection c;
                        c = (Connection)server.connections.elementAt(i);
```

Example 9-3: Using synchronized, wait(), and notify() (continued)

```
                        // if the connection thread isn't alive anymore,
                        // remove it from the Vector and List.
                        if (!c.isAlive()) {
                            server.connections.removeElementAt(i);
                            server.connection_list.delItem(i);
                            i--;
                        }
                    }
                }
            }
        }
    }
```

A Multithreaded Client

Example 9-4 shows a new version of our `Client` program from Section 7. The old version used a single thread, expected the server to always send a single-line response to the client's input, and to never send any other text. Our new `Server` class, however, sends two lines of identifying text when it first connects with a client. Our old `Client` would not handle that text correctly.

The new client creates two threads when it starts up. One, the `Reader` thread, is responsible for reading data from the server and printing it to the console. The other, the `Writer` thread, reads user input from the console and writes it to the server. This way, any text the server sends is displayed at the appropriate time.

Note that there is apparently some problem with shared access by these threads to the console. To work around the problem, it is necessary to give the `Reader` thread a higher priority than the `Writer` thread. This is done right after the threads are created in the `Client` constructor method.

Example 9-4: A multithreaded client

```
import java.io.*;
import java.net.*;

public class Client {
    public static final int DEFAULT_PORT = 6789;
    Socket socket;
    Thread reader, writer;

    // Create the client by creating its reader and writer threads
    // and starting them.
    public Client(String host, int port) {
        try {
            socket = new Socket(host, port);
            // Create reader and writer sockets
            reader = new Reader(this);
            writer = new Writer(this);
            // Give the reader a higher priority to work around
            // a problem with shared access to the console.
            reader.setPriority(6);
            writer.setPriority(5);
```

Advanced Threads

Example 9-4: A multithreaded client (continued)

```
            // Start the threads
            reader.start();
            writer.start();
        }
        catch (IOException e) System.err.println(e);
    }

    public static void usage() {
        System.out.println("Usage: java Client <hostname> [<port>]");
        System.exit(0);
    }
    public static void main(String[] args) {
        int port = DEFAULT_PORT;
        Socket s = null;

        // Parse the port specification
        if ((args.length != 1) && (args.length != 2)) usage();
        if (args.length == 1) port = DEFAULT_PORT;
        else {
            try port = Integer.parseInt(args[1]);
            catch (NumberFormatException e) usage();
        }

        new Client(args[0], port);
    }
}

// This thread reads data from the server and prints it on the console
// As usual, the run() method does the interesting stuff.
class Reader extends Thread {
    Client client;
    public Reader(Client c) {
        super("Client Reader");
        this.client = c;
    }
    public void run() {
        DataInputStream in = null;
        String line;
        try {
            in = new DataInputStream(client.socket.getInputStream());
            while(true) {
                line = in.readLine();
                if (line == null) {
                    System.out.println("Server closed connection.");
                    break;
                }
                System.out.println(line);
            }
        }
        catch (IOException e) System.out.println("Reader: " + e);
        finally try if (in != null) in.close(); catch (IOException e) ;
        System.exit(0);
    }
}
```

Example 9-4: A multithreaded client (continued)

```
// This thread reads user input from the console and sends it to the server.
class Writer extends Thread {
    Client client;
    public Writer(Client c) {
        super("Client Writer");
        client = c;
    }
    public void run() {
        DataInputStream in = null;
        PrintStream out = null;
        try {
            String line;
            in = new DataInputStream(System.in);
            out = new PrintStream(client.socket.getOutputStream());
            while(true) {
                line = in.readLine();
                if (line == null) break;
                out.println(line);
            }
        }
        catch (IOException e) System.err.println("Writer: " + e);
        finally if (out != null) out.close();
        System.exit(0);
    }
}
```

Advanced Threads

Part III

Java Language Reference

Part III contains a variety of reference material on the Java language and closely related topics. The *How to Use This Book* section at the beginning of the book explains what material is presented in each of these sections.

Section 10, *Java Syntax*
Section 11, *Events*
Section 12, *Fonts, Colors, and Cursors*
Section 13, *System Properties and Applet Parameters*
Section 14, *Applet Security*
Section 15, *Java-Related HTML and HTTP Syntax*
Section 16, *The Unicode Standard*
Section 17, *JDK Development Tools*

Java Syntax

Primitive Data Types

Java supports a complete set of primitive data types, listed in Table 10-1. In Java, the size of each type is defined by the language, and is *not* implementation dependent, as it is in C.

Table 10-1: Java Primitive Data Types

Type	Contains	Default	Size	Min Value / Max Value
`boolean`	`true` or `false`	`false`	1 bit	N.A. N.A.
`char`	Unicode character	\u0000	16 bits	\u0000 \uFFFF
`byte`	signed integer	0	8 bits	-128 127
`short`	signed integer	0	16 bits	-32768 32767
`int`	signed integer	0	32 bits	-2147483648 2147483647
`long`	signed integer	0	64 bits	-9223372036854775808 9223372036854775807
`float`	IEEE 754 floating-point	`0.0`	32 bits	±3.40282347E+38 ±1.40239846E-45
`double`	IEEE 754 floating-point	`0.0`	64 bits	±1.79769313486231570E+308 ±4.94065645841246544E-324

Character Escape Sequences

Java uses the escape sequences listed in Table 10-2 to represent certain special character values. These escape sequences may appear in any Java `char` or `String` literal.

Table 10-2: Java Escape Characters

Escape Sequence	Character Value
`\b`	Backspace
`\t`	Horizontal tab
`\n`	Newline
`\f`	Form feed
`\r`	Carriage return
`\"`	Double quote
`\'`	Single quote
`\\`	Backslash
`\`*xxx*	The character corresponding to the octal value *xxx*, where *xxx* is between 000 and 0377.
`\u`*xxxx*	The Unicode character with encoding *xxxx*, where *xxxx* is one to four hexidecimal digits. Unicode escapes are distinct from the other escape types listed here; they are described below in more detail.

Java characters, strings, and identifiers (e.g., variable, method, and class names) are composed of 16-bit Unicode characters. The Unicode `\u` escape sequence may be used anywhere in a Java program (not only in `char` and `String` literals) to represent a Unicode character.

Unicode `\u` escape sequences are processed before the other escape sequences described in Table 10-2, and thus the two types of escape sequences can have very different semantics. A Unicode escape is simply an alternative way to represent a character which may not be displayable on non-Unicode systems. The character escapes, however, can represent special characters in a way that prevents the usual interpretation of those characters by the compiler.

Operators

Table 10-3 lists the operators of the Java language, along with their precedence, operand types, and associativity.

Table 10-3: Java Operators

Prec.	Operator	Operand Type(s)	Assoc.	Operation Performed
1	`++`	arithmetic	R	pre-or-post increment (unary)
	`--`	arithmetic	R	pre-or-post decrement (unary)
	`+, -`	arithmetic	R	unary plus, unary minus
	`~`	integral	R	bitwise complement (unary)
	`!`	boolean	R	logical complement (unary)

Table 10-3: Java Operators (continued)

Prec.	Operator	Operand Type(s)	Assoc.	Operation Performed
	(*type*)	any	R	cast
2	*, /, %	arithmetic	L	multiplication, division, remainder
3	+, -	arithmetic	L	addition, subtraction
	+	String	L	string concatenation
4	<<	integral	L	left shift
	>>	integral	L	right shift with sign extension
	>>>	integral	L	right shift with zero extension
5	<, <=	arithmetic	L	less than, less than or equal
	>, >=	arithmetic	L	greater than, greater than or equal
	instanceof	object, type	L	type comparison
6	==	primitive	L	equal (have identical values)
	!=	primitive	L	not equal (have different values)
	==	object	L	equal (refer to same object)
	!=	object	L	not equal (refer to different objects)
7	&	integral	L	bitwise AND
	&	boolean	L	boolean AND
8	^	integral	L	bitwise XOR
	^	boolean	L	boolean XOR
9	|	integral	L	bitwise OR
	|	boolean	L	boolean OR
10	&&	boolean	L	conditional AND
11	||	boolean	L	conditional OR
12	?:	boolean, any, any	R	conditional (ternary) operator
13	=	variable, any	R	assignment
	*=, /=, %=, +=, -=, <<=, >>=, >>>=, &=, ^=, |=,	variable, any	R	assignment with operation

Operator precedence controls the order in which operations are performed. Consider the following example:

```
w = x + y * z;
```

The multiplication operator * has a higher precedence than the addition operator +, so the multiplication is performed before the addition. Furthermore, the assignment operator = has the lowest precedence of any operators, so the assignment is done after all the operations on the right-hand side are performed. Operators with the same precedence (like addition and subtraction) are performed in order according to their associativity (usually left-to-right). Operator precedence can be overridden with the explicit use of parentheses. For example:

```
w = (x + y) * z;
```

The associativity of an operator specifies the order that operations of the same precedence are performed in. In Table 10-3, a value of L specifies left-to-right associativity, and a value of R specifies right-to-left associativity. Left-to-right associativity means that operations are performed left-to-right. For example:

```
w = x + y + z;
```

Is the same as:

```
w = ((x + y) + z);
```

because the addition operator has left-to-right associativity. On the other hand, the following expressions:

```
x = ~-~y;
q = a?b:c?d:e?f:g;
```

Are equivalent to:

```
x = ~(-(~y));
q = a?b:(c?d:(e?f:g));
```

because the unary operators and the ternary conditional `?:` operator have right-to-left associativity.

Java operators are basically identical to C operators, except for the following differences:

- The `+` operator applied to `String` values concatenates them. If only one operand of `+` is a `String`, the other one is converted to a string. The conversion is done automatically for primitive types and by calling the `toString` method of non-primitive types.

- Java does not have the comma operator like C does. It does, however, simulate this operator in the limited context of the `for` loop initialization and increment expressions.

- Since all Java integral types are signed, the >> operator always does a signed right shift, filling in high bits with the sign bit of the operand. The new >>> operator performs an unsigned right shift, filling in high bits of the shifted value with zero bits.

- The `&` and `|` operators perform bitwise AND and OR operations on integral operands, and perform logical AND and OR operators on `boolean` operands. `&&` and `||` also perform logical AND and OR on `boolean` operands, but do not evaluate the right-hand operand, if the result of the operation is fully determined by the left-hand operand.

- The `instanceof` operator returns `true` if the object on the left-hand side is an instance of the class or implements the interface on the right-hand side. Otherwise it returns `false`. If the left-hand side is `null`, it returns `false`.

Modifiers

The visibility modifiers in Java specify the accessibility of classes, methods, and variables from other packages, classes, and methods. They are described in Table 10-4.

Table 10-4: Class, Method, and Variable Visibility Modifiers

Modifier	Meaning
`public`	A `public` class or interface is visible anywhere. A `public` method or variable is visible anywhere its class is visible.
`protected`	A `protected` method or variable is visible throughout the package of its class, and in any subclass of its class. Classes may not be `protected`. A subclass in a different package than its superclass can access the `protected` fields inherited by its instances, but it cannot access those fields in instances of the superclass.
default (no modifiers)	If no modifiers are specified, a class, interface, method, or variable is visible only within its package.
`private protected`	A `private protected` method or variable is only visible within its own class and within any subclasses. Classes may not be `private protected`. A subclass can access the `private protected` fields inherited by its instances, but it cannot access those fields in instances of the superclass.
`private`	A `private` method or variable is only visible within its own class. Classes may not be `private`.

Table 10-5 summarizes the visibility modifiers; it shows the circumstances under which fields of the various visibility types are accessible and the circumstances under which they are inherited by subclasses.

Table 10-5: Java Field Visibility

Situation	public	default	protected	private protected	private
Accessible to non-subclass from same package?	yes	yes	yes	no	no
Accessible to subclass from same package?	yes	yes	yes	no	no
Accessible to non-subclass from different package?	yes	no	no	no	no
Accessible to subclass from different package?	yes	no	no	no	no
Inherited by subclass in same package?	yes	yes	yes	yes	no
Inherited by subclass in different package?	yes	no	yes	yes	no

The other Java modifiers specify a number of attributes of classes, methods, and variables. They are described in Table 10-6.

Table 10-6: Other Modifiers

Modifier	Used On	Meaning
`abstract`	class	The class contains unimplemented methods and cannot be instantiated.
	interface	All interfaces are `abstract`. The modifier is optional in interface declarations.
	method	No body is provided for the method (it is provided by a subclass). The signature is followed by a semicolon. The enclosing class must also be `abstract`.
`final`	class	The class may not be subclassed.
	method	The method may not be overridden (compiler may optimize).
	variable	The variable may not have its value changed (compiler may precompute expressions).
`native`	method	The method is implemented in C, or in some other platform-dependent way. No body is provided; the signature is followed by a semicolon.
`static`	method	The method is a "class method." It is not passed as an implicit `this` object reference, and so it cannot refer to non-static variables or methods of the class. It is implictly `final`. It may be invoked through the class name.
	variable	The variable is a "class variable." There is only one instance of the variable, regardless of the number of class instances created. It may be accessed through the class name.
`synchronized`	method	The method makes non-atomic modifications to the class or instance, and care must be taken to ensure that two threads cannot modify the class or instance at the same time. For a `static` method, a lock for the class is acquired before executing the method. For a non-`static` method, a lock for the specific object instance is acquired.
`transient`	variable	The variable is not part of the persistant state of the object. (This modifier currently has no effect).
`volatile`	variable	The variable changes asynchronously (e.g., it may be a hardware register on a peripheral device). The compiler should not try to save its value in registers.

Reserved Words

Table 10-7 lists reserved words in Java. These are keywords or `boolean` literal values. Note that `byvalue`, `cast`, `const`, `future`, `generic`, `goto`, `inner`, `operator`, `outer`, `rest`, and `var` are reserved by Java but currently unused.

Table 10-7: Java Reserved Words

abstract	default	goto	operator	synchronized
boolean	do	if	outer	this
break	double	implements	package	throw
byte	else	import	private	throws
byvalue	extends	inner	protected	transient
case	false	instanceof	public	true
cast	final	int	rest	try
catch	finally	interface	return	var
char	float	long	short	void
class	for	native	static	volatile
const	future	new	super	while
continue	generic	null	switch	

Reserved Method Names

Table 10-8 lists the method names of the `Object` class. Strictly speaking, these method names are not reserved, but since the methods are inherited by every class, they should not be used as the name of a method, except when intentionally overriding an `Object` method.

Table 10-8: Reserved Method Names

clone	getClass	notifyAll
equals	hashCode	toString
finalize	notify	wait

Java Documentation Comment Syntax

The Java language supports special "doc comments," which begin with `/**` and end with `*/`. These comments are not actually treated specially by the compiler, but can be extracted and automatically turned into HTML documentation by the *javadoc* program.

A doc comment may contain HTML markup tags, such as <PRE> and <TT> for code usage examples, but should not contain HTML structural tags such as <H2> or <HR>. Doc comments are associated with the declaration of the class, variable, or method that they precede.

Doc comments may also use special tags, which all begin with the `@` character and allow *javadoc* to provide additional formatting for the documentation. When you use a special *javadoc* tag, it must be the first thing on its line within the doc comment. Also, if you use more than one tag of the same type, they should be on subsequent lines. For example, a class with multiple authors, or a method with multiple arguments would use multiple `@author` or `@param` tags. The available tags are listed below:

`@see` *`classname`*
: This tag adds a "See Also:" entry to the documentation that contains a hyperlink to the specified class. It may be used before classes, methods, or variables.

`@see` *`full-classname`*
: This tag adds a "See Also:" entry to the documentation that contains a hyperlink to the specified class. It may be used before classes, methods, or variables.

`@see` *`full-classname#method-name`*
: This tag adds a "See Also:" entry to the documentation that contains a hyperlink to the specified method of the specified class. It may be used before classes, methods, or variables.

`@version` *`text`*
: This tag adds a "Version:" entry containing the specified text to the documentation. May only be used before a class definition.

`@author` *`text`*
: This tag adds an "Author:" entry containing the specified text to the documentation. May only be used before a class definition.

`@param` *`parameter-name description`*
: This tag adds the specified parameter and its specified description to the "Parameters:" section of the current method. If the description is longer than one line, it may be continued on the next. May only be used before a method definition.

`@return` *`description`*
: Adds a "Returns:" section containing the specified description to the documentation. May only be used before a method definition.

`@exception` *`full-classname description`*
: Adds a "Throws:" entry to the documentation. The entry contains the specified class name of the exception and the description specified, which should explain the significance of the exception. May only be used before a method definition.

Events

Event Types

Table 11-1 lists the events that can be generated by each Component type in the java.awt package. The first column of the table specifies both the type of the component and the type of the event. The event type values are constants defined by the java.awt.Event class and are stored in the id field of the Event object.

The second through sixth columns indicate whether the when (timestamp), x (mouse X coordinate), y (mouse y coordinate), key (the key that was pressed), and modifiers (modifier keys that were down) fields are set for a given event. If a dot appears in this column, the event sets a value for the corresponding field. The seventh column explains what occurred to trigger the event, and what the value of the arg field of the Event object is.

Events listed for the Component component type apply to all java.awt Component subclasses. The events listed for the Window component type also apply to the Window subclasses, Dialog and Frame.

Table 11-1: Events

Component Event Type (id)	when	x	y	key	mods	Event Meaning arg (Type: value)
Button ACTION_EVENT						User clicked on the button String: the button label
Checkbox ACTION_EVENT						User clicked on checkbox Boolean: new checkbox state

Events

Table 11-1: Events (continued)

Component **Event Type (id)**	when	x	y	key	mods	**Event Meaning** arg **(Type: value)**
Choice ACTION_EVENT						User selected an item String: label of selected item
Component GOT_FOCUS						Got input focus *unused*
Component KEY_ACTION	•	•	•	•	•	User pressed a function key *unused*—key contains key constant
Component KEY_ACTION_RELEASE	•	•	•	•	•	User released a function key *unused*—key contains key constant
Component KEY_PRESS	•	•	•	•	•	User pressed a key *unused*—key contains ASCII key value
Component KEY_RELEASE	•	•	•	•	•	User released a key *unused*—key contains ASCII key value
Component LOST_FOCUS						Lost input focus *unused*
Component MOUSE_ENTER	•	•	•			Mouse entered the Component *unused*
Component MOUSE_EXIT	•	•	•			Mouse left the Component *unused*
Component MOUSE_DOWN	•	•	•		•	User pressed mouse button *unused*
Component MOUSE_UP	•	•	•		•	User released mouse button *unused*
Component MOUSE_MOVE	•	•	•		•	User moved mouse *unused*
Component MOUSE_DRAG	•	•	•		•	User dragged mouse *unused*
List ACTION_EVENT						User double-clicked on an item String: label of activated item
List LIST_SELECT						User selected an item Integer: index of selected item
List LIST_DESELECT						User deselected an item Integer: index of deselected item
MenuItem ACTION_EVENT						User selected an item String: label of selected item
Scrollbar SCROLL_LINE_UP						User requested scroll Integer: position to scroll to
Scrollbar SCROLL_LINE_DOWN						User requested scroll Integer: position to scroll to

Component Event Type (id)	when	x	y	key	mods	Event Meaning arg (Type: value)
Scrollbar SCROLL_PAGE_UP						User requested scroll Integer: position to scroll to
Scrollbar SCROLL_PAGE_DOWN						User requested scroll Integer: position to scroll to
Scrollbar SCROLL_ABSOLUTE						User requested scroll Integer: position to scroll to
TextField ACTION_EVENT						User struck <Return> String: user's input text
Window WINDOW_DESTROY						Window was destroyed *unused*
Window WINDOW_ICONIFY						Window was iconified *unused*
Window WINDOW_DEICONIFY						Window was deiconified *unused*
Window WINDOW_MOVED		•	•			Window was moved *unused*

Key and Modifier Constants

The `java.awt.Event` class contains the field `key`, which is filled in when a keyboard event has occurred, and the field `modifiers`, which list the keyboard modifier keys currently in effect for key and mouse events.

Four modifier constants are defined by the `java.awt.Event` class; they are listed in Table 11-2. They are mask values that are OR'ed into the `modifiers` field. You can test for them using AND. You can also check a given event for the first three of the modifiers with the `Event` methods `shiftDown()`, `controlDown()`, and `metaDown()`.

Table 11-2: Java Keyboard Modifiers

Modifier Constant	Meaning
`Event.SHIFT_MASK`	SHIFT key is held down (or CAPS LOCK on)
`Event.CTRL_MASK`	CONTROL key is held down
`Event.META_MASK`	META key is held down
`Event.ALT_MASK`	ALT key is held down

When a `KEY_PRESS` or `KEY_RELEASE` event occurs, it means that the user pressed a key which is a normal printing character, a control character, or a non-printing character with a standard ASCII value—one of RETURN (ASCII 10 or '\n'), TAB (ASCII 9 or '\t'), ESCAPE (ASCII 27), BACKSPACE (ASCII 8), and DELETE (ASCII 127). In this case, the value of the key field in the event is simply the ASCII value of the key that was pressed or released.

When a KEY_ACTION or KEY_ACTION_RELEASE event occurs, it means that the user pressed some sort of function key, one which does not have an ASCII representation. java.awt.Event defines constants for each of these function keys, which are listed in Table 11-3.

Table 11-3: Java Function Key Constants

Key Constant	Meaning
Event.HOME	HOME key
Event.END	END key
Event.PGUP	PAGE UP key
Event.PGDOWN	PAGE DOWN key
Event.UP	UP arrow key
Event.DOWN	DOWN arrow key
Event.LEFT	LEFT arrow key
Event.RIGHT	RIGHT arrow key
Event.F1, . . . , Event.F12	Function keys 1 through 12

Mouse Buttons

In order to maintain platform independence, Java only recognizes a single mouse button—the Event class does not have any kind of mouseButton field to indicate which button has been pressed on a multibutton mouse. On platforms that support two- or three-button mouses, the right and center buttons generate mouse down, mouse drag, and mouse up events as if the user was holding down modifier keys (as shown in Table 11-4).

Table 11-4: Mouse Button Modifiers

Mouse Button	Flags set in Event.modifiers field
Left button	*none*
Right button	Event.META_MASK
Middle button	Event.ALT_MASK

Using keyboard modifiers to indicate which mouse button is pressed maintains compatibility with platforms that only have one-button mouses, but still allows programs to use the right and middle buttons on platforms that support them. Suppose, for example, you want to write a program that allows the user to draw lines with the mouse using two different colors. You might draw in the primary color if there are no modifier flags set, and draw in the secondary color when the META modifier is set. In this way, users with a two- or three-button mouse can simply use the left and right mouse buttons to draw in the two colors; and users with a one-button mouse can use the META key, in conjunction with the mouse, to draw in the secondary color.

Fonts, Colors, and Cursors

Fonts

Java defines platform-independent standard names for five common fonts that should reasonably be available on any platform. These names, and their corresponding platform-specific fonts, for Solaris and other UNIX/X platforms and for Microsoft Windows platforms, are listed in Table 12-1. Note that the table lists six font names. The last, "ZapfDingbats," is not commonly available on UNIX platforms running the X Window System, and so should not be considered portable. Finally, notice that the table specifies a default that is used when a requested font is undefined or cannot be found.

Table 12-1: Java Font Names

Java Font Name	Corresponding X Font	Corresponding Windows Font
Helvetica	adobe-helvetica	Arial
TimesRoman	adobe-times	Times New Roman
Courier	adobe-courier	Courier New
Dialog	b&h-lucida	MS Sans Serif
DialogInput	b&h-lucidatypewriter	MS Sans Serif
ZapfDingbats	itc-zapfdingbats	WingDings
default	misc-fixed	Arial

Font Styles

Java specifies font styles with integer constants defined in the `Font` class. Table 12-2 lists the available styles and Figure 12-1 shows each of the standard fonts in each of the standard styles.

Table 12-2: Java Font Styles

Constant	Style
`Font.PLAIN`	Plain or roman
`Font.ITALIC`	Italic
`Font.BOLD`	Bold
`Font.BOLD + Font.ITALIC`	Bolditalic

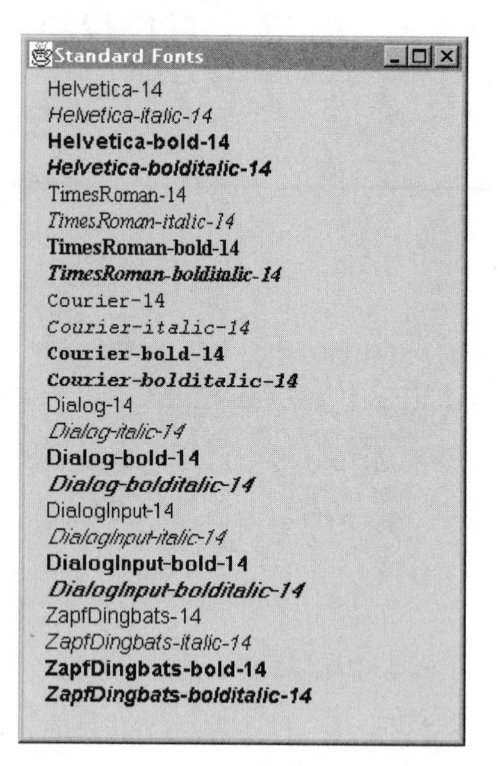

Figure 12-1: Standard Java Fonts and Font Styles

Java Font Properties

To allow customization, programs often call the static method `Font.getFont()` to look up fonts by name from the system properties list. In order to specify fonts on the system properties list, you must specify the font name, style, and point size in a single string. The syntax for doing this is:

```
fontname-style-size
```

The *style* specification should be `plain`, `italic`, `bold`, or `bolditalic`. The *size* specification should be an integer that specifies the desired point size for the font. The *style* specification may optionally be omitted. Or both the *style* and *size* may be omitted to obtain a plain, 12-point font. Here are some example property specifications:

```
mypackage.myprogram.big_font=Dialog-bolditalic-48
mypackage.myprogram.main_font=Helvetica-14
mypackage.myprogram.heading_font=TimesRoman-bold-20
mypackage.myprogram.listing_font=Courier
```

See Section 13, *System Properties and Applet Parameters*, for more information on specifying properties in the system properties list.

Creating Font Name Aliases

You can make one font name an alias for another by setting a property like:

```
awt.font.fontalias=fontname
```

fontname should be one of the standard Java font names described above. *fontalias* should be the alias you want to define, converted to all lowercase letters.

For example, if we wanted to give the illusion that our program supported the New Century Schoolbook font, we might alias it to TimesRoman, by having the program insert a property definition like this:

```
awt.font.schoolbook=TimesRoman
```

into the system properties before we fetch any fonts with `Font.getFont()`. With this done, we can document "Schoolbook" as a supported font name, and users can select fonts with properties like the following:

```
mypackage.myprogram.main_text_font=Schoolbook-14
```

Fonts, Colors, Cursors

Colors

The `java.awt.Color` class defines a number of constant `Color` values. Table 12-3 lists them.

Table 12-3: Java Color Constants

`Color.black`	`Color.green`	`Color.red`
`Color.blue`	`Color.lightGray`	`Color.white`
`Color.cyan`	`Color.magenta`	`Color.yellow`
`Color.darkGray`	`Color.orange`	
`Color.gray`	`Color.pink`	

The Java Color Model

To create a `Color` object, you must specify the red, green, and blue components of the desired color. Java allows you to specify these values as `float` values between 0.0 and 1.0, and even lets you create a color using the HSB (hue, saturation, brightness) color model. But internally, the red, green, and blue values are stored as 8-bit values between 0 and 255. The internal representation of color components is in a single integer, in the form:

```
0xAARRGGBB
```

RR represents the red component, *GG* the green component, and *BB* the blue component. *AA* is the "alpha" component, which is used to represent transparency in image processing. When you create a `Color` object, the alpha component is always set to 0xFF (fully opaque) internally. Transparency can be used for image manipulation, but it is not used by any of Java's drawing operations.

Color Properties

To allow customization, Java programs and applets often call `Color.getColor()` to look up and return a color specified as the value of a named property. To specify a color as the value of a property, convert it to the default 0x*RRGGBB* form and specify it as an integer. Specifying the integer in hexadecimal form is usually the easiest. Here are some example properties:

```
mypackage.myprogram.foreground=0                    0 is black
mypackage.myprogram.highlight=0xFFFF00              yellow
mypackage.myprogram.background=0xE0E0E0             light gray
```

See Section 13 for more information on specifying properties in the system properties list.

Cursors

Java defines a number of standard platform-independent cursors that can be specified as the mouse pointer for a `Frame`. Table 12-4 lists the constants and describes the cursors they represent. Figure 12-2 shows what the cursors look like on a UNIX platform running the X Window System.

Table 12-4: Standard Java Cursors

Cursor Constant	Cursor Description
`Frame.CROSSHAIR_CURSOR`	A simple crosshair.
`Frame.DEFAULT_CURSOR`	The platform-dependent default cursor. Usually an arrow.
`Frame.E_RESIZE_CURSOR`	A cursor useful to indicate that the right edge of something is to be dragged.
`Frame.HAND_CURSOR`	A hand; can be used to indicate that a selection is to be made.
`Frame.MOVE_CURSOR`	A cursor that indicates that something is to be moved.
`Frame.NE_RESIZE_CURSOR`	A cursor useful to indicate that the upper-right corner of something is to be dragged.

Table 12-4: Standard Java Cursors (continued)

Cursor Constant	Cursor Description
`Frame.NW_RESIZE_CURSOR`	A cursor useful to indicate that the upper-left corner of something is to be dragged.
`Frame.N_RESIZE_CURSOR`	A cursor useful to indicate that the top edge of something is to be dragged.
`Frame.SE_RESIZE_CURSOR`	A cursor useful to indicate that the lower-right corner of something is to be dragged.
`Frame.SW_RESIZE_CURSOR`	A cursor useful to indicate that the lower-left corner of something is to be dragged.
`Frame.S_RESIZE_CURSOR`	A cursor useful to indicate that the bottom edge of something is to be dragged.
`Frame.TEXT_CURSOR`	A cursor used to indicate editable text. Often an I-bar of some kind.
`Frame.WAIT_CURSOR`	A cursor used to indicate that the program is busy and that the user should wait. Often a wristwatch or an hourglass.
`Frame.W_RESIZE_CURSOR`	A cursor useful to indicate that the left edge of something is to be dragged.

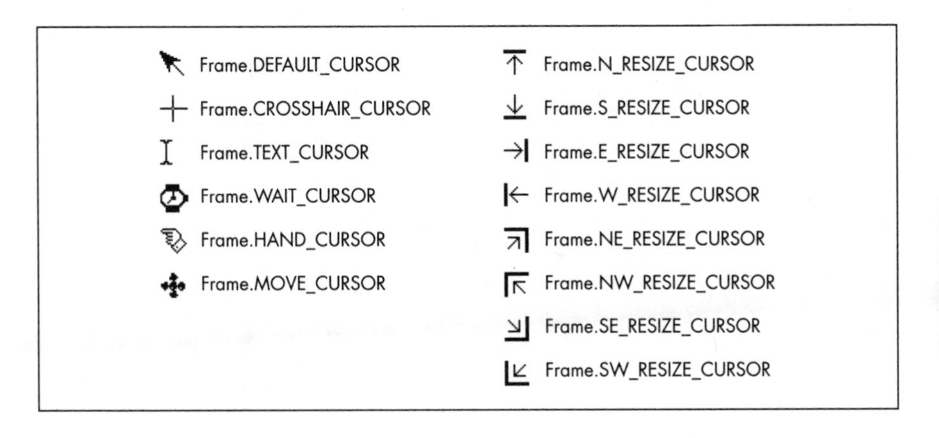

Figure 12-2: Standard Java Cursors

System Properties and Applet Parameters

Java programs and applets cannot read environment variables the way that C programs can. Similar mechanisms exist, however, that allow applications and applets to read the value of a named resource. These resource values allow customization of an application's or applet's behavior based on site-specific parameters, such as the type of host, or based on user preferences.

Named resource values are specified for applications in the "system properties" list. Applications (and applets as well, though this is less common) can read these "system properties" with the `System.getProperties()` method and other methods based on that one, such as `Font.getFont()`, `Color.getColor()`, `Integer.getInteger()`, and `Boolean.getBoolean()`.

The customization mechanism for applets does not use the system properties list. Instead it relies on a very similar list of "applet parameters." An applet can look up a named parameter value with the `Applet.getParameter()` method. Unfortunately, there are no convenient methods for reading color and font specifications from the applet parameters list.

Standard System Properties

When the Java interpreter starts, it inserts fifteen standard properties into the system properties list. These properties, and the meaning of their values, are listed in Table 13-1. The table also specifies whether applets are allowed (at least by default) to read the value of these properties. Certain sensitive values are hidden from "untrusted" applets.

Table 13-1: Standard System Properties

Name	Value	Applet Can Read
java.version	Version of the Java interpreter	yes
java.vendor	Vendor-specific identifier string	yes
java.vendor.url	Vendor's URL	yes
java.home	The directory Java is installed in	no
java.class.version	The version of the Java API	yes
java.class.path	The classpath value	no
os.name	The name of the operating system	yes
os.arch	The host hardware architecture	yes
os.version	Version of the host operating system	yes
file.separator	Platform-dependent file separator (e.g., / or \)	yes
path.separator	Platform-dependent path separator (e.g., : or ;)	yes
line.separator	Platform-dependent line separator (e.g., \n or \r\n)	yes
user.name	The username of the current user	no
user.home	The home directory of the current user	no
user.dir	The current working directory	no

Other Important Properties

There are several other important properties that various portions of the Java API read. These are not standard properties that the interpreter sets to default values, but instead resources that you can set to customize the behavior of some of the standard Java classes. The properties are:

`awt.toolkit`

This property specifies the name of the class that implements the abstract `java.awt.Toolkit` class to be used as the default `Toolkit` for all user interface components. The specified class essentially defines the look and feel of all Java user interfaces. The default value for this property is "sun.awt.motif.MToolkit" on UNIX platforms.

`awt.appletWarning`

This property specifies a warning string that is to appear in a prominent place in all windows created by an applet. The purpose of the warning is to prevent applets from creating windows that masquerade as trusted windows. The default value of this property is "Warning: Applet Window".

`awt.font.`*`fontname`*

When a Java program or applet creates a new font, the system converts the font name to lower case, appends it to the string "awt.font." and looks up the resulting property name. If the property is defined, the system uses the property value instead of the font name when creating the font. This allows programs or users to create aliases for font names, or to modify the fonts used by an application.

In addition to these properties read by portions of the Java API, the JDK *appletviewer* program from Sun reads a number of properties that affect its security policies for untrusted applets. See the *appletviewer* reference pages in Section 17, *JDK Development Tools*, for details, and see Section 14, *Applet Security*, for more information on applet security.

Specifying Property Values

If a Java application reads properties to allow user customization, then you can specify values for those properties to perform that customization. To specify properties that the Java interpreter should insert into the system properties list, use the `-D` option. For example:

```
%java -Dgames.tetris.level=9 -Dgames.tetris.sound=off games.tetris
```

Specifying Properties in a File

A program may support user customization by reading in a file of property specifications when it starts up. Similarly, a Web browser might read a file of properties in order to support customization of the applets it runs. The *appletviewer* application, for example, reads (on UNIX systems) the properties in the file *~/.hotjava/properties* when it starts. To specify properties that are applicable to the *appletviewer*, you simply need to specify them, one to a line, in the form `name=value`. For example:

```
# These are resources from ~/.hotjava/properties
package.restrict.access.netscape=true
package.restrict.access.sun=true
appletviewer.security.mode=host
```

Note that lines beginning with # are comments, and that no `-D` is needed to specify these resources

Sys Properties and Applets

Applet Parameters

Applet parameters are much like system properties. There are a few important differences, however:

- There is no standard list of applet parameters that is set for all applets. An applet may read the system properties to determine things such as the version of the Java interpreter and the type of platform it is being run on.
- Applet parameters are implicitly specified for a particular applet. Therefore there is no need for hierarchical names such as the property name "games.tetris.level." For a corresponding parameter, the name "level" would be sufficient.
- While an application may modify the system properties list, an applet may only read the parameters. An applet cannot set parameter values or add new parameters to the list.

Specifying Parameters for an Applet

To specify parameter values for an applet, you use the HTML <PARAM> tag in the file that references the applet. For example:

```
<APPLET code="games/tetris.class" width=200 height=400>
<PARAM name="level" value="9">
<PARAM name="sound" value="off">
</APPLET>
```

Web browsers and applet viewers may in the future provide a way in which users can interactively modify the parameter settings for a given applet. They may even allow such parameter settings to be saved.

14

Applet Security

Applets loaded over the network are untrusted. The only way to be sure that an untrusted applet cannot perform any malicious actions (e.g., deleting your files, sending out fake email that looks like it came from you, using your computer as a remote file server) is to run it in a very limited environment. For this reason, Web browsers and applet viewers carefully restrict what an applet is allowed to do.

Applet Security Restrictions

When designing an applet, you must bear in mind the list of things that an applet is not allowed to do. Different Web browsers and applet viewers may place slightly different restrictions on applets, and some may even allow the user to relax some of these restrictions, but, in general, applets are not allowed to:

- Read files on the local system.
- Write files to the local system.
- Delete files on the local system, either by calling the `File.delete()` method, or by invoking the system's *rm* or *del* command.
- Rename files on the local system, either by calling the `File.renameTo()` method or by invoking the system's *mv* or *rename* command.
- Create a directory on the local system, either by calling the `File.mkdir()` or `File.mkdirs()` methods, or by invoking the system's *mkdir* command.
- List directory contents.
- Check for the existence of a file.
- Obtain the type, size, or modification time of a file.

- Create a network connection to any computer other than the one from which the applet was itself loaded.
- Listen for or accept network connections on any port of the local system.
- Create a top-level window without a visible warning indicator that the window is "untrusted." This prevents applets from spoofing other, trusted programs into which users may type sensitive data.
- Obtain the user's username or home directory name, or in general, read any of the following system properties: `user.name`, `user.home`, `user.dir`, `java.home`, `java.class.path`.
- Define any system properties.
- Invoke any program on the local system. In other words, an applet cannot call any of the `Runtime.exec()` methods.
- Make the Java interpreter quit; an applet cannot call `System.exit()` or `Runtime.exit()`.
- Load dynamic libraries on the local system. In other words, an applet cannot call the `load()` or `loadLibrary()` methods of the `Runtime` or `System` classes.
- Create or manipulate any thread that is not part of the same `ThreadGroup` as the applet.
- Manipulate any `ThreadGroup` other than its own.
- Create a `ClassLoader` object.
- Create a `SecurityManager` object.
- Specify a `ContentHandlerFactory`, `SocketImplFactory`, or `URLStreamHandlerFactory` for the system. (These classes control how Java handles networking.)
- Access or load classes in any package other than the standard eight of the Java API: `java.applet`, `java.awt`, `java.awt.image`, `java.awt.peer`, `java.io`, `java.lang`, `java.net`, `java.util`.
- Define classes that are part of packages on the local system.

Local Applet Restrictions

When an applet is loaded from the local file system, instead of through a network protocol, Web browsers and applet viewers may relax some, or even many, of the above restrictions. The reason for this is that local applets are assumed to be more trustworthy than anonymous applets from the network.

Intermediate applet security policies are also possible. For example, an applet viewer could be written that would place fewer restrictions on applets loaded from an internal corporate network than on those loaded from the Internet.

Applet Security Implementation

Implementing the security restrictions described above is the responsibility of the `java.lang.SecurityManager` class. This class defines a number of methods that the system calls to check whether a certain operation (such as reading a file) is permitted in the current environment. Applet viewers create a subclass of `SecurityManager` to implement a particular security policy. A security policy is put in place by instantiating a `SecurityManager` object and registering it with `System.setSecurityManager()`. (One of the obvious security restrictions that must be enforced is that untrusted code may not register its own `SecurityManager` object!)

Loading Classes Securely

Another component of Java security is the way Java classes are loaded over the network. The `java.lang.ClassLoader` class defines how this is done. Applet viewers and Web browsers create subclasses of this class that implement security policies and define how class files are loaded via various protocols.

One important function of the class loader is to ensure that loaded classes reside in a separate namespace than classes loaded from the local system. This prevents naming conflicts, and also prevents a malicious applet from replacing standard Java classes with its own versions.

Byte-Code Verification

Another important function of the class loader is to ensure that all untrusted Java code (generally code loaded over the network) is passed through the Java byte-code verification process. This process ensures that the loaded code does not violate Java namespace restrictions or type conversion restrictions. It also checks that the code:

- Is valid Java Virtual Machine code.
- Does not overflow or underflow the stack.
- Does not use registers incorrectly.
- Does not convert data types illegally.

Applet Security

The purpose of these checks is to verify that the loaded code cannot forge pointers or do memory arithmetic, which could give it access to the underlying machine. The checks also ensure that the code cannot crash the Java interpreter or leave it in an undefined state, which might allow malicious code to take advantage of security flaws that could exist in some interpreter implementations. Essentially, the byte-code verification process protects against code from an "untrusted" Java compiler.

Denial of Service Attacks

The one "security hole" that remains when running an untrusted applet is that the applet can perform a "denial of service attack" on your computer. For example, it could frivolously allocate lots of memory, run many threads, or download lots of data. This sort of attack consumes system resources and can slow your computer (or your network connection) considerably. While this sort of attack by an applet is inconvenient, fortunately it cannot do any real damage. (Except to your patience and your deadlines.)

Future Directions: Applet Certification

A possibility being seriously explored for future releases of Java is the ability for applets to carry an attached digital signature and cryptologic checksum. Using public key encryption technology, this would enable a Web browser or applet viewer to verify that an applet is from the source it claims to be from, and that it has not been modified in transmission. With these guarantees, it is possible to load a trusted applet (one that can run without severe security restrictions) over an untrusted network as long as you trust the source of the applet (i.e., whatever individual, corporation, or certification agency has attached their digital signature to the applet).

Java-Related HTML and HTTP Syntax

This section explains what you need to know about HTML and HTTP to work with Java applets.

The <APPLET> Tag

A Java applet is included in a Web page with the <APPLET> tag, which has the following syntax:

```
<APPLET
        [CODEBASE = applet-url]
        CODE = applet-filename
        WIDTH = pixel-width
        HEIGHT = pixel-height
        [ALT = alternate-text]
        [NAME = applet-name]
        [ALIGN = alignment]
        [VSPACE = vertical-pixel-space]
        [HSPACE = horizontal-pixel-space]
>
[<PARAM NAME = parameter VALUE = value>]
[<PARAM NAME = parameter VALUE = value>]
   ...
[alternate-html]
</APPLET>
```

`APPLET` The <APPLET> tag specifies an applet to be run within a Web document. A Web browser that does not support Java and does not understand the <APPLET> tag ignores this tag and any related <PARAM> tags, and simply displays any `alternate-html` that appears between

HTML Syntax

<APPLET> and </APPLET>. A browser that does support Java runs the specified applet, and does *not* display the `alternate-html`.

CODEBASE
: This optional attribute specifies the base URL (absolute or relative) of the applet to be displayed. This should be a directory, not the applet file itself. If this attribute is unspecified, then the URL of the current document is used.

CODE
: This required attribute specifies the file that contains the compiled Java code for the applet. It must be relative to the CODEBASE if that attribute is specified, or relative to the current document's URL. It must not be an absolute URL.

WIDTH
: This attribute specifies the initial width, in pixels, that the applet needs in the browser's window. It is required.

HEIGHT
: This attribute specifies the initial height, in pixels, that the applet needs in the browser's window. It is required.

ALT
: This optional attribute specifies text that should be displayed by browsers that understand the <APPLET> tag but do not support Java.

NAME
: This optional attribute gives a name to the applet instance. Applets that are running at the same time can look each other up by name and communicate with each other.

ALIGN
: This optional attribute specifies the applet's alignment on the page. It behaves just like the ALIGN attribute of the <IMG> tag, and should support at least the same alignment values that the <IMG> tag does. These values include: `top`, `middle`, and `bottom`.

VSPACE
: This optional attribute specifies the margin, in pixels, that the browser should put above and below the applet. It behaves just like the VSPACE attribute of the <IMG> tag.

HSPACE
: This optional attribute specifies the margin, in pixels, that the browser should put on either side of the applet. It behaves just like the HSPACE attribute of the <IMG> tag.

PARAM
: The <PARAM> tag, with its NAME and VALUE attributes, specifies a named parameter and a string value that are passed to the applet. These parameters function like environment variables or command-line arguments do for a regular application. An applet can look up the value of a parameter specified in a <PARAM> tag with the `Applet.getParameter()` method.

: Any number of <PARAM> tags may appear between <APPLET> and </APPLET>.

Example 15-1 shows an HTML fragment that displays Sun's "Steaming cup of Java" animation applet.

Example 15-1: Example HTML page containing an applet

```
<APPLET codebase="betaclasses" code="Animator.class" width=66 height=100>
  <PARAM name="imagesource" value="graphics/100pixel">
  <PARAM name="pause" value="100">
  <PARAM name="repeat" value="true">
  <PARAM name="images" value="1|2|3|1|2|3|1|2|3|4|5|6|7|8|9">
</APPLET>
```

The <EMBED> Tag

It is unlikely that Java will be the only form of "executable content" available on the Web. And it is inconceivable that Java programs will be the only type of content that providers will want to "embed" in their Web pages, as opposed to displaying them in a separate window. The problem is that we don't want to have to invent (and support) a new tag like <APPLET> for each new kind of executable or embeddable content.

Thus, there is a proposal underway to standardize on a new <EMBED> tag. This tag specifies some network resource that is to be downloaded and displayed in the current page. It seems likely that this proposal will be well received, and as it is adopted, that <EMBED> will become a preferred alternative to <APPLET>. To switch from the <APPLET> to the <EMBED> tag, all you need to do is change the NAME attribute to ID and combine the CODEBASE and CODE attributes into a single SRC attribute.

Example 15-2 shows how the HTML fragment of Example 15-1 would appear using the <EMBED> tag.

Example 15-2: A Java applet using <EMBED>

```
<EMBED src="betaclasses/Animator.class" width=66 height=100>
  <PARAM name="imagesource" value="graphics/100pixel">
  <PARAM name="pause" value="100">
  <PARAM name="repeat" value="true">
  <PARAM name="images" value="1|2|3|1|2|3|1|2|3|4|5|6|7|8|9">
</EMBED>
```


Java-Related HTTP

The HTTP protocol specifies the MIME type of each Net resource that it delivers. For example, HTML documents are delivered with a MIME type of "text/html." This type lets the browser know that it should interpret the data as an HTML file (as opposed, for example, to a plain text file, a PostScript file, or a JPEG image).

The same is true of Java applets. Sun's de facto standard has been to send Java applet code with the MIME type "application/octet-stream." If you plan on serving Java applets over the Net, you will probably have to configure your Web server to supply this MIME type. You'll have to edit a file (probably named something like *mime.types*) that maps between filename extensions and MIME types. In this case, you want to serve all files ending in *.class* as type "application/octet-stream."

Currently, the MIME type of applets seems to be something of a moot point. When a Web browser sees an <APPLET> tag in HTML, it assumes that the specified resource is a Java program, and ignores the MIME type supplied by the server. Since the MIME tag is generally ignored, most sites have apparently not customized their Web servers to use the "application/octet-stream" tag, and are serving Java applets as type "text/plain."

When the `<EMBED>` tag comes into common use, the MIME type specified for Java code will no longer be ignored, and sites will have to make their Web servers aware of Java applications. Furthermore, as other types of binary executable content (i.e., other Java-like interpreters) become available on the Web, the MIME tag "application/octet-stream" may no longer seem specific enough. Thus, it seems likely that some Java-specific MIME type will come into use.

The Unicode Standard

Unicode is a 16-bit character encoding established by the Unicode Consortium, which describes the standard this way:

> The Unicode Worldwide Character Standard is a character coding system designed to support the interchange, processing, and display of the written texts of the diverse languages of the modern world. In addition, it supports classical and historical texts of many written languages.
>
> In its current version, the Unicode standard contains 34,168 distinct coded characters derived from 24 supported scripts. These characters cover the principal written languages of the Americas, Europe, the Middle East, Africa, India, Asia, and Pacifica.
>
> Some modern written languages are not yet supported or only partially supported due to a need for further research into the encoding needs of certain scripts.

Unicode is related to, but not the same as ISO 10646, the UCS (Universal Character Set) encoding. The UCS encoding is a four-byte encoding that simply lumps together all known character encodings. For example, it includes the separate Chinese, Japanese, and Korean national encodings for Han ideographic characters. Unicode, by contrast (since it only has two bytes to work with), "unifies" these disparate national encodings into a single set of Han characters that works for all three countries. Unicode is one of the encodings that is adopted as part of UCS—the Unicode character '\u*xxxx*' is equivalent to the UCS character '0000 *xxxx*'.

In the canonical form of the Unicode encoding, which is what Java `char` and `String` types use, every character occupies two bytes. The Unicode characters \u0020 to \u007E are equivalent to the ASCII and ISO8859-1 (Latin-1) characters 0x20 through 0x7E. The Unicode characters \u00A0 to \u00FF are identical to the ISO8859-1 characters 0xA0 to 0xFF. Thus there is a trivial mapping between Latin-1

Unicode

and Unicode characters. A number of other portions of the Unicode encoding are based on pre-existing standards, such as ISO8859-5 (Cyrillic) and ISO8859-8 (Hebrew), though the mappings between these standards and Unicode may not be as trivial as the Latin-1 mapping.

Unicode is a trademark of the Unicode Consortium. Version 1.0 of the standard (the current version is 1.1) is fully defined in two volumes: *The Unicode Standard, Worldwide Character Encoding, Version 1.0, Volume 1* (Addison-Wesley, 1990. ISBN 0-201-56788-1) and *The Unicode Standard, Worldwide Character Encoding, Version 1.0, Volume 2* (Addison-Wesley, 1992. ISBN 0-201-60845-6). Further information about the Unicode standard and the Unicode Consortium can be obtained at *http://unicode.org/*.

Although Java uses Unicode characters internally, note that Unicode support on many platforms is likely to be limited to the use of the `\u`*xxxx* escape sequence in input and output text. One of the difficulties with the use of Unicode is the poor availability of fonts that can display all of the Unicode characters. Windows 95 platforms provide partial support for Unicode, including a partial Unicode font (which omits the Han Chinese/Japanese/Korean characters, and others). Also note that the `java.io.PrintStream` class (of which `System.out` is an instance) discards the top 8 bits of 16-bit Unicode characters. Thus, at least in current implementations, "standard output" supports only ASCII and Latin-1 characters.

Table 16-1 provides an overview of the Unicode 1.1 encoding.

Table 16-1: Outline of the Unicode 1.1 Encoding

Start	End	Description
0000	1FFF	**Alphabets**
0020	007E	Basic Latin (US-ASCII printing characters)
00A0	00FF	Latin-1 Supplement (right half of ISO8859-1)
0100	017F	Latin Extended-A
0180	024F	Latin Extended-B
0250	02AF	IPA Extensions
02B0	02FF	Spacing Modifier Letters
0300	036F	Combining Diacritical marks
0370	03CF	Basic Greek (based on ISO8859-7)
03D0	03FF	Greek Symbols and Coptic
0400	04FF	Cyrillic (based on ISO8859-5)
0500	052F	unassigned
0530	058F	Armenian
0590	05CF	Hebrew Extended-A
05D0	05EA	Basic Hebrew (based on ISO8859-8)
05EB	05FF	Hebrew Extended-B
0600	0652	Basic Arabic (based on ISO8859-6)
0653	06FF	Arabic Extended
0700	08FF	Ethiopic (not finalized)
0900	097F	Devanagari (based on ISCII 1988)
0980	09FF	Bengali (based on ISCII 1988)
0A00	0A7F	Gurmukhi (based on ISCII 1988)
0A80	0AFF	Gujarati (based on ISCII 1988)
0B00	0B7F	Oriya (based on ISCII 1988)
0B80	0BFF	Tamil (based on ISCII 1988)

Table 16-1: Outline of the Unicode 1.1 Encoding (continued)

Start	End	Description
0C00	0C7F	Telugu (based on ISCII 1988)
0C80	0CFF	Kannada (based on ISCII 1988)
0D00	0D7F	Malayalam (based on ISCII 1988)
0D80	0DFF	Sinhala (not finalized)
0E00	0E7F	Thai (based on TIS 620-2529)
0E80	0EFF	Lao (based on TIS 620-2529)
0F00	0F7F	Burmese (not finalized)
0F80	0FDF	Khmer (not finalized)
1000	105F	Tibetan (not finalized)
1060	109F	Mongolian (not finalized)
10A0	10CF	Georgian Extended
10D0	10FF	Basic Georgian
1100	11FF	Hangul Jamo
1200	125F	Ethiopian (not finalized)
1E00	1EFF	Latin Extended Additional
1F00	1FFF	Greek Extended
2000	2FFF	**Symbols and Punctuation**
2000	206F	General Punctuation
2070	209F	Superscripts and Subscripts
20A0	20CF	Currency Symbols
20D0	20FF	Combining Diacritical Marks for Symbols
2100	214F	Letterlike Symbols
2150	218F	Number Forms
2190	21FF	Arrows
2200	22FF	Mathematical Operators
2300	23FF	Miscellaneous Technical
2400	243F	Control Pictures
2440	245F	Optical Character Recognition
2460	24FF	Enclosed Alphanumerics
2500	257F	Box Drawing
2580	259F	Block Elements
25A0	25FF	Geometric Shapes
2600	26FF	Miscellaneous Symbols
2700	27BF	Dingbats
3000	4DFF	**CJK Auxiliary**
3000	303F	CJK Symbols and Punctuation
3040	309F	Hiragana (based on JIS X0208-1990)
30A0	30FF	Katakana (based on JIS X0208-1990)
3100	312F	Bopomofo (based on GB 2312-80)
3190	319F	CJK Miscellaneous (Kaeriten)
3200	32FF	Enclosed CJK Letters and Months
3300	33FF	CJK Compatibility
3400	3D2D	Hangul (based on KSC 5601-1987)
3D2E	44B7	Hangul Supplementary-A
44B8	4DFF	Hangul Supplementary-B
4E00	9FFF	**CJK Unified Ideographs** Han characters used in China, Japan, Korea, Taiwan, and Vietnam

Table 16-1: Outline of the Unicode 1.1 Encoding (continued)

Start	End	Description
A000	DFFF	**Reserved for future assignment**
E000	FFFD	**Restricted use**
E000	F8FF	Private Use Area
F900	FAFF	CJK Compatibility Ideographs
FB00	FB4F	Alphabetic Presentation Forms
FB50	FDFF	Arabic Presentation Forms-A
FE20	FE2F	Combining Half Marks
FE30	FE4F	CJK Compatibility Forms (verticals and overlines)
FE50	FE6F	Small Form Variants
FE70	FEFE	Arabic Presentation Forms-B
FEFF	FEFF	Zero-width no-break space (Byte Order Mark)
FF00	FFEF	Halfwidth and Fullwidth Forms
FFF0	FFFC	Specials
FFFD	FFFD	Replacement Character
FFFE	FFFF	**Excluded from standard**

The UTF-8 Encoding

The canonical two-bytes per character encoding is useful for the manipulation of character data, and is the internal representation used throughout Java. Because a large amount of text used by Java programs is 8-bit text, and because there are so many existing computer systems that support only 8-bit characters, the 16-bit canonical form is not usually the most efficient way to store Unicode text nor the most portable way to transmit it.

Because of this, other encodings called "transformation formats" have been developed. Java provides simple support for the UTF-8 encoding with the `DataInputStream.readUTF()` and `DataOutputStream.writeUTF()` methods. UTF-8 is a variable-width or "multi-byte" encoding format; this means that different characters require different numbers of bytes. In UTF-8, the standard ASCII characters occupy only one byte, and remain untouched by the encoding (i.e., a string of ASCII characters is a legal UTF-8 string). As a tradeoff, however, other Unicode characters occupy two or three bytes.

In UTF-8, Unicode characters between \u0000 and \u007F occupy a single byte, which has a value of between 0x00 and 0x7F, and which always has its high-order bit set to 0. Characters between \u0080 and \u07FF occupy two bytes, and characters between \u0800 and \uFFFF occupy three bytes. The first byte of a two-byte character always has high-order bits 110, and the first byte of a three-byte character always has high-order bits 1110. Since single-byte characters always have 0 as their high-order bit, the one-, two-, and three-byte characters can easily be distinguished from each other.

The second and third bytes of two- and three-byte characters always have high-order bits 10, which distinguishes them from one-byte characters, and also distinguishes them from the first byte of a two- or three-byte sequence. This is important because it allows a program to locate the start of a character in a multibyte sequence.

The remaining bits in each character (i.e., the bits that are not part of one of the required high-order bit sequences) are used to encode the actual Unicode character data. In the single-byte form, there are seven bits available, suitable for encoding characters up to \u007F. In the two-byte form, there are 11 data bits available, which are enough to encode values to \u07FF, and in the three-byte form there are 16 available data bits, which are enough to encode all 16-bit Unicode characters.

Table 16-2 summarizes the encoding.

Table 16-2: The UTF-8 Encoding

Start Charcter	**End Character**	**Required Data Bits**	**Binary Byte Sequence (x = data bits)**
`\u0000`	`\u007F`	7	`0`*xxxxxxx*
`\u0080`	`\u07FF`	11	`110`*xxxxx* `10`*xxxxxx*
`\u0800`	`\uFFFF`	16	`1110`*xxxx* `10`*xxxxxx* `10`*xxxxxx*

The UTF-8 has the following desirable features:

- All ASCII characters are one-byte UTF-8 characters. A legal ASCII string is a legal UTF-8 string.
- Any non-ASCII characters (i.e., any character with the high-order bit set) is part of a multibyte character.
- The first byte of any UTF-8 character indicates the number of additional bytes in the character.
- The first byte of a multibyte character is easily distinguished from the subsequent bytes. Thus, it is easy to locate the start of a character from an arbitrary position in a data stream.
- It is easy to convert between UTF-8 and Unicode.
- The UTF-8 encoding is relatively compact. For text with a large percentage of ASCII characters, it is more compact than Unicode. In the worst case, a UTF-8 string is only 50% larger than the corresponding Unicode string.

JDK Development Tools

appletviewer — The Java Applet Viewer

SYNOPSIS

appletviewer [-debug] *urls*

DESCRIPTION

appletviewer downloads one or more HTML documents specified by URL on the command line. It downloads all the applets referenced in each document and displays them, each in their own window. If none of the named documents has an <APPLET> tag, *appletviewer* does nothing.

OPTIONS

`-debug`

If this option is specified, the *appletviewer* is started within *jdb* (the Java debugger). This allows you to debug the applets referenced by the document or documents.

PROPERTIES

When it starts up, *appletviewer* reads property definitions from the file *~/.hotjava/properties* (UNIX) or *\.hotjava\properties* (Windows). It reads the value of the following properties to determine what security restrictions should be placed on untrusted applets:

`acl.read`
: This is a list of files and directories that an untrusted applet is allowed to read. The elements of the list should be separated with colons on UNIX systems and semicolons on Windows systems. On UNIX systems, the ~ character is replaced with the home directory of the current user. If the plus character appears as an element in the list, it is replaced by the value of the `acl.read.default` property. This provides an easy way to enable read access—by simply setting `acl.read` to "+". By default, untrusted applets are not allowed to read any files or directories.

`acl.read.default`
: This is a list of files and directories that are readable by untrusted applets if the `acl.read` property contains a plus character.

`acl.write`
: This is a list of files and directories that an untrusted applet is allowed to write to. The elements of the list should be separated with colons on UNIX systems and semicolons on Windows systems. On UNIX systems, the ~ character is replaced with the home directory of the current user. If the plus character appears as an element in the list, it is replaced by the value of the `acl.write.default` property. This provides an easy way to enable write access—by simply setting `acl.write` to "+". By default, untrusted applets are not allowed to write to any files or directories.

`acl.write.default`
: This is a list of files and directories that are writable by untrusted applets if the `acl.write` property contains a plus character.

`appletviewer.security.model`
: This property specifies the types of network access an untrusted applet is allowed to perform. The `none` value specifies that the applet can perform no networking at all. The value `host` is the default, and it specifies that the applet can connect only to the host from which it was loaded. The value `unrestricted` specifies that an applet may connect to any host without restrictions.

`firewallHost`
: This is the firewall proxy host to connect to if the `firewallSet` property is `true`.

`firewallPort`
: This is the port of the firewall proxy host to connect to if the `firewallSet` property is `true`.

`firewallSet`
: This tells you whether the applet viewer should use a firewall proxy. Values are `true` or `false`.

`package.restrict.access.`*`package-prefix`*

Properties of this form may be set to `true` to prevent untrusted applets from using classes in any package that has the specified package name prefix as the first component of its name. For example, to prevent applets from using any of the Sun classes (such as the Java compiler and the appletviewer itself) that are shipped with the JDK, you could specify the following property:

```
package.restrict.access.sun=true
```

appletviewer sets this property to `true` by default.

`package.restrict.definition.`*`package-prefix`*

Properties of this form may be set to `true` to prevent untrusted applets from defining classes in a package that has the specified package name prefix as the first component of its name. For example, to prevent an applet from defining classes in any of the standard Java packages, you could specify the following property:

```
package.restrict.definition.java=true
```

appletviewer sets this property to `true` by default.

`proxyHost`

This is the caching proxy host to connect to if the `proxySet` property is `true`.

`proxyPort`

This is the port of the caching proxy host to connect to if the `proxySet` property is `true`.

`proxySet`

This tells you whether the applet viewer should use a caching proxy. Values are `true` or `false`.

ENVIRONMENT

`CLASSPATH`

Specifies an ordered list (colon-separated on UNIX, semicolon-separated on Windows systems) of directories and zip files in which *appletviewer* should look for class definitions. When a path is specified with this environment variable, *appletviewer* always implictly appends the location of the system classes to the end of the path. If this environment variable is not specified, the default path is the current directory and the system classes. Note that *appletviewer* does not support the `-classpath` option that other JDK tools do.

SEE ALSO

java, javac, jdb

java — The Java Interpreter

SYNOPSIS

```
java [ interpreter options ] classname [ program arguments ]
```

DESCRIPTION

java is the Java byte-code interpreter—it runs Java programs.

The program to be run is the class specified by `classname`. This must be a fully qualified name, it must include the package name of the class, but not the *.class* file extension. Note that you specify the package and class name, with components separated by '.', not the directory and filename of the class, which has its components separated by '/' or '\'. If a Java class has no `package` statement, then it is not in any package, and the class name is specified alone. Examples:

```
%java david.games.Checkers
%java test
```

See the description of the `-classpath` option and the `CLASSPATH` environment variable below for information on specifying where *java* should look for classes.

The class specified by `classname` must contain a method `main()` with exactly the following signature:

```
public static void main(String argv[])
```

Any arguments following the `classname` on the *java* command line are placed into an array and passed to the `main()` method when *java* starts up.

If `main()` creates any threads, *java* runs until the last thread exits. Otherwise, the interpreter executes the body of `main()` and exits.

Although only a single class name is specified when invoking *java*, the interpreter automatically loads any additional classes required by the program. These class files must reside in the current directory, with the standard system classes, or in a location specified by the `-classpath` option or the `CLASSPATH` environment variable. Classes are looked up in a file which has the same name as the class with a *.class* extension added. Each such class file is expected to be within a directory hierarchy that corresponds to the package name. Thus, the class `java.lang.String` would be found in *java/lang/String.class.*

`java` can also look up classes within zip files. For UNIX users not familiar with this file format, zip is an archive format, much like tar—a zip file is a single file that contains many other files, which may be individually extracted. The contents of a zip file may be compressed or uncompressed; *java* expects uncompressed zip files. Using zip files is an especially useful way to store classes on systems that do not support long filenames.

By default, *java* runs a byte-code verifier on all dynamically loaded classes (i.e., classes loaded from untrusted sources, such as the network). This verifier performs a number of tests on the byte-code of the loaded class to ensure, for example, that it does not corrupt the internal operand stack and that it performs appropriate run-time checks on such things as array references. The `-verify`, `-noverify`, and `-verifyremote` options control the byte-code verification process.

OPTIONS

`-classpath` *`path`*

The path that *java* uses to look up the specified *`classname`* and all other classes that it loads. Specifying this option overrides the default path and the `CLASSPATH` environment variable.

The class path is an ordered list of directories and zip files within and below which *java* searches for named classes. On UNIX systems, a path is specified as a colon-separated list of directories and zip files. On Windows systems, directories and zip files (which may have drive specifiers that use colons) are separated from each other with semicolons. For example, a UNIX `-classpath` specification might look like this:

```
-classpath /usr/lib/java/classes:.:~/java/classes
```

On a Windows system, the specification might be:

```
-classpath C:\tools\java\classes.zip;.;D:\users\david\classes
```

A period by itself in the path indicates that the current working directory is searched. Directories and zip files are searched in the order they appear. Place the standard Java classes first in the path if you do not want them to be accidentally or maliciously overridden by classes with the same name in other directories.

java expects to find class files in a directory hierarchy (or with a directory name within a zip file) that maps to the fully qualified name; of the class. Thus, on a UNIX system, Java would load the class `java.lang.String` by looking for the file *java/lang/String.class* beneath one of the directories specified in the class path. Similarly, on a Windows 95 or Windows NT system (which support long filenames), *java* would look for the file *java\lang\String.class* beneath a specified directory or within a specified zip file.

If you do not specify `-classpath` or the `CLASSPATH` environment variable, the default class path is:

```
.:$JAVA/classes:$JAVA/classes.zip        UNIX systems
.;$JAVA\classes;$JAVA\classes.zip        Windows systems
```

Where `$JAVA` is the main Java directory.

`-cs`, `-checksource`

This options tells *java* to check the modification times on the specified class file and its corresponding source file. If the object file is out of date, it is automatically recompiled from the source.

`-D`*`propertyname`*`=`*`value`*

Defines *`propertyname`* to equal *`value`* in the system properties list. Your Java program can then look up the specified value by its property name. You may specify any number of `-D` options. For example:

```
%java -Dawt.button.color=gray -Dmy.class.pointsize=14 my.class
```

Man Pages

`-debug`
: Causes *java* to display a password as it starts up. This password can be used to allow the *jdb* debugger to attach itself to this interpreter session. Note that this password should not be considered cryptologically secure.

`-ms` *`initmem`*`[k|m]`
: Specifies how much memory is allocated for the heap when the interpreter starts up. By default, *`initmem`* is specified in bytes. You can specify it in kilobytes by appending the letter `k` or in megabytes by appending the letter `m`. The default initial allocation is 1 MB. For large or memory intensive applications (such as the Java compiler), you can improve run-time performance by starting the interpreter with a larger amount of memory. You must specify an initial heap size of at least 1000 bytes.

`-mx` *`maxmem`*`[k|m]`
: Specifies the maximum heap size the interpreter will use for dynamically allocated objects and arrays. *`maxmem`* is specified in bytes by default. You can specify *`maxmem`* in kilobytes by appending the letter `k` and in megabytes by appending the letter `m`. The default maximum heap size is 16 MB. You must not specify a heap size less than 1000 bytes.

`-noasyncgc`
: Do not do garbage collection asynchronously. With this option specified, *java* only performs garbage collection when it runs out of memory or when the garbage collector is explicitly invoked. Without this option, *java* runs the garbage collector as a separate, low-priority thread.

`-noverify`
: Never run the byte-code verifier.

`-oss` *`stacksize`*`[k|m]`
: Sets the size of each thread's Java code stack. By default, *`stacksize`* is specified in bytes. You can specify it in kilobytes by appending the letter `k` or in megabytes by appending the letter `m`. The default value is 400 KB. You must specify at least 1000 bytes.

`-ss` *`stacksize`*`[k|m]`
: Sets the size of each thread's native code stack. By default, *`stacksize`* is specified in bytes. You can specify it in kilobytes by appending the letter `k` or in megabytes by appending the letter `m`. The default value is 128 KB. You must specify at least 1000 bytes.

`-v`, `-verbose`
: Print a terminal message each time *java* loads a class.

`-verbosegc`
: Print a message whenever the garbage collector frees memory.

`-verify`
: Run the byte-code verifier on all classes that are loaded.

`-verifyremote`

Run the byte-code verifier on all classes that are loaded through a class loader. (This generally means classes that are dynamically loaded from an untrusted location.) This is the default behavior for *java*.

ENVIRONMENT

`CLASSPATH`

Specifies an ordered list (colon-separated on UNIX, semicolon-separated on Windows systems) of directories and zip files in which *java* should look for class definitions. When a path is specified with this environment variable, *java* always implicitly appends the location of the system classes to the end of the path. If this environment variable is not specified, the default path is the current directory and the system classes. This variable is overridden by the `-classpath` option. See `-classpath` above for more information on specifying paths.

SEE ALSO

javac, *jdb*

Man Pages

javac — The Java Compiler

SYNOPSIS

```
javac [ options ] files
```

DESCRIPTION

javac is the Java compiler—it compiles Java source code (in *.java* files) into Java byte-codes (in *.class* files). The Java compiler is itself written in Java.

javac may be passed any number of Java source files, whose names must all end with the *.java* extension. *javac* produces a separate *.class* class file for each class defined in the source files, regardless of how many source files there are. In other words, there need not be a one-to-one mapping between Java source files and Java class files. Note also that the compiler requires that there be only a single public class defined in any one source file, and that the name of the file (minus the *.java* extension) be the same as the name of the class (minus its package name, of course).

By default, *javac* places the class files it generates in the same directory as the corresponding source file. You can override this behavior with the `-d` option.

When a source file references a class that is not defined in another source file on the command line, *javac* searches for the definition of that class using the class path. The default class path contains only the system classes. You may specify additional classes and packages to be searched with the `-classpath` option or the `CLASSPATH` environment variable.

OPTIONS

`-classpath` *`path`*

The path that *javac* uses to look up classes referenced in the specified source code. This option overrides the default path and any path specified by the `CLASSPATH` environment variable. The *`path`* specified is an ordered list of directories and zip files, separated by colons on UNIX systems or semicolons on Windows systems.

To specify additional directories or zip files to be searched, without overriding the default system class path, use the `CLASSPATH` environment variable. See the *java* reference page for more information on specifying paths.

`-d` *`directory`*

The directory in which (or beneath which) class files should be stored. By default, *javac* stores the *.class* files it generates in the same directory as the *.java* file that those classes were defined in. If the `-d` flag is specified, however, the specified *`directory`* is treated as the root of the class hierarchy and *.class* files are placed in this directory, or in the appropriate subdirectory below it, depending on the package name of the class. Thus, the following command:

```
%javac -d java/classes java/src/Checkers.java
```

places the file *Checkers.class* in the directory *java/classes* if the *Check-*

ers.java file has no `package` statement. On the other hand, if the source file specifies that it is in a package:

```
package david.games;
```

then the *.class* file is stored in *java/classes/david/games.*

When the `-d` option is specified, *javac* automatically creates any directories it needs to store its class files in the appropriate place.

`-g`
This option tells *javac* to add line numbers and local variable information to the output class files, for use by debuggers. By default, *javac* only generates the line numbers. With the `-O` option, *javac* does not generate even that information.

`-nowarn`
Tells *javac* not to print warning messages. Errors are still reported as usual.

`-O`
Enable optimization of class files. This option may cause *javac* to compile `static`, `final`, and `private` methods inline, so that they execute faster. The trade-off is that the class files will be larger. This option also prevents *javac* from adding line number debugging information to the class files.

`-verbose`
Tells the compiler to display messages about what it is doing.

ENVIRONMENT

`CLASSPATH`
Specifies an ordered list (colon-separated on UNIX, semicolon-separated on Windows systems) of directories and zip files in which *javac* should look for class definitions. When a path is specified with this environment variable, *javac* always implictly appends the location of the system classes to the end of the path. If this environment variable is not specified, the default path is the current directory and the system classes. This variable is overridden by the `-classpath` option.

SEE ALSO

java, jdb

javadoc — The Java Documentation Generator

SYNOPSIS

```
javadoc [ options ] packagename
javadoc [ options ] filenames
```

DESCRIPTION

javadoc generates API documentation, in HTML format, for the specified package, or for the individual Java source files specified on the command line.

When a package name is specified on the command line, *javadoc* looks for a corresponding package directory relative to the class path. It then parses all of the *.java* source files in that directory and generates an HTML documentation file for each class and an HTML index of the classes in the package. By default, the HTML files are placed in the current directory. The `-d` option allows you to override this default.

Note that the *packagename* argument to *javadoc* is the name of the package (components separated by periods) and not the name of the package directory. You may need to specify the `-classpath` option or the `CLASSPATH` environment variable so that Java can find your package source code correctly, if it is not stored in the same location as the package class files.

javadoc may also be invoked with any number of Java source files specified on the command line. Note that these are filenames, not class names, and are specified with any necessary directory components, and with the *.java* extension. When *javadoc* is invoked in this way, it reads the specified source files and generates HTML files (in the current directory, by default) that describe each public class defined in the specified source files.

The class documentation files that *javadoc* generates describe the class (or interface) and its inheritance hierarchy, and index and describe each of the non-`private` fields in the class. The generated file also contains any "doc comments" that are associated with the class and with its methods, constructors, and variables. A "doc comment," or documentation comment, is a Java comment that begins with `/**` and ends with `*/`. A doc comment may include any HTML markup tags (although it should not include structuring tags like <H1> or <HR>), and may also include tag values that are treated specially by *javadoc*. These special tags and their syntax are documented fully in Section 10, *Java Syntax*.

OPTIONS

`-classpath` *`path`*

The path that *javadoc* uses to look up the specified *packagename*. This option overrides the default path and any path specified by the `CLASSPATH` environment variable. The *`path`* specified is an ordered list of directories and zip files, separated by colons on UNIX systems or semicolons on Windows systems.

To specify additional directories or zip files to search without overriding the default system class path, use the `CLASSPATH` environment variable. See the *java* reference page for more information on specifying paths.

`-d directory`

The directory in which *javadoc* should store the HTML files it generates. The default is the current directory.

`-verbose`

Tells *javadoc* to print messages about what it is doing.

ENVIRONMENT

`CLASSPATH`

Specifies an ordered list (colon-separated on UNIX, semicolon-separated on Windows systems) of directories and zip files in which *javadoc* should look for class definitions. When a path is specified with this environment variable, *javadoc* always implictly appends the location of the system classes to the end of the path. If this environment variable is not specified, then the default path is the current directory and the system classes. This variable is overridden by the `-classpath` option.

BUGS

When *javadoc* cannot find a specified package, it produces a stub HTML file and does not warn you that the package was not found.

SEE ALSO

java, javac

Man Pages

javah — Native Method C File Generator

SYNOPSIS

javah [*options*] *classnames*

DESCRIPTION

javah generates C header and source files (*.h* and *.c* files) that describe the specified classes. These C files provide the information necessary for implementing `native` methods for the specified classes in C.

By default, *javah* generates a header file for the specified class or classes. This header file declares a C `struct` that contains fields that correspond to the instance fields of the Java class. The header also declares a procedure that you must implement for each of the native methods that the Java class contains. (A full description of how to implement Java `native` methods in C is beyond the scope of this reference page.)

If *javah* is run with the `-stubs` option, it generates a *.c* file that contains additional stub procedures necessary for linking the native method into the Java environment. Note that you should not put your native method implementation in this generated stub file.

By default, *javah* creates C files in the current directory and bases their name on the name of the class. If the name of the class includes a package name, then the C files include all the components of the fully qualified class name, with periods replaced by underscores. You can override this default behavior with the `-d` and `-o` options.

OPTIONS

`-classpath` *`path`*

The path that *javah* uses to look up the classes named on the command line. This option overrides the default path, and any path specified by the CLASSPATH environment variable. The *`path`* specified is an ordered list of directories and zip files, separated by colons on UNIX systems or semicolons on Windows systems.

To specify additional directories or zip files for *javah* to search without overriding the default system class path, use the CLASSPATH environment variable. See the *java* reference page for more information on specifying paths.

`-d` *`directory`*

Specifies a directory where *javah* should store the files it generates. By default it stores them in the current directory. This option does not work with `-o`—you must specify any desired directory within the `-o` filename.

`-o` *`outputfile`*

Combine all *.h* or *.c* file output into a single file, *`outputfile`*. This is a convenience when you want to implement native methods for a number of classes in a single package. It allows you to avoid having many short *.h* and *.c* files that must be manipulated separately.

`-stubs`
: Generate *.c* stub files for the class or classes, and do not generate the *.h* header files. Without this option, *javah* generates header files.

`-td` *`directory`*
: The directory where *javah* should store temporary files. The default is */tmp*.

`-v`
: Verbose. Causes *javah* to print messages about what it is doing.

ENVIRONMENT

`CLASSPATH`
: Specifies an ordered list (colon-separated on UNIX, semicolon-separated on Windows systems) of directories and zip files in which *javah* should look for class definitions. When a path is specified with this environment variable, *javah* always implictly appends the location of the system classes to the end of the path. If this environment variable is not specified, the default path is the current directory and the system classes. This variable is overridden by the `-classpath` option.

SEE ALSO

java, javac

Man Pages

javap — The Java Class Disassembler

SYNOPSIS

javap [*options*] *classnames*

DESCRIPTION

javap disassembles the class files specified by the class names on the command line and prints a human-readable version of those classes.

By default, *javap* prints declarations of the non-`private` and non-`protected` fields (i.e., fields with `public` or default visibility), methods, constructors (even implicit constructors), and static initializers in each of the classes specified on the command line. The `-l`, `-p`, and `-c` options specify additional information to be printed.

OPTIONS

`-c`
: Print the Java Virtual Machine instructions for each of the methods in each of the specified classes. This option disassembles all methods, including `private` and `protected` methods.

`-classpath` *`path`*
: The path that *javap* uses to look up the classes named on the command line. This option overrides the default path and any path specified by the `CLASSPATH` environment variable. The *`path`* specified is an ordered list of directories and zip files, separated by colons on UNIX systems or semicolons on Windows systems.

  To specify additional directories or zip files for *javap* to search without overriding the default system class path, use the `CLASSPATH` environment variable. See the *java* reference page for more information on specifying paths.

`-l`
: Prints line numbers and local variable tables in addition to the public fields of the class. Note that line numbers and local variable information is included for use with debuggers. Local variable information is available only if a class was compiled with the `-g` option to *javac*; line number information is available only if a class was compiled *without* the `-O` option.

`-p`
: Prints `private` and `protected` methods and variables of the specified class in addition to the `public` ones. Note that some compilers (though not *javac*) may allow this `private` field information to be "obfuscated" in such a way that `private` fields and method arguments no longer have meaningful names. This makes Java classes harder to disassemble or reverse engineer.

ENVIRONMENT

`CLASSPATH`
: Specifies an ordered list (colon-separated on UNIX, semicolon-separated on Windows systems) of directories and zip files in which *javap* should look for class definitions. When a path is specified with this

environment variable, *javap* always implictly appends the location of the system classes to the end of the path. If this environment variable is not specified, the default path is the current directory and the system classes. This variable is overridden by the `-classpath` option.

SEE ALSO

java, javac

Man Pages

jdb — The Java Debugger

SYNOPSIS

jdb [*java options*] *class*
jdb [-host hostname] -password *password*

DESCRIPTION

jdb is a debugger for Java classes. It is text-based, command-line oriented, and has a command syntax like that of the UNIX *dbx* or *gdb* debuggers.

When *jdb* is invoked with the name of a Java class, it starts another copy of the *java* interpreter, passing any specified *java* options to the interpreter. *jdb* is itself a Java program, running in its own copy of the interpreter. This new interpreter loads the specified class file and stops for debugging before executing the first Java byte-code.

jdb may also be started with the `-password` and optional `-host` arguments. Invoked in this way, *jdb* "attaches itself" to an already running copy of the interpreter. In order for this to work, the Java interpreter running the program to be debugged must have been started with the `-debug` option. When the interpreter is started with this option, it prints a password that must be used with the *jdb* `-password` option.

Once a debugging session is started, you may issue any of the commands described below.

OPTIONS

When invoking *jdb* with a specified class file, any of the *java* interpreter options may be specified. See the *java* reference page for an explanation of these options.

When attaching *jdb* to an already running Java interpreter, the following options are available:

`-host` *`hostname`*
: Specifies the name of the host upon which the desired interpreter session is running.

`-password` *`password`*
: This option is required to attach to a running interpreter. The interpreter must have been started with the `-debug` option, and this `-password` option specifies the password that the interpreter generated. Only a debugger that knows this password is allowed to attach to the interpreter. Note that the passwords generated by *java* should not be considered cryptologically secure.

COMMANDS

jdb understands the following debugging commands:

`!!`
: This is a shorthand command that is replaced with the text of the last command entered. It may be followed with additional text that is appended to that previous command.

`catch [ exception class ]`
: Cause a breakpoint whenever the specified exception is thrown. If no exception is specified, the command lists the exceptions currently being caught. Use `ignore` to stop these breakpoints from occurring.

`classes`
: List all classes that have been loaded.

`clear [ class:line ]`
: Remove the breakpoint set at the specified line of the specified class. Typing `clear` or `stop` with no arguments displays a list of current breakpoints and the line numbers that they are set at.

`cont`
: Resume execution. This command should be used when the current thread is stopped at a breakpoint.

`down [ n ]`
: Move down *n* frames in the call stack of the current thread. If *n* is not specified, move down one frame.

`dump id(s)`
: Print the value of all fields of the specified object or objects. If you specify the name of a class, `dump` displays all class (static) methods and variables of the class, and also displays the superclass and list of implemented interfaces. Objects and classes may be specified by name or by their eight-digit hexadecimal ID number. Threads may also be specified with the shorthand `t@thread-number`.

`exit (or quit)`
: Quit *jdb*.

`gc`
: Run the garbage collector to force unused objects to be reclaimed.

`help (or ?)`
: Display a list of all *jdb* commands.

`ignore exception class`
: Do not treat the specified exception as a breakpoint. This command turns off a `catch` command.

`list [ line number ]`
: List the specified line of source code as well as several lines that appear before and after it. If no line number is specified, use the line number of the current stack frame of the current thread. The lines listed are from the source file of the current stack frame of the current thread. Use the `use` command to tell *jdb* where to find source files.

`load classname`
: Load the specified class into *jdb*.

`locals`
: Display a list of local variables for the current stack frame. Java code must be compiled with the `-g` option in order to contain local variable information.

Man Pages

`memory` Display a summary of memory usage for the Java program being debugged.

`methods` *`class`*
List all methods of the specified class. Use `dump` to list the instance variables or an object or the class (static) variables of a class.

`print` *`id(s)`*
Print the value of the specified item or items. Each item may be a class, object, field, or local variable, and may be specified by name or by eight-digit hexadecimal ID number. You may also refer to threads with the special syntax `t@`*`thread-number`*. The `print` command displays an object's value by invoking its `toString()` method.

`resume` [*`thread(s)`*]
Resume execution of the specified thread or threads. If no threads are specified, all suspended threads are resumed. See also `suspend`.

`run` [*`class`*] [*`args`*]
Run the `main()` method of the specified class, passing the specified arguments to it. If no class or arguments are specified, use the class and arguments specified on the *jdb* command line.

`step` Run the current line of the current thread and stop again.

`stop` [`at` *`class`*`:`*`line`*]
`stop` [`in` *`class`*`.`*`method`*]
Set a breakpoint at the specified line of the specified class or at the beginning of the specified method of the specified class. Program execution stops when it reaches this line or enters the method. If `stop` is executed with no arguments, then it lists the current breakpoints.

`suspend` [*`thread(s)`*]
Suspend the specified thread or threads. If no threads are specified, suspend all running threads. Use `resume` to restart them.

`thread` *`thread`*
Set the current thread to the specified thread. This thread is used implicitly by a number of other *jdb* commands. The thread may be specified by name or number.

`threadgroup` *`name`*
Set the current thread group to the named thread group.

`threadgroups`
List all thread groups running in the Java interpreter session being debugged.

`threads` [*`threadgroups`*]
List all threads in the named thread group. If no thread group is specified, list all threads in the current thread group (specified by `threadgroup`).

`up` [*`n`*]
Move up *n* frames in the call stack of the current thread. If *n* is not specified, move up one frame.

`use [ source-file-path ]`
: Set the path used by *jdb* to look up source files for the classes being debugged. If no path is specified, display the current source path being used.

`where [ thread ] [ all ]`
: Display a stack trace for the specified thread. If no thread is specified, display a stack trace for the current thread. If `all` is specified, display a stack trace for all threads.

ENVIRONMENT

`CLASSPATH`
: Specifies an ordered list (colon-separated on UNIX, semicolon-separated on Windows systems) of directories and zip files in which *jdb* should look for class definitions. When a path is specified with this environment variable, *jdb* always implictly appends the location of the system classes to the end of the path. If this environment variable is not specified, the default path is the current directory and the system classes. This variable is overridden by the `-classpath` option.

SEE ALSO

java

Man Pages

Part IV

API Quick Reference

Part IV is the real heart of this book. It is a *complete* quick reference to the Java API. The *How to Use This Book* section at the beginning of the book contains important information about using this quick reference, and getting the most out of it.

The java.applet Package

The `java.applet` package is a small one. It contains the `Applet` class, which is the superclass of all applets, and three related interfaces. An *applet* is a small, embeddable Java program. Figure 18-1 shows the class hierarchy of this package.

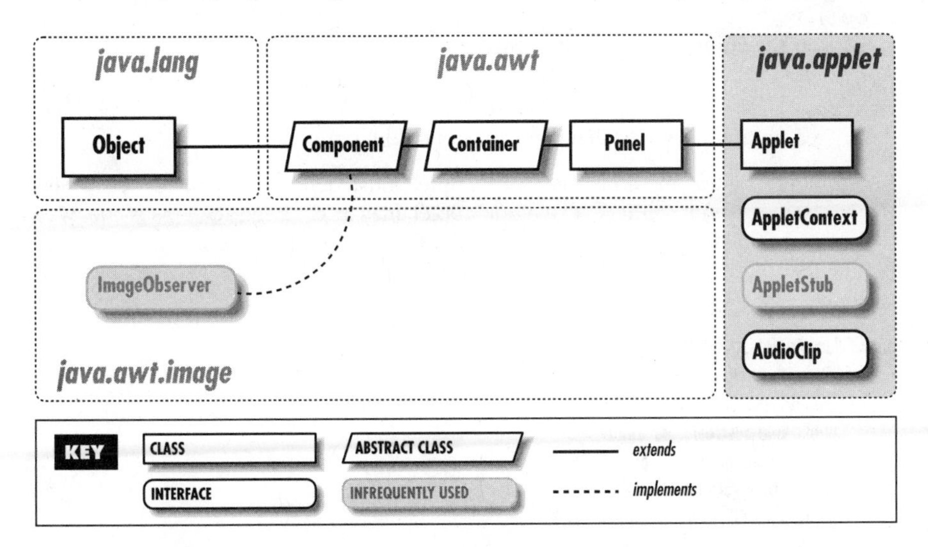

Figure 18-1: The java.applet package

See Section 4, *Applets*, for more information about this package.

java.applet.Applet

This class implements an applet. To create your own applet, you should create a subclass of this class and override some or all of the following methods. Note that you never need to call these methods—they are called when appropriate by a Web browser or other applet viewer.

`getAppletInfo()`
: Return text explaining who wrote the applet, what version it is, what the copyright is, and so on.

`getParameterInfo()`
: Return an arbitrary-length array of 3-element arrays of strings. Each element of this array has three elements and describes one of the parameters that this applet understands. The three elements of each parameter description are strings specifying, respectively, the parameter's name, type, and description.

`init()`
: Perform any initialization for the applet.

`start()`
: This is the method that makes the applet do its thing. Often, it starts a thread that runs the main applet code.

`stop()`
: Stop the applet from executing.

`destroy()`
: Free up any resources that the applet is holding.

In addition to these methods that your applet must define, the `Applet` class also defines some useful methods that your applet may call. `resize()` asks the Web browser or applet viewer to give your applet the amount of space it wants. A number of the other `Applet` methods are simple wrappers around `AppletContext` methods.

```
public class Applet extends Panel {
    // Default Constructor: public Applet()
    // Public Instance Methods
      public void destroy(); // Empty
      public AppletContext getAppletContext();
      public String getAppletInfo();
      public AudioClip getAudioClip(URL url);
      public AudioClip getAudioClip(URL url, String name);
      public URL getCodeBase();
      public URL getDocumentBase();
      public Image getImage(URL url);
      public Image getImage(URL url, String name);
      public String getParameter(String name);
      public String[][] getParameterInfo();
      public void init(); // Empty
```

```
        public boolean isActive();
        public void play(URL url);
        public void play(URL url, String name);
        public void resize(int width, int height);  // Overrides Component.resize()
        public void resize(Dimension d);  // Overrides Component.resize()
        public final void setStub(AppletStub stub);
        public void showStatus(String msg);
        public void start();  // Empty
        public void stop();  // Empty
}
```

java.applet.AppletContext

This interface defines the methods that allow an applet to interact with the context in which it runs (which is usually a Web browser or an applet viewer). The object that implements the `AppletContext` interface is returned by `Applet.getAppletContext()`. You can use it to take advantage of a Web browser's cache, or to display a message to the user in the Web browser's or applet viewer's message area.

The `getAudioClip()` and `getImage()` methods may make use of a Web browser's caching mechanism. `showDocument()` and `showStatus()` give an applet a small measure of control over the appearance of the browser or applet viewer. The `getApplet()` and `getApplets()` methods allow an applet to find out what other applets are running at the same time.

```
public abstract interface AppletContext {
    // Public Instance Methods
        public abstract Applet getApplet(String name);
        public abstract Enumeration getApplets();
        public abstract AudioClip getAudioClip(URL url);
        public abstract Image getImage(URL url);
        public abstract void showDocument(URL url);
        public abstract void showDocument(URL url, String target);
        public abstract void showStatus(String status);
}
```

java.applet.AppletStub

This is an internal interface used when implementing an applet viewer.

```
public abstract interface AppletStub {
    // Public Instance Methods
        public abstract void appletResize(int width, int height);
        public abstract AppletContext getAppletContext();
        public abstract URL getCodeBase();
        public abstract URL getDocumentBase();
```

→

```
        public abstract String getParameter(String name);
        public abstract boolean isActive();
}
```

java.applet.AudioClip

This interface describes the essential methods that an audio clip must have. `AppletContext.getAudioClip()` and `Applet.getAudioClip()` both return an object that implements this interface. The `AudioClip` interface is in the `java.applet` package only because there is not a better place for it.

```
public abstract interface AudioClip {
    // Public Instance Methods
        public abstract void loop();
        public abstract void play();
        public abstract void stop();
}
```

The java.awt Package

The `java.awt` package is the Abstract Windowing Toolkit. The classes of this package may be roughly divided into three categories (see Figure 19-1 and Figure 19-2).

- Graphics: These classes define colors, fonts, images, polygons, and so forth.
- Components: These classes are GUI (graphical user interface) components such as buttons, menus, lists, and dialog boxes.
- Layout Managers: These classes control the layout of components within their container objects.

Note that a separate package, `java.awt.image`, contains classes for image manipulation.

In the first category of classes, `Graphics` is probably the most important. This class defines methods for doing line and text drawing and image painting. It relies on other classes such as `Color`, `Font`, `Image`, and `Polygon`. `Image` is itself an important class, used in many places in `java.awt` and throughout the related package `java.awt.image`. `Event` is another important class that describes a user or window system event that has occurred.

`Component` and `MenuComponent` are root classes in the second category of `java.awt` classes. Their subclasses are GUI components that can appear in interfaces and menus. The `Container` class is one that contains components and arranges them visually. You add components to a container with the `add()` method and specify a layout manager for the container with the `setLayout()` method. Typically, you subclass a container class to provide a definition of the methods that handle `Event` objects generated by the components it contains. These event-handling methods define the dynamic behavior of your interface.

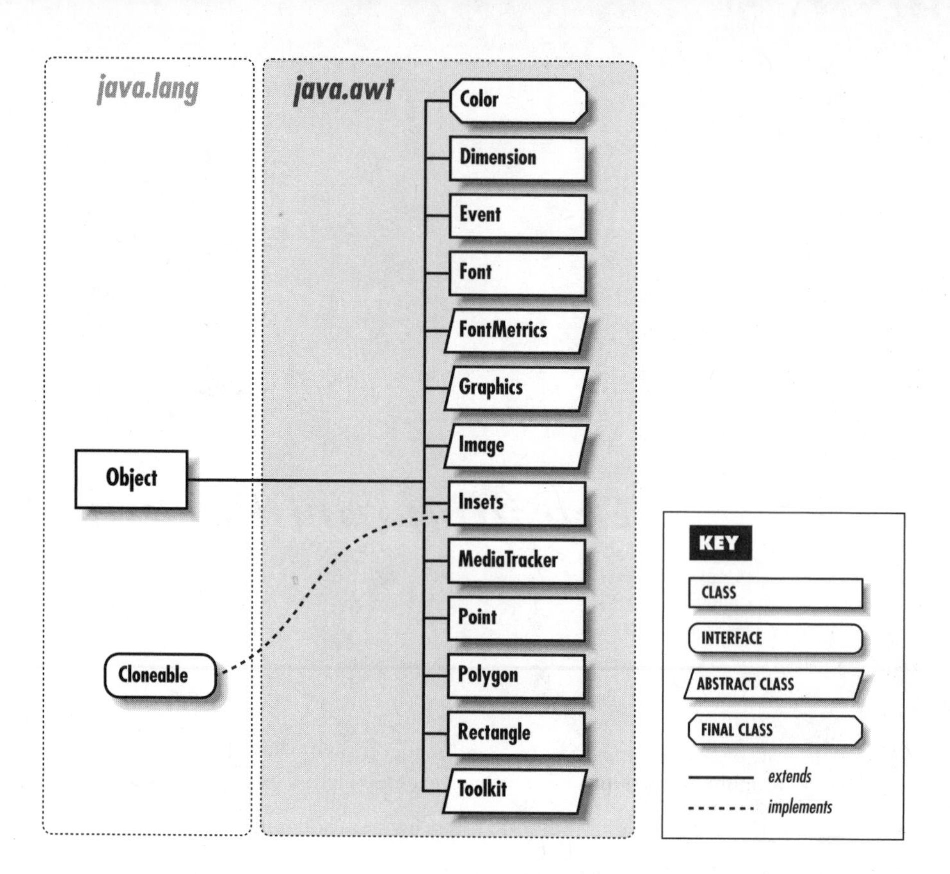

Figure 19-1: Graphics classes of the java.awt package

There are three commonly used `Container` subclasses. `Frame` is a toplevel window that can contain a menu bar and have a custom cursor and an icon. `Dialog` is a dialog window. `Panel` is a container that does not have its own window—it is contained within some other container.

The third category of `java.awt` classes is the layout managers. The subclasses of `LayoutManager` are responsible for arranging the `Component` objects contained within a specified `Container`. `GridBagLayout`, `BorderLayout`, and `GridLayout` are probably the most useful of these layout managers.

See Section 5, *Graphical User Interfaces*, for more detailed information on the `java.awt` package and for examples of using these classes.

java.awt.BorderLayout

This class implements the `LayoutManager` interface to lay out `Component` objects in a `Container`. The `BorderLayout` arranges components that have been added to their `Container` (using the `Container.add()` method) with the names "North," "South," "East," "West," and "Center." These named components are arranged along

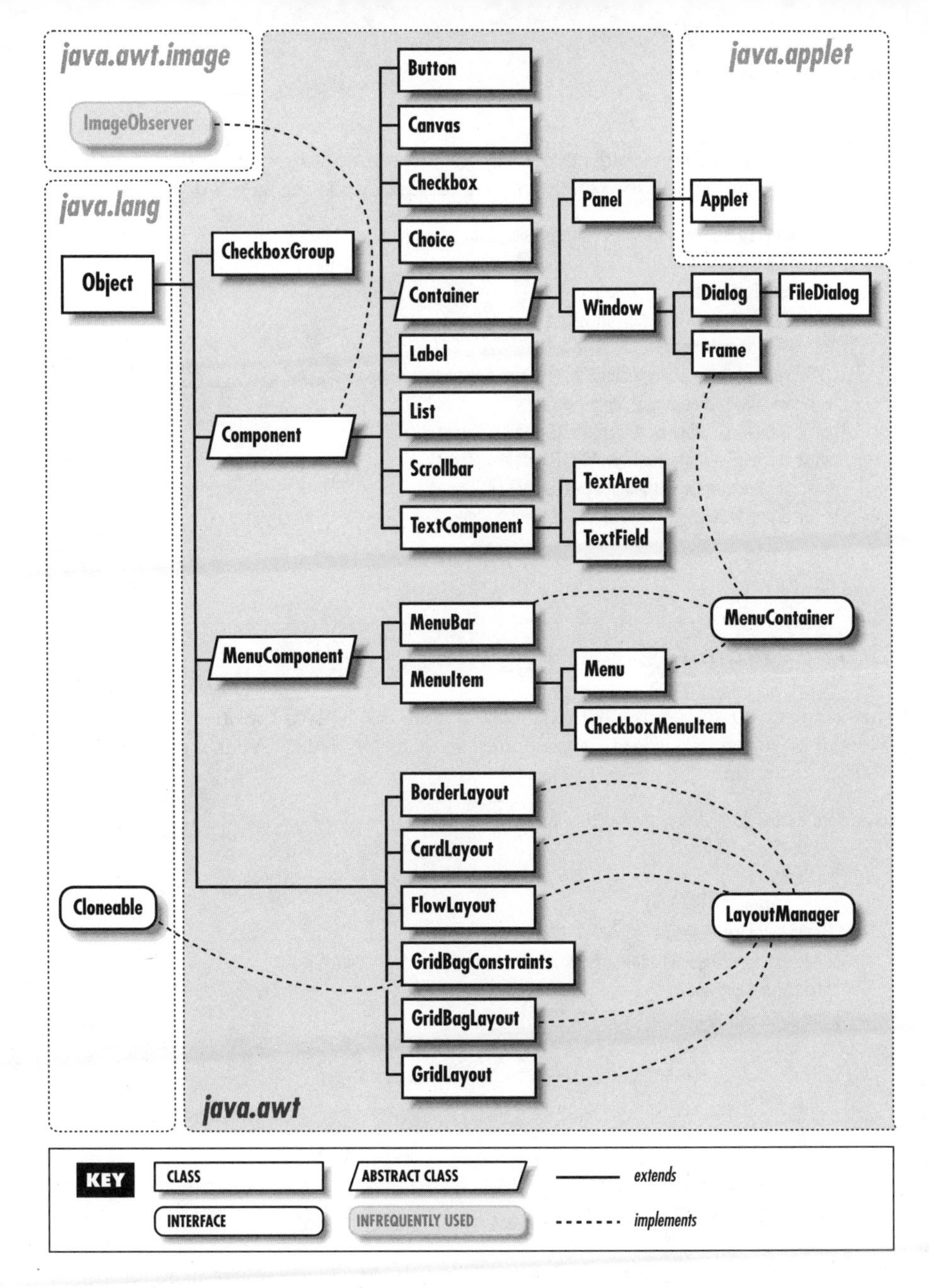

Figure 19-2: Component and layout classes of the java.awt package

the edges and in the center of the container. The *hgap* and *vgap* arguments to the `BorderLayout` constructor specify the desired horizontal and vertical spacing between adjacent components.

→

Note that applications should never call the `LayoutManager` methods of this class directly; the `Container` for which the `BorderLayout` is registered does this.

```
public class BorderLayout extends Object implements LayoutManager {
    // Public Constructors
        public BorderLayout(); // Empty
        public BorderLayout(int hgap, int vgap);
    // Public Instance Methods
        public void addLayoutComponent(String name, Component comp);
        public void layoutContainer(Container target);
        public Dimension minimumLayoutSize(Container target);
        public Dimension preferredLayoutSize(Container target);
        public void removeLayoutComponent(Component comp);
        public String toString(); // Overrides Object.toString()
}
```

java.awt.Button

This class encapsulates a GUI pushbutton that displays a specified textual label. When the button is clicked, it generates an `ACTION_EVENT` event with the button label as its argument.

```
public class Button extends Component {
    // Public Constructors
        public Button();
        public Button(String label);
    // Public Instance Methods
        public synchronized void addNotify(); // Overrides Component.addNotify()
        public String getLabel();
        public void setLabel(String label);
    // Protected Instance Methods
        protected String paramString(); // Overrides Component.paramString()
}
```

java.awt.Canvas

This class is a `Component` that does no default drawing or event-handling on its own. You can subclass it to display any kind of drawing or image, and to handle any kind of user input event. `Canvas` generates `KEY_ACTION`, `KEY_ACTION_RELEASE`, `KEY_PRESS`, `KEY_RELEASE`, `MOUSE_ENTER`, `MOUSE_EXIT`, `MOUSE_DOWN`, `MOUSE_UP`, `MOUSE_MOVE`, and `MOUSE_DRAG` events.

```
public class Canvas extends Component {
    // Default Constructor: public Canvas()
    // Public Instance Methods
```

```
        public synchronized void addNotify(); // Overrides Component.addNotify()
        public void paint(Graphics g); // Overrides Component.paint()
}
```

java.awt.CardLayout

This class is a `LayoutManager` that ensures that only one of the components it manages is visible at a time. The standard `LayoutManager` methods are called by the `Container` object, and should not be called directly by applet or application code. `first()`, `last()`, `next()`, `previous()`, and `show()` make a particular `Component` in the `Container` visible. The names with which the components are added to the container are used only by the `show()` method.

```
public class CardLayout extends Object implements LayoutManager {
    // Public Constructors
        public CardLayout();
        public CardLayout(int hgap, int vgap);
    // Public Instance Methods
        public void addLayoutComponent(String name, Component comp);
        public void first(Container parent);
        public void last(Container parent);
        public void layoutContainer(Container parent);
        public Dimension minimumLayoutSize(Container parent);
        public void next(Container parent);
        public Dimension preferredLayoutSize(Container parent);
        public void previous(Container parent);
        public void removeLayoutComponent(Component comp);
        public void show(Container parent, String name);
        public String toString(); // Overrides Object.toString()
}
```

java.awt.Checkbox

This class encapsulates a GUI checkbox with a textual label. The `Checkbox` maintains a `boolean` state—whether it is checked or not. The checkbox may optionally be part of a `CheckboxGroup`. When a `Checkbox` is selected, it generates an `ACTION_EVENT` event with a `boolean` containing the new checkbox state as its argument.

See also `CheckboxGroup`.

```
public class Checkbox extends Component {
    // Public Constructors
        public Checkbox(); // Empty
        public Checkbox(String label);
        public Checkbox(String label, CheckboxGroup group, boolean state);
    // Public Instance Methods
```

```
        public synchronized void addNotify(); // Overrides Component.addNotify()
        public CheckboxGroup getCheckboxGroup();
        public String getLabel();
        public boolean getState();
        public void setCheckboxGroup(CheckboxGroup g);
        public void setLabel(String label);
        public void setState(boolean state);
    // Protected Instance Methods
        protected String paramString(); // Overrides Component.paramString()
}
```

---

java.awt.CheckboxGroup

A `CheckboxGroup` object enforces mutual exclusion (also known as "radio button" behavior) among any number of `Checkbox` buttons. A `Checkbox` component can specify a `CheckboxGroup` object with `Checkbox.setCheckboxGroup()`. If a `Checkbox` with a given `CheckboxGroup` object is selected, then the `CheckboxGroup` ensures that the previously selected `Checkbox` becomes unselected.

See also `Checkbox`.

```
public class CheckboxGroup extends Object {
    // Public Constructor
        public CheckboxGroup(); // Empty
    // Public Instance Methods
        public Checkbox getCurrent();
        public synchronized void setCurrent(Checkbox box);
        public String toString(); // Overrides Object.toString()
}
```

---

java.awt.CheckboxMenuItem

This class encapsulates a checkbox with a textual label in a GUI menu. It maintains a `boolean` state—whether it is checked or not.

See also `MenuItem`.

```
public class CheckboxMenuItem extends MenuItem {
    // Public Constructor
        public CheckboxMenuItem(String label);
    // Public Instance Methods
        public synchronized void addNotify(); // Overrides MenuItem.addNotify()
        public boolean getState();
        public String paramString(); // Overrides MenuItem.paramString()
        public void setState(boolean t);
}
```

java.awt.Choice

This class encapsulates an "option menu"—a menu of options that drops down from a button. The currently selected option is displayed as the label of the button. The button displays a special icon to indicate that a menu is available from it.

The `addItem()` method adds an item with the specified label to a `Choice` menu. `getSelectedIndex()` returns the numerical position of the selected item in the menu, and `getSelectedItem()` returns the label of the selected item.

When an item is selected from the menu, `Choice` generates an `ACTION_EVENT` event with the label of the selected item as its argument.

```
public class Choice extends Component {
    // Public Constructor
      public Choice();
    // Public Instance Methods
      public synchronized void addItem(String item) throws NullPointerException;
      public synchronized void addNotify(); // Overrides Component.addNotify()
      public int countItems();
      public String getItem(int index);
      public int getSelectedIndex();
      public String getSelectedItem();
      public synchronized void select(int pos) throws IllegalArgumentException;
      public void select(String str);
    // Protected Instance Methods
      protected String paramString(); // Overrides Component.paramString()
}
```

java.awt.Color

The `Color` object describes a color. The `Color()` constructors describe a color as red, green, and blue components between 0 and 255, or as floating-point values between 0.0 and 1.0. The class method `Color.getHSBColor()` creates a color using the hue/saturation/brightness color model.

`brighter()` and `darker()` are useful methods when creating a palette of related colors. The `getColor()` methods look up a color name in the properties database and convert the resulting integer color value into a `Color` object. Two of these methods provide a default value to be used in case the specified color name is not found.

```
public final class Color extends Object {
    // Public Constructors
      public Color(int r, int g, int b);
      public Color(int rgb);
      public Color(float r, float g, float b);
    // Constants
      public final static Color black;
      public final static Color blue;
      public final static Color cyan;
```

→

```
        public final static Color darkGray;
        public final static Color gray;
        public final static Color green;
        public final static Color lightGray;
        public final static Color magenta;
        public final static Color orange;
        public final static Color pink;
        public final static Color red;
        public final static Color white;
        public final static Color yellow;
    // Class Methods
        public static int HSBtoRGB(float hue, float saturation, float brightness);
        public static float[] RGBtoHSB(int r, int g, int b, float[] hsbvals);
        public static Color getColor(String nm);
        public static Color getColor(String nm, Color v);
        public static Color getColor(String nm, int v);
        public static Color getHSBColor(float h, float s, float b);
    // Public Instance Methods
        public Color brighter();
        public Color darker();
        public boolean equals(Object obj);  // Overrides Object.equals()
        public int getBlue();
        public int getGreen();
        public int getRGB();
        public int getRed();
        public int hashCode();  // Overrides Object.hashCode()
        public String toString();  // Overrides Object.toString()
}
```

java.awt.Component

`Component` is the superclass of all GUI components (except menu components) in the `java.awt` package. You may not instantiate a `Component` directly; only one of its subclasses.

`Component` defines many methods. Some of these are intended to be implemented by subclasses. Some are used internally. Some are to be implemented to handle events. And many are useful utility methods for working with GUI components. `getParent()` returns the `Container` that a `Component` is contained in. `setBackground()`, `setForeground()` and `setFont()` set the specified display attributes of a component. `hide()`, `show()`, `enable()`, and `disable()` perform the specified actions for a component. `createImage()` creates an `Image` object from a specified `ImageProducer`, or creates an offscreen image that can be draw into and used for double-buffering during animation.

`Component` generates `GOT_FOCUS` and `LOST_FOCUS` events when it gains and loses the input focus.

```
public abstract class Component extends Object implements ImageObserver {
    // No Constructor
    // Public Instance Methods
      public boolean action(Event evt, Object what);
      public void addNotify();
      public Rectangle bounds();
      public int checkImage(Image image, ImageObserver observer);
      public int checkImage(Image image, int width, int height, ImageObserver observer);
      public Image createImage(ImageProducer producer);
      public Image createImage(int width, int height);
      public void deliverEvent(Event e);
      public synchronized void disable();
      public synchronized void enable();
      public void enable(boolean cond);
      public Color getBackground();
      public synchronized ColorModel getColorModel();
      public Font getFont();
      public FontMetrics getFontMetrics(Font font);
      public Color getForeground();
      public Graphics getGraphics();
      public Container getParent();
      public ComponentPeer getPeer();
      public Toolkit getToolkit();
      public boolean gotFocus(Event evt, Object what);
      public boolean handleEvent(Event evt);
      public synchronized void hide();
      public boolean imageUpdate(Image img, int flags, int x, int y, int w, int h);
      public synchronized boolean inside(int x, int y);
      public void invalidate();
      public boolean isEnabled();
      public boolean isShowing();
      public boolean isValid();
      public boolean isVisible();
      public boolean keyDown(Event evt, int key);
      public boolean keyUp(Event evt, int key);
      public void layout();  // Empty
      public void list();
      public void list(PrintStream out);
      public void list(PrintStream out, int indent);
      public Component locate(int x, int y);
      public Point location();
      public boolean lostFocus(Event evt, Object what);
      public Dimension minimumSize();
      public boolean mouseDown(Event evt, int x, int y);
      public boolean mouseDrag(Event evt, int x, int y);
      public boolean mouseEnter(Event evt, int x, int y);
      public boolean mouseExit(Event evt, int x, int y);
      public boolean mouseMove(Event evt, int x, int y);
      public boolean mouseUp(Event evt, int x, int y);
      public void move(int x, int y);
      public void nextFocus();
      public void paint(Graphics g);  // Empty
      public void paintAll(Graphics g);
```

```
        public boolean postEvent(Event e);
        public Dimension preferredSize();
        public boolean prepareImage(Image image, ImageObserver observer);
        public boolean prepareImage(Image image, int width, int height, ImageObserver observer);
        public void print(Graphics g);
        public void printAll(Graphics g);
        public synchronized void removeNotify();
        public void repaint();
        public void repaint(long tm);
        public void repaint(int x, int y, int width, int height);
        public void repaint(long tm, int x, int y, int width, int height);
        public void requestFocus();
        public synchronized void reshape(int x, int y, int width, int height);
        public void resize(int width, int height);
        public void resize(Dimension d);
        public synchronized void setBackground(Color c);
        public synchronized void setFont(Font f);
        public synchronized void setForeground(Color c);
        public synchronized void show();
        public void show(boolean cond);
        public Dimension size();
        public String toString();  // Overrides Object.toString()
        public void update(Graphics g);
        public void validate();
    // Protected Instance Methods
        protected String paramString();
}
```

java.awt.Container

This class implements a component that can contain other components. You cannot instantiate `Container` directly, but must use one of its subclasses, such as `Panel` or `Frame`, or `Dialog`. Once a `Container` is created, you may set its `LayoutManager` with `setLayout()`, add components to it with `add()`, and remove them with `remove()`. `getComponents()` returns an array of the components contained in a `Container`. `locate()` determines within which contained component a specified point falls. `list()` produces helpful debugging output.

```
public abstract class Container extends Component {
    // No Constructor
    // Public Instance Methods
        public Component add(Component comp);
        public synchronized Component add(Component comp, int pos);
        public synchronized Component add(String name, Component comp);
        public synchronized void addNotify();  // Overrides Component.addNotify()
        public int countComponents();
        public void deliverEvent(Event e);  // Overrides Component.deliverEvent()
        public synchronized Component getComponent(int n) throws ArrayIndexOutOfBoundsException;
        public synchronized Component[] getComponents();
        public LayoutManager getLayout();
        public Insets insets();
```

```
    public synchronized void layout(); // Overrides Component.layout()
    public void list(PrintStream out, int indent); // Overrides Component.list()
    public Component locate(int x, int y); // Overrides Component.locate()
    public synchronized Dimension minimumSize(); // Overrides Component.minimumSize()
    public void paintComponents(Graphics g);
    public synchronized Dimension preferredSize(); // Overrides Component.preferredSize()
    public void printComponents(Graphics g);
    public synchronized void remove(Component comp);
    public synchronized void removeAll();
    public synchronized void removeNotify(); // Overrides Component.removeNotify()
    public void setLayout(LayoutManager mgr);
    public synchronized void validate(); // Overrides Component.validate()
  // Protected Instance Methods
    protected String paramString(); // Overrides Component.paramString()
}
```

java.awt.Dialog

This class encapsulates a dialog box window. A `Dialog` may be modal so that it blocks user input to all other windows until dismissed, may optionally have a title, and may be resizable. A `Dialog` object is a `Container` and `Component` objects can be added to it in the normal way with the `add()` method. The default `LayoutManager` for `Dialog` is `BorderLayout`. You may specify a different `LayoutManager` object with `setLayout()`. Call the `Window.dispose()` method when the `Dialog` is no longer needed so that its window system resources may be reused.

Java programs typically subclass `Dialog` and provide customized event handling for the dialog and the components it contains by overriding the event-handling methods such as `Component.action()`, `Component.mouseDown()`, and `Component.keyDown()`. The `Dialog` class itself generates `WINDOW_DESTROY`, `WINDOW_ICONIFY`, `WINDOW_DEICONIFY`, and `WINDOW_MOVED` events.

```
public class Dialog extends Window {
  // Public Constructors
    public Dialog(Frame parent, boolean modal);
    public Dialog(Frame parent, String title, boolean modal);
  // Public Instance Methods
    public synchronized void addNotify(); // Overrides Window.addNotify()
    public String getTitle();
    public boolean isModal();
    public boolean isResizable();
    public void setResizable(boolean resizable);
    public void setTitle(String title);
```

```
    // Protected Instance Methods
        protected String paramString();  // Overrides Container.paramString()
}
```

java.awt.Dimension

This class has two public instance variables that describe the width and height of something. The `width` and `height` fields are public and may be manipulated directly.

```
public class Dimension extends Object {
    // Public Constructors
        public Dimension();
        public Dimension(Dimension d);
        public Dimension(int width, int height);
    // Public Instance Variables
        public int height;
        public int width;
    // Public Instance Methods
        public String toString();  // Overrides Object.toString()
}
```

java.awt.Event

This class contains public instance variables that describe some kind of GUI event. The class contains a large number of constants. Some of the constants specify the event type and are values for the `id` variable. Other constants are values for keys, like the function keys, that do not have ASCII (or Latin-1) values, and are set on the `key` field. Other constants are mask values that are ORed into the `modifiers` field to describe the state of the modifier keys on the keyboard. The `target` field is very important—it is the object for which the event occurred. The `when` field specifies when the event occurred. The `x` and `y` fields specify the mouse coordinates at which it occurred. Finally, the `arg` field is a value specific to the type of the event. Not all fields have valid values for all types of events.

```
public class Event extends Object {
    // Public Constructors
        public Event(Object target, long when, int id, int x, int y, int key, int modifiers, Object arg);
        public Event(Object target, long when, int id, int x, int y, int key, int modifiers);
        public Event(Object target, int id, Object arg);
    // Constants
    // Event Type Constants
        public final static int ACTION_EVENT;
        public final static int GOT_FOCUS, LOST_FOCUS;
        public final static int KEY_ACTION, KEY_ACTION_RELEASE;
        public final static int KEY_PRESS, KEY_RELEASE;
```

```
    public final static int LIST_SELECT, LIST_DESELECT;
    public final static int LOAD_FILE, SAVE_FILE;
    public final static int MOUSE_DOWN, MOUSE_UP;
    public final static int MOUSE_DRAG;
    public final static int MOUSE_MOVE;
    public final static int MOUSE_ENTER, MOUSE_EXIT;
    public final static int SCROLL_ABSOLUTE;
    public final static int SCROLL_LINE_UP, SCROLL_LINE_DOWN;
    public final static int SCROLL_PAGE_UP, SCROLL_PAGE_DOWN;
    public final static int WINDOW_EXPOSE;
    public final static int WINDOW_ICONIFY, WINDOW_DEICONIFY;
    public final static int WINDOW_DESTROY;
    public final static int WINDOW_MOVED;
  // Keyboard Modifier Constants
    public final static int ALT_MASK;
    public final static int CTRL_MASK;
    public final static int META_MASK;
    public final static int SHIFT_MASK;
  // Function Key Constants
    public final static int F1, F2, F3, F4, F5, F6;
    public final static int F7, F8, F9, F10, F11, F12;
    public final static int LEFT, RIGHT;
    public final static int UP, DOWN;
    public final static int HOME, END;
    public final static int PGUP, PGDN;
  // Public Instance Variables
    public Object arg;
    public int clickCount;
    public Event evt;
    public int id;
    public int key;
    public int modifiers;
    public Object target;
    public long when;
    public int x;
    public int y;
  // Public Instance Methods
    public boolean controlDown();
    public boolean metaDown();
    public boolean shiftDown();
    public String toString();  // Overrides Object.toString()
    public void translate(int x, int y);
  // Protected Instance Methods
    protected String paramString();
}
```

java.awt.FileDialog

This class encapsulates a file selection dialog box. The constants `LOAD` and `SAVE` are values of an optional constructor argument that specifies whether the dialog should be an "Open File" dialog or a "Save As" dialog. You may specify a `FilenameFilter` object to control which files are displayed in the dialog.

```
public class FileDialog extends Dialog {
    // Public Constructors
        public FileDialog(Frame parent, String title);
        public FileDialog(Frame parent, String title, int mode);
    // Constants
        public final static int LOAD;
        public final static int SAVE;
    // Public Instance Methods
        public synchronized void addNotify(); // Overrides Dialog.addNotify()
        public String getDirectory();
        public String getFile();
        public FilenameFilter getFilenameFilter();
        public int getMode();
        public void setDirectory(String dir);
        public void setFile(String file);
        public void setFilenameFilter(FilenameFilter filter);
    // Protected Instance Methods
        protected String paramString(); // Overrides Dialog.paramString()
}
```

java.awt.FlowLayout

This class implements the `LayoutManager` interface to lay out `Component` objects in a `Container`. `FlowLayout` arranges components from left to right in rows. It fits as many components as it can in a row before moving on to the next row. The constructor allows you to specify one of three constants as an alignment value for the rows, and also allows you to specify horizontal spacing between components and vertical spacing between rows.

Note that applications should never call the `LayoutManager` methods of this class directly; the `Container` for which the `FlowLayout` is registered does this.

```
public class FlowLayout extends Object implements LayoutManager {
    // Public Constructors
        public FlowLayout();
        public FlowLayout(int align);
        public FlowLayout(int align, int hgap, int vgap);
    // Constants
        public final static int CENTER;
        public final static int LEFT;
        public final static int RIGHT;
    // Public Instance Methods
        public void addLayoutComponent(String name, Component comp); // Empty
```

```
        public void layoutContainer(Container target);
        public Dimension minimumLayoutSize(Container target);
        public Dimension preferredLayoutSize(Container target);
        public void removeLayoutComponent(Component comp);  // Empty
        public String toString();  // Overrides Object.toString()
}
```

java.awt.Font

This class represents a font in a platform-independent way. The constructor accepts a font name, style, and point size. The style may be one of the constants `PLAIN`, `BOLD`, or `ITALIC`, or the sum `BOLD+ITALIC`. The class method `getFont()` looks up the specified name in the system properties list and returns the font specified as the value of that property. It takes an optional `Font` default to use if the named font property is not found. This allows user customizability.

```
public class Font extends Object {
    // Public Constructor
        public Font(String name, int style, int size);
    // Constants
        public final static int BOLD;
        public final static int ITALIC;
        public final static int PLAIN;
    // Protected Instance Variables
        protected String name;
        protected int size;
        protected int style;
    // Class Methods
        public static Font getFont(String nm);
        public static Font getFont(String nm, Font font);
    // Public Instance Methods
        public boolean equals(Object obj);  // Overrides Object.equals()
        public String getFamily();
        public String getName();
        public int getSize();
        public int getStyle();
        public int hashCode();  // Overrides Object.hashCode()
        public boolean isBold();
        public boolean isItalic();
        public boolean isPlain();
        public String toString();  // Overrides Object.toString()
}
```

java.awt.FontMetrics

This class represents font metrics for a specified `Font`. The methods allow you to determine the overall metrics for the font (ascent, descent, etc.), and also to compute the width of strings that are to be displayed in a particular font.

```
public abstract class FontMetrics extends Object {
    // Protected Constructor
      protected FontMetrics(Font font);
    // Protected Instance Variables
      protected Font font;
    // Public Instance Methods
      public int bytesWidth(byte[] data, int off, int len);
      public int charWidth(int ch);
      public int charWidth(char ch);
      public int charsWidth(char[] data, int off, int len);
      public int getAscent();
      public int getDescent();
      public Font getFont();
      public int getHeight();
      public int getLeading();
      public int getMaxAdvance();
      public int getMaxAscent();
      public int getMaxDecent();
      public int getMaxDescent();
      public int[] getWidths();
      public int stringWidth(String str);
      public String toString();  // Overrides Object.toString()
}
```

java.awt.Frame

This class encapsulates an optionally resizable top-level application window. This window may have a specified title, a menu bar, an icon, and a cursor. `setTitle()` specifies a title, `setMenuBar()` specifies a menu bar, `setCursor()` specifies a cursor, and `setIconImage()` specifies an icon. The constants defined by this class specify various cursor types. The `dispose()` method must be called when the `Frame` is no longer needed so that it can release its window system resources for reuse.

Java programs typically subclass `Frame` and provide customized event handling for the window and the components it contains by overriding the event-handling methods such as `Component.action()`, `Component.mouseDown()`, and `Component.keyDown()`. The `Frame` class itself generates `WINDOW_DESTROY`, `WINDOW_ICONIFY`, `WINDOW_DEICONIFY`, and `WINDOW_MOVED` events.

```
public class Frame extends Window implements MenuContainer {
    // Public Constructors
      public Frame();
      public Frame(String title);
```

```
    // Constants
        public final static int CROSSHAIR_CURSOR;
        public final static int DEFAULT_CURSOR;
        public final static int E_RESIZE_CURSOR;
        public final static int HAND_CURSOR;
        public final static int MOVE_CURSOR;
        public final static int NE_RESIZE_CURSOR;
        public final static int NW_RESIZE_CURSOR;
        public final static int N_RESIZE_CURSOR;
        public final static int SE_RESIZE_CURSOR;
        public final static int SW_RESIZE_CURSOR;
        public final static int S_RESIZE_CURSOR;
        public final static int TEXT_CURSOR;
        public final static int WAIT_CURSOR;
        public final static int W_RESIZE_CURSOR;
    // Public Instance Methods
        public synchronized void addNotify(); // Overrides Window.addNotify()
        public synchronized void dispose(); // Overrides Window.dispose()
        public int getCursorType();
        public Image getIconImage();
        public MenuBar getMenuBar();
        public String getTitle();
        public boolean isResizable();
        public synchronized void remove(MenuComponent m);
        public void setCursor(int cursorType);
        public void setIconImage(Image image);
        public synchronized void setMenuBar(MenuBar mb);
        public void setResizable(boolean resizable);
        public void setTitle(String title);
    // Protected Instance Methods
        protected String paramString(); // Overrides Container.paramString()
}
```

java.awt.Graphics

This abstract class defines a device-independent interface to graphics. It specifies methods for doing line drawing, image painting, area copying, and graphics output clipping. Specific subclasses of `Graphics` are implemented for different platforms and different graphics output devices. A `Graphics` object cannot be created directly through a constructor—it must be obtained with the `getGraphics()` method of a `Component` or an `Image`, or copied from an existing `Graphics` object with `create()`. When a `Graphics` object is no longer needed, you should call `dispose()` to free up window system resources.

```
public abstract class Graphics extends Object {
    // Protected Constructor
        protected Graphics(); // Empty
    // Public Instance Methods
```

→

```
    public abstract void clearRect(int x, int y, int width, int height);
    public abstract void clipRect(int x, int y, int width, int height);
    public abstract void copyArea(int x, int y, int width, int height, int dx, int dy);
    public abstract Graphics create();
    public Graphics create(int x, int y, int width, int height);
    public abstract void dispose();
    public void draw3DRect(int x, int y, int width, int height, boolean raised);
    public abstract void drawArc(int x, int y, int width, int height, int startAngle, int arcAngle);
    public void drawBytes(byte[] data, int offset, int length, int x, int y);
    public void drawChars(char[] data, int offset, int length, int x, int y);
    public abstract boolean drawImage(Image img, int x, int y, ImageObserver observer);
    public abstract boolean drawImage(Image img, int x, int y, int width, int height, ImageObserver observer);
    public abstract boolean drawImage(Image img, int x, int y, Color bgcolor, ImageObserver observer);
    public abstract boolean drawImage(Image img, int x, int y, int width, int height,
                                      Color bgcolor, ImageObserver observer);
    public abstract void drawLine(int x1, int y1, int x2, int y2);
    public abstract void drawOval(int x, int y, int width, int height);
    public abstract void drawPolygon(int[] xPoints, int[] yPoints, int nPoints);
    public void drawPolygon(Polygon p);
    public void drawRect(int x, int y, int width, int height);
    public abstract void drawRoundRect(int x, int y, int width, int height, int arcWidth, int arcHeight);
    public abstract void drawString(String str, int x, int y);
    public void fill3DRect(int x, int y, int width, int height, boolean raised);
    public abstract void fillArc(int x, int y, int width, int height, int startAngle, int arcAngle);
    public abstract void fillOval(int x, int y, int width, int height);
    public abstract void fillPolygon(int[] xPoints, int[] yPoints, int nPoints);
    public void fillPolygon(Polygon p);
    public abstract void fillRect(int x, int y, int width, int height);
    public abstract void fillRoundRect(int x, int y, int width, int height, int arcWidth, int arcHeight);
    public void finalize();
    public abstract Rectangle getClipRect();
    public abstract Color getColor();
    public abstract Font getFont();
    public FontMetrics getFontMetrics();
    public abstract FontMetrics getFontMetrics(Font f);
    public abstract void setColor(Color c);
    public abstract void setFont(Font font);
    public abstract void setPaintMode();
    public abstract void setXORMode(Color c1);
    public String toString(); // Overrides Object.toString()
    public abstract void translate(int x, int y);
}
```

java.awt.GridBagConstraints

This class encapsulates the instance variables that tell a `GridBagLayout` how to position a given `Component` within its `Container`.

`gridx`, `gridy`
: These fields specify the grid position of the component. The `RELATIVE` constant specifies a position to the right or below the previous component.

`gridwidth`, `gridheight`
: These fields specify the height and width of the component in grid cells. The constant `REMAINDER` specifies that the component is the last one and should get all remaining cells.

`fill`
: This field specifies which dimensions of a component should grow when the space available for it is larger than its default size. Legal values are the constants `NONE`, `BOTH`, `HORIZONTAL`, and `VERTICAL`.

`ipadx`, `ipady`
: These fields specify internal padding to add on each side of the component in each dimension. They increase the size of the component beyond its default minimum size.

`insets`
: This `Insets` object specifies margins to appear on all sides of the component.

`anchor`
: This field specifies how the component should be displayed within its grid cells when it is smaller than those cells. The `CENTER` constant and the compass-point constants are legal values.

`weightx`, `weighty`
: These fields specify how extra space in the container should be distributed among its components in the X and Y dimensions. Larger weights specify that a component should receive a proportionally larger amount of extra space. A zero weight specifies that the component should not receive any extra space. These weights specify the resizing behavior of the component and its container.

See also `GridBagLayout`.

```
public class GridBagConstraints extends Object implements Cloneable {
    // Public Constructor
        public GridBagConstraints();
    // Constants
    // anchor Constants
        public final static int CENTER;
        public final static int EAST;
        public final static int NORTH;
        public final static int NORTHEAST;
```

→

```
    public final static int NORTHWEST;
    public final static int SOUTH;
    public final static int SOUTHEAST;
    public final static int SOUTHWEST;
    public final static int WEST;
  // fill Constants
    public final static int HORIZONTAL;
    public final static int VERTICAL;
    public final static int BOTH;
    public final static int NONE;
  // Position and Size Constants
    public final static int RELATIVE;
    public final static int REMAINDER;
  // Public Instance Variables
    public int anchor;
    public int fill;
    public int gridheight;
    public int gridwidth;
    public int gridx;
    public int gridy;
    public Insets insets;
    public int ipadx;
    public int ipady;
    public double weightx;
    public double weighty;
  // Public Instance Methods
    public Object clone(); // Overrides Object.clone()
}
```

java.awt.GridBagLayout

This class implements the `LayoutManager` interface to lay out `Component` objects in a `Container`. It is the most complicated and most powerful `LayoutManager` in the `java.awt` package. It divides the container into a grid of rows and columns (which need not have the same width and height) and places the components into this grid, adjusting the size of the grid cells as necessary to ensure that components do not overlap. Each component controls how it is positioned within this grid by specifying a number of variables (or "constraints") in a `GridBagConstraints` object.

Use `setConstraints()` to specify a `GridBagConstraints` object for each of the components in the container. The variables in this object specify the position of the component in the grid, the number of horizontal and vertical grid cells that the component occupies, and also control other important aspects of component layout. See `GridBagConstraints` for more information on these "constraint" variables. `setConstraints()` makes a copy of the constraints object, so you may reuse a single object in your code.

Note that applications should never call the `LayoutManager` methods of this class directly; the `Container` for which the `GridBagLayout` is registered does this.

Do not confuse this class with the much simpler `GridLayout` which arranges components in a grid of equally sized cells.

```
public class GridBagLayout extends Object implements LayoutManager {
    // Public Constructor
        public GridBagLayout();
    // Constants
        protected final static int MAXGRIDSIZE;
        protected final static int MINSIZE;
        protected final static int PREFERREDSIZE;
    // Public Instance Variables
        public double[] columnWeights;
        public int[] columnWidths;
        public int[] rowHeights;
        public double[] rowWeights;
    // Protected Instance Variables
        protected Hashtable comptable;
        protected GridBagConstraints defaultConstraints;
        protected GridBagLayoutInfo layoutInfo;
    // Public Instance Methods
        public void addLayoutComponent(String name, Component comp);  // Empty
        public GridBagConstraints getConstraints(Component comp);
        public int[][] getLayoutDimensions();
        public Point getLayoutOrigin();
        public double[][] getLayoutWeights();
        public void layoutContainer(Container parent);
        public Point location(int x, int y);
        public Dimension minimumLayoutSize(Container parent);
        public Dimension preferredLayoutSize(Container parent);
        public void removeLayoutComponent(Component comp);  // Empty
        public void setConstraints(Component comp, GridBagConstraints constraints);
        public String toString();  // Overrides Object.toString()
    // Protected Instance Methods
        protected void AdjustForGravity(GridBagConstraints constraints, Rectangle r);
        protected void ArrangeGrid(Container parent);
        protected void DumpConstraints(GridBagConstraints constraints);
        protected void DumpLayoutInfo(GridBagLayoutInfo s);
        protected GridBagLayoutInfo GetLayoutInfo(Container parent, int sizeflag);
        protected Dimension GetMinSize(Container parent, GridBagLayoutInfo info);
        protected GridBagConstraints lookupConstraints(Component comp);
}
```


java.awt.GridLayout

This class implements the `LayoutManager` interface to lay out `Component` objects in a `Container`. It divides the `Container` into a specified number of rows and columns and arranges the components in those rows and columns, left-to-right and top-to-bottom. If either the number of rows or the number of columns is

→

unspecified, it is computed from the other dimension and the total number of components. Do not confuse this class with the more flexible and complicated GridBagLayout.

Note that applications should never call the LayoutManager methods of this class directly; the Container for which the GridLayout is registered does this.

```
public class GridLayout extends Object implements LayoutManager {
    // Public Constructors
        public GridLayout(int rows, int cols);
        public GridLayout(int rows, int cols, int hgap, int vgap) throws IllegalArgumentException;
    // Public Instance Methods
        public void addLayoutComponent(String name, Component comp);  // Empty
        public void layoutContainer(Container parent);
        public Dimension minimumLayoutSize(Container parent);
        public Dimension preferredLayoutSize(Container parent);
        public void removeLayoutComponent(Component comp);  // Empty
        public String toString();  // Overrides Object.toString()
}
```

java.awt.Image

This abstract class represents a displayable image in a platform-independent way. An Image object may not be instantiated directly through a constructor; it must be obtained through a call like Applet.getImage() or Component.createImage(). getSource() method returns the ImageProducer object that produces the image data. getGraphics() returns a Graphics object that can be used for drawing into offscreen images (but not images that are downloaded or generated by an ImageProducer). getProperty() returns the value of a specified property for the image, or the UndefinedProperty constant if the property is not defined.

```
public abstract class Image extends Object {
    // Default Constructor: public Image()
    // Constants
        public final static Object UndefinedProperty;
    // Public Instance Methods
        public abstract void flush();
        public abstract Graphics getGraphics();
        public abstract int getHeight(ImageObserver observer);
        public abstract Object getProperty(String name, ImageObserver observer);
        public abstract ImageProducer getSource();
        public abstract int getWidth(ImageObserver observer);
}
```

java.awt.Insets

This class holds four values that represent the top, left, bottom, and right margins, in pixels, of a Container or other Component. Objects of this type may be specified in a GridBagConstraints layout object, and are returned by Container.-insets(), which queries the margins of a container.

```
public class Insets extends Object implements Cloneable {
    // Public Constructor
        public Insets(int top, int left, int bottom, int right);
    // Public Instance Variables
        public int bottom;
        public int left;
        public int right;
        public int top;
    // Public Instance Methods
        public Object clone(); // Overrides Object.clone()
        public String toString(); // Overrides Object.toString()
}
```

java.awt.Label

This class is a Component that displays a single specified line of read-only text. The constant values specify the text alignment within the component and may be specified to the constructor or to setAlignment().

```
public class Label extends Component {
    // Public Constructors
        public Label();
        public Label(String label);
        public Label(String label, int alignment);
    // Constants
        public final static int CENTER;
        public final static int LEFT;
        public final static int RIGHT;
    // Public Instance Methods
        public synchronized void addNotify(); // Overrides Component.addNotify()
        public int getAlignment();
        public String getText();
        public void setAlignment(int alignment) throws IllegalArgumentException;
        public void setText(String label);
    // Protected Instance Methods
        protected String paramString(); // Overrides Component.paramString()
}
```


java.awt.LayoutManager

This interface defines the methods necessary for a class to be able to arrange Component objects within a Container object. Most programs use one of the existing classes that implements this interface: BorderLayout, CardLayout, FlowLayout, GridBagConstraints, GridBagLayout, or GridLayout.

→

To define a new class that lays out components, you must implement each of the methods defined by this interface. `addLayoutComponent()` should add the specified component (with the specified name) to the Layout. `removeLayoutComponent()` should remove it. `layoutContainer()` should perform the actual positioning of components in the container. `minimumLayoutSize()` should return the absolute minimum container width and height that the `LayoutManager` needs to lay out its components. `preferredLayoutSize()` should return the optimal container width and height for the `LayoutManager` to lay out its components.

Note that a Java applet or application never directly calls any of these `LayoutManager` methods—the `Container` object for which the `LayoutManager` is registered does that.

```
public abstract interface LayoutManager {
    // Public Instance Methods
        public abstract void addLayoutComponent(String name, Component comp);
        public abstract void layoutContainer(Container parent);
        public abstract Dimension minimumLayoutSize(Container parent);
        public abstract Dimension preferredLayoutSize(Container parent);
        public abstract void removeLayoutComponent(Component comp);
}
```

---

java.awt.List

This class is a `Component` that displays a list of strings. The list is scrollable if necessary. The constructor takes optional arguments that specify the number of visible rows in the list and whether selection of more than one item is allowed. The various instance methods allow strings to be added and removed from the `List`, and allow the selected item or items to be queried.

When the user double-clicks on an item, a `List` generates an `ACTION_EVENT` event. When an item is selected, the `List` generates a `LIST_SELECT` event, and when an item is deselected, it generates a `LIST_DESELECT` event. In each of these cases the event argument is the label of the affected item in the `List`.

```
public class List extends Component {
    // Public Constructors
        public List();
        public List(int rows, boolean multipleSelections);
    // Public Instance Methods
        public synchronized void addItem(String item);
        public synchronized void addItem(String item, int index);
        public synchronized void addNotify(); // Overrides Component.addNotify()
        public boolean allowsMultipleSelections();
        public synchronized void clear();
        public int countItems();
        public synchronized void delItem(int position);
        public synchronized void delItems(int start, int end);
        public synchronized void deselect(int index);
        public String getItem(int index);
        public int getRows();
        public synchronized int getSelectedIndex();
```

```
    public synchronized int[] getSelectedIndexes();
    public synchronized String getSelectedItem();
    public synchronized String[] getSelectedItems();
    public int getVisibleIndex();
    public synchronized boolean isSelected(int index);
    public void makeVisible(int index);
    public Dimension minimumSize(int rows);
    public Dimension minimumSize();  // Overrides Component.minimumSize()
    public Dimension preferredSize(int rows);
    public Dimension preferredSize();  // Overrides Component.preferredSize()
    public synchronized void removeNotify();  // Overrides Component.removeNotify()
    public synchronized void replaceItem(String newValue, int index);
    public synchronized void select(int index);
    public void setMultipleSelections(boolean v);
  // Protected Instance Methods
    protected String paramString();  // Overrides Component.paramString()
}
```

java.awt.MediaTracker

This class provides a very convenient way to asynchronously load and keep track of the status of any number of `Image` objects. You can use it to load one or more images and to wait until those images have been completely loaded are are ready to be used.

The `addImage()` method registers an image to be loaded and tracked and assigns it a specified identifier value. `waitForID()` loads all images that have been assigned the specified identifier and returns when they have all finished loading or received an error. `isErrorAny()` and `isErrorID()` check whether any errors have occurred while loading images. `statusAll()` and `statusID()` return the status of all images or of all images with the specified identifier. The return value of these two methods is one of the defined constants.

```
public class MediaTracker extends Object {
  // Public Constructor
    public MediaTracker(Component comp);
  // Constants
    public final static int ABORTED;
    public final static int COMPLETE;
    public final static int ERRORED;
    public final static int LOADING;
  // Public Instance Methods
    public void addImage(Image image, int id);
    public synchronized void addImage(Image image, int id, int w, int h);
    public boolean checkAll();
    public synchronized boolean checkAll(boolean load);
    public boolean checkID(int id);
    public synchronized boolean checkID(int id, boolean load);
    public synchronized Object[] getErrorsAny();
```

→

java.awt

```
        public synchronized Object[] getErrorsID(int id);
        public synchronized boolean isErrorAny();
        public synchronized boolean isErrorID(int id);
        public int statusAll(boolean load);
        public int statusID(int id, boolean load);
        public void waitForAll() throws InterruptedException;
        public synchronized boolean waitForAll(long ms) throws InterruptedException;
        public void waitForID(int id) throws InterruptedException;
        public synchronized boolean waitForID(int id, long ms) throws InterruptedException;
}
```

---

java.awt.Menu

This class encapsulates a pulldown menu pane that appears within a `MenuBar`. Each `Menu` has a label that appears in the `MenuBar` and may optionally be a tear-off menu. The `add()` and `addSeparator()` methods add individual items to a `Menu`.

```
public class Menu extends MenuItem implements MenuContainer {
    // Public Constructors
        public Menu(String label);
        public Menu(String label, boolean tearOff);
    // Public Instance Methods
        public synchronized MenuItem add(MenuItem mi);
        public void add(String label);
        public synchronized void addNotify(); // Overrides MenuItem.addNotify()
        public void addSeparator();
        public int countItems();
        public MenuItem getItem(int index);
        public boolean isTearOff();
        public synchronized void remove(int index);
        public synchronized void remove(MenuComponent item);
        public synchronized void removeNotify(); // Overrides MenuComponent.removeNotify()
}
```

---

java.awt.MenuBar

This class encapsulates a menu bar. `add()` adds `Menu` objects to the menu bar, and `setHelpMenu()` adds a **Help** menu in a reserved location of the menu bar. A `MenuBar` object may be displayed within a `Frame` by passing it to `Frame.setMenuBar()`.

```
public class MenuBar extends MenuComponent implements MenuContainer {
    // Public Constructor
        public MenuBar(); // Empty
    // Public Instance Methods
        public synchronized Menu add(Menu m);
```

```
        public synchronized void addNotify();
        public int countMenus();
        public Menu getHelpMenu();
        public Menu getMenu(int i);
        public synchronized void remove(int index);
        public synchronized void remove(MenuComponent m);
        public void removeNotify(); // Overrides MenuComponent.removeNotify()
        public synchronized void setHelpMenu(Menu m);
}
```

java.awt.MenuComponent

This class is the superclass of all menu-related classes: `MenuItem`, `Menu`, and `MenuBar`. You never need to instantiate a `MenuComponent` directly. `setFont()` specifies the font to be used for all text within the menu component.

```
public abstract class MenuComponent extends Object {
    // Public Constructor
        public MenuComponent(); // Empty
    // Public Instance Methods
        public Font getFont();
        public MenuContainer getParent();
        public MenuComponentPeer getPeer();
        public boolean postEvent(Event evt);
        public void removeNotify();
        public void setFont(Font f);
        public String toString(); // Overrides Object.toString()
    // Protected Instance Methods
        protected String paramString();
}
```

java.awt.MenuContainer

This interface defines the methods necessary for `MenuContainer` types such as the `Menu`, `Frame`, and `MenuBar` objects. Unless you are implementing new menu-like components, you will never need to use it.

```
public abstract interface MenuContainer {
    // Public Instance Methods
        public abstract Font getFont();
        public abstract boolean postEvent(Event evt);
        public abstract void remove(MenuComponent comp);
}
```

java.awt.MenuItem

This class encapsulates a menu item with a specified textual label. A `MenuItem` can be added to a menu pane with the `Menu.add()` method. The `disable()` method makes an item non-selectable; you might use it to "gray-out" a menu item when the command it represents is not valid in the current context. The `enable()` method makes an item selectable again.

When a menu item is selected, `MenuItem` generates an `ACTION_EVENT` event, with the label of the selected item as its argument.

```
public class MenuItem extends MenuComponent {
    // Public Constructor
      public MenuItem(String label);
    // Public Instance Methods
      public synchronized void addNotify();
      public void disable();
      public void enable();
      public void enable(boolean cond);
      public String getLabel();
      public boolean isEnabled();
      public String paramString(); // Overrides MenuComponent.paramString()
      public void setLabel(String label);
}
```

java.awt.Panel

This class is a `Container` that is itself contained within a container. Unlike `Frame` and `Dialog`, `Panel` is a container that does not create a separate window of its own. `Panel` is suitable for holding portions of a larger interface within a parent `Frame` or `Dialog` or within another `Panel`. (Note that `Applet` is a subclass of `Panel`, and thus applets are displayed in a `Panel` that is contained within a Web browser or applet viewer.) The default `LayoutManager` for a `Panel` is `Flow-Layout`.

```
public class Panel extends Container {
    // Public Constructor
      public Panel();
    // Public Instance Methods
      public synchronized void addNotify(); // Overrides Container.addNotify()
}
```

java.awt.Point

This class encapsulates the X and Y coordinates of a two-dimensional point. The `move()` method sets the coordinates, and the `translate()` method adds the specified values to the coordinates. The `x` and `y` fields are public and may be manipulated directly. Point objects are returned by and passed to several java.awt methods.

```
public class Point extends Object {
    // Public Constructor
        public Point(int x, int y);
    // Public Instance Variables
        public int x;
        public int y;
    // Public Instance Methods
        public boolean equals(Object obj);  // Overrides Object.equals()
        public int hashCode();  // Overrides Object.hashCode()
        public void move(int x, int y);
        public String toString();  // Overrides Object.toString()
        public void translate(int x, int y);
}
```

java.awt.Polygon

This class encapsulates a polygon defined as an array of points. The points of the polygon may be specified by the constructor, or with the addPoint() method. getBoundingBox() returns the smallest Rectangle that contains the polygon, and inside() tests whether a specified point is within the Polygon. Note that the arrays of X and Y points and the number of points in the polygon (not necessarily the same as the array size) are defined as public variables. Polygon objects are used when drawing polygons with the Graphics.drawPolygon() and Graphics.-fillPolygon() methods.

```
public class Polygon extends Object {
    // Public Constructors
        public Polygon();  // Empty
        public Polygon(int[] xpoints, int[] ypoints, int npoints);
    // Public Instance Variables
        public int npoints;
        public int[] xpoints;
        public int[] ypoints;
    // Public Instance Methods
        public void addPoint(int x, int y);
        public Rectangle getBoundingBox();
        public boolean inside(int x, int y);
}
```

java.awt

java.awt.Rectangle

This class encapsulates a rectangle defined by the X and Y coordinate of its upper-left corner and a width and height. The instance methods perform various tests and transformations on the rectangle. The x, y, width, and height methods are public

→

and may thus be manipulated directly. `Rectangle` objects are used in several places in the `java.awt` package to specify clipping rectangles and bounding boxes.

```
public class Rectangle extends Object {
    // Public Constructors
        public Rectangle(); // Empty
        public Rectangle(int x, int y, int width, int height);
        public Rectangle(int width, int height);
        public Rectangle(Point p, Dimension d);
        public Rectangle(Point p);
        public Rectangle(Dimension d);
    // Public Instance Variables
        public int height;
        public int width;
        public int x;
        public int y;
    // Public Instance Methods
        public void add(int newx, int newy);
        public void add(Point pt);
        public void add(Rectangle r);
        public boolean equals(Object obj); // Overrides Object.equals()
        public void grow(int h, int v);
        public int hashCode(); // Overrides Object.hashCode()
        public boolean inside(int x, int y);
        public Rectangle intersection(Rectangle r);
        public boolean intersects(Rectangle r);
        public boolean isEmpty();
        public void move(int x, int y);
        public void reshape(int x, int y, int width, int height);
        public void resize(int width, int height);
        public String toString(); // Overrides Object.toString()
        public void translate(int x, int y);
        public Rectangle union(Rectangle r);
}
```

java.awt.Scrollbar

This `Component` encapsulates a scrollbar. `setValue()` sets the displayed value of the scrollbar. `setValues()` sets the displayed value, the page size, and the minimum and maximum values. The constants `HORIZONTAL` and `VERTICAL` are legal values for the scrollbar orientation.

When the user interacts with a `Scrollbar`, it generates one of these events: `SCROLL_LINE_UP`, `SCROLL_LINE_DOWN`, `SCROLL_PAGE_UP`, `SCROLL_PAGE_DOWN`, `SCROLL_ABSOLUTE`. The event argument is an `Integer` object that specifies the number of lines or pages to scroll, or the absolute position to scroll to.

```
public class Scrollbar extends Component {
    // Public Constructors
        public Scrollbar();
        public Scrollbar(int orientation) throws IllegalArgumentException;
        public Scrollbar(int orientation, int value, int visible, int minimum, int maximum);
```

```
    // Constants
        public final static int HORIZONTAL;
        public final static int VERTICAL;
    // Public Instance Methods
        public synchronized void addNotify();  // Overrides Component.addNotify()
        public int getLineIncrement();
        public int getMaximum();
        public int getMinimum();
        public int getOrientation();
        public int getPageIncrement();
        public int getValue();
        public int getVisible();
        public void setLineIncrement(int l);
        public void setPageIncrement(int l);
        public void setValue(int value);
        public void setValues(int value, int visible, int minimum, int maximum);
    // Protected Instance Methods
        protected String paramString();  // Overrides Component.paramString()
}
```

java.awt.TextArea

This class encapsulates a GUI component that allows viewing and optional editing of multiline text. The `appendText()`, `insertText()`, and `replaceText()` provide various techniques for specifying text to appear in the TextArea. Many important `TextArea` methods are defined by the `TextComponent` superclass.

See also `TextComponent` and `TextField`.

```
public class TextArea extends TextComponent {
    // Public Constructors
        public TextArea();
        public TextArea(int rows, int cols);
        public TextArea(String text);
        public TextArea(String text, int rows, int cols);
    // Public Instance Methods
        public synchronized void addNotify();  // Overrides Component.addNotify()
        public void appendText(String str);
        public int getColumns();
        public int getRows();
        public void insertText(String str, int pos);
        public Dimension minimumSize(int rows, int cols);
        public Dimension minimumSize();  // Overrides Component.minimumSize()
        public Dimension preferredSize(int rows, int cols);
        public Dimension preferredSize();  // Overrides Component.preferredSize()
        public void replaceText(String str, int start, int end);
    // Protected Instance Methods
        protected String paramString();  // Overrides TextComponent.paramString()
}
```

java.awt.TextComponent

This class is the superclass of the `TextArea` and `TextField` components. It cannot be instantiated itself, but provides methods that are common to these two Component types. `setEditable()` specifies whether the text in the text component is editable or not. `getText()` returns the text in the component, and `setText()` specifies text to be displayed. `getSelectedText()` returns the currently selected text in the text component, and `getSelectionStart()` and `getSelectionEnd()` return the extents of the selected region of text. `select()` and `selectAll()` select some or all of the text displayed in the text component.

See also `TextField`, and `TextArea`.

```
public class TextComponent extends Component {
    // No Constructor
    // Public Instance Methods
        public String getSelectedText();
        public int getSelectionEnd();
        public int getSelectionStart();
        public String getText();
        public boolean isEditable();
        public synchronized void removeNotify(); // Overrides Component.removeNotify()
        public void select(int selStart, int selEnd);
        public void selectAll();
        public void setEditable(boolean t);
        public void setText(String t);
    // Protected Instance Methods
        protected String paramString(); // Overrides Component.paramString()
}
```

java.awt.TextField

This `Component` encapsulates a line of optionally editable text. Most of its interesting methods are defined by the `TextComponent` superclass. Use `setEchoCharacter()` to specify a character to be echoed when requesting sensitive input such as a password.

See also `TextComponent` and `TextArea`.

```
public class TextField extends TextComponent {
    // Public Constructors
        public TextField();
        public TextField(int cols);
        public TextField(String text);
        public TextField(String text, int cols);
    // Public Instance Methods
        public synchronized void addNotify(); // Overrides Component.addNotify()
        public boolean echoCharIsSet();
        public int getColumns();
        public char getEchoChar();
        public Dimension minimumSize(int cols);
```

```
    public Dimension minimumSize(); // Overrides Component.minimumSize()
    public Dimension preferredSize(int cols);
    public Dimension preferredSize(); // Overrides Component.preferredSize()
    public void setEchoCharacter(char c);
  // Protected Instance Methods
    protected String paramString(); // Overrides TextComponent.paramString()
}
```

java.awt.Toolkit

This abstract class defines methods that, when implemented, create platform-dependent "peers" for each of the `java.awt Component` types. Java supports its platform-independent GUI interface by implementing a subclass of `Toolkit` for each platform. Portable programs should never use these methods to create peers directly—they should use the `Component` classes themselves. A `Toolkit` object cannot be instantiated directly. `Window.getToolkit()` returns the `Toolkit` being used for a particular `Frame` or `Dialog`.

The `Toolkit` class defines a few methods that you can use directly: the static method `getDefaultToolkit()` returns the default `Toolkit` that is in use. `getScreenSize()` returns the screen size in pixels, and `getScreenResolution()` returns the resolution in dots-per-inch. `getFontList()` returns the names of supported fonts on this platform. `sync()` flushes all pending graphics output, which can be useful for animation.

```
public abstract class Toolkit extends Object {
  // Default Constructor: public Toolkit()
  // Class Methods
    public static synchronized Toolkit getDefaultToolkit() throws AWTError;
  // Public Instance Methods
    public abstract int checkImage(Image image, int width, int height, ImageObserver observer);
    public abstract Image createImage(ImageProducer producer);
    public abstract ColorModel getColorModel();
    public abstract String[] getFontList();
    public abstract FontMetrics getFontMetrics(Font font);
    public abstract Image getImage(String filename);
    public abstract Image getImage(URL url);
    public abstract int getScreenResolution();
    public abstract Dimension getScreenSize();
    public abstract boolean prepareImage(Image image, int width, int height, ImageObserver observer);
    public abstract void sync();
  // Protected Instance Methods
    protected abstract ButtonPeer createButton(Button target);
    protected abstract CanvasPeer createCanvas(Canvas target);
    protected abstract CheckboxPeer createCheckbox(Checkbox target);
    protected abstract CheckboxMenuItemPeer createCheckboxMenuItem(CheckboxMenuItem target);
    protected abstract ChoicePeer createChoice(Choice target);
    protected abstract DialogPeer createDialog(Dialog target);
    protected abstract FileDialogPeer createFileDialog(FileDialog target);
```

→

```
        protected abstract FramePeer createFrame(Frame target);
        protected abstract LabelPeer createLabel(Label target);
        protected abstract ListPeer createList(List target);
        protected abstract MenuPeer createMenu(Menu target);
        protected abstract MenuBarPeer createMenuBar(MenuBar target);
        protected abstract MenuItemPeer createMenuItem(MenuItem target);
        protected abstract PanelPeer createPanel(Panel target);
        protected abstract ScrollbarPeer createScrollbar(Scrollbar target);
        protected abstract TextAreaPeer createTextArea(TextArea target);
        protected abstract TextFieldPeer createTextField(TextField target);
        protected abstract WindowPeer createWindow(Window target);
}
```

java.awt.Window

This class encapsulates a top level window with no borders or menu bar. `Window` is a `Container` with `BorderLayout` as its default layout manager. `Window` is rarely used directly; its subclasses `Frame` and `Dialog` are more commonly useful.

`show()` (which overrides `Component.show()`) makes a `Window` visible and brings it to the front of other windows. `toFront()` brings a window to the front, and `toBack()` buries a window beneath others. `pack()` is an important method that sets the window size to match the preferred size of the components contained within the window. `getToolkit()` returns the `Toolkit()` in use for this window. Call `dispose()` when a `Window` is no longer needed to free its window system resources.

The `Window` class generates `WINDOW_DESTROY`, `WINDOW_ICONIFY`, `WINDOW_DEICONIFY`, and `WINDOW_MOVED` events.

```
public class Window extends Container {
    // Public Constructor
        public Window(Frame parent);
    // Public Instance Methods
        public synchronized void addNotify();  // Overrides Container.addNotify()
        public synchronized void dispose();
        public Toolkit getToolkit();  // Overrides Component.getToolkit()
        public final String getWarningString();
        public synchronized void pack();
        public synchronized void show();  // Overrides Component.show()
        public void toBack();
        public void toFront();
}
```

The java.awt.image Package

The `java.awt.image` package is, by any standard, a confusing one. The purpose of the package is to support image processing, and the classes in the package provide a powerful infrastructure for that purpose. (See Figure 20-1.) Most of the classes are part of the infrastructure, however, and are not normally used by ordinary applications that have only simple image manipulation requirements.

To understand this package, it is first important to note that that `Image` class itself is part of the `java.awt` package, not the `java.awt.image` package. Furthermore, the `java.awt.image` classes are not the source of images; they simply serve to manipulate images that come from somewhere else. The `Applet.getImage()` method is perhaps the most common method for obtaining an image in Java—it downloads the image from a specified URL.

The `ImageProducer` interface is one you'll encounter frequently in `java.awt.image`. It represents an image source. If you've created an `Image` object with `Applet.getImage()`, you can obtain the `ImageProducer` for that `Image` (which has not been downloaded yet) with `Image.getSource()`. Conversely, given an `ImageProducer` object, you can create an `Image` from it with the `createImage()` method of any `Component` (such as an `Applet`). Once you have an `ImageProducer` object, you can manipulate it with the other `java.awt.image` classes.

`FilteredImageSource` is the most important class for image manipulation. It is itself a type of `ImageProducer` that, when created, applies a specified `ImageFilter` object to some other specified `ImageProducer` object. The `FilteredImageSource` thus configured can be used as an `ImageProducer` to display a filtered image. `CropImageFilter` is a predefined type of `ImageFilter` that you can use to extract a specified rectangle out of a larger image.

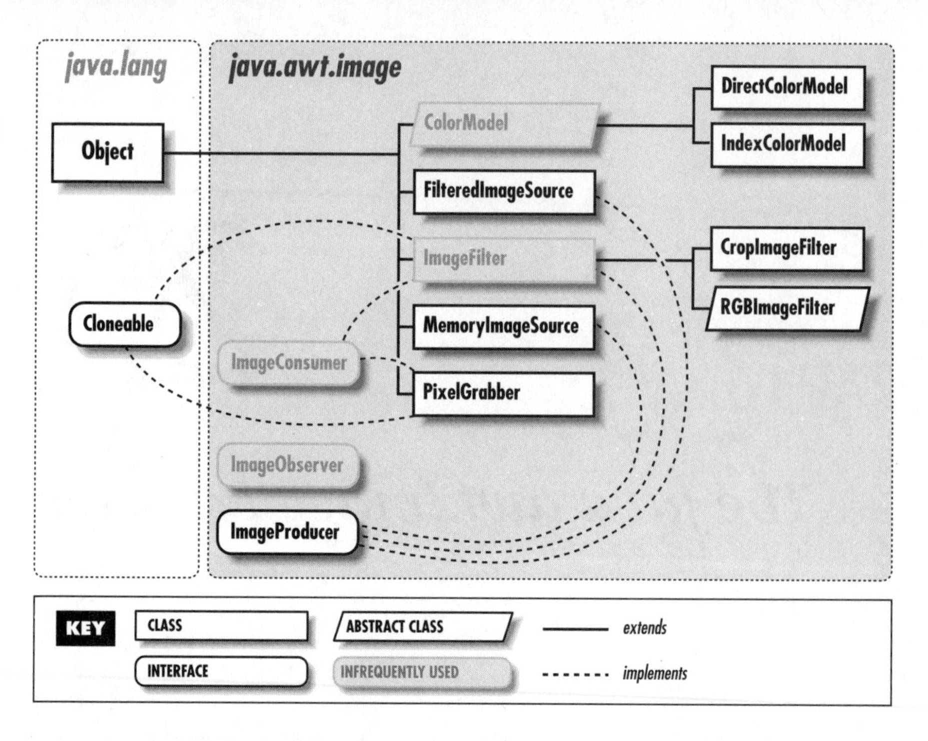

Figure 20-1: The java.awt.image package

`RGBImageFilter` is another subclass of `ImageFilter` that makes it easy to filter the colors of an image. To do so, you must subclass `RGBImageFilter` and provide the definition of a single simple method that manipulates the image colors. In order to manipulate image colors, you will probably need to be familiar with the `ColorModel` class and its two subclasses, `DirectColorModel` and `IndexColorModel`. An instance of `ColorModel` or of one of its subclasses converts a pixel value to the red, green, and blue components of the color it represents.

Finally, two other classes in the `java.awt.image` package are worth noting. `MemoryImageSource` is a type of `ImageProducer` that generates an image from an array of bytes or integers in memory. `PixelGrabber` does the reverse—it captures pixels from an `ImageProducer` and stores them into an array. You can use these classes separately or together to perform your own custom image manipulation.

See Section 8, *Advanced Graphics and Images*, for some examples of image manipulation.

java.awt.image.ColorModel

This abstract class defines a color model—i.e., a scheme for representing a color. Subclasses implement the methods of this interface to convert their particular representation of a pixel value into the default RGB color model. The static method `getRGBDefault()` returns a `ColorModel` object that implements the default color model—RGB plus alpha transparency. You generally never need to call the instance methods of a `ColorModel`—they are called internally by other image manipulation classes.

See also `DirectColorModel`, and `IndexColorModel`.

```
public abstract class ColorModel extends Object {
    // Public Constructor
        public ColorModel(int bits);
    // Protected Instance Variables
        protected int pixel_bits;
    // Class Methods
        public static ColorModel getRGBdefault();
    // Public Instance Methods
        public abstract int getAlpha(int pixel);
        public abstract int getBlue(int pixel);
        public abstract int getGreen(int pixel);
        public int getPixelSize();
        public int getRGB(int pixel);
        public abstract int getRed(int pixel);
}
```

java.awt.image.CropImageFilter

This class implements an `ImageFilter` that crops an image to a specified rectangle. The methods defined by this class are used for communication between the filter and its `FilteredImageSource`, and should never be called directly.

```
public class CropImageFilter extends ImageFilter {
    // Public Constructor
        public CropImageFilter(int x, int y, int w, int h);
    // Public Instance Methods
        public void setDimensions(int w, int h); // Overrides ImageFilter.setDimensions()
        public void setPixels(int x, int y, int w, int h, ColorModel model, byte[] pixels, int off, int scansize);
                        // Overrides ImageFilter.setPixels()
        public void setPixels(int x, int y, int w, int h, ColorModel model, int[] pixels, int off, int scansize);
                        // Overrides ImageFilter.setPixels()
        public void setProperties(Hashtable props); // Overrides ImageFilter.setProperties()
}
```


java.awt.image.DirectColorModel

This class is a `ColorModel` that extracts the red, green, blue, and alpha values directly from the bits of the pixel. The arguments to the constructor methods specify the number of significant bits in the pixel and the mask used to extract each of the color components from the pixel. The default RGB color model is a `DirectColor-Model`.

→

You should not need to instantiate any kind of `ColorModel` object unless you are processing image data, and that data does not use the standard RGB color format.

```
public class DirectColorModel extends ColorModel {
    // Public Constructors
        public DirectColorModel(int bits, int rmask, int gmask, int bmask);
        public DirectColorModel(int bits, int rmask, int gmask, int bmask, int amask);
    // Public Instance Methods
        public final int getAlpha(int pixel);  // Defines ColorModel.getAlpha()
        public final int getAlphaMask();
        public final int getBlue(int pixel);  // Defines ColorModel.getBlue()
        public final int getBlueMask();
        public final int getGreen(int pixel);  // Defines ColorModel.getGreen()
        public final int getGreenMask();
        public final int getRGB(int pixel);  // Overrides ColorModel.getRGB()
        public final int getRed(int pixel);  // Defines ColorModel.getRed()
        public final int getRedMask();
}
```

java.awt.image.FilteredImageSource

This class is an `ImageProducer` that produces image data filtered from some other `ImageProducer`. A `FilteredImageSource` is created with a specified `ImageProducer` and a specified `ImageFilter`. For example, an applet might use the following code to download and crop an image:

```
Image full_image = getImage(getDocumentBase(), "images/1.gif");
ImageFilter cropper = new CropImageFilter(10, 10, 100, 100);
ImageProducer prod = new FilteredImageSource(full_image.getSource(), cropper);
Image cropped_image = createImage(prod);
```

The methods of this class are the standard `ImageProducer` methods that you can invoke to add and remove `ImageConsumer` objects.

```
public class FilteredImageSource extends Object implements ImageProducer {
    // Public Constructor
        public FilteredImageSource(ImageProducer orig, ImageFilter imgf);
    // Public Instance Methods
        public synchronized void addConsumer(ImageConsumer ic);
        public synchronized boolean isConsumer(ImageConsumer ic);
        public synchronized void removeConsumer(ImageConsumer ic);
        public void requestTopDownLeftRightResend(ImageConsumer ic);
        public void startProduction(ImageConsumer ic);
}
```

java.awt.image.ImageConsumer

This interface defines the methods necessary for a class that consumes image data to communicate with a class that produces image data. The methods defined by this interface should never be called by a program directly; instead, they are invoked by an ImageProducer to pass the image data and other information about the image to the ImageConsumer. The constants defined by this interface are values passed to the setHints() and imageComplete() methods.

Unless you want to do low-level manipulation of image data, you never need to use or implement an ImageConsumer.

```
public abstract interface ImageConsumer {
    // Constants
        public final static int COMPLETESCANLINES;
        public final static int IMAGEABORTED;
        public final static int IMAGEERROR;
        public final static int RANDOMPIXELORDER;
        public final static int SINGLEFRAME;
        public final static int SINGLEFRAMEDONE;
        public final static int SINGLEPASS;
        public final static int STATICIMAGEDONE;
        public final static int TOPDOWNLEFTRIGHT;
    // Public Instance Methods
        public abstract void imageComplete(int status);
        public abstract void setColorModel(ColorModel model);
        public abstract void setDimensions(int width, int height);
        public abstract void setHints(int hintflags);
        public abstract void setPixels(int x, int y, int w, int h, ColorModel model, byte[] pixels, int off, int scansize);
        public abstract void setPixels(int x, int y, int w, int h, ColorModel model, int[] pixels, int off, int scansize);
        public abstract void setProperties(Hashtable props);
}
```

java.awt.image.ImageFilter

This class is used in conjunction with a FilteredImageSource. It accepts image data through the ImageConsumer interface and passes it on to an ImageConsumer specified by the controlling FilteredImageSource. ImageFilter is the superclass of all image filters, and performs no filtering itself. You must subclass it to perform the desired filtering. See CropImageFilter and RGBImageFilter. The ImageFilter methods are the ImageConsumer methods invoked by an ImageProducer. You should not call them directly.

See FilteredImageSource for an example of using an ImageFilter.

```
public class ImageFilter extends Object implements ImageConsumer, Cloneable {
    // Public Constructor
        public ImageFilter(); // Empty
    // Protected Instance Variables
        protected ImageConsumer consumer;
    // Public Instance Methods
        public Object clone(); // Overrides Object.clone()
        public ImageFilter getFilterInstance(ImageConsumer ic);
        public void imageComplete(int status);
        public void resendTopDownLeftRight(ImageProducer ip);
        public void setColorModel(ColorModel model);
        public void setDimensions(int width, int height);
```

→

```
        public void setHints(int hints);
        public void setPixels(int x, int y, int w, int h, ColorModel model, byte[] pixels, int off, int scansize);
        public void setPixels(int x, int y, int w, int h, ColorModel model, int[] pixels, int off, int scansize);
        public void setProperties(Hashtable props);
}
```

java.awt.image.ImageObserver

This interface defines a method and associated constants used by classes that want to receive information asynchronously about the status of an image. Many methods that query information about an image take an `ImageObserver` as an argument. If the specified information is not available when requested, it is passed to the `ImageObserver` (by invoking the `imageUpdate()` method) when it becomes available.

Most applications will never need to use or implement this interface.

```
public abstract interface ImageObserver {
    // Constants
        public final static int ABORT;
        public final static int ALLBITS;
        public final static int ERROR;
        public final static int FRAMEBITS;
        public final static int HEIGHT;
        public final static int PROPERTIES;
        public final static int SOMEBITS;
        public final static int WIDTH;
    // Public Instance Methods
        public abstract boolean imageUpdate(Image img, int infoflags, int x, int y, int width, int height);
}
```

java.awt.image.ImageProducer

This interface defines the methods that any class that produces image data must define to enable communication with `ImageConsumer` classes. An `ImageConsumer` registers itself as interested in a producer's image by calling the `addConsumer()` method.

Most applications will never need to use or implement this interface.

```
public abstract interface ImageProducer {
    // Public Instance Methods
        public abstract void addConsumer(ImageConsumer ic);
        public abstract boolean isConsumer(ImageConsumer ic);
        public abstract void removeConsumer(ImageConsumer ic);
        public abstract void requestTopDownLeftRightResend(ImageConsumer ic);
        public abstract void startProduction(ImageConsumer ic);
}
```

java.awt.image.IndexColorModel

This class is a ColorModel that determines the red, green, blue, and alpha values for a pixel by using the pixel value as an index into colormap arrays. If no array of alpha values is specified, then all pixels are considered fully opaque, except for one optionally specified reserved value that is fully transparent. This color model is useful when working with image data that is defined in terms of a color map.

You should not need to instantiate any kind of ColorModel object unless you are processing image data, and that data does not use the standard RGB color format.

```
public class IndexColorModel extends ColorModel {
    // Public Constructors
        public IndexColorModel(int bits, int size, byte[] r, byte[] g, byte[] b);
        public IndexColorModel(int bits, int size, byte[] r, byte[] g, byte[] b, int trans);
        public IndexColorModel(int bits, int size, byte[] r, byte[] g, byte[] b, byte[] a);
        public IndexColorModel(int bits, int size, byte[] cmap, int start, boolean hasalpha);
        public IndexColorModel(int bits, int size, byte[] cmap, int start, boolean hasalpha, int trans);
    // Public Instance Methods
        public final int getAlpha(int pixel);  // Defines ColorModel.getAlpha()
        public final void getAlphas(byte[] a);
        public final int getBlue(int pixel);  // Defines ColorModel.getBlue()
        public final void getBlues(byte[] b);
        public final int getGreen(int pixel);  // Defines ColorModel.getGreen()
        public final void getGreens(byte[] g);
        public final int getMapSize();
        public final int getRGB(int pixel);  // Overrides ColorModel.getRGB()
        public final int getRed(int pixel);  // Defines ColorModel.getRed()
        public final void getReds(byte[] r);
        public final int getTransparentPixel();

}
```

java.awt.image.MemoryImageSource

This class is an ImageProducer that produces an image from data stored in memory. The various constructors specify image data, color model, array offset, scan line length, and properties in slightly different ways. The instance methods implement the standard ImageProducer interface that allows an ImageConsumer object to register interest in the image.

```
public class MemoryImageSource extends Object implements ImageProducer {
    // Public Constructors
        public MemoryImageSource(int w, int h, ColorModel cm, byte[] pix, int off, int scan);
        public MemoryImageSource(int w, int h, ColorModel cm, byte[] pix, int off, int scan, Hashtable props);
        public MemoryImageSource(int w, int h, ColorModel cm, int[] pix, int off, int scan);
        public MemoryImageSource(int w, int h, ColorModel cm, int[] pix, int off, int scan, Hashtable props);
        public MemoryImageSource(int w, int h, int[] pix, int off, int scan);
        public MemoryImageSource(int w, int h, int[] pix, int off, int scan, Hashtable props);
    // Public Instance Methods
        public synchronized void addConsumer(ImageConsumer ic);
```

→

```
        public synchronized boolean isConsumer(ImageConsumer ic);
        public synchronized void removeConsumer(ImageConsumer ic);
        public void requestTopDownLeftRightResend(ImageConsumer ic); // Empty
        public void startProduction(ImageConsumer ic);
}
```

java.awt.image.PixelGrabber

This class is an `ImageConsumer` that extracts a specified rectangular array of pixels (in the default RGB color model) from a specified `Image` or `ImageProducer` and stores them into a specified array (using the specified offset into the array and specified scanline size). You would use this class when you wanted to inspect or manipulate the data of an image or some rectangular portion of an image.

The method `grabPixels()` makes the `PixelGrabber` start grabbing pixels. `status()` returns the status of the pixel-grabbing process. The return value uses the same flag value constants as the `ImageObserver` class does. The remaining methods are the standard `ImageConsumer` methods and should not be called directly.

```
public class PixelGrabber extends Object implements ImageConsumer {
    // Public Constructors
        public PixelGrabber(Image img, int x, int y, int w, int h, int[] pix, int off, int scansize);
        public PixelGrabber(ImageProducer ip, int x, int y, int w, int h, int[] pix, int off, int scansize);
    // Public Instance Methods
        public boolean grabPixels() throws InterruptedException;
        public synchronized boolean grabPixels(long ms) throws InterruptedException;
        public synchronized void imageComplete(int status);
        public void setColorModel(ColorModel model);
        public void setDimensions(int width, int height);
        public void setHints(int hints);
        public void setPixels(int srcX, int srcY, int srcW, int srcH, ColorModel model,
                              byte[] pixels, int srcOff, int srcScan);
        public void setPixels(int srcX, int srcY, int srcW, int srcH, ColorModel model,
                              int[] pixels, int srcOff, int srcScan);
        public void setProperties(Hashtable props);
        public synchronized int status();
}
```

java.awt.image.RGBImageFilter

This abstract class is an `ImageFilter` that provides an easy way to implement filters that modify the colors of an image. To create a color filter that modifies the colors of an image, you should subclass `RGBImageFilter` and provide a definition of `filterRGB()` that converts the input pixel value (in the default RGB color model) to an output value. If the conversion does not depend on the location of the pixel, set the `canFilterIndexColorModel` variable to `true` so that the

`RGBImageFilter` can save time by filtering the colormap of an image that uses an `IndexColorModel` instead of filtering each pixel of the image.

```
public abstract class RGBImageFilter extends ImageFilter {
    // Default Constructor: public RGBImageFilter()
    // Protected Instance Variables
        protected boolean canFilterIndexColorModel;
        protected ColorModel newmodel;
        protected ColorModel origmodel;
    // Public Instance Methods
        public IndexColorModel filterIndexColorModel(IndexColorModel icm);
        public abstract int filterRGB(int x, int y, int rgb);
        public void filterRGBPixels(int x, int y, int w, int h, int[] pixels, int off, int scansize);
        public void setColorModel(ColorModel model);  // Overrides ImageFilter.setColorModel()
        public void setPixels(int x, int y, int w, int h, ColorModel model, byte[] pixels, int off, int scansize);
                        // Overrides ImageFilter.setPixels()
        public void setPixels(int x, int y, int w, int h, ColorModel model, int[] pixels, int off, int scansize);
                        // Overrides ImageFilter.setPixels()
        public void substituteColorModel(ColorModel oldcm, ColorModel newcm);
}
```

The java.awt.peer Package

The `java.awt.peer` package consists entirely of interface definitions. The hierarchy of these interfaces is shown in Figure 21-1. Each `java.awt.peer` interface corresponds to one of the `java.awt Component` or `MenuComponent` classes, and as you can see from the figure, the hierarchy of this package is identical to the hierarchy of those portions of the `java.awt` package.

The interfaces in this package define the methods that must be supported by the GUI components on a specific platform. Porting the `java.awt` GUI components to a new platform is a matter of implementing each of the methods in each of the interfaces in this package on top of the native GUI components of that platform. The `Toolkit` object in the `java.awt` package collects the implementations of these peer interfaces for a given platform. `Toolkit` contains methods that create instances of each of the interfaces in this package. Normal applications never need to instantiate these peers directly; instead they use the `java.awt Component` classes, which create peers as needed.

Because these peer interfaces are rarely used, and because the methods are quite similar to those of the corresponding `java.awt` component, there is no additional commentary for the individual interface definitions below.

java.awt.peer

java.awt.peer.ButtonPeer

```
public abstract interface ButtonPeer extends ComponentPeer {
    // Public Instance Methods
        public abstract void setLabel(String label);
}
```

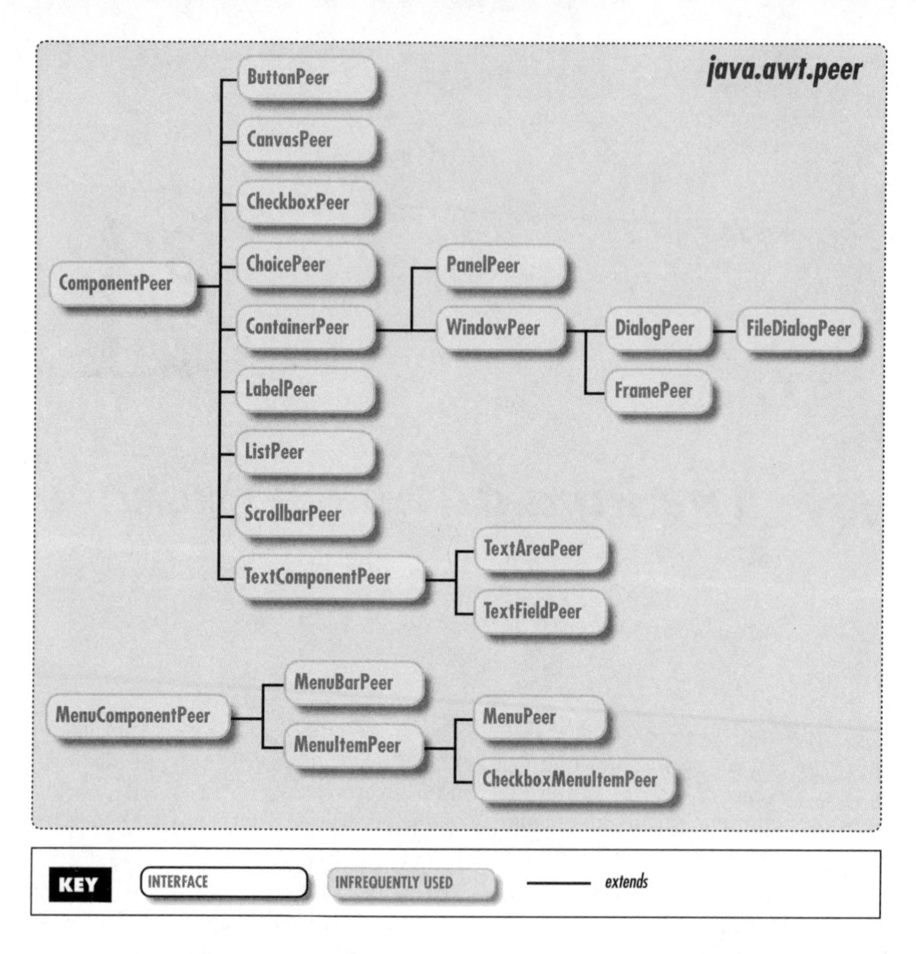

Figure 21-1: The java.awt.peer package

java.awt.peer.CanvasPeer

```
public interface CanvasPeer extends ComponentPeer {
}
```

java.awt.peer.CheckboxMenuItemPeer

```
public abstract interface CheckboxMenuItemPeer extends MenuItemPeer {
    // Public Instance Methods
        public abstract void setState(boolean t);
}
```

java.awt.peer.CheckboxPeer

```
public abstract interface CheckboxPeer extends ComponentPeer {
    // Public Instance Methods
        public abstract void setCheckboxGroup(CheckboxGroup g);
        public abstract void setLabel(String label);
        public abstract void setState(boolean state);
}
```

java.awt.peer.ChoicePeer

```
public abstract interface ChoicePeer extends ComponentPeer {
    // Public Instance Methods
        public abstract void addItem(String item, int index);
        public abstract void select(int index);
}
```

java.awt.peer.ComponentPeer

```
public abstract interface ComponentPeer {
    // Public Instance Methods
        public abstract int checkImage(Image img, int w, int h, ImageObserver o);
        public abstract Image createImage(ImageProducer producer);
        public abstract Image createImage(int width, int height);
        public abstract void disable();
        public abstract void dispose();
        public abstract void enable();
        public abstract ColorModel getColorModel();
        public abstract FontMetrics getFontMetrics(Font font);
        public abstract Graphics getGraphics();
        public abstract Toolkit getToolkit();
        public abstract boolean handleEvent(Event e);
        public abstract void hide();
        public abstract Dimension minimumSize();
        public abstract void nextFocus();
        public abstract void paint(Graphics g);
        public abstract Dimension preferredSize();
        public abstract boolean prepareImage(Image img, int w, int h, ImageObserver o);
        public abstract void print(Graphics g);
        public abstract void repaint(long tm, int x, int y, int width, int height);
        public abstract void requestFocus();
        public abstract void reshape(int x, int y, int width, int height);
        public abstract void setBackground(Color c);
        public abstract void setFont(Font f);
```

→

```
        public abstract void setForeground(Color c);
        public abstract void show();
}
```

java.awt.peer.ContainerPeer

```
public abstract interface ContainerPeer extends ComponentPeer {
    // Public Instance Methods
        public abstract Insets insets();
}
```

java.awt.peer.DialogPeer

```
public abstract interface DialogPeer extends WindowPeer {
    // Public Instance Methods
        public abstract void setResizable(boolean resizable);
        public abstract void setTitle(String title);
}
```

java.awt.peer.FileDialogPeer

```
public abstract interface FileDialogPeer extends DialogPeer {
    // Public Instance Methods
        public abstract void setDirectory(String dir);
        public abstract void setFile(String file);
        public abstract void setFilenameFilter(FilenameFilter filter);
}
```

java.awt.peer.FramePeer

```
public abstract interface FramePeer extends WindowPeer {
    // Public Instance Methods
        public abstract void setCursor(int cursorType);
        public abstract void setIconImage(Image im);
        public abstract void setMenuBar(MenuBar mb);
        public abstract void setResizable(boolean resizeable);
        public abstract void setTitle(String title);
}
```

java.awt.peer.LabelPeer

```
public abstract interface LabelPeer extends ComponentPeer {
    // Public Instance Methods
        public abstract void setAlignment(int alignment);
        public abstract void setText(String label);
}
```

java.awt.peer.ListPeer

```
public abstract interface ListPeer extends ComponentPeer {
    // Public Instance Methods
        public abstract void addItem(String item, int index);
        public abstract void clear();
        public abstract void delItems(int start, int end);
        public abstract void deselect(int index);
        public abstract int[] getSelectedIndexes();
        public abstract void makeVisible(int index);
        public abstract Dimension minimumSize(int v);
        public abstract Dimension preferredSize(int v);
        public abstract void select(int index);
        public abstract void setMultipleSelections(boolean v);
}
```

java.awt.peer.MenuBarPeer

```
public abstract interface MenuBarPeer extends MenuComponentPeer {
    // Public Instance Methods
        public abstract void addHelpMenu(Menu m);
        public abstract void addMenu(Menu m);
        public abstract void delMenu(int index);
}
```

java.awt.peer.MenuComponentPeer

```
public abstract interface MenuComponentPeer {
    // Public Instance Methods
        public abstract void dispose();
}
```

java.awt.peer.MenuItemPeer

```
public abstract interface MenuItemPeer extends MenuComponentPeer {
    // Public Instance Methods
        public abstract void disable();
        public abstract void enable();
        public abstract void setLabel(String label);
}
```

java.awt.peer.MenuPeer

```
public abstract interface MenuPeer extends MenuItemPeer {
    // Public Instance Methods
        public abstract void addItem(MenuItem item);
        public abstract void addSeparator();
        public abstract void delItem(int index);
}
```

java.awt.peer.PanelPeer

```
public interface PanelPeer extends ContainerPeer {
}
```

java.awt.peer.ScrollbarPeer

```
public abstract interface ScrollbarPeer extends ComponentPeer {
    // Public Instance Methods
        public abstract void setLineIncrement(int l);
        public abstract void setPageIncrement(int l);
        public abstract void setValue(int value);
        public abstract void setValues(int value, int visible, int minimum, int maximum);
}
```

java.awt.peer.TextAreaPeer

```
public abstract interface TextAreaPeer extends TextComponentPeer {
    // Public Instance Methods
        public abstract void insertText(String txt, int pos);
        public abstract Dimension minimumSize(int rows, int cols);
```

```
        public abstract Dimension preferredSize(int rows, int cols);
        public abstract void replaceText(String txt, int start, int end);
}
```

java.awt.peer.TextComponentPeer

```
public abstract interface TextComponentPeer extends ComponentPeer {
    // Public Instance Methods
        public abstract int getSelectionEnd();
        public abstract int getSelectionStart();
        public abstract String getText();
        public abstract void select(int selStart, int selEnd);
        public abstract void setEditable(boolean editable);
        public abstract void setText(String l);
}
```

java.awt.peer.TextFieldPeer

```
public abstract interface TextFieldPeer extends TextComponentPeer {
    // Public Instance Methods
        public abstract Dimension minimumSize(int cols);
        public abstract Dimension preferredSize(int cols);
        public abstract void setEchoCharacter(char c);
}
```

java.awt.peer.WindowPeer

```
public abstract interface WindowPeer extends ContainerPeer {
    // Public Instance Methods
        public abstract void toBack();
        public abstract void toFront();
}
```

The java.io Package

The java.io package contains a relatively large number of classes, but, as you can see from Figure 22-1, the classes form a fairly structured hierarchy—most of them are subclasses of InputStream or OutputStream. Each of these stream types has a very specific purpose, and despite its size, java.io is a straightforward package to understand and to use.

Before we consider the stream classes in the package, we'll consider the important non-stream classes. File represents a file or directory name in a system independent way, and provides methods for listing directories, querying file attributes, and for renaming and deleting files. FilenameFilter is an interface that defines a method that accepts or rejects specified filenames. It is used by the java.awt.FileDialog dialog box and by the File class to specify what types of files should be included in directory listings. RandomAccessFile allows you to read or write from or to arbitrary locations of a file. Often, though, you'll prefer sequential access to a file and should use one of the stream classes.

InputStream and OutputStream are abstract classes that define methods for reading and writing data. Their subclasses allow data to be read from and written to a variety of sources and sinks. FileInputStream and FileOutputStream read from and write to files. ByteArrayInputStream and ByteArrayOutputStream read from and write to an array of bytes in memory. Similarly, StringBufferInputStream reads data from a StringBuffer object. PipedInputStream reads data from a PipedOutputStream, and PipedOutputStream writes data to a PipedInputStream. These classes work together to implement a "pipe" for communication between threads.

FilterInputStream and FilterOutputStream are special—they filter input and output data. When a FilterInputStream is created, an InputStream is specified for it to filter. When you call the read() method of a FilterInputStream, it calls the read() method of its specified stream, processes the data it reads somehow, and then returns it. Similarly, you specify an OutputStream to be

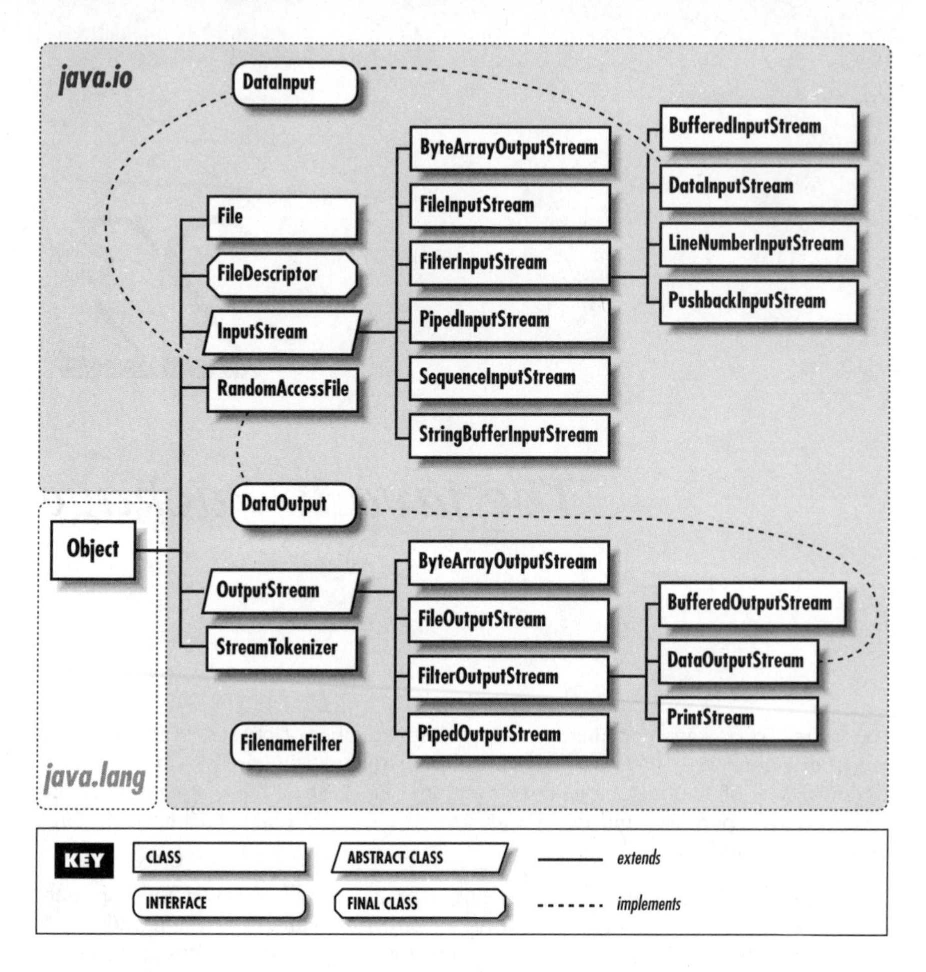

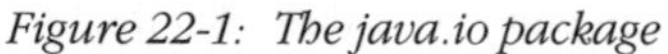

Figure 22-1: The java.io package

filtered when you create a `FilterOutputStream`. Calling the `write()` method of a `FilterOutputStream` causes it to process your data in some way and then pass that processed data to the `write()` method of its `OutputStream`.

`FilterInputStream` and `FilterOutputStream` do not perform any filtering themselves; this is done by their subclasses. `BufferedInputStream` and `BufferedOutputStream` provide input and output buffering and can increase I/O efficiency. `DataInputStream` reads raw bytes from a stream and interprets them in various formats. It has methods to read lines of text, and various methods to read Java primitive data types in their standard binary formats. This is probably the most commonly used input stream class. `DataOutputStream` allows you to write Java primitive data types in binary format. It isn't as commonly used as the `PrintStream`, however, which allows you to write lines of text and Java primitive data types in textual format.

One final note about filtered input and output streams is that they can be combined to any length. For example, you could connect a `FileInputStream` to a `BufferedInputStream` to provide buffering, and then connect the resulting stream to a `DataInputStream` so that you can easily read lines of text from it.

See Section 6, *Input and Output*, for some examples of input and output using the classes in `java.io`.

java.io.BufferedInputStream

This class is a `FilterInputStream` that provides input data buffering—efficiency is increased by reading in large amounts of data and storing them in an internal buffer. When data is requested, it is usually available from the buffer. Thus, most calls to read data do not have to make a (slow) call to actually read data from a disk. Create a `BufferedInputStream` by specifying the `InputStream` that is to have buffering applied in the call to the constructor.

```
public class BufferedInputStream extends FilterInputStream {
    // Public Constructors
        public BufferedInputStream(InputStream in);
        public BufferedInputStream(InputStream in, int size);
    // Protected Instance Variables
        protected byte[] buf;
        protected int count;
        protected int marklimit;
        protected int markpos;
        protected int pos;
    // Public Instance Methods
        public synchronized int available() throws IOException; // Overrides FilterInputStream.available()
        public synchronized void mark(int readlimit); // Overrides FilterInputStream.mark()
        public boolean markSupported(); // Overrides FilterInputStream.markSupported()
        public synchronized int read() throws IOException; // Overrides FilterInputStream.read()
        public synchronized int read(byte[] b, int off, int len) throws IOException;
                                        // Overrides FilterInputStream.read()
        public synchronized void reset() throws IOException; // Overrides FilterInputStream.reset()
        public synchronized long skip(long n) throws IOException; // Overrides FilterInputStream.skip()
}
```

java.io.BufferedOutputStream

This class is a `FilterOutputStream` that provides output data buffering—output efficiency is increased by storing values to be written in a buffer and actually writing them out only when the buffer fills up or when the `flush()` method is called. Create a `BufferedOutputStream` by specifying the `OutputStream` that is to have buffering applied in the call to the constructor.

```
public class BufferedOutputStream extends FilterOutputStream {
    // Public Constructors
        public BufferedOutputStream(OutputStream out);
        public BufferedOutputStream(OutputStream out, int size);
    // Protected Instance Variables
        protected byte[] buf;
        protected int count;
    // Public Instance Methods
        public synchronized void flush() throws IOException; // Overrides FilterOutputStream.flush()
```

→

```
    public synchronized void write(int b) throws IOException;  // OverridesFilterOutputStream.write()
    public synchronized void write(byte[]b, int off, int len) throws IOException;
                                          // Overrides FilterOutputStream.write()
}
```

---

java.io.ByteArrayInputStream

This class is a subclass of `InputStream` in which input data comes from a specified array of `byte` values. This is useful when you want to read data in memory as if it were coming from a file or pipe or socket. This class is much like `StringBuffer-InputStream`.

```
public class ByteArrayInputStream extends InputStream {
    // Public Constructors
        public ByteArrayInputStream(byte[] buf);
        public ByteArrayInputStream(byte[] buf, int offset, int length);
    // Protected Instance Variables
        protected byte[] buf;
        protected int count;
        protected int pos;
    // Public Instance Methods
        public synchronized int available();  // Overrides InputStream.available()
        public synchronized int read();  // Defines InputStream.read()
        public synchronized int read(byte[] b, int off, int len);  // Overrides InputStream.read()
        public synchronized void reset();  // Overrides InputStream.reset()
        public synchronized long skip(long n);  // Overrides InputStream.skip()
}
```

---

java.io.ByteArrayOutputStream

This class is a subclass of `OutputStream` in which data that is written is stored in an internal `byte` array. The internal array grows as necessary, and can be retrieved with `toByteArray()` or `toString()`. The `reset()` method discards any data currently stored in the internal array and begins storing data from the beginning again.

```
public class ByteArrayOutputStream extends OutputStream {
    // Public Constructors
        public ByteArrayOutputStream();
        public ByteArrayOutputStream(int size);
    // Protected Instance Variables
        protected byte[] buf;
        protected int count;
    // Public Instance Methods
        public synchronized void reset();
        public int size();
        public synchronized byte[] toByteArray();
```

```
        public String toString(); // Overrides Object.toString()
        public String toString(int hibyte);
        public synchronized void write(int b); // Defines OutputStream.write()
        public synchronized void write(byte[] b, int off, int len); // Overrides OutputStream.write()
        public synchronized void writeTo(OutputStream out) throws IOException;
}
```

java.io.DataInput

This interface defines the methods required for streams that can read character data or Java primitive data types in a machine-independent format. It is implemented by `DataInputStream` and `RandomAccessFile`. See `DataInputStream` for more information on the methods.

```
public abstract interface DataInput {
    // Public Instance Methods
        public abstract boolean readBoolean() throws IOException, EOFException;
        public abstract byte readByte() throws IOException, EOFException;
        public abstract char readChar() throws IOException, EOFException;
        public abstract double readDouble() throws IOException, EOFException;
        public abstract float readFloat() throws IOException, EOFException;
        public abstract void readFully(byte[] b) throws IOException, EOFException;
        public abstract void readFully(byte[] b, int off, int len) throws IOException, EOFException;
        public abstract int readInt() throws IOException, EOFException;
        public abstract String readLine() throws IOException;
        public abstract long readLong() throws IOException, EOFException;
        public abstract short readShort() throws IOException, EOFException;
        public abstract String readUTF() throws IOException;
        public abstract int readUnsignedByte() throws IOException, EOFException;
        public abstract int readUnsignedShort() throws IOException, EOFException;
        public abstract int skipBytes(int n) throws IOException, EOFException;
}
```

java.io.DataInputStream

This class is a type of `FilterInputStream` that allows you to read lines of text and Java primitive data types in a portable way. This is perhaps the most commonly used class for file input. Create a `DataInputStream` by specifying the `InputStream` that is to be filtered in the call to the constructor.

Many of this class's methods read and return a single Java primitive type, in binary format, from the stream. `readUnsignedByte()` and `readUnsignedShort()` read unsigned values and return them as `int` values, since unsigned `byte` and `short` types are not supported in Java. `read()` reads data into an array of bytes, blocking until at least some data is available. By contrast, `readFully()` reads data into an array of bytes, but blocks until all of the requested data becomes available.

→

`readLine()` reads characters from the stream until it encounters a newline, a carriage return, or a newline carriage return pair. The returned string is not terminated with a newline or carriage return. `readUTF()` reads a string of Unicode text encoded in the UTF-8 "transformation format." UTF-8 is an ASCII-compatible encoding of Unicode characters that is often used for the transmission and storage of Unicode text. The static version of the `readUTF()` method can be used to read a UTF-8 encoded string from any `InputStream` class. Finally, `skipBytes()` blocks until the specified number of bytes have been read and discarded.

```
public class DataInputStream extends FilterInputStream implements DataInput {
    // Public Constructor
        public DataInputStream(InputStream in);
    // Class Methods
        public final static String readUTF(DataInput in) throws IOException;
    // Public Instance Methods
        public final int read(byte[] b) throws IOException; // Overrides FilterInputStream.read()
        public final int read(byte[] b, int off, int len) throws IOException; // Overrides FilterInputStream.read()
        public final boolean readBoolean() throws IOException;
        public final byte readByte() throws IOException;
        public final char readChar() throws IOException;
        public final double readDouble() throws IOException;
        public final float readFloat() throws IOException;
        public final void readFully(byte[] b) throws IOException, EOFException;
        public final void readFully(byte[] b, int off, int len) throws IOException, EOFException;
        public final int readInt() throws IOException;
        public final String readLine() throws IOException;
        public final long readLong() throws IOException;
        public final short readShort() throws IOException;
        public final String readUTF() throws IOException;
        public final int readUnsignedByte() throws IOException;
        public final int readUnsignedShort() throws IOException;
        public final int skipBytes(int n) throws IOException;
}
```

java.io.DataOutput

This interface defines the methods required for streams that can write character data or Java primitive data types in a machine-independent format. It is implemented by `DataOutputStream` and `RandomAccessFile`. See `DataOutputStream` for more information on the methods.

```
public abstract interface DataOutput {
    // Public Instance Methods
        public abstract void write(int b) throws IOException;
        public abstract void write(byte[] b) throws IOException;
        public abstract void write(byte[] b, int off, int len) throws IOException;
        public abstract void writeBoolean(boolean v) throws IOException;
        public abstract void writeByte(int v) throws IOException;
        public abstract void writeBytes(String s) throws IOException;
        public abstract void writeChar(int v) throws IOException;
        public abstract void writeChars(String s) throws IOException;
```

```
        public abstract void writeDouble(double v) throws IOException;
        public abstract void writeFloat(float v) throws IOException;
        public abstract void writeInt(int v) throws IOException;
        public abstract void writeLong(long v) throws IOException;
        public abstract void writeShort(int v) throws IOException;
        public abstract void writeUTF(String str) throws IOException;
}
```

---

java.io.DataOutputStream

This class is a subclass of `FilterOutputStream` that allows you to write Java primitive data types in a portable way. Create a `DataOutputStream` by specifying the `OutputStream` that is to be filtered in the call to the constructor.

Many of this class's methods write a single Java primitive type, in binary format to the output stream. `write()` writes a single byte, an array, or a sub-array of bytes. `writeUTF()` outputs a Java string of Unicode characters using the UTF-8 "transformation format." UTF-8 is an ASCII-compatible encoding of Unicode characters that is often used for the transmission and storage of Unicode text. `flush()` forces any buffered data to be output. `size()` returns the number of bytes written so far. Note that this class does not provide any methods for writing strings. That is done by `PrintOutputStream`. Note also that the primitive Java types written by this class are written in their binary representation, not in an ASCII representation. Again, values may be written in ASCII form with the `PrintOutputStream` class.

```
public class DataOutputStream extends FilterOutputStream implements DataOutput {
    // Public Constructor
        public DataOutputStream(OutputStream out);
    // Protected Instance Variables
        protected int written;
    // Public Instance Methods
        public void flush() throws IOException;  // Overrides FilterOutputStream.flush()
        public final int size();
    // Overrides FilterOutputStream.write()
        public synchronized void write(int b) throws IOException;
    // Overrides FilterOutputStream.write()
        public synchronized void write(byte[] b, int off, int len) throws IOException;
        public final void writeBoolean(boolean v) throws IOException;
        public final void writeByte(int v) throws IOException;
        public final void writeBytes(String s) throws IOException;
        public final void writeChar(int v) throws IOException;
        public final void writeChars(String s) throws IOException;
        public final void writeDouble(double v) throws IOException;
        public final void writeFloat(float v) throws IOException;
        public final void writeInt(int v) throws IOException;
        public final void writeLong(long v) throws IOException;
```

→

java.io

```
        public final void writeShort(int v) throws IOException;
        public final void writeUTF(String str) throws IOException;
}
```

java.io.File

This class provides a platform-independent definition of file and directory names. It also provides methods to list the files in a directory, to check the existence, readability, writeability, type, size, and modification time of files and directories, to make new directories, to rename files and directories, and to delete files and directories. The constants defined by this class are the platform-dependent directory and path separator characters, available as a `String` or `char`.

`getName()` returns the name of the `File` with any directory names omitted. `getPath()` returns the full name of the file, including the directory name. `getParent()` returns the directory of the `File`. If the `File` is an absolute specification, then `getAbsolutePath()` returns the complete filename. Otherwise, if the `File` is a relative file specification, it returns the relative filename appended to the current working directory.

`isAbsolute()` tests whether the `File` is an absolute specification. `exists()`, `canWrite()`, `canRead()`, `isFile()`, and `isDirectory()` perform the obvious tests on the specified `File`. `length()` returns the length of the file. `lastModified()` returns the modification time of the file (which should be used for comparison with other file times only, and not interpreted as any particular time format).

`list()` returns the name of all entries in a directory that are not rejected by an optional `FilenameFilter`. `mkdir()` creates a directory. `mkdirs()` creates all the directories in a `File` specification. `renameTo()` renames a file or directory. `delete()` deletes a file or directory. Note that there is no method to create a file; that is done with a `FileOutputStream`.

```
public class File extends Object {
    // Public Constructors
        public File(String path) throws NullPointerException;
        public File(String path, String name);
        public File(File dir, String name);
    // Constants
        public final static String pathSeparator;
        public final static char pathSeparatorChar;
        public final static String separator;
        public final static char separatorChar;
    // Public Instance Methods
        public boolean canRead();
        public boolean canWrite();
        public boolean delete();
        public boolean equals(Object obj);  // Overrides Object.equals()
        public boolean exists();
```

```
    public String getAbsolutePath();
    public String getName();
    public String getParent();
    public String getPath();
    public int hashCode(); // Overrides Object.hashCode()
    public boolean isAbsolute();
    public boolean isDirectory();
    public boolean isFile();
    public long lastModified();
    public long length();
    public String[] list();
    public String[] list(FilenameFilter filter);
    public boolean mkdir();
    public boolean mkdirs();
    public boolean renameTo(File dest);
    public String toString(); // Overrides Object.toString()
}
```

---

java.io.FileDescriptor

This class is a platform-independent representation of a low-level handle to an open file or an open socket. The static `in`, `out`, and `err` variables are `FileDescriptor` objects that represent the system standard input, output, and error streams, respectively. There is no public constructor method to create a `FileDescriptor` object. You can obtain one with the `getFD()` method of `FileInputStream`, `FileOutputStream`, and `RandomAccessFile`.

```
public final class FileDescriptor extends Object {
    // Default Constructor: public FileDescriptor()
    // Constants
        public final static FileDescriptor err;
        public final static FileDescriptor in;
        public final static FileDescriptor out;
    // Public Instance Methods
        public boolean valid();
}
```

java.io

---

java.io.FileInputStream

This class is a subclass of `InputStream` that reads data from a file specified by name or by a `File` or `FileDescriptor` object. `FileInputStream` provides only a low-level interface to reading data; you would typically use a `DataInputStream` object to filter input from a `FileInputStream` and provide a higher-level interface for reading strings and binary data. Call `close()` to close the file when input is no

→

longer needed. Note that this class has a finalizer method that calls `close()` if necessary.

```
public class FileInputStream extends InputStream {
    // Public Constructors
        public FileInputStream(String name) throws FileNotFoundException, IOException;
        public FileInputStream(File file) throws FileNotFoundException, IOException;
        public FileInputStream(FileDescriptor fdObj);
    // Public Instance Methods
        public int available() throws IOException;  // Overrides InputStream.available()
        public void close() throws IOException;  // Overrides InputStream.close()
        public final FileDescriptor getFD() throws IOException;
        public int read() throws IOException;  // Defines InputStream.read()
        public int read(byte[] b) throws IOException;  // Overrides InputStream.read()
        public int read(byte[] b, int off, int len) throws IOException;  // Overrides InputStream.read()
        public long skip(long n) throws IOException;  // Overrides InputStream.skip()
    // Protected Instance Methods
        protected void finalize() throws IOException;
}
```

---

java.io.FileOutputStream

This class is a subclass of `OutputStream` that writes data to a file specified by name, or by a `File` or `FileDescriptor` object. FileOutputStream provides only a low-level interface to writing data; you would typically use a `DataOutputStream` or `PrintOutputStream` to filter output to a `FileOutputStream` and provide a higher-level interface for writing data. Use `close()` to close a `FileOutputStream` when no further output will be written to it. Note that this class has a finalizer method that will call `close()` if necessary.

```
public class FileOutputStream extends OutputStream {
    // Public Constructors
        public FileOutputStream(String name) throws IOException;
        public FileOutputStream(File file) throws IOException;
        public FileOutputStream(FileDescriptor fdObj);
    // Public Instance Methods
        public void close() throws IOException;  // Overrides OutputStream.close()
        public final FileDescriptor getFD() throws IOException;
        public void write(int b) throws IOException;  // Defines OutputStream.write()
        public void write(byte[] b) throws IOException;  // Overrides OutputStream.write()
        public void write(byte[] b, int off, int len) throws IOException;  // Overrides OutputStream.write()
    // Protected Instance Methods
        protected void finalize() throws IOException;
}
```

---

java.io.FilenameFilter

This interface defines the `accept()` method that must be implemented by any object that filters filenames (i.e., selects a subset of filenames from a list of filenames). There are no standard FilenameFilter classes implemented by Java, but objects that implement this interface are used by the java.awt.FileDialog object, and by the File.list() method. A typical FilenameFilter object might check that the specified File represents a file (not a directory), is readable (and possibly writable as well), and that its name ends with some desired extension.

```
public abstract interface FilenameFilter {
    // Public Instance Methods
        public abstract boolean accept(File dir, String name);
}
```

java.io.FilterInputStream

This class provides method definitions required to filter data obtained from the InputStream specified when the FilterInputStream is created. It must be subclassed to perform some sort of filtering operation, and may not be instantiated directly. See the subclasses BufferedInputStream, DataInputStream, LineNumberInputStream, and PushbackInputStream.

```
public class FilterInputStream extends InputStream {
    // Protected Constructor
        protected FilterInputStream(InputStream in);
    // Protected Instance Variables
        protected InputStream in;
    // Public Instance Methods
        public int available() throws IOException;  // Overrides InputStream.available()
        public void close() throws IOException;  // Overrides InputStream.close()
        public synchronized void mark(int readlimit);  // Overrides InputStream.mark()
        public boolean markSupported();  // Overrides InputStream.markSupported()
        public int read() throws IOException;  // Defines InputStream.read()
        public int read(byte[] b) throws IOException;  // Overrides InputStream.read()
        public int read(byte[] b, int off, int len) throws IOException;  // Overrides InputStream.read()
        public synchronized void reset() throws IOException;  // Overrides InputStream.reset()
        public long skip(long n) throws IOException;  // Overrides InputStream.skip()
}
```

java.io.FilterOutputStream

This class provides method definitions required to filter the data to be written to the OutputStream specified when the FilterOutputStream is created. It must be subclassed to perform some sort of filtering operation and may not be instantiated directly. See the subclasses BufferedOutputStream, DataOutputStream, and PrintStream.

```
public class FilterOutputStream extends OutputStream {
    // Public Constructor
        public FilterOutputStream(OutputStream out);
    // Protected Instance Variables
        protected OutputStream out;
    // Public Instance Methods
```

→

```
        public void close() throws IOException; // Overrides OutputStream.close()
        public void flush() throws IOException; // Overrides OutputStream.flush()
        public void write(int b) throws IOException; // Defines OutputStream.write()
        public void write(byte[] b) throws IOException; // Overrides OutputStream.write()
        public void write(byte[] b, int off, int len) throws IOException; // Overrides OutputStream.write()
}
```

java.io.InputStream

This abstract class is the superclass of all input streams. It defines the basic input methods that all input stream classes provide.

`read()` reads a single byte or an array or subarray of bytes. `skip()` skips a specified number of bytes of input. `available()` returns the number of bytes that can be read without blocking. `close()` closes the input stream and frees up any system resources associated with it. The stream should not be used after `close()` has been called.

If `markSupported()` returns `true` for a given `InputStream`, then that stream supports the `mark()` and `reset()` methods. `mark()` marks the current position in the input stream so that `reset()` can return to that position as long as no more than the specified number of bytes have been read between the `mark()` and `reset()`.

```
public abstract class InputStream extends Object {
    // Public Constructor
        public InputStream(); // Empty
    // Public Instance Methods
        public int available() throws IOException;
        public void close() throws IOException; // Empty
        public synchronized void mark(int readlimit); // Empty
        public boolean markSupported();
        public abstract int read() throws IOException;
        public int read(byte[] b) throws IOException;
        public int read(byte[] b, int off, int len) throws IOException;
        public synchronized void reset() throws IOException;
        public long skip(long n) throws IOException;
}
```

java.io.LineNumberInputStream

This class is a `FilterInputStream` that keeps track of the number of lines of data that have been read. `getLineNumber()` returns the current line number. `setLineNumber()` sets the line number of the current line. Subsequent lines are numbered starting from that number.

```
public class LineNumberInputStream extends FilterInputStream {
    // Public Constructor
        public LineNumberInputStream(InputStream in);
    // Public Instance Methods
        public int available() throws IOException;  // Overrides FilterInputStream.available()
        public int getLineNumber();
        public void mark(int readlimit);  // Overrides FilterInputStream.mark()
        public int read() throws IOException;  // Overrides FilterInputStream.read()
        public int read(byte[] b, int off, int len) throws IOException;  // Overrides FilterInputStream.read()
        public void reset() throws IOException;  // Overrides FilterInputStream.reset()
        public void setLineNumber(int lineNumber);
        public long skip(long n) throws IOException;  // Overrides FilterInputStream.skip()
}
```

java.io.OutputStream

This abstract class is the superclass of all output streams. It defines the basic output methods that all output stream classes provide.

`write()` writes a single byte or an array or subarray of bytes. `flush()` forces any buffered output to be written. `close()` closes the stream and frees up any system resources associated with it. The stream may not be used once `close()` has been called.

```
public abstract class OutputStream extends Object {
    // Public Constructor
        public OutputStream();  // Empty
    // Public Instance Methods
        public void close() throws IOException;  // Empty
        public void flush() throws IOException;  // Empty
        public abstract void write(int b) throws IOException;
        public void write(byte[] b) throws IOException;
        public void write(byte[] b, int off, int len) throws IOException;
}
```

java.io.PipedInputStream

This class is an `InputStream` that implements one-half of a pipe, and is useful for communication between threads. A `PipedInputStream` must be connected to a `PipedOutputStream` object, which may be specified when the `PipedInputStream` is created or with the `connect()` method. Data read from a `PipedInputStream` object is received from the `PipedOutputStream` to which it is connected.

See `InputStream()` for information on the low-level methods for reading data from a `PipedInputStream`. A `FilterInputStream` may be used to provide a higher-level interface for reading data from a `PipedInputStream`.

```
public class PipedInputStream extends InputStream {
    // Public Constructors
        public PipedInputStream(PipedOutputStream src) throws IOException;
```

java.io

→

```
    public PipedInputStream(); // Empty
  // Public Instance Methods
    public void close() throws IOException; // Overrides InputStream.close()
    public void connect(PipedOutputStream src) throws IOException;
    public synchronized int read() throws IOException; // Defines InputStream.read()
    public synchronized int read(byte[] b, int off, int len) throws IOException; // Overrides InputStream.read()
}
```

java.io.PipedOutputStream

This class is an `OutputStream` that implements one half of a pipe, and is useful for communication between threads. A `PipedOutputStream` must be connected to a `PipedInputStream`, which may be specified when the `PipedOutputStream` is created or with the `connect()` method. Data written to the `PipedOutputStream` will be available for reading on the `PipedInputStream`.

See `OutputStream()` for information on the low-level methods for writing data to a `PipedOutputStream`. A `FilterOutputStream` may be used to provide a higher-level interface for writing data to a `PipedOutputStream`.

```
public class PipedOutputStream extends OutputStream {
  // Public Constructors
    public PipedOutputStream(PipedInputStream snk) throws IOException;
    public PipedOutputStream(); // Empty
  // Public Instance Methods
    public void close() throws IOException; // Overrides OutputStream.close()
    public void connect(PipedInputStream snk) throws IOException;
    public void write(int b) throws IOException; // Defines OutputStream.write()
    public void write(byte[] b, int off, int len) throws IOException; // Overrides OutputStream.write()
}
```

java.io.PrintStream

This class is a `FilterOutputStream` that implements a number of methods for displaying textual representation of Java primitive data types. The `print()` methods output a standard textual representation of each data type. The `println()` methods do the same, and follow that representation with a newline. The methods convert various Java primitive types to `String` representations and then output the resulting string. When an `Object` is passed to a `print()` or `println()`, it is converted to a `String` by calling its `toString()` method.

`PrintStream` is the `OutputStream` type that makes it easiest to output text. As such, it is the most commonly used of the output streams. The `System.out` variable is a `PrintStream`.

Note that this class does not handle Unicode—it discards the top 8 bits of all 16-bit Unicode characters, and thus displays only Latin-1 (ISO8859-1) characters.

Note that `PrintStream` outputs textual representations of Java data types, while the `DataOutputStream` outputs binary representations of data.

```
public class PrintStream extends FilterOutputStream {
    // Public Constructors
        public PrintStream(OutputStream out);
        public PrintStream(OutputStream out, boolean autoflush);
    // Public Instance Methods
        public boolean checkError();
        public void close(); // Overrides FilterOutputStream.close()
        public void flush(); // Overrides FilterOutputStream.flush()
        public void print(Object obj);
        public synchronized void print(String s);
        public synchronized void print(char[] s);
        public void print(char c);
        public void print(int i);
        public void print(long l);
        public void print(float f);
        public void print(double d);
        public void print(boolean b);
        public void println();
        public synchronized void println(Object obj);
        public synchronized void println(String s);
        public synchronized void println(char[] s);
        public synchronized void println(char c);
        public synchronized void println(int i);
        public synchronized void println(long l);
        public synchronized void println(float f);
        public synchronized void println(double d);
        public synchronized void println(boolean b);
        public void write(int b) throws IOException; // Overrides FilterOutputStream.write()
        public void write(byte[] b, int off, int len) throws IOException; // Overrides FilterOutputStream.write()
}
```

java.io.PushbackInputStream

This class is a `FilterInputStream` that implements a one-byte push back buffer. The `unread()` method "pushes" one character back into the stream—this character is the first one read by the next call to a `read()` method. This class is sometimes useful when writing parsers.

```
public class PushbackInputStream extends FilterInputStream {
    // Public Constructor
        public PushbackInputStream(InputStream in);
    // Protected Instance Variables
        protected int pushBack;
    // Public Instance Methods
        public int available() throws IOException; // Overrides FilterInputStream.available()
        public boolean markSupported(); // Overrides FilterInputStream.markSupported()
```

→

```
        public int read() throws IOException; // Overrides FilterInputStream.read()
        public int read(byte[] bytes, int offset, int length) throws IOException;
                    // Overrides FilterInputStream.read()
        public void unread(int ch) throws IOException;
}
```

java.io.RandomAccessFile

This class allows reading and writing of arbitrary bytes, text, and primitive Java data types from or to any specified location in a file. Because this class provides random, rather than sequential, access to files it is neither a subclass of `InputStream` nor of `OutputStream`, but provides an entirely independent method for reading and writing data from or to files. `RandomAccessFile` implements the same interfaces as `DataInputStream` and `DataOutputStream`, and thus defines the same methods for reading and writing data as those classes do.

In addition, the `seek()` method provides random access to the file—it is used to select the position in the file from which or to which data should be read or written. The *mode* argument to the constructor methods should be "r" for a file that is to be read-only, and "rw" for a file that is to be written (and perhaps read as well).

```
public class RandomAccessFile extends Object implements DataOutput, DataInput {
    // Public Constructors
        public RandomAccessFile(String name, String mode) throws IOException;
        public RandomAccessFile(File file, String mode) throws IOException;
    // Public Instance Methods
        public void close() throws IOException;
        public final FileDescriptor getFD() throws IOException;
        public long getFilePointer() throws IOException;
        public long length() throws IOException;
        public int read() throws IOException;
        public int read(byte[] b, int off, int len) throws IOException;
        public int read(byte[] b) throws IOException;
        public final boolean readBoolean() throws IOException;
        public final byte readByte() throws IOException;
        public final char readChar() throws IOException;
        public final double readDouble() throws IOException;
        public final float readFloat() throws IOException;
        public final void readFully(byte[] b) throws IOException;
        public final void readFully(byte[] b, int off, int len) throws IOException;
        public final int readInt() throws IOException;
        public final String readLine() throws IOException;
        public final long readLong() throws IOException;
        public final short readShort() throws IOException;
        public final String readUTF() throws IOException;
        public final int readUnsignedByte() throws IOException;
        public final int readUnsignedShort() throws IOException;
        public void seek(long pos) throws IOException;
        public int skipBytes(int n) throws IOException;
```

```
        public void write(int b) throws IOException;
        public void write(byte[] b) throws IOException;
        public void write(byte[] b, int off, int len) throws IOException;
        public final void writeBoolean(boolean v) throws IOException;
        public final void writeByte(int v) throws IOException;
        public final void writeBytes(String s) throws IOException;
        public final void writeChar(int v) throws IOException;
        public final void writeChars(String s) throws IOException;
        public final void writeDouble(double v) throws IOException;
        public final void writeFloat(float v) throws IOException;
        public final void writeInt(int v) throws IOException;
        public final void writeLong(long v) throws IOException;
        public final void writeShort(int v) throws IOException;
        public final void writeUTF(String str) throws IOException;
}
```

java.io.SequenceInputStream

This class provides a way of seamlessly concatenating the data from two or more input streams. It provides an `InputStream` interface to a sequence of `InputStream` objects. Data is read from the streams in the order in which the streams are specified. When the end of one stream is reached, data is automatically read from the next stream. This class might be useful, for example, when implementing an "include file" facility for a parser of some sort.

```
public class SequenceInputStream extends InputStream {
    // Public Constructors
        public SequenceInputStream(Enumeration e);
        public SequenceInputStream(InputStream s1, InputStream s2);
    // Public Instance Methods
        public void close() throws IOException; // Overrides InputStream.close()
        public int read() throws IOException; // Defines InputStream.read()
        public int read(byte[] buf, int pos, int len) throws IOException; // Overrides InputStream.read()
}
```

java.io.StreamTokenizer

This class performs lexical analysis of a specified input stream and breaks the input up into tokens. It can be extremely useful when writing simple parsers.

`nextToken()` returns the next token in the stream—this is either one of the constants defined by the class, (which represent end-of-file, end-of-line, a parsed floating-point number, and a parsed word) or a character value. `pushBack()` "pushes" the token back onto the stream, so that it is returned by the next call to `nextToken()`. The public variables `sval` and `nval` contain the string and numeric values (if applicable) of the most recently read token. They are applicable when the

→

java.io

returned token is TT_WORD and TT_NUMBER. lineno() returns the current line number.

The remaining methods specify flags and characters that control how tokens are recognized. wordChars() specifies a range of characters that should be treated as parts of words. whitespaceChars() specifies a range of characters that serve to delimit tokens. eolIsSignificant() specifies whether end-of-line is significant. If so, the TT_EOL constant is returned for end-of-lines. Otherwise they are treated as whitespace.

ordinaryChars() and ordinaryChar() specify characters that are never part of tokens and should be returned as-is. resetChars() makes all characters "ordinary."

commentChar() specifies a character that begins a comment that lasts until the end of the line. No characters in the comment are returned. slashStarComments() and slashSlashComments() specify whether the StringTokenizer should recognize C and C++-style comments. If so, no part of the comments are returned as tokens.

quoteChar() specifies a character used to delimit strings. When a string token is parsed, the quote character is returned as the token value, and the body of the string is stored in the sval variable.

parseNumbers() specifies that the StringTokenizer should recognize and return double-precision floating-point number tokens.

lowerCaseMode() specifies whether TT_WORD tokens should be converted to all lowercase characters before being stored in sval.

```
public class StreamTokenizer extends Object {
    // Public Constructor
       public StreamTokenizer(InputStream I);
    // Constants
       public final static int TT_EOF;
       public final static int TT_EOL;
       public final static int TT_NUMBER;
       public final static int TT_WORD;
    // Public Instance Variables
       public double nval;
       public String sval;
       public int ttype;
    // Public Instance Methods
       public void commentChar(int ch);
       public void eolIsSignificant(boolean flag);
       public int lineno();
       public void lowerCaseMode(boolean fl);
       public int nextToken() throws IOException;
       public void ordinaryChar(int ch);
       public void ordinaryChars(int low, int hi);
       public void parseNumbers();
       public void pushBack();
       public void quoteChar(int ch);
       public void resetSyntax();
```

```
    public void slashSlashComments(boolean flag);
    public void slashStarComments(boolean flag);
    public String toString(); // Overrides Object.toString()
    public void whitespaceChars(int low, int hi);
    public void wordChars(int low, int hi);
}
```

java.io.StringBufferInputStream

This class is a subclass of `InputStream` in which input data comes from the characters of a specified `String` object. This is useful when you want to read data in memory as if it were coming from a file or pipe or socket. This class is much like `ByteArrayInputStream`.

```
public class StringBufferInputStream extends InputStream {
    // Public Constructor
        public StringBufferInputStream(String s);
    // Protected Instance Variables
        protected String buffer;
        protected int count;
        protected int pos;
    // Public Instance Methods
        public synchronized int available(); // Overrides InputStream.available()
        public synchronized int read(); // Defines InputStream.read()
        public synchronized int read(byte[] b, int off, int len); // Overrides InputStream.read()
        public synchronized void reset(); // Overrides InputStream.reset()
        public synchronized long skip(long n); // Overrides InputStream.skip()
}
```

The java.lang Package

The `java.lang` package contains the classes that are most central to the Java language. As you can see from Figure 23-1, the class hierarchy is broad rather than deep, which means that the classes are independent of each other.

`Object` is the ultimate superclass of all Java classes and is therefore at the top of all class hierarchies. `Class` is a class that describes a Java class. There is one `Class` object for each class that is loaded into Java.

`Boolean`, `Character`, `Double`, `Float`, `Integer`, and `Long` are class wrappers around primitive Java data types. These classes are useful when you need to pass a value by reference, and also contains useful utility methods.

`String` and `StringBuffer` are objects that represent strings. `String` is an immutable type; `StringBuffer` may have its string changed in place.

`Runtime` provides a number of low-level methods associated with the Java runtime system. `System` provides similar low-level system methods. All the `System` methods are class methods, and this class may not be instantiated. `Math` is a similar class that supports only class methods—its methods provide floating-point math support.

`Process` defines a platform-independent interface to processes running externally to the Java interpreter. The `Thread` class provides support for multiple threads of control running within the same Java interpreter.

`Throwable` is the root class of the exception and error hierarchy. `Throwable` objects are used with the Java `throw` and `catch` statements.

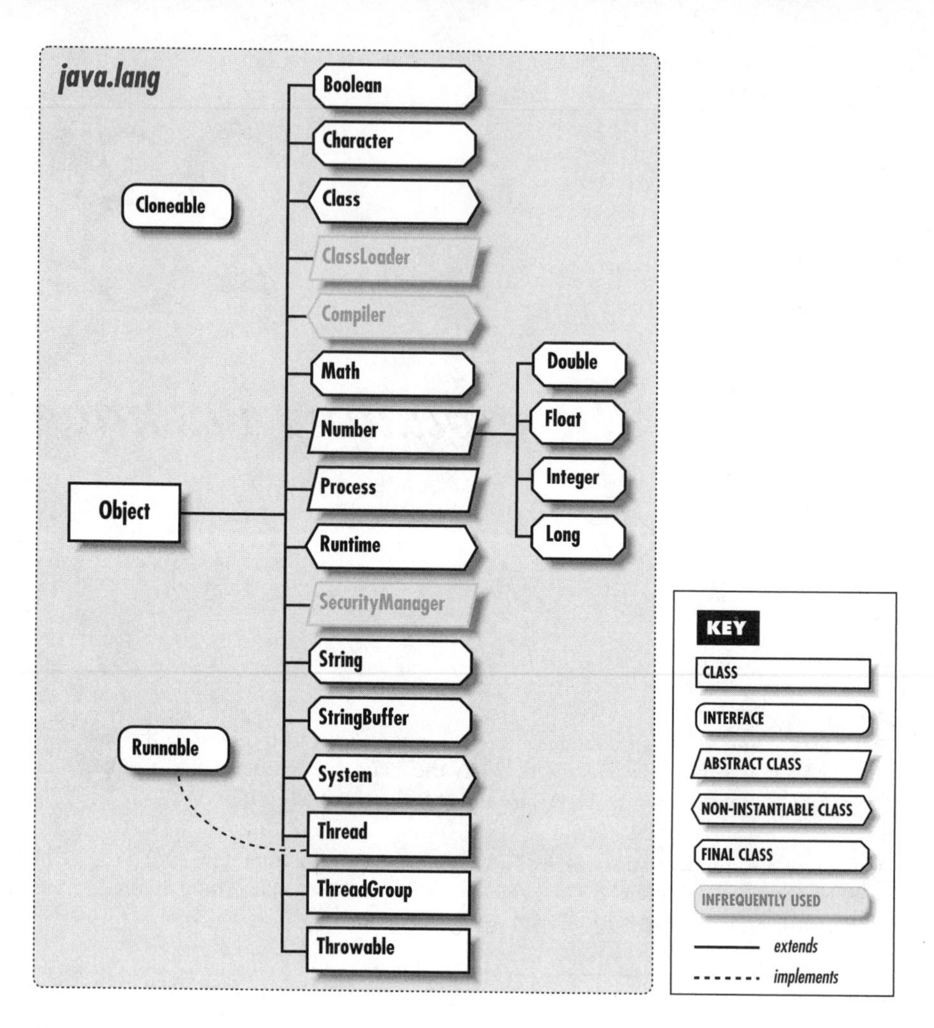

Figure 23-1: The java.lang package

java.lang.Boolean

This class provides an object wrapper around the `boolean` primitive type. It is useful when you need to pass a boolean value by reference. Note the `TRUE` and `FALSE` constants, which are `Boolean` objects; they are not the same as the `true` and `false` `boolean` values.

`booleanValue()` returns the `boolean` value of a `Boolean` object. The class method `getBoolean()` retrieves the `boolean` value of a named property. The class method `valueOf()` parses a string and returns the `Boolean` value it represents.

```
public final class Boolean extends Object {
    // Public Constructors
        public Boolean(boolean value);
        public Boolean(String s);
    // Constants
```

```
    public final static Boolean FALSE;
    public final static Boolean TRUE;
  // Class Methods
    public static boolean getBoolean(String name);
    public static Boolean valueOf(String s);
  // Public Instance Methods
    public boolean booleanValue();
    public boolean equals(Object obj);  // Overrides Object.equals()
    public int hashCode();  // Overrides Object.hashCode()
    public String toString();  // Overrides Object.toString()
}
```

---

java.lang.Character

This class provides an object wrapper around the primitive `char` data type. It is useful when you need to pass a `char` value by reference. `charValue()` returns the `char` value of a `Character` object. A number of class methods provide the Java/Unicode equivalent of the C *<ctype.h>* character macros for checking the type of characters and converting to uppercase and lowercase letters. `digit()` returns the integer equivalent of a given character for a given radix (e.g., radix 16 for hexadecimal). `forDigit()` returns the character that corresponds to the specified value for the specified radix.

```
public final class Character extends Object {
  // Public Constructor
    public Character(char value);
  // Constants
    public final static int MAX_RADIX;
    public final static int MIN_RADIX;
  // Class Methods
    public static int digit(char ch, int radix);
    public static char forDigit(int digit, int radix);
    public static boolean isDigit(char ch);
    public static boolean isLowerCase(char ch);
    public static boolean isSpace(char ch);
    public static boolean isUpperCase(char ch);
    public static char toLowerCase(char ch);
    public static char toUpperCase(char ch);
  // Public Instance Methods
    public char charValue();
    public boolean equals(Object obj);  // Overrides Object.equals()
    public int hashCode();  // Overrides Object.hashCode()
    public String toString();  // Overrides Object.toString()
}
```

java.lang.Class

This class represents a Java class—there is a `Class` object for each class that is loaded into Java. There is no constructor for this class, but the class method `forName()` returns a `Class` object for a named class, or dynamically loads the class, if necessary. Once a class has been loaded, and its `Class` object created, `newInstance()` creates an instance of a given class—this is the only way to create an object in Java without using `new`. These two methods allow the dynamic loading and instantiation of classes in Java.

`getName()` returns the name of the class. `getSuperclass()` returns its superclass. `isInterface()` tests whether the `Class` object represents an interface. `getInterfaces()` returns an array of the interfaces that this class implements.

```
public final class Class extends Object {
    // No Constructor
    // Class Methods
        public static Class forName(String className) throws ClassNotFoundException;
    // Public Instance Methods
        public ClassLoader getClassLoader();
        public Class[] getInterfaces();
        public String getName();
        public Class getSuperclass();
        public boolean isInterface();
        public Object newInstance() throws InstantiationException, IllegalAccessException;
        public String toString(); // Overrides Object.toString()
}
```

java.lang.ClassLoader

This abstract class defines the necessary hook for Java to load classes over the network, or from other sources. Normal applications do not need to use or subclass this class.

```
public abstract class ClassLoader extends Object {
    // Protected Constructor
        protected ClassLoader();
    // Protected Instance Methods
        protected final Class defineClass(byte[] data, int offset, int length) throws ClassFormatError;
        protected final Class findSystemClass(String name) throws ClassNotFoundException, NoClassDefFoundError;
        protected abstract Class loadClass(String name, boolean resolve) throws ClassNotFoundException;
        protected final void resolveClass(Class c);
}
```

java.lang.Cloneable

This interface defines no methods or variables, but indicates that the class that implements it may be cloned (i.e., copied) by calling the `Object` method `clone()`.

Calling `clone()` for an object that does not implement this interface causes a `CloneNotSupportedException` to be thrown.

```
public interface Cloneable {

}
```

---

java.lang.Compiler

The static methods of this class provide an interface to the Java compiler.

```
public final class Compiler extends Object {
    // No Constructor
    // Class Methods
        public static Object command(Object any);
        public static boolean compileClass(Class clazz);
        public static boolean compileClasses(String string);
        public static void disable();
        public static void enable();
}
```

---

java.lang.Double

This class provides an object wrapper around the `double` primitive data type. This is useful when you need to pass a `double` by reference. `valueOf` converts a string to a `Double`, `doubleValue()` returns the primitive `double` value of a `Double` object, and there are other methods for returning a `Double` value as a variety of other primitive types.

This class also provides some useful constants and static methods for testing `double` values. `MIN_VALUE` and `MAX_VALUE` are the smallest (closest to zero) and largest representable `double` values. `isInfinite()` in class method and instance method forms tests whether a `double` or a `Double` has an infinite value. Similarly `isNaN()` tests whether a `double` or `Double` is not-a-number—this is a comparison that cannot be done directly because the `NaN` constant never tests equal to any other value, including itself. `doubleToLongBits()` and `longBitsToDouble()` allow you to manipulate the bit representation of a `double` directly.

```
public final class Double extends Number {
    // Public Constructors
        public Double(double value);
        public Double(String s) throws NumberFormatException;
    // Constants
        public final static double MAX_VALUE;
        public final static double MIN_VALUE;
        public final static double NEGATIVE_INFINITY;
        public final static double NaN;
        public final static double POSITIVE_INFINITY;
    // Class Methods
        public static long doubleToLongBits(double value);
        public static boolean isInfinite(double v);
```

→

```
    public static boolean isNaN(double v);
    public static double longBitsToDouble(long bits);
    public static String toString(double d);
    public static Double valueOf(String s) throws NumberFormatException;
  // Public Instance Methods
    public double doubleValue();  // Defines Number.doubleValue()
    public boolean equals(Object obj);  // Overrides Object.equals()
    public float floatValue();  // Defines Number.floatValue()
    public int hashCode();  // Overrides Object.hashCode()
    public int intValue();  // Defines Number.intValue()
    public boolean isInfinite();
    public boolean isNaN();
    public long longValue();  // Defines Number.longValue()
    public String toString();  // Overrides Object.toString()
}
```

java.lang.Float

This class provides an object wrapper around the `float` primitive data type. This is useful when you need to pass a `float` by reference. `valueOf` converts a string to a `Float`, `floatValue()` returns the primitive `float` value of a `Float` object, and there are methods for returning a `Float` value as a variety of other primitive types.

This class also provides some useful constants and static methods for testing `float` values. `MIN_VALUE` and `MAX_VALUE` are the smallest (closest to zero) and largest representable `double` values. `isInfinite()` in class method and instance method forms tests whether a `float` or a `Float` has an infinite value. Similarly `isNaN()` tests whether a `float` or `Float` is not-a-number—this is a comparison that cannot be done directly because the `NaN` constant never tests equal to any other value, including itself. `floatToIntBits()` and `intBitsToFloat()` allow you to manipulate the bit representation of a `float` directly.

```
public final class Float extends Number {
  // Public Constructors
    public Float(float value);
    public Float(double value);
    public Float(String s) throws NumberFormatException;
  // Constants
    public final static float MAX_VALUE;
    public final static float MIN_VALUE;
    public final static float NEGATIVE_INFINITY;
    public final static float NaN;
    public final static float POSITIVE_INFINITY;
  // Class Methods
    public static int floatToIntBits(float value);
    public static float intBitsToFloat(int bits);
    public static boolean isInfinite(float v);
    public static boolean isNaN(float v);
    public static String toString(float f);
```

```
    public static Float valueOf(String s) throws NumberFormatException;
  // Public Instance Methods
    public double doubleValue(); // Defines Number.doubleValue()
    public boolean equals(Object obj); // Overrides Object.equals()
    public float floatValue(); // Defines Number.floatValue()
    public int hashCode(); // Overrides Object.hashCode()
    public int intValue(); // Defines Number.intValue()
    public boolean isInfinite();
    public boolean isNaN();
    public long longValue(); // Defines Number.longValue()
    public String toString(); // Overrides Object.toString()
}
```

---

java.lang.Integer

This class provides an object wrapper around the `int` primitive data type. It is useful when you need to pass `int` values by reference. This class also contains useful minimum and maximum constants and useful conversion methods. `parseInt()` and `valueOf` convert a string to an `int` or to an `Integer`, respectively. Each can take a radix argument to specify the base that the value is represented in. `toString( )` converts in the other direction and may also take a radix argument. Other routines return the value of an `Integer` as various primitive types, and finally, the `getInteger()` methods return the integer value of a named property or the value of the specified default.

```
public final class Integer extends Number {
  // Public Constructors
    public Integer(int value);
    public Integer(String s) throws NumberFormatException;
  // Constants
    public final static int MAX_VALUE;
    public final static int MIN_VALUE;
  // Class Methods
    public static Integer getInteger(String nm);
    public static Integer getInteger(String nm, int val);
    public static Integer getInteger(String nm, Integer val);
    public static int parseInt(String s, int radix) throws NumberFormatException;
    public static int parseInt(String s) throws NumberFormatException;
    public static String toString(int i, int radix);
    public static String toString(int i);
    public static Integer valueOf(String s, int radix) throws NumberFormatException;
    public static Integer valueOf(String s) throws NumberFormatException;
  // Public Instance Methods
    public double doubleValue(); // Defines Number.doubleValue()
    public boolean equals(Object obj); // Overrides Object.equals()
    public float floatValue(); // Defines Number.floatValue()
    public int hashCode(); // Overrides Object.hashCode()
    public int intValue(); // Defines Number.intValue()
```


→

```
        public long longValue(); // Defines Number.longValue()
        public String toString(); // Overrides Object.toString()
}
```

java.lang.Long

This class provides an object wrapper around the `long` primitive data type. It is useful when you need to pass `long` values by reference. This class also contains useful minimum and maximum constants and useful conversion methods. `parseLong()` and `valueOf` convert a string to a `long` or to a `Long`, respectively. Each can take a radix argument to specify the base that the value is represented in. `toString` converts in the other direction and may also take a radix argument. Other routines return the value of a `Long` as various primitive types, and finally, the `getLong()` methods return the `long` value of a named property or the value of the specified default.

```
public final class Long extends Number {
    // Public Constructors
        public Long(long value);
        public Long(String s) throws NumberFormatException;
    // Constants
        public final static long MAX_VALUE;
        public final static long MIN_VALUE;
    // Class Methods
        public static Long getLong(String nm);
        public static Long getLong(String nm, long val);
        public static Long getLong(String nm, Long val);
        public static long parseLong(String s, int radix) throws NumberFormatException;
        public static long parseLong(String s) throws NumberFormatException;
        public static String toString(long i, int radix);
        public static String toString(long i);
        public static Long valueOf(String s, int radix) throws NumberFormatException;
        public static Long valueOf(String s) throws NumberFormatException;
    // Public Instance Methods
        public double doubleValue(); // Defines Number.doubleValue()
        public boolean equals(Object obj); // Overrides Object.equals()
        public float floatValue(); // Defines Number.floatValue()
        public int hashCode(); // Overrides Object.hashCode()
        public int intValue(); // Defines Number.intValue()
        public long longValue(); // Defines Number.longValue()
        public String toString(); // Overrides Object.toString()
}
```

java.lang.Math

This class defines constants for the mathematical values *e* and π, and defines static methods for floating point trigonometry, exponentiation, and other operations. It is the equivalent of the C <*math.h*> functions. It also contains methods for computing minimum and maximum values and for generating pseudo-random numbers.

```
public final class Math extends Object {
    // No Constructor
    // Constants
        public final static double E;
        public final static double PI;
    // Class Methods
        public static double IEEEremainder(double f1, double f2);
        public static int abs(int a);
        public static long abs(long a);
        public static float abs(float a);
        public static double abs(double a);
        public static double acos(double a);
        public static double asin(double a);
        public static double atan(double a);
        public static double atan2(double a, double b);
        public static double ceil(double a);
        public static double cos(double a);
        public static double exp(double a);
        public static double floor(double a);
        public static double log(double a) throws ArithmeticException;
        public static int max(int a, int b);
        public static long max(long a, long b);
        public static float max(float a, float b);
        public static double max(double a, double b);
        public static int min(int a, int b);
        public static long min(long a, long b);
        public static float min(float a, float b);
        public static double min(double a, double b);
        public static double pow(double a, double b) throws ArithmeticException;
        public static synchronized double random();
        public static double rint(double a);
        public static int round(float a);
        public static long round(double a);
        public static double sin(double a);
        public static double sqrt(double a) throws ArithmeticException;
        public static double tan(double a);
}
```

java.lang

java.lang.Number

This is an abstract class that is the superclass of `Integer`, `Long`, `Float`, and `Double`. It defines conversion functions that those types all implement.

```
public abstract class Number extends Object {
    // Public Constructor
        public Number(); // Empty
    // Public Instance Methods
        public abstract double doubleValue();
```

→

```
        public abstract float floatValue();
        public abstract int intValue();
        public abstract long longValue();
}
```

java.lang.Object

This is the root class in Java. All classes are subclasses of `Object`, and thus all objects can invoke the `public` and `protected` methods of this class. `equals()` tests whether two objects have the same value (i.e., not whether two variables refer to the same object, but whether two distinct objects contain the same values). For classes that implement the `Cloneable` interface, `clone()` makes a copy of an `Object`. `getClass()` returns the `Class` object associated with any `Object`, and the `notify()`, `notifyAll()`, and `wait()` methods are used for thread synchronization on a given `Object`.

A number of these `Object` methods should be overridden by subclasses of `Object`. Subclasses should provide their own definition of the `toString()` method so that they can be used with the string concatenation operator and with the `PrintStream.println()` method. Defining the `toString()` method for all objects also helps with debugging.

Classes that contain references to other objects should override the `equals()` and `clone()` methods (for `Cloneable` objects). The `equals()` method should recursively call the `equals()` methods of all the objects the class refers to. Similarly, the `clone()` method should recursively call the `clone()` method of all objects the class refers to.

Classes that allocate system resources other than memory (such as file descriptors or windowing system graphic contexts) should override the `finalize()` method to release these resources when the object is no longer referred to.

Some classes may also want to override the `hashCode()` method to provide an appropriate hash code to be used when storing instances in a `Hashtable` data structure.

```
public class Object {
    // Public Constructor
        public Object(); // Empty
    // Public Instance Methods
        public boolean equals(Object obj);
        public final Class getClass();
        public int hashCode();
        public final void notify() throws IllegalMonitorStateException;
        public final void notifyAll() throws IllegalMonitorStateException;
        public String toString();
        public final void wait(long timeout) throws InterruptedException, IllegalMonitorStateException;
        public final void wait(long timeout, int nanos) throws InterruptedException, IllegalMonitorStateException;
        public final void wait() throws InterruptedException, IllegalMonitorStateException;
    // Protected Instance Methods
```

```
    protected Object clone() throws CloneNotSupportedException, OutOfMemoryError;
    protected void finalize() throws Throwable;  // Empty
}
```

java.lang.Process

This class describes a process started by a `Runtime.exec()` method call that is running externally to the Java interpreter. Note that a `Process` is a very different thing than a `Thread`, though they can be operated on in similar ways. The `Process` class itself is abstract and may not be instantiated. The `System.exec()` methods return an internal subclass that implements the `Process` methods in a platform-dependent way.

```
public abstract class Process extends Object {
    // Default Constructor: public Process()
    // Public Instance Methods
        public abstract void destroy();
        public abstract int exitValue() throws IllegalThreadStateException;
        public abstract InputStream getErrorStream();
        public abstract InputStream getInputStream();
        public abstract OutputStream getOutputStream();
        public abstract int waitFor() throws InterruptedException;
}
```

java.lang.Runnable

This interface specifies the `run()` method that is required for use with the `Thread` class. Any class that implements this interface can provide the "body" of a thread. See `Thread` for more information.

```
public abstract interface Runnable {
    // Public Instance Methods
        public abstract void run();
}
```

java.lang.Runtime

This class encapsulates a number of platform-dependent system functions. The static method `getRuntime()` returns the `Runtime` object for the current platform, and this object can be used to perform system functions in a platform-independent way.

`exec()` starts a new process running externally to the interpreter. Note that any processes run outside of Java may be system-dependent.

`exit()` causes the Java interpreter to exit and return a specified return code.

`freeMemory()` returns the approximate amount of free memory. `totalMemory()` returns the total amount of memory available to the Java interpreter. `gc()` forces the garbage collector to run synchronously, which may free up more memory. Similarly, `runFinalization()` forces the `finalize()` methods of unreferenced objects to be run immediately. This may free up system resources that those objects were holding.

`getLocalizedInputStream()` and `getLocalizedOutputStream()` return input and output streams that automatically translate the local character encoding to Unicode and Unicode to the local character encoding.

`load()` loads a dynamic library with a fully specified path name. `loadLibrary()` loads a dynamic library with only the library name specified; it looks in platform-dependent locations for the specified library. These libraries generally contain native code definitions for native methods.

`traceInstructions()` and `traceMethodCalls()` enable and disable tracing by the interpreter.

Note that some of the `Runtime` methods are more commonly called via the static methods of the `System` class.

```
public class Runtime extends Object {
    // No Constructor
    // Class Methods
        public static Runtime getRuntime();
    // Public Instance Methods
        public Process exec(String command) throws IOException;
        public Process exec(String command, String[] envp) throws IOException;
        public Process exec(String[] cmdarray) throws IOException;
        public Process exec(String[] cmdarray, String[] envp) throws IOException;
        public void exit(int status);
        public long freeMemory();
        public void gc();
        public InputStream getLocalizedInputStream(InputStream in);
        public OutputStream getLocalizedOutputStream(OutputStream out);
        public synchronized void load(String filename) throws UnsatisfiedLinkError;
        public synchronized void loadLibrary(String libname) throws UnsatisfiedLinkError;
        public void runFinalization();
        public long totalMemory();
        public void traceInstructions(boolean on);
        public void traceMethodCalls(boolean on);
}
```

java.lang.SecurityManager

This abstract class defines the methods necessary to implement a security policy for the execution of untrusted code. Before performing a large number of potentially sensitive operations, Java calls methods of the `SecurityManager` object currently in effect to determine whether the operation is permitted. These methods throw a `SecurityException` if the operation is not permitted.

Normal applications do not need to use or subclass the `SecurityManager` class. It is only used for Web browsers, applet viewers, or other programs that may run untrusted code.

```
public abstract class SecurityManager extends Object {
    // Protected Constructor
        protected SecurityManager() throws SecurityException;
    // Protected Instance Variables
        protected boolean inCheck;
    // Public Instance Methods
        public void checkAccept(String host, int port) throws SecurityException;
        public void checkAccess(Thread g) throws SecurityException;
        public void checkAccess(ThreadGroup g) throws SecurityException;
        public void checkConnect(String host, int port) throws SecurityException;
        public void checkConnect(String host, int port, Object context);
        public void checkCreateClassLoader() throws SecurityException;
        public void checkDelete(String file) throws SecurityException;
        public void checkExec(String cmd) throws SecurityException;
        public void checkExit(int status) throws SecurityException;
        public void checkLink(String lib) throws SecurityException;
        public void checkListen(int port) throws SecurityException;
        public void checkPackageAccess(String pkg);
        public void checkPackageDefinition(String pkg);
        public void checkPropertiesAccess() throws SecurityException;
        public void checkPropertyAccess(String key) throws SecurityException;
        public void checkPropertyAccess(String key, String def) throws SecurityException;
        public void checkRead(FileDescriptor fd) throws SecurityException;
        public void checkRead(String file) throws SecurityException;
        public void checkRead(String file, Object context) throws SecurityException;
        public void checkSetFactory();
        public boolean checkTopLevelWindow(Object window);
        public void checkWrite(FileDescriptor fd) throws SecurityException;
        public void checkWrite(String file) throws SecurityException;
        public boolean getInCheck();
        public Object getSecurityContext();
    // Protected Instance Methods
        protected int classDepth(String name);
        protected int classLoaderDepth();
        protected ClassLoader currentClassLoader();
        protected Class[] getClassContext();
        protected boolean inClass(String name);
        protected boolean inClassLoader();
}
```

java.lang

---

java.lang.String

The `String` class represents a string of characters. A `String` object is created by the Java compiler whenever it encounters a string in double-quotes—this method of creation is usually simpler than using a constructor. The methods of this class provide the equivalents of the C library *<string.h>* functions. `String` objects are immutable—you may not change their contents. Use a `StringBuffer` if you want to

→

manipulate the contents of a string. The + operator can be used to concatenate String objects.

```
public final class String extends Object {
    // Public Constructors
        public String();
        public String(String value);
        public String(char[] value);
        public String(char[] value, int offset, int count) throws StringIndexOutOfBoundsException;
        public String(byte[] ascii, int hibyte, int offset, int count) throws StringIndexOutOfBoundsException;
        public String(byte[] ascii, int hibyte);
        public String(StringBuffer buffer);
    // Class Methods
        public static String copyValueOf(char[] data, int offset, int count);
        public static String copyValueOf(char[] data);
        public static String valueOf(Object obj);
        public static String valueOf(char[] data);
        public static String valueOf(char[] data, int offset, int count);
        public static String valueOf(boolean b);
        public static String valueOf(char c);
        public static String valueOf(int i);
        public static String valueOf(long l);
        public static String valueOf(float f);
        public static String valueOf(double d);
    // Public Instance Methods
        public char charAt(int index) throws StringIndexOutOfBoundsException;
        public int compareTo(String anotherString);
        public String concat(String str);
        public boolean endsWith(String suffix);
        public boolean equals(Object anObject);  // Overrides Object.equals()
        public boolean equalsIgnoreCase(String anotherString);
        public void getBytes(int srcBegin, int srcEnd, byte[] dst, int dstBegin);
        public void getChars(int srcBegin, int srcEnd, char[] dst, int dstBegin);
        public int hashCode();  // Overrides Object.hashCode()
        public int indexOf(int ch);
        public int indexOf(int ch, int fromIndex);
        public int indexOf(String str);
        public int indexOf(String str, int fromIndex);
        public String intern();
        public int lastIndexOf(int ch);
        public int lastIndexOf(int ch, int fromIndex);
        public int lastIndexOf(String str);
        public int lastIndexOf(String str, int fromIndex);
        public int length();
        public boolean regionMatches(int toffset, String other, int ooffset, int len);
        public boolean regionMatches(boolean ignoreCase, int toffset, String other, int ooffset, int len);
        public String replace(char oldChar, char newChar);
        public boolean startsWith(String prefix, int toffset);
        public boolean startsWith(String prefix);
        public String substring(int beginIndex);
        public String substring(int beginIndex, int endIndex) throws StringIndexOutOfBoundsException;
        public char[] toCharArray();
```

```
    public String toLowerCase();
    public String toString(); // Overrides Object.toString()
    public String toUpperCase();
    public String trim();
}
```

java.lang.StringBuffer

This class represents a string of characters. It differs from the `String` class in that its contents may be modified. A `StringBuffer` object grows in length as necessary. The string stored in a `StringBuffer` object may be modified in place with the `setCharAt()`, `append()`, and `insert()` methods.

After a string is processed in a `StringBuffer` object, it may be efficiently converted to a `String` object for subsequent use. The `StringBuffer.toString()` method does not copy the internal array of characters; instead it shares that array with the new `String` object, and makes a new copy for itself only when further modifications are made to the `StringBuffer` object.

```
public final class StringBuffer extends Object {
    // Public Constructors
        public StringBuffer();
        public StringBuffer(int length);
        public StringBuffer(String str);
    // Public Instance Methods
        public synchronized StringBuffer append(Object obj);
        public synchronized StringBuffer append(String str);
        public synchronized StringBuffer append(char[] str);
        public synchronized StringBuffer append(char[] str, int offset, int len);
        public StringBuffer append(boolean b);
        public synchronized StringBuffer append(char c);
        public StringBuffer append(int i);
        public StringBuffer append(long l);
        public StringBuffer append(float f);
        public StringBuffer append(double d);
        public int capacity();
        public synchronized char charAt(int index) throws StringIndexOutOfBoundsException;
        public synchronized void ensureCapacity(int minimumCapacity);
        public synchronized void getChars(int srcBegin, int srcEnd, char[] dst, int dstBegin)
                                        throws StringIndexOutOfBoundsException;
        public synchronized StringBuffer insert(int offset, Object obj) throws StringIndexOutOfBoundsException;
        public synchronized StringBuffer insert(int offset, String str) throws StringIndexOutOfBoundsException;
        public synchronized StringBuffer insert(int offset, char[] str) throws StringIndexOutOfBoundsException;
        public StringBuffer insert(int offset, boolean b) throws StringIndexOutOfBoundsException;
        public synchronized StringBuffer insert(int offset, char c) throws StringIndexOutOfBoundsException;
        public StringBuffer insert(int offset, int i) throws StringIndexOutOfBoundsException;
        public StringBuffer insert(int offset, long l) throws StringIndexOutOfBoundsException;
        public StringBuffer insert(int offset, float f) throws StringIndexOutOfBoundsException;
        public StringBuffer insert(int offset, double d) throws StringIndexOutOfBoundsException;
        public int length();
        public synchronized void setCharAt(int index, char ch) throws StringIndexOutOfBoundsException;
```

→

```
        public synchronized void setLength(int newLength) throws StringIndexOutOfBoundsException;
        public String toString(); // Overrides Object.toString()
}
```

java.lang.System

This class defines methods that provide a platform-independent interface to system functions. All of the methods and variables of this class are static. The class may not be instantiated.

The `in`, `out`, and `err` variables are the system standard input, output, and error streams.

`arraycopy()` copies an array or a portion of an array into a destination array.

`currentTimeMillis()` returns the current time in milliseconds since midnight GMT on January 1, 1970.

`getProperty()` looks up a named property on the system properties list, returning the optionally specified default value if no property definition was found. `getProperties()` returns the entire properties list. `setProperties()` sets a `Properties` object on the properties list.

`exit()`, `gc()`, `load()`, `loadLibrary()` and `runFinalization()` invoke the methods of the same name in the `Runtime` object. See `Runtime` for details.

```
public final class System extends Object {
    // No Constructor
    // Class Variables
        public static PrintStream err;
        public static InputStream in;
        public static PrintStream out;
    // Class Methods
        public static void arraycopy(Object src, int src_position, Object dst, int dst_position, int length)
                                throws ArrayIndexOutOfBoundsException, ArrayStoreException;
        public static long currentTimeMillis();
        public static void exit(int status);
        public static void gc();
        public static Properties getProperties();
        public static String getProperty(String key);
        public static String getProperty(String key, String def);
        public static SecurityManager getSecurityManager();
        public static String getenv(String name); // Obsolete; throws an error
        public static void load(String filename) throws UnsatisfiedLinkError;
        public static void loadLibrary(String libname) throws UnsatisfiedLinkError;
        public static void runFinalization();
        public static void setProperties(Properties props);
        public static void setSecurityManager(SecurityManager s) throws SecurityException;
}
```

java.lang.Thread

This class encapsulates all the information about a single thread of control running on the Java interpreter. To create a thread, you must pass a `Runnable` object (i.e., an object that implements the `Runnable` interface by defining a `run()` method) to the `Thread` constructor, or you must subclass `Thread` so that it defines its own `run()` method.

The `run()` method of the `Thread` or of the specified `Runnable` object is the "body" of the thread. It begins executing when the `start()` method of the `Thread` object is called. The thread runs until the `run()` method returns or until the `stop()` method of its `Thread` object is called. The static methods of this class operate on the currently running thread. The instance methods may be called from one thread to operate on a different thread.

`start()` starts a thread running. `stop()` stops it by throwing a `ThreadDeath` error. `suspend()` temporarily halts a thread. `resume()` allows it to resume. `sleep()` makes the current thread stop for a specified amount of time. `yield()` makes the current thread give up control to any other threads of equal priority that are waiting to run. `join()` waits for a thread to die.

```
public class Thread extends Object implements Runnable {
    // Public Constructors
        public Thread();
        public Thread(Runnable target);
        public Thread(ThreadGroup group, Runnable target);
        public Thread(String name);
        public Thread(ThreadGroup group, String name);
        public Thread(Runnable target, String name);
        public Thread(ThreadGroup group, Runnable target, String name);
    // Constants
        public final static int MAX_PRIORITY;
        public final static int MIN_PRIORITY;
        public final static int NORM_PRIORITY;
    // Class Methods
        public static int activeCount();
        public static Thread currentThread();
        public static void dumpStack();
        public static int enumerate(Thread[] tarray);
        public static boolean interrupted();  // Not implemented; throws NoSuchMethodError
        public static void sleep(long millis) throws InterruptedException;
        public static void sleep(long millis, int nanos) throws InterruptedException;
        public static void yield();
    // Public Instance Methods
        public void checkAccess() throws SecurityException;
        public int countStackFrames() throws IllegalThreadStateException;
        public void destroy();  // Not implemented; throws NoSuchMethodError
        public final String getName();
        public final int getPriority();
        public final ThreadGroup getThreadGroup();
        public void interrupt();  // Not implemented; throws NoSuchMethodError
        public final boolean isAlive();
```

→

java.lang

```
        public final boolean isDaemon();
        public boolean isInterrupted();  // Not implemented; throws NoSuchMethodError
        public final synchronized void join(long millis) throws InterruptedException;
        public final synchronized void join(long millis, int nanos) throws InterruptedException;
        public final void join() throws InterruptedException;
        public final void resume();
        public void run();
        public final void setDaemon(boolean on) throws IllegalThreadStateException;
        public final void setName(String name);
        public final void setPriority(int newPriority) throws IllegalArgumentException;
        public synchronized void start() throws IllegalThreadStateException;
        public final void stop();
        public final synchronized void stop(Throwable o);
        public final void suspend();
        public String toString();  // Overrides Object.toString()
}
```

java.lang.ThreadGroup

This class defines a group of threads and allows operations on the group as a whole. A `ThreadGroup` may contain `Thread` objects, as well as "child" `ThreadGroup` objects. All `ThreadGroup` objects are created as children of some other `ThreadGroup`, and thus there is a parent/child hierarchy of `ThreadGroup` objects.

Some programs may find it convenient to define their own `ThreadGroup`, but generally thread groups will only be used by system-level applications.

```
public class ThreadGroup extends Object {
    // Public Constructors
        public ThreadGroup(String name);
        public ThreadGroup(ThreadGroup parent, String name) throws NullPointerException;
    // Public Instance Methods
        public synchronized int activeCount();
        public synchronized int activeGroupCount();
        public final void checkAccess() throws SecurityException;
        public final synchronized void destroy() throws IllegalThreadStateException;
        public int enumerate(Thread[] list);
        public int enumerate(Thread[] list, boolean recurse);
        public int enumerate(ThreadGroup[] list);
        public int enumerate(ThreadGroup[] list, boolean recurse);
        public final int getMaxPriority();
        public final String getName();
        public final ThreadGroup getParent();
        public final boolean isDaemon();
        public synchronized void list();
        public final boolean parentOf(ThreadGroup g);
        public final synchronized void resume();
        public final void setDaemon(boolean daemon);
        public final synchronized void setMaxPriority(int pri);
```

```
        public final synchronized void stop();
        public final synchronized void suspend();
        public String toString(); // Overrides Object.toString()
        public void uncaughtException(Thread t, Throwable e);
}
```

java.lang.Throwable

This is the root class of the Java exception and error hierarchy. All exceptions and errors that are thrown are subclasses of `Throwable`. The `getMessage()` method retrieves the error message usually associated with the exception or error. `printStackTrace()` prints a stack trace that shows where the exception occurred. `fillInStackTrace()` extends the stack trace when the exception is partially handled, and then re-thrown.

```
public class Throwable extends Object {
    // Public Constructors
        public Throwable();
        public Throwable(String message);
    // Public Instance Methods
        public Throwable fillInStackTrace();
        public String getMessage();
        public void printStackTrace();
        public void printStackTrace(PrintStream s);
        public String toString(); // Overrides Object.toString()
}
```

The java.net Package

The java.net package provides a powerful and flexible infrastructure for networking. Figure 24-1 shows the class hierarchy for this package. Many of the classes in this package are part of the networking infrastructure and are not used by normal applications; these complicated classes can make the package a difficult one to understand. In this overview we describe only the classes that an application might normally use.

The URL class represents an Internet Uniform Resource Locator. It provides a very simple interface to networking—the object referred to by the URL can be downloaded with a single call, or streams may be opened to read from or write to the object.

At a slightly more complex level, the URLConnection object may be obtained from a given URL object. The URLConnection class provides additional methods that allow you to work with URLs in more sophisticated ways.

If you want to do more than simply download an object referenced by a URL, you can do your own networking with the Socket class. This class allows you to connect to a specified port on a specified Internet host and read and write data using the InputStream and OutputStream classes of the java.io package. If you want to implement a server to accept connections from clients, you can use the related ServerSocket class. Both Socket and ServerSocket use the InetAddress address class, which represents an Internet address.

Finally, the java.net package allows you to do very low-level networking with DatagramPacket objects which may be sent and received over the network through a DatagramSocket object.

See Section 7, *Networking*, for some example applications that use classes from java.net.

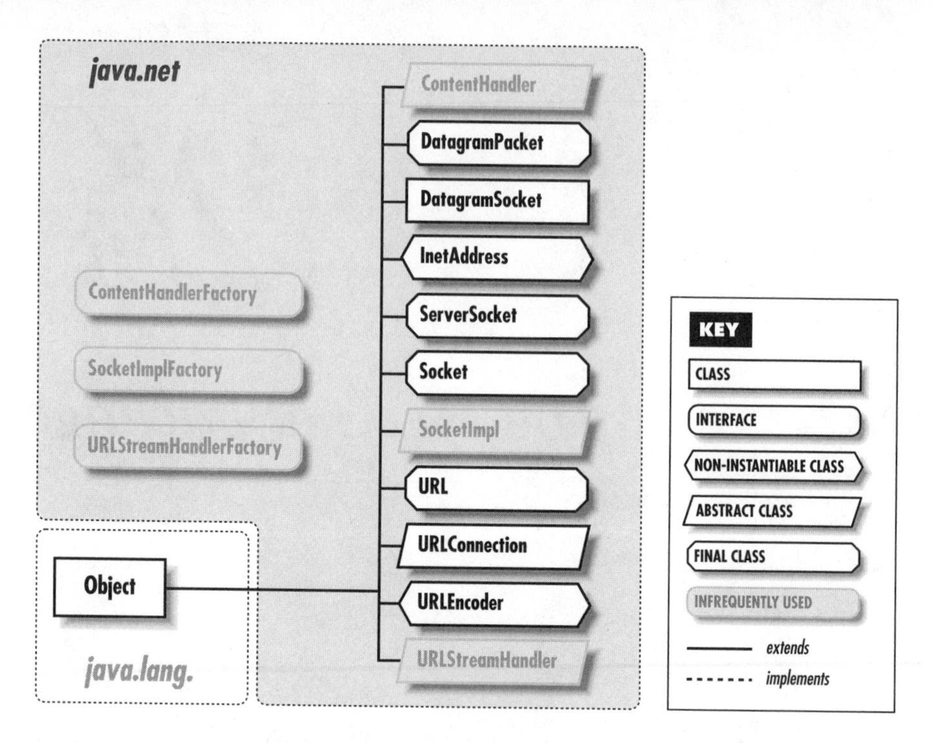

Figure 24-1: The java.net package

java.net.ContentHandler

This abstract class defines a method that reads data from a `URLConnection` and returns an object representing that data. Each subclass that implements this method is responsible for handling a different type of content (i.e., a different MIME type). Applications never create `ContentHandler` objects directly—they are created, when necessary, by the registered `ContentHandlerFactory` object. Applications should also never call `ContentHandler` methods directly—they should call `URL.getContent()` or `URLConnection.getContent()` instead. The only time you would need to subclass `ContentHandler` is if you were writing a Web browser or similar application that needed to parse and understand some new content type.

```
public abstract class ContentHandler extends Object {
    // Default Constructor: public ContentHandler()
    // Public Instance Methods
        public abstract Object getContent(URLConnection urlc) throws IOException;
}
```

java.net.ContentHandlerFactory

This interface defines a method that creates and returns an appropriate `ContentHandler` object for a specified MIME type. A system-wide `ContentHandler-`

Factory interface may be specified by using the URLConnection.setContentHandlerFactory() method.

Normal applications never need to use or implement this interface.

```
public abstract interface ContentHandlerFactory {
    // Public Instance Methods
        public abstract ContentHandler createContentHandler(String mimetype);
}
```

java.net.DatagramPacket

This class implements a "packet" of data that may be sent or received over the network through a DatagramSocket. One of the DatagramPacket constructors specifies an array of binary data to be sent with its destination address and port. A packet created with this constructor may then be sent with the send() method of a DatagramSocket. The other DatagramPacket constructor specifies an array of bytes into which data should be received. The receive() method of DatagramSocket waits for data and stores it in a DatagramPacket created in this way. The contents and sender of a received packet may be queried with the DatagramPacket instance methods.

```
public final class DatagramPacket extends Object {
    // Public Constructors
        public DatagramPacket(byte[] ibuf, int ilength);
        public DatagramPacket(byte[] ibuf, int ilength, InetAddress iaddr, int iport);
    // Public Instance Methods
        public InetAddress getAddress();
        public byte[] getData();
        public int getLength();
        public int getPort();
}
```

java.net.DatagramSocket

This class defines a socket that can receive and send unreliable datagram packets over the network. A datagram is a very low-level networking interface: it is simply an array of bytes sent over the network. A datagram does not implement any kind of stream-based communication protocol, and there is no semi-permanent "connection" established between the sender and the receiver. Datagram packets are called "unreliable" because the protocol does not make any attempt to ensure that they arrived or to resend them if they did not. Thus, packets sent through a DatagramSocket are not guaranteed to arrive in the order sent, or to arrive at all. On the other hand, this low-overhead protocol makes datagram transmission very fast.

If a port is specified when the DatagramSocket is created, that port is be used; otherwise, the system assigns a port. getLocalPort() returns the port number in use. send() sends a DatagramPacket through the socket. The packet must contain the destination address to which it should be sent. receive() waits for data to arrive at the socket and stores it, along with the address of the sender, into the

→

specified DatagramPacket. close() closes the socket and frees the port it used for reuse. Once close() has been called, the DatagramSocket should not be used again.

See Socket and URL for higher-level interfaces to networking.

```
public class DatagramSocket extends Object {
    // Public Constructors
      public DatagramSocket() throws SocketException;
      public DatagramSocket(int port) throws SocketException;
    // Public Instance Methods
      public synchronized void close();
      public int getLocalPort();
      public synchronized void receive(DatagramPacket p) throws IOException;
      public void send(DatagramPacket p) throws IOException;
    // Protected Instance Methods
      protected synchronized void finalize();
}
```

java.net.InetAddress

This class represents an Internet address, and is used when creating DatagramPacket or Socket objects. The class does not have a public constructor function, but instead supports three static methods which return one or more instances of InetAddress. getLocalHost() returns an InetAddress for the local host. getByName() returns the InetAddress of a host specified by name. getAllByName() returns an array of InetAddress that represents all of the available addresses for a host specified by name. Instance methods are getHostName(), which returns the hostname of an InetAddress, and getAddress(), which returns the Internet IP address as an array of bytes, with the highest-order byte as the first element of the array.

```
public final class InetAddress extends Object {
    // No Constructor
    // Class Methods
      public static synchronized InetAddress[] getAllByName(String host) throws UnknownHostException;
      public static synchronized InetAddress getByName(String host) throws UnknownHostException;
      public static InetAddress getLocalHost() throws UnknownHostException;
    // Public Instance Methods
      public boolean equals(Object obj);  // Overrides Object.equals()
      public byte[] getAddress();
      public String getHostName();
      public int hashCode();  // Overrides Object.hashCode()
      public String toString();  // Overrides Object.toString()
}
```

java.net.ServerSocket

This class is used by servers to listen for connection requests from clients. When you create a `ServerSocket`, it listens for connections on the specified port for an optionally specified amount of time. When a connection request arrives and the `ServerSocket` is returned, `getInetAddress()` returns the address of the connecting client, and `accept()` accepts the requested connection and returns a `Socket` for future communication between client and server.

```
public final class ServerSocket extends Object {
    // Public Constructors
        public ServerSocket(int port) throws IOException;
        public ServerSocket(int port, int count) throws IOException;
    // Class Methods
        public static synchronized void setSocketFactory(SocketImplFactory fac)
                                        throws IOException, SocketException;
    // Public Instance Methods
        public Socket accept() throws IOException;
        public void close() throws IOException;
        public InetAddress getInetAddress();
        public int getLocalPort();
        public String toString();  // Overrides Object.toString()
}
```

java.net.Socket

This class implements a socket for interprocess communication over the network. The constructor methods create the socket and connect it to the specified host and port. You may also optionally specify whether communication through the socket should be based on an underlying reliable connection-based stream protocol, or on an underlying unreliable (but faster) datagram protocol. A stream protocol is the default.

Once the socket is created, `getInputStream()` and `getOutputStream()` return `InputStream` and `OutputStream` objects that you can use just as you would for file input and output. `getInetAddress()` and `getPort()` return the address and port that the socket is connected to. `getLocalPort()` returns the local port that the socket is using.

```
public final class Socket extends Object {
    // Public Constructors
        public Socket(String host, int port) throws UnknownHostException, IOException;
        public Socket(String host, int port, boolean stream) throws IOException;
        public Socket(InetAddress address, int port) throws IOException;
        public Socket(InetAddress address, int port, boolean stream) throws IOException;
    // Class Methods
        public static synchronized void setSocketImplFactory(SocketImplFactory fac)
                                        throws IOException, SocketException;
    // Public Instance Methods
        public synchronized void close() throws IOException;
```

→

```
        public InetAddress getInetAddress();
        public InputStream getInputStream() throws IOException;
        public int getLocalPort();
        public OutputStream getOutputStream() throws IOException;
        public int getPort();
        public String toString();  // Overrides Object.toString()
}
```

java.net.SocketImpl

This abstract class defines the methods necessary to implement communication through sockets. Different subclasses of this class may provide different implementations suitable in different environments (such as behind firewalls). These socket implementations are used by the `Socket` and `ServerSocket` classes.

Normal applications never need to use or implement this interface.

```
public abstract class SocketImpl extends Object {
    // Default Constructor: public SocketImpl()
    // Protected Instance Variables
        protected InetAddress address;
        protected FileDescriptor fd;
        protected int localport;
        protected int port;
    // Public Instance Methods
        public String toString();  // Overrides Object.toString()
    // Protected Instance Methods
        protected abstract void accept(SocketImpl s) throws IOException;
        protected abstract int available() throws IOException;
        protected abstract void bind(InetAddress host, int port) throws IOException;
        protected abstract void close() throws IOException;
        protected abstract void connect(String host, int port) throws IOException;
        protected abstract void connect(InetAddress address, int port) throws IOException;
        protected abstract void create(boolean stream) throws IOException;
        protected FileDescriptor getFileDescriptor();
        protected InetAddress getInetAddress();
        protected abstract InputStream getInputStream() throws IOException;
        protected int getLocalPort();
        protected abstract OutputStream getOutputStream() throws IOException;
        protected int getPort();
        protected abstract void listen(int count) throws IOException;
}
```

java.net.SocketImplFactory

This interface defines a method that creates `SocketImpl` objects. `SocketImplFactory` objects may be registered to create `SocketImpl` objects for the `Socket` and `ServerSocket` classes.

Normal applications never need to use or implement this interface.

```
public abstract interface SocketImplFactory {
    // Public Instance Methods
        public abstract SocketImpl createSocketImpl();
}
```

java.net.URL

This class represents a URL (a Uniform Resource Locator) and allows the data referred to by the URL to be downloaded. A URL may be specified as a single string or with separate protocol, host, port, and file specifications. Relative URLs may also be specified with a `String` and the `URL` object that it is relative to.

`getFile()`, `getHost()`, `getPort()`, `getProtocol()`, and `getRef()` return the various portions of the URL specified by a `URL` object. `sameFile()` determines whether a `URL` object refers to the same file as this one.

The data or object referred to by a URL may be downloaded from the Internet in three ways: through a `URLConnection` created with `openConnection()`, through an `InputStream` created by `openStream()`, or through `getContent()`, which returns the URL contents directly.

```
public final class URL extends Object {
    // Public Constructors
        public URL(String protocol, String host, int port, String file) throws MalformedURLException;
        public URL(String protocol, String host, String file) throws MalformedURLException;
        public URL(String spec) throws MalformedURLException;
        public URL(URL context, String spec) throws MalformedURLException;
    // Class Methods
        public static synchronized void setURLStreamHandlerFactory(URLStreamHandlerFactory fac) throws Error;
    // Public Instance Methods
        public boolean equals(Object obj);  // Overrides Object.equals()
        public final Object getContent() throws IOException;
        public String getFile();
        public String getHost();
        public int getPort();
        public String getProtocol();
        public String getRef();
        public int hashCode();  // Overrides Object.hashCode()
        public URLConnection openConnection() throws IOException;
        public final InputStream openStream() throws IOException;
        public boolean sameFile(URL other);
        public String toExternalForm();
        public String toString();  // Overrides Object.toString()
```

→

```
    // Protected Instance Methods
        protected void set(String protocol, String host, int port, String file, String ref);
}
```

java.net.URLConnection

This abstract class defines a network connection to an object specified by a URL. `URL.openConnection()` returns a `URLConnection` instance. You would use a `URLConnection` object when you want more control over the downloading data than is through the simpler URL methods.

`connect()` actually performs the network connection. Other methods that depend on being connected will call this method. `getContent()` returns the data referred to by the URL, parsed into an appropriate type of `Object`. If the URL protocol supports read and write operations then `getInputStream()` and `getOutputStream()` respectively return input and output streams to the object referred to by the URL.

`getContentLength()`, `getContentType()`, `getContentEncoding()`, `getExpiration()`, `getDate()`, and `getLastModified()` return the appropriate information about the object referred to by the URL, if that information can be determined (e.g., from HTTP header fields). `getHeaderField()` returns an HTTP header field specified by name or by number. `getHeaderFieldInt()` and `getHeaderFieldDate()` return the value of a named header field parsed as an integer or a date.

There are a number of options that you may specify to control how the `URLConnection` behaves. These options are set with the various `set()` methods, and may be queried with corresponding `get()` methods. The options must be set before the `connect()` method is called.

`setDoInput()` and `setDoOutput()` allow you to specify whether you use the `URLConnection` for input and/or output. The default is input-only.

`setAllowUserInteraction()` specifies whether user-interaction (such as typing a password) is allowed during the data transfer. The initial default is `false`. `setDefaultAllowUserInteraction()` is a class method that allows you to change the default value for user interaction.

`setUseCaches()` allows you to specify whether a cached version of the URL may be used. You can set this to `false` to force a URL to be reloaded. `setDefaultUseCaches()` sets the default value for `setUseCaches()`.

`setIfModifiedSince()` allows you to specify that a URL should not be fetched (if it is possible to determine its modification date) unless it has been modified since a specified time.

```
public abstract class URLConnection extends Object {
    // Protected Constructor
        protected URLConnection(URL url);
    // Protected Instance Variables
```

```
    protected boolean allowUserInteraction;
    protected boolean connected;
    protected boolean doInput;
    protected boolean doOutput;
    protected long ifModifiedSince;
    protected URL url;
    protected boolean useCaches;
  // Class Methods
    public static boolean getDefaultAllowUserInteraction();
    public static String getDefaultRequestProperty(String key);
    protected static String guessContentTypeFromName(String fname);
    protected static String guessContentTypeFromStream(InputStream is) throws IOException;
    public static synchronized void setContentHandlerFactory(ContentHandlerFactory fac) throws Error;
    public static void setDefaultAllowUserInteraction(boolean defaultallowuserinteraction);
    public static void setDefaultRequestProperty(String key, String value); // Empty
  // Public Instance Methods
    public abstract void connect() throws IOException;
    public boolean getAllowUserInteraction();
    public Object getContent() throws IOException, UnknownServiceException;
    public String getContentEncoding();
    public int getContentLength();
    public String getContentType();
    public long getDate();
    public boolean getDefaultUseCaches();
    public boolean getDoInput();
    public boolean getDoOutput();
    public long getExpiration();
    public String getHeaderField(String name);
    public String getHeaderField(int n);
    public long getHeaderFieldDate(String name, long Default);
    public int getHeaderFieldInt(String name, int Default);
    public String getHeaderFieldKey(int n);
    public long getIfModifiedSince();
    public InputStream getInputStream() throws IOException, UnknownServiceException;
    public long getLastModified();
    public OutputStream getOutputStream() throws IOException, UnknownServiceException;
    public String getRequestProperty(String key);
    public URL getURL();
    public boolean getUseCaches();
    public void setAllowUserInteraction(boolean allowuserinteraction);
    public void setDefaultUseCaches(boolean defaultusecaches);
    public void setDoInput(boolean doinput);
    public void setDoOutput(boolean dooutput);
    public void setIfModifiedSince(long ifmodifiedsince);
    public void setRequestProperty(String key, String value);
    public void setUseCaches(boolean usecaches);
    public String toString(); // Overrides Object.toString()
}
```

java.net.URLEncoder

This class defines a single static method which is used to convert a string to its URL-encoded form. That is, spaces are converted to '+', and non-alphanumeric characters other than underscore are output as two hexadecimal digits following a percent sign. Note that this technique only works for 8-bit characters. This method is used to "canonicalize" a URL specification so that it uses only characters from an extremely portable subset of ASCII which can be correctly handled by computers around the world.

```
public class URLEncoder extends Object {
    // No Constructor
    // Class Methods
      public static String encode(String s);
}
```

java.net.URLStreamHandler

This abstract class defines the method that creates a `URLConnection` for a given URL. A separate subclass of this class may be defined for various URL protocol types. A `URLStreamHandler` is created by a `URLStreamHandlerFactory`.

Normal applications never need to use or subclass this class.

```
public abstract class URLStreamHandler extends Object {
    // Default Constructor: public URLStreamHandler()
    // Protected Instance Methods
      protected abstract URLConnection openConnection(URL u) throws IOException;
      protected void parseURL(URL u, String spec, int start, int limit);
      protected void setURL(URL u, String protocol, String host, int port, String file, String ref);
      protected String toExternalForm(URL u);
}
```

java.net.URLStreamHandlerFactory

This interface defines a method that creates a `URLStreamHandler` object for a specified protocol.

Normal applications never need to use or implement this interface.

```
public abstract interface URLStreamHandlerFactory {
    // Public Instance Methods
      public abstract URLStreamHandler createURLStreamHandler(String protocol);
}
```

The java.util Package

The `java.util` package defines a number of useful classes. This package should not be considered a "utility" package separate from the rest of the language; in fact, Java depends directly on several of the classes in this package. Figure 25-1 shows the class hierarchy of this package.

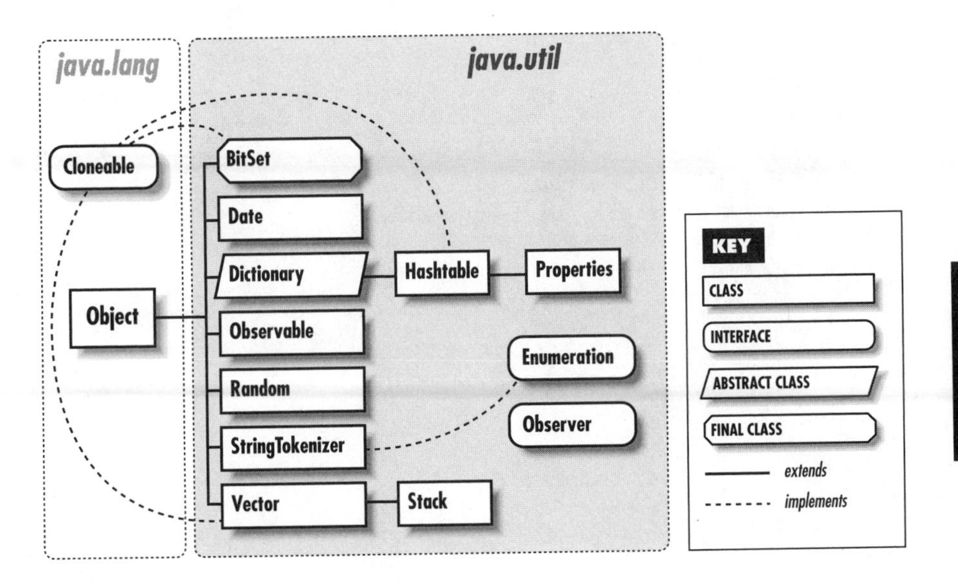

Figure 25-1: The java.util package

java.util

The Hashtable class is one of the most useful in the package—it implements a hashtable or associative array. It allows arbitrary objects to be stored and retrieved by arbitrary keys. The Properties subclass of Hashtable is used to store the Java system properties list.

Vector is another extremely useful class. It implements an array of objects that grows as necessary as objects are added.

The Enumeration interface provides a simple and consistent way to loop through all the elements contained within some kind of object or data structure.

The remaining classes are also useful. BitSet implements an arbitrary-size array of bits. Date represents a date/time value and provides many useful methods for manipulating dates and times. Random generates and returns pseudo-random numbers in a variety of forms. StringTokenizer parses a string into tokens. Stack implements a last-on-first-off stack on which objects may be pushed and from which they may be popped. And the Observer interface and Observable class provide infrastructure for implementing the object-oriented model-view paradigm in Java.

java.util.BitSet

This class defines an arbitrarily large set of bits. Instance methods allow you to set, clear, and query individual bits in the set, and also to perform bitwise boolean arithmetic on the bits in BitSet objects. This class can be used as an extremely compact array of boolean values, although reading and writing those values is slower than normal array access.

```
public final class BitSet extends Object implements Cloneable {
    // Public Constructors
        public BitSet();
        public BitSet(int nbits);
    // Public Instance Methods
        public void and(BitSet set);
        public void clear(int bit);
        public Object clone(); // Overrides Object.clone()
        public boolean equals(Object obj); // Overrides Object.equals()
        public boolean get(int bit);
        public int hashCode(); // Overrides Object.hashCode()
        public void or(BitSet set);
        public void set(int bit);
        public int size();
        public String toString(); // Overrides Object.toString()
        public void xor(BitSet set);
}
```

java.util.Date

This class represents dates and times. It lets you work with them in a system-independent way. You can create a Date by specifying the number of milliseconds from the epoch (midnight GMT, January 1st, 1970), or by specifying the year, month, date, and optionally, the hour, minute, and second. Years are specified as the number of years since 1900. If you call the Date constructor with no arguments, the Date is initialized to the current time and date. The instance methods of the class allow you to get and set the various date and time fields, to compare dates and times, and to convert dates to and from string representations.

```
public class Date extends Object {
    // Public Constructors
        public Date();
        public Date(long date);
        public Date(int year, int month, int date);
        public Date(int year, int month, int date, int hrs, int min);
        public Date(int year, int month, int date, int hrs, int min, int sec);
        public Date(String s);
    // Class Methods
        public static long UTC(int year, int month, int date, int hrs, int min, int sec);
        public static long parse(String s);
    // Public Instance Methods
        public boolean after(Date when);
        public boolean before(Date when);
        public boolean equals(Object obj); // Overrides Object.equals()
        public int getDate();
        public int getDay();
        public int getHours();
        public int getMinutes();
        public int getMonth();
        public int getSeconds();
        public long getTime();
        public int getTimezoneOffset();
        public int getYear();
        public int hashCode(); // Overrides Object.hashCode()
        public void setDate(int date);
        public void setHours(int hours);
        public void setMinutes(int minutes);
        public void setMonth(int month);
        public void setSeconds(int seconds);
        public void setTime(long time);
        public void setYear(int year);
        public String toGMTString();
        public String toLocaleString();
        public String toString(); // Overrides Object.toString()
}
```

java.util

java.util.Dictionary

This abstract class is the superclass of Hashtable. Other hashtable-like data structures might also extend this class. See Hashtable for more information.

```
public abstract class Dictionary extends Object {
    // Public Constructor
        public Dictionary(); // Empty
    // Public Instance Methods
```

→

```
        public abstract Enumeration elements();
        public abstract Object get(Object key);
        public abstract boolean isEmpty();
        public abstract Enumeration keys();
        public abstract Object put(Object key, Object value) throws NullPointerException;
        public abstract Object remove(Object key);
        public abstract int size();
}
```

java.util.Enumeration

This interface defines the methods necessary to enumerate, or iterate through a set of values, such as the set of values contained in a hashtable or binary tree. It is particularly useful for data structures, like hashtables, for which elements cannot simply be looked up by index, as they can in arrays. An `Enumeration` is often not instantiated directly, but instead is created by the object that is to have its values enumerated. A number of classes, such as `Vector` and `Hashtable`, have methods that return `Enumeration` objects.

To use an `Enumeration` object, you use its two methods in a loop: `hasMoreElements()` returns `true` if there are more values to be enumerated, and can be used to determine whether a loop should continue. Within a loop, a call to `nextElement()` returns a value from the enumeration. An `Enumeration` makes no guarantees about the order in which the values are returned. The values in an `Enumeration` may be iterated through only once—there is no way to reset it to the beginning.

```
public abstract interface Enumeration {
    // Public Instance Methods
        public abstract boolean hasMoreElements();
        public abstract Object nextElement() throws NoSuchElementException;
}
```

java.util.Hashtable

This class implements a hashtable data structure, which allows you to associate values with a key and to efficiently look up the value associated with a given key. A hashtable is essentially an associative array, which stores objects with non-numeric array indices.

`put()` associates a value with a key in a `Hashtable`. `get()` retrieves a value for a specified key. `remove()` deletes a key/value association. `keys()` and `elements()` return `Enumeration` objects that allow you to iterate through the complete set of keys and values stored in the table.

```
public class Hashtable extends Dictionary implements Cloneable {
    // Public Constructors
        public Hashtable(int initialCapacity, float loadFactor) throws IllegalArgumentException;
        public Hashtable(int initialCapacity);
        public Hashtable();
    // Public Instance Methods
        public synchronized void clear();
        public synchronized Object clone();  // Overrides Object.clone()
        public synchronized boolean contains(Object value) throws NullPointerException;
        public synchronized boolean containsKey(Object key);
        public synchronized Enumeration elements(); // Defines Dictionary.elements()
        public synchronized Object get(Object key);  // Defines Dictionary.get()
        public boolean isEmpty();  // Defines Dictionary.isEmpty()
        public synchronized Enumeration keys();  // Defines Dictionary.keys()
        public synchronized Object put(Object key, Object value) throws NullPointerException;
                                          // Defines Dictionary.put()
        public synchronized Object remove(Object key);  // Defines Dictionary.remove()
        public int size(); // Defines Dictionary.size()
        public synchronized String toString();  // Overrides Object.toString()
    // Protected Instance Methods
        protected void rehash();
}
```

java.util.Observable

This class is the superclass of all "observable" objects to be used in an object-oriented model/view paradigm. The class methods allow you to add and delete `Observer` objects to and from an `Observable`'s list, and to notify all of the `Observer` objects on the list. `Observer` objects are "notified" by invoking their `update()` method. `Observable` also maintains an internal "changed" flag, which may be set and cleared by the `Observable`, and which may be queried with `hasChanged()` by any interested observer.

```
public class Observable extends Object {
    // Default Constructor: public Observable()
    // Public Instance Methods
        public synchronized void addObserver(Observer o);
        public synchronized int countObservers();
        public synchronized void deleteObserver(Observer o);
        public synchronized void deleteObservers();
        public synchronized boolean hasChanged();
        public void notifyObservers();
        public synchronized void notifyObservers(Object arg);
    // Protected Instance Methods
        protected synchronized void clearChanged();
        protected synchronized void setChanged();
}
```

java.util.Observer

This interface defines the `update()` method required for an object to "observe" subclasses of `Observable`. An `Observer` registers interested in an `Observable()` by calling the `Observable.addObserver()` method. `Observer` objects that have been registered in this way will have their `update()` method invoked by the `Observable` when that object has changed.

```
public abstract interface Observer {
    // Public Instance Methods
        public abstract void update(Observable o, Object arg);
}
```

java.util.Properties

This class is an extension of `Hashtable` which allows key/value pairs to be read from and written to a stream. The `Properties` class is used to implement the system properties list, which supports user customization by allowing programs to look up the value of named resources.

Any `Properties` object may be created with another `Properties` object specified that contains default values. Keys (property names) and values are associated in a `Properties` object with the `Hashtable` method `put()`. Values are looked up with `getProperty()`—if this method does not find the key in the current `Properties` object, then it looks in the default `Properties` object that was passed to the constructor method. A default value may also be specified in case the key is not found at all.

`propertyNames()` returns an enumeration of all property names (keys) stored in the `Properties` object and (recursively) also all property names stored in the default `Properties` object associated with it. `list()` prints the properties stored in a `Properties` object. It is useful for debugging. `save()` writes a `Properties` object to a stream. `load()` reads key/value pairs from a stream and stores them in a `Properties` object.

```
public class Properties extends Hashtable {
    // Public Constructors
        public Properties();
        public Properties(Properties defaults);
    // Protected Instance Variables
        protected Properties defaults;
    // Public Instance Methods
        public String getProperty(String key);
        public String getProperty(String key, String defaultValue);
        public void list(PrintStream out);
        public synchronized void load(InputStream in) throws IOException;
        public Enumeration propertyNames();
        public synchronized void save(OutputStream out, String header);
}
```

java.util.Random

This class implements a pseudo-random number generator. The instance methods return random values for various Java primitive types. `nextDouble()` and `nextFloat()` return a value between 0.0 and 1.0. `nextLong()` and `nextInt()` return `long` and `int` values distributed across the range of those data types. `nextGaussian()` returns pseudo-random values with a Gaussian distribution—the mean of the values is 0.0, and the standard deviation is 1.0. You can use the `setSeed()` method or the optional constructor argument to initialize the pseudo-random number generator with some variable seed value other than the current time (the default), or with a constant to ensure a repeatable sequence of pseudo-randomness.

```
public class Random extends Object {
    // Public Constructors
        public Random();
        public Random(long seed);
    // Public Instance Methods
        public double nextDouble();
        public float nextFloat();
        public synchronized double nextGaussian();
        public int nextInt();
        public long nextLong();
        public synchronized void setSeed(long seed);
}
```

java.util.Stack

This class implements a last-in-first-out stack of objects. `push()` puts an object on the top of the stack. `pop()` removes and returns the top object from the stack. `peek()` returns the top object without removing it.

```
public class Stack extends Vector {
    // Default Constructor: public Stack()
    // Public Instance Methods
        public boolean empty();
        public Object peek() throws EmptyStackException;
        public Object pop() throws EmptyStackException;
        public Object push(Object item);
        public int search(Object o);
}
```


java.util.StringTokenizer

This class, when instantiated with a `String`, breaks the string up into tokens separated by any of the characters in the specified string of delimiters. (For example, words separated by space and tab characters are tokens.) The `hasMoreTokens()` and `nextToken()` methods can be used to obtain the tokens in order.

→

When you create a StringTokenizer you may specify a string of delimiter characters to use for the entire string, or you may rely on the default whitespace delimiters. You may also specify whether the delimiters themselves should be returned as tokens. You may optionally specify a new string of delimiter characters when you call nextToken().

countTokens() returns the number of tokens in the string. Note that StringTokenizer implements the Enumeration interface, so you may also access the tokens with the familiar hasMoreElements() and nextElement() methods.

```
public class StringTokenizer extends Object implements Enumeration {
    // Public Constructors
        public StringTokenizer(String str, String delim, boolean returnTokens);
        public StringTokenizer(String str, String delim);
        public StringTokenizer(String str);
    // Public Instance Methods
        public int countTokens();
        public boolean hasMoreElements();
        public boolean hasMoreTokens();
        public Object nextElement() throws NoSuchElementException;
        public String nextToken() throws NoSuchElementException;
        public String nextToken(String delim);
}
```

java.util.Vector

This class implements an array of objects that grows in size as necessary. It is useful when you need to keep track of a number of objects but do not know in advance how many there will be. There are a number of methods for storing objects in and removing objects from the Vector. Other methods look up the object at specified positions in the Vector, or search for specified objects within the Vector. elements() returns an Enumeration of the objects stored in the Vector. size() returns the number of objects currently stored in the Vector. capacity() returns the number of elements that may be stored before the vector's internal storage must be reallocated.

```
public class Vector extends Object implements Cloneable {
    // Public Constructors
        public Vector(int initialCapacity, int capacityIncrement);
        public Vector(int initialCapacity);
        public Vector();
    // Protected Instance Variables
        protected int capacityIncrement;
        protected int elementCount;
        protected Object[] elementData;
    // Public Instance Methods
        public final synchronized void addElement(Object obj);
        public final int capacity();
        public synchronized Object clone(); // Overrides Object.clone()
        public final boolean contains(Object elem);
        public final synchronized void copyInto(Object[] anArray);
        public final synchronized Object elementAt(int index) throws ArrayIndexOutOfBoundsException;
```

```
public final synchronized Enumeration elements();
public final synchronized void ensureCapacity(int minCapacity);
public final synchronized Object firstElement() throws NoSuchElementException;
public final int indexOf(Object elem);
public final synchronized int indexOf(Object elem, int index);
public final synchronized void insertElementAt(Object obj, int index)
                                        throws ArrayIndexOutOfBoundsException;
public final boolean isEmpty();
public final synchronized Object lastElement() throws NoSuchElementException;
public final int lastIndexOf(Object elem);
public final synchronized int lastIndexOf(Object elem, int index);
public final synchronized void removeAllElements();
public final synchronized boolean removeElement(Object obj);
public final synchronized void removeElementAt(int index)
                                        throws ArrayIndexOutOfBoundsException;
public final synchronized void setElementAt(Object obj, int index)
                                        throws ArrayIndexOutOfBoundsException;
public final synchronized void setSize(int newSize);
public final int size();
public final synchronized String toString();  // Overrides Object.toString()
public final synchronized void trimToSize();
}
```

Java Errors and Exceptions

This section lists the errors and exceptions thrown by the Java interpreter and by the methods of the Java API. The classes listed here are all subclasses of `java.lang.Error` and `java.lang.Exception`, but they are part of several different packages. Figure 26-1 and Figure 26-2 show the exception and error class hierarchy and also indicate the package each class belongs to.

An `Error` generally signals that a non-recoverable error has occurred. They should not be caught and usually cause the Java interpreter to display a message and exit. An exception is the `ThreadDeath` error which causes the thread in which it is thrown to stop running, but which does not print an error message or affect other threads.

An `Exception` signals an abnormal condition that must be specially handled to prevent program termination. Exceptions may be caught and handled. Exceptions that are not subclasses of `RuntimeException` must be caught or declared in the `throws` clause of any method that can throw them. These exception classes represent routine abnormal conditions that should be anticipated and caught to prevent program termination.

All errors and exceptions are subclasses of `Throwable`. As such, they may all have a message associated with them, which can be retrieved with the `getMessage()` method. You can use this to print a message describing the error or exception. You can also use `java.lang.Throwable` methods to display a stack trace of where the exception or error occurred.

Note that the classes listed in this section are alphabetized by class name, not by package name. Because both package name and class name appear in the headings, it may appear that they are out of order.

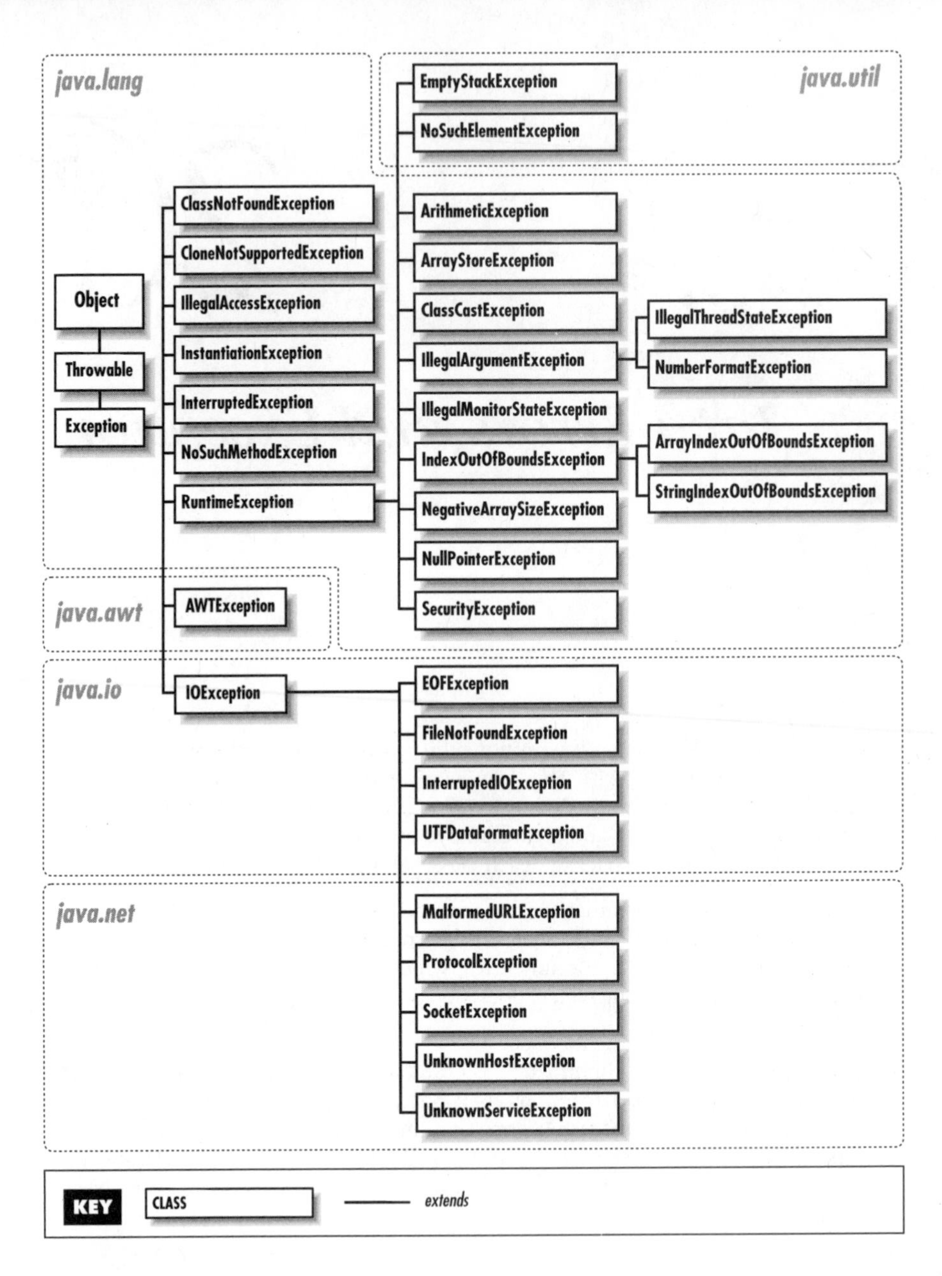

java.lang
java.util
EmptyStackException
NoSuchElementException
ClassNotFoundException
CloneNotSupportedException
IllegalAccessException
InstantiationException
InterruptedException
NoSuchMethodException
RuntimeException
Object
Throwable
Exception
ArithmeticException
ArrayStoreException
ClassCastException
IllegalArgumentException
IllegalThreadStateException
NumberFormatException
IllegalMonitorStateException
IndexOutOfBoundsException
ArrayIndexOutOfBoundsException
StringIndexOutOfBoundsException
NegativeArraySizeException
NullPointerException
SecurityException
java.awt
AWTException
java.io
IOException
EOFException
FileNotFoundException
InterruptedIOException
UTFDataFormatException
java.net
MalformedURLException
ProtocolException
SocketException
UnknownHostException
UnknownServiceException
KEY
CLASS
extends

Figure 26-1: Java exception classes

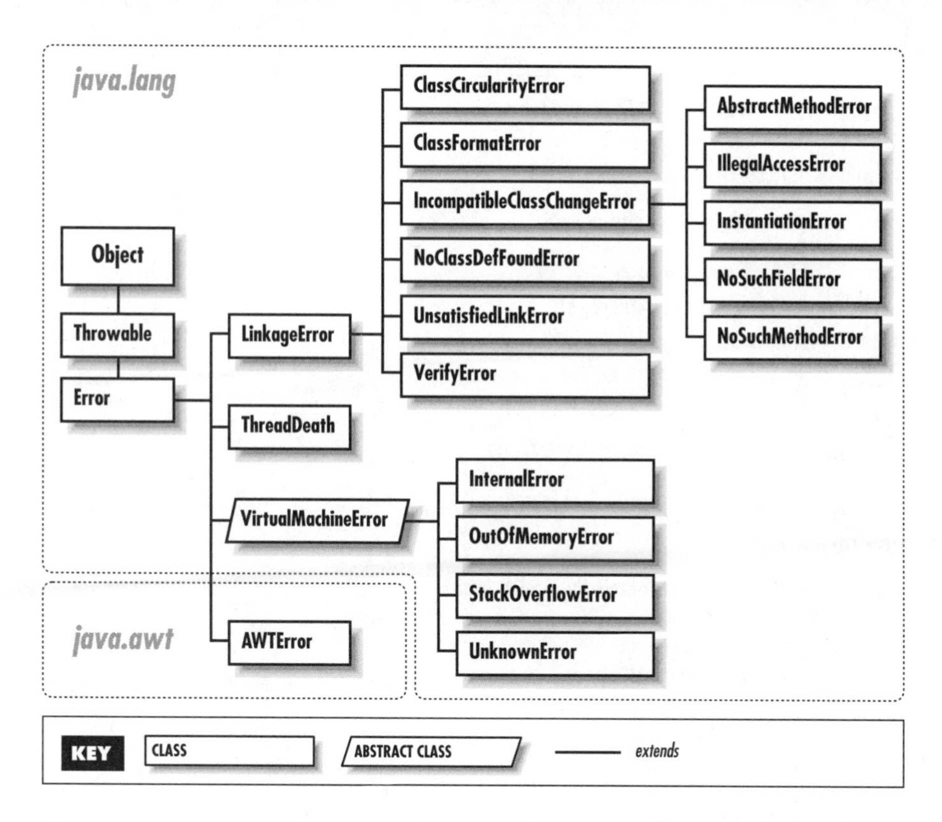

Figure 26-2: Java error classes

---

java.awt.AWTError

Signals that an error has occurred in the `java.awt` package.

```
public class AWTError extends Error {
    // Public Constructor
        public AWTError(String msg);
}
```

---

java.awt.AWTException

Signals that an exception has occurred in the `java.awt` package.

```
public class AWTException extends Exception {
    // Public Constructor
        public AWTException(String msg);
}
```

Errors and Exceptions

java.lang.AbstractMethodError

Signals an attempt to invoke an abstract method.

```
public class AbstractMethodError extends IncompatibleClassChangeError {
    // Public Constructors
       public AbstractMethodError();
       public AbstractMethodError(String s);
}
```

java.lang.ArithmeticException

A `RuntimeException` that signals an exceptional arithmetic condition, such as integer division by zero.

```
public class ArithmeticException extends RuntimeException {
    // Public Constructors
       public ArithmeticException();
       public ArithmeticException(String s);
}
```

java.lang.ArrayIndexOutOfBoundsException

Signals that an array index less than zero or greater than or equal to the array size has been used.

```
public class ArrayIndexOutOfBoundsException extends IndexOutOfBoundsException {
    // Public Constructors
       public ArrayIndexOutOfBoundsException();
       public ArrayIndexOutOfBoundsException(int index);
       public ArrayIndexOutOfBoundsException(String s);
}
```

java.lang.ArrayStoreException

Signals an attempt to store the wrong type of object into an array.

```
public class ArrayStoreException extends RuntimeException {
    // Public Constructors
       public ArrayStoreException();
       public ArrayStoreException(String s);
}
```

java.lang.ClassCastException

Signals an invalid cast of an object to a type of which it is not an instance.

```
public class ClassCastException extends RuntimeException {
    // Public Constructors
        public ClassCastException();
        public ClassCastException(String s);
}
```

java.lang.ClassCircularityError

Signals that a circular dependency has been detected while performing initialization for a class.

```
public class ClassCircularityError extends LinkageError {
    // Public Constructors
        public ClassCircularityError();
        public ClassCircularityError(String s);
}
```

java.lang.ClassFormatError

Signals an error in the binary format of a class file.

```
public class ClassFormatError extends LinkageError {
    // Public Constructors
        public ClassFormatError();
        public ClassFormatError(String s);
}
```

java.lang.ClassNotFoundException

Signals that a class to be loaded could not be found.

```
public class ClassNotFoundException extends Exception {
    // Public Constructors
        public ClassNotFoundException();
        public ClassNotFoundException(String s);
}
```

java.lang.CloneNotSupportedException

Signals that the `clone()` method has been called for an object of a class that does not implement the `Cloneable` interface.

```
public class CloneNotSupportedException extends Exception {
    // Public Constructors
      public CloneNotSupportedException();
      public CloneNotSupportedException(String s);
}
```

java.io.EOFException

An `IOException` that signals the end-of-file.

```
public class EOFException extends IOException {
    // Public Constructors
      public EOFException();
      public EOFException(String s);
}
```

java.util.EmptyStackException

Signals that a `Stack` object is empty.

```
public class EmptyStackException extends RuntimeException {
    // Public Constructor
      public EmptyStackException(); // Empty
}
```

java.lang.Error

A `Throwable` that forms the root of the error hierarchy. Subclasses of `Error`, unlike subclasses of `Exception`, should generally not be caught, and generally cause termination of the program. `getMessage()` returns a message associated with the error. See `Throwable` for other methods.

Subclasses of `Error` need not be declared in the `throws` clause of a method definition.

```
public class Error extends Throwable {
    // Public Constructors
      public Error();
      public Error(String s);
}
```

java.lang.Exception

A `Throwable` that forms the root of the exception hierarchy. Programs may catch subclasses of `Exception`, but generally should not catch subclasses of `Error`. `getMessage()` returns a message associated with the exception. See `Throwable` for other methods.

Subclasses of `Exception` that are not subclasses of `RuntimeException` must be declared in the `throws` clause of any method that can throw them.

```
public class Exception extends Throwable {
    // Public Constructors
        public Exception();
        public Exception(String s);
}
```

java.io.FileNotFoundException

An `IOException` that signals that a specified file was not found.

```
public class FileNotFoundException extends IOException {
    // Public Constructors
        public FileNotFoundException();
        public FileNotFoundException(String s);
}
```

java.io.IOException

Signals that an exceptional condition has occurred during input or output. This class has several more specific subclasses. See `EOFException`, `FileNotFoundException`, `InterruptedIOException`, and `UTFDataFormatException`.

```
public class IOException extends Exception {
    // Public Constructors
        public IOException();
        public IOException(String s);
}
```

Errors and Exceptions

java.lang.IllegalAccessError

Signals an attempted use of a class, method, or variable that is not accessible.

```
public class IllegalAccessError extends IncompatibleClassChangeError {
    // Public Constructors
        public IllegalAccessError();
        public IllegalAccessError(String s);
}
```

java.lang.IllegalAccessException

Signals that a class or initializer is not accessible. Thrown by `Class.newInstance()`.

```
public class IllegalAccessException extends Exception {
    // Public Constructors
        public IllegalAccessException();
        public IllegalAccessException(String s);
}
```

java.lang.IllegalArgumentException

Signals an illegal argument to a method. See subclasses `IllegalThreadStateException` and `NumberFormatException`.

```
public class IllegalArgumentException extends RuntimeException {
    // Public Constructors
        public IllegalArgumentException();
        public IllegalArgumentException(String s);
}
```

java.lang.IllegalMonitorStateException

Signals an illegal monitor state. It is thrown by the object `notify()` and `wait()` methods used for thread synchronization.

```
public class IllegalMonitorStateException extends RuntimeException {
    // Public Constructors
        public IllegalMonitorStateException();
        public IllegalMonitorStateException(String s);
}
```

java.lang.IllegalThreadStateException

Signals that a thread is not in the appropriate state for an attempted operation to succeed.

```
public class IllegalThreadStateException extends IllegalArgumentException {
    // Public Constructors
        public IllegalThreadStateException();
        public IllegalThreadStateException(String s);
}
```

java.lang.IncompatibleClassChangeError

This is the superclass of a group of related error types. It signals some kind of illegal use of a legal class.

```
public class IncompatibleClassChangeError extends LinkageError {
    // Public Constructors
        public IncompatibleClassChangeError();
        public IncompatibleClassChangeError(String s);
}
```

java.lang.IndexOutOfBoundsException

Signals that an index is out of bounds. See the subclasses `ArrayIndexOutOfBoundsException` and `StringIndexOutOfBoundsException`.

```
public class IndexOutOfBoundsException extends RuntimeException {
    // Public Constructors
        public IndexOutOfBoundsException();
        public IndexOutOfBoundsException(String s);
}
```

java.lang.InstantiationError

Signals an attempt to instantiate an interface or abstract class.

```
public class InstantiationError extends IncompatibleClassChangeError {
    // Public Constructors
        public InstantiationError();
        public InstantiationError(String s);
}
```

java.lang.InstantiationException

Signals an attempt to instantiate an interface or an abstract class.

```
public class InstantiationException extends Exception {
    // Public Constructors
        public InstantiationException();
        public InstantiationException(String s);
}
```

java.lang.InternalError

Signals an internal error in the Java interpreter.

```
public class InternalError extends VirtualMachineError {
    // Public Constructors
        public InternalError();
        public InternalError(String s);
}
```

java.lang.InterruptedException

Signals that the thread has been interrupted.

```
public class InterruptedException extends Exception {
    // Public Constructors
        public InterruptedException();
        public InterruptedException(String s);
}
```

java.io.InterruptedIOException

An `IOException` that signals that an input or output operation was interrupted. The `bytesTransferred` variable contains the number of bytes read or written before the operation was interrupted.

```
public class InterruptedIOException extends IOException {
    // Public Constructors
        public InterruptedIOException();
        public InterruptedIOException(String s);
    // Public Instance Variables
        public int bytesTransferred;
}
```

java.lang.LinkageError

The superclass of a group of errors that signal problems linking a class or resolving dependencies between classes.

```
public class LinkageError extends Error {
    // Public Constructors
        public LinkageError();
        public LinkageError(String s);
}
```

java.net.MalformedURLException

Signals that an unparsable URL specification has been passed to a method.

```
public class MalformedURLException extends IOException {
    // Public Constructors
        public MalformedURLException(); // Empty
        public MalformedURLException(String msg);
}
```

java.lang.NegativeArraySizeException

Signals an attempt to allocate an array with fewer than zero elements.

```
public class NegativeArraySizeException extends RuntimeException {
    // Public Constructors
        public NegativeArraySizeException();
        public NegativeArraySizeException(String s);
}
```

java.lang.NoClassDefFoundError

Signals that the definition of a specified class could not be found.

```
public class NoClassDefFoundError extends LinkageError {
    // Public Constructors
        public NoClassDefFoundError();
        public NoClassDefFoundError(String s);
}
```

java.util.NoSuchElementException

Signals that there are no elements in an object (such as a `Vector`) or that there are no *more* elements in an object (such as an `Enumeration`).

```
public class NoSuchElementException extends RuntimeException {
    // Public Constructors
        public NoSuchElementException();
        public NoSuchElementException(String s);
}
```

java.lang.NoSuchFieldError

Signals that a specified field could not be found.

```
public class NoSuchFieldError extends IncompatibleClassChangeError {
    // Public Constructors
        public NoSuchFieldError();
        public NoSuchFieldError(String s);
}
```

java.lang.NoSuchMethodError

Signals that a specified method could not be found.

```
public class NoSuchMethodError extends IncompatibleClassChangeError {
    // Public Constructors
        public NoSuchMethodError();
        public NoSuchMethodError(String s);
}
```

java.lang.NoSuchMethodException

Signals that a specified method could not be found.

```
public class NoSuchMethodException extends Exception {
    // Public Constructors
        public NoSuchMethodException();
        public NoSuchMethodException(String s);
}
```

java.lang.NullPointerException

Signals an attempt to access a field or invoke a method of a `null` object.

```
public class NullPointerException extends RuntimeException {
    // Public Constructors
        public NullPointerException();
        public NullPointerException(String s);
}
```

java.lang.NumberFormatException

Signals an illegal number format.

```
public class NumberFormatException extends IllegalArgumentException {
    // Public Constructors
        public NumberFormatException();
        public NumberFormatException(String s);
}
```

java.lang.OutOfMemoryError

Signals that the interpreter has run out of memory (and that garbage collection is unable to free any memory).

```
public class OutOfMemoryError extends VirtualMachineError {
    // Public Constructors
        public OutOfMemoryError();
        public OutOfMemoryError(String s);
}
```

java.net.ProtocolException

Signals a protocol error in the `Socket` class.

```
public class ProtocolException extends IOException {
    // Public Constructors
        public ProtocolException(String host);
        public ProtocolException(); // Empty
}
```

java.lang.RuntimeException

This exception type is not used directly, but serves as a superclass of a group of run-time exceptions that need not be declared in the `throws` clause of a method definition. These exceptions need not be declared because they are run-time conditions that can generally occur in any Java method. Thus declaring them would be unduly burdensome, and Java does not require it.

```
public class RuntimeException extends Exception {
    // Public Constructors
        public RuntimeException();
        public RuntimeException(String s);
}
```

java.lang.SecurityException

Signals that an operation is not permitted for security reasons.

```
public class SecurityException extends RuntimeException {
    // Public Constructors
        public SecurityException();
        public SecurityException(String s);
}
```

java.net.SocketException

Signals an exceptional condition while using a socket.

```
public class SocketException extends IOException {
    // Public Constructors
        public SocketException(String msg);
        public SocketException(); // Empty
}
```

java.lang.StackOverflowError

Signals that a stack overflow has occurred within the Java interpreter.

```
public class StackOverflowError extends VirtualMachineError {
    // Public Constructors
        public StackOverflowError();
        public StackOverflowError(String s);
}
```

java.lang.StringIndexOutOfBoundsException

Signals that the index used to access a character of a `String` or `StringBuffer` is less than zero or is too large.

```
public class StringIndexOutOfBoundsException extends IndexOutOfBoundsException {
    // Public Constructors
        public StringIndexOutOfBoundsException();
        public StringIndexOutOfBoundsException(String s);
        public StringIndexOutOfBoundsException(int index);
}
```

java.lang.ThreadDeath

Signals that a thread should terminate. This error is thrown in a thread when the `Thread.stop()` method is called for that thread. This is an unusual `Error` type that simply causes a thread to be terminated, but does not print an error message or cause the interpreter to exit. You may catch `ThreadDeath` errors to do any necessary cleanup for a thread, but if you do, you must re-throw the error, so that the thread actually terminates.

```
public class ThreadDeath extends Error {
    // Default Constructor: public ThreadDeath()
}
```

java.io.UTFDataFormatException

An `IOException` that signals that a malformed UTF-8 string has been encountered by a class that implements the `DataInput` interface. UTF-8 is an ASCII-compatible "transformation format" for Unicode characters that is often used to store and transmit Unicode text.

```
public class UTFDataFormatException extends IOException {
    // Public Constructors
        public UTFDataFormatException();
        public UTFDataFormatException(String s);
}
```

java.lang.UnknownError

Signals that an unknown error has occurred at the level of the Java Virtual Machine.

```
public class UnknownError extends VirtualMachineError {
    // Public Constructors
        public UnknownError();
        public UnknownError(String s);
}
```

Errors and Exceptions

java.net.UnknownHostException

Signals that the name of a specified host could not be resolved.

```
public class UnknownHostException extends IOException {
    // Public Constructors
        public UnknownHostException(String host);
        public UnknownHostException(); // Empty
}
```

java.net.UnknownServiceException

Signals an attempt to use an unsupported service of a network connection.

```
public class UnknownServiceException extends IOException {
    // Public Constructors
        public UnknownServiceException(); // Empty
        public UnknownServiceException(String msg);
}
```

java.lang.UnsatisfiedLinkError

Signals that Java cannot satisfy all of the links in a class that it has loaded.

```
public class UnsatisfiedLinkError extends LinkageError {
    // Public Constructors
        public UnsatisfiedLinkError();
        public UnsatisfiedLinkError(String s);
}
```

java.lang.VerifyError

Signals that a class has not passed the byte-code verification procedures.

```
public class VerifyError extends LinkageError {
    // Public Constructors
        public VerifyError();
        public VerifyError(String s);
}
```

java.lang.VirtualMachineError

An abstract error type that serves as superclass for a group of errors related to the Java Virtual Machine. See `InternalError`, `UnknownError`, `OutOfMemoryError`, and `StackOverflowError`.

```
public abstract class VirtualMachineError extends Error {
    // Public Constructors
        public VirtualMachineError();
        public VirtualMachineError(String s);
}
```

Part V

API Cross References

Part V consists of cross-reference indexes to the API quick reference of Part IV. The *How to Use This Book* section at the beginning of the book explains how these indexes help you find information you can't look up directly in Part IV.

Class Defined-In Index

This index tells you in which package a given class is defined. It is useful when you encounter an unfamiliar class (specified without its fully-qualified package name) in Java source code, in the API quick reference, or in another one of the quick reference indexes. Once you've looked up the package name of a class, you'll know where in Part IV to find the class's documentation.

AbstractMethodError: java.lang
AppletContext: java.applet
AppletStub: java.applet
Applet: java.applet
ArithmeticException: java.lang
ArrayIndexOutOfBoundsException: java.lang
ArrayStoreException: java.lang
AudioClip: java.applet
AWTError: java.awt
AWTException: java.awt
BitSet: java.util
Boolean: java.lang
BorderLayout: java.awt
BufferedInputStream: java.io
BufferedOutputStream: java.io
ButtonPeer: java.awt.peer
Button: java.awt
ByteArrayInputStream: java.io
ByteArrayOutputStream: java.io
CanvasPeer: java.awt.peer
Canvas: java.awt
CardLayout: java.awt
Character: java.lang
CheckboxGroup: java.awt
CheckboxMenuItemPeer: java.awt.peer
CheckboxMenuItem: java.awt
CheckboxPeer: java.awt.peer
Checkbox: java.awt
ChoicePeer: java.awt.peer
Choice: java.awt
ClassCastException: java.lang
ClassCircularityError: java.lang
ClassFormatError: java.lang
ClassLoader: java.lang
ClassNotFoundException: java.lang
Class: java.lang
Cloneable: java.lang
CloneNotSupportedException: java.lang
ColorModel: java.awt.image
Color: java.awt
Compiler: java.lang
ComponentPeer: java.awt.peer
Component: java.awt
ContainerPeer: java.awt.peer
Container: java.awt
ContentHandlerFactory: java.net
ContentHandler: java.net

Class Defined-In

Method Defined-In Index

This index allows you to look up a method name and find all the classes and interfaces that define that method. This is often useful when you want to look up documentation for some method of a class, but you don't know whether it is defined directly by the class or if it's inherited from one of the various superclasses.

Note that constructors are not included in this index; they are obviously defined in a class of the same name. Use Section 27, *Class Defined-In Index*, if you are unfamiliar with a class you find here and need to look up the package it is part of.

Method Defined-In

Subclass Index

This index allows you to look up a class (or interface) and find a list of classes (or interfaces) that extend it. The API documentation lets you look up the superclass of a class; this index lets you look up its subclasses. This index is useful in the same way that a class-hierarchy diagram is.

If you do not know what package a class listed here is defined in, use Section 27, *Class Defined-In Index*, to look it up.

ColorModel: DirectColorModel, IndexColorModel

Component: Button, Canvas, Checkbox, Choice, Container, Label, List, Scrollbar, TextComponent

ComponentPeer: ButtonPeer, CanvasPeer, CheckboxPeer, ChoicePeer, ContainerPeer, LabelPeer, ListPeer, ScrollbarPeer, TextComponentPeer

Container: Panel, Window

ContainerPeer: PanelPeer, WindowPeer

Dialog: FileDialog

DialogPeer: FileDialogPeer

Dictionary: Hashtable

Error: AWTError, LinkageError, ThreadDeath, VirtualMachineError

Exception: AWTException, ClassNotFoundException, CloneNotSupportedException, IllegalAccessException, InstantiationException, InterruptedException, IOException, NoSuchMethodException, RuntimeException

FilterInputStream: BufferedInputStream, DataInputStream, LineNumberInputStream, PushbackInputStream

FilterOutputStream: BufferedOutputStream, DataOutputStream, PrintStream

Hashtable: Properties

IllegalArgumentException: IllegalThreadStateException, NumberFormatException

ImageFilter: CropImageFilter, RGBImageFilter

IncompatibleClassChangeError: AbstractMethodError, IllegalAccessError, InstantiationError, NoSuchFieldError, NoSuchMethodError

IndexOutOfBoundsException: ArrayIndexOutOfBoundsException, StringIndexOutOfBoundsException

InputStream: ByteArrayInputStream, FileInputStream, FilterInputStream, PipedInputStream, SequenceInputStream, StringBufferInputStream

IOException: EOFException, FileNotFoundException, InterruptedIOException, MalformedURLException, ProtocolException, SocketException, UnknownHostException, UnknownServiceException, UTFDataFormatException

LinkageError: ClassCircularityError, ClassFormatError, IncompatibleClassChangeError, NoClassDefFoundError, UnsatisfiedLinkError, VerifyError

MenuComponent: MenuBar, MenuItem

MenuComponentPeer: MenuBarPeer, MenuItemPeer

MenuItem: CheckboxMenuItem, Menu

MenuItemPeer: CheckboxMenuItemPeer, MenuPeer

Number: Double, Float, Integer, Long

Object: BitSet, Boolean, BorderLayout, CardLayout, Character, CheckboxGroup, Class, ClassLoader, Color, ColorModel, Compiler, Component, ContentHandler, DatagramPacket, DatagramSocket, Date, Dictionary, Dimension, Event, File, FileDescriptor, FilteredImageSource, FlowLayout, Font, FontMetrics, Graphics, GridBagConstraints, GridBagLayout, GridLayout, Image, ImageFilter, InetAddress, InputStream, Insets, Math, MediaTracker, MemoryImageSource, MenuComponent, Number, Observable, OutputStream, PixelGrabber, Point, Polygon, Process, Random, RandomAccessFile, Rectangle, Runtime, SecurityManager, ServerSocket, Socket, SocketImpl, StreamTokenizer, String, StringBuffer, StringTokenizer, System, Thread, ThreadGroup, Throwable, Toolkit, URL, URLConnection, URLEncoder, URLStreamHandler, Vector

OutputStream: ByteArrayOutputStream, FileOutputStream, FilterOutputStream, PipedOutputStream

Panel: Applet

RuntimeException: ArithmeticException, ArrayStoreException, ClassCastException, EmptyStackException, IllegalArgumentException, IllegalMonitorStateException, IndexOutOfBoundsException, NegativeArraySizeException, NoSuchElementException, NullPointerException, SecurityException

TextComponent: TextArea, TextField

TextComponentPeer: TextAreaPeer, TextFieldPeer

Throwable: Error, Exception

Vector: Stack

VirtualMachineError: InternalError, OutOfMemoryError, StackOverflowError, UnknownError

Window: Dialog, Frame

WindowPeer: DialogPeer, FramePeer

30

Implemented-By Index

This index allows you to look up an interface and find a list of classes that implement the interface. This is useful when you know you want to work with an instance of the interface, but don't know what possible classes you can use.

Note that not all interfaces in the Java API appear in this index—those that are not implemented by a public class in the API do not appear. It is the nature of interfaces to be useful for referring to instances of non-public classes. Since interfaces are frequently used in this way by the Java API, many interfaces do not appear here. For example, while a fair number of Java classes implement an `Enumeration` object, only one of the classes that implements that interface is public.

Implemented-By

31

Returned-By Index

This index allows you to look up a class or interface type and find out which methods return objects of that type. This index is useful when you know you want to work with an object of a particular type, but you're not sure of the best way to obtain an object of that type.

Constructor methods have been omitted from this index, as it is obvious what type of object they return. Methods with no return value, and those that return a primitive type have been omitted. Methods that return `String` or `Dimension` have also been omitted since there are too many of them to be useful for this index.

Return types and method names are specified without package names in this index. If you do not know what package a class listed here is defined in, use Section 27, *Class Defined-In Index*, to look it up.

Applet:
AppletContext.getApplet()
AppletContext:
Applet.getAppletContext()
AppletStub.getAppletContext()
AudioClip:
Applet.getAudioClip()
AppletContext.getAudioClip()
Boolean:
Boolean.valueOf()
ButtonPeer:
Toolkit.createButton()
CanvasPeer:
Toolkit.createCanvas()
Checkbox:
CheckboxGroup.getCurrent()
CheckboxGroup:
Checkbox.getCheckboxGroup()
CheckboxMenuItemPeer:
Toolkit.createCheckboxMenuItem()
CheckboxPeer:
Toolkit.createCheckbox()
ChoicePeer:
Toolkit.createChoice()
Class:
Class.forName()
Class.getSuperclass()
ClassLoader.defineClass()
ClassLoader.findSystemClass()
ClassLoader.loadClass()
Object.getClass()

Returned-By

Passed-To Index

This index allows you to look up a class or interface type and find out which methods take objects of that type as arguments. This index is useful when you want to use an object of a particular type, and need to find out what possible operations you can perform on it. (You should of course also look up the methods defined by the object's class and all of its superclasses.)

Primitive types, and the `String` class, have been omitted from this index, as there are far too many methods that accept arguments of those types to be included in an index like this one.

Argument types and method names are specified without package names in this index. If you do not know what package a class listed here is defined in, use Section 27, *Class Defined-In Index*, to look it up.

Passed-To

33

Thrown-By Index

This index allows you to look up the name of an exception or an error and find a list of all methods (with their classes) that throw that exception or error. This can sometimes be useful when debugging Java programs.

Methods are specified without package names in this index. If you do not know what package a class listed here is defined in, use Section 27, *Class Defined-In Index*, to look it up.

PipedInputStream.close()
PipedInputStream.connect()
PipedInputStream.read()
PipedOutputStream.PipedOutput-Stream()
PipedOutputStream.close()
PipedOutputStream.connect()
PipedOutputStream.write()
PrintStream.write()
Properties.load()
PushbackInputStream.available()
PushbackInputStream.read()
PushbackInputStream.unread()
RandomAccessFile.RandomAccess-File()
RandomAccessFile.close()
RandomAccessFile.getFD()
RandomAccessFile.getFilePointer()
RandomAccessFile.length()
RandomAccessFile.read()
RandomAccessFile.readBoolean()
RandomAccessFile.readByte()
RandomAccessFile.readChar()
RandomAccessFile.readDouble()
RandomAccessFile.readFloat()
RandomAccessFile.readFully()
RandomAccessFile.readInt()
RandomAccessFile.readLine()
RandomAccessFile.readLong()
RandomAccessFile.readShort()
RandomAccessFile.readUTF()
RandomAccessFile.readUnsigned-Byte()
RandomAccessFile.readUnsigned-Short()
RandomAccessFile.seek()
RandomAccessFile.skipBytes()
RandomAccessFile.write()
RandomAccessFile.writeBoolean()
RandomAccessFile.writeByte()
RandomAccessFile.writeBytes()
RandomAccessFile.writeChar()
RandomAccessFile.writeChars()
RandomAccessFile.writeDouble()
RandomAccessFile.writeFloat()
RandomAccessFile.writeInt()
RandomAccessFile.writeLong()
RandomAccessFile.writeShort()
RandomAccessFile.writeUTF()
Runtime.exec()
SequenceInputStream.close()
SequenceInputStream.read()
ServerSocket.ServerSocket()
ServerSocket.accept()
ServerSocket.close()
ServerSocket.setSocketFactory()
Socket.Socket()
Socket.close()
Socket.getInputStream()
Socket.getOutputStream()
Socket.setSocketImplFactory()
SocketImpl.accept()
SocketImpl.available()
SocketImpl.bind()
SocketImpl.close()
SocketImpl.connect()
SocketImpl.create()
SocketImpl.getInputStream()
SocketImpl.getOutputStream()
SocketImpl.listen()
StreamTokenizer.nextToken()
URL.getContent()
URL.openConnection()
URL.openStream()
URLConnection.connect()
URLConnection.getContent()
URLConnection.getInputStream()
URLConnection.getOutputStream()
URLConnection.guessContentType-FromStream()
URLStreamHandler.open-Connection()

IllegalAccessException:
Class.newInstance()

IllegalArgumentException:
Choice.select()
GridLayout.GridLayout()
Hashtable.Hashtable()
Label.setAlignment()
Scrollbar.Scrollbar()
Thread.setPriority()

IllegalMonitorStateException:
Object.notify()
Object.notifyAll()
Object.wait()

IllegalThreadStateException:
Process.exitValue()
Thread.countStackFrames()
Thread.setDaemon()
Thread.start()
ThreadGroup.destroy()

InstantiationException:
Class.newInstance()

InterruptedException:
MediaTracker.waitForAll()
MediaTracker.waitForID()

Thrown-By

Object.wait()
PixelGrabber.grabPixels()
Process.waitFor()
Thread.join()
Thread.sleep()

MalformedURLException:
URL.URL()

NoClassDefFoundError:
ClassLoader.findSystemClass()

NoSuchElementException:
Enumeration.nextElement()
StringTokenizer.nextElement()
StringTokenizer.nextToken()
Vector.firstElement()
Vector.lastElement()

NullPointerException:
Choice.addItem()
Dictionary.put()
File.File()
Hashtable.contains()
Hashtable.put()
ThreadGroup.ThreadGroup()

NumberFormatException:
Double.Double()
Double.valueOf()
Float.Float()
Float.valueOf()
Integer.Integer()
Integer.parseInt()
Integer.valueOf()
Long.Long()
Long.parseLong()
Long.valueOf()

OutOfMemoryError:
Object.clone()

SecurityException:
SecurityManager.SecurityManager()
SecurityManager.checkAccept()
SecurityManager.checkAccess()
SecurityManager.checkConnect()
SecurityManager.checkCreateClass-Loader()
SecurityManager.checkDelete()
SecurityManager.checkExec()
SecurityManager.checkExit()
SecurityManager.checkLink()
SecurityManager.checkListen()
SecurityManager.checkProperties-Access()
SecurityManager.checkProperty-Access()
SecurityManager.checkRead()
SecurityManager.checkWrite()
System.setSecurityManager()
Thread.checkAccess()
ThreadGroup.checkAccess()

SocketException:
DatagramSocket.DatagramSocket()
ServerSocket.setSocketFactory()
Socket.setSocketImplFactory()

StringIndexOutOfBoundsException:
String.String()
String.charAt()
String.substring()
StringBuffer.charAt()
StringBuffer.getChars()
StringBuffer.insert()
StringBuffer.setCharAt()
StringBuffer.setLength()

Throwable:
Object.finalize()

UnknownHostException:
InetAddress.getAllByName()
InetAddress.getByName()
InetAddress.getLocalHost()
Socket.Socket()

UnknownServiceException:
URLConnection.getContent()
URLConnection.getInputStream()
URLConnection.getOutputStream()

UnsatisfiedLinkError:
Runtime.load()
Runtime.loadLibrary()
System.load()
System.loadLibrary()

Glossary

This glossary lists all of the keywords in the Java language and gives examples of using them. It also defines a number of object-oriented programing concepts and other terms that arise frequently when programming with Java.

`abstract`

The `abstract` keyword is used to declare abstract methods and classes. An abstract method has no implementation defined—it is declared with arguments and a return type as usual, but the body enclosed in curly braces is replaced with a semicolon. An abstract method cannot be declared `static`, `private`, or `final`. The implementation of an abstract method is provided by a subclass of the class in which it is defined. If an abstract method appears in a class, the class is also abstract. Abstract classes cannot be instantiated. Only a non-abstract subclass that provides an implementation for all the abstract methods may be instantiated. A class cannot be declared both `final` and `abstract`.

```
abstract public class Graphics {
   public abstract void draw_rectangle(int x, int y, int w, int h);
   public abstract void draw_circle(int x, int y, int r);
}
```

API (Application Programming Interface)

An API consists of the functions and variables that programmers are allowed to use in their applications. The Java API consists of all `public` and `protected` methods of all `public` classes in the `java.applet`, `java.awt`, `java.awt.image`, `java.awt.peer`, `java.io`, `java.-lang`, `java.net`, and `java.util` packages.

assignable

An object is assignable to a variable if it has the same type as the variable or if it is a subclass of the type of the variable. If the variable is of an interface type, then the object is assignable to the variable if it is an instance of a class that implements the interface. A primitive type is assignable to a variable if it can be converted to the variable's type without casting.

AWT (Abstract Windowing Toolkit)

This is the name for Java's platform-independent windowing, graphics, and user-interface toolkit.

`boolean`

`boolean` is a primitive Java data type that contains a truth value. The two possible values of a `boolean` variable are `true` and `false`. In Java, `boolean` values cannot be cast to or from any other type, including numeric types. The result of a comparison operator is a `boolean` value and control structures like `if` statements and `while` loops use a `boolean` value to determine how they execute.

```
boolean b;
int i = 5;

b = (i > 3);        // comparisons yield boolean values
if (b) i = 0;       // booleans are used in if statements
b = (i != 0)        // "convert" a number to a boolean by comparing it
i = b?1:0;          // "convert" a boolean to a number with the ?: operator
```

`break`

The `break` statement, without a label, transfers control out of ("breaks out of" or terminates) the nearest enclosing `for`, `while`, `do`, or `switch` statement. If the `break` keyword is followed by an identifier that is the label of an arbitrary enclosing statement, then execution transfers out of that enclosing statement. After the `break` statement is executed, any required `finally` clauses are executed, and control resumes at the statement following the terminated statement.

```
main_loop: for(int i=0; i < 10; i++) {
  try {
              for(int j=0; j < 10; j++) {
                if (j > i) break;// terminate just this loop
                if (a[i][j] == null)
              break main_loop;// do the finally clause and
              }// terminate both loops.
  }
  finally { cleanup(a, i, j); }
}
```

`byte`

`byte` is a primitive Java data type. It is an 8-bit two's-complement signed number (in all implementations). The minimum value is -128 and the maximum value is 127. It can be cast to and from other numeric types.

```
byte[] octet_buffer = new byte[1024];
byte lookup_table[] = {1, 2, 4, 8, 16, 32, 64};
```

`byvalue`

`byvalue` is a reserved keyword in Java. It is not currently used but may be defined by future versions of the language.

`case`

`case` is used to provide numeric labels for statements within a `switch` statement block. See `switch` for an example.

`cast`

`cast` is a reserved keyword in Java. It is not currently used, but may be defined by future versions of the language.

`catch`

The `catch` statement introduces an exception handling block of code following a `try` statement. The `catch` keyword is followed by an exception type and argument name in parentheses, and a block of code within curly braces. When an exception object that is assignable to the specified type is thrown, the object is assigned to the named argument, and the code within the block is executed to handle the exceptional condition. See `try` for an example.

`char`

`char` is a primitive Java data type. A variable of type `char` holds a single 16-bit Unicode character. `char` values may be cast to and from numeric values, but because character data is implicitly unsigned, casts of `char` to `byte` or `short` may result in a negative number. Note that strings in Java are *not* `null`-terminated arrays of `char`.

```
String s = "This is a test";
char last = s.charAt(s.length() - 1);
```

class

An encapsulated collection of data and methods to operate on the data. A class may be instantiated to produce an object that is an instance of the class. See `class` for a description of declaring a class in Java.

`class`

The `class` keyword is used to declare a class, thereby defining a new object type. Its syntax is similar to the `struct` keyword in C. (Note, though, that Java does not support C `struct` or `union` keywords.) The `class` keyword is preceded by zero or more class modifiers. It is followed by: the name of the class, an optional `extends` clause, an optional `implements` clause, an open curly brace, a series of variable and method declarations, and a close curly brace.

```
public class Screwdriver extends Tool implements Torque {
   private int head_type, shaft_length, handle_diameter;
   public void apply_torque(Torqueable screw) {
               // method definition here
   }
   // more variable and methods declarations here.
}
```

class method

A method declared `static`. Methods of this type are not passed implicit `this` references and may only refer to class variables and invoke other class methods of the current class. A class method may be invoked through the class name, rather than through an instance of the class.

class variable

A variable declared `static`. Variables of this type are associated with the class, rather than with a particular instance of the class. There is only one copy of a static variable, regardless of the number of instances of the class that are created.

component

Any of the GUI primitives implemented in the `java.awt` package as subclasses of `Component`. The classes `Button`, `Choice`, and `TextField` (among many others) are components.

`const`

`const` is a reserved keyword in Java. It is not currently used, but may be defined by future versions of the language.

constructor

A method that is invoked automatically when a new instance of a class is created. Constructors are used to initialize the variables of the newly created object. The constructor method has the same name as the class.

Container

One of the `java.awt` classes that can "contain" GUI components. Components contained in a container appear within the boundaries of the container. The classes `Dialog`, `Frame`, `Panel`, and `Window` are containers.

`continue`

The `continue` keyword is optionally followed by an identifier that names the label of an enclosing iteration statement. A `continue` statement stops the iteration in progress and causes execution to resume after the last statement in the `while`, `do`, or `for` loop just before the loop iteration is to begin again. If the `continue` statement specifies an enclosing labelled loop, execution skips to the end of that loop (even though the label appears at the top of the loop). Otherwise, execution skips to the end of the nearest enclosing loop. If there are any `finally` clauses between the `continue` statement and the end of the appropriate loop, these clauses are executed before control is transferred to the end of the loop.

```
big_loop: while(!done) {
  if (test(a,b) == 0) continue;// control goes to point 2.
  try {
            for(int i=0; i < 10; i++) {
              if (a[i] == null)
            continue;// control goes to point 1.
              else if (b[i] == null)
            continue big_loop;// control goes to point 2,
            // after doing the finally block.
              doit(a[i],b[i]);
              // point 1. Increment and start loop again with the test.
            }
  }
  finally { cleanup(a,b); }
  // point 2. Start loop again with the !done test.
}
```

data hiding

An object-oriented programming technique that makes an object's data `private` or `protected` (i.e., hidden) and allows programmers to access and manipulate that data only through method calls. Done well, data hiding can reduce bugs and it promotes reusability and modularity of classes. This technique is also commonly known as encapsulation.

`default`

The `default` keyword is used only within a `switch` statement block. It labels the statements to be executed by default, i.e., when the value of the `switch` expression does not match any of the `case` labels within the `switch` statement block. See `switch` for an example.

`do`

The `do` keyword introduces a `do/while` loop and has exactly the same syntax as in C. The `do/while` construct is far less common than the regular `while` loop. Don't forget that a semicolon is required after the condition in a `do/while` loop.

```
int i = 10;
do {
  do_it(i--);
} while (i != 0);
```

`double`

`double` is a Java primitive data type. A `double` value is a 64-bit ("double-precision") floating-point number represented in IEEE 754 format. The maximum positive and negative values that can be represented by a `double` are ±1.79769313486231570E+308, and the smallest (closest to zero) representable values are ±4.94065645841246544E-324. The constants `java.lang.Double.MAX_VALUE` and `java.lang.Double.-MIN_VALUE` also have these values. When writing a floating-point literal value, you can indicate that it should be treated as a `double` (instead of a `float`) by appending a `d` or `D`. There are four `double` values with special behavior:

positive infinity

This is a special value generated when a positive floating-point value becomes larger than the largest representable value. In arithmetic and comparison operations it behaves like infinity should—it is greater than any other number. The constant `java.lang.Double.POSITIVE_INFINITY` has this value.

negative infinity

This value is like positive infinity, except generated when a negative floating-point number overflows. It is more negative than any other number. The constant `java.lang.Double.NEGA-TIVE_INFINITY` has this value.

negative zero

This value is generated when a very small negative value underflows and becomes effectively zero. Direct comparison (with `==`) of negative zero to "regular" (i.e., positive) zero does not distinguish the two. One way to distinguish these two zero values, however, is to divide by them: one divided by positive zero yields positive infinity, while one divided by negative zero yields negative infinity.

not a number

This value, also commonly known as NaN, is interpreted literally as "not a number." NaN is generated by mathematical operations that do not have defined values, such as zero divided by zero. Most operations that involve NaN as an argument return NaN as their value. The constant `java.lang.Double.NaN` is NaN. Note, though, that comparing NaN for equality with itself always returns `false`, so in order to test whether a number is NaN, use the method `java.lang.Double.isNaN()`.

`else`

The `else` keyword introduces the (optional) alternative clause of an `if` statement. If the expression evaluated by the `if` statement is `false`, then the statements within the `else` block are executed. With nested `if` statements, it is important to pay attention to be sure which `if` an `else` clause refers to. In Java, as in most languages, an `else` clause is part of the nearest `if` statement that does not have an `else`. Of course the easiest way to make this clear is to use curly braces to mark the `if` and `else` blocks, even when they contain only a single statement.

```
if (i == j)
  if (j == k)
                System.out.println("i == k");
  else  // this else goes with if (j == k)
                System.out.println("i != k");
else // this else goes with  if (i == j)
  System.out.println("i != j");
```

encapsulation

See data hiding.

exception

A signal that some unexpected condition has occurred in the program. In Java, exceptions are objects that are subclasses of `Exception` or `Error` (which themselves are subclasses of `Throwable`). Exceptions in Java are "raised" with the `throw` keyword and received with the `catch` keyword. See `throw`, `throws`, and `catch`.

`extends`

The `extends` keyword is used in a `class` declaration to specify the superclass of the class being defined. `extends` must be followed by the name of a class. This class is known as the superclass. The class being defined has access to all the `public` and `protected` variables and methods of the superclass (or, if the class being defined is in the same package, it has access to all non-`private` variables and methods). If a class definition omits the `extends` clause, its superclass is taken to be `java.lang.Object`.

An `extends` clause may also be used in `interface` declarations. In this case, the `extends` clause is followed by one or more comma-separated interface names. The interface being defined implicitly includes all the constants and abstract methods of each of the interfaces it extends. A class that implements this newly defined interface must provide an implementation for all the abstract methods of each of the interfaces that were extended, as well as any abstract methods defined in the new interface.

```
public class Complex extends Number {
   double x, y;
   ....
}
public class bicycle extends vehicle implements wheel {
   ...
}
public interface bicycle_wheel extends wheel, spokes, rubber_tire {
   ...
}
```

`false`

`false` is one of the two possible `boolean` values. Strictly speaking `false` is not a keyword of the Java language, but a literal value like an integer or a character value.

```
boolean done = false;
while(!done) {
   if (test()) done = true;
}
```

`final`

The `final` keyword is a modifier that may be applied to classes, methods, and variables. It has a similar, but not identical meaning in each case. When `final` is applied to a class, it means that the class may never be subclassed. `java.lang.System` is an example of a `final` class.

When the `final` modifier is applied to a method, it means that the method may never be overridden (i.e., hidden by a subclass method with the same name, arguments, and return type). `static` and `private` methods are implicitly `final`, as are all methods of a `final` class. If a method is implicitly or explicitly `final`, the compiler can perform certain optimizations, such as inlining the method, and the interpreter can invoke the method without the overhead of dynamic method lookup.

If `final` is applied to a variable, it means that the variable has a constant value. The definition of a `final` variable must include an initializer to assign a value to the variable; no assignments after initialization are permitted. `static final` variables are used in Java as constants, in much the same way that `#define` is used in C to define constants. If a `final` variable has a constant expression as its initializer, the compiler can treat the variable as a constant itself and perform computations with it at compile-time, rather than at run-time.

```
// A final class: can't be subclassed.
public final class Buffer {
   // A constant: this variable can't be assigned to.
   // Note the capital letters--a convention for constants.
   protected static final int DEFAULT_SIZE = 2048;

   // A final method: a subclass couldn't override this method
   // even if the class were non-final and allowed subclassing.
   public final read(Stream s, int n)
}
```

finalize

finalize is not actually a Java keyword, but a reserved method name. If a class contains an instance method named finalize that has no arguments and returns no value then this method is a finalizer:

```
void finalize()
```

The finalizer is called when an object is no longer being used (i.e., when there are no further references to it), but before the object's memory is actually reclaimed by the system. A finalizer should perform cleanup tasks and free system resources that are not handled by Java's garbage collection system. These may include closing open files or network connections, removing any lock files created on the system, and so on. A finalizer should invoke any superclass finalizer methods by calling super.finalize() as its last statement.

finalizer

A method that is called just before an object is reclaimed by the garbage collector. A finalizer method should release any system resources (other than memory) held by the object. See finalize.

finally

This keyword introduces the finally block of a try/catch/finally construct. catch and finally blocks provide exception handling and routine cleanup for the code in a try block. The finally block is optional, and appears after the try block and after zero or more catch blocks. The code in a finally block is executed once, regardless of how the code in the try block executes. In normal execution, control reaches the end of the try block and then proceeds to the finally block, which generally performs any necessary cleanup.

If control leaves the try block because of a return, continue, or break statement, the contents of the finally block are executed before control transfers to its new destination.

If an exception occurs in the try block, and there is a catch block to handle the exception, control transfers first to the catch block, and then to the finally block. If there is not a local catch block to handle the exception, control transfers first to the finally block, and then propagates up to the nearest catch block that can handle the exception.

Note that if a finally block itself transfers control with a return, continue, or break statement, or by raising an exception, the pending control transfer is abandoned, and this new transfer is processed.

See try for an example.

float

float is a Java primitive data type. A float value is a 32-bit ("single-precision") floating-point number represented in IEEE 754 format. The maximum positive and negative values that can be represented by a float are ±3.40282347E+38, and the smallest (i.e., closest to zero) representable values are ±1.40239846E-45. The class java.lang.Float serves as an object wrapper for primitive float types, and defines these minimum and maximum values as constants. When writing a floating-point literal value, you can indicate that it should be treated as a float (instead of a double) by appending f or F. There are four special values for the type `float`: positive infinity, negative infinity, negative zero, and NaN or not-a-number. These special `float` values have a different representation than the corresponding `double` values, but have the same meanings. See `double` for more information.

`for`

The `for` statement is perhaps the most useful looping construct available in Java. It is identical to the `for` loop in C, with the addition of the C++ ability to declare local loop variables in the initialization section of the loop. Java does not support the C comma operator that allows multiple expressions to be joined into a single expression, but the Java `for` loop does allow multiple comma-separated expressions to appear in the initialization and increment sections (but not the test section) of the loop. Note that because variable declaration syntax also uses the comma, the Java syntax allows you to specify either multiple comma-separated initialization expressions or the declaration (with initializer) of multiple (comma-separated) variables of the same type. You may not mix variable declarations with other expressions.

```
int i;
String s;
for(i=0, s = "testing";// initialize variables
   (i < 10) && (s.length() >= 1);// test for continuation
   i++, s = s.substring(1))// increment variables
{
   System.out.println(s);// loop body
}

// for loop with local loop variable declaration
for(int i = 0, j=10; i < j; i++, j--) System.out.println("k = " + i*j);
```

`future`

`future` is a reserved keyword in Java. It is not currently used but may be defined by future versions of the language.

garbage collection

The process of reclaiming the memory of objects that are no longer in use. An object is no longer in use when there are no references to it from any other objects in the system and no references in any local variables on the method call stack.

GC

An abbreviation for garbage collection or garbage collector. (Or occasionally "graphics context.")

`generic`

`generic` is a reserved keyword in Java. It is not currently used, but may be defined by future versions of the language.

`goto`

`goto` is a reserved keyword in Java. It is not currently used, but may be defined by future versions of the language.

GUI (graphical user interface)

A GUI is a user interface constructed from graphical push buttons, text fields, pulldown menus, dialog boxes, and other standard interface components. In Java, GUIs are implemented with the classes in the `java.awt` package.

`if`

The `if` statement is exactly the same in Java as in C: it executes a given statement (or block of statements) if a given expression is `true`. Alternatively, if the expression evaluates to `false`, then the statement or statements in the optional `else` clause are executed. See `else` for an example; see `switch` for a language construct that chooses among more than two alternatives.

`implements`

The `implements` keyword must be followed by one or more (comma-separated) interface names. It is used in class declarations to indicate that the class implements the named interface or interfaces. The `implements` clause is optional in class declarations; if it appears, it must follow the `extends` clause (if any). If an `implements` clause appears in the declaration of a non-`abstract` class, every method from each specified interface must be implemented by the class or by one of its superclasses.

```
public class GinsuKnife extends Knife implements Slices, Dices {
  ...
}
```

`import`

The `import` statement makes Java classes available to the current class under an abbreviated name. (Java classes are always available by their fully qualified name, assuming that the appropriate class file can be found relative to the `CLASSPATH` environment variable and that the class file is readable. `import` doesn't make the class available; it just saves typing and makes your code more legible). Any number of `import` statements may appear in a Java program. They must appear, however, after the optional `package` statement at the top of the file, and before the first class or interface definition in the file.

There are three forms of the `import` statement:

```
import package ;
import package.class ;
import package.* ;
```

The first form allows the specified package to be known by the name of its last component. For example:

```
import java.awt.image;
```

allows `java.awt.image.ImageFilter` to be called `image.ImageFilter`.

The second form allows the specified class in the specified package to be known by its class name alone. Thus:

```
import java.util.Hashtable;
```

allows you to type `Hashtable` instead of `java.util.Hashtable`.

Finally, the third form of the `import` statement makes all classes in a package available by their class name. For example, the following `import` statement is implicit (you need not specify it yourself) in every Java program:

```
import java.lang.*;
```

It makes the core classes of the language available by their unqualified class name. If two packages imported with this form of the statement contain classes with the same name, those classes must be referred to by their qualified name to resolve the conflict.

inheritance

An important feature of object-oriented programming: Subclasses inherit the non-`private` variables and methods of all their superclasses. That is, an object implicitly contains all the non-`private` variables of its superclass, and can invoke all the non-`private` methods of its superclass.

`inner`

`inner` is a reserved keyword in Java. It is not currently used, but may be defined by future versions of the language.

instance

An object. When a class is instantiated to produce an object, we say that the object is an instance of the class.

`instanceof`

`instanceof` is a Java operator that returns `true` if the object on its left-hand side is an instance of the class (or implements the interface) specified on its right-hand side. `instanceof` returns `false` if the object is not an instance of the specified class or does not implement the specified interface. It also returns `false` if the specified object is `null`.

```
if (tools[i] instanceof Screwdriver) {
   Screwdriver s = (Screwdriver) tools[i];
   s.torque(screws[j]);
}
else if (tools[i] instanceof Hammer) {
   ((Hammer)tools[i]).drive(nails[j]);
}
```

instance method

A non-`static` method of a class. Such a method is passed an implicit `this` reference to the object that invoked it. See also class method, `static`.

instance variable

A non-`static` variable of a class. Copies of such variables occur in every instance of the class that is created. See also class variable, `static`.

`int`

`int` is a primitive Java data type. It is a 32-bit two's-complement signed number (in all implementations). The minimum value is -2147483648 and the maximum value is 2147483647. It can be cast to and from other numeric types.

```
int j;
for(int i = 0; i < 10; i++) out.print(i + ", ");
```

`interface`

The `interface` keyword is used to declare an interface. Declaring an interface is very similar to declaring a class, except for the following differences:

- The only modifiers that may be used with an interface are `public` and `abstract`. All interfaces are implicitly `abstract`, so use of this modifier is optional.
- The `extends` clause of an interface specification may contain one or more (comma-separated) interface names. The interface being declared implicitly contains the constants and methods of each of the interfaces it extends.
- No `implements` clause is permitted in an interface declaration.
- An interface body may not contain any constructors, static class initializers, instance variables, or class methods.
- All variables declared in an interface are implicitly `static` and `final`, and these modifiers may optionally appear in the declaration. All variables must be initialized to a constant expression. All variables in a public interface are implicitly `public`. The `public` modifier is optional. Variables in an interface may not be `transient` or `volatile`.
- All methods in an interface are implicitly `abstract` and must have a semicolon in place of a body. The `abstract` modifier is optional. All methods in a public interface are implicitly `public`. The `public` modifier is optional. Methods in an interface may not be `final`, `native`, `static`, or `synchronized`.

```
public interface Hammer extends Tool {
   // Some constants describing possible shaft
   // materials for a Hammer
   static final byte WOODEN = 1;
   static final byte STEEL  = 2;
   static final byte FIBER  = 3;
   // abstract methods defined by this interface
   public abstract drive(Nail n) ;
   public abstract pull(Nail n) ;
}
```

ISO8859-1

An eight-bit character encoding standardized by the ISO. This encoding is also known as Latin-1 and contains characters from the Latin alphabet suitable for English and most languages of western Europe.

ISO 10646

A four-byte character encoding that includes all of the world's national standard character encodings. Also known as UCS. The two-byte Unicode character set maps to the range 0x00000000 to 0x0000FFFF of ISO 10646.

JDK (Java Developers Kit)

A package of software distributed by Sun Microsystems for Java developers. It includes the Java interpreter, Java classes, and Java development tools: compiler, debugger, disassembler, appletviewer, stub file generator, and documentation generator.

Latin-1
: A nickname for ISO8859-1.

`long`
: `long` is a primitive Java data type. It is a 64-bit two's-complement signed number (in all implementations). The minimum value is -9223372036854775808 and the maximum value is 9223372036854775807. It can be cast to and from other numeric types.

method
: The object-oriented programming term for a function or procedure.

NaN (not-a-number)
: This is a special value of the `double` and `float` data types that represents an undefined result of a mathematical operation, such as zero divided by zero. See `double`.

`native`
: `native` is a modifier that may be applied to method declarations. It indicates that the method is implemented (elsewhere) in C, or in some other platform-dependent fashion. A `native` method should have a semicolon instead of a body. A `native` method cannot be `abstract`, but all other method modifiers may be used with `native` methods.

`new`
: `new` is a unary operator that creates a new object or array (or raises an `OutOfMemoryException` if there is not enough memory available). The `new` syntax to create a new object is:

new *classname* (*argument-list*)

When invoked like this, `new` creates a dynamic instance of the specified class (which must be a non-`abstract` class), initializes all of its instance variables to their default values (`0`, `0.0`, `\u0000`, `false`, or `null`), and then invokes the appropriate constructor to do any further initialization of the object. The "appropriate constructor" is the one that expects arguments with types matching those specified in the argument list (which may be empty). The `new` operator and the `newInstance()` method of the `java.lang.Class` class are the only ways to create new objects.

```
Complex c = new Complex(2.0, 3.0);
Button b = new Button("Quit");
```

The `new` operator can also be used to allocate arrays with the following syntax:

new *typename* [*dimension*] *other-dimensions*

When invoked in this form, `new` allocates an array with *`dimension`* elements. (*`dimension`* may be a constant integer, or an expression that evaluates to an integer.) For single-dimensional arrays, each element of the array is of the type specified by *`typename`*, and may be a primitive type, a class (abstract or not) or an interface. Once the array has been allocated, the elements of the array are initialized to their default values.

Note that objects are not created as the array elements, and that no object constructors are called. If additional dimensions are specified for the array, these subarrays are recursively created.

```
byte[] buffer = new byte[1024];
Font[][] fonts = new Font[5][4];
String[][][] = new String[20][][];
```

`null`

`null` is a special value that indicates that a variable does not refer to any object. The value `null` may be assigned to any class or interface variable. It cannot be cast to any integral type, and should not be considered equal to zero, as in C.

object

An instance of a class. A class models a group of things; an object models a particular member of that group.

`operator`

`operator` is a reserved keyword in Java. It is not currently used, but may be defined by future versions of the language.

`outer`

`outer` is a reserved keyword in Java. It is not currently used, but may be defined by future versions of the language.

overload

To provide definitions of more than one method with the same name but with different argument lists or return values. We call this process "method overloading" and say that the method name is "overloaded." When an overloaded method is called, the compiler determines which one is intended by examining the supplied argument types.

override

To define a method that exactly matches (i.e., same name, same argument types, and same return type) a method defined in a superclass. When an overridden method is invoked, the interpreter uses "dynamic method lookup" to determine which definition of the method is applicable to the current object.

`package`

The `package` statement must be the first statement in a Java file. It specifies which package the code in the file is part of. Java code that is part of a particular package has access to all classes (`public` and non-`public`) in the package, and all non-`private` methods and fields in all those classes. When Java code is part of a named package, the compiled class file must be placed at the appropriate position in the `CLASSPATH` directory hierarchy before it can be accessed by the Java interpreter or other utilities.

If the `package` statement is omitted from a file, the code in that file is part of an unnamed default package. This is convenient for small test programs, or during development because it means that the code can be interpreted from the current directory.

primitive type

One of the Java data types: `boolean`, `char`, `byte`, `short`, `int`, `long`, `float`, `double`. Primitive types are manipulated, assigned, and passed to methods "by value"—i.e., the actual bytes of the data are copied. See also "reference type."

`private`

The `private` keyword is a visibility modifier that can be applied to method and field variables of classes. A `private` field is not visible outside of its class definition.

`private protected`

When the `private` and `protected` visibility modifiers are both applied to a variable or method in a class, they indicate that the field is visible only within the class itself and within subclasses of the class. Note that subclasses can only access `private protected` fields within themselves or within other objects that are subclasses; they cannot access those fields within instances of the superclass.

`protected`

The `protected` keyword is a visibility modifier that can be applied to method and field variables of classes. A `protected` field is only visible within its class, within subclasses, or within the package of which its class is a part. Note that subclasses in different packages can only access `protected` fields within themselves or within other objects that are subclasses; they cannot access protected fields within instances of the superclass.

`public`

The `public` keyword is a visibility modifier that can be applied to classes and interfaces and to the method and field variables of classes and interfaces. A `public` class or interface is visible everywhere. A non-`public` class or interface is visible only within its package. A `public` method or variable is visible everywhere that its class is visible. When none of the `private`, `protected` or `public` modifiers is specified, a field is visible only within the package of which its class is a part.

reference type

Any object or array. Reference types are manipulated, assigned, and passed to methods "by reference." In other words, the underlying value is not copied; only a reference to it is. See also "primitive type."

`rest`

`rest` is a reserved keyword in Java. It is not currently used, but may be defined by future versions of the language.

`return`

The `return` statement in a method, constructor, or static class initializer causes control to return to the caller. Before control returns to the caller, the `finally` clauses (if any) of any `try` statements that the `return` is nested within are executed.

Static initializers, constructors, and methods that are declared to return `void` use the `return` statement alone:

```
if (done) return;
```

Methods that return a value follow the `return` statement with an expression. The value of this expression must be assignable to the return type of the method, and is returned as the value of the method call.

```
return sorted_array;
```

shadow

To declare a variable with the same name as a variable defined in a superclass. We say that the variable "shadows" the superclass's variable. You can use the `super` keyword to refer to the shadowed variable, or can refer to it by casting the object to the type of the superclass.

`short`

`short` is a primitive Java data type. It is a 16-bit two's-complement signed number (in all implementations). The minimum value is -32768 and the maximum value is 32767. It can be cast to and from other numeric types.

```
public class MousePosition { short x, y; }
```

`static`

The `static` keyword is a modifier that may be applied to method and variable declarations within a class. A `static` variable is also known as a "class variable" as opposed to non-`static` "instance variables." While each instance of a class has a full set of its own instance variables, there is only one copy of each `static` class variable, regardless of the number of instances of the class (perhaps zero) that are created. `static` variables may be accessed by class name or through an instance. Non-`static` variables can only be accessed through an instance.

A `static` method is also known as a "class method." Class methods are not passed an implicit `this` pointer to an instance of the class, and thus can not use or call non-`static` variables and methods of the class. A class method may be invoked through an instance of the class, or through the class itself, even if no instances of the class have been created. A non-`static` "instance method" can only be invoked through an instance of the class.

```
public class TypeA {
   public static int j;
   public static void f(int i) {}
   public static void g(int i) {
      f(i+j);        // a static method can call another static method
   }                 // and use static variables.
}
TypeA.g(A.j);        // We can refer to static methods and variables by class name.
TypeA a = new TypeA();
a.g(a.j);            // Or through an instance.
```

static initializer

A block of code that appears, within curly braces, following the `static` keyword, in a class definition. When a class is first loaded by Java, the class initializers are invoked, in the order in which they appear, in order to initialize the class. This may involve initializing the value of class variables or loading a library of native methods, for example.

subclass

A class that extends another. The subclass inherits the `public` and `protected` methods and variables of its superclass. See `extends`.

`super`

The keyword `super` refers to the same value as `this`—the instance of the class for which the current method (these keywords are only valid within non-`static` methods) was invoked. While the type of `this` is the type of the class in which the method appears, the type of `super` is the type of the superclass of the class in which the method appears. `super` is usually used to refer to superclass variables that have been shadowed by variables in the current class. Using `super` in this way is equivalent to casting `this` to the type of the superclass.

There are two additional special uses of the `super` keyword. The first is to invoke a function in the immediate superclass that has been overridden in the current class. Note that because of the definition of function overriding and dynamic method lookup, casting `this` to the type of the superclass and invoking the method through that cast object still invokes the overriding method in the subclass. To invoke overridden methods in the immediate superclass, you need to use `super`.

The second special use of the `super` keyword is as the first statement (and only the first statement) of a constructor. If `super` appears as the first statement of a constructor and is followed by a parenthesized (possibly empty) argument list, then it is interpreted as a call to a constructor of the immediate superclass. If `super` doesn't appear as the first statement of a constructor body, the Java compiler inserts an implicit call—`super()`—to the immediate superclass constructor.

```
class A {
  public A() { System.out.println("Constructor A(void)"); }
  public A(int i) { System.out.println("Constructor A(int)"); }
  public String name = "A";
  public void f() { System.out.println("A: " + name); }
}

class B extends A {
  public B() {
              // implicit super(); call automatically inserted here.
    System.out.println("Constructor B(void)");
  }
  public B(int i) {
    super(i);    // explicit call to a (non-default) superclass constructor.
    System.out.println("Constructor B(int)");
  }
  public String name = "B";// shadows name in class A.
  public void f() {// overrides method f() in class A.
    System.out.println("B: " + name);
  }
```

```
    public void test() {
      String name = "local";

      System.out.println(name);// local name
      System.out.println(this.name);// name in B
      System.out.println(super.name);// name in A
      System.out.println(((A)this).name);// name in A

      f();            // calls f() in class B.
      this.f();       // calls f() in class B.
      super.f();      // calls f() in class A.
      ((A)this).f(); // calls f() in class B (dynamic lookup)
    }
}
```

superclass

A class that is extended by some other class. The superclass's `public` and `protected` methods and variables are available to the subclass. See `extends`.

`switch`

The `switch` statement is exactly the same in Java as it is in C. It is a way of selecting among an arbitrary number of code fragments based on the value of an expression. The `switch` keyword is followed by an integral-valued expression in parentheses and a block of code in curly braces. The statement block should contain one or more `case` and `default` keywords which serve to label sections of the code. When the `switch` statement is executed, the expression in parentheses is evaluated, and control jumps to the statement which has a `case` label that has the same value as the expression, or to the statement with the `default` label if no `case` label matches. The `break` statement is usually used within the body of a `switch` statement to terminate the statement when the appropriate code fragment has been executed. Without `break` statements, control would "fall through" from one labelled fragment to the next.

```
switch (font.getStyle()) {
  case Font.ITALIC:
                s = "italic"; break;
  case Font.BOLD:
                s = "bold"; break;
  case Font.BOLD + Font.ITALIC:
                s = "bolditalic"; break;
  default:
  case Font.PLAIN:
                s = ""; break;
}
```

`synchronized`

The `synchronized` keyword is used in two related ways in Java: as a modifier and as a statement. First, it is a modifier that can be applied to class or instance methods. It indicates that the method modifies the internal state of the class or the internal state of an instance of the class in a way that is not thread-safe. Before running a `synchronized` class method, Java obtains a lock on the class, to ensure that no other threads can be modifying the class concurrently. Before running a synchronized instance method, Java obtains a lock on the instance that invoked the method, ensuring that no other thread can be modifying the object at the same time.

Java also supports a synchronized statement that serves to specify a "critical section" of code. The synchronized keyword is followed by an expression in parentheses and a statement or block of statements. The expression must evaluate to an object or array. Java obtains a lock on the specified object or array before executing the statements.

this

Within an instance method or constructor of a class, this refers to "this object"—the instance currently being operated on. It is useful to refer to an instance variable of the class that has been shadowed by a local variable or method argument. It is also useful to pass the current object as an argument to static methods or methods of other classes.

There is one additional use of this. When this appears as the very first statement in a constructor method, it refers to one of the other constructors of the class.

```
class Point {
   public int x,y;
   public Point(x,y) { this.x = x; this.y = y; }
   public Point() { this(0,0); }
}
```

thread

A single independent stream of execution within a program. Since Java is a "multithreaded" programming language, more than one thread may be running within the Java interpreter at a time. Threads in Java are represented and controlled through the Thread object.

throw

The throw statement signals that an exceptional condition has occurred by throwing a specified exception object. This statement causes program execution to stop and resume at the nearest containing catch statement that can handle the specified exception object. Note that the throw keyword must be followed by an exception object, not an exception class.

```
if (font == null) throw new NullPointerException("null font specified");
```

throws

The throws keyword is used in a method declaration to list the exceptions that the method can throw. Any exceptions that a method can raise that are not subclasses of Error or RuntimeException must either be caught within the method or declared in the method's throws clause.

```
public void readfile(File f) throws FileNotFoundException {
   ...
}
```

transient

The transient keyword is a modifier that may be applied to variables in a class. It specifies that the variable is not part of the persistent state of the object. (This modifier is not currently used by any part of Java.)

`true`

`true` is one of the two possible `boolean` values. Strictly speaking, `true` is not a keyword of the Java language, but a literal value like an integer or a character value.

`try`

The `try` keyword is used to indicate a block of code to which subsequent `catch` and `finally` clauses apply. The `try` statement itself performs no special action. See `catch` and `finally` for more information on the `try/catch/finally` construct.

```
try {
  // do stuff here that may raise exceptions or
  // terminate in various ways
}
catch (SomeException e1) {
  // Handle one kind of exception here
}
catch (AnotherException e2) {
  // Handle another kind here.
}
finally {
  // Always execute this code, no matter what happens.
}
```

UCS (universal character set)

A synonym for ISO-10646.

Unicode

A 16-bit character encoding that includes all of the world's commonly used alphabets and ideographic character sets in a "unified" form (i.e., a form from which duplications among national standards have been removed). ASCII and Latin-1 characters may be trivially mapped to Unicode characters. Java uses Unicode for its `char` and `String` types.

UTF-8 (UCS transformation format 8-bit form)

This is an encoding for Unicode characters (and more generally, UCS characters) commonly used for transmission and storage. It is a multibyte format in which different characters require different numbers of bytes to be represented.

`var`

`var` is a reserved keyword in Java. It is not currently used, but may be defined by future versions of the language.

`void`

The `void` keyword is used to indicate that a method returns no value. The only methods that are declared without a return type or `void` specified are constructor functions. Java differs from C in that methods that take no arguments are declared with empty parentheses, not with the `void` keyword. Also unlike C, Java does not have any `void *` type, nor does it require a `(void)` cast in order to correctly ignore the result returned by a call to a non-`void` method.

```
public class Complex extends Number {
  double x, y;
  // A constructor: not void, but we don't have to declare
```

```
    // the implicit return value
    Complex(double x, double y) { ... }
    // A method with no arguments and no return value.
    // Note void as return type, but not between the parentheses.
    void swap_components() { ... }
}
```

`volatile`

The `volatile` keyword is a modifier that may be applied to variables. It specifies that the variable changes asynchronously (e.g., it may be a memory-mapped hardware register on a peripheral device), and that the compiler should not attempt to perform optimizations with it. For example, it should read the variable's value from memory every time and not attempt to save a copy of it in registers.

`while`

The `while` loop performs exactly in Java as it does in C. The expression in parentheses is evaluated, and if the `boolean` result is `true`, the statements within curly braces are executed. This process repeats until the value of the expression becomes `false`.

Index

B

G

H

I

O

P

Q

R

S

T

About the Author

David Flanagan is a consulting computer programmer, user interface designer, and trainer. His previous books with O'Reilly & Associates include *X Toolkit Intrinsics Reference Manual* and *Motif Tools: Streamlined GUI Design and Programming with the Xmt Library*. David has a degree in computer science and engineering from the Massachusetts Institute of Technology.

Colophon

Our look is the result of reader comments, our own experimentation, and feedback from distribution channels. Distinctive covers complement our distinctive approach to technical topics, breathing personality and life into potentially dry subjects.

The illustrations featured on the cover of *Java in a Nutshell* are American football referees (or "refs," as they are frequently called). The referee poses, from left to right, are: first down, offsides, touchdown, pass interference, and timeout.

Edie Freedman designed this cover from illustrations drawn by Arthur Saarinen. The referees were created in Adobe Illustrator. Supporting artwork was done in QuarkXPress.

The fonts used in the book are Garamond and Garamond book. Text was prepared using the troff text formatter and FrameMaker. Figures were created by Chris Reilley in Macromedia Freehand 5.0 and Adobe Photoshop.

INTERNET
Books from O'Reilly & Associates, Inc.
WINTER 1995-96

The Whole Internet User's Guide & Catalog

By Ed Krol
2nd Edition April 1994
574 pages, ISBN 1-56592-063-5

Still the best book on the Internet! This is the second edition of our comprehensive—and bestselling—introduction to the Internet, the international network that includes virtually every major computer site in the world. In addition to email, file transfer, remote login, and network news, this book pays special attention to some new tools for helping you find information. Useful to beginners and veterans alike, this book will help you explore what's possible on the Net. Also includes a pull-out quick-reference card.

"An ongoing classic."
—*Rochester Business Journal*

"The book against which all subsequent Internet guides are measured, Krol's work has emerged as an indispensable reference to beginners and seasoned travelers alike as they venture out on the data highway."
—*Microtimes*

"*The Whole Internet User's Guide & Catalog* will probably become the Internet user's bible because it provides comprehensive, easy instructions for those who want to get the most from this valuable electronic tool."
—David J. Buerger, Editor, *Communications Week*

The Whole Internet for Windows 95

By Ed Krol & Paula Ferguson
1st Edition October 1995 (est.)
650 pages (est.), ISBN 1-56592-155-0

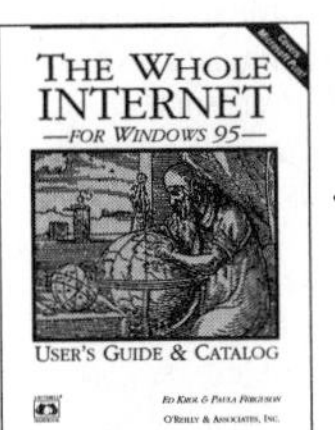

The best book on the Internet...now updated for Windows 95! *The Whole Internet for Windows 95* is the most comprehensive introduction to the Internet available today. For Windows users who in the past have struggled to take full advantage of the Internet's powerful utilities, Windows 95's built-in Internet support is a cause for celebration. And when you get online with Windows 95, this new edition of *The Whole Internet* will guide you every step of the way.

This book shows you how to use Microsoft Internet Explorer (the World Wide Web multimedia browser) and Microsoft Exchange (an email program). It also covers Netscape Navigator, the most popular Web browser on the market, and shows you how to use Usenet readers, file transfer tools, and database searching software.

But it does much more. You'll also want to take advantage of alternative popular free software programs that are downloadable from the Net. This book shows you where to find them and how to use them to save you time and money.

Using Email Effectively

By Linda Lamb & Jerry Peek
1st Edition April 1995
160 pages, ISBN 1-56592-103-8

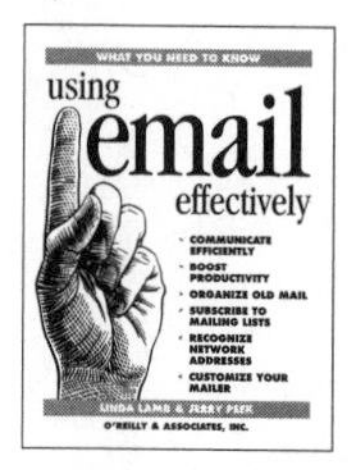

After using email for a few years, you learn from your own mistakes and from reading other people's mail. You learn how to include a message but leave in only the sections that make your point, how to recognize if a network address "looks right," how to successfully subscribe and unsubcribe to a mailing list, how to save mail so that you can find it again. This book shortens the learning-from-experience curve for all mailers, so you can quickly be productive and send email that looks intelligent to others.

Bandits on the Information Superhighway

By Daniel J. Barrett
1st Edition February 1996
246 pages, ISBN 1-56592-156-9

Most people on the Internet behave honestly, but there are always some troublemakers. *Bandits* provides a crash course in Internet "street smarts," describing practical risks that every user should know about. Filled with anecdotes, technical tips, and the advice of experts from diverse fields, *Bandits* helps you identify and avoid risks online, so you can have a more productive and enjoyable time on the Internet.

The USENET Handbook

By Mark Harrison
1st Edition May 1995
388 pages, ISBN 1-56592-101-1

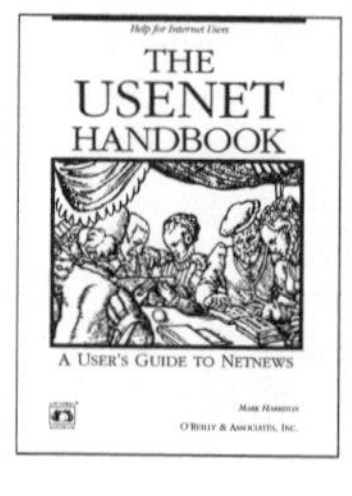

How to get the most out of network news! This book unlocks USENET, the world's largest discussion forum. It includes tutorials on the most popular newsreaders for UNIX and Windows (*tin, nn,* GNUS, and Trumpet). It's also a guide to the culture of the Net, giving you an introduction to etiquette, the private language, and some of the history.

World Wide Web Journal

Edited by O'Reilly & Associates and Web Consortium (W3C)
Special Issue January 1996
748 pages, ISBN 1-56592-169-0

The *World Wide Web Journal* is a quarterly publication that provides timely, in-depth coverage of the issues, techniques, and research developments in the World Wide Web. This special issue contains the Conference Proceeding papers that were chosen for the 4th International World Wide Web Conference in Boston, MA.

MH & xmh: Email for Users & Programmers

By Jerry Peek
3rd Edition April 1995
782 pages, ISBN 1-56592-093-7

This book explains how to make MH do things you never thought an email program could do. It covers all the MH commands as well as three interfaces to MH: *xmh* (for the X environment), *exmh* (written with tcl/tk), and *mh-e* (for GNU Emacs users). Also features configuration tips, customization and programming examples, and a description of the Multipurpose Internet Mail Extensions (MIME) and how to use it with MH.

The Computer User's Survival Guide

By Joan Stigliani
1st Edition October 1995
296 pages, ISBN 1-56592-030-9

The bad news: You can be hurt by working at a computer. The good news: Many of the factors that pose a risk are within your control. This book looks squarely at all the factors that affect your health on the job, including positioning, equipment, work habits, lighting, stress, radiation, and general health.

Internet In A Box,™ Version 2.0

Published by SPRY, Inc.
(Product good only in U.S. and Canada)
2nd Edition June 1995
UPC 799364 012001
Two diskettes & a 528-page version of ***The Whole Internet Users Guide & Catalog*** *as documentation*

Now there are more ways to connect to the Internet—and you get to choose the most economical plan based on your dialing habits.

What will **Internet In A Box** *do for me?*

Internet In A Box is for PC users who want to connect to the Internet. Quite simply, it solves Internet access problems for individuals and small businesses without dedicated lines and/or UNIX machines. Internet In A Box provides instant connectivity, a multimedia Windows interface, and a full suite of applications. This product is so easy to use, you need to know only two things to get started: how to load software onto your PC and how to use a mouse.

New features of version 2.0 include:

- More connectivity options with the CompuServe Network.
- With Spry Mosaic and Progressive Image Rendering, browsing the Internet has never been easier.
- SPRY Mail provides MIME support and a built-in spell checker. Mail and News are now available within the Mosaic Toolbar.
- You'll enjoy safe and secure shopping online with Secure HTTP.
- SPRY News offers offline support for viewing and sending individual articles.
- A Network File Manager means there's an improved interface for dealing with various Internet hosts.

Marketing on the Internet

By Linda Lamb, Tim O'Reilly, Dale Dougherty, & Brian Erwin
1st Edition June 1996 (est.)
170 pages (est.), ISBN 1-56592-105-4

Marketing on the Internet tells you what you need to know to successfully use this new communication and sales channel to put product and sales information online, build relationships with customers, send targeted announcements, and answer product support questions. In short, how to use the Internet as part of your overall marketing mix. Written from a marketing, not technical perspective.

WebSite™ 1.1

By O'Reilly & Associates, Inc.
Documentation by Susan Peck
2nd Edition January 1996
ISBN 1-56592-173-9, UPC 9-781565-921733
Includes four diskettes, 494-page book, and WebSite T-shirt

WebSite 1.1 now makes it easier than ever to start publishing on the Internet. WebSite is a 32-bit multi-threaded World Wide Web server that combines the power and flexibility of a UNIX server with the ease of use of a Windows application. Its intuitive graphical interface and easy install make it a natural for both Windows NT and Windows 95 users.

WebSite provides a tree-like display of all the documents and links on your server, with a simple solution for finding and fixing broken links. Using CGI, you can run a desktop application like Excel or Visual Basic from within a Web document on WebSite. Its access authentication lets you control which users have access to different parts of your Web server. WebSite is a product of O'Reilly & Associates, Inc. It is created in cooperation with Bob Denny and Enterprise Integration Technologies, Inc. (EIT).

New features of WebSite 1.1 include: HTML editor, multiple indexes, WebFind wizard, CGI with Visual Basic 4 framework and server push support, graphical interface for creating virtual servers, Windows 95 style install, logging reports for individual documents, HTML-2 and -3 support, external image map support, self-registration of users, and EMosaic 2.1 Web browser.

Designing for the Web: Basics for a New Medium

By Jennifer Niederst with Edie Freedman
1st Edition April 1996 (est.)
150 pages (est.), ISBN: 1-56592-165-8

This book is for designers who need to hone their skills for the Web. It explains how to work with HTML documents from a designer's point of view, outlines special problems with presenting information online, and walks through incorporating images into Web pages, with emphasis on resolution and improving efficiency. Also discusses the different browsers available and how to make sure a document is most effective for a broad spectrum of browsers and platforms.

Providing Web Content

Using HTML: The Definitive Guide

By Chuck Musciano & Bill Kennedy
1st Edition April 1996 (est.)
350 pages (est.), ISBN 1-56592-175-5

Using HTML helps you become fluent in HTML, fully versed in the language's syntax, semantics, and elements of style. The book covers the most up-to-date version of the HTML standard, plus all the common extensions and, in particular, Netscape extensions. The authors cover each and every element of the currently accepted version of the language in detail, explaining how each element works and how it interacts with all the other elements. They've also included a style guide that helps you decide how to best use HTML to accomplish a variety of tasks, from simple online documentation to complex marketing and sales presentations.

CGI Scripting on the World Wide Web

By Shishir Gundavaram
1st Edition March 1996 (est.)
375 pages (est.), ISBN 1-56592-168-2

This book offers a comprehensive explanation of CGI and related techniques for people who hold on to the dream of providing their own information servers on the Web. Gundavaram starts at the beginning, explaining the value of CGI and how it works, then moves swiftly into the subtle details of programming. The book offers a comprehensive look at the job of providing information dynamically on the Web.

Perl 5 Desktop Reference

By Johan Vromans
1st Edition February 1996
56 pages, ISBN: 1-56592-187-9

This is the standard quick-reference guide for the Perl programming language. It provides a complete overview of the language, from variables to input and output, from flow control to regular expressions, from functions to document formats —all packed into a convenient, carry-around booklet.

Java in a Nutshell: A Desktop Quick Reference for Java Programmers

By David Flanagan
1st Edition February 1996
450 pages (est.), ISBN 1-56592-183-6

Java in a Nutshell is a complete quick reference guide to the Java API, the hot new programming language from Sun Microsystems. This comprehensive volume contains descriptions of all of the Java classes and their related calls and an introduction to important Java concepts.

Exploring Java

By Pat Niemeyer & Josh Peck
1st Edition April 1996 (est.)
250 pages (est.), ISBN 1-56592-184-4

The first book in our new Java documentation series, *Exploring Java* introduces the basics of Java, the new object-oriented programming language for networked applications. This book shows you how to get up to speed writing Java applets and other applications, including networking programs, content and protocol handlers, and security managers.

Learning Perl

By Randal L. Schwartz, Foreword by Larry Wall
1st Edition November 1993
274 pages, ISBN 1-56592-042-2

Learning Perl is a step-by-step, hands-on tutorial designed to get you writing useful Perl scripts as quickly as possible. In addition to countless code examples, there are numerous programming exercises, with full answers. For a comprehensive and detailed guide to advanced programming with Perl, read the companion book, *Programming perl*.

Programming perl

By Larry Wall & Randal L. Schwartz
1st Edition January 1991
482 pages, ISBN 0-937175-64-1

An authoritative guide to the hottest new UNIX utility in years, coauthored by its creator, Larry Wall. Perl is a language for easily manipulating text, files, and processes. *Programming perl* covers Perl syntax, functions, debugging, efficiency, the Perl library, and more.

TO ORDER: **800-889-8969** (CREDIT CARD ORDERS ONLY); **ORDER@ORA.COM**

Internet Security

PGP: Pretty Good Privacy

By Simson Garfinkel
1st Edition December 1994
430 pages, ISBN 1-56592-098-8

PGP is a freely available encryption program that protects the privacy of files and electronic mail. It uses powerful public key cryptography and works on virtually every platform. This book is both a readable technical user's guide and a fascinating behind-the-scenes look at cryptography and privacy. It describes how to use PGP and provides background on cryptography, PGP's history, battles over public key cryptography patents and U.S. government export restrictions, and public debates about privacy and free speech.

"I even learned a few things about PGP from Simson's informative book."—Phil Zimmermann, Author of PGP

"Since the release of PGP 2.0 from Europe in the fall of 1992, PGP's popularity and usage has grown to make it the de-facto standard for email encyrption. Simson's book is an excellent overview of PGP and the history of cryptography in general. It should prove a useful addition to the resource library for any computer user, from the UNIX wizard to the PC novice."
—Derek Atkins, PGP Development Team, MIT

Building Internet Firewalls

By D. Brent Chapman & Elizabeth D. Zwicky
1st Edition September 1995
544 pages, ISBN 1-56592-124-0

Everyone is jumping on the Internet bandwagon, despite the fact that the security risks associated with connecting to the Net have never been greater. This book is a practical guide to building firewalls on the Internet. It describes a variety of firewall approaches and architectures and discusses how you can build packet filtering and proxying solutions at your site. It also contains a full discussion of how to configure Internet services (e.g., FTP, SMTP, Telnet) to work with a firewall, as well as a complete list of resources, including the location of many publicly available firewall construction tools.

Practical UNIX and Internet Security

By Simson Garfinkel & Gene Spafford
2nd Edition April 1996 (est.)
800 pages (est.), ISBN 1-56592-148-8

A complete revision of the first edition, this new guide spells out the threats, system vulnerabilities, and counter-measures you can adopt to protect your UNIX system, network, and Internet connection. It's complete—covering both host and network security—and doesn't require that you be a programmer or a UNIX guru to use it. This edition contains hundreds of pages of new information on Internet security, including new security tools and approaches. Covers many platforms, both System V and Berkeley-based (i.e. Sun, DEC, HP, IBM, SCO, NeXT, Linux, and other UNIX systems).

Computer Crime

By David Icove, Karl Seger & William VonStorch
1st Edition August 1995
464 pages, ISBN 1-56592-086-4

Computer crime is a growing threat. Attacks on computers, networks, and data range from terrorist threats to financial crimes to pranks. *Computer Crime: A Crimefighters Handbook* is aimed at those who need to understand, investigate, and prosecute computer crimes of all kinds.

This book discusses computer crimes, criminals, and laws, and profiles the computer criminal (using techniques developed for the FBI and other law enforcement agencies). It outlines the the risks to computer systems and personnel, operational, physical, and communications measures that can be taken to prevent computer crimes. It also discusses how to plan for, investigate, and prosecute computer crimes, ranging from the supplies needed for criminal investigation, to the detection and audit tools used in investigation, to the presentation of evidence to a jury.

Contains a compendium of computer-related federal statutes, all statutes of individual states, a resource summary, and detailed papers on computer crime.

Internet Administration

Getting Connected: 56K and Up

By Kevin Dowd
1st Edition May 1996 (est.)
450 pages (est.), ISBN 1-56592-154-2

A complete guide for businesses, schools, and other organizations who want to connect their computers to the Internet. This book covers everything you need to know to make informed decisions, from helping you figure out which services you really need to providing down-to-earth explanations of telecommunication options, such as frame relay, ISDN, and leased lines. Once you're online, it shows you how to set up basic Internet services, such as a World Wide Web server. Tackles issues for the PC, Macintosh, and UNIX platforms.

DNS and BIND

By Paul Albitz & Cricket Liu
1st Edition October 1992
418 pages, ISBN 1-56592-010-4

DNS and BIND contains all you need to know about the Internet's Domain Name System (DNS) and the Berkeley Internet Name Domain (BIND), its UNIX implementation. The Domain Name System is the Internet's "phone book"; it's a database that tracks important information (in particular, names and addresses) for every computer on the Internet. If you're a system administrator, this book will show you how to set up and maintain the DNS software on your network.

sendmail

By Bryan Costales, with Eric Allman & Neil Rickert
1st Edition November 1993
830 pages, ISBN 1-56592-056-2

This Nutshell Handbook® is far and away the most comprehensive book ever written on sendmail, the program that acts like a traffic cop in routing and delivering mail on UNIX-based networks. Although sendmail is used on almost every UNIX system, it's one of the last great uncharted territories—and most difficult utilities to learn—in UNIX system administration. This book provides a complete sendmail tutorial, plus extensive reference material on every aspect of the program. It covers IDA sendmail, the latest version (V8) from Berkeley, and the standard versions available on most systems.

Managing Internet Information Services

By Cricket Liu, Jerry Peek, Russ Jones, Bryan Buus, & Adrian Nye
1st Edition December 1994
668 pages, ISBN 1-56592-062-7

This comprehensive guide describes how to set up information services and make them available over the Internet. It discusses why a company would want to offer Internet services, provides complete coverage of all popular services, and tells how to select which ones to provide. Most of the book describes how to set up Gopher, World Wide Web, FTP, and WAIS servers and email services.

Networking Personal Computers with TCP/IP

By Craig Hunt
1st Edition July 1995
408 pages, ISBN 1-56592-123-2

This book offers practical information as well as detailed instructions for attaching PCs to a TCP/IP network and its UNIX servers. It discusses the challenges you'll face and offers general advice on how to deal with them, provides basic TCP/IP configuration information for some of the popular PC operating systems, covers advanced configuration topics and configuration of specific applications such as email, and includes a chapter on NetWare, the most popular PC LAN system software.

TCP/IP Network Administration

By Craig Hunt
1st Edition August 1992
502 pages, ISBN 0-937175-82-X

A complete guide to setting up and running a TCP/IP network for practicing system administrators. *TCP/IP Network Administration* covers setting up your network, configuring important network applications including sendmail, and issues in troubleshooting and security. It covers both BSD and System V TCP/IP implementations.

At Your Fingertips—

A COMPLETE GUIDE TO O'REILLY'S ONLINE SERVICES

O'Reilly & Associates offers extensive product and customer service information online. We invite you to come and explore our little neck-of-the-woods.

For product information and insight into new technologies, visit the O'Reilly Resource Center

Most comprehensive among our online offerings is the O'Reilly Resource Center. You'll find detailed information on all O'Reilly products, including titles, prices, tables of contents, indexes, author bios, software contents, and reviews. You can also view images of all our products. In addition, watch for informative articles that provide perspective on the technologies we write about. Interviews, excerpts, and bibliographies are also included.

After browsing online, it's easy to order, too, with GNN Direct or by sending email to **order@ora.com**. The O'Reilly Resource Center shows you how. Here's how to visit us online:

☞*Via the World Wide Web*

If you are connected to the Internet, point your Web browser (e.g., `mosaic, netscape,` or `lynx`) to:

`http://www.ora.com/`

For the plaintext version, `telnet` to:

`www.ora.com` (login: `oraweb`)

☞*Via Gopher*

If you have a Gopher program, our Gopher server has information in a menu format that some people prefer to the Web.

Connect your `gopher` to: `gopher.ora.com`

Or, point your Web browser to:
`gopher://gopher.ora.com/`

Or, you can `telnet` to: `gopher.ora.com`
(login: `gopher`)

A convenient way to stay informed: email mailing lists

An easy way to learn of the latest projects and products from O'Reilly & Associates is to subscribe to our mailing lists. We have email announcements and discussions on various topics, for example "ora-news," our electronic news service. Subscribers receive email as soon as the information breaks.

☞*To join a mailing list:*

Send email to:

listproc@online.ora.com

Leave the message "subject" empty if possible.

If you know the name of the mailing list you want to subscribe to, put the following information on the first line of your message: `subscribe` "listname" "your name" `of` "your company."

For example: `subscribe ora-news`
`Kris Webber of Fine Enterprises`

If you don't know the name of the mailing list, listproc will send you a listing of all the mailing lists. Put this word on the first line of the body: `lists`

To find out more about a particular list, send a message with this word as the first line of the body: `info` "listname"

For more information and help, send this message: `help`

For specific help, email to:
listmaster@online.ora.com

The complete O'Reilly catalog is now available via email

You can now receive a text-only version of our complete catalog via email. It contains detailed information about all our products, so it's mighty big: over 200 kbytes, or 200,000 characters.

To get the whole catalog in one message, send an empty email message to: **catalog@online.ora.com**

If your email system can't handle large messages, you can get the catalog split into smaller messages. Send email to: **catalog-split@online.ora.com**

To receive a print catalog, send your snail mail address to: **catalog@ora.com**

Check out Web Review, our new publication on the Web

Web Review is our new magazine that offers fresh insights into the Web. The editorial mission of Web Review is to answer the question: How and where do you BEST spend your time online? Each issue contains reviews that look at the most interesting and creative sites on the Web. Visit us at **http://gnn.com/wr/**

Web Review is the product of the recently formed Songline Studios, a venture between O'Reilly and America Online.

Get the files you want with FTP

We have an archive of example files from our books, the covers of our books, and much more available by anonymous FTP.

`ftp` to:

`ftp.ora.com` (login: `anonymous` – use your email address as the password.)

Or, if you have a WWW browser, point it to:

`ftp://ftp.ora.com/`

FTPMAIL

The ftpmail service connects to O'Reilly's FTP server and sends the results (the files you want) by email. This service is for people who can't use FTP—but who can use email.

For help and examples, send an email message to:

`ftpmail@online.ora.com`

(In the message body, put the single word: `help`)

Helpful information is just an email message away

Many customer services are provided via email. Here are a few of the most popular and useful:

info@online.ora.com
For a list of O'Reilly's online customer services.

info@ora.com
For general questions and information.

bookquestions@ora.com
For technical questions, or corrections, concerning book contents.

order@ora.com
To order books online and for ordering questions.

catalog@online.ora.com
To receive an online copy of our catalog.

catalog@ora.com
To receive a free copy of *ora.com*, our combination magazine and catalog. Please include your snail mail address.

international@ora.com
Comments or questions about international ordering or distribution.

proposals@ora.com
To submit book proposals.

info@gnn.com
To receive information about America Online's GNN (Global Network Navigator).™

O'Reilly & Associates, Inc.

103A Morris Street, Sebastopol, CA 95472

Inquiries: **707-829-0515**, **800-998-9938**

Credit card orders: **800-889-8969**
(Weekdays 6 A.M.- 5 P.M. PST)

FAX: **707-829-0104**

O'Reilly & Associates—
LISTING OF TITLES

INTERNET

CGI Scriptin on the World Wide Web (Winter '95-96 est.)
Designing for the Web (Winter '95-96 est.)
Exploring Java (Spring '96 est.)
Getting Connected (Spring '96 est.)
Java in a Nutshell
Smileys
The USENET Handbook
The Whole Internet User's Guide & Catalog
The Whole Internet for Windows 95
The World Wide Web Journal

SOFTWARE

Internet In A Box™
WebSite™ 1.1
WebBoard™

WHAT YOU NEED TO KNOW SERIES

Bandits on the Information Superhighway
Using Email Effectively
Marketing on the Internet (Spring '96 est.)
When You Can't Find Your System Administrator

HEALTH, CAREER & BUSINESS

Building a Successful Software Business
The Computer User's Survival Guide
Dictionary of PC hardware and Data Communication Terms (Winter '95-96 est.)
The Future Does Not Compute
Love Your Job!
TWI Day Calendar - 1996

USING UNIX

BASICS

Learning GNU Emacs
Learning the bash Shell
Learning the Korn Shell
Learning the UNIX Operating System
Learning the vi Editor
MH & xmh: Email for Users & Programmers
SCO UNIX in a Nutshell
UNIX in a Nutshell: System V Ed.
Using and Managing UUCP (Spring'96 est.)
Using csh and tcsh

ADVANCED

Exploring Expect
The Frame Handbook
Learning Perl
Making TeX Work
Perl 5 Quick Reference Guide
Programming perl
Running Linux
Running Linux Companion CD-ROM (Winter '95-96 est.)
sed & awk
UNIX Power Tools (with CD-ROM)

SYSTEM ADMINISTRATION

Building Internet Firewalls
Computer Crime: A Crimefighter's Handbook
Computer Security Basics
DNS and BIND
Essential System Administration
Linux Network Administrator's Guide
Managing Internet Information Services
Managing NFS and NIS
Networking Personal Computers with TCP/IP
Practical UNIX & Internet Security (Spring '96 est.)
PGP: Pretty Good Privacy
sendmail
System Performance Tuning
TCP/IP Network Administration
termcap & terminfo
Volume 8 : X Window System Administrator's Guide

PROGRAMMING

Applying RCS and SCCS
C++: The Core Language
Checking C Programs with lint
DCE Security Programming
Distributing Applications Across DCE and Windows NT
Encyclopedia of Graphics File Formats
Guide to Writing DCE Applications
High Performance Computing
lex & yacc
Managing Projects with make
Microsoft RPC Programming Guide
Migrating to Fortran 90
Multi-Platform Code Management
ORACLE Performance Tuning
ORACLE PL/SQL Programming
Porting UNIX Software
POSIX Programmer's Guide
POSIX.4: Programming for the Real World
Power Programming with RPC
Practical C Programming
Practical C++ Programming
Programming with curses
Programming with GNU Software (Winter '95-96 est.)
Programming with Pthreads (Winter '95-96 est.)
Software Portability with imake
Understanding DCE
Understanding Japanese Information Processing
Using C on the UNIX System

BERKELEY 4.4 SOFTWARE DISTRIBUTION

4.4BSD System Manager's Manual
4.4BSD User's Reference Manual
4.4BSD User's Supp. Documents
4.4BSD Programmer's Reference Manual
4.4BSD Programmer's Supplementary Documents
4.4BSD-Lite CD Companion
4.4BSD-Lite CD Companion: International Version

X WINDOW SYSTEM

Volume 0: X Protocol Reference Manual
Volume 1: Xlib Programming Manual
Volume 2: Xlib Reference Manual:
Volume 3: X Window System User's Guide
Volume. 3M: X Window System User's Guide, Motif Ed
Volume 4M: X Toolkit Intrinsics Programming Manual, Motif Ed.
Volume 5: X Toolkit Intrinsics Reference Manual
Volume 6A: Motif Programming Manual
Volume 6B: Motif Reference Manual
Volume 6C: Motif Tools
Volume 8 : X Window System Administrator's Guide
Volume 9: X Window Programming Extentions (Spring '96 est.)
Programmer's Supplement for Release 6
X User Tools (with CD-ROM)
The X Window System in a Nutshell

THE X RESOURCE

A QUARTERLY WORKING JOURNAL FOR X PROGRAMMERS

The X Resource: Issues 16 and Issue 17

TRAVEL

Travelers' Tales France
Travelers' Tales Hong Kong
Travelers' Tales India
Travelers' Tales Mexico
Travelers' Tales Spain
Travelers' Tales Thailand
Travelers' Tales: A Woman's World

O'Reilly & Associates—
INTERNATIONAL DISTRIBUTORS

Customers outside North America can now order O'Reilly & Associates books through the following distributors. They offer our international customers faster order processing, more bookstores, increased representation at tradeshows worldwide, and the high-quality, responsive service our customers have come to expect.

Europe, Middle East, and Africa

(except Germany, Switzerland, and Austria)

INQUIRIES

International Thomson Publishing Europe
Berkshire House
168-173 High Holborn
London WC1V 7AA, United Kingdom
Telephone: 44-71-497-1422
Fax: 44-71-497-1426
Email: itpint@itps.co.uk

ORDERS

International Thomson Publishing Services, Ltd.
Cheriton House, North Way
Andover, Hampshire SP10 5BE, United Kingdom
Telephone: 44-264-342-832 (UK orders)
Telephone: 44-264-342-806 (outside UK)
Fax: 44-264-364418 (UK orders)
Fax: 44-264-342761 (outside UK)

GERMANY, SWITZERLAND, AND AUSTRIA

International Thomson Publishing GmbH
O'Reilly-International Thomson Verlag
Königswinterer Straße 418
53227 Bonn, Germany
Telephone: 49-228-97024 0
Fax: 49-228-441342
Email: anfragen@ora.de

Asia *(except Japan)*

INQUIRIES

International Thomson Publishing Asia
221 Henderson Road
#08-03 Henderson Industrial Park
Singapore 0315
Telephone: 65-272-6496
Fax: 65-272-6498

ORDERS

Telephone: 65-268-7867
Fax: 65-268-6727

JAPAN

O'Reilly & Associates, Inc.
103A Morris Street
Sebastopol, CA 95472 U.S.A.
Telephone: 707-829-0515
Telephone: 800-998-9938 (U.S. & Canada)
Fax: 707-829-0104
Email: order@ora.com

AUSTRALIA

WoodsLane Pty. Ltd.
7/5 Vuko Place, Warriewood NSW 2102
P.O. Box 935, Mona Vale NSW 2103
Australia
Telephone: 02-970-5111
Fax: 02-970-5002
Email: woods@tmx.mhs.oz.au

NEW ZEALAND

WoodsLane New Zealand Ltd.
21 Cooks Street (P.O. Box 575)
Wanganui, New Zealand
Telephone: 64-6-347-6543
Fax: 64-6-345-4840
Email: woods@tmx.mhs.oz.au

THE AMERICAS

O'Reilly & Associates, Inc.
103A Morris Street
Sebastopol, CA 95472 U.S.A.
Telephone: 707-829-0515
Telephone: 800-998-9938 (U.S. & Canada)
Fax: 707-829-0104
Email: order@ora.com